S0-BYZ-873

murach's
ASP.NET
web programming with
VB.NET

Anne Prince

Doug Lowe

MIKE MURACH & ASSOCIATES, INC

2560 West Shaw Lane, Suite 101 • Fresno, CA 93711-2765
www.murach.com • murachbooks@murach.com

Authors:	Doug Lowe
	Anne Prince
Copy editor:	Mike Murach
Cover design:	Zylka Design
Production:	Tom Murach
	Karen Schletewitz

Four books for every Visual Basic.NET programmer

Murach's Beginning Visual Basic .NET

Murach's VB.NET Database Programming with ADO.NET

Murach's ASP.NET Web Programming with VB.NET

Murach's SQL for SQL Server

Two books for every Java programmer

Murach's Beginning Java 2

Murach's Java Servlets and JSP

Four books for every IBM mainframe programmer

Murach's Structured COBOL

Murach's CICS for the COBOL Programmer

Murach's OS/390 and z/OS JCL

DB2 for the COBOL Programmer, Part 1

Printed in the United States of America

10 9 8 7 6 5 4 3 2 1
ISBN: 1-890774-20-0

Contents

Expanded contents

Section 1 The essence of ASP.NET web programming

Section 2   More ASP.NET essentials

Chapter 10   How to develop user controls

Section 3   ASP.NET database programming skills

Chapter 11   An introduction to relational databases and ADO.NET

Chapter 12 How to work with ADO.NET data commands

Chapter 13 How to use datasets with bound and unbound controls

Chapter 14 How to use the Repeater, DataList, and DataGrid controls

Section 4 Other ASP.NET skills

Chapter 15 How to secure a web application

Chapter 16 How to create and use web services

Chapter 19   How to use email, custom error pages, and back-button control

Chapter 20   How to deploy ASP.NET web applications

Introduction

As we see it, Microsoft's ASP.NET has the potential to help you develop web applications faster and better than ever before. If, for example, you've been using classic ASP for developing web applications, you'll soon see that ASP.NET has many new and improved features. And if you've been using Java servlets and JSP for developing web applications, you'll see that ASP.NET offers many features that just aren't available on the Java platforms.

Whether or not you're new to web programming, though, this book will get you off to a fast start. In fact, by the end of chapter 3, you'll know how to use Visual Studio to develop multi-page applications. And by the end of chapter 4, you'll know how to get database data for your applications and how to use cookies. *No other ASP.NET book gets you started that fast.*

On the other hand, this is much more than a beginning book. By the time you're done, you'll have all the skills you need for developing e-commerce web applications at a professional level. You'll also find that this book does double duty as the best on-the-job reference book that money can buy. *No other ASP.NET book teaches you so much or so thoroughly.*

What this book does

- Section 1 is designed to get you off to a fast start. So the first three chapters show you how to use Visual Studio and ASP.NET to design and code both one-page and multi-page web applications. Along the way, you'll learn how to use view state and session state, two of the critical ASP.NET features. Then, chapter 4 shows you how to retrieve database data for your applications and how to use cookies, and chapter 5 shows you how to test and debug your web applications. At that point, you're ready to write some serious web applications of your own.

- Once you've mastered the skills in section 1, you're ready for rapid progress. So section 2 expands on what you've learned by presenting the other essentials that every ASP.NET programmer needs to know. That includes the essential HTML skills, how to use the Web Server controls and validation controls that weren't presented in section 1, and more about managing the state of an application. Then, the last chapter in this section shows you how to create user controls, which can help you reuse and simplify the code of an application.

- Going beyond the data retrieval techniques presented in section 1, section 3 shows you how to use ADO.NET and the Web Server controls for working with the data in a database. Here, you'll learn the database programming techniques that are commonly used with web applications. Whether you're new to database programming or have experience with it, this will get your web applications working with databases in a thoroughly professional way.

- Finally, section 4 completes the set of skills that every ASP.NET web programmer should have. Here, you'll learn how to provide security for your applications and how to use custom server controls, email, Crystal Reports, and custom error pages with your applications. You'll also learn how to create and use web services, how to deal with the nasty problem of Back button control, and how to deploy your web applications.

Why you'll learn faster and better with this book

Like all our books, this one has features that you won't find in competing books. That's why we believe you'll learn faster and better with our book than with any other. Here are just a few of those features.

- Unlike many of the competing ASP.NET books, this one shows you how to get the most from Visual Studio as you develop your applications. We've found that this Integrated Development Environment is one of the keys to development productivity, but many books ignore or neglect it.

- To show you how all of the pieces of a web application interact, this book presents 23 complete applications ranging from the simple to the complex. This includes the forms, the code, and whatever else is needed to give you the complete picture of how the applications work. As we see it, the only way to master web programming is to study applications like these. And yet, you won't find them in most other books.

- All of the applications in this book use the code-behind programming technique to separate the application's logic from its presentation details. Although this is one of the most important ASP.NET programming techniques, most ASP.NET books treat it as an afterthought.

- If you page through this book, you'll see that all of the information is presented in "paired pages," with the essential syntax, guidelines, and examples on the right page and the perspective and extra explanation on the left page. This helps you learn faster by reading less...and this is the best reference format for refreshing your memory about how to do something.

Who this book is for

If you have basic Visual Basic programming skills, the kind you should get from any beginning book, you're ready for this book. The trouble is that too many beginning books trivialize Visual Basic programming so you don't learn all of the basics that you need for developing real-world applications.

So, if you don't know all of the basics or if you're upgrading to Visual Basic .NET, we would like to recommend *Murach's Beginning Visual Basic .NET*. This book will quickly get you up-to-speed on the basic VB.NET skills, and it's a terrific reference book that you can use whenever you need to refresh those skills. If, for example, you don't know how to use a sorted list or how to create and use business and database classes, this book will fix that fast. In short, our beginning VB.NET book is the perfect companion to our ASP.NET book.

Once you understand the basics of Visual Basic .NET, we're confident that this ASP.NET book will teach you ASP.NET faster and better than any competing book. That's true whether you're coming from a background in Windows development, classic ASP web development, or Java and servlets development.

Two other companion books

A second book that we recommend for all ASP.NET web programmers is *Murach's VB.NET Database Programming with ADO.NET*. This is the book that you need for mastering all aspects of database programming with ADO.NET. Although section 3 of this ASP.NET book presents some of the essential database skills for web programming, our ADO.NET book raises you to another level of expertise.

Then, the third book that we recommend for all ASP.NET programmers is *Murach's SQL for SQL Server*. To start, it shows you how to write SQL statements in all their variations so you can code the right statements for your ADO.NET command objects. This often gives you the option of having Microsoft SQL Server do more so your VB.NET applications do less. Beyond that, this book shows you how to design and implement databases and how to use advanced features like stored procedures and triggers.

What software you need for this book

Most likely, you already have the software for Visual Basic .NET installed on your PC. But here's a quick summary of what you need for developing ASP.NET web applications with Visual Basic .NET. To make sure you install this software in the right sequence, please refer to appendix A.

- To develop any VB.NET application, your computer needs Windows 2000 or Windows XP Professional on your PC. (You can make do with Windows XP Home Edition, but only if you have access to a separate IIS server computer to test your applications.)

- To run ASP.NET applications on your own computer, you need to install the IIS web server on your computer. IIS comes with all versions of Windows 2000 and with Windows XP Professional (but not the Home Edition).

- To use Visual Basic .NET, you need to install either Visual Studio .NET or Visual Basic .NET on your computer. Although Visual Studio .NET includes additional languages and features, you can do almost everything that this book requires with the Standard Edition of Visual Basic .NET, which is far less expensive. The only limitations to Visual Basic .NET are that it doesn't include (1) Web Control Project libraries, which are covered in chapter 17; (2) Crystal Reports, which is covered in chapter 18; and (3) Setup projects, which are covered in chapter 20. Since all of the applications in this book were tested on both the 2002 and 2003 versions of Visual Studio and Visual Basic .NET, you can use either version with this book.

- To run database applications on your PC (as opposed to using a database server on a network), you also need to install MSDE on your PC. MSDE is the desktop database engine that comes with Visual Studio 2002, and it can be downloaded for free if you're using Visual Studio 2003 (see appendix A).

Downloadable files that can help you learn

If you go to our web site at www.murach.com, you can download the source code, files, and databases for all of the applications presented in this book. Then, you can test and review these applications on your own PC to see exactly how they work. We recommend this for anyone who is using this book.

You can also download instructional aids like chapter summaries, learning objectives, review questions, exercises, and projects. These files, though, are designed primarily for students or trainees who are using this book for a class. As a result, your instructor can direct your use of these materials.

Support materials for trainers and instructors

If you're a trainer or instructor who would like to use this book for a course, we offer an Instructor's CD that includes everything that you need for an effective course. Besides the student downloadables that are listed above, this CD includes a complete set of PowerPoint slides, solutions to the exercises and projects, and multiple-choice tests.

To download a sample of this Instructor's Guide and to find out how to get the complete Guide, please go to our web site at www.murach.com and click on the Instructors link. Or, if you prefer, you can call Kelly at 1-800-221-5528 or email kelly@murach.com.

Please let us know how this book works for you

When we started working with ASP.NET, we quickly realized that it offered a powerful new way to develop web applications. However, we also found that it presented many complexities that weren't adequately treated by the documentation or the available books. That's why we knew that we had to take a new approach to this subject if we wanted to make a better book.

Now that we're done, we hope that the many months we put into the development of this book will mean that you can become a proficient ASP.NET programmer in just a few weeks. So, if you have any comments about our book, we would appreciate hearing from you. And good luck with your web programming.

Doug Lowe, Author
doug@murach.com

Anne Prince, Author
anne@murach.com

Section 1

The essence of ASP.NET web programming

When you complete the five chapters in this section, you'll have the essential skills that you need for designing, coding, and testing ASP.NET web applications. After chapter 1 introduces you to the concepts and terms that you need for web programming, chapters 2 and 3 teach you the essential skills for designing web forms and writing the code that makes them work. This gets you off to a fast start.

Then, chapter 4 shows you how to use web forms with the data in databases. It also shows you how to use cookies to store data on the user's machine so it can be retrieved the next time the user accesses your application. From that point on, you'll be able to develop realistic web applications.

Finally, in chapter 5, you'll learn how to use the features for testing and debugging ASP.NET applications. Those features include the integrated debugger provided by Visual Studio .NET as well as the Trace feature provided by ASP.NET.

When you finish all five chapters, you'll be able to develop real-world applications of your own. You'll have a solid understanding of how ASP.NET works. And you'll be ready to learn all of the other ASP.NET features and techniques that are presented in the rest of this book.

1

An introduction to ASP.NET web programming

This chapter introduces you to the basic concepts of web programming and ASP.NET. Here, you'll learn what web applications are and how they work. You'll also be introduced to the files that make up a web application written with VB.NET so you can begin to see how they work together. And you'll learn some basic concepts for developing ASP.NET applications. That will give you the background you need to develop ASP.NET applications of your own.

An introduction to web applications

A *web application* consists of a set of *web pages* that are generated in response to user requests. The Internet has many different types of web applications, such as search engines, online stores, auctions, news sites, discussion groups, games, and so on.

A typical web application

Figure 1-1 shows two pages of a typical web application. In this case, the application is for an online store that lets users purchase a variety of Halloween products, including costumes, masks, and decorations. I developed this application specifically for this book, and you'll see parts of it throughout this book. You can also download this application from our web site as described in appendix A of this book.

The first web page in this figure lists the products that are available from the Halloween store. To display additional information about a product, you can click on the link for the product name. Although it's not shown here, the page that's displayed when you do that lets you add the product to a shopping cart. Then, a shopping cart like the one shown in the second page in this figure is displayed. As you can see, this page lists the selected products and lets the user change the quantity or remove the item from the cart. The user can also click on the Continue Shopping button to return to the page that lists the products or on the Check Out button to enter shipping and payment information. Notice that the user can also display the shopping cart or the check out page by clicking on the links near the top of the first page.

Naturally, the complete Halloween Store application contains pages other than the two shown here. I've already mentioned two of those pages: the one that displays the information for a specific product and the one that lets the user enter shipping and payment information. It also includes a page that thanks the user after they complete an order.

An important point to notice about these pages is that they both contain controls that let the user interact with the page. A page that contains controls like these is called a *web form*. As you'll learn later in this chapter, web forms are a key part of web applications.

The first page of a Halloween Store application

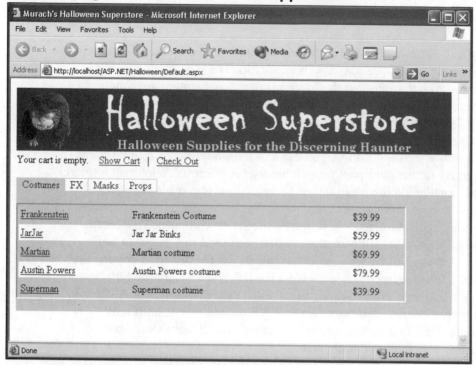

The Shopping Cart page of the Halloween Store application

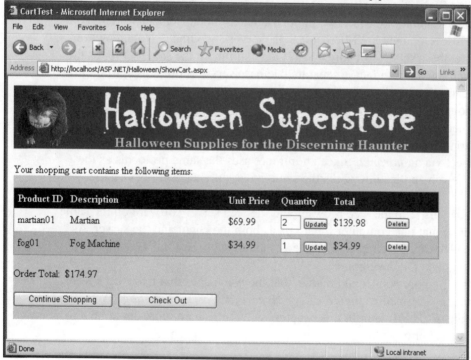

Figure 1-1   Two pages of a typical web application

Hardware and software components for web applications

Figure 1-2 shows the basic hardware and software components that are required for a web application. A web application is a type of *client/server application*, which means that the functions of the application are split between a *client* computer and a *server* computer. The client and server computers are connected to one another via the Internet, and they communicate with each other using *HTTP*, or *Hypertext Transfer Protocol*.

To access a web application, you use a *web browser* that runs on a client computer. By far the most popular web browser is Microsoft's Internet Explorer. The most popular alternative to Internet Explorer is Netscape's Navigator, commonly known as Netscape.

The web application itself is stored on the server computer. This computer runs special *web server* software that enables it to send web pages to web browsers. Although many web servers are available, the two most popular are Microsoft's *Internet Information Services* (or *IIS*) and The Apache Software Foundation's *Apache HTTP Server*, usually just called *Apache*. For ASP.NET applications, the server computer must run IIS. In addition, it must have Microsoft's .NET Framework software installed. You'll learn more about the .NET Framework later in this chapter.

Because most web applications work with data that's stored in a database, most server computers also run a *database management system* (or *DBMS*). Although ASP.NET applications require Microsoft's web server software, you can use any vendor's DBMS. Two popular database management systems for ASP.NET development are Microsoft SQL Server and Oracle. Note, however, that the database server software doesn't have to run on the same server as the web server software. In fact, a separate database server is often used to improve an application's overall performance.

Although this figure shows the client and server computers connected via the Internet, this isn't the only way a client can connect to a server in a web application. If the client and the server are on the same local area network, they can connect via an *intranet*. Since an intranet uses the same protocols as the Internet, a web application works the same on an intranet as it does on the Internet.

You can also run the web browser and the web server software on the same computer so that one computer functions as both the client and the server. As you'll see later in this chapter, a single-computer setup like this is commonly used for application development.

Before I go on, you should realize that the web pages that make up a web application are defined using *HTML*, or *Hypertext Markup Language*. You'll see an example of HTML later in this chapter, and you'll learn more about how to code it in chapter 6.

Components of a web application

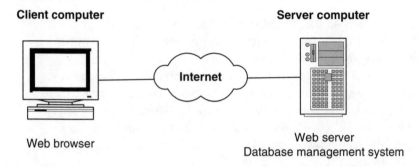

Client computer

Web browser

Server computer

Web server
Database management system

Description

- Web applications are a type of *client/server application*. In a client/server application, a user at a *client* computer accesses an application at a *server* computer. In a web application, the client and server computers are connected via the Internet.

- In a web application, the user works with a *web browser* at the client computer. The web browser provides the user interface for the application. The most popular web browser is Microsoft's Internet Explorer. However, other web browsers such as Netscape Navigator may also be used.

- The application runs on the server computer under the control of *web server* software. For ASP.NET web applications, the server must run Microsoft's web server, called *Internet Information Services*, or *IIS*. The web server must also have Microsoft's .NET Framework installed. Web applications built with other technologies (such as JSP or ColdFusion) often use Apache rather than IIS and don't need the .NET Framework.

- For most web applications, the server computer also runs a *database management system*, or *DBMS*, such as Microsoft's SQL Server. The DBMS provides access to information stored in a database. To improve performance on larger applications, the DBMS can be run on a separate server computer.

- The user interface for a web application is implemented as a series of *web pages* that are displayed in the web browser. Each web page is defined by a *web form* using *HTML*, or *Hypertext Markup Language*, which is a standardized set of markup tags.

- The web browser and web server exchange information using *HTTP*, or *Hypertext Transfer Protocol*.

Figure 1-2   Hardware and software components for web applications

How static web pages work

Many of the web pages on the Internet are *static web pages*. Static pages are HTML documents that are the same each time they're viewed. In other words, they don't change in response to user input.

Figure 1-3 shows how a web server handles static web pages. The process begins when a user at a web browser requests a web page. This can occur when the user enters a web address, called a *URL* (*Uniform Resource Locator*), into the browser's address box or when the user clicks a link that leads to another page. In either case, the web browser uses HTTP to send an *HTTP request* to the web server. The HTTP request includes information such as the name and address of the web page being requested, the address of the browser making the request, and the address of the web server that will process the request.

When the web server receives an HTTP request from a browser, the server retrieves the requested HTML file from disk and sends the file back to the browser in the form of an *HTTP response*. The HTTP response includes the HTML document that the user requested along with the address of the browser and the web server.

When the browser receives the HTTP response, it formats and displays the HTML document. Then, the user can view the content. If the user requests another page, either by clicking a link or typing another web address in the browser's address box, the process begins again.

How a web server processes static web pages

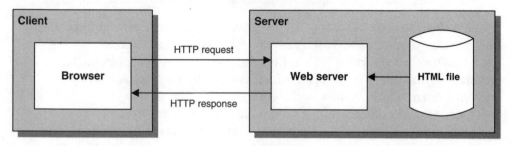

Description

- A *static web page* is an HTML document that is the same each time it's viewed. In other words, a static web page doesn't change in response to user input. Everyone who views a static web page sees exactly the same content.

- Static web pages are usually simple HTML files that are stored on the web server. When a browser requests a static web page, the web server simply retrieves the file from disk and sends it back to the browser. Static web pages usually have a file extension of .htm or .html.

- A web browser requests a page from a web server by sending the server an HTTP message known as an *HTTP request*. The HTTP request includes, among other things, the name of the HTML file being requested and the Internet address of both the browser and the web server.

- A user working with a browser can initiate an HTTP request in several ways. One way is to type the address of a web page, called a *URL*, or *Uniform Resource Locator*, into the browser's address area and then press the Enter key. Another way is to click a link that refers to a web page.

- A web server replies to an HTTP request by sending a message known as an *HTTP response* back to the browser. The HTTP response contains the addresses of the browser and the server as well as the HTML document that's being returned.

Figure 1-3   How static web pages work

How dynamic web pages work

A web application consists of one or more web pages that are not static, but that can change in some way each time the page is displayed. Instead of being stored on disk in the form of HTML files, the pages of a web application are generated dynamically by the application. As a result, the generated web pages are often referred to as *dynamic web pages*.

One of the key differences between static web pages and dynamic web pages is that dynamic web pages are defined by web forms. As I mentioned earlier, a web form contains a collection of *web controls*, such as labels, text boxes, and buttons. Users work with these controls to interact with the application.

Figure 1-4 shows the basic processing for a web application. Typically, the user enters information into one or more form controls and then clicks on a button. That causes the browser to send an HTTP request to the server that contains the address of the web page being requested, along with the information the user entered into the form. When the web server receives this request, it determines that it's a request for a web application rather than for a static web page. As a result, the web server passes the request on to an *application server* for processing. The application server, in turn, manages the execution of the web application.

To determine if the request is for a static page or a dynamic page generated by a web application, the web server looks up the extension of the requested page in a list of *application mappings*. These mappings indicate what program a file extension is associated with. For example, a static web page typically has an extension of htm or html. In contrast, a dynamic page created by an ASP.NET application has an extension of aspx. As a result, when the web server receives an HTTP request for an aspx file, the server knows to pass this request along to ASP.NET.

When the application is executed, it processes the information the user entered and generates an HTML document. The actual content of the HTML document depends on the application. If the application displays data from a database, for example, it queries the database to obtain the requested information. Then, it generates a page with that information, which is returned by the application server to the web server. The web server, in turn, sends the page back to the browser in the form of an HTTP response, and the browser displays the page. This entire process that begins with the browser requesting a web page and ends with the page being sent back to the client is called a *round trip*.

How a web server processes dynamic pages

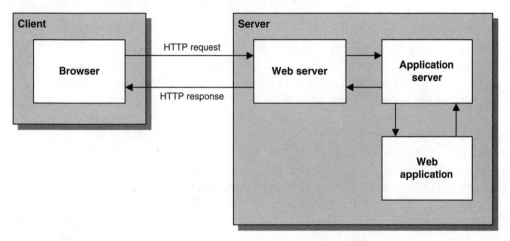

Description

- A *dynamic web page* is an HTML document that's generated by a web application. Often, the web page changes according to information that's sent to the web application by the web browser.

- When a web server receives a request for a dynamic web page, the server passes the request to an *application server*. Then, the application server executes the web application, which generates an HTML document. Next, the document is returned to the application server, which passes it back to the web server. The web server, in turn, sends the document back to the browser.

- The browser doesn't know or care whether the HTML was retrieved from an HTML file or generated by a web application. Either way, the browser simply displays the HTML that was returned as a result of the request.

- After the page is displayed, the user can interact with it using the controls it contains. Some of those controls let the user *post* the page back to the server, in which case it's processed again using the data the user entered.

- To determine what application server is used to process a request, the web server looks up the extension of the requested file in a list of *application mappings*. Each application mapping specifies the name of the application that should be run to process files with that extension. If the file extension is aspx, the request is passed on to ASP.NET for processing.

- If the file extension isn't found in the list of application mappings, the requested file is simply returned to the browser without any additional processing.

- The process that begins with the user requesting a web page and ends with the server sending a response back to the client is called a *round trip*.

- After a web application generates an HTML document, it ends. Then, unless the data the application contains is specifically saved, that data is lost.

Figure 1-4   How dynamic web pages work

The importance of state in web applications

Although it wasn't apparent in the previous figure, after an application generates a web page, the application ends. That means that the current status of any data maintained by the application, such as variables or control properties, is lost. In other words, HTTP doesn't maintain the *state* of the application. This is illustrated in figure 1-5.

Here, you can see that a browser on a client requests a page from a web server. After the server processes the request and returns the page to the browser, the application that created the page terminates. Then, if the browser makes additional requests, the server has no way to associate the browser with its previous requests. Because of that, HTTP is known as a *stateless protocol*.

Although HTTP doesn't maintain state, ASP.NET provides several ways to do that. Three of the most common techniques for maintaining state are listed in this figure. First, you can use *view state* to maintain the values of form control properties. For example, you can use it to preserve the Text property of label controls that change as the program executes or to maintain a list of items in a list box or a drop-down list. Because ASP.NET implements view state by default, you don't need to write any special code to use it.

You can also use *session state* to maintain data between executions of an application. When a user starts a session, ASP.NET creates a *session state object* that's sent back and forth between the server and the browser. This object contains a session ID that the server can use to identify the session. In addition, you can add your own items to this object so that their previous values are available each time the program is executed.

Application state is an ASP.NET feature that lets you save state information so it can be shared by all the users of an application. For example, you can use application state to maintain global counters or to maintain a list of the users who are currently logged on to the application.

Why state is difficult to track in web applications

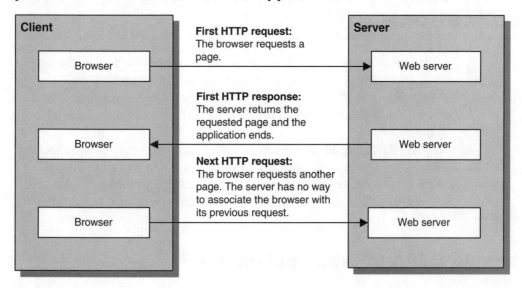

Concepts

- *State* refers to the current status of the properties, variables, and other data maintained by an application for a single user. The application must maintain a separate state for each user currently accessing the application.

- HTTP is a *stateless protocol*. That means that it doesn't keep track of state between round trips. Once a browser makes a request and receives a response, the application terminates and its state is lost.

Three features provided by ASP.NET for maintaining state

- ASP.NET uses *view state* to maintain the value of form control properties that the application changes between executions of the application. View state is implemented by default, so no special coding is required.

- When a user starts a new session, ASP.NET creates a *session state object* that contains a session ID. This ID is passed from the server to the browser and back to the server so that the server can associate the browser with an existing session. To maintain *session state*, you can add program values to the session state object. Then, those values are maintained between executions of the application.

- When an application begins, ASP.NET creates an *application state object*. To maintain *application state*, you can add program values to the application state object. These values are available to all users of the application and are maintained until the application ends.

Figure 1-5   The importance of state in web applications

An introduction to ASP.NET web applications

As you have learned, a web application consists of one or more web forms. Each web form defines a web page that can be displayed in a web browser. In the topics that follow, you'll review a simple web application that consists of two web forms. You'll also learn about the source files that make up a VB.NET web application.

As you study this application, please remember that this is only an introduction to ASP.NET web programming. It is intended to give you a general idea of how ASP.NET programming works. Since all of the ASP.NET coding will be explained in detail in the chapters that follow, you're aren't expected to learn it now.

A simple ASP.NET web application

Figure 1-6 presents two pages of a simple Costume Store application that was developed in Visual Basic. This is a simplified version of the Halloween Store application you saw earlier in this chapter. Throughout this book, I'll build on this application by adding the features you learn in each chapter.

When this application starts, the Costume page shown at the top of this figure is displayed. To order a costume, the user selects the costume from the drop-down list. Then, the price for that costume is displayed. Next, the user enters a quantity in the text box that's provided and clicks the Order Costume button. The application responds by displaying a confirmation message as shown in the Confirmation page in this figure. Notice that this message includes information about the item that was ordered and when it will be shipped. To do that, the application must pass information from the first page to the second page. As you'll see in the code for this application, that's accomplished by storing the order information in session state. From the Confirmation page, the user can click the Return to Order Page button to order another costume or end the application by closing the browser window.

Obviously, this application is much simpler than an actual production application. For example, a production application would let the user order more than one costume, and it would let the user edit and confirm the order before processing it. In addition, it would require the user to enter additional information, such as address, phone number, e-mail address, and credit card number.

Even though this application has been simplified, it illustrates the basic elements of ASP.NET programming. In particular, it illustrates a web form with several web controls, and it shows how a web application can respond to an event such as the user selecting an item from a drop-down list or clicking on a button control. You'll see the code that implements these elements in the topics that follow.

The Costume page after an order is entered

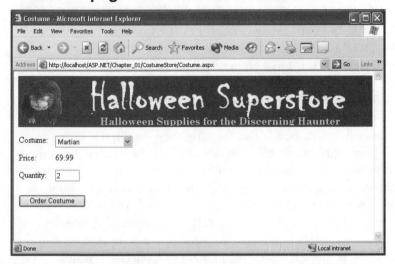

The Confirmation page for the order

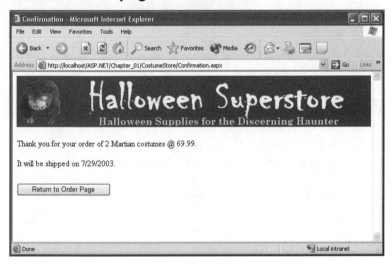

Description

- This application accepts a costume order from the user. To enter an order, the user selects a costume from the drop-down list on the Costume page, enters a quantity, and clicks on the Order Costume button. Then, the order is written to a file and the Confirmation page is displayed.

- The costume information is retrieved from a file and stored in a sorted list. The sorted list is used to load the drop-down list. Then, when the user selects a costume, the price of that costume is retrieved from the sorted list and displayed on the form.

- This application uses view state to maintain the items in the drop-down list when the user posts the page to the server by selecting a costume. It uses session state to store the costume and order data between executions of the application.

Figure 1-6   A simple ASP.NET web application

The aspx code for the web forms

Figure 1-7 presents the code in the aspx files for the Costume and Confirmation forms. Note that all of this code was generated by Visual Studio as I designed the form. Because of that, I'll just point out the most important features of this code here. Then, you can learn more about coding HTML in chapter 6.

The first line of code for each page is a Page directive that's generated automatically by Visual Studio. This directive specifies four *attributes*, two of which associate the aspx file with the file that contains the Visual Basic code for the form. The Codebehind attribute specifies the name of the file that contains the Visual Basic code. Visual Studio uses this option to associate the web page with this file. The Inherits attribute specifies the name of the class within the Visual Basic file that the web page inherits when the page is executed. You'll learn more about this file and the other files that make up an ASP.NET application later in this chapter.

The actual content of the page is contained in the document body, which begins with the <body> *tag* and ends with the </body> tag. Within the document body is a web form, which begins with a <form> tag and ends with a </form> tag. Notice that the <form> tag includes a runat attribute that's assigned a value of "server." That indicates that the form will be processed on the server by ASP.NET. A <form> tag with this attribute is required for all ASP.NET web pages.

The tags within the form that begin with <asp:> define the web controls that appear on the page. For example, the <asp:label> tags define label controls, the <asp:textbox> tags define text box controls, and the <asp:button> tags define button controls. Notice that the tags for these controls include the runat attribute with a value of "server." Once again, this attribute indicates that the control will be processed on the server by ASP.NET. Part of this processing includes *rendering* the control. That means that the control is converted to standard HTML so it can be displayed by a browser.

The aspx code for the Costume form

```
<%@ Page Language="vb" AutoEventWireup="false" Codebehind="Costume.aspx.vb"
Inherits="CostumeStore.Costume"%>
<!DOCTYPE HTML PUBLIC "-//W3C//DTD HTML 4.0 Transitional//EN">
<HTML>
    <HEAD>
        <title>Costume</title>
        <meta name="GENERATOR" content="Microsoft Visual Studio .NET 7.1">
        <meta name="CODE_LANGUAGE" content="Visual Basic .NET 7.1">
        <meta name="vs_defaultClientScript" content="JavaScript">
        <meta name="vs_targetSchema"
            content="http://schemas.microsoft.com/intellisense/ie5">
    </HEAD>
    <body MS_POSITIONING="GridLayout">
        <form id="Form1" method="post" runat="server">
            <asp:image id="Image1" style="Z-INDEX: 107; LEFT: 9px;
                POSITION: absolute; TOP: 9px" runat="server"
                ImageUrl="banner.jpg"></asp:image>
            <asp:label id="Label1" style="Z-INDEX: 101; LEFT: 10px;
                POSITION: absolute; TOP: 122px" runat="server">
                Costume:</asp:label>
            <asp:dropdownlist id="ddlCostumes" style="Z-INDEX: 102;
                LEFT: 82px; POSITION: absolute; TOP: 124px"
                runat="server" Width="152px" AutoPostBack="True">
                </asp:dropdownlist>
            <asp:label id="Label2" style="Z-INDEX: 109; LEFT: 10px;
                POSITION: absolute; TOP: 156px" runat="server">
                Price:</asp:label>
            <asp:label id="lblPrice" style="Z-INDEX: 110; LEFT: 82px;
                POSITION: absolute; TOP: 156px" runat="server"></asp:label>
            <asp:label id="Label3" style="Z-INDEX: 105; LEFT: 10px;
                POSITION: absolute; TOP: 189px" runat="server">
                Quantity:</asp:label>
            <asp:textbox id="txtQuantity" style="Z-INDEX: 104;
                LEFT: 82px; POSITION: absolute; TOP: 189px"
                runat="server" Width="48px"></asp:textbox>
            <asp:requiredfieldvalidator id="RequiredFieldValidator2"
                style="Z-INDEX: 106; LEFT: 134px; POSITION: absolute;
                TOP: 192px" runat="server"
                ErrorMessage="You must enter a quantity."
                ControlToValidate="txtQuantity">
                </asp:requiredfieldvalidator>
            <asp:comparevalidator id="CompareValidator1" style="Z-INDEX: 108;
                LEFT: 299px; POSITION: absolute; TOP: 192px" runat="server"
                ErrorMessage="Quantity must be greater than 0."
                ControlToValidate="txtQuantity" ValueToCompare="0"
                Type="Integer" Operator="GreaterThan"></asp:comparevalidator>
            <asp:button id="btnOrder" style="Z-INDEX: 103; LEFT: 10px;
                POSITION: absolute; TOP: 237px" runat="server"
                Text="Order Costume"></asp:button>
        </form>
    </body>
</HTML>
```

Figure 1-7   The aspx code for the web forms (part 1 of 2)

Although this has been a quick introduction to the aspx code for a web form, you should begin to see how this code defines a web page. In particular, you should see how the <asp:> tags correspond to the controls that are displayed on the web page. If you don't understand all of this code, however, don't worry. Until you start developing more complicated forms, you can let Visual Studio generate the required code for you.

The aspx code for the Confirmation form

```
<%@ Page Language="vb" AutoEventWireup="false"
Codebehind="Confirmation.aspx.vb" Inherits="CostumeStore.Confirmation"%>
<!DOCTYPE HTML PUBLIC "-//W3C//DTD HTML 4.0 Transitional//EN">
<HTML>
    <HEAD>
        <title>Confirmation</title>
        <meta name="GENERATOR" content="Microsoft Visual Studio .NET 7.1">
        <meta name="CODE_LANGUAGE" content="Visual Basic .NET 7.1">
        <meta name="vs_defaultClientScript" content="JavaScript">
        <meta name="vs_targetSchema"
              content="http://schemas.microsoft.com/intellisense/ie5">
    </HEAD>
    <body MS_POSITIONING="GridLayout">
        <form id="Form1" method="post" runat="server">
            <asp:Image id="Image1" style="Z-INDEX: 105; LEFT: 8px;
                POSITION: absolute; TOP: 8px" runat="server"
                ImageUrl="banner.jpg"></asp:Image>
            <asp:Label id="lblCostume" style="Z-INDEX: 102; LEFT: 9px;
                POSITION: absolute; TOP: 128px"
                runat="server"></asp:Label>
            <asp:button id="btnReturn" style="Z-INDEX: 101; LEFT: 9px;
                POSITION: absolute; TOP: 214px" runat="server"
                Text="Return to Order Page"></asp:button>
        </form>
    </body>
</HTML>
```

Description

- An aspx file defines an HTML document. The first line of the HTML document is a Page directive that specifies the ASP.NET options.

- The Codebehind option names the file that contains the Visual Basic code for the page. This option is used by Visual Studio to associate the page with the class that contains the Visual Basic code for the page.

- The Inherits option names the page class that the page inherits at runtime. This class is part of the DLL file that's created when you compile the project. See figure 1-10 for details.

- The rest of the aspx file contains the HTML that determines how the page will appear in the browser. The HTML can include standard HTML tags and special ASP.NET tags. The ASP.NET tags begin with *asp:* and define ASP.NET Web Server controls.

- The Web Server controls are implemented by classes that are defined by the .NET Framework. ASP.NET *renders* these controls to standard HTML so the controls can be displayed in the browser.

- The runat="server" attribute that appears in the form and asp tags indicates that the form and its controls are to be processed at the server by ASP.NET.

Figure 1-7   The aspx code for the web forms (part 2 of 2)

The Visual Basic code for the web forms

Figure 1-8 presents the Visual Basic code for the Costume and Confirmation forms. This code is stored in files called *code-behind files*. These files contain the code that's executed in response to the user interacting with the forms. Notice that I've highlighted the code that's specific to ASP.NET. All of the other code is standard Visual Basic code that you should be able to understand. As a result, the paragraphs that follow focus on the ASP.NET code.

The first line of code for each web form is a class statement that names the class. In this case, the classes are given the same names as the forms they're associated with: Costume and Confirmation. The second line of code for each form indicates that the form inherits the System.Web.UI.Page class. This class provides all of the basic functionality of ASP.NET pages. As a result, all ASP.NET pages must inherit this class to operate properly.

Each time the page is requested, ASP.NET initializes it and raises the Load event. The procedure that responds to this event starts by calling the GetCostumes procedure to load the costumes into the sorted list. However, because the costumes are stored in session state by this application, the GetCostumes procedure starts by checking whether the costumes are already stored in session state. Because each item in session state is stored as an object, it does that by testing whether the Costumes object is equal to Nothing. If it is, the GetCostumes method of the OrderIO class is executed to get the costumes, and the costumes are saved in the Costumes object of session state. But if the Costumes object already exists, it's simply assigned to the Costumes variable.

To refer to the session state object, you use the Session property of the page. However, because the page is the default object within a code-behind file, you don't have to refer to the page explicitly. In the code-behind files in this figure, you can see references to both the Order object and the Costumes object that are stored in the session state object. As a result, those objects are passed from one page to another as the application is executed.

After it loads the sorted list of costumes, the Load procedure checks if the page is being loaded for the first time or if it's being *posted* back to the server from the client. To do that, it uses the IsPostBack property of the page. If this property is false, it means that the page is being loaded for the first time. In that case, the Load procedure calls the LoadCostumeDropDownList procedure, which loads the drop-down list with the values in the sorted list. After that, the Load procedure sets the Text property of the Price label to the price of the costume that's selected in the drop-down list. Note that the procedure for loading the drop-down list only needs to be called the first time the page is requested because the list is stored in view state. As a result, it is restored automatically for subsequent requests of the page.

The last two procedures for the Costume form respond to user actions. If the user selects a different costume from the drop-down list, the procedure for the SelectedIndexChanged event gets the price for the selected costume and assigns it to the Text property of the Price label. If the user clicks the Order Costume button, the code in its Click event procedure processes the order. This code

The Visual Basic code for the Costume form

```
Public Class Costume
    Inherits System.Web.UI.Page

    Dim Costumes As SortedList()

    Private Sub Page_Load(ByVal sender As System.Object, _
            ByVal e As System.EventArgs) Handles MyBase.Load
        'Put user code to initialize the page here
        Me.GetCostumes()
        If Not IsPostBack Then
            Me.LoadCostumeDropDownList()
            lblPrice.Text = Costumes.GetByIndex(ddlCostumes.SelectedIndex)
        End If
    End Sub

    Private Sub GetCostumes()
        If Session("Costumes") Is Nothing Then
            Costumes = OrderIO.GetCostumes()
            Session("Costumes") = Costumes
        Else
            Costumes = Session("Costumes")
        End If
    End Sub

    Private Sub LoadCostumeDropDownList()
        Dim Costume As DictionaryEntry
        For Each Costume In Costumes
            ddlCostumes.Items.Add(Costume.Key)
        Next
    End Sub

    Private Sub ddlCostumes_SelectedIndexChanged _
            (ByVal sender As System.Object, ByVal e As System.EventArgs) _
            Handles ddlCostumes.SelectedIndexChanged
        lblPrice.Text = Costumes.GetByIndex(ddlCostumes.SelectedIndex)
    End Sub

    Private Sub btnOrder_Click(ByVal sender As System.Object, _
            ByVal e As System.EventArgs) Handles btnOrder.Click
        Dim Order As New Order
        Order.Product = ddlCostumes.SelectedItem.Text
        Order.Quantity = txtQuantity.Text
        Order.UnitPrice = lblPrice.Text
        Session("Order") = Order
        OrderIO.WriteOrder(Order)
        Response.Redirect("Confirmation.aspx")
    End Sub

End Class
```

Figure 1-8   The Visual Basic code for the web forms (part 1 of 2)

creates an Order object from the Order class; sets the Product, Quantity, and UnitPrice properties of the Order object using the data in the controls on the form; saves the Order object in session state; and executes the WriteOrder method of the OrderIO class to write data in the Order object to a text file.

After the order has been processed, the last line in the Click event procedure uses the Redirect method of the HttpResponse object to display the Confirmation form. To refer to the HttpResponse object, you use the Response property of the page. But here again, the page is the default object within a code-behind file so you don't have to refer to it explicitly.

In the code for the Confirmation form, you can see the same type of ASP.NET code in use. Here again, the form inherits the System.Web.UI.Page class, which provides all of the basic functionality for the page. Then, in the Load procedure, the Order object that's stored in session state is assigned to a new Order variable. And in the Click event procedure for the Return button, the application is redirected to the Costume page.

* * *

I hope this example has given you some insight into the way code-behind files are coded. Keep in mind, though, that this is just an introduction to the ASP.NET code. As a result, all of the ASP.NET code that has been introduced here will be explained in detail in the next two chapters.

On the other hand, this book does assume that you already have a solid background in Visual Basic .NET coding. As a result, it doesn't try to teach common Visual Basic coding features or techniques like the use of the sorted list for the costumes in this application. So, if you have trouble understanding any of the Visual Basic code that is used by the examples in this book, we recommend that you get a copy of *Murach's Beginning Visual Basic .NET*. It not only shows you how to use all of the Visual Basic features that we use in this book, but it is also an excellent reference book.

The Visual Basic code for the Confirmation form

```
Public Class Confirmation
    Inherits System.Web.UI.Page

    Private Sub Page_Load(ByVal sender As System.Object, _
            ByVal e As System.EventArgs) Handles MyBase.Load
        'Put user code to initialize the page here
        Dim Order As Order
        Order = Session("Order")
        lblConfirm.Text = "Thank you for your order of " _
                        & Order.Quantity & " " & Order.Product _
                        & " costume" & IIf(Order.Quantity > 1, "s", "") _
                        & " @ " & Order.UnitPrice & ".<br><br>" _
                        & "It will be shipped on " & Now().Date.AddDays(1) _
                        & "."
    End Sub

    Private Sub btnReturn_Click(ByVal sender As System.Object, _
            ByVal e As System.EventArgs) Handles btnReturn.Click
        Response.Redirect("Costume.aspx")
    End Sub

End Class
```

Description

- The Visual Basic code for a form is stored in a file called a *code-behind file*. This code includes event procedures that are called by ASP.NET when the user interacts with the controls on the page.

- Each time a page is executed, ASP.NET executes the procedure for the Load event of the form. Within this event procedure, you can test the IsPostBack property of the page to determine if the page is being loaded for the first time or if it's being posted back to the server.

- You can use the Session property of the page to save items in and retrieve items from the session state object.

- You can use the Redirect method of the HttpResponse object that's associated with the page to display a form other than the one that's currently displayed. To refer to this object, you use the Response property of the page.

- A web form inherits the System.Web.UI.Page class defined by the .NET Framework. This class defines the basic functionality for all web pages.

Note

- Since the page is the default object within a code-behind file, you don't need to refer to it explicitly to use its properties and methods.

Figure 1-8   The Visual Basic code for the web forms (part 2 of 2)

The Visual Basic code for the other classes

Besides form classes, an ASP.NET application can include other classes like business and data access classes. For example, the Costume Store application uses the two classes shown in figure 1-9. The first class, Order, defines four public variables that hold the data for an order. Each time the user orders a costume, the application creates an object from this class and stores it in session state. Then, the Confirmation form uses the data in this object to format the confirmation message it displays.

In contrast, the OrderIO class defines two shared methods. The first method, GetCostumes, gets the name and price for each costume from a binary file and stores this data in a sorted list. This sorted list is then returned to the Costume form where it is used to load the drop-down list. The second method, WriteOrder, writes the information for an order to a text file. To get the order information, it receives an Order object that's passed to it from the Costume form.

If you haven't worked with binary or text files before, you may not understand the code in these two procedures. Then, you have another reason for getting a copy of *Murach's Beginning Visual Basic .NET*, which has a full chapter on how to use these types of files.

Keep in mind, though, that you can use a shared method without understanding its code. To use one, you just need to know how to call the method and pass the required parameters to it. To use the WriteOrder method, for example, the Click event procedure in the Costume form uses this code:

```
OrderIO.WriteOrder(Order)
```

This passes an object named Order to the WriteOrder method of the OrderIO class. As long as you understand this syntax, you can master the ASP.NET coding that's presented in this book without understanding the code for the methods in the business and I/O classes. Then, you can learn the details of how those methods work when you have some spare time.

The Visual Basic code for the Order class

```
Public Class Order
    Public Name As String
    Public Product As String
    Public Quantity As String
    Public UnitPrice As Decimal
End Class
```

The Visual Basic code for the OrderIO class

```
Imports System.IO
Public Class OrderIO

    Public Shared Function GetCostumes() As SortedList
        Dim Costumes As New SortedList()
        Dim CostumeStream As New FileStream _
            ("c:\MurachData\Costumes.dat", FileMode.Open, FileAccess.Read)
        Dim CostumeReader As New BinaryReader(CostumeStream)
        Dim sName As String
        Dim dPrice As Decimal
        Do Until CostumeReader.PeekChar = -1
            sName = CostumeReader.ReadString
            dPrice = CostumeReader.ReadDecimal
            Costumes.Add(sName, dPrice)
        Loop
        CostumeReader.Close()
        Return Costumes
    End Function

    Public Shared Sub WriteOrder(ByVal Order As Order)
        Dim OrderStream As New FileStream _
            ("c:\MurachData\Orders.txt", FileMode.Append, FileAccess.Write)
        Dim OrderWriter As New StreamWriter(OrderStream)
        Dim sOrder As String
        sOrder = ControlChars.Quote & Order.Name & ControlChars.Quote & ","
        sOrder &= ControlChars.Quote & Order.Product & ControlChars.Quote & ","
        sOrder &= Order.Quantity & ","
        sOrder &= Order.UnitPrice
        OrderWriter.WriteLine(sOrder)
        OrderWriter.Close()
    End Sub

End Class
```

Description

- An ASP.NET application may include other Visual Basic classes, such as business or data access classes. Business classes typically represent business entities, like orders, or implement business rules. Data access classes work directly with files or databases.

Figure 1-9   The Visual Basic code for the Order and OrderIO classes

How the files of an ASP.NET application are stored and compiled

The first diagram in figure 1-10 shows the source files that make up an ASP.NET application. You saw all of these files for the Costume Store application I just presented. The aspx files contain the HTML code that defines the pages. The code-behind files contain the Visual Basic code that provides the forms' functionality. These files have a file extension of .aspx.vb. Any other Visual Basic classes used by the application are stored in files with the extension .vb.

Before I go on, you should realize that it isn't necessary to store the HTML and Visual Basic code in separate files. Instead, ASP.NET lets you combine the HTML and Visual Basic code into a single aspx file. However, storing the HTML and Visual Basic code in separate files can simplify application development because it lets you separate the presentation elements for a page from its logic elements. In fact, it's not uncommon to have HTML designers work on the aspx files while Visual Basic programmers work on the corresponding code-behind files.

When you build a web application, all the files that contain Visual Basic code are compiled into a single assembly. That assembly is stored in a DLL file on the web server. The aspx files, however, are not compiled when the application is built. Instead, they're stored in their original format on the web server.

The second diagram in this figure illustrates what happens when a user requests a page of a web application. First, ASP.NET creates a class file from the aspx file for the page. Then, it compiles that class into a DLL. Because the class inherits from the code-behind file for the form, the code for the form that's included in the Visual Basic assembly is compiled along with the page class. At that point, the page is ready for execution.

How the files of an ASP.NET application are stored

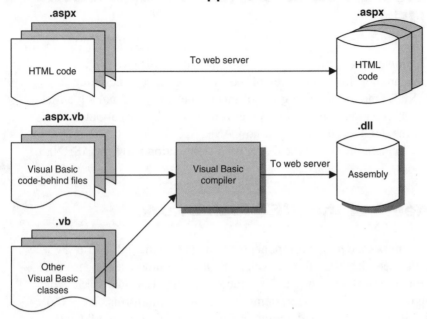

How an ASP.NET application is compiled when it's executed

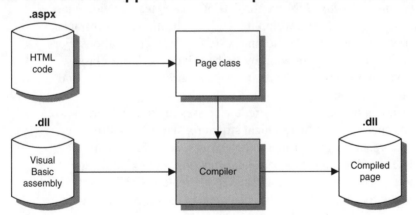

Description

- When you build an ASP.NET application, the Visual Basic .NET compiler compiles the files that contain Visual Basic code to create an assembly. The assembly is stored in a DLL file on the web server.

- The aspx files that contain the HTML code are not compiled along with the Visual Basic code. Instead, those files are stored in their original format on the web server.

- When the user requests an ASP.NET page, ASP.NET creates a class file from the aspx file for the page. Then, it compiles that class file and the code it inherits from the Visual Basic assembly into a single assembly that's stored on disk in a DLL file. ASP.NET then executes the DLL to generate the page.

Figure 1-10 How the files of an ASP.NET application are stored and compiled

An introduction to the .NET Framework and ASP.NET

The *.NET Framework* defines the environment that you use to execute applications that are developed with any of the .NET languages, including Visual Basic .NET. One of the main goals of this framework is to make it easier to develop web applications. In the topics that follow, you'll learn about the components of the .NET Framework and how ASP.NET fits into it. You'll also learn about the architecture of a typical ASP.NET application and how ASP.NET applications work.

The components of the .NET Framework

Figure 1-11 shows the major components that make up the .NET Framework. As you can see, the .NET Framework provides a common set of services that application programs written in a .NET language such as Visual Basic .NET can use to run on various operating systems and hardware platforms. The .NET Framework is divided into two main components: the .NET Framework Class Library and the Common Language Runtime.

The *.NET Framework Class Library* consists of classes that provide many of the functions that you need for developing .NET applications. For instance, the ASP.NET classes are used for developing ASP.NET web applications. For standard Windows applications, you work with the Windows Forms classes. Other classes let you work with databases, manage security, access files, and perform many other functions.

Although it's not apparent in this figure, the classes in the .NET Framework Class Library are organized in a hierarchical structure. Within this structure, related classes are organized into groups called *namespaces*. Each namespace contains the classes used to support a particular function. For example, the System.Web namespace contains the classes used to create ASP.NET web applications, and the System.Data namespace contains the classes used to access data.

The *Common Language Runtime*, or *CLR*, provides the services that are needed for executing any application that's developed with one of the .NET languages. This is possible because all of the .NET languages compile to a common *Intermediate Language*. The CLR also provides the *Common Type System* that defines the data types that are used by all the .NET languages. That way, you can use the same data types regardless of what .NET language you're using to develop your application. Unlike Windows applications, though, all of the forms in a web application must be developed using the same language.

To run an ASP.NET application, the web server must have the .NET Framework installed. However, the client computers that access the web server do not need the .NET Framework. Instead, the client computers can run any client operating system with a modern web browser.

The .NET Framework

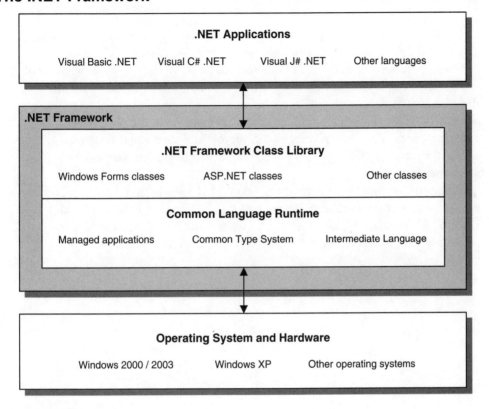

Description

- .NET applications work by using services of the *.NET Framework*. The .NET Framework, in turn, accesses the operating system and computer hardware.

- The .NET Framework consists of two main components: the .NET Framework Class Library and the Common Language Runtime.

- The *.NET Framework Class Library* provides pre-written code in the form of classes that are available to all of the .NET programming languages. These classes are organized into groups called *namespaces*. The classes that support ASP.NET web programs are stored in the System.Web namespace.

- The *Common Language Runtime*, or *CLR*, is the foundation of the .NET Framework. It manages the execution of .NET programs by coordinating essential functions such as memory management, code execution, security, and other services. Because .NET applications are managed by the CLR, they are called *managed applications*.

- The *Common Type System* is a component of the CLR that ensures that all .NET applications use the same basic data types regardless of what programming languages are used to develop the applications.

- All .NET programs are compiled into *Microsoft Intermediate Language* (*MSIL*) or just *Intermediate Language* (*IL*), which is stored on disk in an assembly. This assembly is then run by the CLR.

Figure 1-11   The components of the .NET Framework

How ASP.NET applications work

Earlier in this chapter, you learned how web applications work in general. Now, figure 1-12 presents a more detailed view of how ASP.NET applications work. When IIS first receives an HTTP request for an ASP.NET page, the web server passes the request on to ASP.NET. ASP.NET then compiles the page into a DLL file that includes the class files that support the page.

Next, ASP.NET executes the DLL to create an instance of the page class. The resulting page object then processes the appropriate events and generates the HTML for the page. Finally, the HTML is returned to IIS and sent back to the browser as an HTTP response.

Note that the assembly that contains the compiled page is stored on disk and remains on disk after it's executed. Because of that, the page is only compiled the first time it's requested. Each time it's requested after that, the assembly is retrieved from disk and executed.

The components of an ASP.NET web application

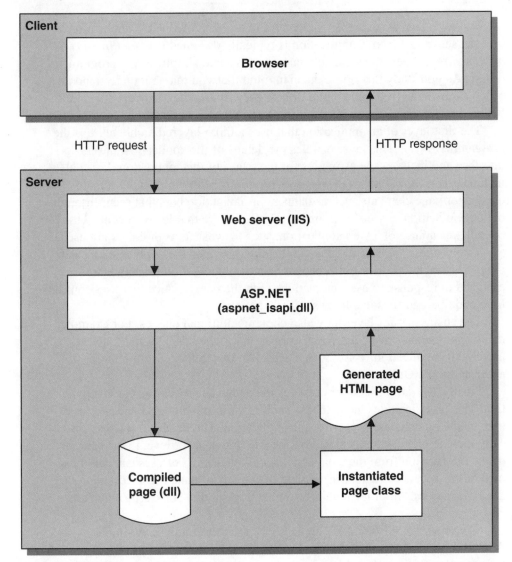

Description

- When IIS receives an HTTP request for an ASP.NET page, it forwards the request to ASP.NET. ASP.NET then creates and executes a compiled page that combines the page class with the compiled Visual Basic code.

- When the compiled page is executed, an instance of the ASP.NET page class is generated. Then, ASP.NET raises the appropriate events, which are processed by the event handlers in the page. Finally, the page generates the HTML that's passed back to IIS.

- The ASP.NET page is compiled only the first time it's requested. After that, the page is run directly from the DLL file.

Figure 1-12   How ASP.NET applications work

The architecture of a typical ASP.NET application

Figure 1-13 illustrates the architecture of a typical ASP.NET application. As you can see, an ASP.NET application is typically designed using a *three-layered architecture* that separates the software elements and simplifies the program design. As you study this figure, keep in mind that you may not understand all of the elements in this architecture or how they fit together. However, it should begin to make sense as you learn to develop ASP.NET applications of your own.

The first layer of an application that uses a three-layered architecture is the *presentation layer*. This layer handles the details of the application's user interface and includes the aspx files for the pages of the application. It can also include *user controls* and *style sheets*. User controls let you create separate classes for page elements such as banners or navigation bars that recur throughout an application. Style sheets are an HTML feature that lets you control the overall appearance of a web application, such as what fonts or colors are used.

The *business rules layer* of an application provides the application's basic logic. That includes the event procedures in the code-behind files that are executed in response to user interactions with the page. Notice that user controls have code-behind files just like aspx files do.

The business rules layer may also contain additional classes. For example, many applications have classes that correspond to the basic business objects used by the application. You saw one class like this in the Costume Store application: the Order class.

Finally, the *database layer* provides the database processing for an application. This layer includes the database itself and often includes database classes that handle all database access for the application. The database classes typically include methods that connect to the database and retrieve, insert, add, or delete information from the database. Then, the business classes can call these methods to access the database, leaving the details of database access to the database classes. All of the database applications in this book use a database class.

Of course, not all ASP.NET applications are this complex. A simple ASP.NET application may consist of a single aspx file that defines the layout of a page and a single code-behind file that contains the Visual Basic code for the page. In addition, not all applications use a database. Some, like the one shown in this chapter, use files. In that case, the database layer consists of the files and the classes that provide access to those files.

The architecture of a typical ASP.NET web application

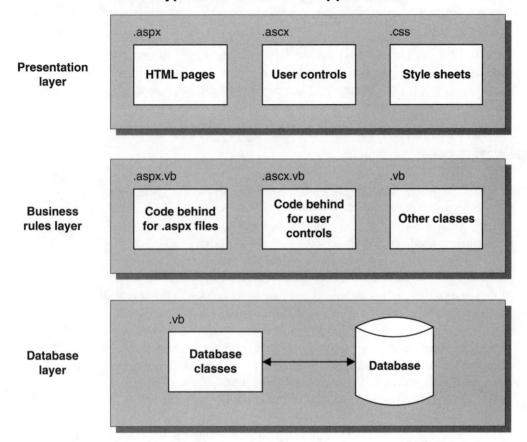

Description

- The *presentation layer* for a typical ASP.NET application consists of HTML pages (.aspx files) that define the layout of each web page; user controls (.ascx files) that define page elements such as banners, navigation menus, and data entry forms; and style sheets (.css files) that control the overall appearance of the pages.

- The *business rules layer* for a typical ASP.NET application consists of Visual Basic class files that provide the code-behind functions for each page (.aspx.vb) and user control (.ascx.vb). These classes provide the code necessary to implement the application's processing requirements. This layer can also include other classes (.vb), such as classes that represent business entities or that implement business rules.

- The *database layer* consists of the database itself (such as Microsoft SQL Server) as well as classes that work directly with the database.

Figure 1-13   The architecture of a typical ASP.NET application

ASP.NET application development

The topics that follow introduce you to ASP.NET application development. First, you'll learn about three possible development environments. Then, you'll learn about the system requirements for developing ASP.NET applications. Finally, you'll learn how to use URLs to access an ASP.NET application.

Three environments for developing ASP.NET applications

Figure 1-14 shows three possible ways to set up a development environment for coding and testing ASP.NET applications. As you'll see, each setup has its advantages and disadvantages. The environment you choose will depend on your development needs and on the resources that are available to you.

The simplest development environment is a standalone environment. In this environment, a single computer serves as both the client and the server. Because of that, it must run an operating system that supports ASP.NET application development, and it must have the .NET Framework and Visual Studio .NET installed. In addition, it must have IIS installed to provide for web server functions. If the applications will access data in a database, it must also have a DBMS installed. Often, the DBMS that's used on a standalone system is a scaled-back version of SQL Server called *MSDE* (*Microsoft SQL Server Desktop Engine*). MSDE comes with Visual Studio 2002 and can be downloaded from Microsoft's web site for use with Visual Studio 2003.

A standalone environment is ideal if you're working alone on an application and you don't have an available server computer. However, you might also use this environment if two or more programmers are working on the same application. In that case, the programmers each work in a standalone environment, but master copies of the source files for the application are typically stored on a server and *source control software* is used to coordinate access to the master files. Note that the files don't need to be stored on a web server. They simply need to be stored on a server that's accessible over a network.

The second development environment shown in this figure works with separate client and server computers that are connected via a *LAN (local area network)*. Here, the client computer has Windows, the .NET Framework, and Visual Studio .NET installed, while the server runs Windows 2000 Server with the .NET Framework and IIS. In addition, it uses SQL Server to handle database access. This environment is ideal if you have more than one programmer working on an application, but all of the programmers are located at the same site.

If your development team is scattered over several sites, you should opt for the third environment in this figure. Here, the clients are connected to the server via the Internet rather than a LAN. The main difference between this type of setup and the LAN setup is that the Internet development setup requires that you install *FrontPage Server Extensions* (*FPSE*) on the server. This feature provides the services needed for Visual Studio .NET to manage application files using Internet protocols rather than LAN protocols.

Standalone development

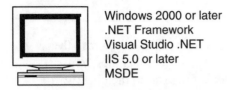

Windows 2000 or later
.NET Framework
Visual Studio .NET
IIS 5.0 or later
MSDE

Local area network development

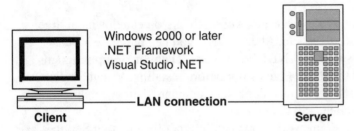

Windows 2000 or later
.NET Framework
Visual Studio .NET

————LAN connection————

Client

Windows 2000 Server or later
.NET Framework
IIS 5.0 or later
SQL Server

Server

Internet development

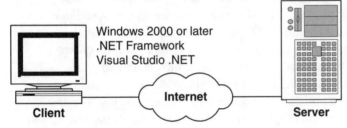

Windows 2000 or later
.NET Framework
Visual Studio .NET

Internet

Client

Windows 2000 Server or later
.NET Framework
IIS 5.0 or later
FrontPage Server Extensions
SQL Server

Server

Description

- When you use standalone development, a single computer serves as both the client and the server. This setup is typically used by programmers who are working on an application independently and don't have access to a server computer.

- When you use a *local area network* (*LAN*), a client computer communicates with a server computer over the LAN. This setup is typically used when two or more programmers who are located at the same site are working on the same application.

- When you use Internet development, a client computer communicates with a server computer over the Internet. This setup is typically used when the programmers working on an application are located at different sites. This setup requires that FrontPage Server Extensions be installed on the server. See figure 1-15 for details.

Note

- When you use a standalone environment, master copies of the source files may be stored on a server where they can be accessed by other programmers. In that case, *source control software* is often used to coordinate access to the master copies.

Figure 1-14   Three environments for developing ASP.NET applications

Software requirements for developing ASP.NET applications

To develop ASP.NET applications, you need a client and a server with the software shown in figure 1-15. On both the client and server machines, you need Windows 2000 or later. In addition, you need a browser on the client so you can test your applications. I recommend that you install both Internet Explorer and Netscape Navigator so you can test your applications with both of these popular browsers.

On the server, you need the .NET Framework, which you can download free of charge from the Microsoft web site. Alternatively, you can purchase Visual Studio .NET, which comes with the .NET Framework. Then, the setup program will instruct you to install the .NET Framework before installing Visual Studio .NET. This is most appropriate for standalone development where a single computer acts as both the client and the server.

In addition to the .NET Framework, you need Internet Information Services on the server to manage your web pages. Note that you should install IIS before you install the .NET Framework or Visual Studio .NET. If you install it after installing the .NET Framework, you'll need to repair the framework. And if you install it after installing Visual Studio .NET, you'll need to reinstall Visual Studio. For more information, see appendix A. Also note that IIS only comes with Windows Professional Edition. As a result, you won't be able to create ASP.NET applications if you have the Home Edition.

Because most ASP.NET applications require database access, you also need a database server such as Microsoft SQL Server. As I mentioned in the last topic, Visual Studio .NET comes with a scaled-back version of SQL Server called MSDE, and that's the database you're most likely to use in a standalone environment. However, MSDE isn't designed to actually run a production database application.

You can also install Microsoft FrontPage Server Extensions on the server. This program is used to manage the files in your web applications. It comes with IIS and is installed and configured along with IIS by default. You typically use FPSE when you develop web applications on a server that you connect to over the Internet.

If you're developing applications on a local server or on your own PC, you can use *file-share access* instead of FPSE. Unlike FPSE, file-share access lets you use standard Windows-based commands to create the files and directories you need. In this case, you need to have appropriate access privileges, but that usually isn't a problem. Because file-share access is the default when you create a web application in Visual Basic .NET, you need to change that default as described in this figure if you want to use FPSE.

Software requirements for ASP.NET application development

Client

- Windows 2000 or later
- A standard browser such as Internet Explorer or Netscape Navigator
- .NET Framework
- Visual Studio .NET

Server

- Windows 2000 Server or later
- Microsoft .NET Framework
- Internet Information Services 5.0 or later
- Microsoft SQL Server or an equivalent database server (database processing only)
- Microsoft FrontPage Server Extensions (Internet development only)

How to install IIS and the .NET Framework on your own PC

- IIS comes with Windows 2000 and later operating systems (Professional Edition only). IIS should be installed prior to installing the .NET Framework and Visual Studio .NET.

- To install IIS for Windows 2000 or later, display the Windows Control Panel, double-click Add/Remove Programs, then click Add/Remove Windows Components. Then, select Internet Information Services (IIS) from the list of components that are displayed and complete the installation.

- You can obtain the .NET Framework from Microsoft free of charge by downloading it from Microsoft's web site at www.microsoft.com/net. Or you can purchase it as part of Visual Studio .NET.

- A complete procedure for installing IIS, the .NET Framework, and Visual Studio .NET is presented in appendix A of this book.

When to use Microsoft FrontPage Server Extensions

- You can use *Microsoft FrontPage Server Extensions* (*FPSE*) to manage the files in your ASP.NET web applications. By default, FPSE is installed and configured along with IIS.

- FPSE must be used when you develop web applications on a server that you connect to via the Internet. It provides the services needed for Visual Studio .NET to manage application files using Internet protocols.

- If you're developing a web application on a local server, you typically use *file-share access* to manage the files in the application. This is the default for web applications developed in Visual Basic .NET.

- To change the default file access method in VB.NET, choose Tools→Options to display the Options dialog box. Then, open the Projects folder and select the Web Settings category to display the available options.

- To change the file access method for a project, right-click on the project in the Solution Explorer, choose Properties from the shortcut menu, open the Common Properties folder in the resulting dialog box, and select the Web Settings category to choose an option.

Figure 1-15   Software requirements for developing ASP.NET applications

How to use URLs to access ASP.NET applications

In the next chapter, you'll learn how to run an ASP.NET application from within the Visual Studio environment. To thoroughly test an ASP.NET application, however, you'll also need to run it directly from a browser. To do that, you enter the URL for the starting page of the application in the Address box if you're using Internet Explorer or in the Location box if you're using Netscape.

Figure 1-16 shows the components of a URL. The first component is the protocol, in this case, HTTP. In most cases, you can omit the protocol and HTTP is assumed.

The second component is the address of the IIS server where the application resides, called the *host*. If you're using a standalone development environment, you can specify the host as *localhost*. Otherwise, you usually use an address that includes a *domain name*. At the top of this figure, for example, you can see a URL that includes the domain name msdn.microsoft.com.

The alternative to using a domain name is to specify the *IP* (*Internet Protocol*) *address* that identifies the host. This is an address like 64.71.179.86 that uniquely identifies a web site. You can use an IP address to access a site before a domain name has been assigned to it. But otherwise, you rarely need to use an IP address.

After the host, you specify the path where the application resides within IIS. Notice that front slashes are used to separate the components of a path in a URL, although backslashes are used to separate them in a DOS path. After the path, you specify the name of the file you want to display in the browser. If the file has an extension of aspx like the ones shown here, IIS will pass the request on to ASP.NET for processing.

Before I go on, you should realize that you don't need to include a file name in the URL for most web applications. In that case, the file named Default.aspx is automatically displayed. This is illustrated by the URL in the browser in this figure. To provide for this in your own applications, you provide pages named Default.aspx for each directory in an application.

The first page of a web site that uses ASP.NET

The components of an HTTP URL

```
http://localhost/ASP.NET/Chapter_01/CostumeStore/Costume.aspx
```

protocol   host   path   file name

Description

- To start an ASP.NET application from a browser, you enter a URL for the starting page of the application in the Address box (for the Internet Explorer) or the Location box (for Netscape). Then, you press Enter to run the application and display the page.

- When IIS is running on your local machine, you can use the "localhost" keyword to specify the *host*, which is the server that's hosting your web site.

- When IIS is running on another machine, you normally use the *domain name* to identify your web site, but you can also use the *IP* (*Internet Protocol*) *address*. The browser uses this information to identify the server that's hosting the web site.

- The path identifies the location of the web page on the web server, and the file name names the page.

- If you omit the file name from the URL, IIS will look for a file with the name Default.aspx. Because of that, you'll typically include a form with this name in your applications.

Figure 1-16   How to use URLs to access ASP.NET applications

Perspective

Now that you've read this chapter, you should have a general idea of what ASP.NET is and how ASP.NET applications work. You should also have a general understanding of what files make up an ASP.NET web application. With that as background, you're ready to learn how to develop ASP.NET applications of your own. And that's what you'll learn how to do in the next three chapters.

Terms

web application	tag
web page	rendering a control
web form	code-behind file
client/server application	.NET Framework
client	.NET Framework Class Library
server	namespace
web browser	CLR (Common Language
web server	Runtime)
IIS (Internet Information Services)	managed application
DBMS (database management system)	Common Type System
intranet	Microsoft Intermediate Language
HTML (Hypertext Markup Language)	(MSIL)
HTTP (Hypertext Transfer Protocol)	Intermediate Language (IL)
static web page	three-layered architecture
HTTP request	presentation layer
HTTP response	user control
URL (Uniform Resource Locator)	style sheet
dynamic web page	business rules layer
application server	database layer
web control	data access layer
posting a web page	LAN (local area network)
application mapping	source control software
round trip	MSDE (Microsoft SQL Server
state	Desktop Engine)
stateless protocol	FPSE (FrontPage Server Exten-
view state	sions)
session state	file-share access
session state object	host
application state	domain name
application state object	IP (Internet Protocol) address
attribute	

2

How to develop a one-page web application

In the last chapter, you were introduced to the basic concepts of web programming and ASP.NET. Now, this chapter shows you how to develop a simple one-page web application using Visual Studio .NET, which is Microsoft's integrated development environment. This environment provides all the tools you need to design, code, and test ASP.NET applications.

If you've used Visual Studio .NET to develop Windows applications, you'll soon see that you develop web applications in much the same way. As a result, you should be able to move quickly through this chapter. On the other hand, if you're new to this environment, you're going to need to practice the skills that this chapter presents. Once you get used to it this environment, though, I think you're going to appreciate the powerful development tools that it offers.

How to work with ASP.NET applications

In case you haven't used Visual Studio .NET before, this chapter starts by introducing you to the concepts of applications, projects, and solutions. Then, you'll learn how to create a new ASP.NET application in Visual Studio and how to open and close existing applications.

Applications, projects, and solutions

To organize the files of an ASP.NET application, Visual Studio .NET uses projects and solutions. Figure 2-1 explains how projects and solutions work. Each *project* is a container that holds the aspx files, the code-behind files, and any other files that are needed to create a single ASP.NET application. A project can have more than one ASP.NET page, but all of the pages in a project belong to the same application.

A *solution* is a container that can hold one or more projects. A solution usually contains just one project. In that case, there's not much distinction between the project and the solution. Most of the solutions presented in this book will consist of just one project.

Although single-project solutions are the norm, multi-project solutions are sometimes used to develop related applications. For example, an online store might have one ASP.NET application that allows customers to place orders online and a second ASP.NET application that processes the orders or allows management to update product information. Each of these applications would have its own project, but the projects could be combined into a single solution. That way, you could work on them together in Visual Studio .NET.

To work with the files in a project, you use the *Solution Explorer*. You'll learn how to use some of the basic functions of the Solution Explorer in this chapter and in the next chapter. For now, you should realize that by default, not all of the files for a project are listed in the Solution Explorer. For example, you'll notice in this figure that the .aspx.vb files for the two forms aren't listed. To include these files in the display, you can click the Show All Files button at the top of the Solution Explorer window.

This figure also summarizes some of the other folders and files that are included in a project. These files and folders are added automatically when a project is created. You'll learn about the Global.asax, Styles.css, and Web.config files later in this book, so I won't describe them here.

The References folder contains references to the assemblies that contain the namespaces that are available to the project. Remember that the namespaces contain the classes that the application requires. Although you can't see the namespaces here, they include the System.Web namespace that contains all the other namespaces that are needed to develop an ASP.NET application.

The AssemblyInfo.vb file contains information about the assemblies in a project, such as their names and versions. This file receives information whenever the project is compiled.

The Visual Basic window with a project open

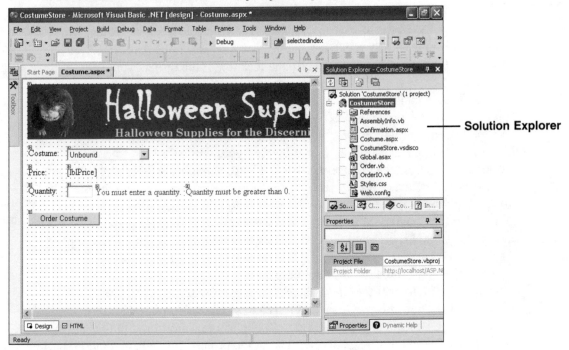

Solution Explorer

Description

- Solutions and projects are containers that help you organize the files that make up an application. A *solution* is a container that can hold one or more projects. A *project* is a container that holds the files that make up an ASP.NET application. That includes Visual Basic source files, HTML files, and class files as well as other files.

- Every solution has a *solution file* that keeps track of the projects that make up the solution and various settings for the solution. Every project has a *project file* that keeps track of the files and settings for the project.

- You can use the *Solution Explorer* to display and manage the files and projects in a solution. To display all of the files for a solution, including the .aspx.vb files, click the Show All Files button at the top of the Solution Explorer.

Other project folders and files

Folder/file	Description
References	Contains references to the assemblies for the namespaces that the application can use.
AssemblyInfo.vb	Contains information about the assembly that's created when you compile the project.
Global.asax	Provides event handlers for application-wide events (see chapter 9).
Styles.css	Contains style rules that you can use to format your web forms (see chapter 6).
Web.config	Contains settings that affect how an ASP.NET application operates. You can also use this file to store application-specific information (see chapters 9, 12, 15, and 19).

Figure 2-1   Applications, projects, and solutions

How to create a new ASP.NET web application

Figure 2-2 shows the New Project dialog box for creating a new project. To create a project for an ASP.NET web application, you select the ASP.NET Web Application template. Then, you specify the location of the project you want to create.

The location includes the address of the web server, followed by the path where you want the project stored. You can select the address of the web server from the Location drop-down list. For a stand-alone development environment, this address is http://localhost as shown in this figure. For a LAN or Internet development environment, the server is listed by its domain name.

After you select the web server, you can enter the appropriate path for the project. In this example, the project will be stored in the directory with this path: ASP.NET\Chapter_02\RegisterUser. Note that the project is given the same name as the lowest level directory you specify, in this case, RegisterUser.

When you create a new project for an ASP.NET application, all of the files for that project are stored on the web server in the location you specify. The actual disk location for those files is determined by how IIS is configured. Because of that, this directory can be referred to as a *virtual directory*.

By default, IIS is configured so that web applications are stored in the C:\Inetpub\wwwroot directory. So the files for the project shown here would be stored in this directory:

```
C:\Inetpub\wwwroot\ASP.NET\Chapter_02\RegisterUser
```

Note, however, that the solution file isn't stored in this directory. Instead, it's stored in the default directory for Visual Studio projects. When you first install Visual Studio .NET, that directory is My Documents\Visual Studio Projects. If that's not what you want, you should change the default directory before you create the new project.

The New Project dialog box

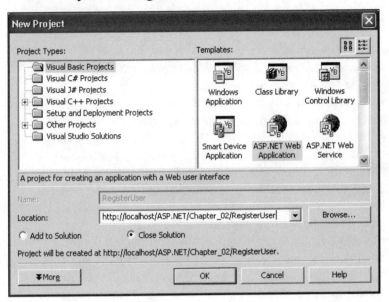

How to create a new ASP.NET application

1. Click the New Project button on the Start page, or use the File→New→Project command to display the New Project dialog box.

2. Select the Visual Basic Projects folder in the Project Types list to display the templates that are available for Visual Basic. Then, select the ASP.NET Web Application template.

3. Select the IIS server where the project will reside from the Location drop-down list. For a stand-alone development environment, the server will be listed as http://localhost. For a LAN or Internet development environment, the server will be listed by its domain name.

4. Enter the path where you want to store the project after the name of the IIS server.

5. Click the OK button to start the new project. Visual Studio creates the directory you specify in the \Inetpub\wwwroot directory of the IIS server and stores all the project files in that directory. This becomes the *virtual directory* for the project. Visual Studio also creates the directory you specify in the default directory for Visual Studio projects and stores the solution file there.

Notes

*   To change the default directory for Visual Studio projects, use the Tools→Options command to display the Options dialog box. Then, open the Environment folder, select the Projects and Solutions category, and change the Visual Studio projects location option.

*   When you create a new ASP.NET application, it consists of a single web form named WebForm1. See chapter 3 for information on how to change the name of this file and the class it defines.

Figure 2-2   How to create a new ASP.NET web application

How to open or close an existing ASP.NET web application

Figure 2-3 describes two ways that you can open an existing ASP.NET application. The easiest way is to open the solution that contains the application. Then, all of the projects in that solution are opened.

You can also open a project directly from the web server where it resides. When you do that, the Open Project From Web dialog box shown at the top of this figure is displayed. This dialog box lets you identify the server where the project resides. After you identify the server, the Open Project dialog box is displayed with a list of the folders and files that are available on that server. Then, you can use standard Windows techniques to locate and open the project. In this figure, you can see the folders that are available on my web server, which include folders for some of the books I've worked on.

When you open a project rather than a solution, Visual Studio looks for the solution file in the default directory for Visual Studio projects. If it doesn't find the solution there, it creates a new solution. Then, when you save the solution, you'll be prompted for the location where you want to save it. This technique is particularly useful if two or more programmers need access to the same project. Then, each programmer can create a separate solution file that points to the project.

Although you can open either a project or a solution, you can't close a project. Instead, you have to close the solution that contains it as indicated in the figure.

The Open Project From Web dialog box

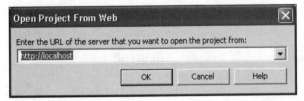

The Open Project dialog box

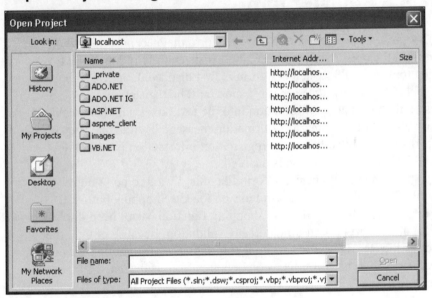

How to open an existing ASP.NET application

- Use the File→Open Solution command to open the solution. Then, Visual Studio automatically opens the projects contained in the solution.

- Use the File→Open→Project From Web command. Then, identify the server where the project resides in the Open Project From Web dialog box. The projects on that server are displayed in the Open Project dialog box so you can select the one you want to open.

- When you open a project rather than a solution, Visual Studio looks for the solution file in the default directory for Visual Studio projects. If it doesn't find the file there, it creates a new one. Then, when you save the solution, Visual Studio asks you where you want to save the solution file.

- After you've worked on one or more projects, the names of those projects will be listed on the Projects tab of the Start page and in the File→Recent Projects submenu. Then, you can click a project name to open the project.

How to close an application

- Use the File→Close Solution command.

Figure 2-3   How to open or close an existing ASP.NET web application

How to design a form for a web application

When you first create a web application, it contains a single, blank form named WebForm1. Then, you can use the techniques presented in the topics that follow to design this web form.

The design of a Register form

Figure 2-4 presents the design of a Register form that accepts registration information from the user. As you can see, it consists entirely of labels, text boxes, and buttons. Note that when this form is first displayed, the Go Shopping button is disabled. That way, the user can't shop until he registers.

To register, the user enters information into the text boxes and then clicks the Register button. At that point, a confirmation message like the one shown in this figure is displayed. In addition, the registration information is written to a text file and the Go Shopping button is enabled.

Before I show you how to design a form like this, I want to point out two things about this form. First, if the user clicks on the Go Shopping button, a message is displayed indicating that the shopping function hasn't been implemented. Second, this form doesn't include any validation. Because of that, the user could click the Register button without entering any information. Although this isn't realistic, it will help you focus on how this form is designed and implemented.

The Register page displayed in a browser

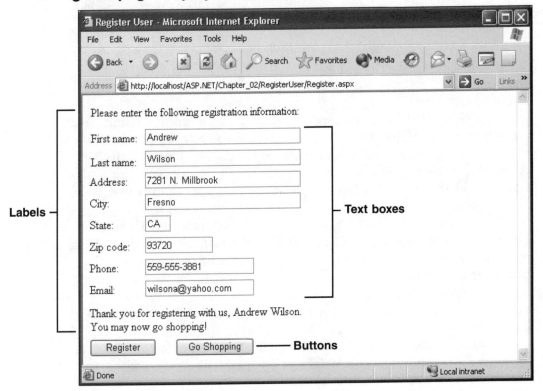

Description

- The Register page accepts name and address information from the user and writes it to a text file.
- The user enters the name and address information into text boxes that are identified by label controls.
- Label controls are also used to display user instructions at the top of the page, to display a confirmation message when the user is registered, and to display a message when the user clicks the Go Shopping button indicating that the shopping function hasn't been implemented.
- After entering name and address information, the user can click the Register button to accept the information. Then, the confirmation message is displayed and the Go Shopping button is enabled so the user can click on it. (This button is disabled when the form is first displayed so that the user can't click on it before registering.)
- To end the application, the user can click the Close button in the upper right corner of the browser window.

Figure 2-4   The design of a Register form

How to use the Web Forms Designer to work with controls

Figure 2-5 shows the *Web Forms Designer* that you use to design a web form. To do that, you start by adding controls from the *Toolbox*. Then, you can move and size the controls as necessary. The basic techniques for doing that are described in this figure.

The ASP.NET Server controls you can use on a web form are available from the Web Forms and HTML tabs of the Toolbox. The controls you're most likely to use as you develop a web application are the *Web Server controls* in the Web Forms tab. These controls are new to .NET and provide functionality that wasn't available with traditional HTML elements. In addition, you can work with them using properties, methods, and events just like other .NET objects.

The controls in the HTML tab provide access to the traditional HTML elements. You can work with these controls, called *HTML Server controls*, using properties, methods, and events just like you do the Web Server controls. Because these controls don't provide the same functionality as the Web Server controls, however, you're likely to use them only if you're converting applications that use traditional HTML elements. Because of that, I'll focus on the Web Server controls in this book.

In addition to the Web Server controls and HTML Server controls, you can use the *validation controls* in the Web Forms tab of the Toolbox to validate the data on the form. You can use these controls to validate data in either Web Server or HTML Server controls. You'll be introduced to these controls in the next chapter.

When you add any of these controls to a form, Visual Studio generates the required HTML for you. Although this is fine for simple forms, you may need to modify the generated HTML for more complicated forms. You may also need to code some of the HTML directly, which you'll learn how to do in chapter 6.

Before I go on, you should notice the grid of dots that makes up the background of the web form in this figure. This grid indicates that the form is displayed in *grid layout mode*. In this mode, you can place controls exactly where you want them on the form using *absolute positioning*.

The alternative to grid layout mode is *flow layout mode*. With this mode, controls are positioned relative to one another. Because of that, the position of the controls can change when the form is displayed depending on the size of the browser window and the resolution of the display.

Throughout this section of the book, all of the forms you'll see will be designed using grid layout mode since that's the default. Because each mode has its advantages and disadvantages, however, you'll want to learn how to work with both of them. You can do that in chapter 7.

A web form after controls have been added

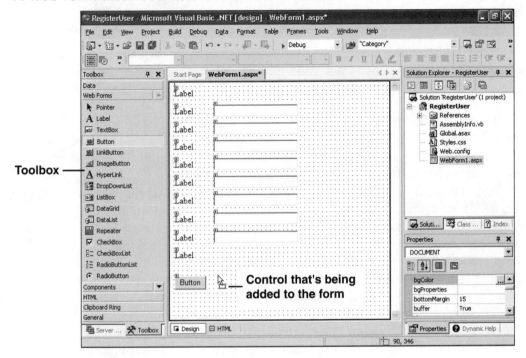

Toolbox ——

Control that's being added to the form

Description

- To design web forms in Visual Studio, you use the *Web Forms Designer*. This designer lets you design a form by adding controls from the *Toolbox*.

- To display a web form in a Web Forms Designer window, double-click on the form in the Solution Explorer, or select the form and then click on the View Designer button at the top of the Solution Explorer.

- To add a control, you can (1) drag it from the Toolbox, (2) select it in the Toolbox and then click and drag in the form, or (3) double-click on it in the Toolbox.

- To select a control, click on it. To move a control, drag it. To size a control, drag one of the handles that appear around it when you select it.

- The *Web Server controls* on the Web Forms tab of the Toolbox and the *HTML Server controls* on the HTML tab of the Toolbox have properties, methods, and events just like other .NET objects. The HTML Server controls map directly to traditional HTML elements and have limited functionality compared to the Web Server controls.

- You can use the *validation controls* that are on the Web Forms tab of the Toolbox to perform common validation checks on Web Server or HTML Server controls.

- The Web Forms Designer works in one of two layout modes. *Grid layout mode* lets you position elements on the page by dragging them. *Flow layout mode* uses traditional HTML formatting where the browser determines the exact position of each element. See chapter 7 for more information on using these modes.

Figure 2-5   How to use the Web Forms Designer to work with controls

How to set the properties for web forms and controls

After you have placed controls on a form, you need to set each control's properties so the control looks and works the way you want it to when the form is displayed. In addition, you need to set some of the properties for the form itself.

To set the properties of a form or control, you work in the Properties window as shown in figure 2-6. To display the properties for a specific control, click on it in the Web Forms Designer window to select the control. To display the properties for the form, click any blank area of the form.

In the Properties window, you can select a property by clicking it. When you do, a brief description of that property is displayed at the bottom of the Properties window. To change a property setting, you change the entry to the right of the property name by typing a new value or choosing a new value from a drop-down list. In some cases, a button with an ellipsis (...) on it will appear when you click on a property. In that case, you can click this button to display a dialog box that helps you set the property.

Some properties are also displayed in groups. In that case, a plus sign appears next to the group name. This is illustrated by the Font property shown in this figure. To display the properties in this group, you can click the plus sign next to the group name.

To display properties alphabetically or by category, you can click the appropriate button at the top of the Properties window. At first, you may want to display the properties by category so you have an idea of what the different properties do. Once you become more familiar with the properties, though, you may be able to find the ones you're looking for faster if you display them alphabetically.

As you work with properties, you'll find that most are set the way you want them by default. In addition, some properties such as Height and Width are set interactively as you size and position the controls in the Web Forms Designer window. As a result, you usually only need to change a few properties for each object.

A form after the properties have been set

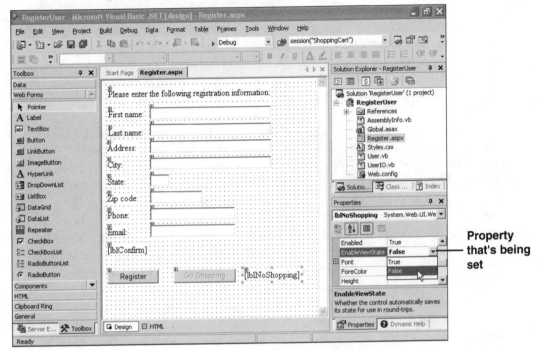

Description

- The Properties window displays the properties for the object that's currently selected in the Web Forms Designer window. To display the properties for another object, click on that object or select the object from the drop-down list at the top of the Properties window.

- To change a property, enter a value into the text box or select a value from its drop-down list if it has one. If a button with an ellipsis (…) appears at the right side of a property's text box, you can click on the ellipsis to display a dialog box that lets you set options for the property.

- To change the properties for two or more controls at the same time, select the controls. Then, the common properties of the controls are displayed in the Properties window.

- When you click on a property in the Properties window, a brief description of the property appears in a pane at the bottom of the window.

- You can use the first two buttons at the top of the Properties window to sort the properties by category or alphabetically.

- You can use the plus and minus signs displayed to the left of some of the properties and categories in the Properties window to expand and collapse the list of properties.

Note

- If a description isn't displayed when you click on a property in the Properties window, right-click on the window and select Description from the shortcut menu.

Figure 2-6   How to set the properties for web forms and controls

Common properties for web forms and controls

Figure 2-7 presents the properties for web forms and Web Server controls that you're most likely to use as you develop web forms. In the last chapter, for example, you saw how you can use the IsPostBack property to determine when a form is being loaded for the first time and when it's being posted back to the server. You can use this property to determine when initialization code is performed.

The PageLayout property of a web form determines how the form is displayed in the designer window. As you have learned, it's displayed in grid layout mode by default. If you want to use flow layout mode instead, you can change this property to FlowLayout.

If you've worked with Windows controls, you'll notice that many of the properties shown here for Web Server controls provide similar functionality. For example, you can use the ID property to name a control that you need to refer to in code, and you can use the Text property to determine what's displayed in the control. However, the AutoPostBack, EnableViewState, and CausesValidation properties are unique to Web Server controls.

The AutoPostBack property determines whether the page is posted back to the server when the user changes the value of the control. Note that this property is only available with certain controls, such as the check box, drop-down list, and radio button controls. Also note that this property isn't available with button controls. That's because these controls are almost always used to post a page back to the server, so that's how they're designed by default.

The EnableViewState property determines whether a Web Server control retains its data from one posting to the next. For that to happen, the EnableViewState property for both the form and the control must be set to True, which is the default. Although you usually don't change the default settings for this property as you develop an application, you will occasionally want to turn this property off for one or more controls by setting it to False. You'll learn more about the use of this property in a moment.

The CausesValidation property is available for button controls and determines whether the validation controls on the form are activated when the user clicks the button. This allows you to check for valid data before the form is posted back to the server. You'll learn more about how to use the validation controls in the next chapter and in chapter 8.

Common web form properties

Property	Description
EnableViewState	Determines whether the page maintains the view state of the controls the page contains between HTTP requests. The default value is True. This overrides the EnableViewState properties of individual controls.
IsPostBack	Gets a Boolean value that indicates whether the page is being posted back from the client (True) or is being loaded for the first time (False).
PageLayout	The layout that's displayed in the Web Forms Designer window. The possible values are GridLayout and FlowLayout. GridLayout is the default.
Title	The text that's displayed in the title bar of the browser when the web page is displayed.

Common Web Server control properties

Property	Description
AutoPostBack	Determines whether the page is posted back to the server when the value of the control changes. Available with controls such as a check box, drop-down list, radio button, or text box. The default value is False.
CausesValidation	Determines whether page validation occurs when you click on the button, link button, or image button. The default value is True.
EnableViewState	Determines whether the control maintains its view state between HTTP requests. The default value is True.
Enabled	Determines whether the control is functional. The default value is True.
ID	The name that's used to refer to the control.
TabIndex	Determines the order in which the controls on the form receive the focus when the Tab key is pressed.
Text	The text that's displayed in the control.
Visible	Determines whether a control is displayed or hidden.

Description

- The IsPostBack property is often used in the Load procedure of a form to determine whether or not the form is being loaded for the first time. This property is set by ASP.NET when it receives a request for the form.

- The AutoPostBack property isn't available with the button controls, since these controls are designed to post the page back to the server by default.

- If the user clicks on a button control whose CausesValidation property is set to True, the data validation that's specified in each of the validation controls on the page is done and the appropriate error messages are displayed.

- By default, Web Server controls retain their view state between HTTP requests. That means that all of the property values a control contains that are changed by the application are maintained when a page is sent back to the client. If that's not what you want, you can set the control's EnableViewState property to False.

Figure 2-7   Common properties for web forms and controls

The property settings for the Register controls

Now that you've learned the basic skills for designing a web form, figure 2-8 presents the property settings for the controls on the Register form. As you can see, the Text properties for all of the labels on the form have been changed to reflect what's displayed on the page. The Text properties for the last two label controls have been changed to initial values of empty strings, but these values will be changed by code as the application is executed.

Because the last two label controls will be referred to from the code for this form, their ID properties have been changed to reflect their contents. That's true for the text box and button controls as well. In addition, the Text properties of the button controls have been changed to "Register" and "Go Shopping," and the Enabled property of the Go Shopping button has been set to False.

In addition to the properties shown here, you should know that the Title property of the form has been changed to "Register User." This is the text that's displayed in the title bar of the browser. By default, this property is set to the name of the form.

The TabIndex properties of the text boxes and buttons have also been changed. By default, this property is set to zero for each control. Then, the first time the user presses the Tab key, the focus moves to the address bar of the browser. Next, it moves to the controls in the order that they were added to the form. If you don't add the controls in the tab order you want to use, then, you can set their TabIndex properties to define the tab order. Note that if you change the TabIndex property of any of the controls to a non-zero value, any controls that still have a zero value will be placed last in the tab order.

Finally, with one exception, the EnableViewState property of the form and all of its controls has been left at its default setting of True. That way, the application will work if any of those controls require the use of view state. The one exception is Label11, which has its EnableViewState property set to False. You'll learn more about this property in the next figure.

The property settings for the controls on the Register form

Default ID	Property	Value
Label1	Text	Please enter the following registration information:
Label2	Text	First name:
Label3	Text	Last name:
Label4	Text	Address:
Label5	Text	City:
Label6	Text	State:
Label7	Text	Zip code:
Label8	Text	Phone:
Label9	Text	Email:
Label10	ID	lblConfirm
	Text	""
Label11	ID	lblNoShopping
	EnableViewState	False
	Text	""
TextBox1	ID	txtFirstName
TextBox2	ID	txtLastName
TextBox3	ID	txtAddress
TextBox4	ID	txtCity
TextBox5	ID	txtState
TextBox6	ID	txtZipCode
TextBox7	ID	txtPhone
TextBox8	ID	txtEMail
Button1	ID	btnRegister
	Text	Register
Button2	ID	btnShop
	Text	Go Shopping
	Enabled	False

Additional property settings

- The TabIndex properties for all of the text boxes and buttons are set so that the controls will receive focus from top to bottom and left to right.
- The Title property for the form is set to Register User.

Figure 2-8   The property settings for the controls on the Register form

How to set the EnableViewState property

By default, the EnableViewState property for a page and every control on the page is set to True. In that case, before a requested page is sent back to the client, the values of any control properties that have been changed by code are stored in view state and sent back to the client as part of the HTTP response. This is done automatically by ASP.NET.

Then, if the user posts the page back to the server, the view state data is returned as part of the HTTP request. When that happens, ASP.NET starts by initializing the page, which returns the page and control properties to their initial values. But after that, ASP.NET restores the properties to their view state values.

Once you understand how this works, it's relatively easy to determine when the EnableViewState property for a control needs to be on and when it needs to be off. This is summarized in figure 2-9. If one or more properties for a control are changed by code and you don't want them reset to their initial values, you want view state on. But if one or more properties are changed by code and you want them reset to their initial values, you turn view state off.

Using those guidelines, only the Go Shopping button of the Register form requires view state, and only the no shopping label should have view state turned off. For the other controls, view state doesn't matter. In particular, you should note that you don't need view state to retain the values that the user enters into text boxes. As you will see, ASP.NET handles that by returning the user entries in the HTML for a page.

Incidentally, view state is also used to save the values of page properties. For instance, the value of the IsPostBack property is saved in view state, which indicates whether a page is being posted back to the server. That's true regardless of whether the EnableViewState property of the page is set to True or False. That's because this property affects only the control properties that are saved in view state. It doesn't affect the page properties that are saved. As a result, the IsPostBack property will work properly even if you disable view state for the page.

How view state is used by the Register form

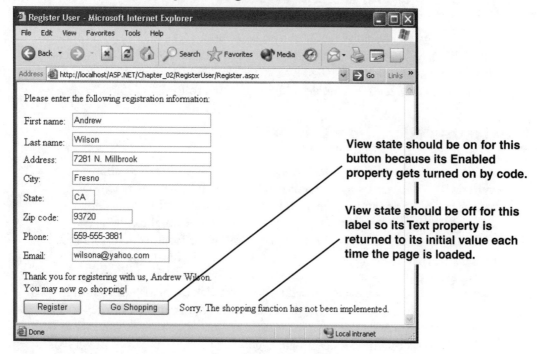

When view state should be on for a control

• When one or more properties are changed by code, and you don't want those properties reset to their initial values when the page is loaded.

When view state should be off for a control

• When one or more of the properties are changed by code, but you want the properties reset to their initial values each time the page is loaded.

When view state doesn't matter for a control

• When its properties aren't changed by code or when its properties are reset by code each time the page is processed.

• When you just want to save the data entered by a user. That's because this data is automatically sent with the HTTP request and returned with the HTTP response.

Description

• If view state is enabled, the values of any control properties that have been changed are stored in view state and sent to the client as part of the HTTP response.

• If the user posts the page back to the server, the view state data is returned as part of the HTTP request. Then, ASP.NET uses this data to restore these control properties.

Figure 2-9   How to set the EnableViewState property

How to add code to a form

To add the functionality required by a web form, you add code to its code-behind file to respond to events on the form. You can also create additional class files that contain code that's called by the code-behind file or another class file. That's what you'll learn how to do in the topics that follow.

How to use the Code Editor

To create and edit Visual Basic code, you use the *Code Editor* shown in figure 2-10. The easiest way to display the Code Editor window is to double-click the form or a control in the Web Forms Designer window to display the code-behind file for the form. If you double-click the form, the code is positioned in the *event procedure* for the Load event of the form, which is included by default. If you double-click a control, Sub and End Sub statements for the default event of the control are generated. If you double-click on a button control, for example, an event procedure for the Click event of that control is created. Then, you can enter the code for that procedure between the generated Sub and End Sub statements.

To create procedures for additional events, you can use the drop-down lists at the top of the Code Editor window. The list at the left side of the window includes all of the available objects. When you select one of these objects, the list at the right side of the window lists all the events for that object. When you select an event, Visual Studio generates Sub and End Sub statements for the event procedure.

You can also code *general procedures* by entering code directly into the Code Editor window. To create a *Sub procedure*, for example, you enter Sub and End Sub statements. And to create a *Function procedure*, or just *function*, you enter Function and End Function statements. Then, you enter the code required to implement the procedure between these statements, and you call the procedure from another procedure.

As you work with the Code Editor, you'll notice that it provides some powerful features that can help you code more quickly and accurately. One of the most useful of these features is the Auto List Members feature. This feature displays a list of members that are available for an object when you type the object name and a period. Then, you can highlight the member you want by clicking on it, typing the first few letters of its name, or using the arrow keys to scroll through the list. In this figure, for example, you can see the members that are listed for a label after the first two characters of the member name were entered. When you press the Tab key, the member you selected is inserted into your code. This feature is especially useful when you can't remember the name or spelling of a more obscure member.

In addition to the code you enter for a form, Visual Studio generates declaration statements for the controls you add to the form. If you're using Visual Studio 2002, these statements appear at the beginning of the class. If you're using Visual Studio 2003, however, these statements are hidden in the Web

A project with the Code Editor window displayed

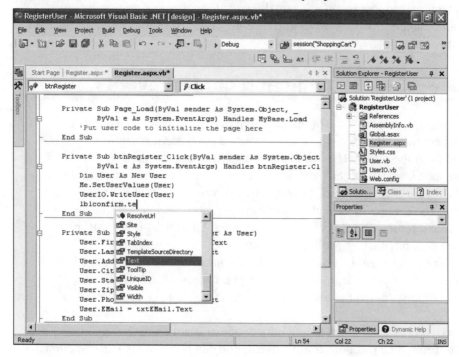

Description

- You develop the code for a web application using Visual Studio's *Code Editor*. To open a Code Editor window, select a Visual Basic file (.aspx.vb or .vb) in the Solution Explorer and then click the View Code button at the top of the Solution Explorer.

- You can also open a Code Editor window for a form class by double-clicking the form or a server control in a Web Forms Designer window. If you double-click a control, Sub and End Sub statements are generated for the default event for that control. Then, you can enter the code for the procedure between these statements.

- To create an *event procedure* from the Code Editor window, select an object from the drop-down list in the upper left corner of the window, and select an event from the drop-down list in the upper right corner of the window. (To create an event procedure for the page, select the (Page Events) item from the first drop-down list to list the page events.)

- To create a *general procedure*, type the Sub and End Sub or Function and End Function statements directly into the Code Editor window.

- The Code Editor includes powerful text editing features such as automatic indentation, syntax checking, and statement completion.

- The Web Form Designer Generated Code section includes declarations for the controls you add to the form and an event procedure for the Init event of the page. (If you're using Visual Studio 2002, the control declarations are listed at the beginning of the class rather than in the Generated Code section.) This code is typically hidden and you won't usually modify it.

Figure 2-10   How to use the Code Editor

Form Designer Generated Code section. To view these statements, you can click the plus sign next to this section. If you do, you'll see that this section includes some additional code that's used to initialize the page. You should be sure not to modify this code.

How to use ASP.NET page and control events

Figure 2-11 presents some of the common events for working with web pages and controls. The Init and Load events of a page occur whenever a page is requested from the server. The Init event occurs first, and it's used by ASP.NET to restore the view state of the page and its controls. Because of that, you don't usually add your own code to this event. Instead, you'll add it to the Load event procedure. You can use this event to perform operations such as setting control properties and retrieving values from session state. You can also use this event to perform data binding, as you'll see in chapter 4.

The PreRender event is raised after all the control events for the page have been processed. As you'll learn in chapter 9, you can use this event to store items in session state. It's the last event to occur before a page is rendered to HTML.

The last page event shown here, Unload, occurs just before the page is discarded. From the procedure for this event, you can perform cleanup functions such as closing files and database connections and discarding object references. Although garbage collection will take care of this automatically if you don't, it may not take care of it immediately. That means that resources may be retained unnecessarily, which can be a problem on a busy server. Because of that, we recommend that you do this cleanup work explicitly whenever an application uses resources that might be retained otherwise.

The control events shown here occur on some of the common Web Server controls. When the user clicks a button, for example, the Click event of that control is *fired*. Then, the page is posted back to the server, the procedures for the Init and Load events of the page are executed, followed by the procedure for the Click event of the control that was clicked.

In this figure, you can see the procedure for the Click event of the Register button on the Register form. This procedure starts by declaring a variable from a class named User. Then, it calls a procedure in the form class named SetUserValues, and it calls a procedure in a UserIO class named WriteUser. You'll see the code for these procedures when I present the complete code for the Register form. Next, the Click event procedure sets the Text property of the label control so it displays an appropriate message. Finally, it sets the Enabled property of the Go Shopping button to True so the user can click on it.

The TextChanged event occurs when the user changes the value in a text box. In most cases, you won't code an event procedure for the TextChanged event. However, you might code a procedure for the CheckedChanged event that responds when the user clicks a radio button or checks a check box. You might also code a procedure for the SelectedIndexChanged event that responds when the user selects an item from a drop-down list.

Common ASP.NET page events

Event	Occurs...
Init	When a page is requested from the server. ASP.NET uses this event to restore the view state of the page and its controls.
Load	When a page is requested from the server. This event occurs after the Init event, and you typically use it to perform initialization operations such as data retrieval and binding. You can also use this event to set control properties or to retrieve data from session state.
PreRender	After all the control events for the page have been processed but before the HTML that will be sent back to the browser is generated. You can use this event to save items in session state.
Unload	When a page is discarded. You typically use this event to close files, close database connections, discard object references, etc.

Common ASP.NET control events

Event	Occurs when...
Click	The user clicks a button, link button, or image button control.
TextChanged	The user changes the value in a text box.
CheckedChanged	The user selects a radio button in a group of radio buttons or selects or unselects a check box.
SelectedIndexChanged	The user selects an item from a list box, a drop-down list, a check box list, or a radio button list.

Code for the Click event of the Register button on the Register page

```
Private Sub btnRegister_Click(ByVal sender As System.Object, _
        ByVal e As System.EventArgs) Handles btnRegister.Click
    Dim User As New User
    Me.SetUserValues(User)
    UserIO.WriteUser(User)
    lblConfirm.Text = "Thank you for registering with us, " _
                & txtFirstName.Text & " " & txtLastName.Text _
                & ".<br> You may now go shopping!"
    btnShop.Enabled = True
End Sub
```

Description

- All of the events associated with an ASP.NET web page and its Web Server controls are executed on the server. Because of that, the page must be posted back to the server to process any event for which you've coded an event procedure.

- The page events listed here are executed each time a web page is requested from the server. That can happen as a result of the user requesting the page from a browser or as a result of the page being posted back to the server.

Figure 2-11   How to use ASP.NET page and control events

How to add a new class to a project

In chapter 1, you saw the code for the Order and OrderIO classes that were used by the Costume Store application. In just a minute, you'll see the code for the User and UserIO classes used by the Register User application. To create classes like these, you start by adding a *class file* to your project. To do that, you use the Add New Item dialog box shown in figure 2-12.

When you complete this dialog box, the new class file will appear in the Solution Explorer with the extension *vb*. This class file will include Class and End Class statements like the ones shown here. Then, you can enter the code for the class between these statements.

How to use an existing class with a project

One way to use an existing class is to add it to a project. If that class file is part of another project, you can do that by using the Add Existing Item command as described in this figure. Then, the class file you select is copied to your project.

Another way to use an existing class is to store it in a *class library*. Then, to use the class, you just add a reference to its class library. One of the advantages of using class libraries is that the source code is stored in a single location. Then, if you need to modify a class, you can just modify the code in the class library and it will be available to any projects that use that library. In contrast, if you copy a class to each project that uses it, you have to modify the code in each project.

The dialog box and starting code for a new class

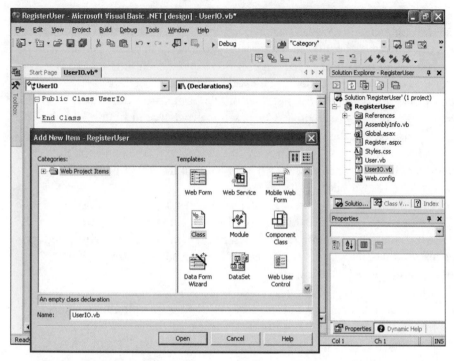

How to add a new class

- Right-click on the project in the Solution Explorer and select the Add→Add Class command to display the Add New Item dialog box. The Class template is selected by default. Enter the name you want to use for the new class and click the Open button.

- When you complete the Add New Item dialog box, a *class file* is added to the project. It will appear in the Solution Explorer with *vb* as the extension.

- The Class and End Class statements are automatically added to the class. Then, you can code the properties and methods for the class between those statements.

How to use an existing class

- To add a class from another project, use the Add→Add Existing Item command in the shortcut menu for the project you want to add the class to. Then, locate and select the class file in the dialog box that's displayed. The file is copied to your project.

- To use a class that's part of a class library, add a reference to the class library. To do that, right-click the References folder and select Add Reference to display the Add Reference dialog box. Then, click the Browse button in the .NET tab and locate and select the DLL for the class library. To use the classes in the class library without qualification, add an Imports statement for the class library.

Figure 2-12   How to add a class to a project

The Visual Basic code for the Register form

Figure 2-13 presents the Visual Basic code for the Register form. This code consists of three event procedures and a general procedure. The first event procedure is for the Load event of the page. It is executed each time a page is requested. As you can see, no code has been added to this procedure.

When the user clicks on the Register button, the event procedure for the Click event of this button is executed. You saw this procedure in figure 2-11. It creates a User object, sets the values of this object, writes the user information to a file, assigns a value to the Text property of the Confirm label, and enables the Go Shopping button. When a Click event procedure like this finishes, the page is automatically sent back to the browser.

The last event procedure is executed when the user clicks the Go Shopping button. This procedure sets the Text property of the NoShopping label to indicate that the shopping function hasn't been implemented. Here again, when this procedure is done, the page is sent back to the browser, which means that the no shopping message is displayed.

Note, however, that the NoShopping label is the one that has its EnableViewState property set to False. As a result, the no shopping message is reset to its initial value of an empty string if the user posts back this page by clicking on the Register button. Then, when the page is sent back to the browser, the message isn't displayed.

Of course, this isn't the only way to get that result. Another way is to leave view state on and reset the message property to an empty string in the Load procedure. I did, however, want to illustrate a case in which it makes sense to turn view state off.

The Visual Basic code for the Register form

```
Public Class WebForm1
    Inherits System.Web.UI.Page

    Private Sub Page_Load(ByVal sender As System.Object, _
            ByVal e As System.EventArgs) Handles MyBase.Load
        'Put user code to initialize the page here
    End Sub

    Private Sub btnRegister_Click(ByVal sender As System.Object, _
            ByVal e As System.EventArgs) Handles btnRegister.Click
        Dim User As New User
        Me.SetUserValues(User)
        UserIO.WriteUser(User)
        lblConfirm.Text = "Thank you for registering with us, " _
                    & txtFirstName.Text & " " & txtLastName.Text _
                    & ".<br> You may now go shopping!"
        btnShop.Enabled = True
    End Sub

    Private Sub SetUserValues(ByVal User As User)
        User.FirstName = txtFirstName.Text
        User.LastName = txtLastName.Text
        User.Address = txtAddress.Text
        User.City = txtCity.Text
        User.State = txtState.Text
        User.ZipCode = txtZipCode.Text
        User.PhoneNumber = txtPhone.Text
        User.EMail = txtEMail.Text
    End Sub

    Private Sub btnShop_Click(ByVal sender As System.Object, _
            ByVal e As System.EventArgs) Handles btnShop.Click
        lblNoShopping.Text = "Sorry. The shopping function has not " _
                        & "been implemented."
    End Sub

End Class
```

Notes

- The Load procedure is executed each time the page is requested. In this case, though, no code has been added to this procedure.

- When either one of the Click event procedures finishes, the page is sent back to the browser.

Figure 2-13   The Visual Basic code for the Register form

The Visual Basic code for the User and UserIO classes

Figure 2-14 presents the code for the User and UserIO classes. The User class consists of a series of public variables that hold information about a user. It's used to create an object for each new user that enters data on the Register form.

In contrast, the UserIO class contains one shared method named WriteUser that writes the information in a User object to a text file. As a result, a User object must be passed to this method. If you have experience working with text files, you shouldn't have any trouble understanding the code for this method. But even if you don't understand the code, you can use this method as long as you know how to call the method and pass the parameter from the Register form.

The Visual Basic code for the User class

```
Public Class User
    Public FirstName As String
    Public LastName As String
    Public Address As String
    Public City As String
    Public State As String
    Public ZipCode As String
    Public PhoneNumber As String
    Public EMail As String
End Class
```

The Visual Basic code for the UserIO class

```
Imports System.IO
Public Class UserIO

    Public Shared Sub WriteUser(ByVal User As User)
        Dim UserStream As New FileStream("C:\MurachData\Users.txt", _
            FileMode.Append, FileAccess.Write)
        Dim UserWriter As New StreamWriter(UserStream)
        Dim sUser As String
        sUser = ControlChars.Quote & User.firstname & ControlChars.Quote & ","
        sUser &= ControlChars.Quote & User.LastName & ControlChars.Quote & ","
        sUser &= ControlChars.Quote & User.Address & ControlChars.Quote & ","
        sUser &= ControlChars.Quote & User.City & ControlChars.Quote & ","
        sUser &= ControlChars.Quote & User.State & ControlChars.Quote & ","
        sUser &= ControlChars.Quote & User.ZipCode & ControlChars.Quote & ","
        sUser &= ControlChars.Quote & User.PhoneNumber & ControlChars.Quote _
            & ","
        sUser &= ControlChars.Quote & User.EMail & ControlChars.Quote
        UserWriter.WriteLine(sUser)
        UserWriter.Close()
    End Sub

End Class
```

Notes

- The User class defines the data for each User object.
- The UserIO class consists of one shared method named WriteUser that writes the data for a User object to a text file.
- When you use one of the methods in an I/O class that has been written by someone else, you don't have to understand the code. You just need to know how to call the method and pass the required parameters.

Figure 2-14   The Visual Basic code for the User and UserIO classes

How to test a web application

After you design the forms and develop the code for a web application, you need to test it to be sure it works properly. Then, if you discover any errors in the application, you can debug it, correct the errors, and test it again.

In chapter 5, you'll learn all the skills you need to test and debug a web application. For now, I want to show you how to run a web application in your default browser to see if it works properly. Then, I'll present a session of the Register User application so you can see how it works. Finally, I'll show you the HTML code that's sent to the browser so you can begin to see how that works.

How to run an application in the default browser

The easiest way to run an ASP.NET application is to click the Start button in the Standard toolbar as shown in figure 2-15. This compiles the application and displays the starting page in your default browser.

By default, the starting page is the page that's added to a project when you first create it. If that's not what you want, you can set another page as the starting page. To do that, just right-click on the page to display the shortcut menu shown in this figure, and select the Set As Start Page command. Since the Register User application is a one-page application, though, you won't need to do that for this application.

To test an application, you try everything that it's intended to do. For the Register User application, for example, you'll want to check that the correct message is displayed when the user clicks one of the buttons and that the Go Shopping button is enabled and disabled when appropriate. You'll also want to make sure that the user information is written to the text file correctly. To do that, you can use a text editor like NotePad to open the text file and display the data. When you're satisfied that the application works under all conditions, you can end it by closing the browser window.

As you're testing an application, exceptions may occur that aren't handled by the application. Then, ASP.NET displays an error page in the browser window. In many cases, the information in this page will be enough for you to determine the cause of the exception. In other cases, you'll need to use Visual Studio's or ASP.NET's debugging features to locate the source of the error. You'll learn how to use these features in chapter 5.

An ASP.NET project with the shortcut menu for a web form displayed

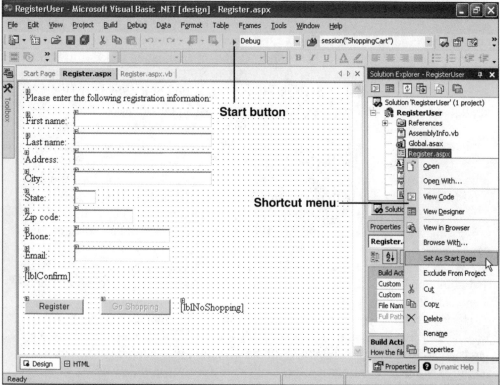

How to test an application in the default browser

- Click on the Start button in the Standard toolbar. Then, the project is compiled and the starting page is displayed in your default browser.

- If an error occurs, an error page that includes information about the cause of the error is displayed in the browser. You can use this information to locate and correct the error.

- When you're done testing the application, you can close it by closing the browser window.

How to change the starting page for an application

- By default, the first page that's added to an application is set as the starting page. To change the starting page, right-click on it in the Solution Explorer and select the Set As Start Page command from the shortcut menu.

Figure 2-15   How to run an application in the default browser

The Register form in action

At this point, you should have a general idea of how to design a form and set control properties; you should know how to write code to respond to page and control events; and you should know how to run an application to see if it works properly. To make sure you understand how ASP.NET processes an application, however, I'd like to take you through a typical execution of the Register User application. That will help you as you test your own applications.

Figure 2-16 describes the processing that takes place as you execute this application. After you start the application (step 1), ASP.NET responds by creating an instance of the Register page. ASP.NET also sets the IsPostBack property of this page to False since the page is being loaded for the first time, and it raises the Load event of the page (step 2). Since the Load procedure doesn't contain any code, the HTML for the page is generated without any additional processing. Then, ASP.NET sends the HTML to the browser and disposes of the page (step 3).

When the browser receives the HTML page, it interprets and displays it. At that point, the page looks like the first one in this figure. Here, the text boxes are empty and the Go Shopping button is disabled.

From this page, you can enter the registration information and click the Register button as shown in the second page (step 4). When you do, the browser sends an HTTP request that includes the information you entered back to the server. When the server receives this request, it forwards it to ASP.NET.

Then, ASP.NET creates another instance of the page. This time, ASP.NET sets the IsPostBack property of the page to True because it detects that the request is for the same page that it previously sent to the browser, and it raises the Load event (step 5). After the Load event is executed (step 6), ASP.NET raises the Click event of the Register button and that procedure is executed (step 7).

How the Register form works

1. Start the application from Visual Studio.

2. ASP.NET creates an instance of the Register page class, sets its IsPostBack property to False, and raises its Load event.

3. The Load event procedure is executed. Since this procedure doesn't contain any code, the HTML for the page is generated and sent to the browser without any other processing:

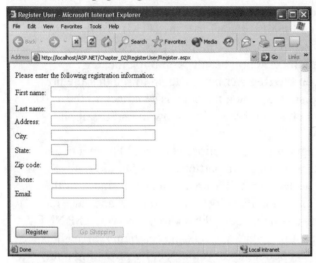

4. Enter the data and click the Register button to post the page to the server:

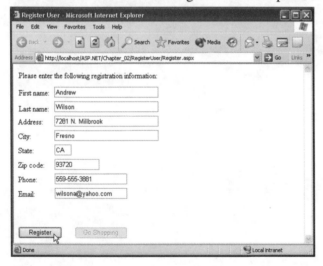

5. ASP.NET creates a new instance of the Register page class, sets its IsPostBack property to True, and raises its Load event.

6. The Load event procedure is executed. Since this procedure doesn't contain any code, processing continues.

7. ASP.NET raises the Click event for the Register button, and the procedure for this event is executed. This procedure sets the Text property of the confirmation label to confirm the registration, and it enables the Go Shopping button.

Figure 2-16   The Register form in action (part 1 of 2)

After these procedures are executed, the HTML for the page is generated and sent back to the browser (step 8). As you can see, the page now includes a message that thanks you for registering and indicates that you can now go shopping. The Go Shopping button is also enabled, so you can click it to post the page back to the server (step 9).

When you click the Go Shopping button, ASP.NET creates another instance of the page, sets its IsPostBack property to True, and executes the Load event procedure (step 10). Then, it executes the event procedure for the Click event of the Go Shopping button (step 11). Finally, it generates the HTML for the page and sends it back to the browser (step 12). This time, the page includes a message indicating that the shopping function hasn't been implemented.

At that point, you can click on the Register button again to see that the no shopping message is no longer displayed when the page is sent back to the browser (step 13). Then, you can close the browser window to end the application (step 14).

Now that you've seen the Register form in action, you should have a better feel for how ASP.NET processes web pages. In particular, you should realize that each time a web page is requested, ASP.NET creates a new instance of that page, initializes it, which includes setting its IsPostBack property, and raises it Load event. In addition, if the page is being posted back to the server, ASP.NET raises the event that caused the post to occur. As you can see, then, ASP.NET is a powerful program that simplifies application development by providing many of the management functions for you.

How the Register form works (continued)

8. The HTML code is generated for the page, and the page is sent back to the browser:

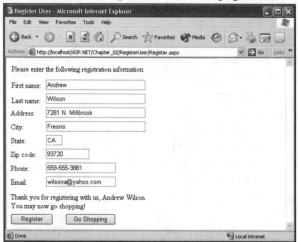

9. Click the Go Shopping button to post the page to the server.

10. ASP.NET creates a new instance of the Register page class, sets its IsPostBack property to True, and raises its Load event. As before, the Load event procedure contains no code, so processing continues.

11. ASP.NET raises the Click event for the Go Shopping button, and the procedure for this event is executed. This procedure sets the Text property for the no shopping label to indicate that the shopping function hasn't been implemented.

12. The HTML code is generated for the page, and the page is sent back to the browser:

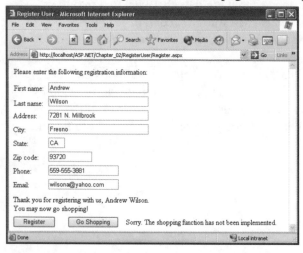

13. Click the Register button to post the page back to the server one more time. When the page is redisplayed, you'll see that the no shopping message is no longer displayed. That's because view state has been turned off for that label so the label is reinitialized to an empty string.

14. To end the application, you can click the Close button for the browser window.

Figure 2-16   The Register form in action (part 2 of 2)

The HTML that's sent to the browser

As you test a web application, it can sometimes be helpful to see the HTML that's generated for a page. For example, figure 2-17 presents the HTML for two instances of the Register page. The first one was created the first time I requested this page. The second one was created after I entered information and clicked the Register button. To view the HTML for a page, you can use the Source command in your browser's View menu.

If you're not familiar with HTML, you may not understand a lot of the code that's shown here. However, you should notice three things. First, this code doesn't include any ASP.NET tags. That's because these tags are rendered to standard HTML by the page so the controls they represent can be displayed in the browser. In the first screen, for example, I've highlighted the code for the First Name text box. As you can see, this text box is implemented using a standard <input> tag.

Second, you can see that the view state data is stored in a hidden input field named _ViewState. Notice that the value of this field is encrypted so you can't read it. Also notice that the value in the second page is larger than the value in the first page. That's because the first time the page is requested, this field contains only the view state data for the page since none of the control properties have changed. When the Register button is clicked, however, the Enabled property of the Go Shopping button and the Text property of the Confirm label have been changed by code so the values of these properties are also stored in view state.

Third, the second page illustrates how the data that you enter into a page is returned to the browser. Here, you can see that the data that I entered into the first two text boxes are included in the HTML for the second page. This also illustrates that you don't need view state to save the information that's entered into text boxes by the user.

Keep in mind that all of this HTML is generated automatically by ASP.NET. As a result, you don't have to worry about it. You just develop the application by using Visual Studio .NET in the way I've just described, and the rest of the work is done for you. That's a major benefit that you get from using Visual Studio and ASP.NET.

The HTML for the first request of the Register form

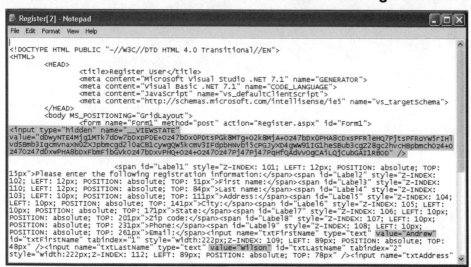

The HTML after the user enters data and clicks the Register button

Description

- To view the HTML for a page, use the View→Source command in the browser's menu.

- The HTML that the browser receives consists entirely of standard HTML tags. All of the ASP.NET tags are converted to standard HTML when the page is generated.

- View state data is stored in a hidden input field within the HTML. This data is encrypted so you can't read it.

- Values that the user enters into a page are returned to the browser as part of the HTML for the page.

Figure 2-17   The HTML that's sent to the browser

Perspective

The purpose of this chapter has been to teach you the basic skills for creating simple one-page ASP.NET applications using Visual Studio .NET. If you already have experience using Visual Studio to develop Windows applications, you shouldn't have any trouble using the skills presented here. You just need to become familiar with the properties and events you can use to work with web pages and controls.

If you haven't had any previous experience with Visual Studio or Visual Basic .NET, though, you may want to learn more about it before you continue. We think the best way to do that is to get our book, *Murach's Beginning Visual Basic .NET*. This book not only teaches you how to use Visual Studio .NET, but also how to use all the features of the Visual Basic .NET language.

Terms

solution	absolute positioning
project	flow layout mode
solution file	Code Editor
project file	event procedure
Solution Explorer	general procedure
virtual directory	Sub procedure
Web Forms Designer	Function procedure
Toolbox	function
Web Server control	fire an event
HTML Server control	class file
validation control	class library
grid layout mode	

About the Student Workbook for this book

If you're an instructor or a student or even if you're learning on your own, you may be interested in the Student Workbook that you can download from our web site. It consists of chapter summaries, learning objectives, exercises that let you practice what you've learned, and student projects that ask you to develop new ASP.NET projects from scratch. To give you some idea of what you can expect from the Student Workbook, the chapter summary, objectives, and exercises for chapter 2 follow.

In the complete Student Workbook, you'll find materials like these for all of the chapters. You'll also see that the exercises get more difficult as the book progresses, and you'll see that many of the exercises start from partial solutions so you can get more practice in less time.

To download the Student Workbook, please go to our web site at www.murach.com, click on the Downloads button, and continue from there. This download includes all of the files that you need for doing the exercises and projects.

Summary

- The files of an application are organized in *solutions* and *projects*. A solution is a container that can hold one or more projects, while a project is a container that holds the files that make up the application. You can use the *Solution Explorer* to manage the projects and files in a solution.

- By default, IIS stores web applications in the \Inetpub\wwwroot directory of the IIS server. Since this directory is determined by IIS, it's called a *virtual directory*.

- You use the *Web Forms Designer* to design web forms in Visual Studio. This designer lets you design a form by adding controls from the *Toolbox*.

- *Web Server controls* have properties, methods, and events just like other .NET controls. In contrast, *HTML Server controls* map directly to traditional HTML controls.

- *Grid layout mode* lets you exactly position the elements of a page, while *flow layout mode* lets the browser control the positioning of each element.

- You can use the Properties window to display and modify the properties of the selected form or control. The AutoPostBack, CausesValidation, and EnableViewState properties are unique to Web Server controls.

- You can use the IsPostBack property of a web page to determine if the page is being requested for the first time or if it's being posted back from the client.

- By default, Web Server controls retain view state between HTTP requests so all properties that are changed by the code of a web form retain their values when the page is sent back from the client. If you want the properties restored to their initial values, though, you can turn off the EnableViewState property of a control.

- You use Visual Studio's *Code Editor* to create *event procedures* that respond to the events of a web form.

- You can use the Load event of a web page to perform initialization operations, set control properties, and retrieve data from session state.

- Three commonly-used events for Web Server controls are the Click event for buttons, the CheckedChanged event for radio buttons and check boxes, and the SelectedIndexChanged event for list boxes and drop-down lists.

- You can add a new class to a project by adding a *class file* to your project, and you can use an existing class by copying a class file from another project. You can also use an existing class that's stored in a *class library* by adding a reference to the class library.

- You can test an ASP.NET application in a default browser by clicking the Start button in the Standard toolbar.

- To view the HTML for a page, you can use the Source command in the View menu of the browser. This HTML includes a hidden input field that contains the view state data that's passed to the browser. It also includes any data entered by the user.

Objectives

The objectives for each chapter describe what you should be able to do when you complete the chapter. Here, the applied objectives are most important because they ask you to apply want you've learned to the development of web applications. In contrast, the knowledge objectives just ask you to show that you understand the required concepts and terms. The best way to make sure that you can do the applied objectives is to do the exercises and projects for each chapter.

Applied objectives

- Given the specifications for a web form, use the Web Forms Designer to design the form.

- Given the specifications for a one-page web application, write the code for the web form.

- Run and test a web form.

Knowledge objectives

- Distinguish between a project and a solution.

- Describe the use of each of these Visual Studio windows: Web Forms Designer, Code Editor, and Solution Explorer.

- Distinguish between Web Server controls and HTML Server controls.

- Distinguish between flow layout mode and grid layout mode.

- Describe the use of the IsPostBack property for a web form and the AutoPostBack, CausesValidation, and EnableViewState properties for a Web Server control.

- Explain how view state affects the property values of a control, and describe a case in which you would want view state for a control turned off.

- Describe the use of the Init, Load, and Unload events for a web page, and describe the use of the Click, TextChanged, CheckedChanged, and SelectedIndexChanged events for a Web Server control.

- Describe two ways that you can use an existing class with a new web application.

- Describe how the HTML that's sent to a browser handles view state and user input.

Before you do the exercises for this book

Before you do the exercises for this book, you need to install IIS, the .NET Framework, and Visual Basic .NET. Then, you need to download the folders and files for this book from our web site and install them on your C drive. At that time, you can also download the Student Workbook for this book. For complete installation instructions, please refer to appendix A.

Exercise 2-1   Create the Register User application

This exercise will guide you through the process of designing, coding, and testing the Register User application presented in this chapter. This will give you some practice with the use of aspx files, code-behind files, and other class files.

Create a new application

1. Change the Visual Studio projects location to C:\Murach\ASP.NET \Exercises\Chapter_02 (Tools→Options). Then, start a new ASP.NET Web Application project in the ASP.NET Exercises\Chapter_02\RegisterUser directory of your IIS server as shown in figure 2-2.

Design the Register web form

2. In the Solution Explorer, notice that the default web form is named WebForm1 with aspx as its extension. For this exercise, this is the Register form. You'll learn how to rename it in chapter 3.

3. Drag and drop the controls needed from the Web Forms Designer in the Toolbox so the page looks similar to the Register form in figure 2-6.

4. Set the properties of the labels, text boxes, and buttons on the Register form as in figure 2-8. Be sure to disable view state for the No Shopping label.

Add the business and I/O classes to the project

5. Add a new class called User to the project as in figure 2-12. Then, code the User class so it contains the eight public variables shown in figure 2-14.

6. Add an existing class called UserIO to the project as shown in figure 2-12. This class is located in the C:\Murach\ASP.NET\Exercises\Chapter_02 \RegisterUser directory. Then, view the code for this class to make sure that it's the same as the code in figure 2-14.

Write the code for the Register web form

7. Return to the Register form and then double-click on the Register button to open the code-behind file for the form as shown in figure 2-10 and create a Click event procedure for the Register button.

8. Code the Click event procedure for this button so the application reads the user's values from the Register form and writes this information to a text file using the WriteUser method of the UserIO class. To simplify the code, you may want to write a Sub procedure to set the user values as done by the code in figure 2-13. This Click

event procedure should also display a confirmation message and enable the Go Shopping button.

9. Code the Click event procedure for the Go Shopping button as shown in figure 2-13 so a message appears that states the Go Shopping function hasn't been implemented.

Test and run the Register application

10. Compile and run the application in the default browser as shown in figure 2-15. If you get compile errors, fix the errors and try again.

11. When the application runs, test and debug it. If the application works right, you should see a message that says that the shopping function hasn't been implemented when you click the Go Shopping button. Then, if you click the Register button, that message should disappear.

Exercise 2-2   Work with view state

In this exercise, you'll learn how disabling or enabling view state can affect the execution of the Register form. This assumes that the messages are displayed correctly by that application as described in step 11 of exercise 2-1.

1. Open the aspx file for the Register form so you can modify its control properties. Then, enable view state for the No Shopping label by setting its EnableViewState property to True.

2. Run the application, enter your data into the text boxes, click the Register button, and click the Go Shopping button. You will then see the message that says that the shopping function hasn't been implemented. Now, click the Register button again. This time, you'll see that the text of the No Shopping label still appears on the form. That's because the code change that was made to the Text property of that label is restored.

3. Close the web browser to end the application.

4. Open the code-behind file for the Register form. Then, modify the Click event procedure for the Register button so the No Shopping label isn't displayed when the user clicks the Register button. To do this, you should add a statement that sets the Text property of the No Shopping label to an empty string ("").

5. Run the application again. Notice that it now operates the way it did when view state was disabled on the No Shopping label. This shows that you can often use code to avoid dealing with the EnableViewState property.

6. If you want to see another example of how view state can affect an application, turn off view state for the Go Shopping button. Then, test the application to see whether the button stays enabled after you click it.

3

How to develop a multi-page web application

Now that you've learned the basic skills for developing web applications, you're ready to learn how to develop applications that consist of two or more pages. As you'll see, you just need a few new skills to do that. Because most web forms are more complicated than the Register form you saw in the last chapter, however, this chapter also presents some additional skills for designing and coding web forms. Specifically, it shows you how to use drop-down lists and list boxes, how to use validation controls, and how to use session state.

Two pages of a multi-page web application

To illustrate the skills you'll learn in this chapter, I'll use an enhanced version of the Costume Store application you saw in chapter 1. This application, called the Halloween Store application, lets the user select products from several categories and displays those products in a shopping cart that the user can modify. I'll describe the two pages of this application in the topics that follow.

The Order page

Figure 3-1 presents the Order page of the Halloween Store application. This page includes two drop-down lists that let the user select a category and product. The categories are retrieved from a binary file the first time the page is requested and stored in an array list. The categories in this file are: Costumes, FX, Masks, and Props. Then, the array list is used to load the Category drop-down list. Because the view state for this control is enabled, the categories in this list will be saved between requests for the page.

The products are also retrieved from a binary file the first time the page is requested. The product information is then stored in a sorted list, which is saved in session state. That's necessary because each time the user selects a different category, the Product drop-down list must be updated so it includes only the products in the selected category. You'll see how that works later in this chapter.

Once a category and product are selected, the user can enter a quantity and click the Add to Cart button. If the user clicks the Add to Cart button without entering a quantity or if the user enters something other than an integer for the quantity, an error message is displayed. To accomplish that, two validation controls are included on the form. The required field validator makes sure that the user enters a quantity, and the compare validator makes sure that the user enters an integer. You'll learn how to use both of these validation controls in this chapter.

If the user enters a valid quantity, a sorted list that contains the user's shopping cart is updated with the product information. If the product isn't already in the shopping cart, that means that an item is added to the sorted list. If the product already exists in the shopping cart, however, the quantity the user entered is added to the quantity that's already in the shopping cart. Because the shopping cart must be retrieved and updated each time a product is added or updated, its sorted list is saved in session state. This shopping cart list is also retrieved by the Shopping Cart page of this application, which I'll describe next.

Before I describe the Shopping Cart page, though, you should realize that the check out function of this application hasn't been implemented. So if the user clicks the Check Out button, a message is displayed to that effect. In a complete application, of course, clicking this button would cause additional pages to be displayed to complete the order. Those pages aren't required to illustrate the skills presented in this chapter, though, so they've been omitted to keep the application as simple as possible.

The design of the Order page

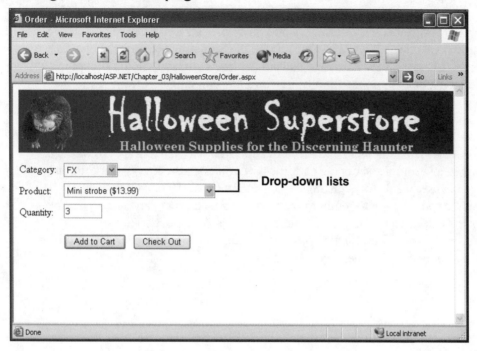

Description

- The Order page of the Halloween Store application accepts an order for any items in the store.

- To order an item, the user starts by selecting a category from the first drop-down list. Then, the products in that category are displayed in the second drop-down list. The user can then select a product and enter a quantity.

- When the user clicks the Add to Cart button, the selected product is added to the shopping cart if it isn't already in the shopping cart. If the product is already in the shopping cart, the quantity is added to the existing shopping cart item. Then the Shopping Cart page is displayed.

- The category information is retrieved from a binary file and stored in an array list. The array list is used to load the Category drop-down list.

- The product information is retrieved from a binary file and stored in a sorted list. The sorted list is saved in session state and is used to load the Product drop-down list when the category changes.

- The shopping cart information is stored in a sorted list. The sorted list is saved in session state so it can be retrieved and updated each time a product is added.

- This form uses validation controls to be sure that an integer is entered for the quantity.

- If the user clicks the Check Out button, a message is displayed that indicates that the check out function hasn't been implemented.

Figure 3-1   The Order page of the Halloween Store application

The Shopping Cart page

After the user selects a category and product from the Order page, enters a quantity, and clicks the Add to Cart button, the Shopping Cart page shown in figure 3-2 is displayed. This page lists all the items currently in the shopping cart in a list box. To do that, it must retrieve the shopping cart from session state.

To work with the items in the shopping cart, the user can use the two buttons to the right of the list box. To remove an item from the shopping cart, the user can select the item and then click the Remove Item button. To remove all the items from the shopping cart, the user can click the Empty Cart button.

If the user wants to add items to the shopping cart, he can click the Continue Shopping button to return to the Order page. Alternatively, the user can click the Check Out button to complete the order. As I mentioned earlier, however, the check out function hasn't been implemented. So clicking on this button simply causes a message to be displayed.

The design of the Shopping Cart page

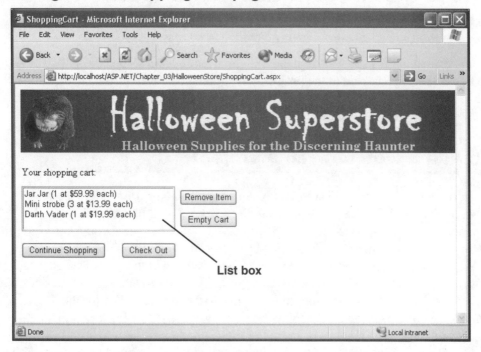

List box

Description

- The Shopping Cart page displays the items in the shopping cart in a list box. To load the list box, it uses the shopping cart information that's saved in session state by the Order page.

- The user can select any item in the shopping cart and then click the Remove Item button to remove the item from the cart. To remove all the items from the cart, the user can click the Empty Cart button.

- After reviewing the cart, the user can click the Continue Shopping button to return to the Order page and select additional products.

- If the user clicks the Check Out button, a message is displayed that indicates that the check out function hasn't been implemented.

Figure 3-2   The Shopping Cart page of the Halloween Store application

Five new skills for multi-page web applications

To create a multi-page web application, you need to learn some new skills like how to add a web form to the project, how to rename a web form, and how to display another page in the browser. You'll learn these skills in the topics that follow.

How to add a web form to a project

To add a new web form to a project, you use the Add New Item dialog box shown in figure 3-3. Notice that when you display this dialog box, the Web Form template is already selected. Then, you simply enter the name you want to use for the new form and click the Open button to add it to your project.

When you first add a new web form, it's displayed in a Web Forms Designer window as you can see here. Then, you can use the Toolbox to add controls to the form, and you can use the Properties window to set the properties for the form and controls. You can also display the Code Editor window for the form so you can add the code it requires.

To add an existing web form to a project, you can use the second procedure in this figure. You might want to do that if you need to create a form that's similar to a form in another project. Note that when you add the aspx file for a form to a project, the associated .aspx.vb and .aspx.resx files are added as well. (The resx file contains information about the .NET resources used by the form. This information is stored in XML format.)

The dialog box and starting page for a new form

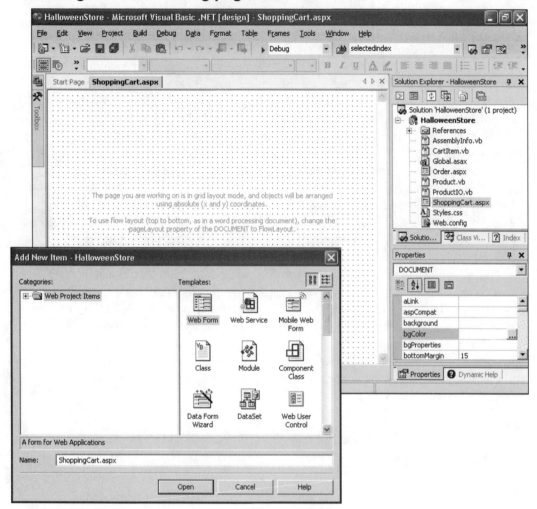

How to add a new web form

- Right-click on the project in the Solution Explorer and select Add→Add Web Form to display the Add New Item dialog box. The Web Form template is selected by default. Then, enter a name for the form and click the Open button.
- When you complete the Add New Item dialog box, an .aspx file is added to the project, and the form is displayed in the Web Forms Designer in grid layout mode.

How to add an existing web form

- Right-click on the project in the Solution Explorer and select Add→Add Existing Item to display the Add Existing item dialog box. Select All Files from the Files of type drop-down list. Then, locate and select the aspx file you want to add. That file and its associated .aspx.vb and .aspx.resx files are copied to the project.

Figure 3-3   How to add a web form to a project

How to rename a web form

When you add a web form to a project as described in the last topic, the form file is given the name you specify in the Add New Item dialog box. In addition, the class that contains the VB code for the form is given the same name, which is usually what you want. In some cases, though, you may need to rename the form file or the form class. In particular, you'll want to rename the default form so its name is more descriptive. Figure 3-4 shows you how.

As you can see, you can rename a web form file in one of three ways. First, you can click on it in the Solution Explorer so its properties are displayed in the Properties window. Then, you can change the File Name property. Second, you can use the Rename command in the shortcut menu for the file to change the file name directly in the Solution Explorer window as shown here. You can also change the name in the Solution Explorer by clicking on the file to select it and then clicking on it again. Regardless of the technique you use, you should be sure not to change or omit the file extension when you rename the file.

When you change the name of a form file, you might think that Visual Studio would change the name of the class that contains the Visual Basic code for the form. However, it doesn't. To do that, you have to open the Code Editor window for the form and change the name on the Class statement. In most cases, then, that's what you'll want to do. The exception is if you name the form file Default so that it will be displayed if the user enters a URL for the application that doesn't include a file name. Then, you might want to give the class a name that's more descriptive.

How to change the starting page for a multi-page web application

By default, the starting page for a web application is the form that's added to the project when you first create it. If that isn't what you want, you can set another form as the starting page. To do that, just right-click on the form and select the Set As Start Page command from the shortcut menu. I mentioned this in the last chapter, and this is illustrated in figure 2-15.

A web form file being renamed in the Solution Explorer window

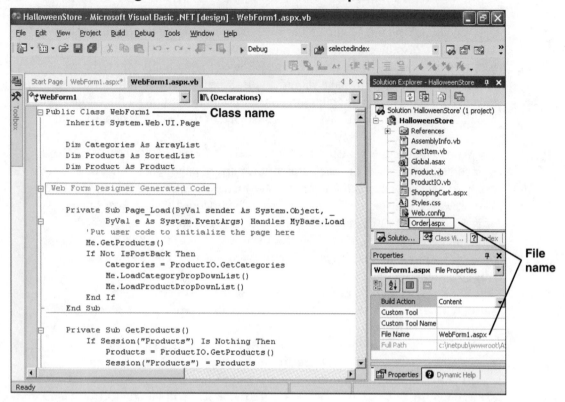

Three ways to rename a web form file

- Highlight the form in the Solution Explorer to display its properties and then change the File Name property. Be sure not to change or omit the file extension.

- Right-click on the form in the Solution Explorer and then select the Rename command from the shortcut menu that's displayed. Then, change the name directly in the Solution Explorer window.

- Click on the form in the Solution Explorer to select it. Then, click on it again and change the name directly in the Solution Explorer window.

How to rename the class that contains the Visual Basic code for a web form

- Display the code for the form in the Code Editor window. Then, change the name that's used for the form on the Class statement at the beginning of the file.

Note

- In most cases, you'll give a web form an appropriate name when you add it to the project. Since the form that's added by default when you create a project is named WebForm1, however, you'll usually want to change this name so it's more descriptive.

Figure 3-4   How to rename a web form

How to display another web page in the browser

When you develop an application with two or more pages, you'll need to know how to display one page from another page. When the user clicks the Add to Cart button on the Order page of the Halloween Store application, for example, the Shopping Cart page should be displayed. Similarly, when the user clicks the Continue Shopping button on the Shopping Cart page, the Order page should be displayed. To do that, you can use one of the two methods presented in figure 3-5.

When you use the Transfer method of the HttpServerUtility class, ASP.NET immediately terminates the execution of the current page. Then, it loads and executes the page specified on the Transfer method and returns it to the browser. The drawback to using this method is that when the new page is sent to the browser, the browser has no way of knowing that the application returned a different page. As a result, the URL for the original page is still displayed in the browser's address box. This can be confusing to the user and prevents the user from bookmarking the page.

The Redirect method of the HttpResponse class works somewhat differently. When this method is executed, it sends a special message called an *HTTP redirect message* back to the browser. This message causes the browser to send a new HTTP request to the server to request the new page. Then, the server processes the page and sends it back to the browser.

Note that because of the way the Redirect method works, it requires an extra round trip to the browser. If this extra round trip will cause a performance problem, you may want to use the Transfer method instead. For most applications, however, the user friendliness of the Redirect method outweighs the small performance gain you get when you use the Transfer method.

The Transfer method of the HttpServerUtility class

Method	Description
Transfer(URL)	Terminates the execution of the current page and transfers control to the page at the specified URL.

The Redirect method of the HttpResponse class

Method	Description
Redirect(URL)	Redirects the client to the specified URL and terminates the execution of the current page.

Code that transfers control to another page

```
Server.Transfer("ShoppingCart.aspx")
```

Code that redirects the client to another page

```
Response.Redirect("ShoppingCart.aspx")
```

Description

- The Transfer method is a member of the HttpServerUtility class, which contains helper methods for processing web requests. To refer to this class, you use the Server property of the page.

- The Redirect method is a member of the HttpResponse class, which contains information about the response. To refer to this class, you use the Response property of the page.

- Both the Transfer and Redirect methods cause the page specified by the URL to be displayed in the browser. See figure 3-6 for more information on coding URLs.

- When you use the Transfer method, the current page is terminated and a new page is processed in its place. This processing is efficient because it takes place on the server. However, the browser isn't updated to reflect the address of the new page.

- When you use the Redirect method, the server sends a special message called an *HTTP redirect message* to the browser. When the browser receives this message, it sends an HTTP request to the server to request the new page. The server then processes the new page and sends it back to the browser. Because this involves a round trip to the browser, it's less efficient than the Transfer method.

- In general, you should use the Redirect method to display another web page. You should use the Transfer method only if the application's performance is critical.

Note

- Session state is not affected by either the Transfer or the Redirect method.

Figure 3-5   How to display another web page in the browser

How to code absolute and relative URLs

In chapter 1, you learned about the basic components of a URL. The URLs you saw in that chapter were all *absolute URLs*. An absolute URL includes the domain name or IP address. When coded within a Transfer or Redirect method, an absolute URL lets you display a page at another web site. For example, the first two statements in figure 3-6 display a page at the web site with the domain name www.murach.com. The first statement displays a page named Default.aspx in the root directory of the web site. The second statement displays a page named Search.aspx in the Books directory of the web site.

To display a page within the same web site, you can use a *relative URL*. This type of URL specifies the location of the page relative to the directory that contains the current page. This is illustrated by the third and fourth statements in this figure. The third statement displays a page that's stored in the same directory as the current page. The fourth statement displays a page in the Login subdirectory of the directory that contains the current page.

The next two statements show how you can use a relative URL to navigate up the directory structure from the current directory. To navigate up one directory, you code two periods followed by a slash as shown in the fifth statement. To navigate up two directories, you code two periods and a slash followed by two more periods and a slash as shown in the sixth statement. To navigate up additional directories, you code two periods and a slash for each directory.

To navigate to the root directory for the host, you code a slash as shown in the next to last statement. You can also navigate to a directory within the root directory by coding the path for that directory following the slash as shown in the last statement.

Examples of absolute and relative URLs

Statements that use absolute URLs

```
Response.Redirect("http://www.murach.com/Default.aspx")
Response.Redirect("http://www.murach.com/Books/Search.aspx")
```

Statements that use relative URLs that are based on the current directory

```
Response.Redirect("Checkout.aspx")
Response.Redirect("Login/Register.aspx")
```

Statements that use relative URLs that navigate up the directory structure

```
Response.Redirect("../Register.aspx")
Response.Redirect("../../Register.aspx")
Response.Redirect("/Register.aspx")
Response.Redirect("/Login/Register.aspx")
```

Description

- When you code an *absolute URL*, you code the complete URL including the domain name or IP address for the site. Absolute URLs let you display pages at other web sites.

- When you code a *relative URL*, you base it on the current directory, that is, the directory that contains the current page.

- To go to the root directory for the host, you code a slash. Then, you can code one or more directories after the slash.

- To go up one level from the current directory, you code two periods and a slash. To go up two levels, you code two periods and a slash followed by two more periods and a slash. And so on.

Figure 3-6   How to code absolute and relative URLs

How to use drop-down lists and list boxes

Many applications require the display of one or more lists. For example, the Halloween Store application uses three lists: one for the categories, one for the products, and one for the shopping cart. To display lists like these, you can use either a *drop-down list control* or a *list box control*. The control you use depends mostly on how much room you have on the page for the control and how you want the user to interact with the list. Regardless of the control you choose, you use the same techniques to work with the control and the list it contains.

How to add list items

Figure 3-7 shows you how to add items to a list. To do that, you use the Add method of the collection that contains the list items. To refer to this collection, you use the Items property of the control.

The Add method lets you add list items in one of two ways. The easiest way is to specify the string value that you want to appear in the list. Then, this value is assigned to the Text property of the list item, which is the value that's displayed in the list. This is illustrated in the first example in this figure. Here, three string values are added to the list of items in a list box.

In addition to a Text property, a list item also has a Value property that you can use to store a value that's associated with the list item. To assign a value to this property, you can use the second technique shown in this figure. Here, a ListItem object is created for each item. Note that the values on the constructor for each item specify the values that are assigned to the Text and Value properties. After the ListItem object is created, it's added to the collection.

How to remove list items

Figure 3-7 also shows how to remove items from a list. To remove the item at a specified index location, you use the RemoveAt method as illustrated in the first example. Here, the item that's selected in a list box is removed from the list box. To do that, the index location is specified using the SelectedIndex property of the list box. You'll learn more about this property in the next figure.

The second example shows how you can remove all of the items from a list. To do that, you use the Clear method.

Although it's not shown in this figure, you should know that you can also use the Remove method to remove items from a drop-down list or list box. You'll learn about this method in chapter 7.

Common methods for adding and removing items from a drop-down list or list box

Method	Description
Add(string)	Adds a new item to the end of the collection, and assigns the specified string value to the Text property of the item.
Add(ListItem)	Adds the specified list item to the end of the collection.
RemoveAt(integer)	Removes the item at the specified index location from the collection.
Clear	Removes all the items from the collection.

Common properties of list items

Property	Description
Text	The text that's displayed for the list item.
Value	A value associated with the list item.

How to add list items

Code that loads items into a list box using strings

```
lstCreditCards.Items.Add("Visa")
lstCreditCards.Items.Add("MasterCard")
lstCreditCards.Items.Add("American Express")
```

Code that loads items into a drop-down list using ListItem objects

```
ddlMonths.Items.Add(New ListItem("January", 1))
ddlMonths.Items.Add(New ListItem("February", 2))
...
ddlMonths.Items.Add(New ListItem("December", 12))
```

How to remove list items

Code that removes the item at the specified index from a list box

```
lstCart.Items.RemoveAt(lstCart.SelectedIndex)
```

Code that removes all items from a list box

```
lstCart.Items.Clear()
```

Description

- A *drop-down list control* lets a user choose an item from a drop-down list of items. A *list box control* lets a user choose one or more items from a list of items.
- The items in a list are defined by ListItem objects that are contained in a ListItemCollection object. Items in this collection are numbered from zero.
- To get the ListItemCollection object associated with a drop-down list or list box, you use the Items property of the control.
- When you use the Add method of a list item collection to add a string to the collection, the Text property of the list item is set to the string value you specify. To set both the Text and Value properties of a list item, you must create a ListItem object and then add that object to the collection.

Figure 3-7   How to add and remove list items

How to work with drop-down lists and list boxes in code

Figure 3-8 presents some common properties of drop-down lists and list boxes that you can use to work with these controls in code. You saw how to use the Items property in the last figure. It returns the collection of list items in the control.

The Rows property applies only to a list box control. It determines the number of rows that are displayed in the list box at one time. Then, if the list contains more than that number of rows, a scroll bar is added so the user can scroll through the list.

The SelectedItem property lets you get the ListItem object for the item that's currently selected in the list. This is illustrated in the first example in this figure. Here, the SelectedItem property is used to get the item that's selected in a drop-down list. Then, the Value property is used to get the value of that item.

The SelectedIndex property contains the index value of the item that's currently selected in the list. You saw one way to use this property in the last figure: to remove the item that's selected in a list box. You can also use it to determine if an item is selected in a list box. This is illustrated in the second example in this figure. Here, the SelectedIndex property of a list box is tested to see if it's greater than -1. If it is, it means that an item is selected. Note that a drop-down list always has an item selected, so the value of its SelectedIndex property is always greater than -1.

When the user selects a different item from a drop-down list or list box, the SelectedIndexChanged event of that control is raised. You can respond to this event by coding an event procedure like the one shown in the third example in this figure. Note that for this to work, you have to set the AutoPostBack property of the control to True so the page is posted back to the server when the selected item changes. In addition, the EnableViewState property has to be set to True, which is the default setting.

When to use view state

As I said in the last chapter, you normally keep the default settings of True for the EnableViewState properties for a form and its controls. As a result, you don't need to know which controls on a form require that the EnableViewState property be set to True. In case you're interested, though, figure 3-8 gives some guidelines for when you need to use view state with drop-down lists and list boxes.

To start, view state has to be enabled for a drop-down list or list box if you want to respond to the SelectedIndexChanged event of the control. That way, ASP.NET can determine when the selected item changes. In general, you also need to use view state when you use code to load items into a list. For example, both the drop-down lists and the list box used by the Halloween Store application require the use of view state. Of course, if a list is loaded each time a page is processed, you don't need to use view state, but that's usually inefficient.

Common properties of drop-down list and list box controls

Property	Description
Items	The collection of ListItem objects that represents the items in the control.
Rows	The number of items that are displayed in a list box at one time. If the list contains more rows than can be displayed, a scroll bar is added automatically.
SelectedItem	The ListItem object for the currently selected item.
SelectedIndex	The index of the currently selected item. If no item is selected in a list box, the value of this property is -1.

Code that retrieves the value of the selected item in a drop-down list

```
Dim sID As String
sID = ddlProducts.SelectedItem.Value
```

Code that tests for a selected item in a list box

```
If lstCart.SelectedIndex > -1 Then
    .
    .
End If
```

Code that uses the SelectedIndexChanged event of a drop-down list

```
Private Sub ddlCategories_SelectedIndexChanged _
        (ByVal sender As System.Object, ByVal e As System.EventArgs) _
        Handles ddlCategories.SelectedIndexChanged
    Me.LoadProductDropDownList()
End Sub
```

How to work with drop-down lists and list boxes in code

- To work with the items in a drop-down list or list box, you use the Items property of the control. This property returns a ListItemCollection object that contains all of the items in the list.

- To get the value of a selected item, you use the SelectedItem property of the control to get the ListItem object for the item. Then, you can use the Value property of that item to get its value.

- The SelectedIndexChanged event is raised when the user selects a different item from a drop-down list or list box. If you want to perform processing when this event occurs, you must set the AutoPostBack and EnableViewState properties of the control to True.

When to use view state with drop-down lists and list boxes

- Use view state to save list items that are loaded in code. The exception is if the control is loaded each time the page is processed and returned to the browser.

- Use view state if you want ASP.NET to raise the SelectedIndexChanged event when the user selects an item from the list.

- You can also load list items using the ListItem Collection Editor (see chapter 7). In that case, the Text and Value properties for the list items are included in the HTML for the page, and view state isn't required.

Figure 3-8   How to work with drop-down lists and list boxes

How to add validation controls to a form

As you learned in the last chapter, a *validation control* is a special type of ASP.NET control that's used to validate input data. Each validation control is associated with an input control. Then, if the user enters invalid data into the input control, the validation control displays an error message on the page. The topics that follow introduce you to the validation controls that are available with ASP.NET and show you how to use the two most common validation controls.

An introduction to the validation controls

Figure 3-9 summarizes the validation controls that are available with ASP.NET. The first five controls are called *validators*. These are the controls you use to check that the user has entered valid data. In contrast, you use the validation summary control to display a summary of all the errors on a page.

The easiest way to add a validation control to a web form is to drag it from the Web Forms tab of the Toolbox. In most cases, you'll position the validation controls next to the controls they validate as shown in the example in this figure. That way, if one of these controls detects an error, the error message that's generated will be displayed next to the control that contains the invalid data.

As you can see, two validation controls have been added to the Order form shown in this example. Note that both of these controls are associated with the Quantity text box. The first one is a *required field validator* that checks that the user entered a value into this text box. The second one is a *compare validator* that checks that the user entered an integer greater than zero. The required field validator is necessary because if the user doesn't enter a value into the control, the validation test done by the compare validator will pass. That's true of the other validators as well. If an input control requires an entry, then, you should include a required field validator in addition to any other validators you use.

Before I go on, you should realize that the validation controls typically work by running script on the client. Because of that, the page isn't posted back to the server unless all of the validators pass their tests. In most cases, that's what you want. If you need to perform more complex validation, however, you may need to control where and when the validation is performed. You'll learn more about that in chapter 8. For now, you should realize that the validation tests are always done on the server, even if they're done on the client. That way, the validators can be used with browsers that don't support scripts.

The validation controls on the Order form of the Halloween Store application

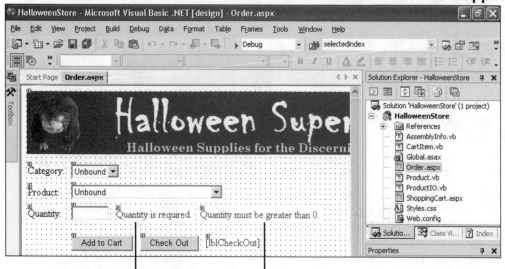

Required field validator   Compare validator

The validation controls provided by ASP.NET

Control	Description
Required field validator	Checks that an entry has been made.
Compare validator	Checks an entry against a constant value or the value of another control. Can also be used to check for a specific data type.
Range validator	Checks that an entry is within a specified range.
Regular expression validator	Checks that an entry matches a pattern, such as a telephone number or an e-mail address.
Custom validator	Checks an entry using validation code that you write yourself.
Validation summary	Displays a summary of error messages from the other validation controls.

Description

- You can use *validation controls* to test user input and produce error messages. The validation is performed when the focus leaves the control that's being validated. The exception is the required field validator, which performs its validation when the user clicks on a button control whose CausesValidation property is set to True.

- Each validation control is associated with a specific Web Server or HTML Server control. You can associate one or more validation controls with a single server control.

- The validation controls work by running client-side script. Then, if the validation fails, the page isn't posted back to the server. (The validation is also performed on the server in case the client doesn't support scripts.)

Figure 3-9   An introduction to the validation controls

How to use the required field validator

To use the required field validator, you set the properties shown in the table at the top of figure 3-10. These are the properties that are used by all the validators.

To start, you associate the validation control with a specific input control on the form through its ControlToValidate property. Then, when the user clicks on a button whose CausesValidation property is set to True, the validator checks to be sure that a value has been entered into the input control. If so, the page is posted to the server, assuming that any other validators on the form passed their validation tests. If any of the validators don't pass their validation tests, however, the appropriate error messages are displayed.

When an error occurs, the Display property of the validation control determines how the message in the ErrorMessage property is displayed. The possible values for the Display property are Static, which lets you allocate space for the error message in the page layout; Dynamic, which causes space to be added for displaying the error message when an error occurs; and None. Note that when you use grid layout, changing the Display property to Dynamic has no effect. If you change it to None, however, you can use a validation summary control to display a list of the error messages in a predefined location.

The third table in figure 3-10 shows how these properties are set for the required field validator on the Order form. As you can see, this validator will validate the Quantity text box and will display the message "Quantity is required." if the user doesn't enter a quantity. Because the form is designed in grid layout mode, the Display property is left at its default value of Static.

How to use the compare validator

The compare validator lets you compare the value entered into an input control with a constant value. You can also use the compare validator to make sure that the value is a particular data type. To use this control, you set the additional properties shown in the second table in figure 3-10.

You specify the value you want to compare the input data with in the ValueToCompare property. Then, you set the Operator property to indicate the type of comparison you want to perform, and you set the Type property to the type of data you're comparing. In the third table in this figure, for example, you can see the property settings for the compare validator on the Order form. This validator tests that the user enters an integer value greater than zero into the Quantity text box. If the user enters a number that isn't greater than zero, or if the user enters a non-numeric value, the error message will be displayed.

To test just for a data type, you set the Type property to the type of data you're testing for, and you set the Operator property to DataTypeCheck. If you want to test that the user enters a date, for example, you set the Type property to Date and the Operator property to DataTypeCheck. Then, any valid date the user enters is acceptable.

Common validation control properties

Property	Description
ControlToValidate	The ID of the control to be validated.
Display	Determines how an error message is displayed. Specify Static to allocate space for the message in the page layout, Dynamic to have the space allocated when an error occurs, or None to display the errors in a validation summary control.
ErrorMessage	The message that's displayed in the validation control when the validation fails.

Additional properties of a compare validator

Property	Description
ValueToCompare	The value that the control specified in the ControlToValidate property should be compared to.
Operator	The type of comparison to perform (Equal, NotEqual, GreaterThan, GreaterThanEqual, LessThan, LessThanEqual, or DataTypeCheck).
Type	The data type to use for the comparison (String, Integer, Double, Date, or Currency).

The property settings for the validation controls on the Order form

Default ID	Property	Value
RequiredFieldValidator1	ControlToValidate	txtQuantity
	Display	Static
	ErrorMessage	Quantity is required.
CompareValidator1	ControlToValidate	txtQuantity
	Display	Static
	ValueToCompare	0
	Operator	Greater Than
	Type	Integer
	ErrorMessage	Quantity must be greater than 0.

Description

- The required field validator is typically used with text box controls, but can also be used with list controls. See chapter 8 for details.

- . If the user doesn't enter a value into the input control that a compare validator is associated with, the validation test passes. Because of that, you should also provide a required field validator if a value is required.

- When you use grid layout, the error message associated with a validator always appears in the same location as the validator. Because of that, changing the Display property to Dynamic has no effect.

Figure 3-10   How to use the required field and compare validators

How to use session state

In chapter 1, you learned that HTTP is a stateless protocol. You also learned that ASP.NET uses *session state* to keep track of each user session and that you can use session state to maintain program values across executions of an application. Now, you'll learn more about how session state works and how you use it.

How session state works

Figure 3-11 shows how session state solves the problem of state management for ASP.NET applications. As you can see, session state tracks individual user sessions by creating a *session state object* for each user's session. This object contains a session ID that uniquely identifies the session. This session ID is passed back to the browser along with the HTTP response. Then, if the browser makes another request, the session ID is included in the request so ASP.NET can identify the session. ASP.NET then matches the session with the session state object that was previously saved.

By default, ASP.NET sends the session ID to the browser as a *cookie*. Then, when the browser sends another request to the server, it automatically includes the cookie that contains the session ID with the request. ASP.NET can also implement session state by including the session ID in the URL. You'll learn more about how cookies work in the next chapter, and you'll learn more about how to use URLs to implement session state in chapter 9.

Although ASP.NET automatically uses session state to track user sessions, you can also use it to store your own data across executions of an application. This figure lists three typical reasons for doing that. First, you can use session state to maintain information about the user. After a user logs on to an application, for example, you can use the logon information to retrieve information about the user from a file or a database. Then, you can store that information in the session state object so it's available each time the application is executed.

Second, you can use session state to save objects that the user is working with. For example, consider a maintenance application that lets the user change customer records. In that case, you can save the customer record that's currently being modified in the session state object so it's available the next time the application is executed.

Third, you can use session state to keep track of the operation a user is currently performing. If a maintenance application lets the user add or change customer records, for example, you can save an item in the session state object that indicates if the user is currently adding or changing a record. That way, the application can determine how to proceed each time it's executed.

How ASP.NET maintains the state of a session

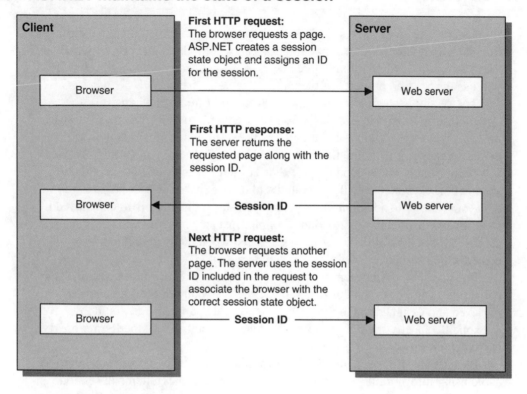

Description

- ASP.NET uses *session state* to track the state of each user of an application. To do that, it creates a *session state object*.
- The session state object includes a session ID that's sent back to the browser as a *cookie*. Then, the browser automatically returns the session ID cookie to the server with each request so the server can associate the browser with an existing session state object.
- If you want your application to work on browsers that don't support cookies, you can configure ASP.NET to encode the session ID in the URL for each page of the application. For more information, see chapter 9.
- You can use the session state object to store and retrieve items across executions of an application.

Typical uses for session state

- **To keep information about the user**, such as the user's name or whether the user has registered.
- **To save objects the user is working with**, such as a shopping cart or a customer record.
- **To keep track of pending operations**, such as what steps the user has completed while placing an order.

Figure 3-11   How session state works

How to work with data in session state

Figure 3-12 shows how you can use the session state object to store application data. To do that, you use the properties and methods of this object, which is created from the HttpSessionState class. To access this object from a web form, you use the Session property of the page.

The session state object contains a collection of items that consist of the item names and their values. One way to add an item to this collection is to use the Item property as shown in the first example. (In this case, since Item is the default property, it is omitted.) Here, an object named ShoppingCart is assigned to a session state item named Cart. If the Cart item doesn't exist when this statement is executed, it will be created. Otherwise, its value will be updated.

Another way to add an item to the session state collection is to use the Add method, as illustrated in the second example. Just as when you use the Item property, if the item already exists, it's updated when the Add method is executed. Otherwise, it's added to the collection.

You can also use the Item property to retrieve an item from the session state collection as shown in the third example. Here, the value of the Cart item is retrieved and assigned to the ShoppingCart variable. Once again, you don't have to explicitly specify the Item property in this example because the Item property is the default property.

Because the session state object uses valuable server memory, you should avoid using it to store large items. Or, if you must store large items in session state, you should remove the items as soon as you're done with them. To do that, you use the Remove method as illustrated in the fourth example in this figure.

The first four examples in this figure use the Session property of the page to access the session state object. Because Session is a property of the System.Web.UI.Page class, however, you can only use this property from a class that inherits the System.Web.UI.Page class. In other words, you can only use it from a code-behind file for a page. To access session state from a class that doesn't inherit the System.Web.UI.Page class, such as a database or business class, you use the Session property of the HttpContext object for the current request. To get this HttpContext object, you use the Current property of the HttpContext class as illustrated in the last example in this figure.

Common properties and methods of the HttpSessionState class

Property	Description
SessionID	The unique ID of the session.
Item(name)	The value of the session state item with the specified name. (Item is the default property of the HttpSessionState class, so you can omit it when you access a session state item.)
Count	The number of items in the session state collection.

Method	Description
Add(name, value)	Adds an item to the session state collection.
Clear	Removes all items from the session state collection.
Remove(name)	Removes the item with the specified name from the session state collection.

A statement that adds or updates a session state item

```
Session("Cart") = ShoppingCart
```

Another way to add or update a session state item

```
Session.Add("Cart", ShoppingCart)
```

A statement that retrieves the value of a session state item

```
ShoppingCart = Session("Cart")
```

A statement that removes an item from session state

```
Session.Remove("Cart")
```

A statement that retrieves the value of a session state item from a class that doesn't inherit System.Web.UI.Page

```
ShoppingCart = HttpContext.Current.Session("Cart")
```

Description

- The session state object is created from the HttpSessionState class, which defines a collection of session state items.
- To access the session state object from the code-behind file for a web form, use the Session property of the page.
- To access the session state object from a class other than the code-behind file for a web form, use the Current property of the HttpContext class to get the HttpContext object for the current request. This object contains information about the HTTP request. Then, use the Session property of the HttpContext object to get the session state object.
- By default, session state objects are maintained in server memory. As a result, you should avoid storing large items in session state.

Figure 3-12   How to work with data in session state

The Visual Basic code for the Halloween Store application

Now that you've learned the skills for developing multi-page web applications, you're ready to see the code for the Halloween Store application. This application consists of the Order and Shopping Cart forms you saw earlier in this chapter, plus three classes. The Product class defines the data for a single product; the ProductIO class contains methods that get the products and product categories used in the drop-down lists; and the CartItem class defines the data for an item in the shopping cart.

As you will see, the most difficult parts of the code for this application aren't the ones that involve ASP.NET code. Instead, they're the ones that deal with the array list and the sorted lists that are required for an application like this. This once again emphasizes the need for strong VB.NET skills.

The code for the Order form

Figure 3-13 presents the code for the Order form. This form starts by declaring three variables: (1) an array list named Categories that will hold the product categories; (2) a sorted list named Products that will hold the products; and (3) a variable named Product that is created from the Product class and will be used to hold the data for a single product.

Each time the page is loaded, the Load procedure starts by executing the GetProducts procedure to get the products. As you can see, this procedure starts by checking if the products are stored in session state. If not, the GetProducts method of the ProductIO class is executed to retrieve the products from a file, which are then stored in the Products sorted list. This sorted list, in turn, is saved in a session state item named Products. On the other hand, if this sorted list is already stored in session state, it is simply retrieved from session state and stored in the Products sorted list.

If you look ahead to the code for the ProductIO class in figure 3-15, you can see the loop in the GetProducts method that retrieves the product data from a binary file. Here, the last line in the loop adds an item to the sorted list that consists of the key for the item and a value that is a Product object. If you look at the Product class in this figure, you can see that it defines three public variables that hold the name, category, and unit price for a product.

After the products are retrieved, the Load procedure checks if the page is being posted back to the server. If it isn't, that means that the page is being accessed for the first time. As a result, the GetCategories method of the ProductIO class is executed to get the categories from a binary file and store them in the Categories array list. Next, the LoadCategoryDropDownList procedure is executed to add one item to the Category drop-down list for each element in the array list. In this case, each element is a String variable.

Last, the Load procedure executes the LoadProductDropDownList procedure. This procedure starts by clearing the Product drop-down list. That's necessary because this list changes each time the user selects a different category. Then, the

The code for the Order form

```vbnet
Public Class WebForm1
    Inherits System.Web.UI.Page

    Dim Categories As ArrayList
    Dim Products As SortedList
    Dim Product As Product

    Private Sub Page_Load(ByVal sender As System.Object, _
            ByVal e As System.EventArgs) Handles MyBase.Load
        'Put user code to initialize the page here
        Me.GetProducts()
        If Not IsPostBack Then
            Categories = ProductIO.GetCategories
            Me.LoadCategoryDropDownList()
            Me.LoadProductDropDownList()
        End If
    End Sub

    Private Sub GetProducts()
        If Session("Products") Is Nothing Then
            Products = ProductIO.GetProducts()
            Session("Products") = Products
        Else
            Products = Session("Products")
        End If
    End Sub

    Private Sub LoadCategoryDropDownList()
        Dim sCategory As String
        For Each sCategory In Categories
            ddlCategories.Items.Add(sCategory)
        Next
    End Sub

    Private Sub LoadProductDropDownList()
        ddlProducts.Items.Clear()
        Dim ProductEntry As DictionaryEntry
        For Each ProductEntry In Products
            Product = ProductEntry.Value
            If Product.Category = ddlCategories.SelectedItem.Text Then
                ddlProducts.Items.Add(New ListItem(Product.Name & " ($" _
                    & Product.UnitPrice & ")", ProductEntry.Key))
            End If
        Next
    End Sub
```

Figure 3-13   The Visual Basic code for the Order form (part 1 of 2)

procedure adds an item to this list for each item in the Products sorted list that's in the selected category.

To understand this code, you need to know that each item in a sorted list is a DictionaryEntry structure that consists of a key and a value. This means that the loop in this procedure is done once for each dictionary entry, and the value of each entry is stored in a Product variable, which represents a Product object. Then, the procedure checks the Category property of the Product object to see if it's equal to the Text property of the item that's selected in the Category drop-down list. If it is, the procedure adds a new item to the Product drop-down list. The Text property of this list item consists of the concatenation of the product name, the unit price, and two strings, and the Value property of this list item is set to the key value of the sorted list item, which is the product ID.

If the user clicks the Add to Cart button, the Click event procedure for that button is executed as shown on page 2 of this listing. It starts by getting the Value property of the item that's selected in the Product drop-down list, which contains the product ID. Then, it declares a new CartItem variable from the CartItem class and a sorted list named ShoppingCart. If you look ahead to figure 3-15, you can see that the CartItem class defines three public variables that hold the name, unit price, and quantity for a shopping cart item.

Next, this procedure checks if a session state item named Cart already exists. If so, it retrieves that item and stores it in the sorted list variable named ShoppingCart. Otherwise, it creates a new sorted list named ShoppingCart.

After the shopping cart list is retrieved or created, the Add procedure checks if the list already contains an entry for the selected product. To do that, it uses the ContainsKey method to look for an entry with the product ID of the product. If an entry is found with this product ID, it's assigned to the CartItem variable. Then, the quantity the user entered is added to the existing quantity for this item. Finally, the shopping cart list is updated with this item.

If the product isn't found in the shopping cart, the Product object is retrieved from the Products sorted list and stored in the Product variable. Then, the product name and unit price are retrieved from the Product object and assigned to the Name and UnitPrice properties of the CartItem object. In addition, the quantity entered by the user is assigned to the Quantity property of the CartItem object, and the CartItem object is added to the shopping cart.

Once the shopping cart list is updated with the product data, the procedure saves it in session state. Then, the last statement in the Add procedure redirects the browser to the ShoppingCart page, which uses the session state data. You'll see how this works right after you look at the last two procedures.

The procedure for the SelectedIndexChanged event of the Category drop-down list is executed when a user selects a different category. This procedure executes the LoadProductDropDownList procedure to update the Product drop-down list so it displays only the products for the selected category. You can refer back to page 1 of this listing if you need to review how this works.

The last procedure for this form is executed when the user clicks the Check Out button. Because the check out function isn't implemented, though, this procedure simply assigns a message to a label that appears to the right of the Check Out button.

The code for the Order form

```vb
Private Sub btnAdd_Click(ByVal sender As System.Object, _
        ByVal e As System.EventArgs) Handles btnAdd.Click
    Dim sID As String
    sID = ddlProducts.SelectedItem.Value
    Dim CartItem As New CartItem
    Dim ShoppingCart As SortedList
    If Session("Cart") Is Nothing Then
        ShoppingCart = New SortedList
    Else
        ShoppingCart = Session("Cart")
    End If
    If ShoppingCart.ContainsKey(sID) Then
        CartItem = ShoppingCart(sID)
        CartItem.Quantity += txtQuantity.Text
        ShoppingCart(sID) = CartItem
    Else
        Product = Products(sID)
        CartItem.Name = Product.Name
        CartItem.UnitPrice = Product.UnitPrice
        CartItem.Quantity = txtQuantity.Text
        ShoppingCart.Add(sID, CartItem)
    End If
    Session("Cart") = ShoppingCart
    Response.Redirect("ShoppingCart.aspx")
End Sub

Private Sub ddlCategories_SelectedIndexChanged _
        (ByVal sender As System.Object, ByVal e As System.EventArgs) _
        Handles ddlCategories.SelectedIndexChanged
    Me.LoadProductDropDownList()
End Sub

Private Sub btnCheckOut_Click(ByVal sender As System.Object, _
        ByVal e As System.EventArgs) Handles btnCheckOut.Click
    lblCheckOut.Text = "The check out function has not been implemented."
End Sub

End Class
```

Figure 3-13   The Visual Basic code for the Order form (part 2 of 2)

The code for the Shopping Cart form

Figure 3-14 presents the code for the Shopping Cart form. This form starts by declaring a variable that will hold the sorted list for the shopping cart. Then, each time the page is loaded, the Load procedure retrieves the shopping cart list from session state and stores it in this variable.

If the page is being loaded for the first time, the Load procedure also executes the DisplayShoppingCart procedure. This procedure starts by clearing the list box that will display the shopping cart items. Then, it adds an item to the list box for each item in the shopping cart list. To do that, it retrieves the value of each item in the list and stores it in the CartItem variable. After that, it uses the properties of the CartItem object to format the text that's displayed for each item.

If the user clicks the Remove button, the Click event procedure for this button starts by checking to see whether an item in the shopping cart list box is selected. If so, the selected item is deleted from the shopping cart. Then, the DisplayShoppingCart procedure is executed to redisplay the shopping cart list without the deleted item. When the Remove procedure ends, the Shopping Cart form is sent back to the browser.

Please note that the Remove procedure doesn't need to specifically update the session state object before it ends. That's because the Load procedure sets the ShoppingCart variable to the Cart item in the session state object. But that means that the variable doesn't actually hold the data, it points to the Cart item. Then, when the code in the Remove procedure removes an element from the ShoppingCart list, it is actually removed from the Cart item in the session state object. This principle also works for the procedures that are executed for the click events of the Empty and Continue buttons.

If the user clicks the Empty button, the Click event procedure for this button is executed. This procedure clears the shopping cart and the shopping cart list box. Note, however, that the last line in this procedure could call the DisplayShoppingCart procedure instead of clearing the list box, although that would be less efficient. Similarly, the Remove procedure could use the Remove method of the list box to remove the item at the selected index instead of calling the DisplayShoppingCart procedure. This just shows that there is usually more than one way that procedures like these can be coded.

The last two event procedures handle the Click events of the Continue Shopping and Check Out buttons. If the user clicks the Continue Shopping button, the browser is redirected to the Order page so the user can select another product. If the user clicks the Check Out button, a message is displayed indicating that this function hasn't been implemented.

The code for the Shopping Cart form

```
Public Class ShoppingCart
    Inherits System.Web.UI.Page

    Dim ShoppingCart As SortedList

    Private Sub Page_Load(ByVal sender As System.Object, _
            ByVal e As System.EventArgs) Handles MyBase.Load
        'Put user code to initialize the page here
        ShoppingCart = Session("Cart")
        If Not IsPostBack Then
            Me.DisplayShoppingCart()
        End If
    End Sub

    Private Sub DisplayShoppingCart()
        lstCart.Items.Clear()
        Dim CartItem As CartItem
        Dim CartEntry As DictionaryEntry
        For Each CartEntry In ShoppingCart
            CartItem = CartEntry.Value
            lstCart.Items.Add(CartItem.Name & " (" & CartItem.Quantity _
                & " at $" & CartItem.UnitPrice & " each)")
        Next
    End Sub

    Private Sub btnRemove_Click(ByVal sender As System.Object, _
            ByVal e As System.EventArgs) Handles btnRemove.Click
        If lstCart.SelectedIndex > -1 Then
            ShoppingCart.RemoveAt(lstCart.SelectedIndex)
            Me.DisplayShoppingCart()
        End If
    End Sub

    Private Sub btnEmpty_Click(ByVal sender As Object, _
            ByVal e As System.EventArgs) Handles btnEmpty.Click
        ShoppingCart.Clear()
        lstCart.Items.Clear()
    End Sub

    Private Sub btnContinue_Click(ByVal sender As System.Object, _
            ByVal e As System.EventArgs) Handles btnContinue.Click
        Response.Redirect("Order.aspx")
    End Sub

    Private Sub btnCheckOut_Click(ByVal sender As System.Object, _
            ByVal e As System.EventArgs) Handles btnCheckOut.Click
        lblCheckOut.Text = "The check out function has not been implemented."
    End Sub

End Class
```

Figure 3-14   The Visual Basic code for the Shopping Cart form

The code for the Product, ProductIO, and CartItem classes

Figure 3-15 presents the code for the Product, ProductIO, and CartItem classes. Since you've already seen how the Product and CartItem classes are used, I'll focus on the ProductIO class here.

The ProductIO class consists of two methods. The first one, GetCategories, gets the categories that are displayed in the Category drop-down list from a binary file. This method is called by the Load procedure of the Order form the first time the form is loaded. Notice that this method returns the categories in an array list, which is a one-dimensional collection of elements. In this case, these elements are String objects that contain the names of the categories. Also notice that before the array list is returned, it's sorted. That way, the categories will appear alphabetically in the drop-down list.

The second method, GetProducts, gets the products that are displayed in the Product drop-down list from a binary file. This method is similar to the GetCategories method. The main difference is that the products are stored in a sorted list instead of an array list. Because of that, the list is sorted automatically. As you have already learned, each element in a sorted list consists of a key and a value. In this case, the key is the product ID and the value is a Product object that consists of name, category, and unit price.

The code for the Product class

```
Public Class Product
    Public Name As String
    Public Category As String
    Public UnitPrice As Decimal
End Class
```

The code for the ProductIO class

```
Imports System.IO
Public Class ProductIO

    Public Shared Function GetCategories() As ArrayList
        Dim CategoryList As New ArrayList
        Dim CategoryStream As New FileStream("C:\MurachData\Categories.dat", _
                            FileMode.Open, FileAccess.Read)
        Dim CategoryReader As New BinaryReader(CategoryStream)
        Dim sCategory As String
        Do Until CategoryReader.PeekChar = -1
            sCategory = CategoryReader.ReadString
            CategoryList.Add(sCategory)
        Loop
        CategoryReader.Close()
        CategoryList.Sort()
        Return CategoryList
    End Function

    Public Shared Function GetProducts() As SortedList
        Dim Products As New SortedList
        Dim ProductStream As New FileStream("C:\MurachData\Products.dat", _
                            FileMode.Open, FileAccess.Read)
        Dim ProductReader As New BinaryReader(ProductStream)
        Dim sID As String
        Do Until ProductReader.PeekChar = -1
            Dim Product As New Product
            sID = ProductReader.ReadString
            Product.Category = ProductReader.ReadString
            Product.Name = ProductReader.ReadString
            Product.UnitPrice = ProductReader.ReadDecimal
            Products.Add(sID, Product)
        Loop
        ProductReader.Close()
        Return Products
    End Function

End Class
```

The code for the CartItem class

```
Public Class CartItem
    Public Name As String
    Public UnitPrice As Decimal
    Public Quantity As Decimal
End Class
```

Figure 3-15   The Visual Basic code for the Product, ProductIO, and CartItem classes

Perspective

In this chapter, you learned the basic skills you need for developing multi-page web applications. In addition, you learned how to use four new web controls: drop-down lists, list boxes, required field validators, and compare validators. You also learned how to use session state to store data between executions of the pages of an application. With these skills, you should be able to develop simple multi-page web applications of your own.

Note, however, that developing web applications with Visual Basic .NET also requires a solid set of Visual Basic skills. In fact, the most difficult code for the application in this chapter isn't the ASP.NET code. Instead, it's the code that deals with the sorted lists, the DictionaryEntry structures, the binary files, and the Product and CartItem objects. But that type of code is commonly required in a web application like this.

So, if you're having trouble with that type of code, you will eventually want to enhance your VB.NET programming skills. We think the best way to do that is to use our *Beginning Visual Basic .NET* book, but that can wait. As long as you understand the ASP.NET aspects of the applications in this book, you can focus on that for right now and master the Visual Basic coding later on.

Terms

HTTP redirect message
absolute URL
relative URL
drop-down list control
list box control
validation control
validator
required field validator
compare validator
session state
session state object
cookie

4

How to use datasets and cookies

As you develop ASP.NET applications, you'll frequently work with data that's retrieved from a database and stored in a dataset. That's why this chapter introduces you to the use of databases and datasets. Then, in section 3, you can expand on this knowledge as you learn to develop more complex database applications.

Since many of the ASP.NET applications you develop will use cookies, this chapter also shows you how to use them. A cookie typically contains a small amount of user information like an email address that's stored on the user's PC. Then, a web application can use this information to identify the user and get the user's information from a database. In other words, you commonly use cookies in conjunction with databases.

How to retrieve data from a database into a dataset

Before you can use the data in a database, you usually need to retrieve it from the database and store it in a dataset. Then, you can use Visual Basic to work with the data in the dataset. In the topics that follow, you'll learn how to get the data into a dataset.

Three of the tables in the Halloween database

Figure 4-1 presents three of the tables that are in the Halloween database that's used by the Halloween Store application that you've been studying. These tables should serve as the basis for a quick review of the database concepts and terms that you should know for this chapter. Then, as you go through this chapter, you will see how these tables are used by the Halloween Store application.

If you look at the database diagram in this figure, you can see that it gives the names of the columns that are available in each row of each table. For instance, the Categories table contains three columns, and the Customers table contains eight columns. As you would guess, the Categories table contains the data for the product categories. The Products table contains the data for the products that are presented by the application. And the Customers table contains the data for each customer that orders from the Halloween store.

The key symbol for each table in the diagram indicates which of the columns has the key value that uniquely identifies each row of the table. In the Products table, for example, the ProductID column contains the key. And in the Customers table, the Email column contains the key.

The line that connects the Categories and Products table means that there is a relationship between these tables. In particular, these tables are related by the values in the CategoryID column, which is in both tables. The infinity symbol to the right of the connecting line means that there may be more than one row in the Products table that has the same CategoryID value as the related row in the Categories table.

To get data from a database, a program issues SQL Select statements like those in this figure. The first statement, for example, gets the CategoryID and ShortName columns from the Categories table. And the Order By clause in this statement sorts the rows by the value in the ShortName column before the rows are returned by the statement. The asterisk (*) in the third Select statement in this figure means that all of the columns in each row of the Customers table are returned by the statement.

The tables in the Halloween database

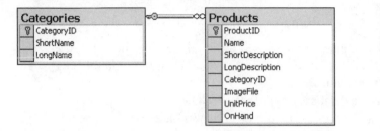
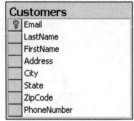

SQL statements that retrieve data from the tables

A Select statement that retrieves two columns from the Categories table

```
Select CategoryID, ShortName
    From Categories Order By ShortName
```

A Select statement that retrieves six columns from the Products table

```
Select ProductID, CategoryID, Name, LongDescription, ImageFile, UnitPrice
    From Products Order By Name
```

A Select statement that retrieves all columns from the Customers table

```
Select * From Customers
```

Description

- A database consists of one or more tables, and each table consists of columns and rows.

- SQL statements are used to work with the data in a table. Select statements are used to retrieve data from one or more tables, and Insert, Update, and Delete statements are used to add, update, and delete one or more rows in a table.

- The database diagram shown above was created by using the Database Designer. This tool is available from the Server Explorer window of Visual Studio .NET.

Figure 4-1   Three of the tables in the Halloween database

How to use ADO.NET to retrieve data from a database into a dataset

A *dataset* acts as a container for data used by an application. In many cases, a dataset contains data that's retrieved from a database. Then, you use the data in the dataset in your web applications.

To retrieve data from a database, you use the ADO.NET classes provided by the *.NET data providers*. To get data from a SQL Server database, for example, you use the SQL Server data provider. Figure 4-2 lists the core classes provided by this data provider.

To establish a connection with a database, you use a *connection* object. To identify the data you want to retrieve, you use a *command* object. And to manage the process of retrieving data from the database and storing it in a dataset, you use a *data adapter* object.

The code in this figure illustrates how you create and use these objects. The first group of statements creates a connection object. The first statement declares a variable to hold the connection. The second statement creates a string variable that specifies the *connection string* that will be used to connect to the database. Then, the third statement assigns this string to the ConnectionString property of the connection.

The next group of statements creates a command object. The first statement declares a variable to hold the command. Then, the second statement creates a string variable that contains the Select statement that will be used to retrieve the data from the database. The third statement assigns this string to the CommandText property of the command. And the fourth statement assigns the connection object created by the first group of statements to the Connection property of the command.

The next two statements create the data adapter object. The first statement declares a variable to hold the data adapter. Then, the second statement assigns the command object created by the second group of statements to the SelectCommand property of the data adapter.

The last two statements create the dataset, retrieve data from the database, and store it in the dataset. Notice that a single method of the data adapter, Fill, is used to retrieve and store the data. This statement causes the Select statement in the command object specified by the SelectCommand property of the data adapter to be passed to the database specified by the Connection property of that command. Then, after the Select statement is executed, the result set it produces is sent back to the data adapter, which stores the result in a *data table* within the dataset. In this case, the data is stored in a data table named Products.

Of course, the data provider objects have properties and methods other than the ones shown in this example. You'll learn about many of those properties and methods later in this book. For simple applications, though, the ones shown here are all you'll need.

Core classes provided by the SQL Server data provider

Class	Description
SqlConnection	Establishes a connection to a database.
SqlCommand	Represents an individual SQL statement that can be executed against the database.
SqlDataAdapter	Provides the link between the command and connection objects and a dataset object.

Code that retrieves data from a database and stores it in a dataset

```
Dim conHalloween as SqlConnection
Dim sConnection As String = "Data Source=DOUG\VSDOTNET;" _
    & "Initial Catalog=Halloween;Integrated Security=SSPI"
conHalloween.ConnectionString = sConnection

Dim cmdProducts As New SqlCommand
Dim sSelect As String = "Select ProductID, CategoryID, Name, " _
                    & "ShortDescription, LongDescription, UnitPrice " _
                    & "From Products Order By Name"
cmdProducts.CommandText = sSelect
cmdProducts.Connection = conHalloween

Dim daProducts As New SqlDataAdapter
daProducts.SelectCommand = cmdProducts

Dim dsProducts As New DataSet
daProducts.Fill(dsProducts, "Products")
```

Description

- The *ADO.NET* classes that you use to work with a database are provided by the *.NET data providers*. In addition to the SQL Server data provider shown above, ADO.NET provides OLE DB, ODBC, and Oracle data providers.

- A *dataset* stores data from the database so it can be accessed by the application. To retrieve data from the database, you use the data provider objects.

- A *data adapter* manages the flow of data between a database and a dataset. To do that, it uses *commands* that define the SQL statements to be issued. The commands connect to the database using a *connection*.

- The *connection string* for a connection includes information such as the name of the server, the name of the database, and login information.

- All of the ADO.NET objects are implemented by classes in the System.Data namespace of the .NET Framework. The classes for the SQL Server data provider are stored in the System.Data.SqlClient namespace. You should add an Imports statement for this namespace in any class that uses it.

Figure 4-2   How to use ADO.NET to retrieve data from a database into a dataset

Three methods of the HalloweenDB class

As you learned in chapter 1, the code for database operations is commonly stored in a database class in the database layer of an application. Because we've used this architecture for the Halloween Store application, the methods for database retrieval are stored in the HalloweenDB class. Three of the methods of this class are illustrated in figure 4-3.

The first method, GetCategories, creates a dataset that contains information that's retrieved from the Categories table of the Halloween database. As you can see in the Select statement that's assigned to the CommandText property of the command object, the data includes the CategoryID and the ShortName columns. Here again, the categories are sorted by the ShortName column.

To get a connection to the database, this method calls the Connection procedure shown at the bottom of this page. This procedure creates a connection object with the appropriate connection information and then passes that connection back to the GetCategories method. The connection is then assigned to the Connection property of the command object.

Next, the GetCategories method creates a data adapter object and assigns the command object to its SelectCommand property. Then, it executes the Fill method of the data adapter to retrieve the data specified by the Select statement. That data is then stored in the dataset in a data table named Categories, and the dataset is returned to the calling procedure.

The next method, GetProducts, is similar. It retrieves product information from the Products table in the Halloween database. This data is sorted by the product name and stored in a dataset in a data table named Products. Notice that before this method fills the dataset, it sets the MissingSchemaAction property of the data adapter to MissingSchemaAction.AddWithKey. That way, the schema of the data table that's created will identify the ProductID column as the primary key of the Products table. As you'll see later on, the Order form of the application uses this key to retrieve the row with a given key value.

The third method in the HalloweenDB class retrieves data from the Customers table of the Halloween database. Like the GetCategories and GetProducts methods, this method stores the data in a data table within a dataset. It also retrieves the primary key of the table just like the GetProducts method does. In this case, the primary key is the EMail column.

If, at this point, you're confused by this code because you're new to database programming, please keep in mind that it isn't essential that you understand all of the code right now. At the least, though, you should be able to call these methods using standard Visual Basic code. You should also realize that all three of the Get methods return a dataset that contains one table.

The code for the HalloweenDB class

```vb
Imports System.Data.SqlClient
Public Class HalloweenDB

    Public Shared Function GetCategories() As DataSet
        Dim dsCategories As New DataSet
        Dim cmdCategories As New SqlCommand
        Dim sSelect As String = "Select CategoryID, ShortName " _
                        & "From Categories Order By ShortName"
        cmdCategories.CommandText = sSelect
        cmdCategories.Connection = Connection()
        Dim daCategories As New SqlDataAdapter
        daCategories.SelectCommand = cmdCategories
        daCategories.Fill(dsCategories, "Categories")
        Return dsCategories
    End Function

    Public Shared Function GetProducts() As DataSet
        Dim dsProducts As New DataSet
        Dim cmdProducts As New SqlCommand
        Dim sSelect As String = "Select ProductID, CategoryID, Name, " _
                        & "LongDescription, ImageFile, UnitPrice " _
                        & "From Products Order By Name"
        cmdProducts.CommandText = sSelect
        cmdProducts.Connection = Connection()
        Dim daProducts As New SqlDataAdapter
        daProducts.SelectCommand = cmdProducts
        daProducts.MissingSchemaAction = MissingSchemaAction.AddWithKey
        daProducts.Fill(dsProducts, "Products")
        Return dsProducts
    End Function

    Public Shared Function GetCustomers() As DataSet
        Dim dsCustomers As New DataSet
        Dim cmdCustomers As New SqlCommand
        Dim sSelect As String = "Select * From Customers"
        cmdCustomers.CommandText = sSelect
        cmdCustomers.Connection = Connection()
        Dim daCustomers As New SqlDataAdapter
        daCustomers.SelectCommand = cmdCustomers
        daCustomers.MissingSchemaAction = MissingSchemaAction.AddWithKey
        daCustomers.Fill(dsCustomers, "Customers")
        Return dsCustomers
    End Function

    Private Shared Function Connection() As SqlConnection
        Dim conHalloween As New SqlConnection
        Dim sConnectionString As String = "Data Source=Doug\VSDOTNET;" _
            & "Initial Catalog=Halloween;Integrated Security=SSPI"
        conHalloween.ConnectionString = sConnectionString
        Return conHalloween
    End Function

End Class
```

Figure 4-3   Three methods of the HalloweenDB class

How to work with a dataset

Once you've retrieved the data from a database into a dataset, your web applications can use the data in the dataset. The next few topics show how.

How a dataset is organized

Figure 4-4 illustrates the basic organization of an ADO.NET dataset. As you can see, a dataset can contain one or more data tables, and each data table can contain one or more *data columns* and *data rows*. In addition, each data table can contain one or more *constraints* that can define a *unique key* within the table or a *foreign key* of another table in the dataset. If a dataset contains two or more data tables, the dataset can also define the relationships between those tables.

If you're familiar with the structure of a relational database, you'll notice that the structure of a dataset is similar. However, you should realize that each data table in a dataset corresponds to the result set that's returned from a Select statement, not necessarily to an actual table in a database. For example, a Select statement may join data from several tables in a database to produce a single result set. In this case, the data table in the dataset represents data from each of the tables involved in the join.

You should also know that each group of objects in the diagram in this figure is stored in a collection. All of the data columns in a data table, for example, are stored in a collection of data columns, and all of the data rows are stored in a collection of data rows. You'll learn more about how to use these collections in the next topic.

The basic dataset object hierarchy

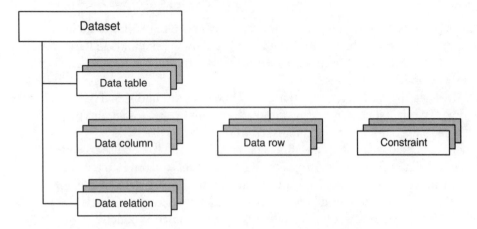

Description

- A dataset object consists of a hierarchy of one or more *data table* and *data relation* objects.

- A data table object consists of one or more *data column* objects and one or more *data row* objects. The data column objects define the data in each column of the table, including its name, data type, and so on, and the data row objects contain the data for each row in the table.

- A data table can also contain one or more *constraint* objects that are used to maintain the integrity of the data in the table. A *unique key constraint* ensures that the values in a column, such as the primary key column, are unique. And a *foreign key constraint* determines how the rows in one table are affected when corresponding rows in a related table are updated or deleted.

- The data relation objects define how the tables in the dataset are related. They are used to manage constraints and to simplify the navigation between related tables.

- All of the objects in a dataset are stored in collections. For example, the data table objects are stored in a data table collection, and the data row objects are stored in a data row collection. You can refer to these collections through properties of the containing objects.

Figure 4-4   How a dataset is organized

How to create and work with untyped datasets

An *untyped dataset* is one that's based on the generic ADO.NET DataSet class. That's the case for the datasets that are created by the methods in the HalloweenDB class. Now, figure 4-5 presents the basic skills for creating and working with an untyped dataset.

To create an untyped dataset, you use the New keyword and specify DataSet as the type. The first statement in this figure, for example, creates an untyped dataset and assigns it to a variable named dsProducts.

After you create a dataset, you fill it with data. To do that, you use the Fill method of the data adapter that defines the data you want to store in the dataset. This is illustrated by the second example in this figure. Here, a data adapter named daProducts is used to load the untyped dataset created in the first ex- ample. In this case, the data is loaded into a data table named Products.

To work with an untyped dataset, you use the properties and methods of the DataSet class. Right now, I want to focus on the properties you use to access the collections of objects contained within a dataset. This figure lists some of those properties and describes the collections they access. To access the collection of data tables in a dataset, for example, you use the Tables property of the dataset. To access the collection of data rows in a data table, you use the Rows property of the data table.

The third and fourth examples in this figure help illustrate how this works. Both examples refer to a data table in the dsProducts dataset. The code in the third example refers to the data table by name. To do that, it passes a string that contains the table name to the Tables property. The code in the fourth example refers to the data table by index. In this case, an index value of 0 is specified, so the first data table is retrieved. You use similar techniques to refer to items in other collections.

The syntax for creating an untyped dataset

```
dataset = New DataSet()
```

Common properties used to access data collections

Object	Property	Collection	Description
Dataset	Tables	DataTableCollection	A collection of the data tables in the dataset.
Data table	Rows	DataRowCollection	A collection of the data rows in a data table.
	Columns	DataColumnCollection	A collection of the data columns in a data table.

A statement that creates an untyped dataset

```
Dim dsProducts As New DataSet()
```

A statement that fills an untyped dataset

```
daProducts.Fill(dsProducts, "Products")
```

Code that refers to a table in the dataset by name

```
dsProducts.Tables("Products")
```

Code that refers to a table in the dataset by index

```
dsProducts.Tables(0)
```

Description

- An *untyped dataset* is one that's created from the generic ADO.NET DataSet class. You use the properties and methods of this class to work with an untyped dataset and the objects it contains.

- The information within a dataset is stored in collections. To refer to a collection, you can use a property of the parent object. To refer to the collection of data tables in a dataset, for example, you use the Tables property of the dataset as shown above.

- To refer to a specific object in a collection, you can use a string with the object's name or its index value. All of the ADO.NET collections are zero-based.

- To load a dataset with data, you use the Fill method of the data adapter that defines the data you want to retrieve into the dataset. On this method, you specify the name of the dataset and the name of the data table within the dataset where you want the data stored.

Figure 4-5   How to create and work with untyped datasets

How to bind a list control to a data table

To display the data from a data source such as a data table in a control, you *bind* the control to the data source. For example, you can bind a list control, such as a drop-down list or a list box, to a data table. Then, all of the items in the data table are displayed in the list.

To bind a list control to a data table, you set the properties of the control shown in figure 4-6. The DataSource and DataMember properties identify the dataset and data table that contain the data to be displayed in the list. Then, the DataTextField property identifies the column in the data table to be displayed in the list, and the DataValueField property identifies the column in the data table whose value is stored in the list. That makes it possible to display data from one column and retrieve the corresponding data from another.

The first example in this figure illustrates how this works. Here the DataSource property of a drop-down list is set to a dataset named dsProducts, and the DataMember property is set to a data table named Products. Then, the DataTextField property is set to the column named Name so the values in this column will be displayed in the list. Because the DataValueField property is set to the ProductID column, however, the value of this column will be stored in the list.

The last property, DataTextFormatString, lets you specify the format for numeric values displayed in the list. You can use many of the standard numeric formatting codes within the format specification. For example, to display a column named UnitPrice in currency format, you set the DataTextFormatString property to {0:C}. For more information on how to code a format specification, see the online help topic for this property.

If you've developed Windows applications that use bound controls, you may be surprised to discover that just setting the binding properties for a control doesn't bind the control. To do that, you have to execute the DataBind method. This is illustrated in the two statements in this figure.

Here, the first statement binds the drop-down list whose binding properties were set in the example. The second statement shows how you can bind all of the controls on a page at once. To do that, you execute the DataBind method of the page. As you can see, you can use the Me keyword to refer to the current page. You can also omit the Me keyword if you'd like to, but I recommend you include it so it's clear what you're binding.

You should also realize that you have to rebind a control each time its data source changes. If a row is added to a data table that a drop-down list is bound to, for example, the new row won't appear in the list until it's rebound to the table.

The properties for binding a list control to a data table

Property	Description
DataSource	The dataset.
DataMember	The name of a data table in the dataset.
DataTextField	The column in the data table whose value is displayed in the list.
DataValueField	The column in the data table whose value is stored in the list.
DataTextFormatString	The format of the items displayed in the list.

Code for setting the binding properties for a drop-down list

```
ddlProducts.DataSource = dsProducts
ddlProducts.DataMember = "Products"
ddlProducts.DataTextField = "Name"
ddlProducts.DataValueField = "ProductID"
```

A statement that binds the control

```
ddlProducts.DataBind()
```

A statement that binds all the controls on a page

```
Me.DataBind()
```

Description

- You can display the data in a data table in a list control by *binding* the control to the table. Before you can bind a control to a table, you must set the binding properties shown above.

- The DataTextField and DataValueField properties make it possible to display the values from one column in a list control but store the values of another column. The DataValueField property typically specifies a column that contains a key value. Then, when a user selects an item from the list, you can use the key value of that item to get the related row from the data table.

- To bind a control to a data table, you use the DataBind method of the control. To bind all of the controls on a page at once, you use the DataBind method of the Page.

- You must bind the controls to the data table as the program executes. You must do that any time the data table changes.

Figure 4-6   How to bind a list control to a data table

How to retrieve and work with a data row

Figure 4-7 shows how to retrieve and work with the data in a data row. To start, you declare a variable that will hold the data row from the DataRow class. Then, you retrieve a row into that variable. To do that, you can retrieve a row using its index as illustrated in the first example. Here, the Tables property of the dataset is used to get the table that contains the row, and the Rows property of the table is used to get the row with the specified index.

The rest of the code in this example retrieves values from individual columns of the row and assigns them to the appropriate properties of controls on a form. To do that, it uses the Item property of the data row and specifies the name of the column as an argument. Note that because the Item property is the default property of a row, it can be omitted as shown in this figure.

Another way to retrieve a row from a data table is to use the table's primary key as shown in the second example. To do that, the primary key for the table must be included in the table's *schema*. The schema of a table includes, among other things, the definition of each column. When you load a table with data using the Fill method of a data adapter, the schema is retrieved from the database along with the data, but the primary key isn't retrieved by default. To retrieve the primary key, you set the MissingSchemaAction property of the data adapter to MissingSchemaAction.AddWithKey as illustrated by the second method that you saw in figure 4-3. Then, when you execute the Fill method, the primary key for the table is retrieved along with the other schema information.

To retrieve a row for a table using its primary key value, you use the Find method of the data row collection. This is illustrated by the second and third examples in this figure. In the second example, the row with the primary key value specified by the ProductID variable is retrieved. In the third example, the row with the value of an item selected from a list control is retrieved.

If a row with the key value you specify on a Find method doesn't exist, this method returns a null. Then, you can test the variable that the row is assigned to for a null to determine if the row was found.

You can also test to be sure that a row with the specified key value exists before you retrieve it. To do that, you use the Contains method of the data row collection as illustrated in the last example in this figure. Here, an If statement tests that a row with the value specified by the ProductID variable exists in the Products table. If the row exists, the Contains method returns a value of True. Otherwise, it returns a value of False.

Code that retrieves a row using its index and assigns column values to form controls

```
Dim drProduct As DataRow
Dim iCurrentRow As Integer
    .
    .
drProduct = dsProducts.Tables("Products").Rows(iCurrentRow)
lblName.Text = drProduct("Name")
lblShortDescription.Text = drProduct("ShortDescription")
lblLongDescription.Text = drProduct("LongDescription")
lblUnitPrice.Text = drProduct("UnitPrice")
```

Code that retrieves a row with the specified key value

```
Dim drProduct As DataRow
drProduct = dsProducts.Tables("Products").Rows.Find(ProductID)
```

Code that retrieves a row with the value of a selected list control item

```
Dim drProduct As DataRow
drProduct = dsProducts.Tables("Products").Rows.Find _
        (ddlProduct.SelectedItem.Value)
```

Code that tests if a row with the specified key value exists

```
If dsProducts.Tables("Products").Rows.Contains(ProductID) Then ...
```

Description

- You can use the Rows property of a data table to retrieve a row using its index. Then, you can assign that row to a variable that's declared with the DataRow type.

- To get the value of a column in a row, use the Item property of the row and specify the name of the column as the argument. Since Item is the default property of a data row, you can omit it as shown above.

- You can use the Find method of a data row collection to get the row with the specified key. If the row doesn't exist, this method returns a null.

- To determine if a row with the specified key value exists before you retrieve it, you can use the Contains method of the data row collection. This method returns a Boolean value that indicates whether or not the row exists.

- To use the Find or Contains method, a primary key must be defined for the data table. To retrieve the primary key from the database, set the MissingSchemaAction property of the data adapter to MissingSchemaAction.AddWithKey before you use the data adapter to fill the dataset.

Figure 4-7   How to retrieve and work with a data row

How to use cookies

In the last chapter, you learned that ASP.NET uses cookies to track user sessions. Now, you'll learn how to create your own cookies to save data between user sessions.

An introduction to cookies

Figure 4-8 presents some basic information about cookies and shows some examples. If you look at the examples, you'll see that each cookie has a name and a value. The name of the first cookie, for example, is ASP.NET_SessionId, and its value is

```
jsswpu5530hcyx2w3jfa5u55
```

This is a typical value for the cookie that's generated by ASP.NET to keep track of a session. The other cookies shown here are typical of cookies you create yourself. You'll learn how to create cookies like this in the next figure.

Once you create a cookie, you include it in the HTTP response that the server sends back to the browser. Then, the browser stores the cookie either in its own memory or in a text file on the client machine's hard disk. A cookie that's stored in the browser's memory is called a *session cookie* because it exists only for that session. When the browser session ends, the contents of any session cookies are lost. ASP.NET uses session cookies to track session ID's. In contrast, *persistent cookies* are written to disk, so they are maintained after the browser session ends. Whether you use session cookies or persistent cookies, once a cookie is sent to a browser, it's returned to the server automatically with each HTTP request to that server.

This figure also lists three typical uses for cookies. First, you can use cookies to save information that identifies each user so the users don't have to enter that information each time they visit your web site. You can also use cookies to store information that lets you personalize the web pages that are displayed. Finally, you can use cookies to save information that lets you display advertising that targets the users.

When you use cookies to store this type of information, you should keep in mind that some users may have disabled cookies on their browsers. In that case, you won't be able to save cookies on the user's computer. Unfortunately, ASP.NET doesn't provide a way for you to determine whether a user has disabled cookies. As a result, if you use cookies in an application, you may need to notify the user that cookies must be enabled to use it.

Examples of cookies

```
ASP.NET_SessionId=jsswpu5530hcyx2w3jfa5u55
EMail=Doug@Murach.com
user_ID=4993
password=opensesame
```

How cookies work

- A cookie is a name/value pair that's stored in a browser or on the user's hard disk.
- A web application creates a cookie and sends it to a browser via an HTTP response.
- Every time the browser sends an HTTP request to the server, it attaches any cookies that are associated with that server.
- Some users disable cookies in their browsers. As a result, you can't always count on users having cookies enabled.
- Browsers can be configured to limit the number of cookies they will accept from each site, the total number of cookies accepted from all sites, and the maximum size of each cookie. Typical limits are 20 cookies from each site, 300 cookies altogether, and 4K as the maximum cookie size.

Two types of cookies

- A *session cookie* is kept in the browser's memory and exists only for the duration of the browser session.
- A *persistent cookie* is kept on the user's hard disk and is retained until the cookie's expiration date arrives.

Typical uses for cookies

- **To allow users to skip login and registration forms** that gather data like the user's name, password, or address.
- **To personalize pages** that display information like weather reports, sports scores, or stock quotations.
- **To focus advertising** like banner ads to target the user's interests.

Description

- By default, ASP.NET uses a cookie to store the session ID for a session.
- You can also create and send your own cookies to a user's browser. For example, you might store a user's ID and password in a persistent cookie so that you can automatically log the user on to your application the next time that user visits your site.

Figure 4-8   An introduction to cookies

How to create cookies

To create a cookie, you use the HttpCookie class. The two constructors for this class are presented at the top of figure 4-9. The first constructor lets you specify the name of the cookie. The second constructor lets you specify a name and a value.

This figure also presents some properties of the HttpCookie class. If you don't set the value of a cookie when you create it, for example, you can do that using the Value property. In addition, you can use the Expires property to set the expiration date for a persistent cookie. This is illustrated by the first example in this figure. Here, the first statement creates a cookie named UserName. Then, the second statement assigns the value of a variable named sUserName to the Value property of the cookie. Finally, the third statement sets the expiration date to one year from the current date.

The second example shows how to create a session cookie. Here, both the cookie's name and value are specified on the constructor. Because the Expires property isn't set, it's given a default value of 12:00 a.m. on January 1, 0001. Because this value has already passed, the cookie is deleted when the session ends.

Two ways to create a cookie

```
cookie = New HttpCookie(name)
cookie = New HttpCookie(name, value)
```

Common properties of the HttpCookie class

Property	Description
Expires	A DateTime value that indicates when the cookie should expire.
Name	The cookie's name.
Secure	A Boolean value that indicates whether the cookie should be sent only when a secure connection is used. See chapter 15 for information on secure connections.
Value	The string value assigned to the cookie.

Code that creates a persistent cookie

```
Dim NameCookie As New HttpCookie("UserName")
NameCookie.Value = sUserName
NameCookie.Expires = Now().AddYears(1)
```

Code that creates a session cookie

```
Dim NameCookie As New HttpCookie("UserName", sUserName)
```

Description

- Cookies are defined by the HttpCookie class. When you create a cookie, you must specify its name. You can also specify a cookie's value when you create it.

- To create a persistent cookie, set the Expires property to the time when you want the cookie to expire. If you don't set this property, a session cookie is created.

Figure 4-9   How to create cookies

How to work with cookies

After you create a cookie, you work with it using the properties and methods of the HttpCookieCollection class shown in figure 4-10. This class defines a collection of HttpCookie objects. To refer to a cookie in a cookies collection, for example, you use the Item property of the collection. And to add a cookie to the collection, you use the Add method of the collection.

The key to working with cookies is realizing that you must deal with two instances of the HttpCookieCollection class. The first one contains the collection of cookies that have been sent to the server from the client. You access this collection using the Cookies property of the HttpRequest object. The second one contains the collection of cookies that will be sent back to the browser. You access this collection using the Cookies property of the HttpResponse object.

To send a new cookie to the client, you create the cookie and then add it to the collection of cookies in the HttpResponse object. This is illustrated in the first example in this figure. Here, a cookie named UserName is created and added to the HttpResponse object. Note that to refer to the HttpResponse object, you use the Response property of the page.

The second example shows you how to retrieve the value of a cookie that's sent from the browser. Here, the Request property of the page is used to refer to the HttpRequest object. Then, the Item property (the default) of the Cookies collection of the request object is used to get the cookie, and the Value property of the cookie is used to get the cookie's value.

The last example in this figure illustrates how you can delete a persistent cookie. To do that, you create a cookie with the same name as the cookie you want to delete, and you set its Expires property to a time in the past. In this example, I set the date to one second before the current time. Then, you add the cookie to the Response object so that it's sent back to the browser. When the browser receives the cookie, it replaces the existing cookie with the new cookie. Then, when the client's system detects that the cookie has expired, it deletes it.

Common properties and methods of the HttpCookieCollection class

Property	Description
Item(name)	The cookie with the specified name.
Count	The number of cookies in the collection.

Method	Description
Add(cookie)	Adds a cookie to the collection.
Clear	Removes all cookies from the collection.
Remove(name)	Removes the cookie with the specified name from the collection.

Code that creates a new cookie and adds it to the HttpResponse object

```
Dim NameCookie As New HttpCookie("UserName", sUserName)
NameCookie.Expires = Now().AddYears(1)
Response.Cookies.Add(NameCookie)
```

Code that retrieves the value of a cookie from the HttpRequest object

```
Dim sUserName As String
sUserName = Request.Cookies("UserName").Value
```

Code that deletes a persistent cookie

```
Dim NameCookie As New HttpCookie("UserName")
NameCookie.Expires = Now().AddSeconds(-1)
Response.Cookies.Add(NameCookie)
```

Description

- Cookies are managed in collections defined by the HttpCookieCollection class.
- To access the cookies collection for a request or response, use the Cookies property of the HttpRequest or HttpResponse object. To refer to these objects, use the Request and Response properties of the page.
- To delete a persistent cookie, create a cookie with the same name as the cookie you want to delete and set its Expires property to a time that has already passed.

Figure 4-10   How to work with cookies

How to enable or disable cookies

If an application relies on the use of cookies, you'll want to be sure that cookies are enabled in your browser as you test the application. Conversely, to test an application that's intended to work even if cookies have been disabled, you'll need to disable cookies in your browser. To do that, you can use the techniques presented in figure 4-11.

If you're using Internet Explorer 6.0, you use the Privacy tab of the Internet Options dialog box shown in this figure to enable or disable cookies. The default setting is Medium, which enables both session and persistent cookies. To disable both types of cookies, you can select a privacy setting that blocks all cookies as shown here. Alternatively, you can use the dialog box that's displayed when you click the Advanced button to override the default settings so that your browser accepts session cookies but disables persistent cookies.

For earlier versions of Internet Explorer, you control cookies through the Security tab of the Internet Options dialog box. This tab works much like the Privacy tab for Internet Explorer 6.0. Here, the recommended security level is Medium. The default settings for this level enable session and persistent cookies. To disable both session and persistent cookies, you can set the security level to High. You can also use the Custom tab to modify the defaults for the High security level so it allows session cookies.

This figure also describes how to enable or disable cookies if you're using Netscape. The technique you use to do that depends on the version of Netscape you're using. If you're using version 7.1, you use the Cookies option in the Privacy and Security category of the Preferences dialog box to work with cookies. If you're using an earlier version, you use the Advanced option to work with cookies.

An Internet Explorer dialog box with disabled cookies

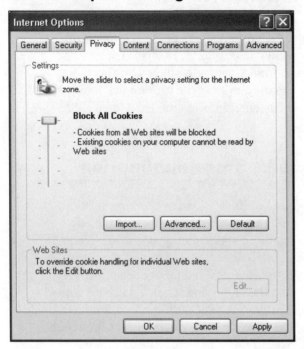

How to enable or disable cookies for Internet Explorer

1. Pull down the Tools menu and select the Internet Options command.
2. For Internet Explorer 6.0, select the Privacy tab. For Internet Explorer 5.5 or earlier, select the Security tab.
3. Use the slider control to set the security level to accept or block cookies.

How to enable or disable cookies for Netscape

1. Pull down the Edit menu and select the Preferences command.
2. For Netscape 7.1, expand the Privacy and Security category and then select Cookies. For Netscape 7.0 or earlier, select the Advanced option.
3. Choose an option to enable or disable cookies.

Description

* If you're using Internet Explorer, you can also enable or disable persistent cookies and session cookies separately. To do that with Internet Explorer 6.0, click the Advanced button and select from the advanced privacy settings that are displayed. To change these settings from earlier versions of Internet Explorer, select the Custom Level button in the Security tab.

Figure 4-11   How to enable or disable cookies

A Halloween Store application

The remaining topics of this chapter present an enhanced version of the Halloween Store application that you saw in chapter 3. In this version, the category and product data is retrieved from a database rather than from text files. In addition, a persistent cookie is used to store the user's email address. Then, that address is used to retrieve customer information from the database the next time the user places an order.

The design of the Halloween Store application

Figure 4-12 presents the three pages of the Halloween Store application. The first two pages, Order and Shopping Cart, are similar to the Order and Shopping Cart pages of the Halloween Store application you saw in chapter 3. Because of that, I'll just focus on the differences here.

To start, this application retrieves the category and product data that's displayed in the two drop-down lists on the Order page from a database named Halloween. This data is saved in data tables named Categories and Products within two separate datasets. Then, the Category drop-down list is bound to the Categories data table. Because the Product drop-down list displays only some of the data in the Products table, however, it isn't bound to this table. Instead, this drop-down list is loaded with data from the appropriate rows.

Notice that the Product drop-down list doesn't include the price of the products. Instead, the price is displayed in a separate label when the user selects a product from this list. In addition, a description of the product and a picture of the product are displayed.

A new button, Show Cart, has also been added to the Order form. This button lets the user display the Shopping Cart page without having to enter an order for another product. Note that this button is enabled only if the shopping cart contains one or more items. That's true of the Check Out button as well, which displays the Check Out page you'll see next.

The Order and Shopping Cart pages of the Halloween Store application

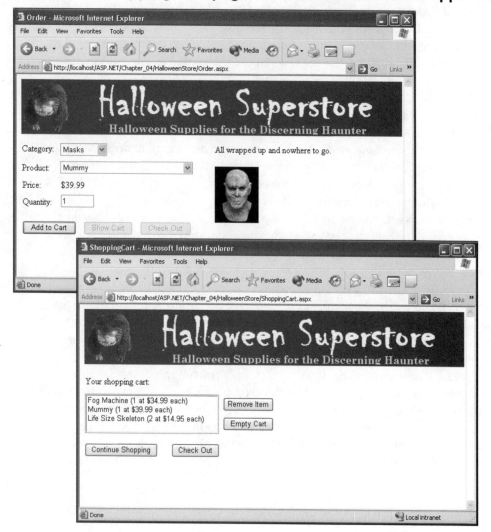

Enhancements to the Order and Shopping Cart pages

- The category and product data is retrieved from the Halloween database and stored in datasets. The Category drop-down list is bound to the dataset that contains the categories, and the Product drop-down list is loaded from the dataset that contains the products.

- When the user selects a product, the price, description, and image are displayed.

- The Show Cart button lets the user display the Shopping Cart page without adding a product to it. It's enabled only if the shopping cart contains one or more items.

- The Check Out buttons on both pages let the user display the Check Out page. It's enabled only if the shopping cart contains one or more items.

Figure 4-12   The design of the Halloween Store application (part 1 of 2)

The Check Out page of the Halloween Store application lets the user enter name and address information for an order. This page uses a persistent cookie to save the email address for a new user on the user's hard disk. It also saves the user information in a table of customers in the Halloween database. Then, the next time the user requests the page, it can use the cookie to retrieve the customer information from the database and display it on this page.

This page also updates the cookie and the data in the Halloween database if necessary when the user clicks the Continue Checkout button. If the user changes the email address that's retrieved from the database, for example, the value of the cookie is updated, a new row with the new email address is written to the Halloween database, and the row with the old email address is deleted. Similarly, if the user changes any of the other information on this page, the row for that user in the Halloween database is updated.

For this to work, three items are saved in session state. First, the customers that are retrieved from the Halloween database and stored in a dataset are saved in session state. That way, this data can be retrieved the first time the page is loaded and then used on subsequent requests to get the data for a user.

If a cookie with the user's email address already exists, this address is also saved in session state. Then, this item is used to determine if the user changes the address. Similarly, if a row with the email address is found, that row is saved in session state. Then, the data in that row can be used to determine if the user changes any of the information on the page.

Before I go on, you should realize that this application doesn't save the order information. Instead, after it processes the cookie and the customer data, it displays a message indicating that the remaining functions haven't been implemented. Later in this book, after you learn more about database processing, you'll see a complete application that implements all the functions of a production application.

The Check Out page of the Halloween Store application

Description

- The Check Out page lets the user enter name and address information for an order.

- This page retrieves customer data from the Halloween database and stores it in a dataset. Then, if a request for the page includes the user's email address, it retrieves the related row from the dataset and displays the data on the form.

- If the dataset doesn't contain a row for the user, the user can enter the required information and then click the Continue Checkout button. Then, a cookie is created and a row is added to the Halloween database if it doesn't already exist. In addition, a message is displayed indicating that the remaining checkout functions haven't been implemented.

- If the user changes an existing email address, the cookie is updated, a row with the new email address is added to the Halloween database, and the old row is deleted.

- If the user changes any other information in an existing row, the row in the Halloween database is updated.

- If the user clicks the Cancel Order button, the shopping cart is removed from session state and the Order page is redisplayed. If the user clicks the Continue Shopping button, the Order page is redisplayed without removing the shopping cart.

- A required field validator is included for each text box on the form.

Figure 4-12   The design of the Halloween Store application (part 2 of 2)

The Visual Basic code for the Customer class

In addition to the CartItem class that you saw in the last chapter, the Halloween Store application in this chapter uses a Customer class. This class, which defines the properties of a Customer object, is shown in figure 4-13. Please note that the properties in this object correspond to the columns in each row of the Customers table in the Halloween database and also to the columns in each row of the resulting dataset.

Three more methods of the HalloweenDB class

Figure 4-13 also shows three more methods of the HalloweenDB class that you need for updating the Customers table in the database. Note, however, that these methods use some code that hasn't been presented yet. As a result, you just need to know what these methods do and how you call them.

Even if you don't understand all of the code, you should be able to tell that the AddCustomer method adds a row for the customer specified by the Customer object that's passed to it. The UpdateCustomer method updates the customer row with the information in the Customer object that's passed to it. And the DeleteCustomer method deletes the customer with the email address that's passed to it.

Incidentally, even though these methods are coded as functions, they don't return any value. In practice, though, you would code them so they returned a value like the number of rows inserted, updated, or deleted.

The code for the Customer class

```
Public Class Customer
    Public EMail As String
    Public FirstName As String
    Public LastName As String
    Public Address As String
    Public City As String
    Public State As String
    Public ZipCode As String
    Public PhoneNumber As String
End Class
```

Three more methods for the HalloweenDB class

```
    Public Shared Function AddCustomer(ByVal Customer As Customer)
        Dim conHalloween As SqlConnection = Connection()
        Dim cmdCustomer As New SqlCommand
        cmdCustomer.Connection = conHalloween
        cmdCustomer.CommandText = "Insert Into Customers Values ('" _
            & Customer.EMail & "', '" & Customer.LastName & "', '" _
            & Customer.FirstName & "', '" & Customer.Address & "', '" _
            & Customer.City & "', '" & Customer.State & "', '" _
            & Customer.ZipCode & "', '" & Customer.PhoneNumber & "')"
        conHalloween.Open()
        cmdCustomer.ExecuteNonQuery()
        conHalloween.Close()
    End Function

    Public Shared Function UpdateCustomer(ByVal Customer As Customer)
        Dim conHalloween As SqlConnection = Connection()
        Dim cmdCustomer As New SqlCommand
        cmdCustomer.Connection = conHalloween
        cmdCustomer.CommandText = "Update Customers Set " _
            & "LastName = '" & Customer.LastName & "', FirstName = '" _
            & Customer.FirstName & "', Address = '" & Customer.Address _
            & "', City = '" & Customer.City & "', State = '" _
            & Customer.State & "', ZipCode = '" & Customer.ZipCode & "', " _
            & "PhoneNumber = '" & Customer.PhoneNumber & "'" _
            & "Where EMail = '" & Customer.EMail & "'"
        conHalloween.Open()
        cmdCustomer.ExecuteNonQuery()
        conHalloween.Close()
    End Function

    Public Shared Function DeleteCustomer(ByVal EMail As String)
        Dim conHalloween As SqlConnection = Connection()
        Dim cmdCustomer As New SqlCommand
        cmdCustomer.Connection = conHalloween
        cmdCustomer.CommandText = "Delete From Customers " _
            & "Where EMail = '" & EMail & "'"
        conHalloween.Open()
        cmdCustomer.ExecuteNonQuery()
        conHalloween.Close()
    End Function

End Class
```

Figure 4-13   Visual Basic code for the Customer and HalloweenDB classes

The Visual Basic code for the Order form

Figure 4-14 presents the code for the Order form of the Halloween Store application. Because the basic logic of this form is the same as the logic of the Order form you saw in the last chapter, I'll focus mostly on the statements that work with the datasets that contain the Categories and Products data tables. Those statements are highlighted in this figure.

To start, two module-level variables named dsCategories and dsProducts are declared to hold the two datasets. Then, each time the page is loaded, the GetProducts procedure is executed to get the products dataset and assign it to the dsProducts variable. If the products aren't already in session state, the GetProducts method of the HalloweenDB class is executed to get the products. Otherwise, the products are simply retrieved from session state.

Next, the Load procedure executes the SetButtons procedure shown on page 2 of this listing. This procedure enables or disables the Show Cart and Check Out buttons depending on whether there's anything in the shopping cart. If the shopping cart doesn't exist or it doesn't contain any items, these buttons are disabled. Otherwise, they're enabled.

If the page is being loaded for the first time, the Load procedure continues by executing the GetCategories method of the HalloweenDB class. The dataset that's returned by this method is then assigned to the dsCategories variable. Next, the BindCategoryDropDownList procedure is executed to bind the Category drop-down list. As you can see, the DataSource property of this control is set to the dataset that contains the categories, and the DataMember property is set to the Categories data table within that dataset. Then, the DataTextField property is set to the ShortName column of this data table so this column will be displayed in the list. And the DataValueField property is set to the CategoryID column so this value will be stored in the list. You'll see how the CategoryID is used in a moment. The last statement in this procedure binds the drop-down list to the data table using the binding properties.

Next, the Load procedure calls the LoadProductDropDownList procedure to load the Product drop-down list. To do that, this procedure loops through the rows in the Products table. For each row, it checks if the CategoryID column is equal to the value of the item that's selected in the Category drop-down list. Since the DataValueField of this control was set to the CategoryID column, the value of the selected item is its category ID. If the category IDs are equal, this procedure creates a new list item with a Text property that's equal to the name column of the product and a Value property that's equal to the ProductID column. Finally, the Load procedure calls the DisplayProductData procedure shown on page 2 of this listing.

The code for the Order form   **Page 1**

```
Public Class Order
    Inherits System.Web.UI.Page

    Dim dsCategories As DataSet
    Dim dsProducts As DataSet

    Private Sub Page_Load(ByVal sender As System.Object, _
            ByVal e As System.EventArgs) Handles MyBase.Load
        'Put user code to initialize the page here
        Me.GetProducts()
        Me.SetButtons()
        If Not IsPostBack Then
            dsCategories = HalloweenDB.GetCategories()
            Me.BindCategoryDropDownList()
            Me.LoadProductDropDownList()
            Me.DisplayProductData()
        End If
    End Sub

    Private Sub GetProducts()
        If Session("Products") Is Nothing Then
            dsProducts = HalloweenDB.GetProducts()
            Session("Products") = dsProducts
        Else
            dsProducts = Session("Products")
        End If
    End Sub

    Private Sub BindCategoryDropDownList()
        ddlCategories.DataSource = dsCategories
        ddlCategories.DataMember = "Categories"
        ddlCategories.DataTextField = "ShortName"
        ddlCategories.DataValueField = "CategoryID"
        ddlCategories.DataBind()
    End Sub

    Private Sub LoadProductDropDownList()
        ddlProducts.Items.Clear()
        Dim drProduct As DataRow
        For Each drProduct In dsProducts.Tables("Products").Rows
            If drProduct("CategoryID") = ddlCategories.SelectedItem.Value Then
                ddlProducts.Items.Add(New ListItem(drProduct("Name"), _
                    drProduct("ProductID")))
            End If
        Next
    End Sub
```

Figure 4-14   The Visual Basic code for the Order form (part 1 of 3)

The DisplayProductData procedure displays the unit price, description, and image for the selected product. To do that, it starts by declaring a variable to hold a data row. Then, it uses the Find method of the data rows collection of the Products table to retrieve the row for the selected product. Note that for this to work, the Products table must contain a primary key. That's why the MissingSchemaAction property of the data adapter that was used to load the table was set to MissingSchemaAction.AddWithKey.

After the row for the selected product is retrieved and assigned to the data row variable, the values of the UnitPrice and LongDescription columns are assigned to the Text properties of the appropriate labels on the form. In addition, the value of the ImageFile column is used to create a URL that points to a file that contains a picture of the product. This URL is then assigned to the ImageUrl property of the image control.

When the user clicks the Add to Cart button, the Add procedure updates the shopping cart with the selected product. To add an item to the shopping cart, this procedure starts by declaring a variable that will hold the data row for the product. Then, it uses the Find method to retrieve the row, and it assigns it to this variable. Next, it sets the Name and UnitPrice properties of the cart item to the values of the Name and UnitPrice columns of this row, and it sets the Quantity property to the Text property of the Quantity text box. Finally, it adds the item to the shopping cart.

The code for the Order form

```vb
Private Sub DisplayProductData()
    Dim drProduct As DataRow
    drProduct = dsProducts.Tables("Products").Rows.Find _
        (ddlProducts.SelectedItem.Value)
    lblLongDesc.Text = drProduct("LongDescription")
    lblPrice.Text = FormatCurrency(drProduct("UnitPrice"))
    imgPicture.ImageUrl = "Images\" & drProduct("ImageFile")
End Sub

Private Sub SetButtons()
    If Session("Cart") Is Nothing Then
        btnShow.Enabled = False
        btnCheckOut.Enabled = False
    Else
        If Session("Cart").Count = 0 Then
            btnShow.Enabled = False
            btnCheckOut.Enabled = False
        Else
            btnShow.Enabled = True
            btnCheckOut.Enabled = True
        End If
    End If

End Sub

Private Sub btnAdd_Click(ByVal sender As System.Object, _
        ByVal e As System.EventArgs) Handles btnAdd.Click
    Dim sID As String
    sID = ddlProducts.SelectedItem.Value
    Dim CartItem As New CartItem
    Dim ShoppingCart As SortedList
    If Session("Cart") Is Nothing Then
        ShoppingCart = New SortedList
    Else
        ShoppingCart = Session("Cart")
    End If
    If ShoppingCart.ContainsKey(sID) Then
        CartItem = ShoppingCart(sID)
        CartItem.Quantity += txtQuantity.Text
        ShoppingCart(sID) = CartItem
    Else
        Dim drProduct As DataRow
        drProduct = dsProducts.Tables("Products").Rows.Find(sID)
        CartItem.Name = drProduct("Name")
        CartItem.UnitPrice = drProduct("UnitPrice")
        CartItem.Quantity = txtQuantity.Text
        ShoppingCart.Add(sID, CartItem)
    End If
    Session("Cart") = ShoppingCart
    Response.Redirect("ShoppingCart.aspx")
End Sub
```

Figure 4-14   The Visual Basic code for the Order form (part 2 of 3)

On page 3 of the listing for the Order form, you can see the code for the SelectedIndexChanged events of the two drop-down lists and the code for the Click events of the Check Out and Show Cart buttons. These procedures are identical to the ones you saw in chapter 3, so you shouldn't have any trouble understanding how they work.

The Visual Basic code for the Shopping Cart form

Because the code for the Shopping Cart is almost identical to the code shown in the last chapter, it's not shown again here. The only difference is that if the user clicks the Empty button to empty the shopping cart, the Check Out button is disabled. In addition, if the user clicks the Remove button to remove an item from the shopping cart, the Check Out button is disabled if the item that was removed was the last item in the cart.

The code for the Order form   **Page 3**

```vbnet
    Private Sub ddlCategories_SelectedIndexChanged _
            (ByVal sender As System.Object, ByVal e As System.EventArgs) _
            Handles ddlCategories.SelectedIndexChanged
        Me.LoadProductDropDownList()
        Me.DisplayProductData()
    End Sub

    Private Sub ddlProducts_SelectedIndexChanged _
            (ByVal sender As System.Object, ByVal e As System.EventArgs) _
            Handles ddlProducts.SelectedIndexChanged
        Me.DisplayProductData()
    End Sub

    Private Sub btnCheckOut_Click(ByVal sender As System.Object, _
            ByVal e As System.EventArgs) Handles btnCheckOut.Click
        Response.Redirect("CheckOut.aspx")
    End Sub

    Private Sub btnShow_Click(ByVal sender As System.Object, _
            ByVal e As System.EventArgs) Handles btnShow.Click
        Response.Redirect("ShoppingCart.aspx")
    End Sub

End Class
```

Figure 4-14   The Visual Basic code for the Order form (part 3 of 3)

The Visual Basic code for the Check Out form

Figure 4-15 presents the code for the Check Out form. Because this form is new, I'll describe it in detail. However, I've highlighted the code that works with the dataset that contains the Customers data table and the code that works with the cookie that contains the user's email address. So if you want to focus on how that code works, you can skip the other code.

This form starts by declaring three variables. The first one, dsCustomers, will be used to hold the dataset that contains the Customers data table. The second one, sEmail, will be used to hold the email address in an existing cookie that's passed with the request for the page. And the third one, bCookieExists, will be used to indicate whether or not a cookie already exists.

Each time this page is loaded, the Load procedure executes the GetCustomers procedure. This procedure starts by checking session state to see if it already contains a session state item named Customers. If so, that item is assigned to the dsCustomers variable. Otherwise, the GetCustomers method of the HalloweenDB class is executed to get the customers. The dataset that's returned by this method is then assigned to the dsCustomers variable, and this variable is saved in session state.

If the page is being loaded for the first time, the Load procedure continues by executing the GetCustomerData procedure. This procedure starts by checking the Cookies collection of the request object to see if it contains a cookie named EMail. If not, the bCookieExists variable is set to False and the procedure ends. Otherwise, the bCookieExists variable is set to True and the value of the cookie is assigned to the sEmail variable. Then, this variable is saved in session state.

Next, the GetCustomerData procedure uses the Contains method to check if the Customers data table contains a row with the user's email address. (Remember that the email address is the key of the Customers table.) If it does, this procedure uses the Find method to assign the row to a data row variable. Then, it assigns the column values of this row to the text boxes on the form. Finally, it saves the row in session state.

If the user clicks the Continue button from this form, the client is redirected to the Order page so the user can select additional products. Note that when this happens, any data the user has entered on the form is lost. If that's not what you want, you could save the customer data in session state and then redisplay it the next time the page is requested.

The code for the Check Out form   **Page 1**

```
Public Class CheckOut
    Inherits System.Web.UI.Page

    Dim dsCustomers As DataSet
    Dim sEmail As String
    Dim bCookieExists As Boolean

    Private Sub Page_Load(ByVal sender As System.Object, _
            ByVal e As System.EventArgs) Handles MyBase.Load
        'Put user code to initialize the page here
        Me.GetCustomers()
        If Not IsPostBack Then
            Me.GetCustomerData()
        End If
    End Sub

    Private Sub GetCustomers()
        If Session("Customers") Is Nothing Then
            dsCustomers = HalloweenDB.GetCustomers
            Session("Customers") = dsCustomers
        Else
            dsCustomers = Session("Customers")
        End If
    End Sub

    Private Sub GetCustomerData()
        If Request.Cookies("EMail") Is Nothing Then
            bCookieExists = False
        Else
            bCookieExists = True
            sEmail = Request.Cookies("EMail").Value
            Session("EMail") = sEmail
            If dsCustomers.Tables("Customers").Rows.Contains(sEmail) Then
                Dim drCustomer As DataRow
                drCustomer = dsCustomers.Tables("Customers").Rows.Find(sEmail)
                txtEmail.Text = drCustomer("EMail")
                txtFirstName.Text = drCustomer("FirstName")
                txtLastName.Text = drCustomer("LastName")
                txtAddress.Text = drCustomer("Address")
                txtCity.Text = drCustomer("City")
                txtState.Text = drCustomer("State")
                txtZipCode.Text = drCustomer("ZipCode")
                txtPhone.Text = drCustomer("PhoneNumber")
                Session("CustomerRow") = drCustomer
            End If
        End If
    End Sub

    Private Sub btnContinue_Click(ByVal sender As System.Object, _
            ByVal e As System.EventArgs) Handles btnContinue.Click
        Response.Redirect("Order.aspx")
    End Sub
```

Figure 4-15   The Visual Basic code for the Check Out form (part 1 of 3)

The client is also redirected to the Order page if the user clicks the Cancel button. But first, the shopping cart is removed from session state. Then, a new, empty shopping cart is created when the Order page is loaded.

The most complicated procedure of this form is the one that's executed when the user clicks the Check Out button. This procedure starts by checking whether a new cookie needs to be created. That's the case if a cookie wasn't included in the page request (Not bCookieExists) or if the user changed the email address from its original value. Then, the AddCookie procedure is executed. This procedure creates a cookie named EMail with the value the user entered in the Email text box. Then, it sets the Expires property of the cookie so the cookie will expire in one year. Finally, it adds the cookie to the Cookies collection of the response object so it will be sent back to the browser with the response. Note that if a cookie with the name EMail already exists on the user's machine, it will be replaced with the new cookie. Otherwise, a new cookie will be created.

The next two statements in the CheckOut procedure create a new Customer object and call a procedure named SetCustomerValues that assigns values to the Customer object using the data the user entered into the text boxes on the form. Then, the CheckOut procedure checks if a row exists in the Customers data table with the email address the user entered. If not, the AddCustomer method of the HalloweenDB class is executed to add a new row to the Customer table of the database. Next, this procedure gets the original email address from session state. If this address isn't equal to the email address entered by the user and it isn't an empty string, the DeleteCustomer method of the HalloweenDB class is executed to delete the row with this email address from the Customers table. This happens if the user changed the email address in the row that was originally retrieved from the Customers data table.

If the Customers table does contain a row with the email address entered by the user, the CheckOut procedure executes the CustomerModified procedure to determine if the user changed any of the other data on the page. You'll see the code for this procedure in a moment. If any of the data was changed, the CheckOut procedure creates a new Customer object, assigns values to it using the data entered by the user, and then executes the UpdateCustomer method of the HalloweenDB class to update the existing row in the Customers table.

The code for the Check Out form   **Page 2**

```vbnet
Private Sub btnCancel_Click(ByVal sender As System.Object, _
        ByVal e As System.EventArgs) Handles btnCancel.Click
    Session.Remove("Cart")
    Response.Redirect("Order.aspx")
End Sub

Private Sub btnCheckOut_Click(ByVal sender As System.Object, _
        ByVal e As System.EventArgs) Handles btnCheckOut.Click
    If Not bCookieExists Or sEmail <> txtEmail.Text Then
        Me.AddCookie()
    End If
    Dim Customer As New Customer
    Me.SetCustomerValues(Customer)
    If Not dsCustomers.Tables("Customers").Rows.Contains _
            (txtEmail.Text) Then
        HalloweenDB.AddCustomer(Customer)
        sEmail = Session("EMail")
        If sEmail <> txtEmail.Text And sEmail <> "" Then
            HalloweenDB.DeleteCustomer(sEmail)
        End If
    Else
        If CustomerModified() Then
            Dim Customer As New Customer
            Me.SetCustomerValues(Customer)
            HalloweenDB.UpdateCustomer(Customer)
        End If
    End If
    lblCheckOut.Text _
        = "The remaining check out functions have not been " _
        & "implemented.<br>Click Cancel Order to start a new order, " _
        & "or Continue Shopping<br>to modify your order."
End Sub

Private Sub AddCookie()
    Dim EMailCookie As New HttpCookie("EMail", txtEmail.Text)
    EMailCookie.Expires = Now().AddYears(1)
    Response.Cookies.Add(EMailCookie)
End Sub

Private Sub SetCustomerValues(ByVal Customer As Customer)
    Customer.EMail = txtEmail.Text
    Customer.FirstName = txtFirstName.Text
    Customer.LastName = txtLastName.Text
    Customer.Address = txtAddress.Text
    Customer.City = txtCity.Text
    Customer.State = txtState.Text
    Customer.ZipCode = txtZipCode.Text
    Customer.PhoneNumber = txtPhone.Text
End Sub
```

Figure 4-15   The Visual Basic code for the Check Out form (part 2 of 3)

The code for the CustomerModified procedure is shown on page 3 of this listing. It starts by declaring a variable to hold a data row. Then, it assigns the row that was originally retrieved from the Customers table and saved in session state to this variable. Next, it compares each column in this row except the EMail column against the related text box on the page to determine if the user changed the value of the column. (The EMail column isn't checked because if it has changed, the customer row isn't updated. Instead, a new customer row is added and the old row is deleted.) If any of the values were changed, the Boolean variable that's returned by the procedure is set to True. That way, the CheckOut procedure will update the customer row.

* * *

Now that you've reviewed this application, I hope it has helped you appreciate the complexity of a typical business application. In particular, a real-world business application needs to provide for all of the possible user requirements. That's why this application lets the customers change their email addresses or change any of their data. Although this has made the logic of the application more difficult to follow, this has also made the application more realistic.

You should realize, though, that one part of this application isn't realistic. Specifically, all of the rows in the Customers table in the database are retrieved into the dataset, when only the row for the current customer is needed. In practice, then, you would use other techniques for getting just the customer row that's needed, and you'll learn some of those techniques in section 3 of this book.

The code for the Check Out form   **Page 3**

```
Private Function CustomerModified() As Boolean
    Dim drCustomer As DataRow
    drCustomer = Session("CustomerRow")
    If drCustomer("LastName") <> txtLastName.Text Then
        CustomerModified = True
    ElseIf drCustomer("FirstName") <> txtFirstName.Text Then
        CustomerModified = True
    ElseIf drCustomer("Address") <> txtAddress.Text Then
        CustomerModified = True
    ElseIf drCustomer("City") <> txtCity.Text Then
        CustomerModified = True
    ElseIf drCustomer("State") <> txtState.Text Then
        CustomerModified = True
    ElseIf drCustomer("ZipCode") <> txtZipCode.Text Then
        CustomerModified = True
    ElseIf drCustomer("PhoneNumber") <> txtPhone.Text Then
        CustomerModified = True
    End If
End Function

End Class
```

Figure 4-15   The Visual Basic code for the Check Out form (part 3 of 3)

Perspective

The goal of this chapter has been to show you how to use both cookies and the data from a database in a real-world application. Keep in mind, though, that this is just a brief introduction to the use of databases and datasets. So in section 3 of this book, you'll learn some of the other skills that you need for working with databases and datasets. Later on, if you would like a thorough treatment of database programming, we recommend *Murach's VB.NET Database Programming with ADO.NET*.

Terms

ADO.NET
.NET data provider
dataset
data adapter
command
connection
connection string
data table
data relation
data column
data row
constraint
unique key constraint
foreign key constraint
untyped dataset
binding a control
schema
session cookie
persistent cookie

5

How to test and debug an ASP.NET application

If you've done much programming, you know that testing and debugging are often the most difficult and time-consuming phase of program development. Fortunately, Visual Studio includes an integrated debugger that can help you locate and correct even the most obscure bugs. In addition, ASP.NET includes a Trace feature that displays useful information as your ASP.NET pages execute. In this chapter, you'll learn how to use both of these powerful debugging tools. But first, you'll learn how to test an application to determine if it works properly.

How to test an ASP.NET application

To test an ASP.NET application, you typically start by running it from within Visual Studio so that you can locate and correct any errors you encounter. Then, you run it directly from a browser window to be sure it works correctly from outside of Visual Studio. You'll learn the techniques for performing both of these types of testing in the topics that follow. In addition, you'll learn how to use the Server Error page that's displayed if an error occurs while you're testing an application.

How to test an ASP.NET application from Visual Studio

Figure 5-1 presents four techniques you can use to test an ASP.NET application from Visual Studio. To thoroughly test and debug an application, you run it in your default browser. You learned about this technique in chapter 2. You can also run an application in your default browser without debugging, but there's usually no reason to do that.

Visual Studio also provides an internal browser that you can use to test an application. When you use the internal browser, the pages are displayed in a Browse window within Visual Studio. Note that you typically start the internal browser from the starting page for an application. That way, you can be sure that any session state items this page creates are available to the other pages. Also note that when you use the internal browser, the debugger isn't available. Because of that, this technique is most appropriate for making sure that the pages look the way you want them to and that the basic functions of the application work properly.

When you test an application, you'll want to be sure to test it from any browser that might be used to run the application. That includes not only browsers from different manufacturers, but different versions of those browsers that are currently in use. One way to do that is to start each browser from outside Visual Studio. You'll learn how to do that in the next topic. Another way is to use the Browse With command from within Visual Studio.

When you select the Browse With command, the dialog box that's displayed lists the available browsers. Then, you can select the browser you want to use and click the Browse button to start the application. If the browser you want to use doesn't appear in the list, you can click the Add button to add it to the list. You can also use the Browse With dialog box to change the default browser for Visual Studio. Then, that browser is used whenever you run an application.

The Order form displayed in the internal browser

How to test an application in the default browser

- Select the Debug→Start command or click the Start button in the Standard toolbar. Then, the project is compiled and the starting page is displayed in your default browser.
- To end the application, close the browser, select the Debug→Stop Debugging command, or click the Stop Debugging button in the Debug toolbar.

How to test an application in the default browser without debugging

- Select the Debug→Start Without Debugging command. The project is compiled and the starting page is displayed in your default browser.
- To end the application, close the browser.

How to test an application in the internal web browser

- Right-click on the starting page in the Solution Explorer and select the View in Browser command from the shortcut menu. The project is compiled and the selected page is displayed in a Browse window within Visual Studio. The debugger is not available with this browser.
- To stop the browse, close the Browse window.

How to test an application in a browser other than the default

- Select the Browse With command in the shortcut menu for the starting page to display the Browse With dialog box. Then, select the browser you want to use from the list that's displayed and click the Browse button.
- To change the browser that's used by default when you run an application, select the browser from the Browse With dialog box and then click the Set as Default button.
- To add another browser to the list in the Browse With dialog box, click the Add button and then locate the executable file for the browser.

Figure 5-1   How to test an ASP.NET application from Visual Studio

How to test an ASP.NET application from outside Visual Studio

Once you've thoroughly tested and debugged an application from within Visual Studio, you'll want to run it from outside of Visual Studio to make sure it works properly. Figure 5-2 describes how you do that. To start, you open the browser you want to use. Then, you enter the URL for the starting page of the application and press Enter. When you do, a request for the page is sent to the server and the resulting page is displayed in the browser.

If you haven't already tested the application from within Visual Studio in each browser that might be used to run the application, you should do that from outside Visual Studio. At the least, you'll want to run the application from both Internet Explorer and Netscape. Since you'll see the Internet Explorer window throughout this book, this figure shows you a sample Netscape window. This is the window that's displayed when you enter the URL for the Order page of the Halloween Store application.

In addition to testing an application in different browsers, you may need to test it simultaneously in two browser windows. This is particularly true for applications that retrieve and update data in a database. To understand why, you need to realize that after an application retrieves data from a database and stores it in a dataset, it closes the connection to the database. Because of that, two or more users can retrieve the same data at the same time. This is called *concurrency*, and it can cause problems when the data is updated. You'll learn more about concurrency and how you provide for it in chapter 13. For now, you should just realize that you'll need to test your applications to be sure that they handle concurrency problems appropriately.

The Order form displayed in a Netscape browser window

Description

- To test an ASP.NET application from a browser other than your default browser, or to test an application simultaneously in two browser windows, you have to start the browser from outside of Visual Studio.

- After you start the browser, you enter the URL for the starting page of the application in the Address text box (for the Internet Explorer) or the Location text box (for Netscape). Then, you press Enter to run the application and display the page.

Figure 5-2   How to test an ASP.NET application from outside Visual Studio

How to use an ASP.NET Server Error page

As you test an ASP.NET application, you may encounter runtime errors that prevent an application from executing. When that happens, an exception is thrown. In many cases, the application anticipates these exceptions and provides error-handling code to process them. If an unhandled exception occurs, however, ASP.NET terminates the application and sends a Server Error page like the one shown in figure 5-3 back to the browser.

As you can see, the Server Error page indicates the type of exception that occurred and the statement that caused the error. In many cases, this information is enough to determine what caused the error and what should be done to correct it. For example, the Server Error page in this figure indicates that an input string value was not in the correct format. The problem was encountered in line 128 of the source code for the page:

```
CartItem.Quantity = txtQuantity.Text
```

Based on that information, you can assume that the Text property of the txtQuantity control contains a value that can't be converted to an integer, since the Quantity property of the CartItem object is declared as an integer. This could happen if the application didn't check that the user entered an integer value into this control. (To force this error to occur, I omitted the compare validator for the Quantity text box from the Order page of the Halloween Store application.)

Many of the exceptions you'll encounter will be system exceptions like the one shown here. These exceptions apply to general system operations such as arithmetic operations and the execution of methods and Visual Basic functions. If your applications use ADO.NET, you can also encounter ADO.NET and data provider exceptions. If the connection string for a database is invalid, for example, a data provider exception will occur. And if you try to add a row to a data table with a key that already exists, an ADO.NET error will occur.

In some cases, you won't be able to determine the cause of an error just by analyzing the Server Error page. Then, you can use the Visual Studio debugger to help you locate the problem. You'll learn how to do that next.

An ASP.NET Server Error page

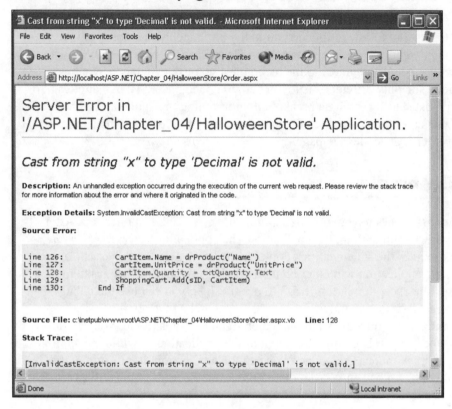

Description

- If an unhandled exception occurs in an ASP.NET application, ASP.NET terminates the application and sends an error page like the one shown above to the browser.

- An ASP.NET Server Error page provides the name of the application, a description of the exception, and the line in the program that caused the error. It also includes a *stack trace* that indicates the processing that led up to the error.

- The information in the Server Error page is often all you need to determine the cause of the error. If not, you should note the line where the error occurred. Then, you can use the debugging techniques presented in this chapter to determine the cause.

Figure 5-3   How to use an ASP.NET Server Error page

How to use the debugger

The topics that follow introduce you to the basic techniques for using the Visual Studio *debugger* to debug an ASP.NET application. Note that these techniques are almost identical to the techniques you use to debug a Windows application. The only difference is that when you debug an ASP.NET application, you must start by setting a breakpoint and running the application. That's because you can't break into the debugger from the browser since the application ends after it generates the page.

How to use breakpoints

Figure 5-4 shows how to use *breakpoints* in an ASP.NET application. After you set a breakpoint and run the application, the application enters *break mode* before it executes the statement that contains the breakpoint. In this case, for example, the application will enter break mode before it executes the statement that caused the exception in figure 5-3 to occur. Then, you can use the debugging features described in the topics that follow to debug the application.

In some cases, you may want to set more than one breakpoint. You can do that either before you begin the execution of the application or while the application is in break mode. Then, when you run the application, it will stop at the first breakpoint. And when you continue execution, the application will execute up to the next breakpoint.

Once you set a breakpoint, it remains active until you remove it. In fact, it remains active even after you close the project. If you want to remove a breakpoint, you can use one of the techniques presented in this figure.

You can also work with breakpoints from the *Breakpoints window*. To disable a breakpoint, for example, you can remove the check mark in front of the breakpoint. Then, the breakpoint isn't taken until you enable it again. You can also move to a breakpoint in the Code Editor window by selecting the breakpoint in the Breakpoints window and then clicking on the Go To Source Code button at the top of this window. In most cases, though, you'll work with breakpoints in the Code Editor window.

The Halloween Store application with a breakpoint

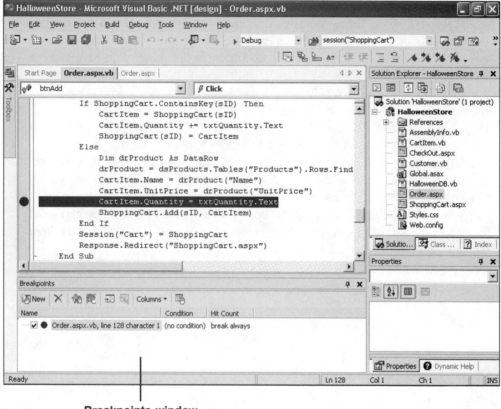

Breakpoints window

How to set and clear breakpoints

- To set a *breakpoint*, click in the margin indicator bar to the left of the statement where you want the break to occur. The statement will be highlighted and a breakpoint indicator (a large dot) will appear in the margin. You can set a breakpoint before you run an application or while you're debugging the application.

- To remove a breakpoint, click the breakpoint indicator. To remove all breakpoints at once, use the Debug→Clear All Breakpoints command.

Description

- When ASP.NET encounters a breakpoint, it enters *break mode* before it executes the statement on which the breakpoint is set. From break mode, you can use the debugger to determine the cause of an error.

- You can only set breakpoints for lines that contain executable statements. You can't set breakpoints on blank lines, comments, or declarative statements.

- The current breakpoints are listed in the *Breakpoints window* (Debug→Windows→ Breakpoints). You can use the toolbar at the top of this window to work with the breakpoints, and you can use the check box next to a breakpoint to enable or disable the breakpoint.

Figure 5-4   How to use breakpoints

How to work in break mode

Figure 5-5 shows the application in figure 5-4 in break mode. In this mode, the next statement to be executed is highlighted. Then, you can use the debugging information that's available to try to determine the cause of an exception or a logical error. For example, you can place the mouse pointer over a variable, property, or expression to display its current value in a *data tip*. In this figure, for example, you can see the current value of the Text property of the txtQuantity text box. You can also see the value of other variables in the Autos window near the bottom left of the Visual Studio window. You'll learn more about the Autos window and some of the other debugging windows in a minute.

If you want to, you can change the values of variables and properties while in break mode. You'll learn how to do that later in this chapter. Note, however, that you can't change the Visual Basic code for an application from break mode. To do that, you must first end the application. Then, you can make the necessary changes and run the application again.

The Halloween Store application in break mode

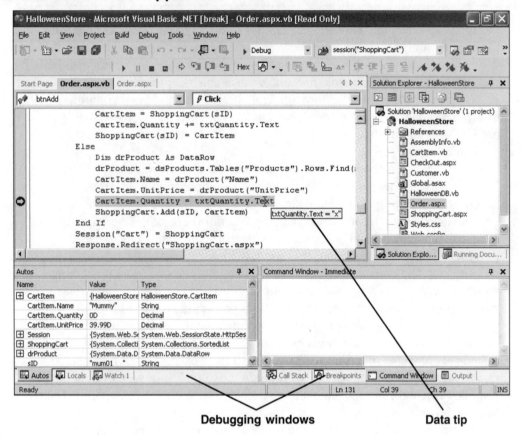

Debugging windows   Data tip

Description

- When you enter break mode, the debugger highlights the next statement to be executed.

- You can use the debugging windows and the buttons in the Debug menu and toolbar to control the execution of the program and determine the cause of an exception.

- To display the value of a variable or property in a *data tip,* position the mouse pointer over the variable or property in the Code Editor window. To display a data tip for an expression, highlight the expression and then point to it. The expression must not contain a function call.

- To continue program execution, press F5 or click the Continue button in the Standard or Debug toolbar. For more options about controlling program execution, see figure 5-6.

Figure 5-5   How to work in break mode

How to control the execution of an application

Once you're in break mode, you can use a variety of commands to control the execution of the application. These commands are summarized in figure 5-6. As you can see, most of these commands are available from the Debug menu or the Debug toolbar, but a couple of them are available only from the shortcut menu for the Code Editor window. You can also use shortcut keys to start a few of these commands. (Note that the shortcut keys in the table are for Visual Studio 2003, and the two differences for Visual Studio 2002 are summarized at the bottom of this figure.)

To *step through* an application one statement at a time, you use the Step Into command. When you use this command, the application executes the next statement, then returns to break mode so you can test the values of properties and variables and perform other debugging functions. The Step Over command is similar to the Step Into command, but it executes the statements in called procedures without interruption (they are "stepped over").

The Step Out command executes the remaining statements in a procedure without interruption. When the procedure finishes, the application enters break mode before the next statement in the calling procedure is executed.

To skip over code that you know is working properly, you can use the Run To Cursor or Set Next Statement command. You can also use the Set Next Statement command to rerun lines of code that were executed before an exception occurred. And if you've been working in the Code Editor window and have forgotten where the next statement to be executed is, you can use the Show Next Statement command to move to it.

If your application gets caught in a processing loop so it keeps executing indefinitely without generating a page, you can force it into break mode by choosing the Debug→Break All command. This command lets you enter break mode any time during the execution of an application.

Commands in the Debug menu and toolbar

Command	Toolbar	Keyboard	Function
Start/Continue	▶	F5	Start or continue execution of the application.
Break All	II	Ctrl+Break	Suspend execution of the application.
Stop Debugging	■		Stop debugging and end execution of the application.
Restart	⟲		Restart the entire application.
Step Into	⤋	F8	Execute one statement at a time.
Step Over	⤈	Shift+F8	Execute one statement at a time except for called procedures.
Step Out	⤉		Execute the remaining lines in the current procedure.
Show Next Statement	⇨		Display the next statement to be executed. Also available from the shortcut menu for the Code Editor window.

Commands in the Code Editor window's shortcut menu

Command	Function
Run to Cursor	Execute the application until it reaches the statement that contains the insertion point.
Set Next Statement	Set the statement that contains the insertion point as the next statement to be executed.

Description

- Once the application enters break mode, you can use the Step Into, Step Over, Step Out, and Run To Cursor commands to execute one or more statements and return to break mode.

- To alter the normal execution sequence of the application, you can use the Set Next Statement command. Just place the insertion point in the statement you want to execute next, issue this command, and click the Continue button to continue application execution.

- To stop an application that's caught in a loop, press Ctrl+Break or switch to the Visual Studio window and use the Debug→Break All command.

Shortcut key differences for Visual Studio 2002

- The shortcut keys in the table above are for Visual Studio 2003. For Visual Studio 2002, the shortcut key for the Step Into command is F11, and the shortcut key for the Step Over command is F10. Otherwise, the shortcut keys are the same for both 2002 and 2003.

Figure 5-6   How to control the execution of an application

How to use the Autos, Locals, and Watch windows to monitor variables

If you need to see the values of several application variables or properties, you can do that using the Autos, Locals, or Watch windows. By default, these windows are displayed in a group in the lower left corner of the IDE when an application enters break mode. If they're not displayed, you can display them by selecting the appropriate command from the Debug→Windows menu. Note that you can display up to four separate Watch windows.

The content of the Autos, Locals, and Watch windows is illustrated in figure 5-7. The difference between the Autos and Locals windows is in the amount of information they display and the scope of that information.

The *Locals window* displays information about the variables and controls within the scope of the current procedure. Since that includes information about all of the controls on the form if the code in a form is currently executing, that information can be extensive.

In contrast, the *Autos window* displays information about the variables, properties, and constants used in the current statement, the three statements before that statement, and the three statements after that statement. Although the information in this window is more limited than the information shown in the Locals window, the Autos window helps you focus on the variables that are relevant to the current statement.

Unlike the Autos and Locals windows, the *Watch windows* let you choose the values that are displayed. The Watch window shown in this figure, for example, displays the values of two properties, a variable, and a data column. The Watch windows also let you watch the values of expressions you specify. Note that an expression doesn't have to exist in the application for you to add it to a Watch window.

To add an item to a Watch window, you can type it directly into the Name column. Alternatively, if the item appears in the Code Editor window, you can highlight it in that window and then drag it to a Watch window. You can also highlight the item in the Code Editor and then right-click on it and select the Add Watch command to add it to the Watch window that's currently displayed.

Besides displaying the values of variables and properties, you can use the Autos, Locals, and Watch windows to change these values. To do that, you simply double-click on the value you want to change and enter a new value. Then, you can continue debugging or continue the execution of the application.

The Autos window

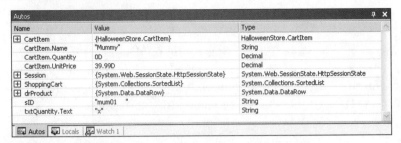

The Locals window

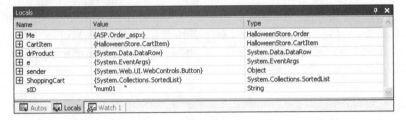

A Watch window

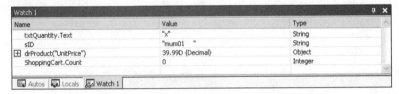

Description

- The *Autos window* displays information about variables, properties, and constants in the current statement and the three statements before and after the current statement.

- The *Locals window* displays information about the variables and controls within the scope of the current procedure.

- The *Watch windows* let you view the values of variables and expressions you specify, called *watch expressions*. You can display up to four Watch windows.

- To add a watch expression, type the variable name or expression into the Name column, highlight the variable or expression in the Code Editor window and drag it to the Watch window, or right-click on the variable or highlighted expression and choose Add Watch.

- To delete a row from a Watch window, right-click the row and choose Delete Watch. To delete all the rows in a Watch window, right-click the window and choose Select All to select the rows, then right-click and choose Delete Watch.

- To display any of these windows, click on its tab if it's visible or select the appropriate command from the Debug→Windows menu.

- To change the value of a property or variable from any of these windows, double-click on the value in the Value column, then type a new value and press the Enter key.

Figure 5-7   How to use the Autos, Locals, and Watch windows to monitor variables

How to use the Command window to work with values

The *Command window*, shown in figure 5-8, is useful for displaying the values of variables or properties that don't appear in the Code Editor window. To display a value, you simply type a question mark followed by the name of the variable or property. The first line of code in this figure, for example, displays the Text property of the item selected from the Categories drop-down list. You can see the result in the second line of this window.

The Command window is also useful for executing Visual Basic statements. For example, you can execute an assignment statement to change the value of a variable or property. After I displayed the Text property of the Quantity text box, for example, I assigned a value of 1 to this property. Similarly, you can execute a Sub procedure or function or display the value returned by the execution of a function. This can be useful for testing the result of a procedure with different arguments.

When you enter commands in the Command window, they're executed in the same context (or scope) as the application that's running. That means that you can't display the value of a variable that's out of scope and you can't execute a private procedure that's in a module or class that isn't currently executing. If you try to do that, the debugger displays a blank line or an error message.

The commands that you enter into the Command window remain there until you exit from Visual Studio or explicitly delete them using the Clear All command in the shortcut menu for the window. That way, you can use standard Windows techniques to edit and reuse the same commands from one execution of an application to another without having to reenter them.

To execute a command that you've already entered in the Command window, just place the insertion point in the command and press the Enter key. This copies the command to the bottom of the window. Then, you can change it if necessary and press Enter to execute it.

The Command window in Immediate mode

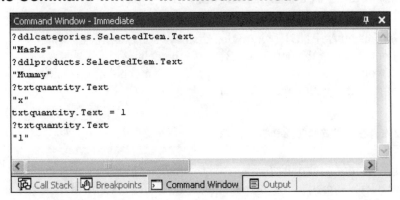

Description

- You can use Immediate mode of the *Command window* to display and assign values from a program during execution. To display this window, click on the Command Window tab or use the Debug→Windows→Immediate command.

- To display a value in the Command window, enter a question mark followed by the expression whose value you want to display. Then, press the Enter key.

- To assign a different value to a variable, property, or object, enter an assignment statement in the Command window. Then, press the Enter key.

- To execute a function or Sub procedure from the Command window, enter its name and any arguments it requires. Then, press the Enter key. If you want to display the result of a function call, precede the function call with a question mark.

- To reissue a command, use the Up and Down arrow keys to scroll through the commands until you find the one you want. Then, place the insertion point in the command and press the Enter key to add the command to the bottom of the Command window. Modify the command if necessary, then press the Enter key to execute it.

- To remove all commands and output from the Command window, use the Clear All command in the shortcut menu for the window.

Figure 5-8   How to use the Command window to work with values

How to use the Trace feature

The *Trace feature* is an ASP.NET feature that displays some useful information that you can't get by using the debugger. Because the debugger works so well, you probably won't need to use the Trace feature very much, but you should at least be aware of the information that it can provide.

How to enable the Trace feature

To use the Trace feature, you must first enable tracing. To do that, you add a Trace attribute to the Page directive for the page, and you assign a value of True to this attribute. This is illustrated in figure 5-9.

When you enable this feature, it is enabled only for the current page, which is usually what you want. To enable tracing for another page, you must modify the Page directive for that page too. Once this feature has been enabled for a page, .NET adds trace output to the page whenever the page is requested.

Because trace output is added to the end of the page using flow layout, it can conflict with pages that are created using grid layout. Specifically, the controls on the page may appear on top of the trace output. To eliminate this problem, you can add <br> tags after the </form> tag for the page but before the </body> tag. Each <br> tag moves the trace output down a line. When you're done with the Trace feature, you'll want to be sure to remove these tags.

The information provided by this feature

In figure 5-9, you can see the start of the output for the Order page of the Halloween Store application after the user has selected a category and a product. After the request details, the trace information provides a list of messages that are generated as the application executes. Here, ASP.NET automatically adds Begin and End messages when major page events such as Init, LoadViewState, and ProcessPostData occur.

By studying the trace information, you can get a better idea of how ASP.NET works. For instance, after its Init procedure initializes the variables for a page, its LoadViewState procedure restores the properties that were changed by code to the values that were saved in view state. Normally, though, you won't need to use this trace information for debugging.

After the trace information, you'll find information about the controls used by the page, the session state objects, the cookies that were included with the HTTP request, the HTTP request headers, and the server variables. In this figure, for example, you can see the session state and cookies data for the Check Out page of the Halloween Store application. In this case, three session objects are included in session state, and two cookies are included with the HTTP request. The Email cookie is the one created by the application, and the SessionID cookie is the one that ASP.NET uses to track the session. This is the type of trace output that can be useful when you encounter an elusive debugging problem.

The beginning of the trace output for the Order page

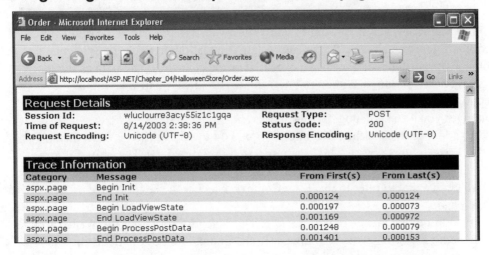

The session and cookies information for the Check Out page

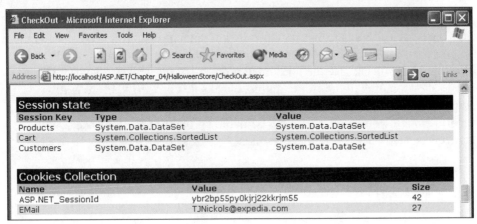

A Page directive that enables tracing for the Order page

```
<%@ Page Language="vb" AutoEventWireup="false" Codebehind="Order.aspx.vb"
Inherits="HalloweenStore.Order" Trace="True"%>
```

Description

- The ASP.NET *Trace feature* traces the execution of a page and displays trace information and other information at the bottom of that page.
- To activate the trace feature for a page, you add a Trace attribute to the Page directive at the top of the .aspx file for the page and set its value to True as shown above.
- If the page uses grid layout, the tracing information may be obscured by controls that use absolute positioning. To avoid this, you can add a series of <br> tags at the bottom of the document body to insert line breaks.

Figure 5-9   How to enable tracing

How to create custom trace messages

In some cases, you may want to add your own messages to the trace information that's generated by the Trace feature. This can help you track the sequence in which the procedures of a form are executed or the changes in the data as the procedures are executed. Although you can also do this type of tracking by stepping through the procedures of a form with the debugger, the trace information gives you a static listing of your messages.

To add messages to the trace information, you use the Write or Warn method of the TraceContext object. This is summarized in figure 5-10. The only difference between these two methods is that messages created with the Warn method appear in red. Notice that to refer to the TraceContext object, you use the Trace property of the page.

In addition to a message, you can specify a category for either the Write or Warn method. This category will appear in the first column of the trace output. One common practice is to specify the procedure name as the category, as in this example:

```
Trace.Write("Page_Load", "Binding categories drop-down list")
```

Then, it's easy for you to see the sequence in which the procedures were executed.

If you want to determine whether tracing is enabled before executing a Write or Warn method, you can use the IsEnabled property of the TraceContext object. The code shown in this figure, for example, checks this property before adding messages that list all of the products that have been loaded into the Products table. Normally, though, you won't check the IsEnabled property because trace statements are executed only if tracing is enabled.

Common members of the TraceContext class

Property	Description
IsEnabled	True if tracing is enabled for the page.

Method	Description
Write(message)	Writes a message to the trace output.
Write(category, message)	Writes a message to the trace output with the specified category.
Warn (message)	Writes a message in red type to the trace output.
Warn(category, message)	Writes a message in red type to the trace output with the specified category.

A statement that writes a custom trace message

```
Trace.Write("Binding categories drop-down list")
```

Code that checks if tracing is enabled before adding trace messages

```
If Trace.IsEnabled Then
    Dim drProduct As DataRow
    For Each drProduct In dsHalloween.Tables("Products").Rows
        Trace.Write(drProduct("Name"))
    Next
End If
```

A portion of a trace that includes a custom message

Trace Information			
Category	**Message**	**From First(s)**	**From Last(s)**
aspx.page	Begin Init		
aspx.page	End Init	0.005462	0.005462
	Binding categories drop-down list	2.803469	2.798006
aspx.page	Begin PreRender	2.937466	0.133997
aspx.page	End PreRender	3.446602	0.509137
aspx.page	Begin SaveViewState	3.462054	0.015452
aspx.page	End SaveViewState	3.463157	0.001103
aspx.page	Begin Render	3.463228	0.000071
aspx.page	End Render	3.582827	0.119598

Custom trace message

Description

- You can use the TraceContext object to write your own messages to the trace output. The TraceContext object is available through the Trace property of a page.

- Use the Write method to write a basic text message. Use the Warn method to write a message in red type.

- Trace messages are written only if tracing is enabled for the page. To determine whether tracing is enabled, you use the IsEnabled property of the TraceContext object.

Figure 5-10   How to create custom trace messages

Perspective

As you can now appreciate, Visual Studio provides a powerful set of tools for debugging ASP.NET applications. By using them, you can set breakpoints at the start of critical portions of code. Then, you can step through the statements that follow each breakpoint, and you can review the values of the related variables and properties after each step. If necessary, you can also change values, alter the execution sequence of the statements, and trace the execution of an application. With tools like these, a difficult debugging job becomes more manageable.

Terms

concurrency
debugger
breakpoint
break mode
Breakpoints window
data tip
stepping through an application
Autos window
Locals window
Watch window
watch expression
Command window
Trace feature

Section 2

More ASP.NET essentials

The five chapters in this section expand upon the essentials that you learned in section 1. To start, chapter 6 presents the essential HTML skills that you will need as an ASP.NET programmer. Then, chapter 7 shows you how to work with all of the server controls that can be used for developing web pages; chapter 8 shows you how to work with all of the validation controls; and chapter 9 presents all the ways that you can manage the state of an application or form. Last, chapter 10 shows you how to develop user controls that can be reused throughout an application.

To a large extent, each of the chapters in this section is an independent unit. As a result, you don't have to read these chapters in sequence. If, for example, you want to know more about state management after you finish section 1, you can go directly to chapter 9. Eventually, though, you're going to want to read all five chapters. So unless you have a compelling reason to skip around, you may as well read the chapters in sequence.

6

HTML essentials for web programming

The web forms you've seen so far in this book have consisted entirely of ASP.NET controls that you drag onto the forms from the Toolbox. In some cases, though, you may want to work directly with the HTML for a form. You may also want to include HTML within the Visual Basic coding for a form. That's why this chapter presents the HTML essentials that every ASP.NET programmer should know.

If you already know how to code HTML, you should be able to go through this chapter quickly. You won't want to skip this chapter altogether, though, because it presents some skills that are specific to Visual Studio .NET.

An introduction to HTML

HTML documents consist of *HTML elements* that define the content and appearance of the page when it's viewed in a web browser. In the two topics that follow, you'll learn the basic rules for coding HTML elements, and you'll learn how to work with HTML using Visual Studio.

Basic rules for coding HTML elements

Figure 6-1 presents the basic rules for coding HTML elements. To start, each HTML element is coded within a *tag* that starts with an opening bracket (<) and ends with a closing bracket (>). For example, <title>, </h1>, and <hr color=red> are all examples of HTML tags.

Most HTML elements are made up of three parts. First, a *start tag* marks the start of the element. The start tag consists of the element name (such as title or h1) plus one or more optional *attributes* that provide additional information for the tag. After the start tag is the *content*, which is the text or other data that makes up the element. Following the content is the *end tag* that marks the end of the element. The end tag consists of a slash followed by the element's name. This is illustrated by the three lines of code in the first example in this figure.

It's important to realize that the content of an element can contain other elements. For example, consider this HTML code:

```
<h1>This is a <b>bold</b>heading</h1>
```

Here, the H1 element contains the text "This is a bold heading." Within this text, the B element indicates that the word "bold" should be boldfaced. You'll learn about these and other formatting elements later in this chapter.

Not all HTML elements have content and end tags. For example, the line of code in the second example in this figure includes two elements without content or end tags. The first element, <br> inserts a line break, and the second element, <hr>, inserts a horizontal rule. Notice that the text in this line of code isn't enclosed in tags. That's because, like the <br> and <hr> tags, it is content for another tag that's coded at a higher level in the document. You'll learn more about that later.

Although all of the tags shown in this figure are lowercase, you should realize that HTML tags aren't case sensitive. So you can use either upper or lowercase letters when you code your tags. Since lowercase is easier to read and type, most programmers use lowercase when coding HTML tags. However, Visual Studio sometimes generates uppercase tags, so you'll see both upper and lowercase tags used in this book.

You can also code *comments* within an HTML document as shown in the third example in this figure. That way, you can document sections of code that might be confusing. In addition, you can use spaces, indentation, and blank lines to make your code easier to read. This is called *white space*, and web browsers ignore it. If you want to include space within a line that the web browser doesn't ignore, you can use the special code   as shown in the last example.

Three HTML elements with start tags, content, and end tags

```
<title>The Halloween Store</title>
<h1>Halloween Costumes</h1>
<b>Choose a costume:</b>
```

Two elements that have no content or end tags

```
A red line appears below.<br><hr color=red>
```

A comment

```
<!-- This text will be ignored. -->
```

A line that has three consecutive spaces

```
Last name:   Wilson
```

Elements and tags

- An *HTML document* includes *HTML elements* that specify the content and appearance of the page when viewed in a web browser.

- Most HTML elements have three parts: a start tag, content, and an end tag. Each *tag* is coded within a set of brackets (< >).

- An element's *start tag* includes the name of the element. The *end tag* includes the element name preceded by a slash. And the *content* includes everything that appears between the start and end tags.

- Some HTML elements have no content or end tag. For example, the <br> element, which forces a line break, and the <hr> element, which inserts a horizontal rule, consist of just a start tag.

- HTML tags aren't case sensitive, so you can use upper or lowercase letters for your tags.

Attributes

- *Attributes* can appear within an element's start tag to supply optional values. For example, you can use the Color attribute within an <hr> element to specify the color of the rule.

- Attribute values that contain spaces or special symbols should be enclosed in quotation marks.

- Use commas to separate attributes from one another.

Comments and white space

- A *comment* is text that appears between the <!-- and --> characters. Web browsers ignore comments, so you can use them to document sections of your HTML code that might otherwise be confusing.

- *White space*, such as tabs, line returns, and consecutive spaces, is ignored by browsers. As a result, you can use space to indent lines of code and line breaks to separate elements from one another. Used properly, white space can make your HTML code easier to read. However, Visual Studio typically removes white space from the HTML it generates.

- To force the browser to display two or more consecutive spaces, use the special code   for each space.

Figure 6-1   Basic rules for coding HTML elements

How to work with HTML using Visual Studio

In chapter 2, you learned how to create a simple web form by dragging ASP.NET controls onto the design surface of the Web Forms Designer. When you do that, Visual Studio generates the code for those controls. To see the code that's generated, you can click the HTML button at the bottom of the designer window to display the form in HTML view. Then, you can work with the HTML as described in figure 6-2.

When you display a web form in HTML view, you'll notice that Visual Studio uses different colors to identify various items of information. For example, element names are displayed in maroon, attribute names are displayed in red, and attribute values are displayed in blue. Visual Studio also makes syntax errors easy to locate by underlining them with a red wavy line.

Visual Studio also provides tools that help you enter and edit HTML code. One of the most useful is the statement completion feature. With this feature, a list of the available elements is displayed when you enter the opening bracket for a start tag. Then, you can select the element you want to add from this list and press the Tab key to add the element name to your document.

After you enter an element name followed by a space, Visual Studio displays a list of the available attributes for that element. In this figure, for example, you can see the list of attributes that's displayed for a Form element. To add an attribute, you just select it from the list and then press the Tab key. Then, you can type an equal sign and enter a value for the attribute. To enter additional attributes, type a comma and a space to redisplay the list. When you're finished entering the attributes for an element, you enter its closing bracket. Then, the end tag for that element, if it has one, is added automatically.

As you work with the Web Forms Designer, you'll frequently switch back and forth between HTML view and Design view. When you make a change to the HTML in HTML view, you can quickly switch to Design view to check the results of your editing. Then, you can switch back to HTML view to continue editing the HTML. When you do that, you'll notice that Visual Studio removes any white space you may have added to align and group elements. Because of that, you probably won't use white space with the web forms that you create from Visual Studio.

A web page in HTML view with a completion list displayed

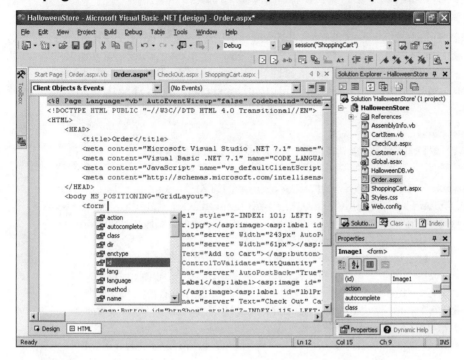

Description

- To edit the HTML document for a web form in Visual Studio, display the form in HTML view by clicking on the HTML button at the bottom of the Web Forms Designer window.

- Visual Studio uses distinctive colors to identify various items in HTML view. In addition, it highlights syntax errors with a red wavy underline so they're easy to locate.

- You can edit an HTML document directly in HTML view. Then, any changes you make will be reflected in the form when you switch back to Design view.

- When you enter the opening bracket (<) for a start tag, Visual Studio displays a list of the available elements. To select an element, type one or more letters of the element or scroll to the element, and then press the Tab key.

- When you enter the name of an HTML element followed by a space, Visual Studio displays a list of the attributes you can use with that element. To select an attribute, type one or more letters of the attribute or scroll to the attribute, and then press the Tab key.

- When you enter the closing bracket (>) for a start tag, Visual Studio automatically adds the end tag.

- You can also add or modify element attributes using the Properties window. To do that, highlight the element to display its attributes in the Properties window and then change the attribute values as appropriate.

- You can also use Visual Studio's drag-and-drop feature to add ASP.NET controls to a form in HTML view. To do that, just drag the control from the Toolbox to the location where you want it to appear in the HTML document.

Figure 6-2   How to work with HTML using Visual Studio

How to code HTML documents

Every HTML document for a web form must be structured in a certain way for it to be interpreted properly by ASP.NET. In the topics that follow, you'll learn about the basic structure of an HTML document. You'll also learn how you code some of the common elements that appear within an HTML document.

The basic structure of an HTML document

Figure 6-3 shows the overall structure of an HTML document for an ASP.NET web page. When you create a web form in Visual Studio, the elements that make up this structure are generated for you automatically. So you don't have to worry about coding them yourself.

The first two elements are an ASP.NET Page directive and an HTML DocType declaration. The Page directive supplies the information ASP.NET needs to process the web form, and the Doctype declaration provides information the browser needs to display the page. You'll learn about both of these elements in the next figure.

After the Page directive and the Doctype declaration is an Html element. This element, known as the *root element*, contains all of the document's remaining elements. According to the HTML standards, the start and end tags for the Html element are optional. As a result, you'll sometimes see HTML documents without the <html> and </html> tags.

The Html element contains two additional elements: a Head element and a Body element. The Head element defines the document head, which contains various information about the document. You'll learn more about this element in figure 6-5. The Body element defines the document body, which contains the HTML content that's displayed when the document is viewed in a browser.

For a web form, the document body typically consists of just a Form element. As you've seen in previous chapters, this element contains all of the ASP.NET controls for the form. You should realize, however, that you can code any of the standard HTML elements within the Form element. You can also code these elements outside the Form element, but within the Body element. That's unusual, however.

Because the Head and Body elements are contained with an Html element, the Html element is called a *parent element* and the Head and Body elements are called *child elements*. The Body element is also a parent element because it contains a Form element. This hierarchy of elements becomes particularly important when you're working with styles, as you'll see later in this chapter.

The structure of an HTML document for an ASP.NET web page

```
<%@ page ...>
<!doctype ...>

<html>

    <head>
        Document head
    </head>

    <body>
        <form>
            Form content
        </form>
    </body>

</html>
```

HTML structural elements

Element	Start tag	End tag	Description
Page directive	<%@ page ...>		Identifies various options applied to the web page. See figure 6-4 for details.
Document type	<!doctype ...>		Identifies the type of HTML document. See figure 6-4 for details.
Html	<html>	</html>	Marks the beginning and end of an HTML document.
Head	<head>	</head>	Marks the beginning and end of the document head. See figure 6-5 for details.
Body	<body>	</body>	Marks the beginning and end of the document body.
Form	<form>	</form>	Marks the beginning and end of the form.

Description

- The Html element contains the content of the document. This element is called the *root element* because it contains all the other elements in the document. Within this element, you code the Head and Body elements.
- The Body element contains the Form element that defines the form. Although other elements can be coded within the Body element, that's uncommon when you create web pages using Visual Studio.
- The Form element contains the controls and other elements that you want to be displayed when the document is viewed in a browser.
- An element that's contained within another element is called a *child element*. The element that contains a child element is called the child's *parent element*.

Note

- All of the tags shown in this figure are generated automatically by Visual Studio .NET when you create a web form.

Figure 6-3   The basic structure of an HTML document for an ASP.NET web page

The Page directive

Figure 6-4 shows the Page directive that appears at the beginning of all ASP.NET pages. Notice that the Page directive begins with the characters <%@ and ends with the characters %>. These special sequences of characters form a *directive block*. Because directive blocks aren't a part of standard HTML, they aren't included in the final HTML that's sent to the browser when the page is displayed. Instead, directive blocks are processed by ASP.NET when the page is compiled.

As you can see in this figure, the Page directive has several attributes. The first attribute, Language, specifies the programming language that's used for the page's code. For Visual Basic projects, the value of this attribute is *vb*.

The next attribute is AutoEventWireup. For web forms created in Visual Studio, this attribute is set to False. That causes the event procedures with Handles clauses for the Init and Load events of the page to be executed automatically when the page is initialized and loaded. In that case, you can change the names of the procedures since they're associated with the appropriate events through the Handles clause. You can also associate procedures with these events without using the Handles clause. To do that, you must name the event procedures Page_Init and Page_Load. Then, you set the AutoEventWireup attribute to True.

The Codebehind and Inherits attributes work together to link the ASP.NET web page to the code-behind file. First, the Codebehind attribute provides the name of the code-behind file. Visual Studio uses this option to associate the page with the file that contains the Visual Basic code for the page. Then, the Inherits attribute provides the name of the class defined by the code-behind file that the page inherits at runtime. This is the name that's specified on the Class statement within the code-behind file.

Another attribute you can include in the Page directive is Trace. You learned about this attribute in chapter 5. It determines whether or not trace information that you can use for debugging is displayed on the web page.

The Doctype declaration

Figure 6-4 also shows the Doctype declaration. This declaration is used by a web browser to determine which version of HTML the document uses. The Doctype declaration generated by Visual Studio specifies transitional HTML version 4.0. That means that the web page uses HTML version 4.0, including certain HTML elements that are expected to be phased out in the future.

The Page directive for the Order page of the Halloween Store application

```
<%@ Page Language="vb" AutoEventWireup="false"
    Codebehind="Order.aspx.vb" Inherits="HalloweenStore.Order"%>
```

Common attributes of the Page directive

Attribute	Description
Language	Specifies the language used to implement the processing for the page. For Visual Basic applications, this attribute is set to *vb*.
AutoEventWireup	Indicates whether the event procedures named Page_Init and Page_Load will be called automatically when the Init and Load events occur for the page (True) or if you must use the Handles keyword to bind procedures to these events (False). The default is True, but Visual Studio sets this attribute to False when it creates a web form.
Codebehind	Specifies the name of the Visual Basic code-behind file. This option is used by Visual Studio to associate the aspx file with the file that contains the Visual Basic code for the page.
Inherits	Specifies the name of the class that the page inherits at runtime. This class is part of the DLL that's created when the project is compiled.
Trace	Indicates whether tracing is enabled. The default is False.

The Doctype declaration for the Order page of the Halloween Store application

```
<!DOCTYPE HTML PUBLIC "-//W3C//DTD HTML 4.0 Transitional//EN">
```

Description

- The Page directive is processed by ASP.NET when the page is compiled. It isn't included in the output that's sent to the browser.
- The Doctype declaration specifies that the root element of the document—that is, the first element after the Doctype declaration—is an HTML element.
- The Public attribute of the Doctype declaration and the string that follows it specify the version of HTML that the document complies with.

Figure 6-4   The Page directive and the Doctype declaration

How to code the document head

Figure 6-5 shows how to code a document head. The document head shown here includes two types of elements: a Title element and several Meta elements. The Title element supplies the text that's displayed in the title bar of the web browser when the page is displayed. By default, Visual Studio sets the title to the name of the class that defines the page, but you can change it to anything you like.

The Meta elements in the remaining lines of the document head supply *meta data* for the page. Each item of meta data has a name and a value. For example, the first Meta element creates a meta data item named GENERATOR whose value is "Microsoft Visual Studio.NET 7.1." Meta data is used by browsers, search engines, and other programs to get information about your pages.

Although you should avoid changing the meta data that's generated by Visual Studio, you may want to add additional meta data items of your own. For example, search engines such as www.google.com base their indexing algorithms in part on keywords that you supply for your pages via a meta data item named Keywords. To illustrate, suppose you added the Meta element shown in the second code example in this figure to the Order page of the Halloween Store application. Then, if a user enters one or more of the keywords listed in this element into a search engine, the search engine includes the page in a list of pages that match the search. Note that although you can enter a Meta element like this one directly into the HTML document, you can also generate it from Visual Studio using the Property Pages dialog box shown in this figure.

A document head

```
<HEAD>
    <title>Order</title>
    <meta name="GENERATOR" content="Microsoft Visual Studio.NET 7.1">
    <meta name="CODE_LANGUAGE" content="Visual Basic 7.1">
    <meta name="vs_defaultClientScript" content="JavaScript">
    <meta name="vs_targetSchema"
        content="http://schemas.microsoft.com/intellisense/ie5">
</HEAD>
```

A Meta tag for a Keywords data item

```
<meta name="keywords" content="halloween, costumes, discount">
```

The Keywords tab of the DOCUMENT Property Pages dialog box

Description

- The document head is generated automatically by Visual Studio, but you can modify it or add additional elements to it if you need to.

- The Title element provides the name that appears in the web browser's title bar.

- The Meta tags provide *meta data* for the page. Meta data provides useful information about the page for browsers, servers, search engines, or other web applications.

- Each Meta tag includes a Content attribute that supplies the value of the meta data and a Name attribute that supplies the name of the meta data.

- To help search engines index your page, you can include keywords in the meta data. To do that, you can enter a Meta tag like the one shown above into the document head.

- You can also create a Meta tag with keywords by entering the keywords into the Keywords tab of the DOCUMENT Property Pages dialog box as shown above. To display this dialog box, right-click the page in Design view and select Properties from the shortcut menu. A Meta tag that contains the keywords you specify is generated for you.

Figure 6-5   How to code the document head

How to code basic text formatting elements

In addition to ASP.NET controls, a web form can contain literal text. Later in this chapter, for example, you'll see a table that includes literal text. And in the next chapter, you'll learn how to type literal text directly on a form when you use flow layout mode. To format text like this, you can use the elements shown in figure 6-6.

To use the elements shown in this figure, you enclose the text you want to format in the start and end tags for the element. The exception is the Br tag. This tag is used to insert a line break and doesn't have an end tag.

The first three elements listed in this figure are the H1, H2, and H3 heading elements. (Although HTML actually has six levels of headings, it's unlikely that you'll use more than three.) The heading elements are designed to create headings with various formats. All three of the headings shown in the output in this figure, for example, are formatted using H2 elements.

The next two elements, P and Br, let you format paragraphs and force line endings. When you use the P element to create standard text paragraphs, the web browser determines where to break lines based on the width of the browser window and the size of the text. If you want to force a line ending at a particular spot, you need to use a Br element. The paragraph that describes the P element in this figure, for example, is formatted using the P element. Because of that, the text flows to the right side of the browser window. In contrast, the paragraph that describes the Br element contains a Br element that forces a line break.

The last three elements let you create bold, italic, or underlined text. These elements are typically used within P elements or literal text to format all or part of the text. The last paragraph shown in the output in this figure, for example, illustrates how individual words can be formatted within literal text.

Before I go on, you should realize that the basic appearance of the text in an HTML document is determined by the browser. Because of that, headings and body text may appear differently in one browser than they do in another. Later in this chapter, though, you'll learn how to use styles to control the overall appearance of the elements in a document.

Basic HTML formatting elements

Element	Start tag	End tag	Description
H1	\<h1>	\</h1>	Level-1 heading
H2	\<h2>	\</h2>	Level-2 heading
H3	\<h3>	\</h3>	Level-3 heading
P	\<p>	\</p>	Standard paragraph
Br	\ 		Line break
B	\<b>	\</b>	Bold
I	\<i>	\</i>	Italic
U	\<u>	\</u>	Underline

HTML that uses some basic formatting elements

```
<h2>The P element</h2>
<p>The P element marks a standard paragraph. Note that the
web browser determines where the individual lines within the
paragraph will break.</p>
<h2>The BR element</h2>
In contrast, the BR element lets you force a<br>
line break wherever you wish.
<h2>The B, I, and U elements</h2>
This is <b>bold</b>.  This is <i>italic</i>. This is <u>underlined</u>.
```

The HTML viewed in a browser window

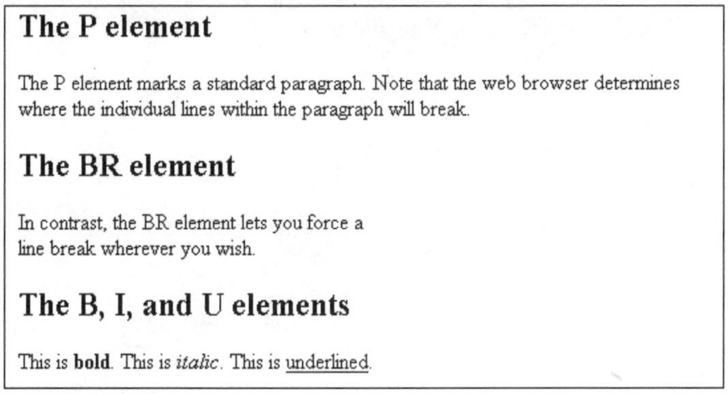

The P element

The P element marks a standard paragraph. Note that the web browser determines
where the individual lines within the paragraph will break.

The BR element

In contrast, the BR element lets you force a
line break wherever you wish.

The B, I, and U elements

This is **bold**. This is *italic*. This is underlined.

Description

- You typically use these elements in a web form to format literal text.
- The default appearance of heading and body text is determined by the browser. However, you can also use styles to determine the default formatting for various elements.
- The P element formats text as a standard paragraph. The browser determines where line endings occur for the text within the paragraph. If you want to force a line break at a specific location within a paragraph, use the Br element.

Figure 6-6   How to code basic text formatting elements

How to code links to other HTML pages

Most web applications consist of a series of web pages. In chapter 3, you learned how you can display one web page from another by using either the Redirect method of the HttpResponse object or the Transfer method of the HttpServerUtility object. Another way to display a different page is to code an Anchor, or A, element, often called a link.

Figure 6-7 shows how to use the Anchor element. As you can see, this element typically consists of just the start and end tags, an Href attribute that specifies the URL of the page you want to link to, and the text that's displayed by the browser to identify the link. When viewed in a browser, the text within the Anchor element is usually underlined. In addition, the mouse pointer typically changes to a hand when hovered over the text for the link. Then, when the user clicks on the link, the browser requests the page specified by the Href attribute.

When you code an Href attribute in an Anchor element, you can use either a relative URL or an absolute URL. The first Anchor element in this figure, for example, uses a relative URL to display the Register page in the Login subdirectory of the directory that contains the current page. The second Anchor element uses an absolute URL to display the Index page on the www.murach.com web site.

In the next chapter, you'll learn how to use the hyperlink control to link to another web page. Because this control provides the same functionality as the Anchor element, you'll typically use it in your web forms instead of Anchor elements. However, Anchor elements can be useful in some situations. In particular, they're useful for creating menus in code. You'll see an example of that in chapter 9.

Examples of Anchor elements

An anchor element that uses a relative URL

```
<a href="Login/Register.aspx">Register as a new user</a>
```

An anchor element that uses an absolute URL

```
<a href="http://www.murach.com/Index.aspx">View Murach's web site</a>
```

The Anchor elements viewed in a browser

Register as a new user

View Murach's web site

The Anchor element

Start tag	End tag	Description
<a>	</a>	Defines a link to another URL. When the user clicks on the text that's displayed by the element, the browser requests the page that's identified by the href attribute of the element.

One attribute of an Anchor element

Attribute	Description
href	The URL for the page to be displayed.

Description

* You can code both relative and absolute URLs in the Href attribute. See figure 3-6 in chapter 3 for the details on coding these URLs.

* Because ASP.NET provides a Hyperlink control, you may not use the Anchor element often. However, you may want to assign a series of Anchor elements that are created in code to the Text property of a label to create a menu. See chapter 9 for an example.

Figure 6-7   How to code links to other HTML pages

How to code tables

HTML *tables* present content in grids of *rows* and *columns*. You can use tables to present tabular information in a way that resembles a spreadsheet. You can also use tables as a way to control the overall layout of page elements such as titles, banners, navigation bars, and content areas.

How to create a table

Figure 6-8 presents the basic HTML elements you use to create a table. To start, you use a Table element to identify the start and end of the table. Within the Table element, you use one or more Tr elements to define each row of the table. (Tr stands for Table Row.) Then, within each Tr element, you use one or more Td elements to create each *cell*. (Td stands for Table Data.)

The code shown in this figure defines a table that contains three rows, each with two cells. Below the code you can see how the table is displayed in a browser. Tables are frequently used to align form content like this, particularly when the form is designed in flow layout mode. You'll learn more about designing forms in this mode in the next chapter.

Notice that the HTML shown here doesn't specify the size of the table or its cells. Because of that, the sizes will change dynamically depending on the data in each cell. If that's not what you want, you can use some of the formatting attributes you'll learn about in the next figure to control the table and cell sizes.

In this example, the first cell in each row contains literal text, and the second cell in each row contains a text box. You should realize, however, that a cell can store any type of data, including other tables. In fact, it's common for a web page to consist of tables nested within other tables.

The HTML code for a table

```
<p>Please enter the following information:</p>
<table cellspacing="5" cellpadding="5" border="1">
  <tr>
    <td align="right">First name:</td>
    <td><asp:TextBox id="TextBox1" runat="server"></asp:TextBox></td>
  </tr>
  <tr>
    <td align="right">Last name:</td>
    <td><asp:TextBox id="TextBox2" runat="server"></asp:TextBox></td>
  </tr>
  <tr>
    <td align="right">Email address:</td>
    <td><asp:TextBox id="TextBox3" runat="server"></asp:TextBox></td>
  </tr>
</table>
```

The table displayed in a browser

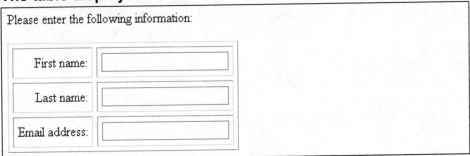

The HTML elements for working with tables

Element	Start tag	End tag	Description
Table	<table>	</table>	Defines the start and end of the table.
Tr	<tr>	</tr>	Defines the start and end of each row.
Td	<td>	</td>	Defines the start and end of each cell within a row.

Description

- A *table* consists of *rows* and *columns*. The intersection of a row and column is a *cell* that can hold content, such as text, images, controls, or even other tables.
- By default, the height and width of the cells in a table change dynamically depending on their content. However, you can specify static cell sizes as well as other table formatting options using the attributes presented in figure 6-9.
- Tables are often used to align form content and to control the overall layout of a page.

Figure 6-8   How to create a table

Common table attributes

Figure 6-9 presents some of the attributes you can use with Table, Tr, and Td elements. To control the border that's displayed around a table and between the cells in a table, for example, you set the Border attribute of the table. Notice that to hide the border, you can set this attribute to 0. To control the amount of space between the cells in a table, you set the Cellspacing attribute of the table. And to control the amount of space between the border and the contents of a cell, you set the Cellpadding attribute of the table.

You can use the Height and Width attributes to set an absolute height or width for the table or for individual cells. These attributes are especially useful when you use a table to control page layout. Then, you'll want the total height and width of the table to be less than the total number of pixels for your target resolution. Since most web sites are designed to be viewed best in an 800x600 pixel window, that usually means coding tables with widths less than 780 and heights less that 580. That leaves an extra 20 pixels for the horizontal and vertical scroll bars. Note that the width of a table includes the width of all of the cells plus the spacing between the cells.

Two of the attributes shown in this figure, Colspan and Rowspan, are essential when working with complicated table layouts. These attributes let you create cells that span two or more columns or rows. You'll see an example of a table that uses the Colspan attribute in the next figure.

Common attributes of the Table element

Attribute	Description
border	Specifies the visual border of the table. To turn the border off, specify a value of 0. To specify the width of the border in pixels, specify a value of 1 or greater.
cellspacing	Specifies the number of pixels between cells.
cellpadding	Specifies the number of pixels between the contents of a cell and the edge of the cell.
width	Specifies the width of the table. To specify the width in pixels, use a number such as 300. To specify a percent of the browser's display space, use a number followed by the percent sign such as 60%.
height	Specifies the height of the table in pixels or as a percentage of the browser's display space. This works like the Width attribute.
bgcolor	Specifies the background color for all of the table's cells.

Common attributes of the Tr element

Attribute	Description
valign	Specifies the vertical alignment of the contents of the row. Acceptable values include Top, Bottom, and Middle.
bgcolor	Specifies the background color for all of the row's cells. This value overrides any color you specify for the table.

Common attributes of the Td element

Attribute	Description
align	Specifies the horizontal alignment of the contents of the cell. Acceptable values include Left, Right, and Center.
colspan	Specifies the number of columns that the cell will span. This attribute is used to create wide cells that span two or more columns.
rowspan	Specifies the number of rows that the cell will span. This attribute is used to create tall cells that span two or more rows.
height	Specifies the height of the cell in pixels.
width	Specifies the width of the cell in pixels.
valign	Specifies the vertical alignment of the contents of the cell. Acceptable values include Top, Bottom, and Middle. This value overrides any alignment you specify for the row.
bgcolor	Specifies the background color for the cell. This value overrides any color you specify for the table or row.

Note

- Colors can be specified using color names or color values, but color names aren't supported by all browsers. To choose a color, select the element, then select the bgcolor property in the Properties window and click the ellipsis button that appears. Then, choose the color you want from the Color Picker dialog box that's displayed.

Figure 6-9   Common table attributes

How to use a table to control the layout of a page

Figure 6-10 shows how to use a table to arrange a page that consists of three areas. A banner area is displayed at the top of the page, a navigation area is displayed at the left side of the page, and a content area occupies the rest of the page. This table consists of two rows. The first one consists of a single cell that contains the banner area. The second one consists of two cells that contain the navigation and content area.

The key to the HTML for this table is the Colspan attribute in the first Td element. It causes the cell in the first row to span both of the cells in the second row. Also notice that the Border and Cellspacing attributes of the table are set to 0 so the cells will appear right next to each other. In addition, each cell has a different background color so you can see the area that it occupies. Although this is a relatively simple layout, it should help you begin to see how you can use tables to divide a page into distinct areas.

A table that sets up a simple page layout

```
<table width=750 border=0 cellspacing=0>
  <tr height=75>
    <td colspan=2 bgcolor=gray>
        Banner area
    </td>
  </tr>
  <tr height=400>
    <td width=150 valign=top bgcolor=silver>
        Navigation area
    </td>
    <td width=600 valign=top bgcolor=white>
        Content area
    </td>
  </tr>
</table>
```

The table viewed in a browser

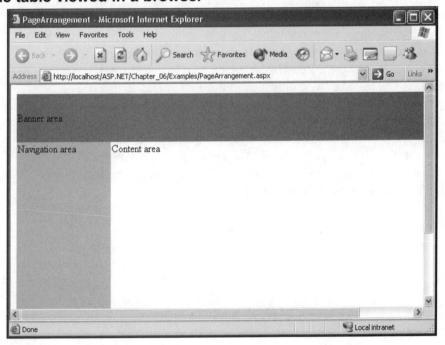

Description

- The Colspan attribute for the cell that makes up the banner area is set to 2 so that it spans both of the columns in the table.
- The Border attribute for the table is set to zero so no border appears around the table, and the Cellspacing attribute for the table is set to zero so there is no space between the cells in the table.
- Each cell is defined with a different color so you can see how the layout appears when displayed in the browser.

Figure 6-10   How to use a table to control the layout of a page

Visual Studio features for working with tables

Although you can create a table by entering code like that shown in figures 6-8 and 6-10, you can also use the features Visual Studio provides to create and work with tables. Figure 6-11 summarizes these features.

First, you can create a table using the Insert Table dialog box shown in this figure. This dialog box lets you specify the number of rows and columns the table should contain. It also lets you set various table attributes, such as width, height, and background color, and cell attributes, such as background color and alignment. When you complete this dialog box, Visual Studio generates the Table, Tr, and Td elements to define the table.

After you create a table, it appears in the Web Forms Designer window. Then, you can adjust its size and shape by dragging its borders. You can also adjust the size of an individual cell by selecting the cell and dragging one of its borders. And you can set the properties for a cell or the entire table by selecting the cell or table and then using the Properties window.

You can also use the commands in the Table menu to work with an existing table. To add a row, column, cell, or table to an existing table, for example, you can use the commands in the Table→Insert menu. And to delete rows, columns, cells, or a table, you can use the commands in the Table→Delete menu. You can also merge two or more adjacent cells using the Merge Cells command.

In practice, I usually use the Visual Studio features to create the initial version of a table. Often, though, I'm not able to adjust the table so it looks the way that I want it to. Then, I switch to HTML view and work with the HTML for the table until it does suit my requirements. This is a primary reason why you need to know how to code the HTML for a table.

The Insert Table dialog box

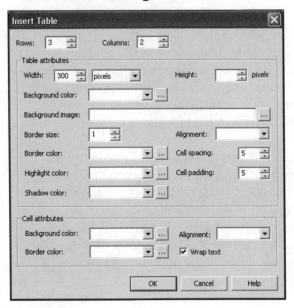

Description

- You can use the commands on the Table menu to insert and format tables. These commands generate the Table, Tr, and Td elements for the table.

- To create a table, use the Table→Insert→Table command to display the Insert Table dialog box. From this dialog box, you can specify the number of rows and columns in the table along with various attributes for the table.

- You can use the other commands in the Table→Insert menu to add a row, column, or cell to an existing table. The commands that are available depend on whether a row, column, or cell is selected.

- To select a row, place the mouse pointer to the left of the row until it turns into a black arrow and then click the left mouse button. To select a column, place the mouse pointer above the row until it turns into a black arrow and then click the left mouse button. To select a cell, place the mouse pointer at the left side of the cell until it turns into a black arrow and then click the left mouse button. To select the entire table, click on its border.

- You can also select a cell, row, column, or table by clicking in a cell and then selecting the appropriate command from the Table→Select menu.

- To delete a cell, column, or row, select it and then use the appropriate command in the Table→Delete menu.

- To change the size of a cell, drag the cell by one of its borders.

- To merge two or more adjacent cells into a single cell, select the cells and then choose the Table→Merge Cells command. Visual Studio .NET adjusts the Colspan and Rowspan attributes to create the resulting merged cell.

Figure 6-11   Visual Studio features for working with tables

How to use styles

With early versions of HTML, the appearance of the HTML elements in a page was determined almost entirely by the browser where the page was displayed. With newer versions of HTML, however, you can use a feature called *cascading style sheets*, or *CSS*, to provide better control over the appearance of your web pages. Like the basic formatting elements you learned about earlier in this chapter, you're most likely to use styles to format the literal text you add to a form.

In the topics that follow, you'll learn about two types of CSS styles: inline styles and external styles. With *inline styles*, you specify style formatting directly in an HTML element. In contrast, *external styles* let you store formatting information in a separate file so you can apply it to all of the pages in a site. When you develop ASP.NET applications, you'll probably work with both types of styles from time to time. However, you should avoid using inline styles whenever possible because they make a web site more difficult to maintain.

How to use inline styles

To use inline styles, you include a Style attribute in the element you want to format. Within this attribute, you specify one or more individual *style properties* that control various style settings. Some of the most common style properties are listed in figure 6-12.

The HTML in this figure illustrates how you can use the Style attribute. Here, the style properties for the H1 element specify that the text it contains should be displayed in a bold, 16-point, white, Arial font against a blue background. Similarly, the style properties for the H2 element specify that the text it contains should be displayed in an italic, 14-point, Times New Roman font.

The three P elements in this figure show how you can use the Text-align property to align text on a page. The first element aligns the text at the left margin, the second element centers the text between the margins, and the third element aligns the text at the right margin. All three of these elements also specify the Courier New font, which is a mono-spaced font. This figure illustrates how these elements and the two heading elements appear in a browser window.

Notice that the syntax for specifying style properties is different from the syntax you use for HTML attributes. Instead of an equals sign, you separate a style name from its value with a colon. And instead of separating items with commas, you separate items with semicolons.

You should also notice that the Font-family property in each of the Style attributes specifies a specific font plus a generic font style. For example, the Font-family property for the H1 element specifies Arial and sans-serif. That way, if the Arial font isn't installed on the computer where the page is displayed, the text will be displayed in the default sans-serif font. When you code the Font-family property, you can specify as many different fonts as you want,

Common properties of the Style attribute

Property	Description
Font-family	A comma-separated list of font names, such as Arial, Times New Roman, and Courier New, and generic font styles, such as serif, sans-serif, and monospace.
Font-size	A specific number of points, a point size relative to the parent element's font size, or a keyword such as small, medium, or large.
Font-style	A keyword that determines how the text is slanted. Possible values are normal, italic, and oblique.
Font-weight	A keyword that determines the boldness of the font. Possible values are normal, bold, bolder, and lighter. Bolder or lighter are relative to the parent element.
Background-color	A color value, such as red, blue, or yellow that controls the background color of an element.
Color	A color value that controls the foreground color of an element.
Text-align	A keyword that determines the alignment of the text in a P element relative to the page margins. Possible values are left, right, center, or justify.

HTML that uses inline styles

```
<h1 style="Font-Weight: bold; Font-Size: 16pt; Color: white; Font-Family:
    Arial, Sans-Serif; Background-Color: blue">The Halloween Store</h1>
<h2 style="Font-Size: 14pt; Font-Style: italic; Font-Family:
    'Times New Roman', Serif">The Halloween Store</h2>
<p style="Font-Size: 10pt; Font-Family: 'Courier New', Monospace;
    Text-Align: left">This text is left-justified and mono-spaced.</p>
<p style="Font-Size: 10pt; Font-Family: 'Courier New', Monospace;
    Text-Align: center">This text is centered and mono-spaced.</p>
<p style="Font-Size: 10pt; Font-Family: 'Courier New', Monospace;
    Text-Align: right">This text is right-justified and mono-spaced.</p>
```

The HTML viewed in a browser window

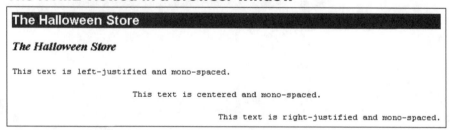

Description

- You typically use styles to format the literal text on a web form.

- You can use the Style attribute to create an *inline style* that affects the appearance of a single element in an HTML document and any child elements it contains. If you specify a style for a child element, it overrides the style specified by the parent element.

- Within the Style attribute, you specify one or more *style properties*, such as Font-size and Font-family. The name of each property is separated from its value by a colon, and the properties are separated from one another with semicolons.

Figure 6-12   How to use inline styles

and the first one that's available will be used. In case none of the fonts you specify are available, however, you should always end the list with a generic font style.

Although it's not illustrated in this figure, you should realize that if an element contains child elements, the style properties applied to the parent element are also applied to the child elements. For example, if you wanted to display most of the text in the body of a document in 10-point Arial, you could add a Style attribute to the Body element with the appropriate style properties. Then, if you wanted to display a child element within the Body element in a different font, you could add a Style attribute to that element to override the style properties in the Body element.

How to use the Span element to apply styles

When you use inline styles, the style properties you specify apply to the entire element. If you want to apply a style to just a portion of an element, you can do that using a Span element. Figure 6-13 illustrates how this element works.

The first example in this figure shows how you might use the Span element to format the text in the Text property of a label control. Notice that the Span element only encloses part of the text, so only that portion of the text is formatted. Similarly, the second example shows how you can format a portion of the text that's displayed for an Anchor element. If you look at how the label and Anchor elements appear in a browser, you shouldn't have any trouble understanding how the Span element works.

Examples of Span elements

A Span element used to format text within the Text property of a label

```
<asp:Label id="Label1" runat="server">This is the
    <span style="background-color: blue; color: white">selected</span>
    item.</asp:Label>
```

A Span element used to format text that's displayed for an Anchor element

```
<a href="inlinestyles.aspx">Click here for a list of
    <span style="FONT-WEIGHT: bold; FONT-SIZE: large; COLOR: red">
    Drastically Reduced</span> items</a>
```

The elements viewed in a browser

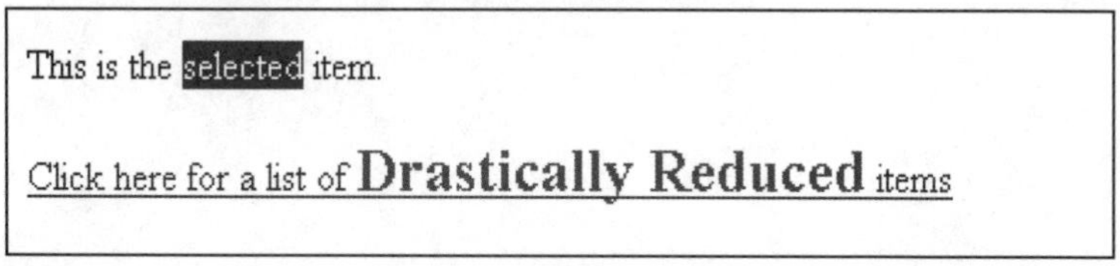

This is the selected item.

Click here for a list of **Drastically Reduced** items

The Span element

Start tag	End tag	Description
<span>	</span>	Delimits HTML content.

One attribute of a Span element

Attribute	Description
style	Specifies one or more style properties that affect the appearance of the text within the Span element.

Description

- The Span element delimits content within an HTML document. It's typically used to apply styles to all or part of the text within another element.
- See figure 6-12 for some common properties of the Style attribute.

Figure 6-13   How to use the Span element to apply styles

How to use the Style Builder

To simplify the task of creating Style attributes, you can use the Style Builder dialog box shown in figure 6-14. This dialog box lets you select the styles you want to use. Then, it generates a Style attribute with the appropriate style properties for the elements you select.

As you can see in this figure, the Style Builder dialog box separates the style properties into several categories. To display a specific category, you simply click on the category name in the list at the left side of the dialog box. In this figure, for example, you can see the properties in the Font category, which are the ones you'll use most often.

The Style Builder dialog box

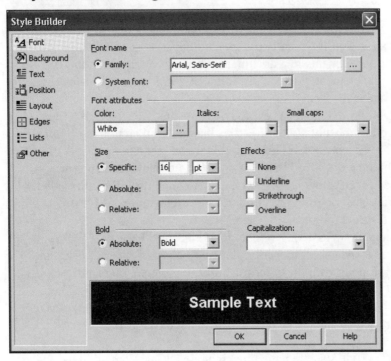

Description

- You can use the *Style Builder* to generate Style attributes for you. The list at the left side of the Style Builder dialog box lets you display different categories of style settings.

- To display the Style Builder dialog box from Design view, select the elements you want the style to apply to. Then, choose the Format→Build Style command, right-click the elements and choose Build Style from the shortcut menu that's displayed, or click the Style property in the Properties window and click the ellipsis button that appears.

- To display the Style Builder dialog box from HTML view, place the cursor anywhere in the element you want the style to apply to. Then, click the Style property in the Properties window and click the ellipsis button that appears.

- You can use the Style Builder to create inline styles, or you can use it to create style rules for external style sheets as described in figure 6-17.

Figure 6-14   How to use the Style Builder

How to use an external style sheet

Although inline styles are a convenient way to make quick changes to a document's appearance, you'll typically use an external style sheet to define the basic formatting for the elements in a document. Then, if you need to modify that style for a specific element, you can use inline styles. Figure 6-15 shows how to use an external style sheet.

An *external style sheet* contains a set of *style rules* that are stored in a file. Each style rule specifies a list of style properties that are applied to one or more HTML elements. The first style rule shown in this figure, for example, specifies that P elements should be displayed in the 11-point Times New Roman font. The other style rules specify how H1, H2, H3, and A elements will be displayed. Notice that two different style rules are defined for A elements. You'll learn more about that in the next figure.

When you create a new ASP.NET web application, Visual Studio .NET automatically creates a style sheet named Styles.css. This style sheet is listed in the Solution Explorer along with the other files for the project. You can display this style sheet in a Code Editor window simply by double-clicking on it. Then, you can use the techniques you'll learn in figure 6-17 to modify the style rules it contains. Alternatively, you can create a new style sheet as described in that figure.

To use an external style sheet, a page must include a Link element in its document head. Unfortunately, Visual Studio .NET doesn't create the Link element automatically, so you have to enter it in yourself. (You can also use the Visual Studio feature you'll learn about in figure 6-17 to create the Link element for you.) As you can see in the example in this figure, the Link element includes a Rel attribute that specifies that the link is for a style sheet, and an Href attribute that specifies the URL of the style sheet. Note that even if you use the style sheet that's added to your project by default, you have to specify the full path for that file in the Href attribute.

The last example in this figure shows how you can create a style rule that applies to more than one element. To do that, you simply code the element names separated by commas at the beginning of the rule. In this example, the style rule applies to both the H2 and H3 elements.

The code for the Murach.css style sheet

```
P  {Font-Family: Times New Roman, Serif; Font-Size: 11pt}

H1 {Font-Family: Arial, Sans-Serif; Font-Size: 14pt; Color: blue;
    Text-Align: center}
H2 {Font-Family: Arial, Sans-Serif; Font-Size: 14pt; Color: blue}
H3 {Font-Family: Arial, Sans-Serif; Font-Size: 12pt; Color: blue}

a {Font-Family: Arial, Sans-Serif; Font-Size: 9pt}
a:hover {Font-Weight: bold}
```

The code in an HTML document that links to the style sheet

```
<head>
    <title>Murach's ASP.NET web programming</title>
    <link rel="stylesheet" href="../styles/murach.css">
</head>
```

The Link element

Tag	Description
`<link>`	Defines the link to an external style sheet.

Attributes of the Link element

Attribute	Description
`href`	The URL of the document to be linked. For a style sheet, the document must have a file extension of css.
`rel`	The type of link. To specify a style sheet, supply a value of Stylesheet.

A style rule for two HTML elements

```
H2, H3 {Font-Family: Arial, Sans-Serif; Font-Size: 14pt; Color: blue}
```

Description

- An *external style sheet* is a file that contains *style rules* for HTML elements. Each style rule associates an HTML element with a list of style properties. Then, the styles are applied automatically whenever an element of the specified type appears in the document.

- To link an HTML document to an external style sheet, you include a Link element that identifies the style sheet within the document's Head element.

- You can create a style rule for two or more elements by coding a comma-separated list of the elements at the beginning of the style rule.

- You can create two or more styles for the same element using classes. See figure 6-16 for details.

Note

- Visual Studio creates an external style sheet named Styles.css for each new web project. You can use this style sheet as is, modify it any way you want, or create your own external style sheet. See figure 6-17 for details.

Figure 6-15   How to use an external style sheet

How to use classes in a style sheet

Another feature of style sheets that you may find useful is *style classes*. With *regular classes*, you can define more than one style rule for the same element, or you can define a generic style rule that can be applied to any element. The first set of examples in figure 6-16 illustrates how this works.

The first statement shows how to define a style rule for a class that can be used with a specific element. To do that, you code the element name, followed by a period and the class name you want to use for the class. Then, you code the style properties just as you would for any other style. To apply a style class to an element, you name the class on the Class attribute for that element as illustrated in the second statement.

The third statement shows how to define a style rule for a class that can be used with any element. To do that, you simply omit the element name from the beginning of the style rule. Then, you can apply the class to any element using its Class attribute.

In addition to the regular classes you define, HTML also provides for *pseudo-classes*. The names of these classes are predefined and, in some cases, can be applied only to specific elements. The Link and Visited classes, for example, can only be applied to an A element, as indicated by the first table in this figure. You can use these classes to specify the style for an A element based on its state. If the user hasn't clicked on the link defined by the element, it's displayed with the style specified by the Link class. Otherwise, it's displayed with the style specified by the Visited class.

Unlike the pseudo-classes you use for A elements, you can apply the Hover, Active, and Focus classes, called *dynamic pseudo-classes*, to any element. In this case, the class that's used is based on a user action. If the user points to the element with the mouse, for example, the element is displayed with the style specified by the Hover class. And if the user moves the focus to the element, it's displayed with the style specified by the Focus class.

The last three style rules in this figure illustrate how you might use pseudo-classes with an A element. Here, the first style rule defines the basic formatting for the element: 9-point Arial. Then, the second style rule specifies that after the user clicks on the link defined by the element, it should be displayed in blue. Finally, if the user points to the link, it should be displayed in bold.

How to use regular classes

A style rule that can be used only with the specified element

```
P.ProductList {Font-Size: X-Large; Font-Family: Arial, Sans-Serif}
```

An element that uses the style rule

```
<p class=ProductList>Martian costume</p>
```

A style rule for a generic class

```
.ProductList {Font-Size: X-Large; Font-Family: Arial, Sans-Serif}
```

Pseudo-classes for the Anchor element

Tag	Class	Description
A	link	The style that's applied to links that haven't been visited by the user.
A	visited	The style that's applied to links that have been visited by the user.

Dynamic pseudo-classes

Class	Description
Hover	The style that's applied while the user points to an element with a pointing device (usually the mouse).
Active	The style that's applied while an element is being activated by the user.
Focus	The style that's applied while an element has the focus.

Style rules that include an A pseudo-class and a dynamic pseudo-class

```
a {Font-Family: Arial, Sans-Serif; Font-Size: 9pt}
a:visited {Color: blue}
a:hover {Font-Weight: bold}
```

Description

- You can use *style classes* to define two or more styles for the same element. You can define your own *regular classes* or use pre-defined *pseudo-classes*.

- To define a regular class that can be used with a specified element, code the name of the element, followed by a period, followed by the class name and style properties. To define a generic class that can be used with any element, omit the element name from the style rule.

- To use a regular class, name it on the Class attribute of the element you want to apply it to.

- To define a pseudo-class, code the name of the element, followed by a colon, followed by the class name and the style properties. The styles defined by these classes are applied automatically when the specified condition occurs.

- The pseudo-classes you're most likely to use are the ones for the Anchor element and the *dynamic pseudo-classes* shown above. You can use the dynamic pseudo-classes with any element. The style rules for dynamic pseudo-classes must always be coded after any other style rules.

Figure 6-16   How to use classes in a style sheet

Visual Studio features for working with style sheets

Although you can create a style sheet using any text editor, Visual Studio provides some features that make it easy to create and work with style sheets. These features are described in figure 6-17. To create a new style sheet, for example, you can use the Style Sheet template in the Add New Item dialog box.

To work with an existing style sheet, you display it in a Code Editor window. Then, you can add a style rule using the Add Style Rule dialog box shown in this figure. As you can see, this dialog box lets you define a style rule for an element, for a class, or for an element with a specified ID. (ID is an attribute you can use to uniquely identify an element.) Note that if you create a style rule for a class, a generic class is defined by default. To define a class for a specific element, check the Optional Element option and then select the element from the drop-down list. A preview of the style rule appears near the lower right corner of the dialog box. Then, you can click on the add button (>) to create the style rule.

When you create a new style rule, Visual Studio adds the rule without any style properties to the style sheet. After I added the style rule shown in this figure, for example, this code was added to the style sheet:

```
P:ProductList
{
}
```

Then, you can add properties to the style rule using the Style Builder you learned about in figure 6-14. To display the Style Builder dialog box, click anywhere in the style rule and then choose the Styles→Build Style command.

You should also notice the CSS Outline window that's displayed at the left side of the Visual Studio window when a style sheet is displayed. This window displays the style rules defined by the style sheet in a tree structure. You can use this tree to navigate to a specific style rule by expanding the folder that contains that rule and then clicking on the rule.

An external style sheet in Visual Studio .NET

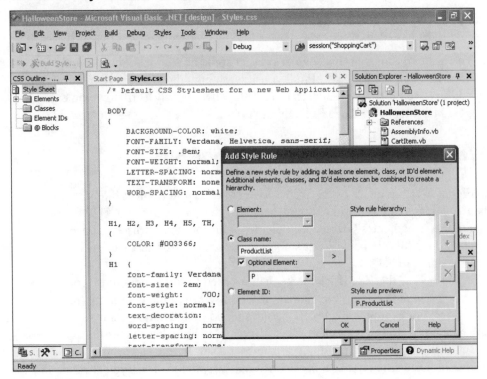

Discussion

- To link a page to a style sheet, display the page in Design view and use the Format→Document Styles command to display the Document Styles dialog box. Then, right-click on the page in this dialog box, select the Add Style Link command to display the Select Style Sheet dialog box, and select a style sheet.

- To create a new style sheet, choose the Project→Add New Item command. Then, select the Style Sheet template from the Add New Item dialog box that's displayed, type the name you want to use for the new style sheet, and click Open.

- To add a style rule to a style sheet, use the Add Style Rule dialog box. To display this dialog box, display the style sheet in a Code Editor window and then choose the Styles→Add Style Rule command.

- To add a style rule for an element, select the element from the Element drop-down list. To add a rule for a class, select the Class name option and then enter the class name. To define the class for a specific element, select the Optional Element check box and then select the element from the drop-down list.

- To add style properties to a style rule, click anywhere in the rule and choose the Styles→Build Style command to display the Style Builder. See figure 6-14 for details on using the Style Builder.

- You can use the CSS Outline window that's displayed at the left side of the Visual Studio window to navigate to the style rule you select.

Figure 6-17   Visual Studio features for working with style sheets

Additional concepts and skills for working with HTML

The last two topics of this chapter present some additional concepts and skills for working with HTML. First, you'll learn how the Web Server controls you add to a web form are rendered in HTML. Then, you'll learn how you can write HTML directly to the HTTP output stream.

How Web Server controls are rendered

Figure 6-18 summarizes the Web Server controls you're most likely to use when you design a web form and indicates how they're *rendered* in HTML. In other words, it indicates how the asp: elements for these controls are converted to standard HTML elements. That's necessary because browsers can only interpret standard HTML.

If you review the HTML elements that are used to implement these controls, you can see that the same element can be used to implement more than one control. For example, the text box, button, and image button controls are all implemented by an Input element. The difference in how these controls appear and act, then, depends on how their attributes are set. In this case, the Type attribute indicates the type of input control that's rendered. The Type attribute of a text box, for example, is set to "text," the Type attribute of a button is set to "submit," and the Type attribute of an image button is set to "image." Because of that, the browser handles each of these controls differently.

If you look through the rest of the controls shown here, you can get a general idea of how each one is implemented in HTML. To fully understand the HTML elements, however, you need to know about the attributes you can set for each one. When you work with Visual Studio, of course, you typically set these attributes by setting properties of the ASP.NET controls. You'll learn how to do that in the next chapter.

A summary of the common Web Server controls

Name	HTML element	Additional information
Label	<span>	The <span> element is typically used to apply special formatting to the text it encloses.
TextBox	<input>	The type="text" attribute identifies this element as a text box.
Button	<input>	The type="submit" attribute identifies this element as a button.
ImageButton	<input>	The type="image" attribute identifies this element as an image button.
LinkButton	<a>	This control is rendered as an Anchor element whose Href attribute points to a function generated in JavaScript that posts the page back to the server.
HyperLink	<a>	This control is rendered as an Anchor element that links to another URL.
CheckBox	<span>	The <span> element contains an <input> element with the type="checkbox" attribute that identifies it as a check box and a <label> element that defines the text associated with the check box.
CheckBoxList	<table>	Each check box in the list is defined by an <input> element with the type="checkbox" attribute that identifies it as a check box and a <label> element that defines the text associated with the check box. By default, each check box and label appear in a separate row of the table.
RadioButton	<span>	The <span> element contains an <input> element with the type="radio" attribute that identifies it as a radio button and a <label> element that defines the text associated with the radio button.
RadioButtonList	<table>	Each radio button in the list is defined by an <input> element with the type="radio" attribute that identifies it as a radio button and a <label> element that defines the text associated with the check box. By default, each radio button and label appear in a separate row of the table.
ListBox	<select>	Each item in the list is defined by an <option> element within the <select> element.
DropDownList	<select>	Each item in the list is defined by an <option> element within the <select> element.
Image	<img>	Displays the specified image.

Description

- All of the Web Server controls are *rendered* as standard HTML that can be interpreted by a browser.

- The radio button list and check box list controls can also be formatted using HTML flow rather than a table.

- For information on the properties that affect the definition of these controls, see chapter 7.

Figure 6-18   How Web server controls are rendered

How to write to the HTTP output stream

As you know, all of the HTML that the browser needs to render a page is included in the HTTP output stream that's sent back to the browser as part of the HTTP response. For a web form, that HTML includes, among other things, the code that's used to define the controls on the form. In some cases, though, you may want to generate additional HTML from your code. To do that, you can use the Write method of the HttpResponse object as shown in figure 6-19.

As you can see in this figure, you simply code the HTML you want to include in the output stream on the Write method. Note that this HTML is added at the beginning of the output stream, which means that it will appear at the top of the browser window. If that's not what you want, you can generate the HTML by adding a label control at the location where you want the output to appear and then setting the Text property of that control to the HTML. You'll learn more about how that works in the next chapter.

You should also realize that if you use grid layout mode to position controls on a web form, those controls can overlay the output from the Write method. In that case, you can add Br tags to the beginning of the HTML that you write to the output stream so the output appears after the controls on the form.

In most cases, you won't use the Write method of the HttpResponse object in a production application. However, you may use it during the testing and debugging phase of program development. Then, you can display messages like those shown here that include the values of variables used by the application. You can do this as an easy alternative to using custom trace messages like those in figure 5-10.

Code that writes HTML output from a code-behind file

```
Response.Write("<b>Order complete</b><br>")
Response.Write("Costume: " & sCostume & "<br>")
Response.Write("Quantity: " & iQuantity & "<br>")
Response.Write("Unit price: " & dUnitPrice & "<br>")
Response.Write("Order total: " & dOrderTotal & "<br>")
```

Sample output from the code above

> **Order complete**
> Costume: Martian
> Quantity: 2
> Unit price: 69.99
> Order total: 139.98

Code that writes HTML output from another class

```
HttpContext.Current.Response.Write("Now updating database<br>")
```

Description

- The Write method of the HttpResponse object provides a convenient way to add HTML output directly to the HTTP output stream. The output can include any valid HTML.
- To access the HttpResponse object from the code-behind file for a page, you use the Response property of the page. To access this object from another class, you use the Response property of the HttpContext object for the current request. To access this object, you use the Current property of the HttpContext class.
- The HTML output you add to the HTTP output stream using the Write method of the HttpResponse object appears at the beginning of the output stream, before any HTML rendered for the controls on the page. As a result, the output from the Write method always appears at the top of the page in the browser window.
- If you use grid layout mode to place the controls on a form, the output from the Write method will appear behind those controls. In that case, you can include Br tags at the beginning of the HTML you write to the output stream to move the output down on the page.
- The Write method isn't typically used to create page output for production applications. Instead, you can set the Text property of a label control to the appropriate HTML so it will appear where you want it on the page. You'll learn more about working with label controls in the next chapter.
- The Write method can be useful for testing and debugging an application.

Figure 6-19   How to write to the HTTP output stream

Perspective

The goal of this chapter has been to teach you the HTML essentials that you need for ASP.NET programming. So at this point, you should feel qualified to make minor modifications to the HTML that's generated by Visual Studio so each form looks just the way you want it to. In some cases, you may even find that it's easier to use HTML for creating an element like a table from scratch than it is to use the features of Visual Studio for generating the HTML.

Above all, you should now be able to understand most of the HTML that's generated for a form. You should also understand much of the code that actually gets sent to the browser. Then, to complete your understanding of the code that gets generated for the controls of a form, the next chapter tells you more about asp: elements.

Of course, there's a lot more to HTML than what's presented in this chapter. So if you want to learn more about HTML, you can get a book that's dedicated entirely to that topic. When you use Visual Studio to develop your forms, though, that shouldn't be necessary.

Terms

HTML document	row
HTML element	column
tag	cell
start tag	cascading style sheets (CSS)
end tag	inline style
content	external style
attribute	style property
comment	Style Builder
white space	external style sheet
root element	style rule
child element	style class
parent element	regular class
directive block	pseudo-class
meta data	dynamic pseudo-class
table	render a control

7

How to work with server controls

So far in this book, you've learned the basic skills for working with some of the most common server controls: labels, text boxes, buttons, drop-down lists, and list boxes. Now, this chapter presents some additional skills for working with these controls. It also presents the skills for working with the other controls, like check boxes and radio buttons. When you complete this chapter, you'll be able to create ASP.NET web forms that use any of the server controls.

An introduction to server controls

In chapter 2, you learned how to add server controls to a web form and set control properties. Now, you'll learn about the different types of server controls and how you use them. You'll also learn about the most common Web Server controls, how you work with them in the Web Forms Designer, and how you handle their events.

Types of server controls

Figure 7-1 describes the four different types of server controls that you can use in your ASP.NET applications. The controls you'll use most often are the Web Server controls and the validation controls. Although most of the Web Server controls have HTML Server control counterparts, the Web Server controls provide added functionality and are designed to work better in Visual Studio. You'll learn how to use many of the Web Server controls later in this chapter, and you'll learn how to use the validation controls in chapter 8. The HTML server controls and the rich controls aren't covered elsewhere in this book, so I want to mention them briefly here.

When you add an HTML control from the HTML tab of the Toolbox, it generates a standard HTML element. Then, you can change that element to a server control by selecting the Run As Server Control command from the shortcut menu for the control. When you do that, a Runat attribute with a value of "Server" is added to the HTML element, along with an Id attribute. The Runat attribute indicates that the control should be processed on the server, and the Id attribute provides a name that you can use to refer to the control from the application. For example, the HTML for a text box control would look something like this:

```
<input id="txtName" type="text" name="Text1"
runat="server">
```

Then, you can work with the control using standard object-oriented techniques. Since these controls don't provide the same functionality as the Web Server controls, however, you won't use them often.

ASP.NET also comes with two rich server controls: the Calendar control and the AdRotator control. The Calendar control displays a calendar that lets the user select a date. That can help a user avoid entering invalid dates. The AdRotator control displays one of a series of images based on a rotation schedule. This control is frequently used for advertisements. If you want to learn more about these controls, you can refer to online help.

HTML Server controls

- Server-based versions of the standard HTML form controls
- Use standard HTML tags with the addition of a Runat attribute set to a value of "Server" and an Id attribute set to the name of the control

Web Server controls

- An improved set of standard controls for web forms
- Use special asp: tags, such as <asp:label> and <asp:dropdownlist >
- Provide more consistent attributes than HTML server controls
- Designed to work better than HTML server controls in Visual Studio
- Can be bound to a data source

Validation controls

- Designed to simplify data validation
- Work by running client-side script
- Can handle most validation requirements
- Can be used with either HTML Server controls or Web Server controls

Rich controls

- The Calendar control lets you display a calendar in a variety of formats
- The AdRotator control displays one of several images based on a schedule

Notes

- The HTML Server controls are available in the HTML tab of the Toolbox. All of the other controls are available in the Web Forms tab of the Toolbox.
- By default, the controls in the HTML tab of the Toolbox are implemented as standard HTML elements that are processed on the client. To convert a control to a control that can be processed on the server, right-click on the control in Design view and select Run As Server Control from the shortcut menu that's displayed.

Figure 7-1   Types of server controls

Common Web Server controls

Figure 7-2 summarizes the Web Server controls you're most likely to use as you develop ASP.NET applications. You've already learned how several of these controls work, and you'll learn about the others in this chapter.

If you've developed Windows applications, you'll notice that many of these controls have Windows counterparts and operate similarly to the Windows controls. Because of that, you shouldn't have much difficulty learning how to use the Web Server controls. As you'll see in this chapter, however, some of the techniques you use to work with these controls are different from the techniques you use to work with their Windows counterparts. In addition, some of the functionality they provide is different. So you'll want to be sure to read about each control even if you're familiar with Windows controls.

A summary of the common Web Server controls

Control	Name	Suggested prefix	Description
 A	Label	lbl	Displays descriptive information.
 abl	TextBox	txt	Lets the user enter or modify a text value.
 abl	Button	btn	Submits a page for processing.
	ImageButton	ibtn	Submits a page for processing.
 abl	LinkButton	lbtn	Submits a page for processing.
 A	HyperLink	hlnk	Lets users move to another page in the application.
 ✓	CheckBox	chk	Turns an option on or off.
	CheckBoxList	cbl	Turns options in a list of options on or off.
 ⊙	RadioButton	rdo	Turns an option on or off. Only one radio button in a group can be on.
	RadioButtonList	rbl	Turns an option in a list of options on or off. Only one radio button in the list can be on.
	ListBox	lst	Lets the user choose one or more items from a list.
	DropDownList	ddl	Lets the user choose an item from a list that drops down from the control.
	Image	img	Displays an image.

Description

- The button, image button, and link button controls all provide the same functionality. They differ only in how they appear on the form.
- The check box list and radio button list controls serve as containers for a collection of check box or radio button items. They're typically used to create a list of check boxes or radio buttons that are bound to a data source. If you need more control over the layout of the check boxes or radio buttons, though, you can use individual controls.

Figure 7-2   Common Web Server controls

How to work in grid layout mode

The applications you've seen so far in this book have been developed in *grid layout mode*. With this layout, you can position controls exactly where you want them on the form using absolute positioning. Figure 7-3 presents some techniques for working with controls in grid layout mode.

To start, you can set options that determine the default grid settings for a new page. To do that, you use the Options dialog box shown in this figure. The Default Grid Setting options in this dialog box determine the spacing between the gridlines in the grid, whether the grid is displayed in the Web Forms Designer, and whether controls you add to a form or move or size on a form are aligned with the grid.

You can also determine whether the grid is displayed and whether controls snap to the grid for individual pages. To do that, you use the Show Grid and Snap to Grid commands in the Format menu or the buttons that are available in the Design toolbar. Note that even if the grid isn't displayed, Visual Studio still aligns the controls with the grid if the Snap to grid option is on.

Once you add controls to a form, you can use the Align and Order submenus of the Format menu to work with the controls. The commands in the Align menu let you align the controls you select along one of their edges, their centers, or to the grid. For example, if you select three text box controls and then select the Format→Align→Lefts command, the controls are aligned on their left sides with the last control you select.

When you use grid layout mode, you can position controls on a form so they overlap. Then, you can use the commands in the Order submenu to determine which control appears on top. If you select a control and then select the Bring to Front command, the control is placed on top of the other control. If you select the Send to Back command, the control is placed behind the other control. These commands change the z-index attribute of the selected control. A control with a higher z-index value appears on top of a control with a lower z-index value.

By default, the first control you add to a form is given a z-index value of 101, and each control you add to the form is given a z-index value of one more than the previous control. Then, if you use the Bring to Front command, the selected control is given a z-index value of one more than the highest z-index value. Similarly, if you use the Send to Back command, the selected control is given a z-index value of one less than the lowest z-index value.

Another command on the Format menu you may want to use is the Lock Element command. This command locks the controls you select so that they can't be moved in the designer window. You may want to use this command after you get the controls positioned the way you want them so you don't move them accidentally.

The dialog box for setting grid options in grid layout mode

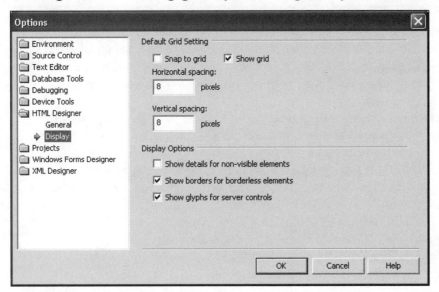

Description

- You can use the Options dialog box to set the default options for *grid layout mode*. To display this dialog box, choose Tools→Options, and then select the HTML Designer folder and the Display option.

- If you select the Snap to grid option, Visual Studio will align any element you add to or move or size on a form to the nearest grid guidelines. This option is off by default.

- If you select the Show grid option, Visual Studio displays the grid guidelines. This option is on by default. Elements will still snap to the grid even if it isn't displayed.

- To change the distance between the grid guidelines, change the Horizontal spacing and Vertical spacing options.

- To set the Snap to grid option for the current page, click the Snap to Grid button in the Design toolbar or select Format→Snap to Grid.

- To display or hide the grid for the current page, click the Show Grid button in the Design toolbar or select Format→Show Grid.

- To align controls manually, select the controls and then use the commands in the Format→Align menu to align the controls at their left, right, top, or bottom edges, along their vertical or horizontal centers, or to the grid. The alignment source is the last control you select.

- You can use the Bring to Front and Send to Back commands in the Format→Order menu to place a control on top of or behind other controls. Then, the z-index attribute of the control is set to indicate its position in the layering. Controls with a higher z-index value are placed on top of controls with a lower z-index value.

- To lock a control in place so it can't be moved on the form, use the Format→Lock Element command. Use the same command to unlock the control.

Figure 7-3   How to work in grid layout mode

How to work in flow layout mode

The alternative to grid layout mode is *flow layout mode*. In this mode, controls are positioned relative to one another. Because of that, the position of the controls can change when the page is displayed depending on the size of the browser window and the resolution of the display. In many cases, that's what you want.

By default, a web page is displayed in grid layout mode. To change to flow layout mode, you change the pageLayout property of the page to FlowLayout. Then, you can use the techniques presented in figure 7-4 to work with the controls on the form. If you spend a few minutes experimenting with these techniques, you shouldn't have any trouble formatting your web pages just the way you want them.

When you drag controls to a form using flow layout, the controls will appear one after the other on the form. If you want to insert space between two controls, you can simply use the space bar. Then, the special code   is inserted for each space in the HTML for the document. If you want to move a control to the next line, you can press Shift+Enter to insert a Br element into the document. You can also place a control in a separate paragraph by pressing Enter after the control to insert <p> and </p> tags around the control. Paragraph tags are also inserted around the remainder of the controls on the form.

Because you're limited to what you can do with spaces, line breaks, and paragraphs, you'll frequently use tables to format a form in flow layout. The code shown in this figure, for example, is for a Costume form like the one you saw in chapter 1. Unlike the earlier form, however, this form was created in flow layout mode. As you can see, it uses a table to align all of the elements except for the image at the top of the form and the button at the bottom of the form. It also uses line breaks to add space above and below the table.

If you compare this code with the code for the form in chapter 1 (see figure 1-7), you'll notice a couple of other differences. First, instead of using label controls to identify the Costume, Price, and Quantity controls, this form uses literal text. To include literal text on a form, you type it directly into the form. Then, you can format the text by selecting it and using the Formatting toolbar or the Format menu. You can also use the HTML formatting elements or styles as you learned in the last chapter.

Second, none of the controls include a Style attribute. When you add a control to a web form in grid layout mode, this attribute is added automatically to indicate the absolute position of the control on the form as well as its position in the layering of the controls. In contrast, since the controls you add in flow layout have relative positions and can't be layered, the Style attribute is omitted.

When do you use grid layout and when do you use flow layout? For small forms that fit on all screens, that's often a matter of personal preference. But if you want the size of the form to adjust to the size and resolution of the browser's screen, you need to use flow layout. Once you get used to flow layout, you'll find that it's just as easy to use as grid layout.

The HTML code for a web form created using flow layout mode

```
<form id="Form1" method="post" runat="server">
    <asp:Image id="Image1" runat="server" ImageUrl="banner.jpg">
    </asp:Image><BR><BR>
    <TABLE id="Table1" cellSpacing="5" cellPadding="0" width="523"
            border="0" style="WIDTH: 523px; HEIGHT: 104px">
        <TR height="30">
            <TD style="WIDTH: 68px">Costume:</TD>
            <TD><asp:DropDownList id="ddlCostumes" runat="server"
                    Width="152px" AutoPostBack="True">
                </asp:DropDownList></TD></TR>
        <TR height="30">
            <TD style="WIDTH: 68px">Price:</TD>
            <TD><asp:Label id="lblPrice" runat="server"></asp:Label></TD>
        </TR>
        <TR height="30">
            <TD style="WIDTH: 68px">Quantity:</TD>
            <TD><asp:TextBox id="txtQuantity" runat="server" Width="48px">
                </asp:TextBox> 
                <asp:RequiredFieldValidator id="RequiredFieldValidator1"
                    runat="server"   ControlToValidate="txtQuantity"
                    ErrorMessage="You must enter a quantity."
                    Display="Dynamic"></asp:RequiredFieldValidator> 
                <asp:CompareValidator id="CompareValidator1" runat="server"
                    ControlToValidate="txtQuantity" Display="Dynamic"
                    ErrorMessage="Quantity must be greater than 0."
                    Operator="GreaterThan" Type="Integer"
                    ValueToCompare="0"></asp:CompareValidator></TD></TR>
    </TABLE><BR>
    <asp:Button id="btnOrder" runat="server" Text="Order Costume">
    </asp:Button>
</form>
```

How to work in flow layout mode

- To change a web form to *flow layout mode*, set the pageLayout property to FlowLayout.

- When you use flow layout mode, you can't position controls by dragging them and you can't layer or lock controls.

- When you add controls to a form in flow layout mode, they will appear one after the other, from left to right and from top to bottom.

- To insert a space after a control, use the space bar. The special code   is inserted into the document.

- To insert a line break after a control, press Shift+Enter. A <br> tag is inserted into the document.

- To place a control in a paragraph, press Enter after you add the control. <p> and </p> tags are inserted around the control and around the remainder of the document.

- To insert literal text, type it directly into the designer window. Then, you can format the text using the controls in the Formatting toolbar and the commands in the Format menu. You can also format it using the HTML formatting elements or styles that you learned about in chapter 6.

- To align text and controls, use tables as described in chapter 6.

Figure 7-4   How to work in flow layout mode

Two ways to handle control events

Like other objects, server controls have events that are fired when certain actions are performed on them. When you click on a button control, for example, the Click event is fired. If your application needs to respond to an event, you code a Sub procedure called an *event handler*. Figure 7-5 shows two ways you can do that.

When you create an event handler using the Code Editor, Visual Studio creates a Sub Procedure to handle the event. The Sub statement includes a Handles clause that names the object and event that it handles. Then, you enter the code you want to be executed when that event occurs within the Sub procedure. This is illustrated by the first example in this figure. Here, the Handles clause of the event handler indicates that the procedure handles the Click event of the control named btnCancel.

You can also create an event handler for a control without using the Handles clause. To do that, you name the event handler on the appropriate event attribute of the control. This is illustrated by the second example in this figure. Here, the asp: tag for the control includes an OnClick attribute. This attribute names the Sub procedure that's executed when the Click event of the control is raised.

Regardless of which technique you use, you can use a single event handler to handle more than one event. If you include a Handles clause on the event handler, you simply list the events it will handle on that clause like this:

```
Sub Procedure NavigationButtons_Click _
    Handles btnPrevious.Click, btnNext.Click
```

Here, the event handler will handle the Click event of two buttons named btnPrevious and btnNext. Notice in this example that I changed the name of the procedure to indicate that it processes more than one event. That's possible because the events are associated with the event handler through the Handles clause and not through the procedure name.

To use a single event handler for more than one event when you don't use the Handles clause, you simply name the event handler on the appropriate event attributes. For example, consider these tags:

```
<asp:Button id="btnPrevious" runat="server" Text="Previous"
        OnClick="NavigationButtons_Click">
<asp:Button id="btnNext" runat="server" Text="Next"
        OnClick="NavigationButtons_Click">
```

Here again, the procedure named NavigationButtons_Click will handle the Click event for both buttons.

This figure also lists some of the most common control events and their associated attributes. As I present each of the Web Server controls in this chapter, I'll illustrate how you can use these events.

Now that you've seen the two techniques for handling control events, you may be wondering which technique is better. In most cases, I recommend you use the Handles clause to create event handlers, since that's the default in Visual Studio. However, you should be familiar with the other technique in case you encounter it in other ASP.NET applications.

Code that handles a Click event using the Handles clause

The asp: tag for a button control

```
<asp:Button id="btnCancel" runat="server" Text="Cancel Order">
```

The event handler for the Click event of the control

```
Private Sub btnCancel_Click(ByVal sender As System.Object,
        ByVal e As System.EventArgs) Handles btnCancel.Click
    Session.Remove("Cart")
    Response.Redirect("Order.aspx")
End Sub
```

Code that handles a Click event using the OnClick attribute

The asp: tag for a button control

```
<asp:Button id="btnCancel" runat="server" Text="Cancel Order"
        OnClick="btnCancel_Click">
```

The event handler for the Click event of the control

```
Protected Sub btnCancel_Click(ByVal sender As System.Object,
        ByVal e As System.EventArgs)
    Session.Remove("Cart")
    Response.Redirect("Order.aspx")
End Sub
```

Common control events

Event	Attribute	Controls
Click	OnClick	Button, image button, link button
Command	OnCommand	Button, image button, link button
TextChanged	OnTextChanged	Text box
SelectedIndexChanged	OnSelectedIndexChanged	Drop-down list, list box, radio button list, check box list
CheckedChanged	OnCheckedChanged	Check box, radio button

Description

- An *event handler* is a Sub procedure that's called when a specified event occurs.
- By default, Visual Studio creates an event handler by including a Handles clause on the Sub procedure. The Handles clause names the control and event that the procedure handles. When you use this technique, you can give the procedure any name you want.
- You can also code an event handler without a Handles clause. Then, you have to name the handler in the appropriate event attribute of the control. For example, you can use the OnClick attribute to name the procedure that's executed when the user clicks a control.
- If you use the Handles clause, the event handler can be declared with Public, Protected, or Private scope. Otherwise, the event handler must be declared with Public or Protected scope.
- A single event handler can be used to handle more than one event. If you define the event handler using a Handles clause, you list the controls and events on that clause. Otherwise, you name the handler on each event attribute of each control you want it to handle.

Figure 7-5   Two ways to handle control events

How to work with button controls

Most web forms have at least one button control that the user can click to submit the form to the server for processing, commonly called a *submit button*. In the topics that follow, you'll learn how to use all three types of button controls that ASP.NET provides: buttons, link buttons, and image buttons.

How to work with button, link button, and image button controls

Figure 7-6 presents the three types of button controls. These controls differ only in how they appear to the user. This is illustrated by the three buttons shown in this figure. As you can see, a *button control* displays text within a rectangular area. A *link button control* displays text that looks like a hyperlink. And an *image button control* displays an image.

At the top of this figure, you can see the asp: elements for the three buttons that are illustrated. For the button and link button, the Text property provides the text that's displayed for the control. For the image button, the ImageUrl property provides the URL address of the image that's displayed on the button. In some cases, though, a browser may not be able to display the image. Because of that, you should also code the AlternateText property so it provides the text that's displayed if the browser isn't able to display the image.

When a user clicks one of the button controls, ASP.NET raises two events: Click and Command. You can see an event handler for the Click event of a button control in this figure. Notice that this event handler receives two arguments. The sender argument represents the control that was clicked. Because this argument has a type of Object, you'll need to convert it to a button control if you want to access the properties and methods of the control. You might want to do that, for example, if you code a procedure that handles the processing for more than one button. Then, you can use the Id property of the control to determine which button was clicked. An easier way to do that, however, is to use the Command event. You'll see how to use this event in figure 7-8.

The second argument that's passed to the event handler of a Click event, e, contains event-specific information. You're most likely to use this argument with an image button control to determine where the user clicked on the image. You'll learn more about that in the next topic.

Incidentally, from this point on in this chapter and this book, the figures will often present the asp: elements for the controls that are used. By studying the code for these controls, you can quickly see how their properties are set. Please keep in mind, though, that you usually add a control to a form by using the Web Forms Designer, and you set the properties for a control by using the Properties window. Then, the code for the asp: element in the aspx file is generated automatically.

HTML for three types of button controls

```
<asp:Button Id="btnOrder" Runat="Server" Text="Place Order"></asp:Button>
<asp:LinkButton Id="btnOrder" Runat="Server">Place Order</asp:LinkButton>
<asp:ImageButton Id="btnCostumes" Runat="Server"
    ImageUrl="Images/costumes.gif" AlternateText="Costumes">
</asp:ImageButton>
```

How the button controls appear in a browser

Common button control properties

Property	Description
Text	(Button and LinkButton controls only.) The text displayed by the button. For a LinkButton control, the text is coded as content between the start and end tags. You can also code the text as the value of the Text attribute of the start tag.
ImageUrl	(ImageButton control only.) The image to be displayed for the button.
AlternateText	(ImageButton control only.) The text to be displayed if the browser can't display the image.
CausesValidation	Determines whether page validation occurs when you click the button. The default is True.
CommandName	A string value that's passed to the Command event when a user clicks the button.
CommandArgument	A string value that's passed to the Command event when a user clicks the button.

An event handler for the Click event of a button control

```
Private Sub btnAccept_Click(ByVal sender As System.Object, _
        ByVal e As System.EventArgs) Handles btnAccept.Click
    Me.AddInvoice
    Response.Redirect("Confirmation.aspx")
End Sub
```

Description

- When a user clicks a *button*, *link button*, or *image button control*, the page is posted back to the server and the Click and Command events are raised. You can code event handlers for either or both of these events.

- Two arguments are passed to the Click event handler: sender and e. Sender is the control that the user clicked, and e contains event-specific information. Since the button and link button controls have no event-specific data, the e argument doesn't contain any useful information for these controls.

- For an image button control, the e argument has X and Y properties that mark the coordinates where the user clicked in the image. See figure 7-7 for more information.

- See figure 7-8 for information on coding an event handler for the Command event.

Figure 7-6   How to work with button, link button, and image button controls

How to use the e argument of an image button control

In some cases, the processing that's performed when the user clicks on an image button will depend on where the user clicks. For example, consider the image button shown at the top of figure 7-7 that represents four navigation buttons. (This image uses the standard icons for First (<<), Previous (<), Next (>), and Last (>>)). This image button could be used to let the user navigate through pages in a section of your web site or to different rows of a data table.

To process an image button like this, you can use the X and Y properties of the e argument that's passed to the Click event handler of the button. These properties indicate the x and y coordinates where the user clicked. The event handler shown in this figure illustrates how this works.

In this example, a Select Case statement is used to determine the value of the X property. If it's between 0 and 23, it indicates that the user clicked the << icon. Then, the event handler executes the code in the procedure named GoToFirstRow. If it's between 24 and 47, it indicates that the user clicked the < icon, and the GoToPreviousRow procedure is executed. If it's between 48 and 71, it indicates that the user clicked the > icon, and the GoToNextRow procedure is executed. Last, if it's between 72 and 95, it indicates that the user clicked the >> icon, and the GoToLastRow procedure is executed. Notice that it's not necessary to check the y coordinate in this example. That's because all of the icons have the same y-coordinate range.

An image used for an image button control

The HTML for the control

```
<asp:ImageButton Id="btnNavigate" Runat="Server"
    ImageUrl="Images/navbuttons.gif">
</asp:ImageButton>
```

An event handler for the Click event of the control

```
Private Sub btnNavigate_Click(ByVal sender As System.Object, _
        ByVal e As System.Web.UI.ImageClickEventArgs) _
        Handles btnNavigate.Click
    Select Case e.X
        Case 0 To 23
            Me.GoToFirstRow
        Case 24 To 47
            Me.GoToPreviousRow
        Case 48 To 71
            Me.GoToNextRow
        Case 72 To 95
            Me.GoToLastRow
    End Select
End Sub
```

Properties of the ImageClickEventArgs class

Property	Description
X	An integer that represents the x coordinate where the user clicked the image button.
Y	An integer that represents the y coordinate where the user clicked the image button.

Description

- When the user clicks an ImageButton control, ASP.NET calls the Click event handler for the control and passes the X and Y coordinates where the user clicked the image as properties of the e argument.

- You can use the X and Y properties to determine the processing that's performed when the user clicks on a particular part of an image.

Figure 7-7   How to use the e argument of an image button control

How to use the Command event

Figure 7-8 shows how you can use the Command event to process a group of button controls using a single event handler. Like the Click event, this event receives both a sender argument and an e argument. In this case, the e argument represents a CommandEventArgs object.

The two properties of the CommandEventArgs class are shown in this figure. You can use these properties to get the CommandName and CommandArgument properties of a control. When you create a button control, you can set the CommandName and CommandArgument properties to any string value. Then, you can examine them in the Command event handler to determine how the application should respond when the user clicks the button.

The examples in this figure illustrate how this works. The first example shows the asp: tags for four button controls. Notice that a different CommandName value is assigned to each one. Although you can also assign CommandArgument values to each control, that's not necessary here.

The second example shows an event handler that processes the Command event of all four controls. To do that, it uses a Select Case statement that tests the value of the CommandName property of the e argument. Since this value indicates the control that was clicked, it can be used to determine the processing that's done. In this case, a Sub procedure that moves to another row in a data table is executed. This is another way to do the processing you saw in figure 7-7 that used an image button control.

Four button controls that use the CommandName attribute

```
<asp:Button id="btnFirst" runat="server" Text="<<" Width="24px"
    CommandName="First"></asp:Button>
<asp:Button id="btnPrevious" runat="server" Text="<" Width="24px"
    CommandName="Previous"></asp:Button>
<asp:Button id="btnNext" runat="server" Text=">" Width="24px"
    CommandName="Next"></asp:Button>
<asp:Button id="btnLast" runat="server" Text=">>" Width="24px"
    CommandName="Last"></asp:Button>
```

An event handler for the Command events of the buttons

```
Private Sub NavigationButtons_Command(ByVal sender As Object,
        ByVal e As System.Web.UI.WebControls.CommandEventArgs)
        Handles btnFirst.Command, btnPrevious.Command,
            btnNext.Command, btnLast.Command
    Select Case e.CommandName
        Case "First"
            Me.GoToFirstRow
        Case "Previous"
            Me.GoToPreviousRow
        Case "Next"
            Me.GoToNextRow
        Case "Last"
            Me.GoToLastRow
    End Select
End Sub
```

Properties of the CommandEventArgs class

Property	Description
CommandName	The value specified in the CommandName property for the control that generated the Command event.
CommandArgument	The value specified in the CommandArgument property for the control that generated the Command event.

Description

- The Command event is raised whenever a user clicks a button control. It's useful when you want to code a single event handler for a group of buttons that perform related functions.
- The e argument that's passed to a Command event handler is a CommandEventArgs object. This object includes properties that let you retrieve the values of the CommandName and CommandArgument properties of the control. You can use these values to determine which control raised the Command event.

Note

- If you code an event handler for both the Click event and the Command event, the Click event handler will be executed first.

Figure 7-8   How to use the Command event

How to work with label and text box controls

Two controls you'll use frequently as you develop web forms are the label and text box controls. You'll learn the details of using these controls in the topics that follow.

How to work with label controls

Label controls let you display text on a web page. The web page shown in figure 7-9, for example, includes four label controls. The first and last label controls provide instructions for the user, and the second and third label controls identify text boxes where the user can enter data.

To specify the text that's displayed in a label control, you set the Text property of the control. Then, this value appears between the start and end tags for the control as illustrated by the two examples in this figure. Notice in the second example that the text includes a Br tag so it will be displayed on two lines. You can also include tags such as B, I, and U to format the text.

As you learned earlier in this chapter, you can also add text to a form by typing it directly into the form in flow layout mode. If you use literal text, however, you should realize that you can't change it as the program executes. If you need to do that, you should display the text in a label control. Then, you can change the Text property of the control as the program executes as illustrated by the code example in this figure.

A web page that uses four label controls

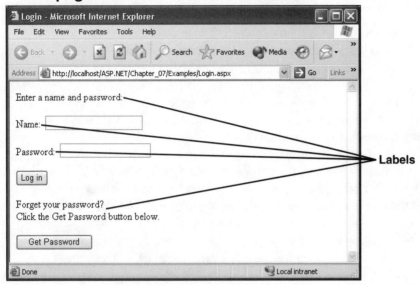

The HTML for the first label control

```
<asp:Label Id="Label1" Runat="Server">Enter a name and password:
</asp:Label>
```

The HTML for the last label control

```
<asp:Label Id="lblMessage" Runat="Server">
    Forget your password?<br>Click the Get Password button below.
</asp:Label>
```

Code that changes the Text property of the last label control

```
lblMessage.Text = "That password is not valid.<br>" _
                & "Click the Get Password button to get your password."
```

Common property of label controls

Property	Description
Text	The text displayed by the label. This text is coded as content between the start and end tags by default, but you can also code the text as the value of the Text attribute of the start tag.

Description

- *Label controls* provide an easy way to include text on an ASP.NET page.
- The text for a label control can include HTML tags. For example, you can include tags that format the text.
- When you use a label control, you can change its Text property as the program executes. In contrast, you can't change literal text that you enter into a form.

Figure 7-9   How to work with label controls

How to work with text box controls

Figure 7-10 shows how to use *text box controls*. These controls let you accept text input from the user. At the top of this figure, for example, you can see the web page from the previous figure after data has been entered into the two text boxes.

This figure also shows the asp: tags for the two text boxes. Notice that the TextMode property of the second text box has been set to Password. That way, the characters that are entered are masked so they aren't displayed.

You can also use the TextMode property to create a multi-line text box. Then, the user can press the Enter key to start a new line in the text box. When you create a multi-line text box, you can also use the Rows property to specify the vertical size of the text box, and you can use the Wrap property to determine if text wraps automatically when it reaches the side of the text box.

To retrieve the value the user enters into a text box, you use the Text property. This is illustrated in the code example in this figure. Here, the values entered into the two text boxes on the web page in this figure are assigned to variables.

Although most text boxes are used to accept data from the user, you may occasionally need to restrict the user from entering data into a text box. To do that, you can set the ReadOnly property of the control to True. Then, the user can see the text in the control but can't change it.

You can use the MaxLength property to specify the maximum number of characters that can be entered into a text box. This is particularly useful if the data the user enters will be stored in a column of a database table. Then, you can limit the entry to the number of characters that are allowed for that column.

Although the width of a text box is set automatically as you size it in Design view, you can also set the width using the Columns property. This property specifies the width of the text box in characters. Note, however, that the width is approximate because it's based on the average width of a character for the font that's used.

The web page in figure 7-9 after the user enters data into the text boxes

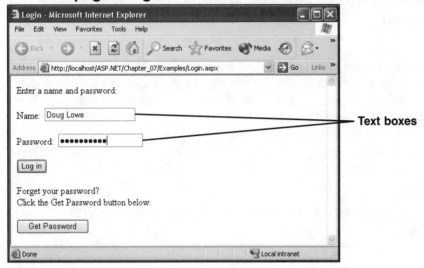

Text boxes

The HTML for the text box controls

```
<asp:TextBox Id="txtName" Runat="Server"></asp:TextBox>
<asp:TextBox Id="txtPassword" Runat="Server" TextMode="password">
</asp:TextBox>
```

Code that retrieves the text entered by a user

```
Dim sName As String = txtName.Text
Dim sPassword As String = txtPassword.Text
```

Common properties of text box controls

Property	Description
TextMode	The type of text box. SingleLine creates a standard text box, MultiLine creates a text box that accepts more than one line of text, and Password causes the characters that are entered to be masked. The default is SingleLine.
Text	The text content of the text box.
MaxLength	The maximum number of characters that can be entered into the text box.
Wrap	Determines whether or not text wraps in a multi-line text box. The default is True.
ReadOnly	Determines whether the user can change the text in the text box. The default value is False, which means that the text can be changed.
Columns	The width of the text box in characters. The actual width is determined based on the font that's used for the text entry.
Rows	The height of a multi-line text box in lines. The default value is 0, which sets the height to a single line.

Description

- *Text box controls* are typically used to accept input from the user. A text box can accept one or more lines of text depending on the setting of the TextMode property.

Figure 7-10   How to work with text box controls

How to work with check box and radio button controls

In addition to entering text into a form, you may want to let users select from one or more options. To do that, you can use *check box* or *radio button controls*. The main difference between these two types of controls is that radio buttons in groups are mutually exclusive and check boxes operate independently. In other words, if the user selects one radio button in a group, all of the other radio buttons in the same group are automatically turned off. In contrast, when a user selects a check box, it has no effect on other check boxes.

Basic skills for working with check box and radio button controls

Figure 7-11 presents part of a web page that includes five check box controls and a group of three radio button controls. The first check box control lets the user indicate if he wants to be added to a mailing list. The other check box controls lets the user select what he wants to be contacted about. The radio button controls let the user select how he wants to be contacted.

To create a group of radio buttons, you simply specify the same name for the GroupName property of each radio button in the group. If you want to create two or more groups of radio buttons on a single form, just use a different group name for each group. Note that if you don't specify a group name for a radio button, that button won't be a part of any group. Instead, it will be processed independently of any other radio buttons on the form.

If you've developed Windows applications, you'll realize that this is in contrast to how Windows radio buttons work. In that case, any radio buttons on a form that aren't specifically included in a group are treated as part of the same group. As a result, if a form has only one group of radio buttons, you can let them default to the same group. Since the Web Server radio button controls don't work that way, however, you'll almost always specify a group name for them.

To determine whether or not a radio button or check box is selected when it's first displayed, you use the Checked property. If you look at the HTML for the check box and radio buttons shown in this figure, for example, you'll see that the Checked properties of the first check box and the last radio button are set to True. When the web page is first displayed, then, these options will be selected as shown. Note that since only one radio button in a group can be selected, you should only set the Checked property to True for one button. If you set this property to True for more than one button in a group, the last one will be selected.

Five check boxes and three radio buttons displayed in a browser

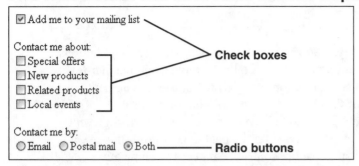

☑ Add me to your mailing list

Contact me about:
☐ Special offers
☐ New products
☐ Related products
☐ Local events

Check boxes

Contact me by:
◯ Email ◯ Postal mail ◉ Both ——— **Radio buttons**

The HTML for the check box and radio buttons

```
<asp:CheckBox id="chkMail" runat="server"
    Text="Add me to your mailing list"
    Checked="True"></asp:CheckBox><BR><BR>
Contact me about:<BR>
<asp:CheckBox id="chkSpecial" runat="server"
    Text="Special offers"></asp:CheckBox><BR>
<asp:CheckBox id="chkNew" runat="server"
    Text="New products"></asp:CheckBox><BR>
<asp:CheckBox id="chkRelated" runat="server"
    Text="Related products"></asp:CheckBox><BR>
<asp:CheckBox id="chkEvents" runat="server"
    Text="Local events"></asp:CheckBox><BR><BR>
Contact me by:<BR>
<asp:RadioButton id="rdoEmail" runat="server" Text="Email"
    GroupName="Contact"></asp:RadioButton> 
<asp:RadioButton id="rdoPostal" runat="server" Text="Postal mail"
    GroupName="Contact"></asp:RadioButton> 
<asp:RadioButton id="rdoBoth" runat="server" Text="Both"
    Checked="True" GroupName="Contact"></asp:RadioButton>
```

Common properties of check box and radio button controls

Property	Description
Text	The text that's displayed next to the check box or radio button.
Checked	Indicates whether the check box or radio button is selected. The default is False.
GroupName	The name of the group that the control belongs to (radio buttons only).

Description

- A *check box control* displays a single option that the user can either check or uncheck. *Radio button controls* present a group of options from which the user can select just one option. All of the radio buttons in a group should have the same group name.

- If you want a check box or radio button to be selected when it's initially displayed, set its Checked property to True. If you set the Checked property of more than one radio button in the same group to True, only the last one will be selected.

Figure 7-11   How to work with check box and radio button controls

Visual Basic code for working with check box and radio button controls

Figure 7-12 shows two ways you can process check boxes and radio buttons in an application. First, you can process these controls in the event handler for the Click event of the form's submit button. Then, you just use If statements to test the Checked properties of the check box and radio button controls.

You can also process check box and radio button controls by writing event handlers for their CheckedChanged events. For a check box control, this event is raised whenever the checked status of the control changes. That typically happens when the user checks or unchecks the control. Then, you can use an If statement to test the Checked property of the control just as you do in the event handler for the Click event of a submit button.

The CheckedChanged event works a bit differently for a radio button control. Instead of being raised any time the status of the control changes, it's raised only when the status changes to checked. Because of that, there's no need to test the Checked property within the event handler for the CheckedChanged event.

Before I go on, you should realize that the CheckChanged event is raised regardless of how the AutoPostBack property of the check box or radio button is set. This property only affects when the event is raised. If the AutoPostBack property of the control is set to True, the form is submitted and the event is raised immediately when the user checks a check box or radio button or unchecks a check box. Then, if the program includes an event handler for this event, it's executed after the Load event handler for the page.

In contrast, if the AutoPostBack property of a control is set to False, the CheckedChanged event isn't raised until another user action causes the page to be submitted to the server. Then, the event handler for this event is processed after the event handler for the Load event of the page. When these two event handlers complete, the event handler for the event that caused the page to be posted is executed.

Note that for this to work, you must set the EnableViewState property of the check box or radio button to True. That way, ASP.NET will be able to determine when the status of the control changes.

In addition to the check box and radio button controls shown here, ASP.NET provides check box list and radio button list controls. These controls can simplify the task of creating groups of controls. You'll learn about these controls and the other list controls next.

Code that processes the first check box and radio buttons in figure 7-11

```
Private Sub btnContinue_Click1(ByVal sender As Object, _
        ByVal e As System.EventArgs) Handles btnContinue.Click
    If chkMail.Checked Then
        Customer.Mail = True
    Else
        Customer.Mail = False
    End If
    If rdoEmail.Checked Then
        Customer.MailType = "Email"
    ElseIf rdoPostal.Checked Then
        Customer.MailType = "Postal"
    ElseIf rdoBoth.Checked Then
        Customer.MailType = "Both"
    End If
End Sub
```

Another way to process the check box and radio buttons

```
Private Sub chkMail_CheckedChanged(ByVal sender As System.Object,
        ByVal e As System.EventArgs) Handles chkMail.CheckedChanged
    If chkMail.Checked Then
        Order.Mail = True
    Else
        Order.Mail = False
    End If
End Sub

Private Sub rdoEmail_CheckedChanged(ByVal sender As System.Object,
        ByVal e As System.EventArgs) Handles rdoEmail.CheckedChanged
    Customer.MailType = "Email"
End Sub

Private Sub rdoPostal_CheckedChanged(ByVal sender As System.Object,
        ByVal e As System.EventArgs) Handles rdoPostal.CheckedChanged
    Customer.MailType = "Postal"
End Sub

Private Sub rdoBoth_CheckedChanged(ByVal sender As System.Object,
        ByVal e As System.EventArgs) Handles rdoBoth.CheckedChanged
    Customer.MailType = "Both"
End Sub
```

Description

- To determine whether a check box or radio button is selected, you test its Checked property.
- To use the CheckedChanged event of a check box or radio button, you must set the EnableViewState property of the control to True so that ASP.NET can determine when the Checked property of the item changes.
- For a check box, the CheckedChanged event is raised whenever the checked status of the control changes. For a radio button, this event is raised only when the status of the control changes to checked.

Figure 7-12   Visual Basic code for working with check box and radio button controls

How to work with list controls

ASP.NET provides several controls that are designed to present lists of information. You'll learn about four of those controls here: drop-down list, list box, radio button list, and check box list. Then, you'll learn about three additional list controls that are specifically designed for working with the data in a database in chapter 14.

Basic skills for working with drop-down list and list box controls

Figure 7-13 presents the basic skills for working with a *list box control* or a *drop-down list control*. The list box control shown here lets the user select from one of four colors. List boxes are typically used in cases like this where there are a small number of items to select from. In contrast, drop-down lists are typically used with larger lists so they don't take up as much space on the page. The drop-down list in this figure, for example, displays a list of the days of the week.

The HTML for the list box and drop-down list is also shown in this figure. Here, you can see that the ListBox element has four ListItem elements that correspond to the four colors in the list. Similarly, the DropDownList element has seven ListItem elements that correspond to the days of the week. The easiest way to add elements like these to a list is to use the ListItem Collection Editor. You'll see how to do that in figure 7-16.

You can also add items to a list using Visual Basic code. In that case, the HTML for the form won't include ListItem elements like those shown here. Instead, ASP.NET will generate the elements when the page is rendered. You'll learn two ways to add items to a list in figure 7-15.

A list box displayed in a browser

The HTML for the list box

```
Color:<BR>
<asp:ListBox id="lstColor" runat="server">
    <asp:ListItem Value="Black" Selected="True">Black</asp:ListItem>
    <asp:ListItem Value="Red">Red</asp:ListItem>
    <asp:ListItem Value="Blue">Blue</asp:ListItem>
    <asp:ListItem Value="Green">Green</asp:ListItem>
</asp:ListBox>
```

A drop-down list displayed in a browser

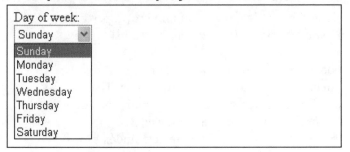

The HTML for the drop-down list

```
Day of week:<br>
<asp:DropDownList id="ddlDay" runat="server">
    <asp:ListItem Value="1">Sunday</asp:ListItem>
    <asp:ListItem Value="2">Monday</asp:ListItem>
    <asp:ListItem Value="3">Tuesday</asp:ListItem>
    <asp:ListItem Value="4">Wednesday</asp:ListItem>
    <asp:ListItem Value="5">Thursday</asp:ListItem>
    <asp:ListItem Value="6">Friday</asp:ListItem>
    <asp:ListItem Value="7">Saturday</asp:ListItem>
</asp:DropDownList>
```

Description

- A *drop-down list control* lets a user choose an item from a drop-down list of items. A *list box control* lets a user choose one or more items from a list of items.

- List boxes and drop-down lists typically contain one or more list items. You can load list items using Visual Basic code or using the ListItem Collection Editor. See figures 7-15 and 7-16 for details.

Figure 7-13   Basic skills for working with drop-down list and list box controls

Properties for working with drop-down lists, list boxes, and list items

Figure 7-14 presents some common properties and methods for working with drop-down lists and list boxes. As you learned in chapter 3, these controls contain a collection of ListItem objects that define the items in the list. To refer to this collection, you use the Items property of the control. You'll see examples that use this property in the next figure.

You can also get the selected item using the SelectedItem property of the control, and you can get or set the index of the selected item using the SelectedIndex property. By default, the SelectedIndex property of a drop-down list is set to zero, which means that the first item is selected. In contrast, the SelectedIndex property of a list box is set to -1 by default, which means that none of the items in the list are selected. Then, you can check if the user has selected an item using code like this:

```
If lstColor.SelectedIndex > -1 Then...
```

You can also select an item by default by setting the SelectedIndex property to the appropriate index value. And you can clear the selection from a list box by setting this property to -1.

The Rows and SelectionMode properties apply only to list box controls. The Rows property determines how many items are displayed at one time. The SelectionMode property determines whether the user can select more than one item from the list. Note that when multiple selections are allowed, the SelectedItem property gets the first selected item, and the SelectedIndex property gets the index of the first selected item.

To work with an item in a drop-down list or list box, you use the properties shown in this figure. The Text property specifies the text that's displayed for the item. The Value property specifies a value that's associated with the item. And the Selected property indicates whether the item is selected. You can look back to figure 7-13 to see how these properties typically appear in the HTML for a list item.

This figure also shows two ways to process a drop-down list or list box control. In the first example, the event handler for the Click event of a submit button is used to retrieve the value of an item selected from a drop-down list. To do that, the SelectedItem property of the control is used to get a ListItem object for the selected item. Then, the Value property of that object is used to get the value of the selected item. Note that if the Value property has a null value, the value of the Text property is returned instead. Also note that if you're using Visual Basic 2003, you can use the SelectedValue property of a drop-down list or list box to get the value of the currently selected item.

The second example is similar except that the event handler is executed in response to the SelectedIndexChanged event of the drop-down list. This event occurs any time the item that's selected changes between posts to the server. Like the CheckedChanged event of a check box or radio button control, you must set the AutoPostBack property of a drop-down list or list box control to True to use the SelectedIndexChanged event.

Common properties of drop-down list and list box controls

Property	Description
Items	The collection of ListItem objects that represents the items in the control. This property returns an object of type ListItemCollection.
Rows	The number of items that are displayed in a list box at one time. If the list contains more rows than can be displayed, a scroll bar is added automatically.
SelectedItem	The ListItem object for the currently selected item, or the ListItem object for the item with the lowest index if more than one item is selected in a list box.
SelectedIndex	The index of the currently selected item, or the index of the first selected item if more than one item is selected in a list box. If no item is selected in a list box, the value of this property is -1.
SelectionMode	Indicates whether a list box allows single selections (Single) or multiple selections (Multiple).
SelectedValue	The value of the currently selected item (Visual Basic 2003 only).

Common properties of list item objects

Property	Description
Text	The text that's displayed for the list item.
Value	A value associated with the list item.
Selected	Indicates whether the item is selected.

Code that retrieves the value of a selected item in a drop-down list

```
Private Sub btnOK_Click(ByVal sender As System.Object, _
        ByVal e As System.EventArgs) Handles btnOK.Click
    Dim iDay = ddlDay.SelectedItem.Value
End Sub
```

Code that uses the SelectedIndexChanged event of a drop-down list

```
Private Sub ddlDay_SelectedIndexChanged _
        (ByVal sender As System.Object, ByVal e As System.EventArgs) _
        Handles ddlDay.SelectedIndexChanged
    Dim iDay = ddlDay.SelectedItem.Value
End Sub
```

Description

- To work with the items in a drop-down list or list box, you use the Items property of the control. This property returns a ListItemCollection object that contains all of the items in the list.

- To get the value of a selected item, you use the SelectedItem property of the control to get the ListItem object for the item. Then, you use the Value property of that item to get its value.

- The SelectedIndexChanged event is raised when the user selects a different item from a drop-down list or list box. If you want to perform processing when this event occurs, you must set the EnableViewState property of the control to True so that ASP.NET can determine when the selected item changes.

Figure 7-14   Properties for working with drop-down lists, list boxes, and list items

Properties and methods for working with list item collections

Figure 7-15 presents some common properties and methods for working with a collection of list item objects. To get the item at a specific index, for example, you use the Item property. And to get a count of the number of items in the collection, you use the Count property.

All but two of the methods shown here let you add and remove items in the collection. The method you're most likely to use is Add, which adds an item to the end of the collection. The examples in this figure show two different ways you can use this method. The first example contains the code that's used to load the colors into the list box you saw in figure 7-13. Here, the Add method is used to add an item with the specified string value. When you code the Add method this way, the value you specify is assigned to the Text property of the item. Then, if you try to get the Value property of the item, the Text property is retrieved instead. In essence, then, this technique assigns the same value to the Text and Value properties.

If you want to assign different values to the Text and Value properties of an item, you use the technique shown in the second example. Here, a new list item object is created with two string values. The first one contains a string that's stored in the Text property, and the second one contains a string that's stored in the Value property. Then, the Add method is used to add the new item to the list item collection of the drop-down list you saw in figure 7-13.

Notice in both of these examples that the Items property is used to refer to the collection of list item objects for the control. You can also use the SelectedIndex property of a control to refer to an item at a specific index. For example, you could use a statement like this to remove the selected item from a drop-down list:

```
ddlDay.Items.RemoveAt(ddlDay.SelectedIndex)
```

The last two methods let you locate a list item based on the value of its Text or Value property. These methods are useful when you need to access a list item and you don't know its index value. You'll see a program that uses the FindByValue method in chapter 12.

Common properties and methods of list item collection objects

Property	Description
Item(integer)	A ListItem object that represents the item at the specified index.
Count	The number of items in the collection.

Method	Description
Add(string)	Adds a new item to the end of the collection, and assigns the specified string value to the Text property of the item.
Add(ListItem)	Adds the specified list item to the end of the collection.
Insert(integer, string)	Inserts an item at the specified index location in the collection, and assigns the specified string value to the Text property of the item.
Insert(integer, ListItem)	Inserts the specified list item at the specified index location in the collection.
Remove(string)	Removes the item from the collection whose Text property is equal to the specified string value.
Remove(ListItem)	Removes the specified list item from the collection.
RemoveAt(integer)	Removes the item at the specified index location from the collection.
Clear	Removes all the items from the collection.
FindByValue(string)	Returns the list item object whose Value property has the specified value.
FindByText(string)	Returns the list item object whose Text property has the specified value.

Code that loads items into a list box using strings

```
lstColor.Items.Add("Black")
lstColor.Items.Add("Red")
lstColor.Items.Add("Blue")
lstColor.Items.Add("Green")
```

Code that loads items into a drop-down list using ListItem objects

```
ddlDay.Items.Add(New ListItem("Sunday", 1))
ddlDay.Items.Add(New ListItem("Monday", 2))
ddlDay.Items.Add(New ListItem("Tuesday", 3))
ddlDay.Items.Add(New ListItem("Wednesday", 4))
ddlDay.Items.Add(New ListItem("Thursday", 5))
ddlDay.Items.Add(New ListItem("Friday", 6))
ddlDay.Items.Add(New ListItem("Saturday", 7))
```

Description

- The ListItemCollection object is a collection of ListItem objects. Each ListItem object represents one item in the list.

- Items in a ListItemCollection object are numbered from 0. So the index for the first item in the list is 0, the index for the second item is 1, and so on.

- When you use the Add method of a list item collection to add strings to the collection, the Text property of the list item is set to the string value you specify. Since the value of the Value property isn't set, the value of the Text property is retrieved if you try to retrieve the value of the Value property.

- To set both the Text and Value properties of a list item, you must create a list item object and then add that item to the collection.

Figure 7-15   Properties and methods for working with list item collections

How to use the ListItem Collection Editor

In the last figure, you saw how to use the Add method of a list item collection to load items into a drop-down list or list box control. If the items are static, however, you might want to use the ListItem Collection Editor to load them instead. Figure 7-16 shows you how to use this editor.

When you first display the ListItem Collection Editor, the list is empty. Then, you can use the Add button below the Members list to add items to the list. When you do, the item appears in the Members list and its properties appear in the Properties list. The three properties here are the same properties you learned about in figure 7-14. Note, however, that when you set the Text property, the Value property defaults to the same value. If that's not what you want, you'll want to be sure to change this value.

The ListItem Collection Editor dialog box

Description

- You can use the ListItem Collection Editor to add items to a drop-down list or a list box. You'll typically use it to create a static list of items.
- To display the Collection Editor dialog box, select the control, then click the ellipsis button that appears when you select the Items property in the Properties window.
- To add an item to the list, click the Add button and then enter the properties for the item in the Properties list. The item appears in the Members list.
- By default, the ListItem Collection Editor sets the Value property of a list item to the value you specify for the Text property.
- To remove an item, select it in the Members list and then click the Remove button.
- You can use the up and down arrow buttons to the right of the Members list to move the selected item up or down in the list.

Figure 7-16   How to use the ListItem Collection Editor

How to work with radio button list and check box list controls

Earlier in this chapter, you learned how to use radio button and check box controls. ASP.NET also provides *radio button list* and *check box list controls* that you can use to create lists of radio buttons or check boxes. Figure 7-17 shows you how to use these controls.

In this figure, you can see part of a web page that contains a radio button list and a check box list. If you look back to figure 7-11, you'll see that these are the same options that were provided on the web page shown there using check boxes and radio buttons.

As you can see from the HTML for the check box list and radio button list shown here, each control consists of a collection of ListItem objects. You can refer to this collection through the Items property of the control just as you can for drop-down list and list box controls. These controls also have SelectedItem and SelectedIndex properties just like drop-down lists and list boxes.

Just like a group of radio buttons, only one item in a radio button list can be selected at one time. Then, you can use the SelectedItem property to get the selected item, and you can use the SelectedIndex property to get or set the index of the selected item. This is illustrated by the first statement in this figure. This statement uses the SelectedItem property to get the selected item. Then, it uses the Value property to get the value of that item. Note that this is much simpler than the code you use to get the value of the selected radio button in a group.

Like a list box, you can select more than one item in a check box list. Because of that, you'll usually determine whether an item in the list is selected using the Selected property of the item. This is illustrated in the second example in this figure. Here, the Items property of a check box list is used to get the item at index 0. Then, the Selected property of that item is used to determine if the item is selected. Notice here that you can't refer to individual check boxes by name when you use a check box list. Because of that, your code may not be as readable as it is when you use individual check box controls. That's why I recommend that you use check box lists only when they provide a distinct advantage over using individual controls.

To determine the layout of the items in a radio button or check box list, you use the three properties shown in this figure. The RepeatLayout property determines whether ASP.NET aligns the buttons or check boxes in a list using a table or HTML flow. I recommend that you use tables since they're more precise.

The RepeatDirection property determines whether the controls are listed horizontally or vertically. For the radio button list in this figure, I set this property to Horizontal. In contrast, I left this property at its default of Vertical for the check box list.

The RepeatColumns attribute specifies the number of columns in the radio button or check box list. By default, the items are displayed in a single column. If a list contains more than just a few items, however, you may want to display the items in two or more columns to save space. The four check boxes in the list shown in this figure, for example, are displayed in two columns.

A check box list and a radio button list displayed in a browser

The HTML for the check box list and radio button list

```
Contact me about:<BR>
<asp:CheckBoxList id="cblContact" runat="server" Width="305px"
    RepeatColumns="2">
    <asp:ListItem Value="Special">Special offers</asp:ListItem>
    <asp:ListItem Value="New">New products</asp:ListItem>
    <asp:ListItem Value="Related">Related products</asp:ListItem>
    <asp:ListItem Value="Events">Local events</asp:ListItem>
</asp:CheckBoxList><BR>
Contact me by:<BR>
<asp:RadioButtonList id="rblMail" runat="server" Width="346px"
    RepeatDirection="Horizontal">
    <asp:ListItem Value="Email">Email</asp:ListItem>
    <asp:ListItem Value="Postal">Postal mail</asp:ListItem>
    <asp:ListItem Value="Both" Selected="True">Both</asp:ListItem>
</asp:RadioButtonList>
```

Properties for formatting radio button list and check box list controls

Property	Description
RepeatLayout	Specifies whether ASP should use table tags (Table) or normal HTML flow (Flow) to format the list when it renders the control. The default is Table.
RepeatDirection	Specifies the direction in which the controls should be repeated. The available values are Horizontal and Vertical. The default is Vertical.
RepeatColumns	Specifies the number of columns to use when repeating the controls. The default is 0.

A statement that gets the value of the selected item in a radio button list

```
sMail = rblMail.SelectedItem.Value
```

A statement that checks if the first item in a check box list is selected

```
If cblContact.Items(0).Selected Then...
```

Description

- A *radio button list control* presents a list of mutually exclusive options. A *check box list control* presents a list of independent options. These controls contain a collection of ListItem objects that you refer to through the Items property of the control.

- These controls also have a SelectedItem property that refers to the currently selected item and a SelectedIndex property that refers to the index of the currently selected item. If more than one item is selected in a check box list, the SelectedItem property refers to the first item, and the SelectedIndex property refers to the index of the first item.

Figure 7-17   How to work with radio button list and check box list controls

How to work with other controls

ASP.NET provides other controls in addition to those you've already seen in this chapter. You'll learn about many of those controls later in this book. For now, I want to present two controls that you'll use in many of the applications you develop: image controls and hyperlink controls.

How to work with image controls

Figure 7-18 presents part of a web page that includes an *image control* that displays a graphic image. In this case, the graphic image is stored in a *GIF* file. Graphic images are also frequently stored in *JPEG* files. JPEG files are typically used for photographs and scanned images, and GIF files are typically used for other types of images.

You can see three common properties of an image control in this figure. The most important property is ImageUrl, which specifies the URL of the image file. Image files are typically stored in a directory named Images or Graphics within the application directory. In that case, you can specify a relative URL for this property. Otherwise, you may have to specify an absolute URL.

If you know that some browsers won't be able to display the image, you should also set the AlternateText property. Then, the text you specify will be displayed in place of the image if the image can't be displayed.

The ImageAlign property determines how the image is aligned relative to the web page or other elements on the page. If you set this property to Left, for example, the image is aligned at the left side of the page and any text on the page will wrap around the right side of the image. For more information on the available alignment options, see the topic on this property in online help.

The last two properties, Width and Height, let you control the size of the displayed image. If you leave both of these properties at their defaults, ASP.NET will display the image at its original size. If you specify just one of these properties, ASP.NET will automatically set the other property so that the proportions of the original image are maintained. If you set both properties, the image will be distorted if necessary to fit the dimensions you specify. Because of that, you'll usually set just one of these properties.

How to work with hyperlink controls

The web page in figure 7-18 also includes a *hyperlink control*. This control navigates to the web page specified in the NavigateUrl property when the user clicks the control. If you want to display text for a hyperlink control, you set the Text property. Then, the text appears with an underline as shown in this figure. Alternatively, you can display an image for this control. To do that, you set the ImageUrl property to the URL of an image you want to display.

An image and a hyperlink displayed in a browser

The HTML for the image and hyperlink controls

```
<asp:Image id="Image2" runat="server"
    ImageUrl="Images\Murach web logo slogan.gif"
    AlternateText="Murach's Practical Programming Books">
</asp:Image><BR><BR>
<asp:HyperLink id="HyperLink1" runat="server"
    NavigateUrl="http://www.murach.com">Click here to order
</asp:HyperLink>
```

Common properties of image controls

Property	Description
ImageUrl	The absolute or relative URL of the image.
AlternateText	The text that's used in place of the image if the browser can't display the image.
ImageAlign	The alignment of the image relative to the web page or other elements on the page.
Width	The width of the image.
Height	The height of the image.

Common properties of hyperlink controls

Property	Description
NavigateUrl	The absolute or relative URL of the page that's displayed when the control is clicked.
Text	The text that's displayed for the control.
ImageUrl	The absolute or relative URL of the image that's displayed for the control.

Description

- An *image control* displays a graphic image, typically in *GIF* (*Graphic Interchange Format*) or *JPEG* (*Joint Photographic Experts Group*) format.

- A *hyperlink control* navigates to another web page when the user clicks the control. You can display either text or an image for the control.

Figure 7-18   How to work with image and hyperlink controls

The Halloween Store application

The last three topics of this chapter present another page of the Halloween Store application. As you'll see, this page uses many of the controls you learned about in this chapter. That should help you see how you can use these controls in a production application.

The design of the second Check Out form

In chapter 4 (figure 4-12), you saw a Check Out page that lets the user enter name and address information for an order. If the user clicked on the Continue Checkout button on this page, a message was displayed indicating that the remaining check out functions hadn't been implemented. The Halloween Store application in this chapter has been enhanced to include those functions. Now when the user clicks the Continue Checkout button, the second Check Out page shown in figure 7-19 is displayed. As you can see, this page lets the user enter shipping and payment information.

In addition to label, text box, image, and button controls, this form uses a group of radio buttons that let the user select a shipping method. To select a credit card type, this form uses a list box. And to select the expiration date for the credit card, this form uses two drop-down lists. You'll see how all of these controls are implemented when you see the aspx and Visual Basic code for this form.

Although it's not shown here, I also added a Confirmation page to the Halloween Store application. This page is displayed when the user clicks the Accept Order button. It simply displays a confirmation message and lets the user return to the Order page. Since it doesn't use any controls or techniques you haven't already seen, I won't present it here.

The second Check Out page of the Halloween Store application

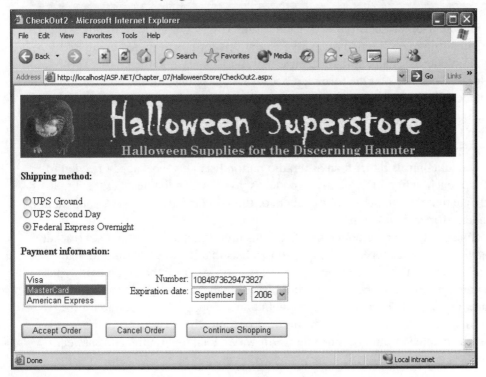

Description

- The second Check Out page of the Halloween Store application lets the user enter shipping and payment information.

- The Check Out page includes three radio buttons that let the user select a shipping method, a list box that lets the user select a credit card type, a text box that lets the user enter a credit card number, and two drop-down lists that let the user select the month and year that the credit card expires.

- If the user clicks the Accept Order button, an invoice and line items are written to the Halloween database and a Confirmation page is displayed. The Confirmation page displays a simple confirmation message and lets the user return to the Order page.

- If the user clicks the Cancel Order button, the shopping cart item is removed from session state and the client is redirected to the Order page.

- If the user clicks the Continue Shopping button, the client is redirected to the Order page.

Figure 7-19   The design of the second Check Out form

The aspx code for the Check Out form

Figure 7-20 presents the aspx code for the Check Out form in figure 7-19. The first thing you should notice here is that this form is designed using flow layout mode. You can tell that because literal text is used to display the two boldfaced headings on the form and because the asp: tags for the controls don't include a Style attribute to indicate the position of the controls. Notice that the headings are formatted using Strong elements. These elements were added when I highlighted the text and clicked the Bold button on the toolbar.

Next, you should notice that I implemented the group of radio buttons as individual controls rather than as a radio button list. That's because I needed to refer to each option individually in code, as you'll see in the next figure. To indicate that these buttons are members of the same group, I set the GroupName property for each to "Ship."

Finally, you should notice that list items aren't included for the list box that lists the credit card types or the drop-down lists that list the months and years. That's because I chose to create these items in code. Since the credit card types and months are static, however, I could have created them using the ListItem Collection Editor. Then, these items would have appeared in the code for the controls. In contrast, the list items in the drop-down list that displays the years must be created at runtime since they will vary depending on the current year.

The aspx code for the Check Out form

```
<form id="Form1" method="post" runat="server">
    <asp:image id="Image1" runat="server" ImageUrl="banner.jpg">
    </asp:image>
    <BR><BR>
    <STRONG>Shipping method:</STRONG>
    <BR><BR>
    <asp:radiobutton id="rdoGround" runat="server" Text="UPS Ground"
        Checked="True" GroupName="Ship"></asp:radiobutton><BR>
    <asp:radiobutton id="rdo2Day" runat="server" Text="UPS Second Day"
        GroupName="Ship"></asp:radiobutton><BR>
    <asp:radiobutton id="rdoFedEx" runat="server"
        Text="Federal Express Overnight" GroupName="Ship">
    </asp:radiobutton>
    <BR><BR>
    <STRONG>Payment information:</STRONG>
    <BR><BR>
    <TABLE id="Table1" style="WIDTH: 676px; HEIGHT: 65px" cellSpacing="5"
        cellPadding="0" width="697" border="0">
        <TR>
            <TD style="WIDTH: 130px" vAlign="top">
                <asp:listbox id="lstCardType" runat="server" Height="55px">
            </TD>
            <TD style="WIDTH: 130px" vAlign="top" align="right">
                <asp:label id="Label1" runat="server">Number:</asp:label>
                <BR>
                <asp:label id="Label2" runat="server">
                    Expiration date:</asp:label>
            </TD>
            <TD style="WIDTH: 416px" vAlign="top">
                <asp:textbox id="txtCardNumber" runat="server"
                    MaxLength="20"></asp:textbox> 
                <asp:RequiredFieldValidator id="RequiredFieldValidator1"
                    runat="server" ControlToValidate="txtCardNumber"
                    ErrorMessage="You must enter a credit card number.">
                </asp:RequiredFieldValidator>
                <asp:dropdownlist id="ddlMonth" runat="server" Width="88px">
                </asp:dropdownlist> 
                <asp:dropdownlist id="ddlYear" runat="server" Width="58px">
                </asp:dropdownlist>
            </TD>
        </TR>
    </TABLE>
    <BR>
    <asp:button id="btnAccept" runat="server" Text="Accept Order">
    </asp:button>   
    <asp:button id="btnCancel" runat="server" Text="Cancel Order"
        CausesValidation="False"></asp:button>   
    <asp:Button id="btnContinue" runat="server" Text="Continue Shopping"
        CausesValidation="False"></asp:Button>
</form>
```

Figure 7-20   The aspx code for the Check Out form

The Visual Basic code for the Check Out form

Figure 7-21 presents the Visual Basic code for the Check Out form. To start, this form declares two module-level variables. The first one will hold a sorted list that contains the shopping cart, and the second one will hold the customer's email address.

Each time this form is loaded, the shopping cart and email address are retrieved from session state and assigned to the module-level variables. Note that in previous versions of this program, the email address wasn't saved in session state unless it already existed in a cookie on the user's computer. For this form to work, then, the code for the first Check Out form was modified so that if a cookie didn't exist or the user entered a new email address, that address is saved in session state.

If the form is being loaded for the first time, this Load procedure also executes the LoadCardData procedure. This procedure loads the list items into the list box and combo box controls. Notice that list item objects are created for the credit card types and the months so that different values can be assigned to their Text and Value properties. In contrast, the statement that adds a list item to the drop-down list that displays the years specifies an integer value that contains the year. This sets the Text, but not the Value, property of the item. That makes sense in this case because the value of the item is the value that's assigned to the Text property.

If the user clicks the Accept Order button, the Click event procedure for that button is executed. This procedure starts by creating an Invoice object from the Invoice class. If you look ahead to page 2 of this figure, you'll see that this class defines the fields that will hold the information entered on the form, plus the customer's email address and some calculated fields. The Click event procedure assigns values to the fields in the Invoice object and then uses this object to create an invoice in the Halloween database.

To assign values to the ShipMethod and Shipping fields, this procedure starts by testing the Checked property of the radio button controls to determine which option is selected. Then, it assigns a string value that indicates the shipping method to be used to the ShipMethod field. It also calculates the shipping amount based on the option that's selected and assigns that amount to the Shipping field.

The Visual Basic code for the Check Out form

```
Public Class CheckOut2
    Inherits System.Web.UI.Page
    Dim ShoppingCart As SortedList
    Dim sEmail As String

    Private Sub Page_Load(ByVal sender As System.Object, _
            ByVal e As System.EventArgs) Handles MyBase.Load
        'Put user code to initialize the page here
        ShoppingCart = Session("Cart")
        sEmail = Session("EMail")
        If Not IsPostBack Then
            Me.LoadCardData()
        End If
    End Sub

    Private Sub LoadCardData()
        lstCardType.Items.Add(New ListItem("Visa", "VISA"))
        lstCardType.Items.Add(New ListItem("MasterCard", "MC"))
        lstCardType.Items.Add(New ListItem("American Express", "AMEX"))
        lstCardType.SelectedIndex = 0
        ddlMonth.Items.Add(New ListItem("January", 1))
        ddlMonth.Items.Add(New ListItem("February", 2))
        ddlMonth.Items.Add(New ListItem("March", 3))
        ddlMonth.Items.Add(New ListItem("April", 4))
        ddlMonth.Items.Add(New ListItem("May", 5))
        ddlMonth.Items.Add(New ListItem("June", 6))
        ddlMonth.Items.Add(New ListItem("July", 7))
        ddlMonth.Items.Add(New ListItem("August", 8))
        ddlMonth.Items.Add(New ListItem("September", 9))
        ddlMonth.Items.Add(New ListItem("October", 10))
        ddlMonth.Items.Add(New ListItem("November", 11))
        ddlMonth.Items.Add(New ListItem("December", 12))
        Dim iCount As Integer
        Dim iYear As Integer = Now.Year
        Do Until iCount = 6
            ddlYear.Items.Add(iYear)
            iCount += 1
            iYear += 1
        Loop
    End Sub

    Private Sub btnAccept_Click(ByVal sender As System.Object, _
            ByVal e As System.EventArgs) Handles btnAccept.Click
        Dim Invoice As New Invoice
        Invoice.CustEMail = sEmail
        Dim iQuantity As Integer = Me.Quantity
        If rdoGround.Checked Then
            Invoice.ShipMethod = "UPS Ground"
            Invoice.Shipping = 3.95 + (iQuantity - 1) * 1.25
        ElseIf rdo2Day.Checked Then
            Invoice.ShipMethod = "UPS Second Day"
            Invoice.Shipping = 7.95 + (iQuantity - 1) * 2.5
        ElseIf rdoFedEx.Checked Then
            Invoice.ShipMethod = "Federal Express"
            Invoice.Shipping = 19.95 + (iQuantity - 1) * 4.95
        End If
```

Figure 7-21   The Visual Basic code for the Check Out form and Invoice class (part 1 of 2)

At the top of page 2 of this listing, you can see the code that assigns values to the CreditCardType, ExpirationMonth, and ExpirationYear fields. These values are retrieved from the list controls on the form. Notice that each assignment statement uses the SelectedItem property of the control to retrieve the selected item and the Value property of the selected item to get its value.

The next two procedures are called by the Click event procedure for the Accept Order button. The first one calculates the total quantity for an order. To do that, it loops through the items in the shopping cart and sums the quantity. The second procedure is similar. It calculates a subtotal for the order by summing the unit price of each item by its quantity.

After values are assigned to all the fields of the Invoice object, the Accept procedure calls a method of the HalloweenDB class named AddInvoice. As you can see, both the Invoice object and the shopping cart are passed to this method. Then, this method adds an invoice to the Invoices table of the Halloween database using the information in the Invoice object. It also adds a line item to the LineItems table of the Halloween database for each item in the shopping cart. Although the code for this method isn't presented here, it looks much like the method you saw in chapter 4 that added a customer to the Customers table.

Finally, the Accept procedure removes the shopping cart from session state and redirects the browser to the Confirmation page. As I've already mentioned, the Confirmation page simply displays a message confirming the order and lets the user return to the Order page. The shopping cart is removed from session state so that if the user returns to the Order page, a new, empty shopping cart will be created.

The last two procedures for this form handle the Click events for the Cancel and Continue Shopping buttons. If the user clicks the Cancel button, the Cancel procedure removes the shopping cart from session state and then redirects the browser to the Order page. If the user clicks the Continue Shopping button, the browser is redirected to the Order page but the shopping cart is left in session state.

The Visual Basic code for the Check Out form   **Page 2**

```
        Dim dSubtotal As Decimal = Me.SubTotal
        Invoice.Subtotal = dSubtotal
        Dim dSalestax As Decimal = dSubtotal * 0.075
        Invoice.SalesTax = dSalestax
        Invoice.Total = dSubtotal + dSalestax
        Invoice.CreditCardType = lstCardType.SelectedItem.Value
        Invoice.CardNumber = txtCardNumber.Text
        Invoice.ExpirationMonth = ddlMonth.SelectedItem.Value
        Invoice.ExpirationYear = ddlYear.SelectedItem.Value
        HalloweenDB.AddInvoice(Invoice, ShoppingCart)
        Session.Remove("Cart")
        Response.Redirect("Confirmation.aspx")
    End Sub

    Private Function Quantity() As Integer
        Dim CartItem As CartItem
        Dim CartEntry As DictionaryEntry
        For Each CartEntry In ShoppingCart
            CartItem = CartEntry.Value
            Quantity += CartItem.Quantity
        Next
    End Function

    Private Function SubTotal() As Decimal
        Dim CartItem As CartItem
        Dim CartEntry As DictionaryEntry
        For Each CartEntry In ShoppingCart
            CartItem = CartEntry.Value
            SubTotal += CartItem.Quantity * CartItem.UnitPrice
        Next
    End Function

    Private Sub btnCancel_Click(ByVal sender As System.Object, _
            ByVal e As System.EventArgs) Handles btnCancel.Click
        Session.Remove("Cart")
        Response.Redirect("Order.aspx")
    End Sub

    Private Sub btnContinue_Click(ByVal sender As System.Object, _
            ByVal e As System.EventArgs) Handles btnContinue.Click
        Response.Redirect("Order.aspx")
    End Sub
End Class
```

The Visual Basic code for the Invoice class

```
Public Class Invoice
    Public CustEMail As String
    Public Subtotal As Decimal
    Public ShipMethod As String
    Public Shipping As Decimal
    Public SalesTax As Decimal
    Public Total As Decimal
    Public CreditCardType As String
    Public CardNumber As String
    Public ExpirationMonth As Integer
    Public ExpirationYear As Integer
End Class
```

Figure 7-21   The Visual Basic code for the Check Out form and Invoice class (part 2 of 2)

Perspective

In this chapter, you've learned how to use 13 of the Web Server controls that ASP.NET provides. These controls, along with the validation controls you'll learn about in the next chapter and the data controls you'll learn about in chapter 14, are the ones you'll use most often as you develop ASP.NET applications.

With that as background, if you need to use any of the other controls, you should be able to figure out how to do that on your own. In most cases, it's just a matter of becoming familiar with the properties, methods, and events of the control. You can do that by reviewing the online documentation for the control and the class it's based on.

Terms

grid layout mode
flow layout mode
event handler
button control
link button control
image button control
label control
text box control
check box control
radio button control
drop-down list control
list box control
radio button list control
check box list control
image control
GIF (Graphic Interchange Format)
JPEG (Joint Photographic Experts Group)
hyperlink control

8

How to use validation controls

In chapter 3, you learned the basic skills for using two of the validation controls ASP.NET provides: the required field validator and the compare validator. In this chapter, you'll learn additional techniques for using these controls. In additional, you'll learn how to use the other validation controls ASP.NET provides. As you'll see, you can use these controls to perform the data validation required by most web forms.

An introduction to the validation controls

ASP.NET provides six *validation controls* that you can use to validate the data on a web form. You'll learn the basic skills for using these controls in the topics that follow. You'll also learn how ASP.NET processes these controls.

How to use the validation controls

Figure 8-1 summarizes the validation controls that are available with ASP.NET. As you learned in chapter 3, the first five controls are called *validators*. These are the controls you use to check that the user has entered valid data into the input controls on a web form. In contrast, you use the validation summary control to display a summary of all the errors on a page.

This figure also illustrates how the validation controls appear in the Web Forms Designer. Here, you can see the Order form of the Halloween Store application that was developed in flow layout mode for the application in chapter 7. This form uses two validation controls. The first one is a required field validator that checks that the user entered a value into the Quantity text box, and the second one is a compare validator that checks that the user entered an integer greater than zero into that text box.

Notice in this example that the required field validator appears directly to the right of the text box, but the compare validator appears below it. That's because the compare validator doesn't fit on the same line as the required field validator within the table cell. As you'll see later in this chapter, however, these validators are defined so an error message will be displayed to the right of the text box regardless of which validator detects the error.

The validation controls on the Order form of the Halloween Store application

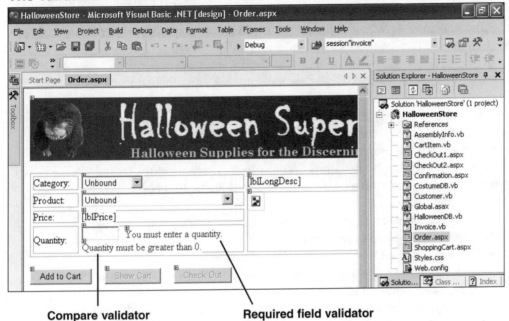

Compare validator   **Required field validator**

The validation controls provided by ASP.NET

Control	Name	Description
	RequiredFieldValidator	Checks that an entry has been made.
	CompareValidator	Checks an entry against a constant value or the value of another control. Can also be used to check for a specific data type.
	RangeValidator	Checks that an entry is within a specified range.
	RegularExpressionValidator	Checks that an entry matches a pattern that's defined by a regular expression.
	CustomValidator	Checks an entry using validation code that you write yourself.
	ValidationSummary	Displays a summary of error messages from the other validation controls.

Description

- ASP.NET provides *validation controls* that you can use to validate the data that a user enters into a page and produce error messages. You can use these controls with any of the Web Server or HTML Server input controls.

- Each *validator* is associated with a single input control, but you can associate two or more validators with the same input control. See figure 8-7 for details on how to do that.

Figure 8-1   How to use the validation controls

Common validator properties

After you add a validator to a web form, you set its properties to determine which input control it validates and how errors are displayed. Figure 8-2 presents the properties you use to do that. The most important property is ControlToValidate, which associates the validator with an input control on the page.

The Display property determines how the error message for a validator is displayed. The option you choose depends on whether two or more validators are associated with the same input control and whether or not you use a validation summary control. The default is Static, which causes the error message to appear in the same location as the validator. You'll learn more about the other options in later topics.

You use the ErrorMessage and Text properties to specify messages that are displayed when the validator detects an error. You can set one or both of these properties depending on whether you use a validation summary control. If you don't use a validation summary control, you can set either of these properties to the error message you want to display in the validator.

When ASP.NET performs the validation test specified by a validator, it sets the IsValid property of the validator to indicate whether or not the data is valid. Then, you can refer to this property in code to test the result of the validation. In most cases, though, you won't test the result of individual validators. Instead, you'll test that all of the validators on the page passed their validation tests. You'll learn how to do that in the next figure.

The last property shown in this figure is the Enabled property. If this property is set to True, the validation test specified by the validator is performed. If you want to skip the validation that's done by a validator, you can set this property to False. You'll learn more about why you might want to do that later in this chapter.

Common validator properties

Property	Description
ControlToValidate	The ID of the control to be validated.
Display	Determines how the error message is to be displayed. Specify Static to allocate space for the message in the page layout, Dynamic to have space allocated only when an error occurs, or None to display errors only in a validation summary control. The default is Static.
ErrorMessage	The message that's displayed in the validation control and/or the validation summary control when the validation fails. To display a different message in each control, set this property to the message you want to display in the validation summary control and set the Text property to the message you want to display in the validation control.
Text	The message that's displayed in the validation control when the validation fails. To display a message in a validation summary control as well, set the ErrorMessage property.
IsValid	Indicates whether the control specified in the ControlToValidate property passed the validation.
Enabled	Indicates whether the validation control is enabled.

Description

- Each validator has an IsValid property that indicates whether its validation was successful. You'll typically use this property when you initiate validation manually as described in figure 8-9.
- You typically set the Display property to Dynamic if you use two or more validators to validate the same control. Then, the validators that pass their validation tests don't take up space on the page. For more information, see figure 8-7.
- In addition to the properties shown above, validators have properties that affect the appearance of the message that's displayed. For example, the ForeColor property is set to Red by default so the message is displayed in red.
- You can also format the error message that's displayed by including HTML in the values you assign to the Text and ErrorMessage properties.

Figure 8-2   Common validator properties

How ASP.NET processes validation controls

Now that you have a general idea of how validation controls work, figure 8-3 explains how they're processed by ASP.NET. To start, you should realize that the validation tests are typically done on the client before the page is posted to the server. That way, a round trip to the server isn't required to display error messages if any invalid data is detected.

In most cases, client-side validation is done when the focus leaves an input control that has validators associated with it. That can happen when the user presses the Tab key to move to the next control or clicks another control to move the focus to that control. The required field validator works a bit differently, however. When you use this validator, the validation isn't done until the user clicks a submit button whose CausesValidation property is set to True. The exception is if the user enters a value into an input control and then tries to clear the value. In that case, an error will be detected when the focus leaves the control.

To perform client-side validation, a browser must support *Dynamic HTML*, or *DHTML*. Because most browsers in use today support DHTML, validation can usually be done on the client. In case the page is being displayed in a browser that doesn't support DHTML, however, validation is always done on the server when a page is submitted. ASP.NET does this validation after it initializes the page.

When ASP.NET performs the validation tests specified by the validators, it sets the IsValid property of each validator to indicate if the test was successful. In addition, after all the validators are tested, it sets the IsValid property of the page to indicate if all the input data is valid. You can test this property in the event handler for the event that caused the page to be posted to the server.

At the top of this figure, for example, you can see how this property is tested in the event handler for the Click event of a submit button. Note that it isn't necessary to test the IsValid property of the page if the validation has been performed on the client. That's because, in that case, the page isn't submitted until all of the data is valid. In most cases, though, you'll test this property just in case validation wasn't done on the client.

By the way, you can also bypass client-side validation and just perform the validation on the server. To do that, you set the EnableClientScript property of the validation controls to False. Then, the scripts that are typically used to perform the validation on the client aren't generated, and validation is done only on the server. You'll learn about one situation in which you may want to disable client-side validation later in this chapter.

Typical code for processing a page that contains validation controls

```
Private Sub btnAccept_Click(ByVal sender As System.Object, _
        ByVal e As System.EventArgs) Handles btnAccept.Click
    If Page.IsValid Then
        .
        .
        .
    End If
End Sub
```

Description

- When a page is posted to the server, ASP.NET processes any validation controls it contains after the page is initialized. If any of the controls indicate invalid data, the IsValid property of the page is set to False. You can test this property to determine what processing is done.

- If a browser supports *DHTML* (*Dynamic HTML*), validation controls can also perform their validation using client-side script. That way, the validation is performed and error messages are displayed without the page being posted to the server.

- In most cases, the validation controls work the same regardless of whether they are processed on the client or on the server.

- Validation is performed on the server regardless of whether it's performed on the client. That way, the validation is done whether or not the browser supports DHTML.

- If you want to perform validation only on the server, you can set the EnableClientScript properties of the validation controls to False. Then, no client-side scripts are generated for validating the data.

- Although most browsers support DHTML, your code should still check that a page is valid in case an older browser is used.

- The validation for an input control is performed on the client when the focus leaves that control. The exception is the validation for a required field validator. In that case, validation is performed only when you click a submit button whose CausesValidation property is set to True, or if you enter a value into a control and then subsequently clear and leave the control.

- Validation is performed on the server when you click a submit button whose CausesValidation property is set to True. To create a button, such as a Cancel button, that doesn't initiate validation, set this property to False.

Figure 8-3   How ASP.NET processes validation controls

How to use the basic validation controls

In the topics that follow, you'll learn about the three validation controls you'll use most often as you develop web applications. These are the required field validator, the compare validator, and the range validator.

How to use the required field validator

Figure 8-4 shows how to use the *required field validator*. This validator checks that the user entered a value into an input control. If the user doesn't enter a value, the IsValid property of the validator is set to False and its error message is displayed.

The three examples in this figure illustrate how you use the required field validator. In the first example, this validator is used to check for a required entry in a text box. To do that, its ControlToValidate property is set to the ID property of the text box. Then, if the user doesn't enter anything into the text box, the text in the ErrorMessage property is displayed.

The second and third examples show how you can use the InitialValue property of the required field validator to check that the user changed the initial value of a control. By default, this property is set to an empty string, which is what you want if the input control is empty. If you specify an initial value for an input control, however, you'll want to set the InitialValue property of the required field validator to the same value.

In the second example, this technique is used with a text box. Here, the initial value indicates the format for a date entry. If the user doesn't change this value, the validation test will fail.

The third example uses the InitialValue property with a list box. Here, the InitialValue property is set to None, which is the value of the first item in the list. That way, if the user doesn't select another item, the validation test will fail. You can also use this technique with a drop-down list or a radio button list.

Additional property of a required field validator

Property	Description
InitialValue	The initial value of the control that's validated. If the value isn't changed, the validation fails. The default is an empty string.

A required field validator that checks for a required entry

```
Name: 
<asp:TextBox id="txtName" runat="server" Width="213px"></asp:TextBox> 
<asp:RequiredFieldValidator id="RequiredFieldValidator1" runat="server"
    ControlToValidate="txtName" ErrorMessage="You must enter a name."
</asp:RequiredFieldValidator>
```

A required field validator that checks that an initial value is changed

```
Birth date: 
<asp:TextBox id="txtBirthdate" runat="server" Width="224px"
    Text="mm/dd/yyyy"></asp:TextBox> 
<asp:RequiredFieldValidator id="RequiredFieldValidator2" runat="server"
    ControlToValidate="txtBirthDate" InitialValue="mm/dd/yyyy"
    ErrorMessage="You must enter a birth date.">
</asp:RequiredFieldValidator>
```

A required field validator that checks that an option is chosen from a list box

```
<asp:ListBox id="lstCardType" runat="server">
    <asp:ListItem Value="None" Selected="True">
        --Select a credit card--</asp:ListItem>
    <asp:ListItem Value="VISA">Visa</asp:ListItem>
    <asp:ListItem Value="MC">MasterCard</asp:ListItem>
    <asp:ListItem Value="AMEX">American Express</asp:ListItem>
</asp:ListBox>
<asp:RequiredFieldValidator id="RequiredFieldValidator1" runat="server"
    InitialValue="None" ControlToValidate="lstCardType"
    ErrorMessage="You must select a credit card.">
</asp:RequiredFieldValidator>
```

How the input controls are initially displayed in a browser

```
Name: [                    ]

Birth date: [mm/dd/yyyy]

┌──────────────────────┐
│--Select a credit card--│
│Visa                  │
│MasterCard            │
│American Express      │
└──────────────────────┘
```

Description

- The *required field validator* checks that the user entered information into an input control. It's typically used with text box controls, but can also be used with list controls.

- ASP.NET uses the InitialValue property to determine if the user entered a value. If the initial value of the control that's being validated is something other than an empty string, you'll want to set the InitialValue property to the same value.

Figure 8-4   How to use the required field validator

How to use the compare validator

Figure 8-5 shows how you use the *compare validator*. This validator lets you compare the value entered into an input control with a constant value or the value of another control. You can also use the compare validator to make sure that the value is a particular data type.

To define a compare validator, you use the four additional properties shown in this figure. To compare the input data with a constant value, you specify the value in the ValueToCompare property. Then, you set the Operator property to indicate the type of comparison you want to perform, and you set the Type property to the type of data you're comparing. The first example illustrates how this works. Here, the value entered into a text box is tested to be sure that it's greater than zero. Then, if the user enters a number that isn't greater than zero, or if the user enters a value that isn't an integer, the error message will be displayed.

To test for just a data type, you set the Type property to the type of data you're testing for, and you set the Operator property to DataTypeCheck. This is illustrated by the second example. Here, the value entered into a text box is tested to be sure that it's an integer.

The third example illustrates how to compare the value of an input control with the value of another control. To do that, you set the Operator and Type properties just as you do when you compare an input value with a constant. Instead of setting the ValueToCompare property, however, you set the ControlToCompare property to the ID of the control whose value you want to compare. This is illustrated in the third example, which tests that a date that's entered into one text box is after the date entered into another text box.

At this point, you should realize that if the user doesn't enter a value into a control, the compare validator associated with that control will pass its validation test. Because of that, you must use a required field validator along with the compare validator if you want to be sure that the user enters a value into the input control. You'll learn more about combining validation controls like this in figure 8-7.

You should also realize that if you compare the value of a control against the value of another control, the validation test will pass if the user doesn't enter a value into the other control or the value of the other control can't be converted to the correct type. To avoid that problem, you'll want to be sure that the other control is validated properly.

Additional properties of a compare validator

Property	Description
ValueToCompare	The value that the control specified in the ControlToValidate property should be compared to.
Operator	The type of comparison to perform (Equal, NotEqual, GreaterThan, GreaterThanEqual, LessThan, LessThanEqual, or DataTypeCheck).
Type	The data type to use for the comparison (String, Integer, Double, Date, or Currency).
ControlToCompare	The ID of the control that the value of the control specified in the ControlToValidate property should be compared to.

A compare validator that checks for a value greater than zero

```
Quantity: 
<asp:TextBox id="txtQuantity" runat="server" Width="50px">
</asp:TextBox> 
<asp:CompareValidator id="CompareValidator1" runat="server"
    ErrorMessage="Quantity must be greater than zero."
    ValueToCompare="0" Operator="GreaterThan"
    Type="Integer" ControlToValidate="txtQuantity">
</asp:CompareValidator>
```

A compare validator that checks for a numeric entry

```
Quantity: 
<asp:TextBox id="txtQuantity" runat="server" Width="50px">
</asp:TextBox> 
<asp:CompareValidator id="CompareValidator2" runat="server"
    ErrorMessage="Quantity must be numeric." Operator="DataTypeCheck"
    Type="Integer" ControlToValidate="txtQuantity">
</asp:CompareValidator>
```

A compare validator that compares the values of two controls

```
Start Date: 
<asp:TextBox id="txtStartDate" runat="server" Width="64px">
</asp:TextBox>
End Date: 
<asp:TextBox id="txtEndDate" runat="server" Width="64px">
</asp:TextBox> 
<asp:CompareValidator id="CompareValidator3" runat="server"
    ControlToValidate="txtEndDate" Type="Date"
    Operator="GreaterThan" ControlToCompare="txtStartDate"
    ErrorMessage="End Date must be greater than Start Date.">
</asp:CompareValidator>
```

Description

- The *compare validator* compares the value entered into a control with a constant value or with the value entered into another control. You can also use the compare validator to check that the user entered a specific data type.

- If the user doesn't enter a value into the associated input control, the validation test passes. As a result, you should also provide a required field validator if a value is required.

Figure 8-5   How to use the compare validator

How to use the range validator

The *range validator*, shown in figure 8-6, validates user input by making sure that it falls within a given range of values. To specify the valid range, you set the MinimumValue and MaximumValue properties. You must also set the Type property to the type of data you're checking. The first example in this figure, for instance, checks that the user enters an integer between 1 and 14 into a text box.

The second example in this figure shows how you can set the range for a range validator at runtime. If you look at the HTML in this example, you can see that the MinimumValue and MaximumValue properties weren't set when the range validator was created. Instead, they're set when the page is loaded for the first time. In this case, the MinimumValue property is set to the current date, and the MaximumValue property is set to 30 days after the current date.

Like the compare validator, you should realize that the range validator will pass its validation test if the user doesn't enter anything into the associated control. Because of that, you'll need to use a required field validator along with the range validator if the user must enter a value.

Additional properties of the range validator

Property	Description
MinimumValue	The minimum value allowed for the control.
MaximumValue	The maximum value allowed for the control.
Type	The data type to use for the comparison (String, Integer, Double, Date, or Currency).

A range validator that checks for a numeric range

```
Days: 
<asp:TextBox id="txtDays" runat="server" Width="64px">
</asp:TextBox> 
<asp:RangeValidator id="RangeValidator1" runat="server"
     ControlToValidate="txtDays" Type="Integer"
     MaximumValue="14" MinimumValue="1"
     ErrorMessage="Days must be between 1 and 14.">
</asp:RangeValidator>
```

How to set a range at runtime

A range validator that checks a date range that's set at runtime

```
Arrival Date: 
<asp:TextBox id="txtArrival" runat="server" Width="64px">
</asp:TextBox> 
<asp:RangeValidator id="valArrival" runat="server"
     ControlToValidate="txtArrival" Type="Date"
     ErrorMessage="You must arrive within 30 days.">
</asp:RangeValidator>
```

Code that sets the minimum and maximum values when the page is loaded

```
Private Sub Page_Load(ByVal sender As System.Object, _
        ByVal e As System.EventArgs) Handles MyBase.Load
    'Put user code to initialize the page here
    If Not IsPostBack Then
        valArrival.MinimumValue = Today
        valArrival.MaximumValue = Today.AddDays(30)
    End If
End Sub
```

Description

- The *range validator* checks that the user enters a value that falls within the range specified by the MinimumValue and MaximumValue properties. These properties can be set when the range validator is created or when the page is loaded.

- If the user enters a value that can't be converted to the correct data type, the validation fails.

- If the user doesn't enter a value into the associated input control, the range validator passes its validation test. As a result, you should also provide a required field validator if a value is required.

Figure 8-6   How to use the range validator

Validation techniques

Now that you're familiar with the basic validation controls, you're ready to learn some additional techniques for validating data. First, you should know how to combine validation controls since this is a technique you'll use regularly. Second, you should know how to use the validation summary control to display a summary of all the errors on a page. And third, you should know how to initiate server validation manually so that you can handle those cases where you need to perform some processing before validating the data.

How to combine validation controls

As you know, a compare validator or a range validator will pass its validation test if the user doesn't enter data into the input control it's validating. Because of that, you must use a required field validator along with the compare validator or range validator if an entry is required. Figure 8-7 describes how you combine controls like this.

The HTML in this figure is for the Quantity text box on the Order form you saw back in figure 8-1 and the required field and compare validators associated with it. You should notice two things in this example. First, the ControlToValidate property for both validators is set to the ID property of the text box, which is what you'd expect. Second, the Display property for both validators is set to Dynamic. That way, the validators take up space on the page only if they don't pass their validation tests. Note that this technique works only if you use flow layout to design the form. If you use grid layout, an error message will always appear where you place the validator.

To understand how this works, consider the Order page shown in this figure. Here, the user entered a value of 0 into the text box, so the required field validator passes its validation test. However, the compare validator requires that the value be greater than zero, so this validation test fails and an error message is displayed. Notice that the error message is displayed immediately to the right of the text box, even though the required field validator is positioned between the text box and the compare validator. In contrast, if you set the Display property to Static or let it default to Static, the error message would be displayed exactly where the compare validator was positioned on the form, which isn't usually what you want.

When you combine validation controls, the user must enter a value that passes all the validation tests. Because of that, you can't use the compare or range validators to test that one condition or another is true. To do that, you have to use a custom validator. You'll learn how to use this type of validator later in this chapter.

A table row with a text box and two validators

```
<TR>
    <TD style="WIDTH: 73px">Quantity:</TD>
    <TD style="WIDTH: 261px">
        <asp:TextBox id="txtQuantity" runat="server" Width="60px">
        </asp:TextBox> 
        <asp:RequiredFieldValidator id="RequiredFieldValidator1"
            runat="server" ErrorMessage="You must enter a quantity."
            ControlToValidate="txtQuantity" Display="Dynamic">
        </asp:RequiredFieldValidator>
        <asp:CompareValidator id="CompareValidator1" runat="server"
            ErrorMessage="Quantity must be greater than 0."
            ControlToValidate="txtQuantity" Display="Dynamic"
            Operator="GreaterThan" Type="Integer" ValueToCompare="0">
        </asp:CompareValidator></TD>
</TR>
```

The message from the second validator displayed in a browser

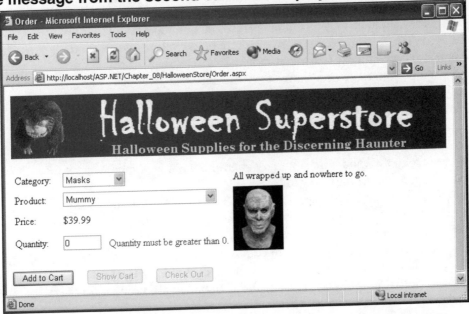

Description

- You can provide more than one validator for a single input control. For example, it's common to combine a required field validator with another validation control.

- To use two or more validators for a single input control, just specify the input control's ID in the ControlToValidate property of each validator.

- When you use two or more validators for an input control, the value entered by the user must pass all validation tests to be considered valid. If any of the validators detects an invalid entry, its IsValid property and the IsValid property of the page are set to False.

- If you use two or more validators for a single input control, you should set the Display property of each control to Dynamic. That way, no space will be reserved for errors that don't occur. Note that this technique works only in flow layout. In grid layout, the error message appears in the same location as the validator it's associated with.

Figure 8-7   How to combine validation controls

How to use the validation summary control

The *validation summary control* lets you summarize all the errors on a page. The summary can be a simple message, such as "There were errors on the page," or a more elaborate message that includes information about each error. The summary can be displayed directly on the page, or, if validation is being performed on the client, in a separate message box.

Figure 8-8 illustrates how you use the validation summary control. The most difficult part of using this control is determining how to code the Text and ErrorMessage properties of a validator so that the error message is displayed the way you want. To display the same message in both the validator and the validation summary control, for example, you set the ErrorMessage property to that message. To display a different message in each control, you set the ErrorMessage property to the message you want to display in the validation summary control, and you set the Text property to the message you want to display in the validator. This technique is illustrated in the example in this figure. Here, the Text properties of two required field validators are set to "*" so that indicators appear next to the controls in error, and the ErrorMessage properties are set to more descriptive error messages.

If you don't want to display individual messages for each error in the validation summary control, you can do that too. Just set the HeaderText property of the control to the generic message you want to display, and then leave the ErrorMessage property of each validator blank. Also, to display an error message in the validation summary control but not in a validator, set the Display property of the validator to None.

By default, the error messages displayed by a validation summary control are formatted as a bulleted list as shown in this figure. However, you can also display the errors in a simple list or paragraph format by setting the DisplayMode property accordingly. In addition, you can display the error messages in a message box rather than on the web page by setting the ShowMessageBox property to True and the ShowSummary property to False.

Properties of the validation summary control

Property	Description
DisplayMode	Specifies how the error messages from the validation controls are to be displayed. The available values are BulletList, List, or SingleParagraph. The default is BulletList.
HeaderText	The text that's displayed before the list of error messages.
ShowSummary	A Boolean value that determines whether the validation summary should be displayed on the web page. The default is True.
ShowMessageBox	A Boolean value that determines whether the validation summary should be displayed in a message box (client-side validation only). The default is False.

Two validators and a validation summary control that are displayed on the web page

```
<asp:RequiredFieldValidator id="RequiredFieldValidator1" runat="server"
    ErrorMessage="You must select a credit card type."
    Display="Dynamic" ControlToValidate="lstCardType"
    InitialValue="None">*</asp:RequiredFieldValidator>
<asp:RequiredFieldValidator id="RequiredFieldValidator2" runat="server"
    ErrorMessage="You must enter a credit card number."
    Display="Dynamic" ControlToValidate="txtCardNumber">*
</asp:RequiredFieldValidator>
<asp:ValidationSummary id="ValidationSummary1" runat="server"
    HeaderText="Please correct the following errors:">
</asp:ValidationSummary>
```

How the controls appear on the web page

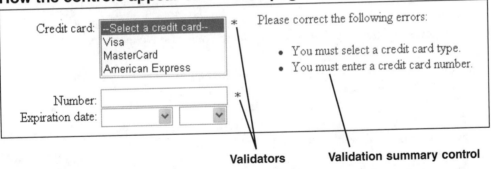

Validators   **Validation summary control**

Description

- The *validation summary control* displays a summary of error messages that were generated by the page's validators. The summary can be displayed on the web page or in a separate message box.

- The error messages displayed in the validation summary control come from the ErrorMessage property of the page's validators. If you want to display a different message in the validator, set the Text property of that control.

- If you don't want to display an error message in the validator, set its Display property to None.

Figure 8-8   How to use the validation summary control

How to initiate server validation manually

Normally, validation occurs on the server when the user clicks a button whose CausesValidation property is set to True. Then, ASP.NET validates the input data by executing the Validate method of the Page class. This method, in turn, executes the Validate method of every enabled validator on the page. This happens automatically after the page is initialized.

In some cases, however, you won't want ASP.NET to validate a page automatically. For example, consider the page shown in figure 8-9. As you can see, this page contains a series of text boxes that let the user enter a billing name and address, another series of text boxes that let the user enter a separate shipping name and address, and a check box that indicates if the shipping address is the same as the billing address. If the user checks the check box, no shipping data needs to be entered, so no validation is required for the text boxes that accept that data. On the other hand, if the user doesn't check the check box, the shipping data should be validated for required entries.

To accomplish that, you start by setting the CausesValidation property of the submit button to False so ASP.NET doesn't perform server validation automatically. Then, you can include code like that shown in this figure in the event handler for the Click event of the submit button. Here, the Checked property of the check box is tested to determine whether shipping data is required. If the check box is checked, the required field validators for the text boxes that accept the shipping data are disabled. On the other hand, if the check box isn't checked, the required field validators are enabled. Then, the Validate method of the page is called to validate the page. Since only the validators that are enabled are tested, the shipping data is validated only if the check box isn't checked.

When you perform server validation manually as shown here, you probably won't want the associated controls to be validated on the client. In this case, for example, you don't want the text boxes that let the user enter shipping data to be validated on the client. Otherwise, error messages could be displayed when they're not appropriate. To avoid that, you can set the EnableClientScript property of these controls to False.

Another situation where you might want to initiate validation manually is if you need to set the properties of a validation control based on data entered by the user. For example, you might use a range validator to test that the value entered into one input control is between the values entered into two other input controls. To do that, you need to set the MinimumValue and MaximumValue properties of the range validator in code before the page is validated.

A web page that accepts a billing and a shipping address

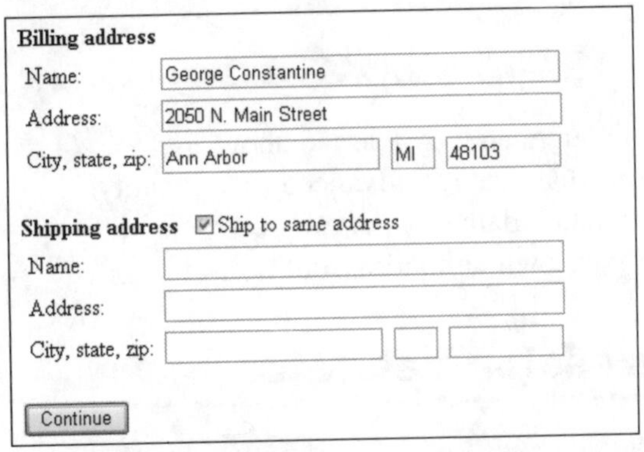

Billing address

Name: George Constantine

Address: 2050 N. Main Street

City, state, zip: Ann Arbor   MI   48103

Shipping address   ☑ Ship to same address

Name:

Address:

City, state, zip:

[Continue]

The event handler for the Continue button

```
Private Sub btnContinue_Click(ByVal sender As System.Object, _
        ByVal e As System.EventArgs) Handles btnContinue.Click
    If chkShipSame.Checked Then
        valShipName.Enabled = False
        valShipAddress.Enabled = False
        valShipCity.Enabled = False
        valShipState.Enabled = False
        valShipZip.Enabled = False
    Else
        valShipName.Enabled = True
        valShipAddress.Enabled = True
        valShipCity.Enabled = True
        valShipState.Enabled = True
        valShipZip.Enabled = True
    End If
    Page.Validate()
End Sub
```

Description

- By default, the data on a page is validated on the server when the user clicks the submit button. If that's not what you want, you can change the CausesValidation property of the submit button to False. Then, you can initiate page validation on the server manually.

- To validate the data on a page, you use the Validate method of the Page. You can also validate individual controls using the Validate method of the associated validation controls.

- Before you initiate page validation, you can enable and disable validation controls so that only the validation done by the enabled controls is tested.

- You can also initiate page validation manually if you need to set validation values based on data entered by the user. For example, you can set the MinimumValue and MaximumValue properties of a range validator based on data entered into two input controls.

- When you initiate page validation manually, you should disable client-side validation for any input controls that are affected by the changes you make in code. To do that, you set the EnableClientScript properties of the controls to False.

Figure 8-9   How to initiate server validation manually

How to use the advanced validation controls

In addition to the validation controls you've already learned about, ASP.NET provides two additional controls that provide advanced functionality. The regular expression validator lets you match data to a pattern you specify, and the custom validator lets you create your own validation routines.

How to use the regular expression validator

A *regular expression* is a string made up of special pattern-matching symbols. You can use regular expressions with the *regular expression validator* to make sure that an input control's data matches a particular pattern, such as a zip code, phone number, or email address. Figure 8-10 shows how to use the regular expression validator.

As you can see, the ValidationExpression property specifies the regular expression the input data must match. The code for the first regular expression validator shown in this figure, for example, specifies that the input data must contain five decimal digits (\d{5}). The regular expression for the second validator is much more complex. It specifies that the input data must be in the format of a U.S. phone number.

In the next topic, you'll learn how to create your own regular expressions. However, you should know that Visual Studio provides several standard expressions you can choose from. These expressions define patterns for validating phone numbers and postal codes for the U.S., France, Germany, Japan, and China; U.S. Social Security numbers; and Internet email addresses and URLs. To use a standard expression, you simply select it from the Regular Expression Editor dialog box shown in this figure. You can also create a custom expression that's based on a standard expression by selecting the standard expression so that its definition appears in the text box at the bottom of the Regular Expression Editor dialog box. Then, you can edit the regular expression any way you'd like.

An additional property of the regular expression validator

Property	Description
ValidationExpression	A string that specifies a regular expression. The regular expression defines a pattern that the input data must match to be valid.

A regular expression validator that validates five-digit numbers

```
Zip code: 
<asp:TextBox id="txtZipCode" Runat="server"></asp:TextBox> 
<asp:RegularExpressionValidator id="RegularExpressionValidator1"
    runat="server" ControlToValidate="txtZipCode"
    ValidationExpression="\d{5}"
    ErrorMessage="Must be a five-digit number.">
</asp:RegularExpressionValidator>
```

A regular expression validator that validates U.S. phone numbers

```
Phone: 
<asp:TextBox id="txtPhone" runat="server"></asp:TextBox> 
<asp:RegularExpressionValidator id="RegularExpressionValidator2"
    runat="server" ControlToValidate="txtPhone"
    ValidationExpression="((\(\d{3}\) ?)|(\d{3}-))?\d{3}-\d{4}"
    ErrorMessage="Must be a valid U.S. Phone Number.">
</asp:RegularExpressionValidator>
```

The Regular Expression Editor dialog box

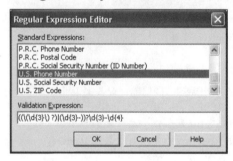

Description

- The *regular expression validator* matches the input entered by the user with the pattern supplied by the ValidationExpression property. If the input doesn't match the pattern, the validation fails.

- The string you specify for the ValidationExpression property must use *regular expression* notation. For more information, see figure 8-11.

- ASP.NET provides several standard regular expressions you can access using the Regular Expression Editor. To display the Regular Expression Editor dialog box, select the validation control, select the ValidationExpression property in the Properties window, and then click the ellipsis button that appears for that property.

- You can also use the Regular Expression Editor to create a custom expression that's based on a standard expression. To do that, select the standard expression and then edit it in the Validation Expression text box.

Figure 8-10   How to use the regular expression validator

How to create your own regular expressions

Figure 8-11 presents the basic elements of regular expressions. Although the .NET Framework provides many other elements that you can use in regular expressions, you can create expressions of considerable complexity using just the ones shown here. In fact, all of the standard expressions provided by ASP.NET use only these elements.

To start, you can specify any ordinary character, such as a letter or a decimal digit. If a character must be an A, for example, you just include that character in the expression. To include a character other than an ordinary character, you must precede it with a backslash. For example, \(specifies that the character must be a left parenthesis, \] specifies that the character must be a right bracket, and \\ specifies that the character must be a backslash. A backslash that's used in this way is called an *escape character*.

You can also specify a *character class*, which consists of a set of characters. For example, \d indicates that the character must be a decimal digit, \w indicates that the character must be a *word character*, and \s indicates that the character must be a *whitespace character*. The uppercase versions of these elements—\D, \W, and \S—match any character that is not a decimal digit, word character, or whitespace character.

To create a list of possible characters, you enclose them in brackets. For example, [abc] specifies that the character must be the letter a, b, or c, and [a-z] specifies that the character must be a lowercase letter. One fairly common construct is [a-zA-Z], which specifies that the character must be a lowercase or uppercase letter.

You can also use *quantifiers* to indicate how many of the preceding element the input data must contain. To specify an exact number, you just code it in brackets. For example, \d{5} specifies that the input data must be a five-digit number. You can also specify a minimum number and a maximum number of characters. For example, \w{6,20} specifies that the input data must contain from six to twenty word characters. You can also omit the maximum number to require just a minimum number of characters. For example, \w{6,} specifies that the input data must contain at least 6 word characters. You can also use the *, ?, and + quantifiers to specify zero or more, zero or one, or one or more characters.

If the input data can match one or more patterns, you can use the vertical bar to separate elements. For example, \w+|s{1} means that the input data must contain one or more word characters or a single whitespace character.

To create groups of elements, you use parentheses. Then, you can apply quantifiers to the entire group or you can separate groups with a vertical bar. For example, (AB)|(SB) specifies that the input characters must be either AB or SB. And (\d{3}-)? Specifies that the input characters must contain zero or one occurrence of a three-digit number followed by a hyphen.

To help you understand how you can use each of these elements, this figure presents several examples. If you study them, you'll quickly see the complex patterns you can provide using these basic elements.

Common regular expression elements

Element	Description
Ordinary character	Matches any character other than ., $, ^, [, {, (, |,), *, +, ?, or \.
\	Matches the character that follows.
\d	Matches any decimal digit (0-9)
\D	Matches any character other than a decimal digit.
\w	Matches any word character (a-z, A-Z, and 0-9).
\W	Matches any character other than a word character.
\s	Matches any white space character (space, tab, new line, etc.).
\S	Matches any character other than a whitespace character.
[abcd]	Matches any character included between the brackets.
[^abcd]	Matches any character that is not included between the brackets.
[a-z]	Matches any characters in the indicated range.
{n}	Matches exactly *n* occurrences of the preceding element or group.
{n,}	Matches at least *n* occurrences of the preceding element or group.
{n,m}	Matches at least *n* but no more than *m* occurrences of the preceding element or group.
*	Matches zero or more occurrences of the preceding element.
?	Matches zero or one occurrence of the preceding element.
+	Matches one or more occurrences of the preceding element.
		Matches any of the elements separated by the vertical bar.
( )	Groups the elements that appear between the parentheses.

Examples of regular expressions

Expression	Example	Description
\d{3}	289	A three digit number.
\w{8,20}	Frankenstein	At least eight but no more than twenty word characters.
\d{2}-\d{4}	10-3944	A two-digit number followed by a hyphen and a four-digit number.
\w{1,8}.\w{1,3}	freddy.jpg	Up to eight letters or numbers, followed by a period and up to three letters or numbers.
(AB)|(SB)-\d{1,5}	SB-3276	The letters AB or SB, followed by a hyphen and a one- to five-digit number.
\d{5}(-\d{4})?	93711-2765	A five-digit number, optionally followed by a hyphen and a four-digit number.
\w*\d\w*	arm01	A text entry that contains at least one numeral.
[xyz]\d{3}	x023	The letter x, y, or z, followed by a three-digit number.

Notes

- A regular expression can include elements other than those shown above. For more information, see the *Regular Expression Language Elements* topic in online help.
- The standard expressions provided by the Regular Expression Editor use only the elements shown above.

Figure 8-11   How to create your own regular expressions

How to use a custom validator

If none of the other validators provide the data validation your program requires, you can use a *custom validator*. Then, you can code your own validation routine that's executed when the page is submitted to the server. This technique is frequently used to validate input data that requires a database lookup.

Figure 8-12 shows how you use a custom validator. In this example, a custom validator is used to check that a value entered by the user is a valid product code in a table of products. To do that, the program includes an event handler for the ServerValidate event of the custom validator. This event occurs whenever validation is performed on the server.

When the ServerValidate event occurs, the event handler receives an argument named args that you can use to validate the data that the user entered. The Value property of this argument contains the input value. Then, the event handler performs the tests that are necessary to determine if this value is valid. In the example in this figure, the event handler calls a method of the HalloweenDB class named CheckProductCode. Although you can't see the code for this method here, you can imagine that it tries to retrieve the row with the specified product code to see if it exists. If it does exist, it returns a value of True. Otherwise, it returns a value of False. In either case, the returned value is assigned to the IsValid property of the args argument. Then, if this property is set to False, the error message specified by the custom validator is displayed.

HTML for a text box and a custom validator

```
Product code: 
<asp:TextBox id="txtProductCode" runat="server" Width="100px">
</asp:TextBox> 
<asp:CustomValidator id="valProductCode" runat="server"
    ControlToValidate="txtProductCode"
    ErrorMessage="Invalid Product Code.">
</asp:CustomValidator>
```

Visual Basic code for the custom validator

```
Private Sub valProductCode_ServerValidate(ByVal source As System.Object, _
    ByVal args As System.Web.UI.WebControls.ServerValidateEventArgs) _
    Handles valProductCode.ServerValidate
    args.IsValid = HalloweenDB.CheckProductCode(args.Value)
End Sub
```

Properties of the ServerValidateEventArgs class

Property	Description
Value	The text string to be validated.
IsValid	A Boolean property that you set to True if the value passes the validation test or to False otherwise.

Description

- You can use a *custom validator* to validate input data using the validation tests you specify.

- You code the validation tests within an event handler for the ServerValidate event of the custom validator. This event is raised whenever validation is performed on the server. Because of that, the form must be submitted before the validation can be done.

- You can use the properties of the args argument that's passed to the ServerValidate event handler to test the input data (args.value) and indicate whether the data passed the validation test (args.IsValid). If you set the IsValid property of the args argument to False, the error message you specified for the custom validator is displayed.

- If the user doesn't enter a value into the associated input control, the custom validator doesn't perform its validation test. As a result, you should also provide a required field validator if a value is required.

Figure 8-12   How to use a custom validator

A validation routine that validates credit card numbers

To give you a better idea of what you can do with a custom validator, figure 8-13 shows the Visual Basic code for a custom validator that validates credit card numbers. To do that, it checks that the credit card number meets a mod-10 algorithm that all credit card numbers adhere to. This test often catches simple typographic errors before taking the time to actually authorize the card. Please note that this test doesn't establish that an account with the specified number exists or that credit is available on the account. It merely establishes that the number meets the required mod-10 algorithm.

To validate a credit card number, the event handler for the ServerValidate event calls a procedure named ValidateCreditCard and passes the card number to it. Then, after this procedure declares three variables, it removes any spaces in the card number using the Replace method of the String class, and it reverses the digits in the number using the StrReverse function. Next, it uses a For Next loop to double the digits in even-numbered positions. To determine if a digit is in an even-numbered position, it uses the Mod operator to divide the position by 2 to see if there's a remainder. If not, it multiplies the number in that position by 2 and then concatenates it to the variable named sDigits. (Note that because the Substring method that gets the number returns a string, it's coded within a CType function so that an integer value is returned.) Otherwise, it just concatenates the number.

After the digits in the even-numbered positions have been multiplied, the procedure uses another For Next loop to add up all the digits. (Again, a CType function is used to convert the result of the Substring method to an integer.) The Mod operator is then used to determine if the result is evenly divisible by 10. If so, the credit card number is valid and a True value is returned to the calling procedure. Otherwise, a False value is returned and the error message associated with the custom validator is displayed.

Visual Basic code for a credit card validator

```
Private Sub valCreditCardNumber_ServerValidate( _
        ByVal source As System.Object, _
        ByVal args As System.Web.UI.WebControls.ServerValidateEventArgs) _
        Handles valCreditCardNumber.ServerValidate
    args.IsValid = ValidateCreditCard(args.Value)
End Sub

Private Function ValidateCreditCard(ByVal CardNumber As String) As Boolean
    Dim iDigitSum As Integer
    Dim sDigits As String
    Dim i As Integer
    'Remove spaces and reverse string
    CardNumber = StrReverse(CardNumber.Replace(" ", Nothing))
    'Double the digits in even-numbered positions
    For i = 0 To CardNumber.Length - 1
        If (i + 1) Mod 2 = 0 Then
            sDigits &= CType(CardNumber.Substring(i, 1), Integer) * 2
        Else
            sDigits &= CardNumber.Substring(i, 1)
        End If
    Next
    'Add the digits
    For i = 0 To sDigits.Length - 1
        iDigitSum += CType(sDigits.Substring(i, 1), Integer)
    Next
    'Check that the sum is divisible by 10
    If iDigitSum Mod 10 = 0 Then
        Return True
    Else
        Return False
    End If
End Function
```

What the mod 10 validation algorithm does

1. Removes any spaces from the number.
2. Reverses the number.
3. Doubles the digits in even-numbered positions. If the original digit is 5 or greater, this will insert an additional digit into the number.
4. Add up the individual digits.
5. Divide the result by 10. If the remainder is 0, the credit card number is valid.

Description

- This code can be used along with a custom validator to ensure that the user enters a credit card number that passes a standard mod-10 algorithm used for all credit card numbers. If the credit card number passes this algorithm, the program would probably continue by checking with the bank to make sure that the account is valid and that the customer has available credit.

- The ServerValidate event handler for the custom validator calls a function named ValidateCreditCard and passes the credit card number entered by the user. This function returns a Boolean value that indicates whether the credit card is valid.

Figure 8-13   A validation routine that validates credit card numbers

Perspective

Now that you've completed this chapter, you should be able to create web forms that provide for a variety of data validation. Keep in mind, though, that after you add validators to a form, you need to test them thoroughly to be sure they detect all invalid entries. Although that can be time-consuming, particularly if you use regular expression validators that require complicated expressions or custom validators that require complicated validation routines, it's an essential part of developing professional web applications.

Terms

validation control
validator
DHTML (Dynamic HTML)
required field validator
compare validator
range validator
validation summary control
regular expression validator
regular expression
escape character
character class
word character
whitespace character
quantifier
custom validator

9

How to manage state

One of the most important aspects of developing an ASP.NET application is managing the state of the application. You've seen some of the features ASP.NET provides for managing state in earlier chapters. Specifically, you've learned how ASP.NET uses view state to preserve the values of form control properties, how to use session state to save data across round trips to the browser, and how to use cookies to save data on the user's computer.

Now, in this chapter, you'll learn more about how to use view state and session state. You'll also learn how to manage the state of an application using application state and URLs. When you complete this chapter, you'll have all the skills you need to manage the state of the applications you develop.

Five ways to manage state

In all but the simplest of ASP.NET applications, you need to keep track of the state of an application across round trips to the browser. Figure 9-1 shows five ways you can manage state information. Although programmers have devised other ways to manage state, the techniques listed here are the most common.

View state is an ASP.NET feature that provides for retaining the values of page properties and form control properties that change as the program executes. For example, you can use it to preserve the Text property of label controls or the list of items in a list box or a drop-down list. Many of the applications presented so far in this book have relied on view state, so you should be familiar with its basic operation. Still, there are some details of how view state works and some features it provides that you haven't seen yet. You'll learn about those details and features in this chapter.

ASP.NET uses *session state* to track the state of each user of an application. As you've seen throughout this book, you can also use session state to save application data across round trips to the browser. In this chapter, you'll learn some additional techniques and features for using session state.

Application state is an ASP.NET feature that lets you save state information so it can be shared by all the users of an application. For example, you can use application state to maintain global counters or to maintain a list of the users who are currently logged on to the application. Note that because two or more users can access application state at the same time, threading problems can occur. You'll learn how to avoid these problems later in this chapter.

The data you save in session state and application state is stored on the server. In contrast, *cookies* let you maintain information in a file on the user's computer. That way, the data is maintained across sessions. As you learned in chapter 4, cookies are particularly useful for storing user information that can be used to automatically log the user into an application or to customize what the user sees.

The last state management technique described in this figure is *URL encoding*. With this technique, the state information is stored in a query string that's added to the end of the URL that's used to access a page of your application. Since using query strings is a common state management technique, you've probably seen them used on search sites such as Google (www.google.com) and shopping sites such as Ebay (www.ebay.com) and Amazon (www.amazon.com).

As you learn about the various state management techniques in this chapter, keep in mind that they aren't exclusive of one another. In fact, you'll often use two or more of these techniques to maintain various types of state information for a complicated application. For example, the Halloween Store application you saw in chapter 7 used view state, session state, and cookies. Later in this chapter, you'll see how you can also use application state and URL encoding in this application.

View state

- **How it works:** Maintains the values of page properties and form control properties that are changed by the application across round trips to the browser by saving the data in a hidden form field named _VIEWSTATE. You can also add your own values to view state.
- **Advantage:** Implemented automatically, so no special coding is required. Doesn't require server resources.
- **Disadvantage:** Can increase the amount of data sent to and from the browser. Because view state is enabled for a page and its controls by default, it may be used unnecessarily.

Session state

- **How it works:** Saves a session ID in a session state object on the server. This ID is passed from the server to the browser and back to the server so that the server can associate the browser with an existing session. You can also save your own items in the session state object.
- **Advantage:** Sends only a small amount of information to the browser, so session state doesn't slow response time.
- **Disadvantage:** Uses server memory between round trips, so session state can degrade overall server performance if used excessively.

Application state

- **How it works:** You can save your own items in the application state object that's created when an application begins. Then, those items are available to all users of the application.
- **Advantage:** Easy to implement.
- **Disadvantage:** Can result in threading problems when two or more users attempt to update application state data at the same time.

Cookies

- **How they work:** Data is saved in the browser or in a file on the user's hard disk and is automatically sent to the server as part of the HTTP request.
- **Advantage:** Information can be saved in one session and retrieved in a later session.
- **Disadvantage:** Can be disabled by the end user.

URL encoding

- **How it works:** Data is passed as query strings added to the end of URLs.
- **Advantage:** Efficient for small amounts of data. Doesn't consume server resources.
- **Disadvantage:** The query strings are visible to end users.

Figure 9-1   Five ways to manage state in an ASP.NET application

How to use view state

For the most part, *view state* is automatic. Because of that, you don't have to add any extra code or set any additional properties to enable it. However, it's important for you to understand how view state works, when you should disable it, and how you do that. You should also know how to add your own data to view state in case you ever need to do that.

How view state works

As figure 9-2 shows, view state works by saving data in the HTML stream that's sent to the browser. This data is saved as a hidden input field named _VIEWSTATE. Because the field is hidden, it isn't displayed in the browser. Because the field is an input field, however, it's automatically sent back to the server when the user posts the page.

Although the view state feature is relatively straightforward, it's easy to become confused about what data is actually saved in view state. It's natural to assume that the view state feature is used to preserve the values of input fields such as text boxes across round trips. As you saw in chapter 2, however, those values are sent back to the server automatically when the user posts the form. As a result, they don't depend on view state at all.

What does depend on view state are the form control properties that you set in code. If you populate a list box in code, for example, you'll want to save the list items in view state so that you don't have to populate the control each time the page is executed. As you learned in chapter 2, however, there are some instances where you won't want to save changes you make to property values in view state. In those instances, you'll want to disable view state. You'll learn more about that in the next topic.

If you're interested, you can look at the hidden input field that's used to store view state information when you run an ASP.NET application. To do that, choose the View→Source command from the menu in the browser window when the form is displayed. Then, just look for the Input tag with a Name attribute of _VIEWSTATE. The Value attribute in this tag contains the view state data for the page. As you can see in this figure, however, this data is encrypted so you won't be able to identify any of it.

The hidden __VIEWSTATE field for a web page

```
Order[1] - Notepad

File  Edit  Format  View  Help

<!DOCTYPE HTML PUBLIC "-//W3C//DTD HTML 4.0 Transitional//EN">
<HTML>
        <HEAD>
                <title>order</title>
                <meta content="Microsoft Visual Studio .NET 7.1" name="GENERATOR">
                <meta content="Visual Basic .NET 7.1" name="CODE_LANGUAGE">
                <meta content="JavaScript" name="vs_defaultclientScript">
                <meta content="http://schemas.microsoft.com/intellisense/ie5"
name="vs_targetSchema">
        </HEAD>
        <body>
                <form name="Form1" method="post" action="order.aspx" language="javascript"
onsubmit="ValidatorOnSubmit();" id="Form1">
<input type="hidden" name="__EVENTTARGET" value="" />
<input type="hidden" name="__EVENTARGUMENT" value="" />
<input type="hidden" name="__VIEWSTATE"
value="dDwtMjAwMZQxMTQwODt0PDtsPGk8MT47PjtsPHQ8O2w8aTwzPjtpPDU+O2k8Nz47aTw5PjtpPDExPjs+O2w8dDxU
PHA8cDxsPERhdGFFNZW1iZXI7ZGF0YWJpbmRpbmc7PjtsPGE7CDxsPGk8MTtpPTHvVR1eHRGaWVsZDtEYXRhVmFsdWVGaWVsZDs+O2w8Q2F0ZWdvcmllcztTaG9wdFdpbmU5hbwU
7Q2F0OZWdvcnlJRDs+Pjs+O3Q8aTw0PjtAPENvc3R1bWVyO200lhc2t2O1Byb3BlcnR5O2VuZ04dw1lcztmeDttDttYXNrcz
twcm9wczs+PjtsPGk88MD47PjsPGk8o247dDxwPHA8bDxUZXh0OaGUgbw9zdCBzaGFnFnYWR1bGGdLzlJGd1ZXNoNOIGFOI
HRoaXMgMgeWvhcidzIHBhcnR5LCBiYWJJ5Ljs+Pjs+Ozs+O3Q8dDw7dDxpPDU+OOA8QXvzdGluIFBvd2Vycz<tGcmUa2Vuc3R1
aW47SmFySmFYO01hcnRpYW47U3VwZXtJtYW47PjtAPHBVdzAxICAgIGA7CA7ZnJhhbmtjMDEgIDtgTiDqyXIwMSAgIDs2AgIC8g0d21hcnRpYW4w
wMSA7C3VwZXtJWMSAgIDs+PjtsPGk8MD47dD47dDxpPj70z47dDpwPHPA8bDxbwNZ1hZ2VVVybDs+O2w8sw1hZ2VZd21hcZz
s+Pj8+O3Q8pCDxwPGw8VGV4dDs+O2w8w8JDc5Ljk5Oz4+Ozt47oZ47Pj47Pj5rAznofI3B+ZCbbFvtsevboifE" />

<script language="javascript">
<!--

        function __doPostBack(eventTarget, eventArgument) {
                var theform;
                if (window.navigator.appName.toLowerCase().indexOf("netscape") > -1) {
                        theform = document.forms["Form1"];
                }
                else {
                        theform = document.Form1;
                }
```

Concepts

- Before ASP.NET sends a page back to the client, it determines what changes the program has made to the properties of the page and each control on the page. These changes are encoded into a string that's assigned to the value of a hidden input field named __VIEWSTATE.

- When the page is displayed in the user's browser, the __VIEWSTATE field isn't visible because it's a hidden field. You can display this field along with the other source code for the web page by choosing View➔Source from the browser's menu.

- When the page is posted back to the server, the __VIEWSTATE field is sent back to the server along with the HTTP request. Then, ASP.NET retrieves the property values from the __VIEWSTATE field and uses them to restore the page and control properties.

- ASP.NET also uses view state to save the values of the page properties it uses, such as IsPostBack.

Note

- View state is not used to preserve data entered by a user into a text box or any other input control. That's because this data is sent back to the server automatically as part of the HTTP request.

Figure 9-2   How view state works

When and how to disable view state

By default, view state is enabled for each control you add to a form. In many cases, that's what you want. Then, if you change a property of a control in code, that property will automatically be saved in view state and restored the next time the page is executed. In some cases, though, you'll want to disable view state to minimize the amount of data that's sent back and forth between the server and the browser. Figure 9-3 gives you some guidelines for when to do that.

First, you should disable view state for a control if you want its initial property values to be restored each time the page that contains the control is loaded. For example, suppose the initial value of the Text property of a label is an empty string. Then, suppose that property is changed so that it displays a message to the user when a particular operation is performed. If you don't want that message to remain on the page after the next operation, you should disable view state for the control so its initial value is restored.

Second, you should disable view state for a control if you assign values to one or more of its properties each time the page that contains the control is loaded. For example, suppose that the Enabled property of a button is set to either True or False each time the page is loaded. In that case, you can disable view state for the button because the value of its Enabled property is always sent as part of the HTML for the page.

Third, you should disable view state for an entire page if you change properties in code but the page never posts back to itself. To illustrate, consider a page that contains a series of links that let the user display information about the products in the Halloween database. One link is created in code for each product, and each link causes another page to be displayed with information about the selected product. Because this page always displays another page, you can disable view state for the page. That way, any properties that are set in code aren't saved in view state unnecessarily.

To disable view state for a control, you simply set its EnableViewState property to False. Similarly, you can disable view state for an entire page by setting the form's EnableViewState property to False. Then, view state is disabled for all of the controls the form contains.

To determine how a page is using view state, you can enable the ASP.NET Trace feature as described in chapter 5. Then, when the page is displayed, you can look at the Control Tree section of the trace output to see which controls are using view state and how many bytes they're using. In this figure, for example, you can see the Control Tree section for the Order page of the Halloween Store application from chapter 8. Here, you can see that 24 bytes of view state are used to store page properties (_PAGE). In addition, 216 bytes are used to store data for the drop-down list that contains the categories because its list is populated in code; 104 bytes are used to store data for the label that displays the product description since its Text property is assigned in code; and so on.

Trace output that shows the view state used by a page and its controls

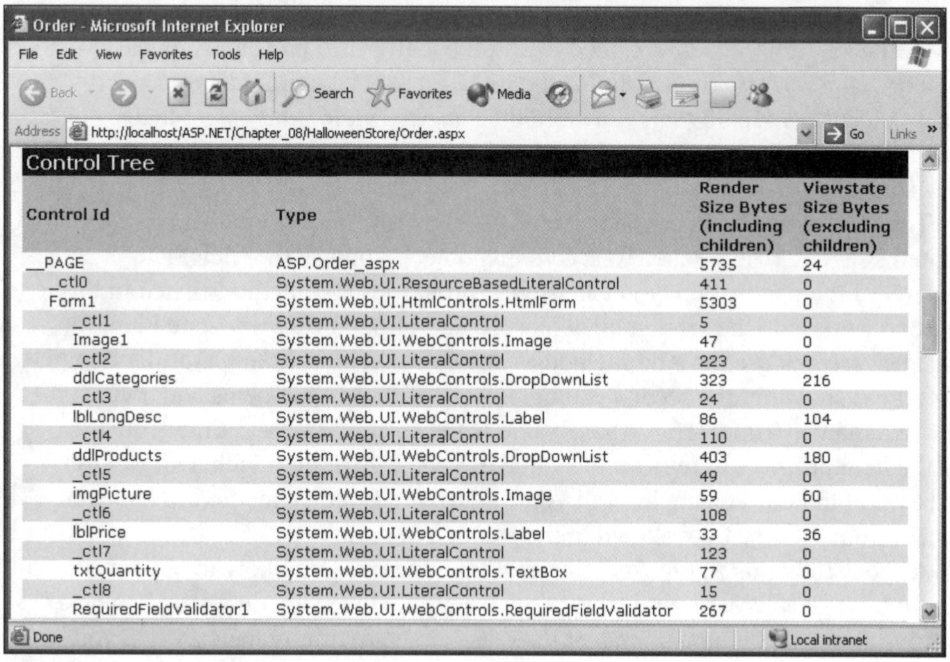

When to disable view state

- You can disable view state for a control if you change the value of a control property in code, but you want the initial value of that property to be restored the next time the page is loaded.

- You can disable view state for a control if you assign a value to a control property each time the page is loaded.

- If more than one property of a control is changed in code, you should disable view state for the control only if none of the properties need to be saved in view state.

- You can disable view state for a page if you change the value of one or more properties in code but the page never posts back to itself.

How to determine the size of view state

- Enable the Trace feature for the page by setting the Trace attribute of the Page directive for the page to True as described in chapter 5.

- Scroll down to the Control Tree section of the trace output to see the number of bytes of view state used by the page and its controls.

How to disable view state

- View state is enabled by default for all Web Server controls. To disable view state for a control, set the control's EnableViewState property to False.

- To disable view state for an entire page, set the EnableViewState property of the page to False. Then, view state is disabled for all the controls on the page.

Figure 9-3   When and how to disable view state

How to work with data in view state

Although view state is designed to automatically save page and control property values across round trips to the browser, you can also add your own data to view state. To do that, you store the data in a *view state object* that's created from the StateBag class. Figure 9-4 shows you how to work with the view state object.

The view state object contains a collection of key/value pairs that represent the items saved in view state. To access this object, you use the ViewState property of the page. Then, you can use the properties and methods listed in this figure to work with the view state object. To add or update a view state item, for example, you can use the Add method as shown in the first example or the Item property as shown in the second example. Both of these statements add a view state item named TimeStamp whose value is the current date and time. You also use the Item property to retrieve the value of a view state item with a given key as shown in the third example. And you can use the Remove method to remove an item from view state as shown in the fourth example.

As you study this figure, keep in mind that you're more likely to use session state to save data across round trips to the browser. However, view state can be a useful way to save small amounts of data, and it's particularly handy when you want to associate the data with a specific page. You'll see an example like that in chapter 19. For now, just realize that you won't typically use view state to store your own data.

Common properties and methods of the StateBag class

Property	Description
Item(name)	The value of the view state item with the specified name. If you set the value of an item that doesn't exist, that item is created. (Item is the default property of the StateBag class, so you can omit it when you access a view state item.)
Count	The number of items in the view state collection.
Keys	A collection of keys for all of the items in the view state collection.
Values	A collection of values for all of the items in the view state collection.

Method	Description
Add(name, value)	Adds an item to the view state collection. If the item you name already exists, its value is updated.
Clear	Removes all items from the view state collection.
Remove(name)	Removes the item with the specified name from the view state collection.

A statement that adds or updates a view state item

```
ViewState.Add("TimeStamp", Now())
```

Another way to add or update a view state item

```
ViewState("TimeStamp") = Now()
```

A statement that retrieves the value of a view state item

```
dtTimeStamp = ViewState("TimeStamp")
```

A statement that removes an item from view state

```
ViewState.Remove("TimeStamp")
```

Description

- View state is implemented using a *view state object* that's defined by the StateBag class. This class defines a collection of view state items.
- Although the form control properties are automatically saved in view state, you can also save other data in view state.
- To access the view state object for a page, you use the ViewState property of the page.

Figure 9-4　How to work with data in view state

How to use session state

In chapter 3, you learned some basic skills for using session state to save data across round trips to the browser. The topics that follow review and expand on that information.

How to work with data in session state

As you know, ASP.NET uses *session state* to track the state of each user of an application. To do that, it creates a *session state object* that contains a unique session ID for each user's session. The session ID is passed back to the browser as part of the response and then returned to the server with the next request. ASP.NET can then use the session ID to get the session state object associated with the request.

To take advantage of session state, you can store data in the session state object. Figure 9-5 shows you how to do that. Since you've already seen how session state is used in the Halloween Store application, you shouldn't have any trouble understanding the first three examples. The first one adds or updates an item named EMail to session state. The second one retrieves the value of the EMail item. And the third one removes the EMail item from session state.

All three of these examples assume that session state is being accessed from within a web form. In that case, you refer to the session state object using the Session property of the page. To access session state from outside of a web form, however, you use the Session property of the HttpContext object for the current request as illustrated in the fourth example.

This figure also lists three typical uses for session state. I described these uses and gave an example of each in chapter 3. You've also seen how session state is used by the Halloween Store application. With that as background, you shouldn't have any trouble understanding when you might use session state.

Common properties and methods of the HttpSessionState class

Property	Description
SessionID	The unique ID of the session.
Item(name)	The value of the session state item with the specified name. If you set the value of an item that doesn't exist, that item is created.
Count	The number of items in the session state collection.

Method	Description
Add(name, value)	Adds an item to the session state collection. If the item you name already exists, its value is updated.
Clear	Removes all items from the session state collection.
Remove(name)	Removes the item with the specified name from the session state collection.

A statement that adds or updates a session state item

```
Session("EMail") = sEmail
```

A statement that retrieves the value of a session state item

```
sEmail = Session("EMail")
```

A statement that removes an item from session state

```
Session.Remove("EMail")
```

A statement that retrieves the value of a session state item from a class that doesn't inherit System.Web.UI.Page

```
sEmail = HttpContext.Current.Session("EMail")
```

Typical uses for session state

- **To keep information about the user**, such as the user's name or whether the user has registered.
- **To save objects the user is working with**, such as a shopping cart or a customer record.
- **To keep track of pending operations**, such as what steps the user has completed while placing an order.

Description

- ASP.NET uses *session state* to track the state of each user of an application. To do that, it creates a *session state object* that contains a session ID. The session ID is passed to the browser and then back to the server with the next request so the server can identify the session associated with that request.
- You can also use the session state object to store and retrieve items across round trips to the browser. To work with the data in session state, you use the HttpSessionState class, which defines a collection of session state items.
- To access the session state object from the code-behind file for a web form, use the Session property of the page. To access the session state object from a class other than the code-behind file for a web form, use the Session property of the HttpContext object for the current request.

Figure 9-5 How to work with data in session state

When to save and retrieve session state items

Many ASP.NET applications use session state in a predictable way during each execution of the application. First, the application retrieves data from session state and stores it in module-level variables. Then, the application uses these variables when it processes the user interface events raised by the user. Finally, the application saves the updated variables back to session state so they can be retrieved the next time the page is posted back to the server.

If an item in session state is used within a single procedure in an application, you can retrieve, process, and save that item within that procedure. However, it's common for an application to use a session state item in two or more procedures. Because of that, it makes sense to retrieve the item when the application first starts and save it just before it ends. To do that, you can use the Load and PreRender events as illustrated in figure 9-6.

The example in this figure illustrates how this works. This program consists of a single page that contains a Post button that the user can click to post the page back to the server. Each time the user clicks this button, the program code updates the label on the page to indicate how many times the button has been clicked.

To implement this program, a session state item named Count is used to maintain a count of the number of times the user clicks the Post button. To do that, the Load event procedure starts by checking if this session state item exists. If not, it means that the page is being requested for the first time, and a value of zero is assigned to a module-level variable named iCount. If the Count item already exists, however, it means that the user clicked the Post button to post the page back to the server. In that case, the value of the Count session state item is retrieved and assigned to the iCount variable.

If the user clicked the Post button, the program continues by executing the code in the event procedure for the Click event of that button. This procedure adds one to the iCount variable and updates the label on the form to indicate how many times the button has been clicked.

Just before ASP.NET generates the HTML for the page, the code in the PreRender event procedure is executed. This procedure saves the value of the iCount variable to session state so it's available the next time the user clicks the Post button. Note that because PreRender is a page event, it's raised each time the page is executed just like the Load event.

It's important to note that the variable that's used to store the value of the session state item in this example is a value-type variable. That means that the value is actually stored in the variable. Because of that, you have to explicitly update the session state item with this value as shown here.

In contrast, if you use a reference-type variable such as a string or other object variable, the session state item is updated automatically when you update the variable that refers to it. That's because the variable contains a pointer to the object, not the data itself. As a result, you don't have to update the session state item explicitly.

The Counter application displayed in a browser

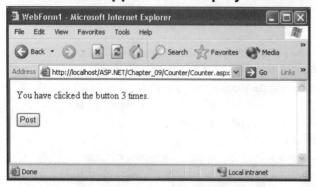

The code for the Counter application

```
Dim iCount As Integer

Private Sub Page_Load(ByVal sender As System.Object, _
        ByVal e As System.EventArgs) Handles MyBase.Load
    'Put user code to initialize the page here
    If Session("Count") Is Nothing Then
        iCount = 0
    Else
        iCount = Session("Count")
    End If
End Sub

Private Sub btnPost_Click(ByVal sender As System.Object, _
        ByVal e As System.EventArgs) Handles btnPost.Click
    iCount += 1
    lblMessage.Text = "You have clicked the button " & iCount & " times."
End Sub

Private Sub Page_PreRender(ByVal sender As Object, _
        ByVal e As System.EventArgs) Handles MyBase.PreRender
    Session("Count") = iCount
End Sub
```

Description

- If a session state item is accessed from two or more event handlers in an application, it's common to structure the application so it retrieves the value of that item in the Load event handler and then saves the updated value back to session state in the PreRender event handler.

- The Load event handler is raised before any of the control events for the page are processed. That way, if you retrieve a session state item in this procedure, it's available to whatever control event is raised.

- The PreRender event is raised after all the control events for the page have been processed, but before ASP.NET begins to generate the HTML that will be sent back to the browser.

- You only need to update a session state item explicitly if it's stored in a value-type variable. If it's stored in a reference-type variable, the session state item is updated automatically when the variable is updated.

Figure 9-6   When to save and retrieve session state items

Options for storing session state and tracking the session ID

By default, ASP.NET stores session state data in server memory and tracks user sessions using cookies. As figure 9-7 shows, however, ASP.NET actually provides three options for storing session state data and two options for tracking user sessions. Although you'll typically use the default options, you should be familiar with the other options in case you ever need to use them. You'll learn how to change these options in the next figure.

The default setting for storing session state data is called *In-process mode*. When you use this mode, session state data is stored in server memory within the same process that your ASP.NET application runs. This is the most efficient way to store session state data, but it only works for applications that are hosted on a single web server.

If your application has so many users that a single web server can't carry the load, you can deploy the application on two or more servers. When you do that, you need to store session state in a location that can be accessed by all of the servers that host the application. Session state provides two options for doing that: State Server mode and SQL Server mode.

State Server mode stores session state data in server memory, but not in the same process as your application. Instead, session state is managed by a separate service that can be accessed by all of the servers that host the application. To understand why this is necessary, you need to realize that when two or more servers host an application, a different server can process the application each time it's executed. So if the session state data was stored on the server that processed the application the first time it was executed, that data wouldn't be available if the application was processed by another server the next time it was executed.

Another way to make session state data available to two or more servers is to use *SQL Server mode*. With this mode, session state data is stored in a SQL Server database rather than in server memory. Although this is the slowest of the three session state modes, it's also the most reliable. That's because if your web server goes down, the session state data will be maintained in the database. In contrast, session state data is lost if the server goes down when you're using In-process or State Server mode. So if reliability is your main concern, you should use SQL Server mode to save session state data.

Fortunately, the programming requirements for all three session state modes are identical. So you can change an application from one mode to another without changing any of the application's code.

You already know that, by default, ASP.NET maintains session state by sending the session ID for a user session to the browser as a cookie. Then, the cookie is returned to the server with the next request so that the server can associate the browser with the session. This is the most reliable and secure way to track sessions. This is *cookie-based session tracking*.

If a user has disabled cookies, however, session state won't work unless you switch to *cookieless session tracking*. Cookieless session tracking works by

Three options for storing session state data

- **In-process mode** (the default) stores session state data in IIS server memory in the same process as the ASP.NET application. It is the most commonly used session state model, but it's suitable only when a single server is used for the application.

- **State Server mode** stores session state data in server memory under the control of a separate service called aspnet_state. The session state service can be accessed by other IIS servers, so it's better than In-process mode when the application is hosted on a web farm that consists of more than one IIS server. In that case, each request for the application can be processed by a different server, so the session state information must be available to all the servers.

- **SQL Server mode** stores session state data in a SQL Server database. Like State Server mode, SQL Server mode is used for applications that require more than one IIS server. It's the slowest of the three storage modes, but it's also the most reliable. As a result, you should use SQL Server mode when reliability is critical.

Two options for tracking the session ID

- By default, ASP.NET uses cookies to keep track of user sessions. However, if the user has disabled cookies, *cookie-based session tracking* won't work.

- With *cookieless session tracking*, the session ID is encoded as part of the URL. As a result, cookieless session state works whether or not the browser allows cookies.

Description

- The programming requirements for all three session state modes are identical, so you don't have to recode the application if you change the mode.

- Cookieless session tracking introduces security risks because the session ID is visible to the user. It also limits the way URL's can be specified in Response.Redirect and Server.Transfer method calls. For these reasons, most developers don't use cookieless sessions. Instead, they inform the user that cookies must be enabled to use the application.

- You can control where session state data is stored and how the session ID is tracked by setting attributes of the <sessionState> element in the application's Web.config file. For more information, see figure 9-8.

Figure 9-7   Options for storing session state data and tracking the session ID

adding the session ID to the URL that's used to request the ASP.NET page. Unfortunately, because the URL is visible to the user and isn't encrypted, the use of cookieless session tracking creates a security risk.

Ideally, ASP.NET would use cookies to track session ID's unless the user's browser didn't support cookies. Then, it would automatically switch to cookieless session tracking for that user. Unfortunately, that's not how it works. Instead, you must choose whether or not to use cookies to track session IDs on an application-wide basis.

Because of the security risk involved, I recommend you use cookieless session tracking only if you must support users who have disabled cookies. Otherwise, you can use cookie-based session tracking and then notify your users that they must enable cookies to use your application.

How to set session state options

Every ASP.NET application includes a configuration file named Web.config that resides in the application's root folder. This file is generated by Visual Studio when you create a new project. Figure 9-8 shows how you can edit this file to change various options for an application, including the session state options I described in figure 9-7. Note that although Web.config is an XML file, you shouldn't have trouble editing it even if you aren't familiar with the details of XML syntax.

To edit the Web.config file, just double-click on it in the Solution Explorer to display it in a Code Editor window. Then, scroll down through the file until you find the <sessionState> element. This element contains a mode attribute that lets you specify the mode to use for session state and a cookieless attribute that lets you specify whether or not cookies are used to maintain session state. Note that if you use State Server mode, you'll need to set the stateConnectionString attribute to the IP address and port number of the server that hosts the session state service. Similarly, if you use SQL Server mode, you'll need to set the sqlConnectionString attribute to the connection string for the SQL Server database that is used to store the session state data.

Attributes of the Web.config file's <sessionState> element

Attribute	Description
mode	The session state mode. Values can be Off, InProc, StateServer, or SQLServer.
cookieless	Specifies whether cookieless sessions are used. The default is False.
timeout	The number of minutes a session should be maintained without any user activity. After the specified number of minutes, the session is deleted. The default is 20.
stateConnectionString	The IP address and port number of the server that runs the aspnet_state process. This attribute is required when State Server mode is used.
sqlConnectionString	A database connection string for the SQL Server database that's used to store the session state data. This attribute is required when SQL Server mode is used.

The <sessionState> element in the Web.config file

```
<?xml version="1.0" encoding="utf-8" ?>
<configuration>

  <system.web>
    .
    .
    .
    <!--   SESSION STATE SETTINGS
           By default ASP.NET uses cookies to identify which requests belong to a
           particular session. If cookies are not available, a session can be
           tracked by adding a session identifier to the URL. To disable cookies,
           set sessionState cookieless="true".
    -->
    <sessionState
           mode="InProc"
           stateConnectionString="tcpip=127.0.0.1:42424"
           sqlConnectionString="data source=127.0.0.1;Trusted_Connection=yes"
           cookieless="false"
           timeout="20"
    />
    .
    .
    .
  </system.web>
</configuration>
```

Description

- The Web.config file contains settings that affect how an ASP.NET web application operates. When you create an ASP.NET web application, Visual Studio generates a Web.config file with default settings.

- To change the options for session state, you change the values that are assigned to the attributes for the <sessionState> element of the Web.config file.

Figure 9-8   How to set session state options

How to use application state

In contrast to session state, which stores data for a single user session, application state lets you store data that is shared by all users of an application. In the topics that follow, you'll learn some basic concepts about ASP.NET applications and application state. You'll also learn how to store and retrieve application state data and how to use an ASP.NET application file named Global.asax to work with application events.

ASP.NET application concepts

Figure 9-9 presents some basic concepts related to ASP.NET applications that you need to understand before you learn how to use application state. To start, an *application* is made up of all the pages, code, and other files that are located under a single virtual directory in an IIS web server. When you create a Visual Studio project, Visual Studio automatically creates a virtual directory for the application and stores all of the application's files in that folder. As a result, you don't have to create the virtual directory yourself unless you move the application to a different web server. Then, you can use the Internet Information Services program as described in figure A-5 of appendix A to create a virtual directory from the folder that contains the application.

The first time a user requests a page that resides in an application's virtual directory, ASP.NET initializes the application. During that process, ASP.NET creates an *application object* from the HttpApplication class. The application object is represented in an ASP.NET project by a special class file named Global.asax. You'll learn how to work with this file in figure 9-11.

The application object represents the entire application and can be accessed by any of the application's pages executed on behalf of any user. This object exists until the application ends, which normally doesn't happen until IIS shuts down. However, the application is automatically restarted each time you rebuild the project or edit the application's Web.config file.

Application state concepts

Figure 9-9 also presents the basic *application state* concepts. Each time it starts an application, ASP.NET creates an *application state object* from the HttpApplicationState class. You can use this object to store data in server memory that can be accessed by any page executed on behalf of any user of the application.

One common use for application state is to store hit counters that track how many times users have retrieved specific pages. This is similar to the counter you saw back in figure 9-6 that tracked the number of times a user clicked a submit button on a page. Because this counter was stored in session state, however, it tracked the count for a single user. When you use application state, you can track the count for all users of an application.

ASP.NET application concepts

- An ASP.NET *application* is the collection of pages, code, and other files within a single virtual directory on an IIS web server. In most cases, an ASP.NET application corresponds to a single Visual Studio web project.

- Visual Studio sets up a virtual directory automatically when you create a project, so you don't have to create it manually unless you want to deploy the application to another server.

How applications begin and end

- An application begins when the first user requests a page that's a part of the application. When that happens, ASP.NET initializes the application before it processes the request for the page.

- As part of its initialization, ASP.NET creates an *application object* from the HttpApplication class. This object exists for the duration of the application. You can access this object via the Global.asax file, as described in figure 9-11.

- Once an application has started, it doesn't normally end until the IIS server is shut down. If you rebuild the project or edit the Web.config file, however, the application will be restarted the next time a user requests a page that's part of the application.

Application state concepts

- ASP.NET creates an *application state object* for each application from the HttpApplicationState class.

- You can store program items in *application state*. Then, those items are available to all users of the application.

Typical uses for application state

- **To store page hit counters** and other statistical data.
- **To store global application data** such as discount terms and tax rates.
- **To track users currently visiting the site** by keeping a list of user names or other identifying data.

Note

- Application state is similar to another ASP.NET feature, called data caching. Data caching is typically used for read-only data retrieved from a database. You'll learn about data caching in chapter 12.

Figure 9-9   An introduction to applications and application state

Another common use for application state is to store application-specific data, such as discount terms and tax rates for an ordering system. Although you could retrieve this type of information from a database each time it's needed, it sometimes makes sense to retrieve it just once when the application starts and then store it in application state. That way, the data is more readily accessible as the application executes.

Finally, application state is commonly used to keep track of which users are logged on to the application. That's particularly useful for applications that provide chat rooms or message boards where you can communicate with other users. Then, the application can display a list of the users who are currently in the chat room or who are using the message board.

How to work with data in application state

Figure 9-10 presents the details of working with application state data. As you can see from the first three examples, the techniques you use to add items to and retrieve items from application state are similar to the techniques you use to work with items in session state. The main difference is that you use the Application property of the page to access the application state object from a code-behind file, and you use the Application property of the HttpContext object for the current request to access the application state object from a class other than a code-behind file.

Because two or more users can access the data in application state at the same time, you'll want to lock the application state object if you intend to modify any of the data it contains. This is illustrated in the last example in this figure. The code in this example increments an application state item named InvoiceNumber by one. Notice that the application state object is locked before the InvoiceNumber item is retrieved. That way, another user can't update this item after you've retrieved it. After the item is updated, the application state object is unlocked. To minimize the length of time the application state object is locked, you should do as little processing as possible between the Lock and Unlock methods.

Common properties and methods of the HttpApplicationState class

Property	Description
Item(name)	The value of the application state item with the specified name. (Item is the default property of the HttpApplicationState class, so you can omit it when you access an application state item.)
Count	The number of items in the application state collection.

Method	Description
Add(name, value)	Adds an item to the application state collection.
Clear()	Removes all items from the application state collection.
Remove(name)	Removes the item with the specified name from the application state collection.
Lock()	Locks the application state collection so only the current user can access it.
Unlock()	Unlocks the application state collection so other users can access it.

A statement that adds an item to application state

```
Application.Add("InvoiceNumber", 0)
```

A statement that retrieves an item from application state

```
iInvoiceNumber = Application("InvoiceNumber")
```

A statement that retrieves the value of an application state item from a class that doesn't inherit System.Web.UI.Page

```
iInvoiceNumber = HttpContext.Current.Application("InvoiceNumber")
```

Code that locks application state while retrieving and updating an item

```
Application.Lock()
Dim iInvoiceNumber As Integer = Application("InvoiceNumber")
iInvoiceNumber += 1
Application("InvoiceNumber") = iInvoiceNumber
Application.Unlock()
```

Description

- You can use the application state object that ASP.NET creates for an application to store items that are common to all users of the application.

- To access the application state object from the code-behind file for an ASP.NET web form, use the Application property of the page.

- To access the application state object from a class other than the code-behind file for a web form, use the Current property of the HttpContext class to get the HttpContext object for the current request. Then, use the Application property of this object to get the application state object.

- Before you retrieve the value of an application state variable that you intend to modify, you should lock the application state object so that other users don't attempt to modify the application state data at the same time. As soon as you finish modifying the application state data, you should release the application state object so that other users can access it.

- Application state objects are maintained in server memory. As a result, you should avoid storing large items in application state.

Figure 9-10   How to work with data in application state

How to work with application events

Now that you know how to work with data in application state, you may be wondering how you initialize the values of application state items when an application starts. To do that, you use the event handler for the Start event of the application as illustrated in figure 9-11. In the code shown in this figure, for example, an application state item named HitCount is created and given an initial value of zero.

Notice in this example that the Application_Start event handler is included in a class file named Global. This class inherits the System.Web.Http-Application class that defines the properties, methods, and events that are available to an ASP.NET application. In essence, the Global object that's created from the Global class when an application starts represents the application itself. To refer to the application state object from this class, you use the Application property of the application object as shown here.

If you look in the Solution Explorer, you'll find the Global class file listed as Global.asax. To work with this file, you simply open it in a Code Editor window. When you do, you'll see that it contains Sub and End Sub statements for several application-wide events. Four of those events are listed in this figure.

As you've already seen, you can use the Application_Start event to initialize the values of application state items when an application starts. If the initial values are retrieved from a file or database, you can use the Application_End event to save data back to a file or database when ASP.NET terminates the application. That way, the application state data is maintained between the time the application ends and starts again.

Two other application events you might use are Session_Start and Session_End. These events occur each time a user session for the application starts and ends. You might use the Session_Start event to initialize the values of session state items or to determine if the user is authorized to use the application. You might also use it to update application state items. You'll see an example of that later in this chapter. You might use the Session_End event to free resources held by the user during the session or to log the user off.

Before I go on, you should realize that you can display the Global.asax file in design view as well as in code view. You can use design view to add components to the file, such as data components that let you retrieve data from a database. In most cases, though, you won't add components to the Global.asax file.

Four common application events

Event	Description
Application_Start	This event is raised when the first page of an application is requested by any user. It is often used to initialize the values of application state items.
Application_End	This event is raised when an application is about to terminate. It can be used to write the values of critical application state items to a database or file.
Session_Start	This event is raised when a user session begins. It can be used to initialize session state items, update application state items, or authorize user access.
Session_End	This event is raised when a user session is about to terminate. It can be used to free resources held by the user or to log the user off the application.

Code that initializes an application state item when an application starts

```
Imports System.Web
Imports System.Web.SessionState

Public Class Global
    Inherits System.Web.HttpApplication

    Sub Application_Start(ByVal sender As Object, ByVal e As EventArgs)
        ' Fires when the application is started
        Application.Add("HitCount", 0)
    End Sub
    .
    .
    .
End Class
```

Description

- The Global.asax file is a class file that provides event handlers for application-wide events. This file is generated automatically when you create an ASP.NET application.

- The Global.asax file includes the Sub…End Sub statements for the application-wide events shown above as well as others. As a result, all you have to do to handle an application event is open this file and add code between the correct Sub and End Sub statements.

- To refer to the application state object from the Global.asax file, you use the Application property of the application.

Figure 9-11   How to work with application events

How to access application state when an HttpContext object isn't available

As you know, you can refer to the application state object from a class other than a code-behind file by using the Application property of the HttpContext object for the current request. A complication arises, however, if you want to refer to the application state object from a class property or method that's called from the Global.asax file. That's because the events in the Global.asax file aren't raised in response to an HTTP request and therefore aren't associated with an HttpContext object. However, you can get around this problem using the technique shown in figure 9-12.

In this figure, a class named HitCount contains two methods named Create and Increment that are used to initialize and update the data in an application state item named HitCount and a property named Value that's used to retrieve the value of that item. Notice that the Create method that initializes the HitCount item is called from the Application_Start event of the Global.asax file. Because of that, it can't refer to the application state object using the HttpContext object. Instead, it refers to the application state object using a variable named AppState that's exposed by the Global.asax file.

The Global.asax file exposes this variable by declaring it at the module level as a public shared variable of type HttpApplicationState. Then, in the Application_Start event handler, this variable is set to the application state object using the Application property of the application. As a result, the Create method in the HitCount class can refer to application state using this variable.

Although the Value property and the Increment method in the HitCount class also use the AppState variable, you should realize that they don't have to. That's because they're not called from the Global.asax file. Instead, they would be called in response to a user event that's handled by a web page, which means that they would be executed in the context of an HttpContext object. So, for example, I could have coded the Return statement in the Value property like this:

```
Return HttpContext.Current.Application("HitCount")
```

For consistency, though, I used the AppState variable throughout this class.

A Global.asax file that exposes application state as a property

```
Public Class Global
    Inherits System.Web.HttpApplication

    Public Shared AppState As HttpApplicationState

    Sub Application_Start(ByVal sender As Object, ByVal e As EventArgs)
        ' Fires when the application is started
        AppState = Application
        HitCount.Create()
    End Sub
    .
    .
    .
End Class
```

A HitCount class that accesses application state via the exposed property

```
Public Class HitCount

    Shared Sub Create()
        Global.AppState("HitCount") = 0
    End Sub

    Public Shared ReadOnly Property Value()
        Get
            Return Global.AppState("HitCount")
        End Get
    End Property

    Public Shared Sub Increment()
        Global.AppState("HitCount") += 1
    End Sub

End Class
```

Discussion

- The events in the Global.asax file aren't associated with HTTP requests and therefore aren't associated with an HttpContext object. Because of that, you can't refer to a property or method of another class from the Global.asax file if that property or method uses the HttpContext object to access application state.

- To get around this limitation, you can expose the application state object as a public property of the Global.asax file. Then, class properties and methods that are referred to from Global.asax event procedures can access application state via this public property.

- To expose the application state object as a property of Global.asax, you declare a public shared variable of type HttpApplicationState. Then, you assign the application state object to this variable in the event handler for the Start event of the application.

Note

- Because the Value property and the Increment method in the HitCount class shown above aren't referred to from the Global.asax file, they could use the HttpContext object to access the application state object. For consistency, however, the procedures all use the public property defined in the Global.asax file.

Figure 9-12   How to access application state when an HttpContext object isn't available

The code for the Global.asax file of the Halloween Store application

To illustrate how you might use application state, figure 9-13 presents the Global.asax file for an enhanced version of the Halloween Store application. If you look at the procedure for the Start event of the application, you can see that three items are added to application state when the application starts. These items are retrieved from the Halloween database using methods of the HalloweenDB class.

The GetSalesTax method retrieves the sales tax percent, which is stored in an application state item named SalesTax. As you'll see in the next figure, this item will be used to calculate the sales tax for an order. The GetHitCount method retrieves an integer that contains the total number of times that the application has been started, or "hit," by a user. This value is stored in an application state item named HitCount. Then, each time a user starts a new session, the procedure for the Start event of the session increments this value by 1. Notice that the application state object is locked before this value is incremented so that another user can't update it at the same time. Finally, the GetOrderCount method retrieves an integer that contains the total number of orders that have been placed. You'll see how this value is used by the application in the next figure.

Because the hit count and order count are maintained in the Halloween database, the database must be updated whenever the application ends. To do that, the procedure for the End event of the application executes a method of the HalloweenDB class named UpdateSiteStats. This method uses the values in the HitCount and OrderCount application state items to update the appropriate columns in the database.

The code for the Global.asax file

```
Imports System.Web
Imports System.Web.SessionState

Public AppState As HttpApplicationState

Public Class Global
    Inherits System.Web.HttpApplication

    Sub Application_Start(ByVal sender As Object, ByVal e As EventArgs)
        ' Fires when the application is started
        Application.Add("SalesTax", HalloweenDB.GetSalesTax)
        Application.Add("HitCount", HalloweenDB.GetHitCount)
        Application.Add("OrderCount", HalloweenDB.GetOrderCount)
    End Sub

    Sub Session_Start(ByVal sender As Object, ByVal e As EventArgs)
        ' Fires when the session is started
        Application.Lock()
        Application("HitCount") += 1
        Application.UnLock()
    End Sub
    .
    .
    .
    Sub Application_End(ByVal sender As Object, ByVal e As EventArgs)
        ' Fires when the application ends
        HalloweenDB.UpdateSiteStats(Application("HitCount"), _
                                    Application("OrderCount"))
    End Sub

End Class
```

Description

- When the application starts, three items are added to the application state object: SalesTax, HitCount, and OrderCount.

- The SalesTax item contains a value that's retrieved from the Halloween database using a method of the HalloweenDB class named GetSalesTax. It's used by the second Check Out form to calculate the sales tax for an order.

- The HitCount item is used to keep track of the number of times the application is started by a user. Its initial value is retrieved from the Halloween database using a method of the HalloweenDB class named GetHitCount. This value is increased by 1 each time a new session is started.

- The OrderCount item is used to keep track of the number of orders that are placed. Its initial value is retrieved from the Halloween database using a method of the HalloweenDB class named GetOrderCount. This value is increased by 1 after a new invoice is created by the second Check Out form.

- If the application ends, a method of the HalloweenDB class named UpdateSiteStats is used to update the number of hits and orders in the Halloween database using the values of the HitCount and OrderCount items.

Figure 9-13   The code for the Global.asax file of the Halloween Store application

The code for using application state in the second Check Out form

In addition to the Global.asax file, the application state items are also used in the second Check Out form of the Halloween Store application. This is the form that accepts the shipping and payment information from the user. Some of the code from this form is shown in figure 9-14.

You may recall that when the user clicks the Accept Order button on the Check Out form, the Accept procedure creates a new Invoice object and assigns values to its properties. One of those properties is SalesTax, which contains the amount of the sales tax for the invoice. To calculate the sales tax, the Accept procedure multiplies the order subtotal by the sales tax percent that's stored in the SalesTax item in application state.

After it sets all the properties of the Invoice object, the Accept procedure adds the invoice to the Halloween database. Then, it executes a procedure named UpdateOrderCount. This procedure starts by locking the application state object so that it can't be updated by another user. Then, the OrderCount item is incremented by 1, and the application state object is unlocked.

The code in the second Check Out form that uses application state

```
Private Sub btnAccept_Click(ByVal sender As System.Object, _
        ByVal e As System.EventArgs) Handles btnAccept.Click
    If IsValid Then
        Dim Invoice As New Invoice
            .
            .
            .
        Dim dSubtotal As Decimal = Me.SubTotal
        Invoice.Subtotal = dSubtotal
        Dim dSalestax As Decimal = dSubtotal * Application("SalesTax")
        Invoice.SalesTax = dSalestax
            .
            .
            .
        HalloweenDB.AddInvoice(Invoice, ShoppingCart)
        Me.UpdateOrderCount()
        Session.Remove("Cart")
        Response.Redirect("Confirmation.aspx")
    End If
End Sub

Private Sub UpdateOrderCount()
    Application.Lock()
    Application("OrderCount") += 1
    Application.UnLock()
End Sub
```

Description

- The SalesTax item that's placed in application state when the application starts is used to calculate the sales tax for an order when the user accepts the order by clicking the Accept Order button.

- After the Accept procedure writes the order to the Halloween database, it calls a procedure named UpdateOrderCount. This procedure increases the value of the OrderCount item in application state by 1.

Figure 9-14   The code for using application state in the second Check Out form

How to use URL encoding

URL encoding is a technique that lets you store information in the URL in addition to the location of the page to be displayed. This information is stored in a *query string* that's added to the end of the URL. In the topics that follow, you'll learn how to code and use query strings, and you'll see another version of the Halloween Store application that uses query strings to implement category and product menus.

How to code and use query strings in URLs

At the top of figure 9-15, you can see two URLs that include query strings. The first one includes a single attribute named category, and the second one includes two attributes named category and product. As you can see, you add a query string by coding a question mark after the URL. Then, you code the name of the first attribute, an equal sign, and the value you want to assign to the attribute. To include another attribute, you code an ampersand (&), followed by the name and value of the attribute.

In most cases, you'll use query strings with Anchor tags to pass information from one page of an application to another. This is illustrated in the second example in this figure. Here, the Href attribute of the Anchor tag indicates that it will link to a page named Product.aspx. In addition, the URL includes a query string that contains a category and a product value. The Product page can then use these values to display information for the specified product.

To retrieve the values included in a query string, you use the QueryString property of the Request object as illustrated in the third example. The two statements in this example retrieve the two values passed by the query string in the second example.

Although you can hard code attribute values into a query string as shown in the second example in this figure, it's much more common to set the attribute values at runtime. To do that, you have to create the Anchor tag dynamically. This is illustrated in the fourth example. Here, the attribute value is retrieved from a row of the Categories data table and stored in a variable. Then, that variable is used within a string expression that defines the Anchor tag. In addition, the category name is retrieved from the data table and included between the start and end tags of the Anchor element. This name will appear as the text for the link. Notice that the resulting string is assigned to the Text property of a label control. That way, the link will appear within the label on the page.

Query strings are often used within Anchor tags to implement menus. For example, you could add an Anchor tag for each row in the Categories table to the Text property of a label. Then, the user could click one of those links to display a list of products in the selected category. Note that although the link could cause another page with the list of products to be displayed, it could also redisplay the current page with the product list. You'll see a version of the Halloween Store application that does just that next.

Two URLs with query strings

```
Order.aspx?category=costumes
Order.aspx?category=props&product=rat01
```

An Anchor tag with a URL that includes a query string

```
<a href='product.aspx?category=fx&product=fog01'>Fog machine</a>
```

Statements that retrieve the values of the query string attributes

```
Dim sCategoryID As String = Request.QueryString("category")
Dim sProductID As String = Request.QueryString("product")
```

Code that creates an Anchor tag with a query string and displays it in a label

```
Dim sCategory, sName As String
sCategory = dsCategories.Tables("Categories").Rows(0)("CategoryID")
sName = dsCategories.Tables("Categories").Rows(0)("ShortName")
lblCatMenu.Text = "<a href='order.aspx?category=" & sCategory & "'>" _
                & sName & "</a>"
```

Code that uses a URL with a query string in a Redirect method

```
Response.Redirect("Confirmation.aspx?email=" & sEmail)
```

Description

- When you use *URL encoding*, a *query string* that consists of attribute/value pairs is added to the end of a URL. Query strings are frequently used in Anchor tags to pass information from one page of an application to another.

- Query strings can also be used in Anchor tags to pass information from one page back to the same page. This technique is often used to implement menus that cause additional information to be displayed on the page when a menu item is clicked.

- Query strings can also be used in the URL that's specified on a Redirect or Transfer method.

- To code a query string, follow the URL with a question mark, the name of the attribute, an equal sign, and a value. To code two or more attributes, separate them with ampersands (&). Be sure not to include any spaces in the query string.

- Most browsers impose a limit of 255 characters in a query string.

- To retrieve the value of a query string attribute, use the QueryString property of the HttpRequest object and specify the attribute name. To refer to the HttpRequest object, use the Request property of the page.

Note

- When you use an Anchor tag or a Redirect or Transfer method that specifies a URL for the current page, a postback doesn't occur. Instead, the page is processed as if it's being requested for the first time. Because of that, this technique can be inefficient.

Figure 9-15   How to code and use query strings in URLs

But first, you should know that you can also use query strings in URLs that you code on a Redirect or Transfer method. This is illustrated in the last example in this figure. Here, the URL contains a query string with a single attribute that contains an email address.

The design of an Order page that uses query strings

Figure 9-16 presents another version of the Order page for the Halloween Store application. As you can see, this page displays a horizontal category menu that lets the user select a product category and a vertical product menu that lets the user select a product within that category. Each menu item is implemented as an Anchor tag that's created at runtime. Then, the items that make up the category menu are assigned to the Text property of a label so they're displayed across the page. The items that make up the product menu are also assigned to the Text property of a label. However, these items are formatted within a table so that the items display down the side of the page.

When this form is first displayed, the products in the first category are listed in the product menu. Then, the user can click another category link to display the products in that category. To display the information for a product, the user can click a product link. Note that when any of these links are clicked, the Order page is redisplayed with the requested information. In other words, the links on the Order page link back to the Order page.

Although you might think that linking back to the current page would cause the IsPostBack property of the page to be set to True, that's not the case. Instead, the page is treated as if it's being loaded for the first time. Because of that, this technique can be inefficient. Each time the Order page is loaded, for example, the Category and Product menus must be recreated.

Note that since the links on this page don't cause a postback to occur, and because the buttons on this page cause other pages to be displayed, this page never posts back to itself. Because of that, I was able to turn view state off for the entire page. If I hadn't done that, all of the menu data and product data would have been stored in view state, which would have been inefficient.

The Order page of the Halloween Store application

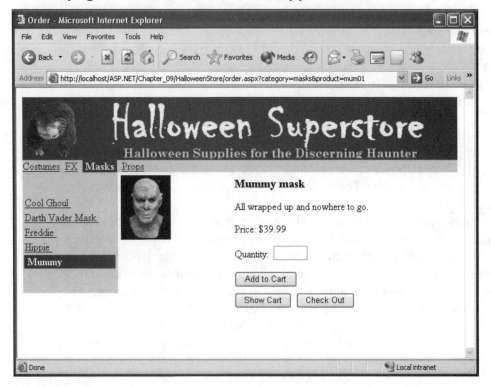

Description

- The Order page of the Halloween Store application has been modified so it provides menus that let the user select a category and product. Each item in a menu appears as a link.
- To create the category menu, the Text property of a label is assigned a series of Anchor tags that represent the categories. Each Anchor tag includes a query string with the category ID.
- To create the product menu, the Text property of a label is defined as a table. Each row of the table consists of a single cell that contains an Anchor tag for a product. Each Anchor tag includes a query string with the category ID and the product ID.
- When this form is first displayed, the products in the first category are listed. Then, if the user selects another category link, the products in that category are listed.
- When the user selects a product link, the information for that product is displayed. Then, the user can enter a quantity and click the Add to Cart button to add that product to the shopping cart.

Note

- Because this page never posts back to itself, the view state for the page has been disabled.

Figure 9-16   The design of the Order page

The code for the Order page

Figure 9-17 presents the code for the Order page. The first thing you should notice here is that the Load procedure doesn't check the IsPostBack property. That's because, as I've already explained, this page is never posted back. Because of that, all six of the procedures executed by the Load procedure are executed each time the page is loaded.

The first procedure, GetCategories, works like the GetProducts procedure you saw in earlier versions of the application. It checks to see if an item named Categories is stored in session state. If not, it calls the GetCategories method of the HalloweenDB class to get a dataset that contains the categories and then stores it in session state. Otherwise, it just retrieves the Categories dataset from session state.

At this point, you may be wondering why this version of the application stores the Categories dataset in session state. The answer is that, in previous versions, you could retrieve the category data only when the IsPostBack property of the page was False. Because of the way this application works, however, the IsPostBack property is always False. So you can't check this property to determine if the page is being loaded for the first time. Instead, you can check for the existence of the Categories item in session state each time the page is loaded. That way, the category data is only retrieved from the database the first time the page is loaded.

After the Load procedure executes the GetCategories and GetProducts procedures, it executes the DisplayCategories procedure. This procedure creates the category menu that's displayed on the page. To do that, it creates an Anchor element for each row in the Categories table, and it assigns the elements to the Text property of a label control. Notice that the URL for each tag includes a query string that contains the category ID.

If you study this code, you should be able to figure out how the Anchor elements are created. The only statements that may be confusing are the two If statements that appear within the For Each...Next statement. These statements create a Span element that applies a style to the category that's currently selected. Since the ID of that category is passed to the page in the category attribute of the query string, the application can test this value against the category ID of the current row. That's what the first part of the first If statement does. Then, if the values are the same, a Span element is added to display the link with white, boldfaced text on a red background. Note that because all of the text that's displayed for the link is enclosed in the Span element, I could also have used the Style attribute of the Anchor tag to format the text.

If the page is being displayed for the first time, no category ID will be sent in the query string. Then, the first category should be highlighted. To accomplish that, the If statement also tests the category attribute for an empty string, and it tests if the bFirstRow variable is true. As you can see, this variable is set to True before the first row is processed and it's set to False after the first row is processed.

The Visual Basic code for the Order page   **Page 1**

```vb
Public Class Order
    Inherits System.Web.UI.Page

    Dim dsCategories As DataSet
    Dim dsProducts As DataSet

    Private Sub Page_Load(ByVal sender As System.Object, _
            ByVal e As System.EventArgs) Handles MyBase.Load
        'Put user code to initialize the page here
        Me.GetCategories()
        Me.GetProducts()
        Me.DisplayCategories()
        Me.DisplayProducts()
        Me.DisplayProductData()
        Me.SetButtons()
    End Sub

    Private Sub GetCategories()
        If Session("Categories") Is Nothing Then
            dsCategories = HalloweenDB.GetCategories
            Session("Categories") = dsCategories
        Else
            dsCategories = Session("Categories")
        End If
    End Sub

    Private Sub GetProducts()
        If Session("Products") Is Nothing Then
            dsProducts = HalloweenDB.GetProducts()
            Session("Products") = dsProducts
        Else
            dsProducts = Session("Products")
        End If
    End Sub

    Private Sub DisplayCategories()
        Dim dr As DataRow
        Dim bFirstRow As Boolean = True
        For Each dr In dsCategories.Tables("Categories").Rows
            lblCatMenu.Text &= "<a href='order.aspx?category=" _
                            & dr("CategoryID") & "'>"
            If Request.QueryString("category") = dr("CategoryID") _
                    Or (Request.QueryString("category") = "" And bFirstRow) Then
                lblCatMenu.Text &= "<span style='background-color: red; " _
                                    & "color: white; font-weight: bold'> "
            End If
            lblCatMenu.Text &= dr("ShortName")
            If Request.QueryString("category") = dr("CategoryID") _
                    Or (Request.QueryString("category") = "" And bFirstRow) Then
                lblCatMenu.Text &= " </span>"
            End If
            lblCatMenu.Text &= "</a>  "
            If bFirstRow Then
                bFirstRow = False
            End If
        Next
    End Sub
```

Figure 9-17   The code for the Order page (part 1 of 3)

The second If statement is similar. If an Anchor element is being created for the category that's currently selected or if the page is being displayed for the first time, the end tag for the Span element is added after the text for the link.

The next procedure that's executed by the Load procedure, DisplayProducts, creates the product menu. The code in this procedure is similar to the code in the DisplayCategories procedure. It creates an Anchor element for each row in the Products table that's in the currently selected category. If a category isn't currently selected—in other words, if the page is being displayed for the first time—the products in the first category are displayed. To accomplish that, the procedure starts by checking the category attribute of the query string for an empty string. If it is an empty string, the category ID of the first row in the Categories table is used to identify the current category. Otherwise, the category ID in the query string is used.

Notice that each Anchor element is coded within a cell in a separate row of a table. That way, each link will appear on a separate line on the page. Also notice that both the category ID and the product ID are included in the query string for each element. That way, the appropriate category and product can be highlighted in the menus when the page is displayed, and the data for the selected product can be displayed.

To display the data for a product, the Load procedure executes the DisplayProductData procedure. This procedure starts by checking the product attribute of the query string for an empty string. If it contains an empty string, it means that the page is either being displayed for the first time or the user clicked on a category link to display the products for that link. Then, the appropriate properties of the controls that display the product data are set so nothing is displayed. In addition, the Visible property of the Add to Cart button is set to False so this button doesn't appear on the page.

If the product attribute does contain a product ID, though, the data row for that product is retrieved from the Products table. Then, the data from that row is used to set the properties of the controls that display the product data.

The Visual Basic code for the Order page

```vb
Private Sub DisplayProducts()
    Dim sCategory As String
    If Request.QueryString("category") = "" Then
        sCategory _
            = dsCategories.Tables("Categories").Rows(0)("CategoryID")
    Else
        sCategory = Request.QueryString("category")
    End If
    Dim dr As DataRow
    lblProductMenu.Text = "<table width='150'>"
    For Each dr In dsProducts.Tables("Products").Rows
        If dr("CategoryID") = sCategory Then
            If Request.QueryString("product") _
                    = dr("ProductID") Then
                lblProductMenu.Text _
                    &= "<tr><td style='background-color: red'>"
            Else
                lblProductMenu.Text &= "<tr><td>"
            End If
            lblProductMenu.Text &= "<a href='order.aspx?category=" _
                                & dr("CategoryID") & "&product=" _
                                & dr("ProductID") & "'>"
            If Request.QueryString("product") _
                    = dr("ProductID") Then
                lblProductMenu.Text &= "<span style='color: white; " _
                                    & "font-weight: bold'> "
            End If
            lblProductMenu.Text &= dr("Name") & " " _
                                & "</span></a></td></tr>"
        End If
    Next
    lblProductMenu.Text &= "</table>"
End Sub

Private Sub DisplayProductData()
    If Request.QueryString("product") = "" Then
        imgProduct.Visible = False
        lblShortDesc.Text = ""
        lblLongDesc.Text = ""
        lblPrice.Text = ""
        lblQuantity.Text = ""
        txtQuantity.Visible = False
        btnAdd.Visible = False
    Else
        Dim drProduct As DataRow
        drProduct = dsProducts.Tables("Products").Rows.Find _
            (Request.QueryString("product"))
        lblShortDesc.Text = drProduct("ShortDescription")
        lblLongDesc.Text = drProduct("LongDescription")
        lblPrice.Text = "Price: " & FormatCurrency(drProduct("UnitPrice"))
        lblQuantity.Text = "Quantity: "
        imgProduct.ImageUrl = "Images\" & drProduct("imagefile")
    End If
End Sub
```

Figure 9-17   The code for the Order page (part 2 of 3)

The last procedure that's called by the Load procedure is the SetButtons procedure. This procedure is similar to the SetButtons procedure in previous versions of the Order form. The only difference is that instead of setting the Enabled properties of the buttons depending on whether there's anything in the shopping cart, the procedure sets the Visible property. That way, the controls don't appear at all if the shopping cart is empty.

If the user clicks the Add to Cart button to add a product to the shopping cart, the procedure for the Click event of this button is executed. This procedure is almost identical to the procedure in previous versions of this form. The only difference is that instead of getting the product ID of the selected product from a drop-down list, this procedure gets it from the product attribute of the query string.

The Visual Basic code for the Order page

```
Private Sub SetButtons()
    If Session("Cart") Is Nothing Then
        btnShow.Visible = False
        btnCheckOut.Visible = False
    Else
        If Session("Cart").Count = 0 Then
            btnShow.Visible = False
            btnCheckOut.Visible = False
        Else
            btnShow.Visible = True
            btnCheckOut.Visible = True
        End If
    End If

End Sub

Private Sub btnAdd_Click(ByVal sender As System.Object, _
        ByVal e As System.EventArgs) Handles btnAdd.Click
    If IsValid Then
        Dim sID As String
        sID = Request.QueryString("product")
        Dim CartItem As New CartItem
        Dim ShoppingCart As SortedList
        If Session("Cart") Is Nothing Then
            ShoppingCart = New SortedList
        Else
            ShoppingCart = Session("Cart")
        End If
        If ShoppingCart.ContainsKey(sID) Then
            CartItem = ShoppingCart(sID)
            CartItem.Quantity += txtQuantity.Text
            ShoppingCart(sID) = CartItem
        Else
            Dim drProduct As DataRow
            drProduct = dsProducts.Tables("Products").Rows.Find(sID)
            CartItem.Name = drProduct("Name")
            CartItem.UnitPrice = drProduct("UnitPrice")
            CartItem.Quantity = txtQuantity.Text
            ShoppingCart.Add(sID, CartItem)
        End If
        Session("Cart") = ShoppingCart
        Response.Redirect("ShoppingCart.aspx")
    End If

End Sub

Private Sub btnCheckOut_Click(ByVal sender As System.Object, _
        ByVal e As System.EventArgs) Handles btnCheckOut.Click
    Response.Redirect("CheckOut1.aspx")
End Sub

Private Sub btnShow_Click(ByVal sender As System.Object, _
        ByVal e As System.EventArgs) Handles btnShow.Click
    Response.Redirect("ShoppingCart.aspx")
End Sub

End Class
```

Figure 9-17   The code for the Order page (part 3 of 3)

Perspective

The goal of this chapter has been to show you how to use the various state management features provided by ASP.NET. Although you learned the basic skills for using view state and session state in earlier chapters, you should now have a better idea of how these features work and how you can use them. You should also understand when and how to use application state and URL encoding. In particular, if you understand the code for the Halloween Store application that is presented in this chapter, you are well on your way to developing web applications that use any form of state management.

Terms

view state
view state object
session state
session state object
application
application object
application state
application state object
In-process mode
State Server mode
SQL Server mode
URL encoding
query string

10

How to develop user controls

In this chapter, you'll learn how to create user controls and use them in the web forms you develop. As you'll see, user controls make it easy to create web forms that include common elements such as banners, navigation menus, and page footers. Then, instead of recreating these elements in each page that needs them, you can simply include the user controls.

An introduction to user controls

A *user control* is a special type of ASP.NET page that can be added to other pages. In the topics that follow, you'll learn some basic concepts related to user controls, and you'll learn the basic procedure for creating user controls.

A web page that contains five user controls

Figure 10-1 presents another version of the Order page of the Halloween Store application that you saw in the last chapter. Although this page is almost identical to the page in that chapter, it was developed by dividing the page into five user controls. The first one contains the banner that's displayed across the top of the page. The second one contains the category menu. The third one contains the product menu. The fourth one contains the product information and the Add to Cart button. And the fifth one contains the footer that's displayed at the bottom of the page.

Notice that the Show Cart and Check Out buttons aren't included in any of the user controls. Although I could have included them in the ProductDisplay control, I decided that they weren't directly related to the other elements of that control. Based on that logic, I could have omitted the Add to Cart button from this control as well. I decided to include it for illustrative purposes, however.

As you decide what to include in each user control, keep in mind that the major benefit of user controls is that they are reusable. That means that you want to design a user control so it can be used in two or more forms. Then, you can change all the forms that contain the user control by simply changing the user control. In contrast, if you don't use a user control, you have to change each form separately.

A procedure for creating and using user controls

Figure 10-1 also presents a procedure for creating and using user controls. To start, you add a new user control to the project. Then, you can use the User Control Designer that's displayed to design the control. As you'll see, this designer works much like the Web Forms Designer you use to design web forms.

Next, you add any code that's necessary to implement the control. For instance, the code for the PageFooter control in this figure must create the message that's displayed in the footer. This code is added to a code-behind file just as it is for a form.

After you create a user control, you can add it to any form in the project. Then, if necessary, you add the code for working with the control to the form.

A web page that contains five user controls

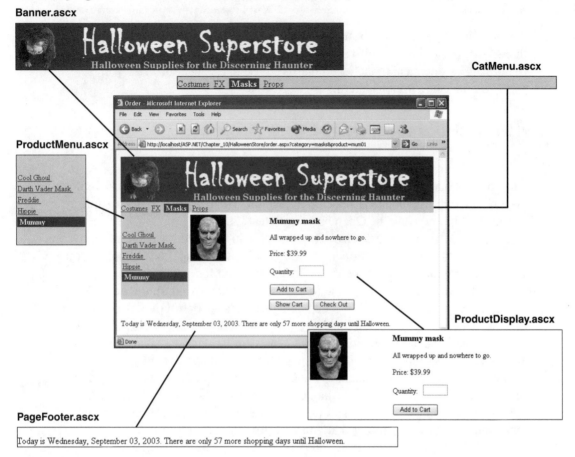

Concepts

- A *user control* is a special type of ASP.NET page that has been converted to a control. A user control is stored in a separate file so that it can be added to any form in a project.

- User controls are typically used to develop common page elements, such as banners, navigation menus, data-entry areas, and display areas. Then, you can use these user controls as building blocks to create complete pages.

- Like a regular ASP.NET web page, a user control can handle events. You code the procedures for handling those events in the code-behind file for the control.

A procedure for creating and using user controls

1. Add a new user control to the project.
2. Design the user control using the User Control Designer.
3. Add the code to implement the control using the Code Editor.
4. Add the control to any form in the project.
5. Add any code to the form that's needed for working with the control.

Figure 10-1   An introduction to user controls

How to create user controls

Now that you know the basic procedure for creating user controls, the topics that follow present the details for doing that. As you'll see, the techniques you use are almost identical to the techniques you use to create a form. So you shouldn't have any trouble creating user controls.

How to add a user control to a project

To add a user control to a project, you use the Project→Add Web User Control command to display the Add New Item dialog box. When you do, the Web User Control template is selected by default. Then, you can enter a name for the control and click the Open button to create it.

After you create a user control, it will appear in the Solution Explorer as shown in figure 10-2. The user control shown here is the PageFooter control you saw in the previous figure. Note that the file extension for a control is .ascx.

This figure also shows the code in the ascx file that Visual Studio generated for the PageFooter control. This code begins with an @Control directive that's similar to the @Page directive for a web form. It includes an AutoEventWireup attribute that indicates whether Handles clauses are needed to associate the Init and Load events of the page with their page handlers. It also includes a Codebehind attribute that associates the control with its code-behind file and an Inherits attribute that provides the name of the class in the code-behind file that the control will inherit at runtime. Finally, it includes a TargetSchema attribute that identifies the web browser that you're designing the control for.

After the @Control directive, you define the elements that the control contains. In this case, the control consists of a single label. To add a control like this, you use the User Control Designer.

How to design a user control

When you first create a user control, it appears in the *User Control Designer* shown in figure 10-2. To add ASP.NET controls to a user control, you simply drag them from the Toolbox. You can also add HTML elements to a control by typing the appropriate tags directly into HTML view. Note, however, that a user control shouldn't contain a Body or Form element. That's because the control will be added to a form, which already contains these elements.

Notice in this figure that the user control is displayed in flow layout mode. In fact, user controls can't be designed in grid layout mode. As a result, you have to use HTML to position the elements of a user control. In most cases, you'll do that using tables.

A user control displayed by the User Control Designer

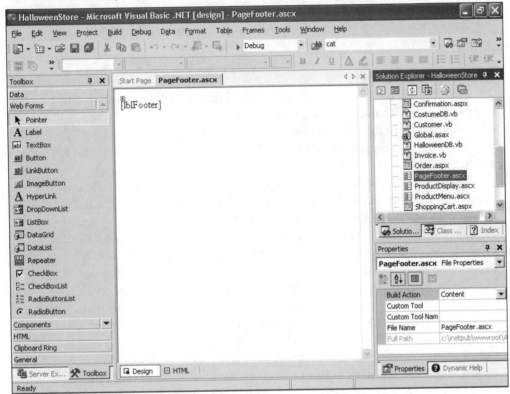

The ascx file for the user control

```
<%@ Control Language="vb" AutoEventWireup="false"
Codebehind="PageFooter.ascx.vb" Inherits="HalloweenStore.PageFooter"
TargetSchema="http://schemas.microsoft.com/intellisense/ie5" %>
<asp:Label id="lblFooter" runat="server"></asp:Label>
```

Description

- To add a user control to a project, use the Project→Add Web User Control command to display the Add New Item dialog box. Then, use the Web User Control template to create a user control with the name you specify.

- When you add a user control, it will appear in the Solution Explorer with the extension .ascx.

- You can use the *User Control Designer* to add ASP.NET controls and HTML elements to the control. A user control should not include a Body or a Form element.

- User controls can be designed only in flow layout mode; grid layout mode isn't available.

- The HTML for a user control begins with an @Control directive that's generated by Visual Studio when you create the user control. This directive includes AutoEventWireup, Codebehind, and Inherits attributes just as the @Page directive of a page does. It also includes a TargetSchema attribute that identifies the web browser that the control is designed for.

Figure 10-2   How to create a user control

How to code a user control

Before you begin coding user controls, you need to be familiar with the sequence of events that are raised for a page that contains user controls. That way, you can be sure to code the user control appropriately. Figure 10-3 presents this sequence of events.

To start, ASP.NET raises the Load event of the page. Then, it raises the Load event for each user control that the page contains. By default, the Load events are raised in the order in which the controls are added to the form. To avoid problems, however, you should code your user controls so they don't depend on other user controls.

After the Load events are raised and processed, ASP.NET raises the control events that result from the user interacting with the page. If the user selects a check box, for example, the CheckedChanged event of that control is raised. Similarly, if the user clicks a button, the Click event of that button is raised. If event procedures are coded for any of the control events, their code is then executed in the sequence that the events occurred. Finally, the PreRender event of the page is raised, followed by the PreRender event of each user control.

This figure also presents the code for the PageFooter user control. The first thing you should notice here is that the class that defines the control inherits the System.Web.UI.UserControl class. Because this class provides many of the same properties, methods, and events as the System.Web.UI.Page class, the code you use to implement a user control is almost identical to the code you would use to implement the same function in a web form. For example, you can use the Load event to execute code each time the control is loaded, and you can use the PreRender event to save data in session state.

The UserControl class also provides many of the same properties as the Page class. For example, you can use the Request and Response properties to work with the HttpRequest and HttpResponse objects, and you can use the Session property to work with the HttpSessionState object. You can also use the IsPostBack property to determine whether the page that contains the user control is being displayed for the first time or if it's being posted back to the server. This is illustrated in the procedure for the Load event shown here. As you can see, the code in this procedure is executed only if the page is being displayed for the first time. Then, the label that the user control contains is formatted so that it displays the current date and the number of days until Halloween.

In addition to the properties, methods, and events a user control inherits from the UserControl class, you can add your own properties, methods, and events to a user control. To do that, you use the same techniques that you use for any other class. Then, you can access those properties, methods, and events from the page that contains the control. You'll learn how to do that later in this chapter.

The sequence of events that are raised for a page with user controls

1. The Load event for the page.
2. The Load event for each user control.
3. Control events caused by user interaction with the page.
4. The PreRender event for the page.
5. The PreRender event for each user control.

The Visual Basic code for the PageFooter user control

```
Public Class PageFooter
    Inherits System.Web.UI.UserControl

    Private Sub Page_Load(ByVal sender As System.Object, _
            ByVal e As System.EventArgs) Handles MyBase.Load
        'Put user code to initialize the page here
        If Not IsPostBack Then
            lblFooter.Text = "Today is " & Now().ToString("D")
            lblFooter.Text &= ". There are only "
            lblFooter.Text &= Me.DaysToHalloween
            lblFooter.Text &= " more shopping days until Halloween."
        End If
    End Sub

    Private Function DaysToHalloween() As Integer
        Return DateDiff(DateInterval.Day, Now(), DateNextHalloween())
    End Function

    Private Function DateNextHalloween() As DateTime
        Dim dtHalloween As DateTime
        dtHalloween = DateTime.Parse("10/31/" & Now.Year)
        If Now > dtHalloween Then
            dtHalloween = DateTime.Parse("10/31/" & Now.Year + 1)
        End If
        Return dtHalloween
    End Function

End Class
```

Description

- You can use the Code Editor to add code to the code-behind file that's generated for a user control. The code-behind file for a user control should only contain code that's directly related to the user control. It shouldn't contain code that depends on code in other user controls.

- You can define properties and methods within a user control and then access them from the page that contains the control. You can also define and raise events within a user control and then respond to them from the page that contains the control. See figure 10-6 for details.

- The class for a user control inherits the System.Web.UI.UserControl class. This class includes many of the same properties as a page, including IsPostBack, Request, Response, Server, and Session. This class also contains a Page property that refers to the Page object that contains the control.

Figure 10-3   How to code a user control

How to use user controls

After you design and code a user control, you can add it to any form in the project that needs it. Then, if necessary, you can add code to the page to work with the control. You'll learn how to do that in the topics that follow. You'll also see the HTML that's generated for a user control so you have a better understanding of how they're implemented by ASP.NET.

How to add a user control to a web form

Figure 10-4 shows how you add a user control to a web form. To do that, you simply drag the control from the Solution Explorer to the location where you want it displayed on the form. Then, ASP.NET generates an HTML tag that declares the control so it can be used on the form. In addition, it generates a tag that defines the control. You'll see these tags in the next figure.

Before I go on, you should realize that user controls are always positioned on a form using flow layout. That's true even if you design the form using grid layout. This is one of the reasons many developers prefer to work in flow layout mode. Then, you can easily position all of the elements on the form using tables as shown in this figure.

The form shown here is the Order form of the Halloween Store application. As you can see, it consists of the five user controls you saw back in figure 10-1 along with two button controls. Notice that the Web Forms Designer doesn't display the actual interface for the user controls. Instead, it displays each control as a simple button. That means that you won't know how a page will actually look until you build and run the project. As you can imagine, that can make designing pages somewhat difficult. However, the benefits of using user controls typically outweigh this shortcoming.

Also notice in this figure that user controls expose properties just like standard ASP.NET controls. You're already familiar with the ID, EnableViewState, and Visible properties, and you'll learn about the DataBindings property in chapter 13.

The Order form with user controls displayed in the Web Forms Designer

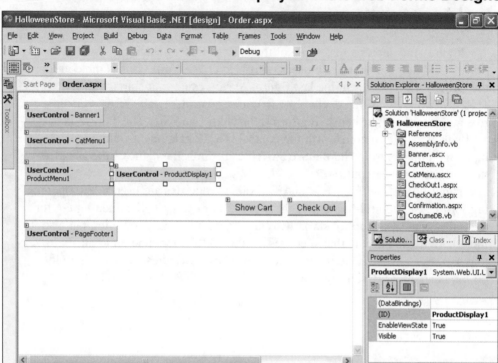

Description

- To add a user control to an ASP.NET page, drag it from the Solution Explorer onto the page. The Web Forms Designer automatically generates the HTML tags necessary to register the user control and insert it into the page.

- User controls are displayed as simple buttons in the Web Forms Designer. As a result, you have to build and run the project to view the final appearance of the page.

- You can set the basic properties of a user control by selecting it in the Web Forms Designer and then using the Properties window.

- User controls are always positioned on a form using flow layout, even if you create the form using grid layout. That means that you can't drag a user control to a specific location on a form.

- In most cases, you'll position user controls on a form using tables. To do that, create the basic table structure with one cell for each user control. Then, drag the user controls to the appropriate cells.

Figure 10-4   How to add a user control to a web form

The HTML that's generated when you add a user control to a form

Figure 10-5 shows an example of the HTML that's generated by the Web Forms Designer when you add user controls to a web form. This is the code for the Order form you saw in the last figure. As you can see, it starts with five @Register directives that declare the five user controls. Each @Register directive includes three attributes: TagPrefix, TagName, and Src. The TagPrefix attribute associates a prefix with the control. The TagName attribute associates a name with the control. And the Src attribute specifies the name of the ascx file that defines the user control.

The values of the TagPrefix and TagName properties are used in the opening tag for the user control to identify the control. For example, the opening tag for the PageFooter user control starts with uc1:PageFooter. Each opening tag also includes a runat attribute that specifies a value of "Server" and an id attribute that assigns a unique ID to the user control. These attributes work just like they do for standard ASP.NET controls.

The HTML for the Order form that uses user controls

```
<%@ Register TagPrefix="uc1" TagName="Banner" Src="Banner.ascx" %>
<%@ Register TagPrefix="uc1" TagName="CatMenu" Src="CatMenu.ascx" %>
<%@ Register TagPrefix="uc1" TagName="ProductMenu" Src="ProductMenu.ascx" %>
<%@ Register TagPrefix="uc1" TagName="ProductDisplay" Src="ProductDisplay.ascx" %>
<%@ Register TagPrefix="uc1" TagName="PageFooter" Src="PageFooter.ascx" %>
<%@ Page Language="vb" AutoEventWireup="false" Codebehind="Order.aspx.vb"
Inherits="HalloweenStore.Order" enableViewState="False"%>
<!DOCTYPE HTML PUBLIC "-//W3C//DTD HTML 4.0 Transitional//EN">
<HTML>
  <HEAD>
    <title>Order</title>
    <meta content="Microsoft Visual Studio .NET 7.1" name="GENERATOR">
    <meta content="Visual Basic .NET 7.1" name="CODE_LANGUAGE">
    <meta content="JavaScript" name="vs_defaultClientScript">
    <meta content="http://schemas.microsoft.com/intellisense/ie5"
        name="vs_targetSchema">
  </HEAD>
  <body>
    <form id="Form1" method="post" runat="server">
      <TABLE id="Table1" style="WIDTH: 700px; HEIGHT: 226px"
          cellSpacing="0" cellPadding="0" width="700" border="0">
        <TR>
          <TD style="WIDTH: 652px" bgColor="#dcdcdc" colSpan="2">
            <uc1:Banner id="Banner1" runat="server"></uc1:Banner></TD></TR>
        <TR>
          <TD bgColor="#dcdcdc" colSpan="2" style="WIDTH: 652px">
            <uc1:CatMenu id="CatMenu1" runat="server"></uc1:CatMenu></TD></TR>
        <TR>
          <TD style="WIDTH: 140px" bgColor="#dcdcdc">
            <uc1:ProductMenu id="ProductMenu1" runat="server"></uc1:ProductMenu>
          </TD>
          <TD style="WIDTH: 543px">
            <uc1:ProductDisplay id="ProductDisplay1" runat="server">
            </uc1:ProductDisplay></TD></TR>
        <TR>
          .
          .
        <TR>
          <TD style="WIDTH: 652px" colSpan="2">
            <uc1:PageFooter id="PageFooter1" runat="server"></uc1:PageFooter>
          </TD></TR>
      </TABLE>
    </form>
  </body>
</HTML>
```

Description

- Visual Studio adds two elements to a page when you add a user control. The @Register directive appears before the Html element and declares the user control. The user control element appears within the Form element to place the control on the form.

- The @Register directive specifies a tag prefix, which is uc1 by default. It also specifies a tag name that corresponds to the class name for the user control.

- The user control element identifies the control by combining the tag prefix and tag name from the @Register directive.

Figure 10-5   The HTML that's generated when you add a user control to a form

How to work with user controls that expose properties, methods, or events

A user control is simply a class that inherits the System.Web.UI.User-Control class. Like any other class, a user control class can expose properties, methods, and events. Then, the page that contains the control can work with the control using those properties, methods, and events.

Figure 10-6 illustrates how this works. At the top of this figure, you can see the code for a user control that displays product data. This code includes a property that's defined as a public variable named Product with a type of DataRow. This variable is used within the Load procedure to assign values to the controls included in the user control that display product information.

Before the Load procedure of the user control is executed, the value of its Product property must be set from the page that contains the control. The second code example shows how to do that. First, you have to declare a variable that refers to the control. That's necessary because Visual Studio doesn't automatically generate this declaration when you add a user control to a form like it does for standard ASP.NET controls.

You should notice four things about the variable declaration in this figure. First, it's declared with the Protected keyword. That way, the control is visible to the aspx file that will inherit it. Second, the WithEvents keyword is included on the declaration. That way, any events that are defined and raised by the user control can be handled by the page. Third, the variable name is the same as the name that's specified on the ID attribute of the tag that defines the user control. And fourth, the type is the same as the class name of the user control.

After you declare a variable for the user control, you can use standard techniques to refer to the properties, methods, and events of the control. In this case, the code in the Load event procedure of the page assigns a value to the Product property of the user control. That way, when the Load event procedure of the user control is executed, it can retrieve the appropriate values from this variable.

When you use properties like this with user controls, be sure to keep in mind the order in which the events for a page and its user controls are raised. In this illustration, for example, the property is used each time the Load event procedure of the user control is executed. Since this event occurs immediately after the Load event of the page, that means that this property must be set in the Load event of the page.

The code for a user control that exposes a property

```
Public Class ProductDisplay
    Inherits System.Web.UI.UserControl

    Public Product As DataRow

    Private Sub Page_Load(ByVal sender As System.Object, _
            ByVal e As System.EventArgs) Handles MyBase.Load
        'Put user code to initialize the page here
        lblName.Text = Product("Name")
        lblShortDesc.Text = Product("ShortDescription")
        lblLongDesc.Text = Product("LongDescription")
        lblPrice.Text = "Price: " & FormatCurrency(Product("UnitPrice"))
        imgProduct.ImageUrl = "Images\" & Product("ImageFile")
    End Sub

End Class
```

Code that sets a user control property from the page that contains the control

```
Protected WithEvents ProductDisplay1 As ProductDisplay

Private Sub Page_Load(ByVal sender As System.Object, _
        ByVal e As System.EventArgs) Handles MyBase.Load
    'Put user code to initialize the page here
    ProductDisplay1.Product = dsProducts.Tables("Products").Rows.Find _
            (ddlProducts.SelectedItem.Value)
End Sub
```

Description

- A user control can include public variables and property procedures that are exposed to the page that contains the control. This lets the page set control values before the code in the control is executed.

- In most cases, you'll set control values from the event procedure for the Load event of the page. That way, the value will be set before the control's Load event is raised, and you'll be able to use the value in the Load event procedure.

- You can also call methods defined by a user control from the page that contains the control, and you can code event procedures that respond to events that are defined and raised by the control.

- When you add a user control to a form, Visual Studio doesn't generate a variable declaration for the control in the form's code-behind file. Because of that, you'll need to code the declaration yourself if you want to refer to the control from the page that contains it.

- The variable name that you use in the declaration for a user control should be the same as the name in the ID attribute of the user control element. The type you specify in the declaration should be the class name of the user control.

- The variable for a user control must be declared using either the Protected or Public keyword. That's because the aspx file inherits the code-behind file, so the control in the code-behind file must be visible to the aspx file.

- If a user control raises events that you want the page to respond to, you should include the WithEvents keyword in the declaration. Then, you can create an event procedure for the event within the code-behind file for the page.

Figure 10-6   How to work with user controls that expose properties, methods, or events

The code for the Order form and its user controls

The remaining figures in this chapter present the code for the Order form of the Halloween Store application that you saw in figure 10-1. As you'll see, most of this code is identical to the code that was used to implement this form without user controls. The main difference is that much of the code has been moved out of the page and into the user controls. In addition, code has been added to implement the PageFooter user control. Since I presented the code for this user control in figure 10-3, however, I won't present it again here.

The code for the Order form

Figure 10-7 presents the code for the Order form. The Load event procedure for this form starts by executing the GetCategories, GetProducts, and SetButtons procedures. The SetButtons procedure sets the Visible properties of the Show Cart and Check Out buttons depending on whether the shopping cart contains any items. It's identical to the code in the previous version of this form.

The GetCategories procedure starts by checking for a session state item named Categories. If this item doesn't exist, the procedure retrieves a dataset that contains the categories using the GetCategories method of the HalloweenDB class. Then, it saves this dataset in session state. Notice that unlike the previous version of this form, the categories dataset isn't retrieved from session state if it already exists. That's because this dataset isn't used by the Order form.

The GetProducts procedure is similar. It gets a dataset of products if one doesn't already exist in session state and then stores that dataset in session state. Like the GetCategories procedure, this procedure doesn't retrieve the products dataset from session state because it isn't used by the form.

At this point, you may be wondering why the categories and products datasets are created by the Order form if they're not used by this form. The answer is that both of these datasets are used by two user controls on the form. The categories dataset is used by the CatMenu and ProductMenu user controls, and the products dataset is used by the ProductMenu and ProductDisplay user controls. To ensure that these datasets are available when the Load events of these controls are executed, they must be created in the Load event of the page.

Earlier in this chapter, I mentioned that the Order form contains two button controls in addition to the user controls. Because of that, the Order form also contains the event procedures for the Click events of these buttons. These procedures simply redirect the browser to another page.

The Visual Basic code for the Order form

```vb
Public Class Order
    Inherits System.Web.UI.Page

    Private Sub Page_Load(ByVal sender As System.Object, _
            ByVal e As System.EventArgs) Handles MyBase.Load
        'Put user code to initialize the page here
        Me.GetCategories()
        Me.GetProducts()
        Me.SetButtons()
    End Sub

    Private Sub GetCategories()
        If Session("Categories") Is Nothing Then
            Dim dsCategories As DataSet
            dsCategories = HalloweenDB.GetCategories
            Session("Categories") = dsCategories
        End If
    End Sub

    Private Sub GetProducts()
        If Session("Products") Is Nothing Then
            Dim dsProducts As DataSet
            dsProducts = HalloweenDB.GetProducts()
            Session("Products") = dsProducts
        End If
    End Sub

    Private Sub SetButtons()
        If Session("Cart") Is Nothing Then
            btnShow.Visible = False
            btnCheckOut.Visible = False
        Else
            If Session("Cart").Count = 0 Then
                btnShow.Visible = False
                btnCheckOut.Visible = False
            Else
                btnShow.Visible = True
                btnCheckOut.Visible = True
            End If
        End If

    End Sub

    Private Sub btnCheckOut_Click(ByVal sender As System.Object, _
            ByVal e As System.EventArgs) Handles btnCheckOut.Click
        Response.Redirect("CheckOut1.aspx")
    End Sub

    Private Sub btnShow_Click(ByVal sender As System.Object, _
            ByVal e As System.EventArgs) Handles btnShow.Click
        Response.Redirect("ShoppingCart.aspx")
    End Sub

End Class
```

Figure 10-7   The code for the Order form

The code for the CatMenu user control

Figure 10-8 presents the code for the CatMenu user control. To create the menu that's displayed by this control, the control uses the categories dataset that's saved in session state by the Order form. The first statement in the Load event procedure of this control retrieves this dataset and stores it in a module-level variable. Then, the Load procedure executes the DisplayCategories procedure. This procedure works just like the one you saw in the last chapter.

The code for the ProductMenu user control

Figure 10-9 presents the code for the ProductMenu user control. This control starts by retrieving both the categories and products datasets from session state each time it's executed. These datasets are then used by the DisplayProducts procedure to create a menu that lists all of the products in the selected category. Since the code for this procedure is identical to the code you saw in the last chapter, you shouldn't have any trouble understanding how it works.

The code for the ProductDisplay user control

Figure 10-10 presents the code for the ProductDisplay user control. This control starts by retrieving the products dataset from session state. This dataset is then used by the DisplayProductData procedure to display the data for the selected product. Again, this code is identical to the code you saw in the last chapter.

This user control also includes an event handler for the Click event of the Add to Cart button that's included in the control. This code is the same as the code in the previous version of this form with one exception. That is, it uses the Page property to refer to the IsValid property of the page. That's necessary because a user control doesn't have an IsValid property. Another way to do this, however, would be to check the IsValid property of each validation control used by the user control. In most cases, though, it's easiest to just check the IsValid property of the page.

The Visual Basic code for the CatMenu user control

```
Public Class CatMenu
    Inherits System.Web.UI.UserControl

    Dim dsCategories As DataSet

    Private Sub Page_Load(ByVal sender As System.Object, _
            ByVal e As System.EventArgs) Handles MyBase.Load
        'Put user code to initialize the page here
        dsCategories = Session("Categories")
        Me.DisplayCategories()
    End Sub

    Private Sub DisplayCategories()
        Dim dr As DataRow
        Dim bFirstRow As Boolean = True
        For Each dr In dsCategories.Tables("Categories").Rows
            lblCatMenu.Text &= "<a href='order.aspx?category=" _
                            & dr("CategoryID") & "'>"
            If Request.QueryString("category") = dr("CategoryID") _
                    Or (Request.QueryString("category") = "" And bFirstRow) Then
                lblCatMenu.Text &= "<span style='background-color: red; " _
                                & "color: white; font-weight: bold'> "
            End If
            lblCatMenu.Text &= dr("ShortName")
            If Request.QueryString("category") = dr("CategoryID") _
                    Or (Request.QueryString("category") = "" And bFirstRow) Then
                lblCatMenu.Text &= " </span>"
            End If
            lblCatMenu.Text &= "</a>  "
            If bFirstRow Then
                bFirstRow = False
            End If
        Next
    End Sub

End Class
```

Figure 10-8   The code for the CatMenu user control

The Visual Basic code for the ProductMenu user control

```
Public Class ProductMenu
    Inherits System.Web.UI.UserControl

    Dim dsCategories As DataSet
    Dim dsProducts As DataSet

    Private Sub Page_Load(ByVal sender As System.Object, _
            ByVal e As System.EventArgs) Handles MyBase.Load
        'Put user code to initialize the page here
        dsCategories = Session("Categories")
        dsProducts = Session("Products")
        Me.DisplayProducts()
    End Sub


    Private Sub DisplayProducts()
        Dim sCategory As String
        If Request.QueryString("category") = "" Then
            sCategory = dsCategories.Tables("Categories").Rows(0)("CategoryID")
        Else
            sCategory = Request.QueryString("category")
        End If
        Dim dr As DataRow
        lblProductMenu.Text = "<table width='150'>"
        For Each dr In dsProducts.Tables("Products").Rows
            If dr("CategoryID") = sCategory Then
                If Request.QueryString("product") = dr("ProductID") Then
                    lblProductMenu.Text _
                        &= "<tr><td style='background-color: red'>"
                Else
                    lblProductMenu.Text &= "<tr><td>"
                End If
                lblProductMenu.Text &= "<a href='order.aspx?category=" _
                                & dr("CategoryID") & "&product=" _
                                & dr("ProductID") & "'>"
                If Request.QueryString("product") = dr("ProductID") Then
                    lblProductMenu.Text &= "<span style='color: white; " _
                                    & "font-weight: bold'> "
                End If
                lblProductMenu.Text &= dr("Name") & " " _
                                & "</span></a></td></tr>"
            End If
        Next
        lblProductMenu.Text &= "</table>"
    End Sub

End Class
```

Figure 10-9 The code for the ProductMenu user control

The Visual Basic code for the ProductDisplay user control

```vb
Public Class ProductDisplay
    Inherits System.Web.UI.UserControl
    Dim dsProducts As DataSet

    Private Sub Page_Load(ByVal sender As System.Object, _
            ByVal e As System.EventArgs) Handles MyBase.Load
        'Put user code to initialize the page here
        dsProducts = Session("Products")
        Me.DisplayProductData()
    End Sub

    Private Sub DisplayProductData()
        If Request.QueryString("product") = "" Then
            imgProduct.Visible = False
            lblShortDesc.Text = ""
            lblLongDesc.Text = ""
            lblPrice.Text = ""
            lblQuantity.Text = ""
            txtQuantity.Visible = False
            btnAdd.Visible = False
        Else
            Dim drProduct As DataRow
            drProduct = dsProducts.Tables("Products").Rows.Find _
                (Request.QueryString("product"))
            lblShortDesc.Text = drProduct("ShortDescription")
            lblLongDesc.Text = drProduct("LongDescription")
            lblPrice.Text = "Price: " & FormatCurrency(drProduct("UnitPrice"))
            lblQuantity.Text = "Quantity: "
            imgProduct.ImageUrl = "Images\" & drProduct("imagefile")
        End If
    End Sub

    Private Sub btnAdd_Click(ByVal sender As System.Object, _
            ByVal e As System.EventArgs) Handles btnAdd.Click
        If Page.IsValid Then
            Dim sID As String
            sID = Request.QueryString("product")
            Dim CartItem As New CartItem
            Dim ShoppingCart As SortedList
            If Session("Cart") Is Nothing Then
                ShoppingCart = New SortedList
            Else
                ShoppingCart = Session("Cart")
            End If
            If ShoppingCart.ContainsKey(sID) Then
                CartItem = ShoppingCart(sID)
                CartItem.Quantity += txtQuantity.Text
                ShoppingCart(sID) = CartItem
            Else
                Dim drProduct As DataRow
                drProduct = dsProducts.Tables("Products").Rows.Find(sID)
                CartItem.Name = drProduct("Name")
                CartItem.UnitPrice = drProduct("UnitPrice")
                CartItem.Quantity = txtQuantity.Text
                ShoppingCart.Add(sID, CartItem)
            End If
            Session("Cart") = ShoppingCart
            Response.Redirect("ShoppingCart.aspx")
        End If
    End Sub
End Class
```

Figure 10-10   The code for the ProductDisplay user control

Perspective

Now that you've completed this chapter and this section, you should have a powerful set of skills for developing web applications. So at this point, you should be able to develop significant web applications on your own. But there's still a lot more to learn.

In particular, you need to know more about working with the data in a database as you develop web applications. Although you learned some basic skills for doing that in chapter 4, the chapters in the next section will raise you to a new level.

Terms

user control
User Control Designer

Section 3

ASP.NET database programming skills

Most ASP.NET applications store their data in databases. As a result, this section is devoted to the essentials of database programming in ASP.NET. When you complete it, you should be able to develop database applications that use the latest data access method, called ADO.NET.

To start, chapter 11 introduces you to the concepts and terms you need to know to develop database applications with ADO.NET, and it presents an overview of the ADO.NET classes. Then, chapter 12 shows you how to work with ADO.NET command objects to perform basic database processing. Next, chapter 13 shows you how to work with ADO.NET datasets using both bound and unbound controls. Finally, chapter 14 shows you how to use three Web Server controls that are specially designed for working with database data: the repeater, the data list, and the data grid.

11

An introduction to relational databases and ADO.NET

This chapter introduces you to the basic concepts and terms that apply to database applications. In particular, it explains what a relational database is and describes how you work with it using SQL. It also presents an overview of the basic ADO.NET classes you use to access relational database data.

To illustrate these concepts and terms, this chapter presents examples that use the *Microsoft SQL Server 2000 Desktop Engine* (*MSDE*). MSDE is a scaled-back version of Microsoft *SQL Server 2000,* and SQL Server 2000 is the database you're most likely to use as you develop database applications with Visual Basic .NET. However, the concepts and terms you'll learn in this chapter apply to other databases as well.

An introduction to relational databases

In 1970, Dr. E. F. Codd developed a model for what was then a new and revolutionary type of database called a *relational database*. This type of database eliminated some of the problems that were associated with standard files and other database designs. By using the relational model, you can reduce data redundancy, which saves disk storage and leads to efficient data retrieval. You can also view and manipulate data in a way that is both intuitive and efficient. Today, relational databases are the de facto standard for database applications.

How a table is organized

The model for a relational database states that data is stored in one or more *tables*. It also states that each table can be viewed as a two-dimensional matrix consisting of *rows* and *columns*. This is illustrated by the relational table in figure 11-1. Each row in this table contains information about a single product.

In practice, the rows and columns of a relational database table are sometimes referred to by the more traditional terms, *records* and *fields*. In fact, some software packages use one set of terms, some use the other, and some use a combination. In this book, we've used the terms *rows* and *columns* for consistency.

If a table contains one or more columns that uniquely identify each row in the table, you can define these columns as the *primary key* of the table. For instance, the primary key of the Products table in this figure is the ProductID column. Here, the primary key consists of a single column. However, a primary key can also consist of two or more columns, in which case it's called a *composite primary key*.

In addition to primary keys, some database management systems let you define additional keys that uniquely identify each row in a table. If, for example, the Name column in the Products table contains a unique name for each product, it can be defined as a *non-primary key*. In SQL Server, this is called a *unique key*, and it's implemented by defining a *unique key constraint* (also known simply as a *unique constraint*). The only difference between a unique key and a primary key is that a unique key can contain a null value and a primary key can't.

Indexes provide an efficient way to access the rows in a table based on the values in one or more columns. Because applications typically access the rows in a table by referring to their key values, an index is automatically created for each key you define. However, you can define indexes for other columns as well. If, for example, you frequently need to sort the rows in the Products table by the CategoryID column, you can set up an index for that column. Like a key, an index can include one or more columns.

The Products table in a Halloween database

Primary key **Columns**

ProductID	Name	ShortDescription	LongDescription	CategoryID	ImageFile	UnitPrice	OnHand
arm01	Severed Arm	Trick Severed Arm	Creates the illusion	props	arm01.jpg	49.99	200
bl01	Black light (24")	24" black light.	Create that creepy	fx	blacklight01.jpg	24.99	200
cat01	Deranged Cat	20" Ugly Cat	This is one ugly cat	props	cat01.jpg	19.99	45
cool01	Cool Ghoul	Cool Ghoul Mask	This guy is one coo	masks	cool01.jpg	69.99	25
fog01	Fog Machine	600W Fog Machine	The perfect fog ma	fx	fog01.jpg	34.99	100
fogj01	Fog Juice (1qt)	1 Qt bottle of Fog	The drink your fog	fx	nopic.jpg	9.99	500
frankc01	Frankenstein	Frankenstein Costu	It's alive!	costumes		39.99	100
fred01	Freddie	Freddie Krueger ma	The ultimate in mor	masks	freddy.jpg	29.99	50
head01	Shrunken Head	Shrunken Head Spil	Spikes driven throu	props	head01.jpg	29.99	100
head02	Severed Head	Severed Head in Po	Incredibly realist se	props	head02.jpg	29.99	100
hippie01	Hippie	Ghoulish Hippie Mas	This guy did too mu	masks	hippie01.jpg	79.99	40
jar01	JarJar	Jar Jar Binks	Meesa happy to se	costumes	jarjar1.jpg	59.99	25
martian01	Martian	Martian costume	Now includes an ex	costumes		69.99	100
mum01	Mummy	Mummy mask	All wrapped up and	masks	mummy.jpg	39.99	30
pow01	Austin Powers	Austin Powers cost	Be the most shaga	costumes	powers1.jpg	79.99	25
rat01	Ugly Rat	16" Rat	This guy will is sure	props	rat01.jpg	14.99	75
rat02	Uglier Rat	20" Rat	Yuch! This one will	props	rat02.jpg	19.99	50
skel01	Life Size Skeleton	Life Size Plastic Ske	This blown plastic s	props	skel01.jpg	14.95	10
skullfog01	Skull Fogger	2,800 Cubic Foot F	This fogger puts ou	fx	skullfog01.jpg	39.95	50
str01	Mini-strobe	Black mini strobe lig	Perfect for creating	fx	strobe1.jpg	13.99	200
super01	Superman	Superman costume	Look, up in the sky	costumes		39.99	100
tlm01	TLM	Thunder & Lightnin	Flash! Boom! Creat	props	tlm1.jpg	99.99	10
vader01	Darth Vader Mask	The legendary Dart	OB1 has taught yo	masks	vader01.jpg	19.99	100

Rows

Concepts

- A *relational database* uses *tables* to store and manipulate data. Each table consists of one or more *records*, or *rows*, that contain the data for a single entry. Each row contains one or more *fields*, or *columns*, with each column representing a single item of data.

- Most tables contain a *primary key* that uniquely identifies each row in the table. The primary key often consists of a single column, but it can also consist of two or more columns. If a primary key uses two or more columns, it's called a *composite primary key*.

- In addition to primary keys, some database management systems let you define one or more *non-primary keys*. In SQL Server, these keys are called *unique keys*, and they're implemented using *unique key constraints*. Like a primary key, a non-primary key uniquely identifies each row in the table.

- A table can also be defined with one or more *indexes*. An index provides an efficient way to access data from a table based on the values in specific columns. An index is auto- matically created for a table's primary and non-primary keys.

Figure 11-1   How a table is organized

How the tables in a database are related

The tables in a relational database can be related to other tables by values in specific columns. The two tables shown in figure 11-2 illustrate this concept. Here, each row in the Categories table is related to one or more rows in the Products table. This is called a *one-to-many relationship*.

Typically, relationships exist between the primary key in one table and the *foreign key* in another table. The foreign key is simply one or more columns in a table that refer to a primary key in another table. In SQL Server, relationships can also exist between a unique key in one table and a foreign key in another table.

Although one-to-many relationships are the most common, two tables can also have a one-to-one or many-to-many relationship. If a table has a *one-to-one relationship* with another table, the data in the two tables could be stored in a single table. Because of that, one-to-one relationships are used infrequently.

In contrast, a *many-to-many relationship* is usually implemented by using an intermediate table, called a *linking table*, that has a one-to-many relationship with the two tables in the many-to-many relationship. In other words, a many-to-many relationship can usually be broken down into two one-to-many relationships.

The relationship between the Categories and Products tables

Primary key

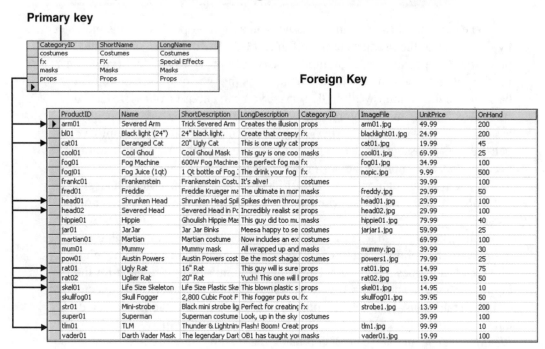

Foreign Key

Concepts

- The tables in a relational database are related to each other through their key columns. For example, the CategoryID column is used to relate the Categories and Products tables above. The CategoryID column in the Products table is called a *foreign key* because it identifies a related row in the Categories table.

- Usually, a foreign key corresponds to the primary key in the related table. In SQL Server, however, a foreign key can also correspond to a unique key in the related table.

- When two tables are related via a foreign key, the table with the foreign key is referred to as the *foreign key table* and the table with the primary key is referred to as the *primary key table*.

- The relationships between the tables in a database correspond to the relationships between the entities they represent. The most common type of relationship is a *one-to-many relationship* as illustrated by the Categories and Products table. A table can also have a *one-to-one relationship* or a *many-to-many relationship* with another table.

Figure 11-2   How the tables in a database are related

How the columns in a table are defined

When you define a column in a table, you assign properties to it as indicated by the design of the Products table in figure 11-3. The two most important properties for a column are Column Name, which provides an identifying name for the column, and Data Type, which specifies the type of information that can be stored in the column. With SQL Server, you can choose from *system data types* like the ones in this figure, and you can define your own data types that are based on the system data types. As you define each column in a table, you generally try to assign the data type that will minimize the use of disk storage because that will improve the performance of the queries later.

In addition to a data type, you must identify whether the column can store a *null value*. A null represents a value that's unknown, unavailable, or not applicable.

You can also assign a *default value* to each column. Then, that value is assigned to the column if another value isn't provided. If a column doesn't allow nulls and doesn't have a default value, you must supply a value for the column when you add a new row to the table. Otherwise, an error will occur.

Each table can also contain a numeric column whose value is generated automatically by the DBMS. In SQL Server, a column like this is called an *identity column*, and you establish it using the Identity, Identity Seed, and Identity Increment properties. Identity columns are often used as the primary key for a table.

A *check constraint* defines the acceptable values for a column. For example, you can define a check constraint for the Products table in this figure to make sure that the UnitPrice column is greater than zero. A check constraint like this can be defined at the column level because it refers only to the column it constrains. If the check constraint for a column needs to refer to other columns in the table, however, it can be defined at the table level.

After you define the constraints for a database, they're managed by the DBMS. If, for example, a user tries to add a row with data that violates a constraint, the DBMS sends an appropriate error code back to the application without adding the row to the database. The application can then respond to the error code.

Another alternative is to validate the data that is going to be added to a database before the program tries to add it. That way, the constraints shouldn't be needed and the program should run more efficiently. In many cases, both data validation and constraints are used. That way, the programs run more efficiently if the data validation routines work, but the constraints are there in case the data validation routines don't work or aren't coded.

The Server Explorer design view window for the Products table

Column Name	Data Type	Length	Allow Nulls
ProductID	varchar	10	
Name	varchar	50	
ShortDescription	varchar	200	
LongDescription	varchar	2000	
CategoryID	varchar	10	
ImageFile	varchar	30	✓
UnitPrice	money	8	
OnHand	int	4	

Columns	
Description	
Default Value	
Precision	0
Scale	0
Identity	No
Identity Seed	
Identity Increment	
Is RowGuid	No
Formula	
Collation	<database default>

Common SQL Server data types

Type	Description
bit	A value of 1 or 0 that represents a True or False value.
char, varchar, text	Any combination of letters, symbols, and numbers.
datetime, smalldatetime	Alphanumeric data that represents a date and time. Various formats are acceptable.
decimal, numeric	Numeric data that is accurate to the least significant digit. The data can contain an integer and a fractional portion.
float, real	Floating-point values that contain an approximation of a decimal value.
bigint, int, smallint, tinyint	Numeric data that contains only an integer portion.
money, smallmoney	Monetary values that are accurate to four decimal places.

Description

- The *data type* that's assigned to a column determines the type of information that can be stored in the column. Depending on the data type, the column definition can also include its length, precision, and scale.

- Each column definition also indicates whether or not the column can contain *null values*. A null value indicates that the value of the column is not known.

- A column can be defined with a *default value*. Then, that value is used for the column if another value isn't provided when a row is added to the table.

- A column can also be defined as an *identity column*. An identity column is a numeric column whose value is generated automatically when a row is added to the table.

- To restrict the values that a column can hold, you define *check constraints*. Check constraints can be defined at either the column level or the table level.

Figure 11-3   How the columns in a table are defined

The design of the Halloween database

Now that you've seen how the basic elements of a relational database work, figure 11-4 shows the design of the Halloween database that's used in the programming examples throughout this book. Although this database may seem complicated, its design is actually much simpler than most databases you'll encounter when you work on actual database applications.

The purpose of the Halloween database is to track orders placed at an online Halloween products store. To do that, the database must track not only invoices, but also products and customers.

The central table for this database is the Invoices table, which contains one row for each order placed by the company's customers. The primary key for this table is the InvoiceNumber column, which is an identity column. As a result, invoice numbers are generated automatically by SQL Server whenever a new invoice is created.

The LineItems table contains the line item details for each invoice. The primary key for this table is a combination of the InvoiceNumber and ProductID columns. The InvoiceNumber column relates each line item to an invoice, and the ProductID column relates each line item to a product. As a result, each invoice can have only one line item for a given product.

The Products and Categories tables work together to store information about the products offered by the Halloween store. The Category table has just three columns: CategoryID, ShortName, and LongName. The CategoryID column is a 10-character code that uniquely identifies each category. The ShortName and LongName columns provide two different descriptions of the category that the application can use, depending on how much room is available to display the category information.

The Products table contains one row for each product. Its primary key is the ProductID column. The Name, ShortDescription, and LongDescription columns provide descriptive information about the product. The ImageFile column provides the name of a separate image file that depicts the product. This column specifies just the name of each image file, not the complete path. The image files are stored in a directory named Images beneath the application's main directory, so the application knows where to find them.

Finally, the Customers table contains a row for each customer who has purchased from the Halloween store. The primary key for this table is the customer's email address. The other columns in this table contain the customer's name, address, and phone number.

The tables that make up the Halloween database

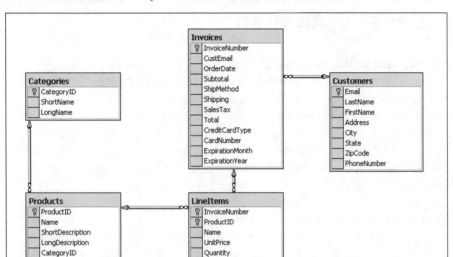

Description

- The Categories table contains a row for each product category. Its primary key is CategoryID, a 10-character code that identifies each category.

- The Products table contains a row for each product. Its primary key is ProductID, a 10-character code that identifies each product. CategoryID is a foreign key that relates each product to a row in the Categories table.

- The Customers table contains a row for each customer. Its primary key is Email, which identifies each customer by his or her email address.

- The Invoices table contains a row for each invoice. Its primary key is InvoiceNumber, an identity field that's generated automatically when a new invoice is created. CustEmail is a foreign key that relates each invoice to a row in the Customers table.

- The LineItems table contains one row for each line item of each invoice. Its primary key is a combination of InvoiceNumber and ProductID. InvoiceNumber is a foreign key that relates each line item to an invoice, and ProductID is a foreign key that relates each line item to a product.

- The relationships between the tables in this diagram appear as links, where the endpoints indicate the type of relationship. A key indicates the "one" side of a relationship, and the infinity symbol (∞) indicates the "many" side.

Figure 11-4   The design of the Halloween database

How to use SQL to work with the data in a relational database

In the topics that follow, you'll learn about the four SQL statements that you can use to manipulate the data in a database: Select, Insert, Update, and Delete. Although you'll learn the basics of coding these statements in the topics that follow, you may want to know more than what's presented here. In that case, we recommend our book, *Murach's SQL for SQL Server*. In addition to the Select, Insert, Update, and Delete statements, that book teaches you how to code the statements you use to define the data in a database, and it teaches you how to use other features of SQL Server that the top professionals use.

Although SQL is a standard language, each DBMS is likely to have its own *SQL dialect*, which includes extensions to the standard language. So when you use SQL, you need to make sure that you're using the dialect that's supported by your DBMS. In this chapter and throughout this book, all of the SQL examples are for Microsoft SQL Server's dialect, which is called *Transact-SQL*.

How to query a single table

Figure 11-5 shows how to use a Select statement to query a single table in a database. In the syntax summary at the top of this figure, you can see that the Select clause names the columns to be retrieved and the From clause names the table that contains the columns. You can also code a Where clause that gives criteria for the rows to be selected. And you can code an Order By clause that names one or more columns that the results should be sorted by and indicates whether each column should be sorted in ascending or descending sequence.

If you study the Select statement below the syntax summary, you can see how this works. Here, the Select statement retrieves three columns from the Products table. It selects a row only if the CategoryID column for the row has a value of "Props." And it sorts the returned rows by UnitPrice, so that the least expensive products are listed first.

This figure also shows the *result table*, or *result set*, that's returned by the Select statement. A result set is a logical table that's created temporarily within the database. When an application requests data from a database, it receives a result set.

Simplified syntax of the Select statement

```
Select column-1 [, column-2]...
From table-1
[Where selection-criteria]
[Order By column-1 [Asc|Desc] [, column-2 [Asc|Desc]]...]
```

A Select statement that retrieves and sorts selected columns and rows from the Products table

```
Select ProductID, Name, UnitPrice
From Products
Where CategoryID = 'Props'
Order By UnitPrice
```

The result set defined by the Select statement

	ProductID	Name	UnitPrice
1	ske101	Life Size Skeleton	14.9500
2	rat01	Ugly Rat	14.9900
3	rat02	Uglier Rat	19.9900
4	cat01	Deranged Cat	19.9900
5	head01	Shrunken Head	29.9900
6	head02	Severed Head	29.9900
7	arm01	Severed Arm	49.9900
8	tlm01	TLM	99.9900

Concepts

- The result of a Select statement is a *result table*, or *result set*, like the one shown above. A result set is a logical set of rows that consists of all of the columns and rows requested by the Select statement.

- To select all of the columns in a table, you can code an asterisk (*) in place of the column names. For example, this statement will select all of the columns from the Products table:

```
Select * From Products
```

Figure 11-5   How to query a single table

How to join data from two or more tables

Figure 11-6 presents the syntax of the Select statement for retrieving data from two tables. This type of operation is called a *join* because the data from the two tables is joined together into a single result set. For example, the Select statement in this figure joins data from the Categories and Products tables into a single result set.

An *inner join* is the most common type of join. When you use an inner join, rows from the two tables in the join are included in the result set only if their related columns match. These matching columns are specified in the From clause of the Select statement. In the Select statement in this figure, for example, rows from the Categories and Products tables are included only if the value of the CategoryID column in the Categories table matches the value of the CategoryID column in one or more rows in the Products table. If there aren't any products for a particular category, that category won't be included in the result set.

Although this figure shows how to join data from two tables, you should know that you can extend this syntax to join data from additional tables. If, for example, you want to include data from the LineItems table in the results shown in this figure, you can code the From clause of the Select statement like this:

```
From Products
    Inner Join Categories
        On Categories.CategoryID = Products.CategoryID
    Inner Join LineItems
        On LineItems.ProductID = Invoices.ProductID
```

Then, in the column list of the Select statement, you can include any of the columns in the LineItems table.

The syntax of the Select statement for joining two tables

```
Select column-list
From table-1
    [Inner] Join table-2
        On table-1.column-1 {=|<|>|<=|>=|<>} table-2.column-2
[Where selection-criteria]
[Order By column-list]
```

A Select statement that joins data from the Products and Categories tables

```
Select ShortName, ProductID, Name, UnitPrice
From Products Inner Join Categories
    On Categories.CategoryID = Products.CategoryID
Order By Categories.CategoryID
```

The result set defined by the Select statement

	ShortName	ProductID	Name	UnitPrice
1	Costumes	frankc01	Frankenstein	39.9900
2	Costumes	jar01	JarJar	59.9900
3	Costumes	martian01	Martian	69.9900
4	Costumes	pow01	Austin Powers	79.9900
5	Costumes	super01	Superman	39.9900
6	FX	skullfog01	Skull Fogger	39.9500
7	FX	str01	Mini-strobe	13.9900
8	FX	fog01	Fog Machine	34.9900
9	FX	fogj01	Fog Juice (1qt)	9.9900
10	FX	bl01	Black light (24")	24.9900
11	Masks	cool01	Cool Ghoul	69.9900

Concepts

- A *join* lets you combine data from two or more tables into a single result set.

- The most common type of join is an *inner join*. This type of join returns rows from both tables only if their related columns match.

Figure 11-6   How to join data from two or more tables

How to add, update, and delete data in a table

Figure 11-7 presents the basic syntax of the SQL Insert, Update, and Delete statements. You use these statements to add new rows to a table, to update the data in existing rows, and to delete existing rows.

To add a single row to a table, you use an Insert statement with the syntax shown in this figure. With this syntax, you specify the name of the table you want to add the row to, the names of the columns you're supplying data for, and the values for those columns. In the example, the Insert statement adds a row to the Categories table and supplies a value for each of the three columns in that table. If a table allows nulls or provides default values for some columns, though, the Insert statement doesn't have to provide values for those columns.

To change the values of one or more columns in one or more rows, you use the Update statement. On this statement, you specify the name of the table you want to update, expressions that indicate the columns you want to change and how you want to change them, and a condition that identifies the rows you want to change. In the example, the Update statement changes the ShortName value for just the one row in the Categories table that has a CategoryID value of "food."

To delete one or more rows from a table, you use the Delete statement. On this statement, you specify the table you want to delete rows from and a condition that indicates the rows you want to delete. In the example, the Delete statement deletes just the one Categories row whose CategoryID field is "food."

How to add a single row

The syntax of the Insert statement for adding a single row

```
Insert [Into] table-name [(column-list)]
    Values (value-list)
```

A statement that adds a single row to a table

```
Insert Into Categories (CategoryID, ShortName, LongName)
    Values ("food", "Spooky Food", "The very best in Halloween cuisine")
```

How to update rows

The syntax of the Update statement

```
Update table-name
    Set expression-1 [, expression-2]...
    [Where selection-criteria]
```

A statement that changes the value of the ShortName column for a selected row

```
Update Categories
    Set ShortName = "Halloween cuisine"
    Where CategoryID = "food"
```

How to delete rows

The syntax of the Delete statement

```
Delete [From] table-name
    [Where selection-criteria]
```

A statement that deletes a specified category

```
Delete From Categories
    Where CategoryID = "food"
```

Description

- You use the Insert, Update, and Delete statements to maintain the data in a database table.

- The Insert statement can be used to add one or more rows to a table. Although the syntax shown above is for adding just one row, there is another syntax for adding more than one row.

- The Update and Delete statements can be used for updating or deleting one or more rows in a table using the syntax shown above.

Figure 11-7   How to add, update, and delete data in a table

An overview of ADO.NET

ADO.NET (*ActiveX Data Objects .NET*) is the primary data access API for the .NET Framework. It provides the classes that you use as you develop database applications with Visual Basic .NET as well as other .NET languages. The topics that follow introduce you to the major ADO.NET classes you'll use to access databases in ASP.NET web applications.

How ADO.NET works

To work with data using ADO.NET, you use a variety of ADO.NET objects. Figure 11-8 shows the primary objects you'll use to develop ASP.NET database applications. Since you were introduced to these objects in chapter 4, you should be familiar with much of the information presented in this figure.

To start, the data used by an application is stored in a *dataset* that contains one or more *data tables*. To load data into a data table, you use a *data adapter*. The main function of the data adapter is to manage the flow of data between a dataset and a database. To do that, it uses *commands* that define the SQL statements to be issued. The command for retrieving data, for example, typically defines a Select statement. Then, the command connects to the database using a *connection* and passes the Select statement to the database. After the Select statement is executed, the result set it produces is sent back to the data adapter, which stores the results in the data table.

To update the data in a database, the data adapter uses a command that defines an Insert, Update, or Delete statement for a data table. Then, the command uses the connection to connect to the database and perform the requested operation.

Although it's not apparent in this figure, the data in a dataset is independent of the database that the data was retrieved from. In fact, the connection to the database is typically closed after the data is retrieved from the database. Then, the connection is opened again when it's needed. Because of that, the application must work with the copy of the data that's stored in the dataset. The architecture that's used to implement this type of data processing is referred to as a *disconnected data architecture*. Although this is more complicated than a connected architecture, the advantages offset the complexity.

One of the advantages of using a disconnected data architecture is improved system performance due to the use of fewer system resources for maintaining connections. Another advantage is that it works well with ASP.NET web applications, which are inherently disconnected. In chapter 4, for example, you saw how an ASP.NET web application can load database data into a dataset once and then save the dataset across round trips in session state.

The ADO.NET classes that are responsible for working directly with a database are provided by the *.NET data providers*. These data providers include the classes you use to create data adapters, commands, and connections. The .NET Framework currently includes four data providers for SQL Server, Oracle, OLE DB, and ODBC. Other third-party providers are also available.

Basic ADO.NET objects

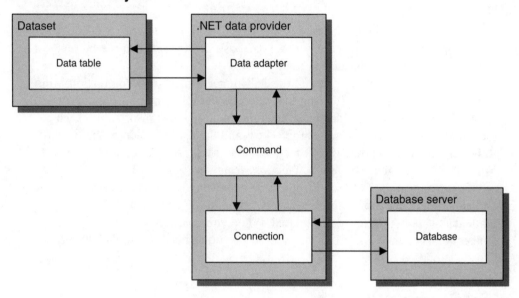

Description

- ADO.NET uses two types of objects to access the data in a database: *datasets*, which can contain one or more *data tables*, and *.NET data provider* objects, which include data adapters, commands, and connections.

- A dataset stores data from the database so it can be accessed by the application. The .NET data provider objects retrieve data from and update data in the database.

- To retrieve data from a database and store it in a data table, a *data adapter* object issues a Select statement that's stored in a *command* object. Next, the command object uses a *connection* object to connect to the database and retrieve the data. Then, the data is passed back to the data adapter, which stores the data in the dataset.

- To update the data in a database based on the data in a data table, the data adapter object issues an Insert, Update, or Delete statement that's stored in a command object. Then, the command object uses a connection to connect to the database and update the data.

- The data provider remains connected to the database only long enough to retrieve or update the specified data. Then, it disconnects from the database and the application works with the data via the dataset object. This is referred to as a *disconnected data architecture.*

- All of the ADO.NET objects are implemented by classes in the System.Data namespace of the .NET Framework. However, the specific classes used to implement the connection, command, and data adapter objects depend on the .NET data provider you use.

- You should add an Imports statement for the namespace that contains the .NET data provider classes to any class that uses the objects it defines. If you're using the SQL Server data provider, for example, you should add an Imports statement for the System.Data.SqlClient namespace.

Figure 11-8   How ADO.NET works

The SqlConnection class

Before you can access the data in a database, you have to create a connection object that defines the connection to the database. To do that, you use the SqlConnection class presented in figure 11-9.

The most important property of the SqlConnection class is ConnectionString. A *connection string* is a text string that provides the information necessary to establish a connection to a database. That means it includes information such as the name of the database you want to access and the database server that contains it. It can also contain authentication information such as a user-id and password. You'll learn more about coding connection strings in chapter 12.

The two methods of the SqlConnection class shown in this figure let you open and close the connection. In general, you should leave a connection open only while data is being retrieved or updated. When you use a data adapter, though, the connection is opened and closed for you so you don't need to use the Open and Close methods.

The SqlCommand class

To execute a SQL statement against a SQL Server database, you create a SqlCommand object that contains the statement. Figure 11-9 presents the SqlCommand class you use to create this object. Notice that the Connection property of this class associates the command with a SqlConnection object, and the CommandText property contains the SQL statement to be executed.

The CommandType property indicates how the command object should interpret the value of the CommandText property. Instead of specifying a SQL statement for the CommandText property, for example, you can specify the name of a stored procedure, which consists of one or more SQL statements that have been compiled and stored with the database. Or you can specify the name of a table. If you specify a SQL statement, you set the value of the CommandType property to CommandType.Text. If you specify the name of a stored procedure, you set it to CommandType.StoredProcedure. And if you specify the name of a table, you set it to CommandType.TableDirect. Then, a Select * statement will be executed on the table.

Earlier in this chapter, you learned that you can use a data adapter to execute command objects. In addition, you can execute a command object directly using one of the three Execute methods shown in this figure. If the command contains a Select statement, for example, you can execute it using either ExecuteReader or ExecuteScalar. If you use ExecuteReader, the results are returned as a DataReader object. If you use ExecuteScalar, only the value in the first column and row of the query results is returned. You're most likely to use this method with a Select statement that returns a single summary value.

If the command contains an Insert, Update, or Delete statement, you'll use the ExecuteNonQuery method to execute it. This method returns an integer value that indicates the number of rows that were affected by the command. For example, if the command deletes a single row, the ExecuteNonQuery method returns 1.

Common property and methods of the SqlConnection class

Property	Description
ConnectionString	Contains information that lets you connect to a SQL Server database, including the server name, the database name, and login information.

Method	Description
Open	Opens a connection to a database.
Close	Closes a connection to a database.

Common properties and methods of the SqlCommand class

Property	Description
Connection	The SqlConnection object used to connect to the database.
CommandText	The text of the SQL command or the name of a stored procedure or database table.
CommandType	A constant in the CommandType enumeration that indicates whether the CommandText property contains a SQL statement (Text), the name of a stored procedure (StoredProcedure), or the name of a database table (TableDirect).
Parameters	The collection of parameters used by the command.

Method	Description
ExecuteReader	Executes a query and returns the result as a SqlDataReader object.
ExecuteNonQuery	Executes the command and returns an integer representing the number of rows affected.
ExecuteScalar	Executes a query and returns the first column of the first row returned by the query.

Common properties of the SqlParameter class

Property	Description
ParameterName	The name of the parameter.
Value	The value assigned to the parameter.
SqlDbType	The SQL data type for the parameter.

Description

- A SqlConnection object is required to establish a connection to a SQL Server database.
- A SqlCommand object is used to execute a SQL command against a SQL Server database.
- A SqlParameter object is used to pass variable information to a SQL command.

Figure 11-9   The SqlConnection, SqlCommand, and SqlParameter classes

The SqlParameter class

The SqlParameter class, also shown in figure 11-9, lets you pass parameter values to a SQL command. Parameters are commonly used to limit the number of rows retrieved by a Select statement. For example, you can retrieve the Product row for a specific product by passing the ProductID as a parameter. Or, you can retrieve all of the products for a given category by passing the CategoryID as a parameter. Parameters are also commonly used to pass column values to Insert and Update statements. You'll learn how to use parameters in chapter 12.

The SqlDataReader class

Figure 11-10 lists the most important properties and methods of the SqlDataReader class. You use this class to create a data reader object, which provides an efficient way to read the rows in a result set returned by a database query. In fact, when you use a data adapter to retrieve data, the data adapter uses a data reader to read through the rows in the result set and store them in a dataset. You'll learn how to use the SqlDataReader class in chapter 12.

A data reader is similar to other types of readers you may have encountered in the .NET Framework, such as a TextReader, a StreamReader, or an XmlReader. Like these other readers, a data reader lets you read rows but not modify them. In other words, a data reader is read-only. In addition, it only lets you read rows in a forward direction. Once you read the next row, the previous row is unavailable.

The SqlDataAdapter class

As you have learned, the job of a data adapter is to provide a link between a database and a dataset. The four properties of the SqlDataAdapter class listed in figure 11-10, for example, identify the four SQL commands that the data adapter uses to transfer data from the database to the dataset and vice versa. The SelectCommand property identifies the command object that's used to retrieve data from the database. And the DeleteCommand, InsertCommand, and UpdateCommand properties identify the commands that are used to update the database based on changes made to the data in the dataset.

To execute the command identified by the SelectCommand property and place the data that's retrieved in a dataset, you use the Fill method. Then, the application can work with the data in the dataset without affecting the data in the database. If the application makes changes to the data in the dataset, it can use the data adapter's Update method to execute the commands identified by the DeleteCommand, InsertCommand, and UpdateCommand properties and post the changes back to the database.

Common properties and methods of the SqlDataReader class

Property	Description
Item	Accesses the column with the specified index or name from the current row.
FieldCount	The number of columns in the current row.

Method	Description
Read	Reads the next row. Returns True if there are more rows. Otherwise, returns False.
Close	Closes the data reader.

Common properties and methods of the SqlDataAdapter class

Property	Description
SelectCommand	A SqlCommand object representing the Select statement used to query the database.
DeleteCommand	A SqlCommand object representing the Delete statement used to delete a row from the database.
InsertCommand	A SqlCommand object representing the Insert statement used to add a row to the database.
UpdateCommand	A SqlCommand object representing the Update statement used to update a row in the database.

Method	Description
Fill	Executes the command identified by the SelectCommand property and loads the result into a dataset object.
Update	Executes the commands identified by the DeleteCommand, InsertCommand, and UpdateCommand properties for each row in the dataset that was deleted, added, or updated.

Description

- A data reader provides read-only, forward-only access to the data in a database. Because it doesn't require the overhead of a dataset, it's more efficient than using a data adapter. However, it can't be used to update data.

- When the Fill method of a data adapter is used to retrieve data from a database, the data adapter uses a data reader to load the results into a dataset.

Figure 11-10   The SqlDataReader and SqlDataAdapter classes

Perspective

This chapter has introduced you to the basic concepts of relational databases and described how you use SQL and ADO.NET classes to work with the data in a relational database. With that as background, you're now ready to learn how to develop ASP.NET database applications. In the next three chapters, then, you'll learn the essential skills for building ASP.NET applications that use ADO.NET.

Terms

Microsoft SQL Server 2000
    Desktop Engine (MSDE)
SQL Server 2000
relational database
table
record
row
field
column
primary key
composite primary key
non-primary key
unique key
unique key constraint
unique constraint
index
foreign key
foreign key table
primary key table
one-to-many relationship
one-to-one relationship
many-to-many relationship
linking table

data type
system data type
null value
default value
identity column
check constraint
SQL dialect
Transact-SQL
result table
result set
join
inner join
ADO.NET (ActiveX Data
    Objects .NET)
dataset
data table
.NET data provider
data adapter
command
connection
disconnected data architecture
connection string

12

How to work with ADO.NET data commands

In chapter 4, you learned how to use a data command with a data adapter to retrieve data from a database and store it in a dataset. The application in that chapter illustrated the most common use for a data adapter: to populate a list control such as a drop-down list or list box. You're also likely to use a data adapter if you need to display, but not update, single rows of data or if you need to display or update two or more rows of data at the same time. You'll see examples of applications that perform these types of operations in the next two chapters.

In contrast, you'll typically use a data command without a data adapter if you only need to retrieve one row from a database at a time. You'll also use data commands without data adapters when you need to insert, update, and delete one row in a database at a time. In this chapter, you'll learn how to use data commands without data adapters, and you'll learn how to create and use the connection objects that the data commands require.

How to connect to a database

Before you can use a data command to work with the data in a database, you have to define the connection to the database. To do that, you create a connection object. You'll learn how to do that in the topic that follows. Then, you'll learn how to use connection pooling to improve the performance of database operations, and you'll learn how to store your connection settings in a central location.

How to create and use connection objects

Figure 12-1 shows how you create and use a connection to access a SQL Server database. As you can see from the syntax at the top of this figure, you can specify a connection string when you create the connection. If you do, this string is assigned to the ConnectionString property. Otherwise, you have to assign a value to this property after you create the connection object. This is illustrated by the first two examples in this figure.

The first example also shows how you can use the Open and Close methods to open and close a connection. Remember, though, that a data adapter automatically opens and closes the connection when it needs to access the database. Because of that, you don't need to use the Open and Close methods if you'll be using a data adapter to load the database data into a dataset or to update the database data with the data in a dataset. If you'll be using data commands to access the database directly as shown in this chapter, however, you'll need to open and close the connection explicitly.

This figure also shows some of the common values that you specify in a connection string for a SQL Server database. The connection string in this figure, for example, specifies the name of the server where the database resides, the name of the database, and the type of security to be used. Because the requirements for each data provider differ, you may need to consult the documentation for that provider to determine what values to specify.

Before I go on, you should realize that the connection strings for production programs are frequently stored in configuration files outside the program rather than in the program itself. That way, they can be accessed by any program that needs them, and they can be modified without having to modify each program that uses them. You'll learn how to store a connection string in a configuration file later in this chapter.

Two ways to create a SqlConnection object

```
connection = New SqlConnection()
connection = New SqlConnection(connectionString)
```

Common properties and methods of a connection object

Property	Description
ConnectionString	Provides information for accessing the database.

Method	Description
Open	Opens the connection using the specified connection string.
Close	Closes the connection.

Common values used in the ConnectionString property for a SQL Server database

Name	Description
Data source/Server	The name of the instance of SQL Server you want to connect to.
Database/Initial catalog	The name of the database you want to access.
Integrated security	Determines whether the connection is secure. Valid values are True, False, and SSPI. SSPI uses Windows integrated security and is equivalent to True.
Persist security info	Determines whether sensitive information, such as the password, is returned as part of the connection. The default is False.
Packet size	The number of bytes in the packets used to communicate with SQL Server.
User ID	The user id that's used to log in to SQL Server.
Password/Pwd	The password that's used to log in to SQL Server.
Workstation ID	The name of the workstation that's connecting to SQL Server.

Code that creates, opens, and closes a SQL connection

```
Dim sConnection As String = "server=DB1\Sql1;database=Halloween;" _
    & "integrated security=SSPI"
Dim conHalloween As New SqlConnection()
conHalloween.ConnectionString = sConnection
conHalloween.Open
...
conHalloween.Close
```

Another way to create a SqlConnection object

```
Dim conHalloween As New SqlConnection(sConnection)
```

Description

- You can set the ConnectionString property after you create a connection or as you create it by passing the string to the constructor of the connection class.
- The values you specify for the ConnectionString property depend on the type of database you're connecting to.

Figure 12-1   How to create and use connection objects

How connection pooling works

Figure 12-2 illustrates how *connection pooling* works. The basic idea behind connection pooling is that a pool of database connections is available to two or more users of a database. When a user attempts to connect to the database, ADO.NET checks to see if an existing connection can be retrieved from a *connection pool*. If so, that connection is used and the user doesn't have to wait for a new connection to be created. When the user is finished with the connection, the connection is returned to the pool so that other users can use it.

ADO.NET creates a separate connection pool for each unique database connection string. In this figure, for example, you can see that separate connection pools are used for two databases named Halloween and Payables. Keep in mind, though, that two or more connection pools can exist for the same database if different connection strings are used to connect to it. If, for example, a large number of users use an application, the name of the application can be included in the connection string. Then, a separate connection pool is created for that application.

Each connection pool contains a limited number of connections. Because of that, if a large number of users attempt to access the database using the same connection string, it's likely that some users will have to wait for a connection to become available. Part of the trick to tuning the performance of ASP.NET database applications, then, is setting the size of the connection pool. If the connection pool is too large, valuable server memory will be wasted on unused connections. But if the connection pool is too small, users will frequently be forced to wait for database connections to become available.

Although connection pooling is provided by the ADO.NET data providers, you can control some of the aspects of connection pooling for a SQL Server or Oracle database. You'll see how to do that in the next figure. Because the OLE DB and ODBC data providers manage connection pooling automatically, you don't have any control over how it works with these providers.

Two connection pools that access different databases

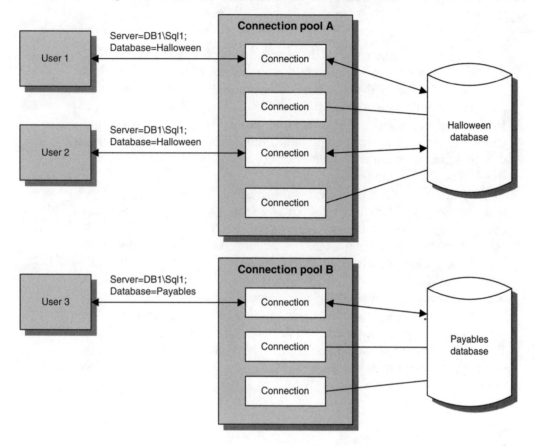

Description

- A *connection pool* consists of zero or more open connections to a database. When a program requests a connection to that database, an open connection is assigned to it if one is available.

- If a program requests a connection and one isn't available in the pool, a new connection is created unless the maximum number of the connections for the pool are already in use. In that case, the program must wait for a connection to become available.

- When a program closes a connection, the connection is returned to the connection pool so that it can be used by another program.

- The connection string determines which connection pool is used. Each application that uses the same connection string uses connections in the same connection pool.

- If an application opens a connection and a connection pool isn't already available for the specified connection string, a new pool is created.

- *Connection pooling* improves the performance of database operations because the programs that use the database typically don't have to wait for a connection to be established.

Figure 12-2   How connection pooling works

Connection string settings that affect connection pooling

To influence the behavior of the connection pools used by the SQL Server and Oracle data providers, you can use the connection string settings shown in figure 12-3. To change the minimum or maximum number of connections in a pool, for example, you use the Min Pool Size and Max Pool Size settings. Because the minimum number of connections in a pool is zero by default, you'll almost always want to change this value. Similarly, you'll want to change the default maximum number of connections in a pool unless a large number of users will use the same pool.

The first example in this figure shows a connection string that includes these two settings. Here, the Min Pool Size setting specifies that the pool should contain at least 10 connections, and the Max Pool Size setting indicates that the pool can contain a maximum of 20 connections. As a result, this pool will initially be created with 10 connections, and it will expand to as many as 20 connections if necessary. When 20 connections are in use, any additional users will have to wait until an existing connection becomes available.

The second example shows how to create a connection string that doesn't participate in connection pooling. To do that, you set the Pooling setting to False. Although this is uncommon, you might want to opt out of connection pooling if an application is only run occasionally or if it has unique connection requirements.

SQL Server and Oracle connection string settings for managing connection pools

Setting	Description
Pooling	Indicates whether the connection should be obtained from the appropriate connection pool. The default is True.
Min Pool Size	The minimum number of connections to maintain in the pool. The default is 0.
Max Pool Size	The maximum number of connections to maintain in the pool. The default is 100.
Connection Lifetime	The number of seconds a connection should be allowed to exist before it's destroyed and recreated. The default setting is 0, which causes the connection to last indefinitely.

A connection string that specifies the size of the pool

```
server=DB1\Sql1;database=Halloween;integrated security=SSPI;
Min Pool Size=10;Max Pool Size=20
```

A connection string that doesn't participate in pooling

```
server=DB1\Sql1;database=Halloween;integrated security=SSPI;Pooling=False
```

Description

- The SQL Server and Oracle data providers for ADO.NET provide for connection pooling automatically. However, you can control how connection pooling works by specifying values within a connection string.

- The OLE DB and ODBC data providers manage connection pooling automatically, so you don't need to manage it yourself.

Figure 12-3   Connection string settings that affect connection pooling

How to use a configuration file to store connection information

To be sure that all of the connections an application uses to connect to a given database are drawn from the same connection pool, each connection must use the same connection string. One way to make that connection string available to all the classes in the application is to store it in the Web.config file that's generated when you create an ASP.NET web project. Then, whenever the application needs a connection string, it can retrieve it from that file. In addition, if you later need to change the connection string, you can change it in the Web.config file and be assured that all the connections will continue to use identical connection strings.

Figure 12-4 shows how you can store a connection string in a Web.config file. Although this file is an XML file, you shouldn't have trouble editing it to add a connection string entry even if you aren't familiar with the details of XML syntax.

To edit the Web.config file, just double-click on it in the Solution Explorer to display it in the Code Editor window. Then, add an <appSettings> section as shown in this figure. This section should consist of an <add> element that includes a key attribute with the name you want to use for the setting and a value attribute that specifies the value of the setting. In this example, the key is given the name ConnectionString and the value is the actual content of the connection string.

After you add the connection string to the Web.config file, you can access it from your program by using the AppSettings property of the ConfigurationSettings class. On this property, you name the setting you want to access. The code shown in this figure, for example, retrieves the setting named ConnectionString and assigns it to a string variable. Then, you can use this variable to create a connection.

Note that you can edit the Web.config file after an application has been deployed to a production server. To do that, you simply open the file with a text editor such as Notepad. Then, when you save your changes, ASP.NET will detect that the file has changed and automatically restart the application so your changes take effect.

Because each application has its own Web.config file, any connection string you add to it can only be accessed by that application. If you want two or more applications to use the same connection string, you can define it in the global configuration file. This configuration file, named Machine.config, is stored in a central location where it's available to any application that runs on the server. You use the same technique to access this file that you use to access the Web.config file. Then, if the setting you specify isn't found in the Web.config file, it's retrieved from the Machine.config file.

A Web.config file with a connection string entry

```
<?xml version="1.0" encoding="utf-8" ?>
<configuration>

    <appSettings>
        <add key="ConnectionString"
            value="server=DB1\Sql1;database=Halloween;integrated security=SSPI" />
    </appSettings>

    <system.web>
    .
    .
    .
    </system.web>

</configuration>
```

Code that retrieves the connection string from the Web.config file

```
Dim sConnection As String
sConnection = ConfigurationSettings.AppSettings("ConnectionString")
```

Description

- When you create an ASP.NET web application, Visual Studio generates a Web.config file that stores application settings in an XML format. This file appears in the Solution Explorer, and you can edit it by double-clicking on it.

- To store a connection string in the Web.config file, you must add an <appSettings> section. This section should appear after the <configuration> tag and before the <system.web> tag.

- To create a configuration element, code an <add> tag within the <appSettings> section. Within this tag, define two attributes: a key attribute that specifies the name you want to use for the element and a value attribute that specifies the contents of the connection string.

- You can use the AppSettings property of the ConfigurationSettings class within the application to access the elements in the <appSettings> section of the Web.config file.

- You can also store connection information in the <appSettings> section of the Machine.config file that's stored in the Config folder subordinate to the .NET Framework installation folder. That way, the connection information is available to any application that runs on that machine.

- When you use the AppSettings property to get connection information, it looks first in the Web.config file for the application. If the <appSettings> section or the element you specify isn't found in this file, it looks in the Machine.config file.

Figure 12-4   How to use a configuration file to store connection information

How to create data commands

After you define the connection to the database, you create the command objects that contain the SQL statements you want to execute against the database. When you create command objects, you can also create parameters that let you work with different data each time the command is executed. You'll learn how to create both commands and parameters in the topics that follow.

How to create a command object

Figure 12-5 shows three ways you can create a command object using the SqlCommand class. First, you can create it without specifying any arguments. Then, you must set the Connection property to identify the connection to be used by the command, and you must set the CommandText property to specify the text of the statement to be executed. This is illustrated by the first example in this figure. Second, you can set the CommandText property by specifying the statement to be executed when you create the object. Then, you must set just the Connection property before you execute the command. Third, you can specify both the connection and the statement when you create the object. This is illustrated by the second example in this figure.

Another property you may need to set is the CommandType property. This property determines how the value of the CommandText property is interpreted. The values you can specify for this property are members of the CommandType enumeration that's shown in this figure. The default value is Text, which causes the value of the CommandText property to be interpreted as a SQL statement. If the CommandText property contains the name of a stored procedure, however, you'll need to set this property to StoredProcedure. And if the CommandText property contains the name of a table, you'll need to set this property to TableDirect. Then, all the rows and columns will be retrieved from the table. Note that this setting is only available for the OLE DB data provider.

The last property that's shown in this figure, Parameters, lets you work with the collection of parameters for a command. As you'll see in the next figure, you can use parameters to restrict the data that's retrieved by a command. For example, you can use a parameter to retrieve a single product row from the Products table or to retrieve all of the rows for a particular category.

In addition to the properties shown in this figure, you can also use the Execute methods of a command object to execute the statement it contains. You'll learn how to use these methods later in this chapter.

Three ways to create a SqlCommand object

```
command = New SqlCommand()
command = New SqlCommand(cmdText)
command = New SqlCommand(cmdText, connection)
```

Common properties of a command

Property	Description
Connection	The connection used to connect to the database.
CommandText	A SQL statement, the name of a stored procedure, or the name of a table.
CommandType	A member of the CommandType enumeration that determines how the value in the CommandText property is interpreted.
Parameters	The collection of parameters for the command.

CommandType enumeration members

Member	Description
Text	The CommandText property contains a SQL statement. This is the default.
StoredProcedure	The CommandText property contains the name of a stored procedure.
TableDirect	The CommandText property contains the name of a table (OleDb only).

Code that creates a SqlCommand object that executes a Select statement

```
Dim sSelect As String = "Select CategoryID, ShortName, LongName " _
    & "From Categories Order By ShortName"
Dim cmdSelect As New SqlCommand()
With cmdSelect
    .Connection = conHalloween
    .CommandText = sSelect
End With
```

Another way to create a SqlCommand object

```
Dim cmdSelect As New SqlCommand(sSelect, conHalloween)
```

Description

- The CommandText and Connection properties are set to the values you pass to the constructor of the command class. If you don't pass these values to the constructor, you must set the CommandText and Connection properties after you create the command object.

- If you set the CommandText property to the name of a stored procedure or table, you must also set the CommandType property.

Figure 12-5   How to create a command object

How to create a parameterized query

A *parameterized query* is a query that depends on the value of one or more *parameters*. For example, an application that maintains the Products table will need to use a parameterized query to retrieve a specific row from the Products table based on the ProductID column. A parameterized query that does just that is shown in the first example in figure 12-6. Here, the parameter is identified by a placeholder named @ProductID.

When you use parameters in a SQL statement for a SQL Server command, you use *named variables* for placeholders like the one shown in this example. Note that the variable name must begin with an at sign (@) and is usually given the same name as the column it's associated with. Similarly, the placeholder for an Oracle parameter must be a name that begins with a colon (:), as illustrated by the second example in this figure. In contrast, the placeholder for a parameter in a SQL statement for an OLE DB or ODBC command is a question mark, as illustrated by the third example.

After you define the SQL statement, you create the parameter objects that will hold the values that are substituted for the placeholders. The next figure shows you how to do that.

A parameterized query for a SQL Server command

```
Select ProductID, Name, ShortDescription, OnHand, UnitPrice
From Products
Where ProductID = @ProductID
```

A parameterized query for an Oracle command

```
Select ProductID, Name, ShortDescription, OnHand, UnitPrice
From Products
Where ProductID = :ProductID
```

A parameterized query for an OLE DB or ODBC command

```
Select ProductID, Name, ShortDescription, OnHand, UnitPrice
From Products
Where ProductID = ?
```

Description

- A *parameterized query* is a query that depends on the values of one or more *parameters*. In most cases, you'll use parameters in the Where clause of a Select statement to identify the rows to be retrieved.

- To create a parameterized query, you code a SQL statement with placeholders for the parameters. Then, you create a parameter object that defines the parameter, and you add it to the parameters collection of the command object that contains the SQL statement.

- The placeholder for a parameter in a SQL Server command is a *named variable* whose name begins with an at sign (@). For an Oracle command, the name of a variable begins with a colon (:). In most cases, you'll give the variable the same name as the column it's associated with.

- The placeholder for a parameter in an OLE DB or ODBC command is a question mark. The question mark simply indicates the position of the parameter.

Figure 12-6   How to create a parameterized query

How to create and use parameter objects

Figure 12-7 shows you how to create and work with parameter objects. Here, you can see three formats for creating a SQL Server parameter. Although there are others, these are the three you're most likely to use. You create a parameter for an OLE DB, ODBC, or Oracle command using similar techniques.

Before you can use a parameter, you must assign a name, a data type, and a value to it. If you don't assign these values when you create the object, you can do that using some of the properties shown in this figure. Notice that you can specify the data type using either the DbType or SqlDbType property for a SQL Server parameter. (Similarly, you can use either the DbType property or the OleDbType, OdbcType, or OracleType property for an OLE DB, ODBC, or Oracle parameter).

The first example in this figure shows how to create a parameter and add it to the collection of parameters for a command. This code creates the parameter named @ProductID that's used by the Select statement you saw in figure 12-6. Like the ProductID column in the Products table, this parameter is assigned a data type of VarChar. Then, the Add method of the parameters collection is used to add the parameter to the collection of parameters for a command named cmdSelect. (This is the command that contains the Select statement.)

In most cases, you'll create a parameter object, assign it to a variable, set its properties, and add it to the parameters collection as shown in this example. You should know, however, that you can also add a parameter to the parameters collection without creating a parameter variable. For example, to create the parameter shown in this figure and add it to the parameters collection, you could use a statement like this:

```
cmdSelect.Parameters.Add("@ProductID", SqlDbType.VarChar)
```

If you do that, of course, you won't be able to refer to the parameter using a variable. So if you need to set additional properties of the parameter, you'll have to access the parameter through the command object.

The second example in this figure shows one way to set the Value property of a parameter. To do that, you use the Parameters property of the command to access the parameters collection and you identify the parameter by name or by index. If the parameter is assigned to a variable, you can use that variable to set its Value property as shown in the third example in this figure. To do that, of course, the variable must be within the scope of the procedure that sets its value, which usually means that it's defined at the module level.

When you assign a name to a SQL Server or Oracle parameter, you should realize that it must be the same name that's specified in the SQL statement. That's because ADO.NET associates the parameters with the placeholders by name. Because of that, if a statement uses two or more parameters, you can add them to the parameters collection in any sequence. In contrast, OLE DB and ODBC parameters must be added to the collection in the same order that they appear in the SQL statement. In that case, ADO.NET associates the parameters with the placeholders in the SQL statement by sequence since the placeholders aren't named.

Three ways to create a SqlParameter object

```
sqlParameter = New SqlParameter()
sqlParameter = New SqlParameter(parameterName, value)
sqlParameter = New SqlParameter(parameterName, dbType)
```

Common properties of a SQL Server parameter

Property	Description
DbType	A member of the DbType enumeration that determines the type of data that the parameter can hold.
IsNullable	A Boolean value that indicates if the parameter accepts nulls. The default is False.
ParameterName	The name of the parameter.
Size	The maximum size of the value that the parameter can hold.
SqlDbType	A member of the SqlDbType enumeration that determines the type of data that the parameter can hold. This property is synchronized with the DbType property.
Value	The value of the parameter.

Code that creates a parameter and adds it to a parameters collection

```
Dim prmProductID As New SqlParameter()
prmProductID.ParameterName = "@ProductID"
prmProductID.SqlDbType = SqlDbType.VarChar
cmdSelect.Parameters.Add(prmProductID)
```

A statement that sets the value of the parameter

```
cmdSelect.Parameters("@ProductID").Value = txtProductID.Text
```

Another way to set the value of the parameter

```
prmProductID.Value = txtProductID.Text
```

Description

- When you create a parameter, you can specify the parameter name along with a value or a data type. If you don't specify these values, you can set the values of the associated properties after you create the parameter.

- When you create parameters for a SQL Server or Oracle command, you must give them the same names you used in the SQL statement. Then, you can add the parameters to the parameters collection in any order you want since ADO.NET refers to them by name.

- Because the parameters for OLE DB and ODBC commands aren't named in the SQL statement, the parameters can be given any name you want. However, they must be added to the parameters collection in the same order that they appear in the statement.

- You can refer to a parameter through the parameters collection of the command or through the variable that the parameter is assigned to.

Figure 12-7   How to create and use parameter objects

How to work with data commands

The method you use to execute the SQL statement associated with a command object depends on the operation the SQL statement performs. The three methods you're most likely to use are ExecuteReader, which lets you retrieve and work with a result set created by a Select statement; ExecuteScalar, which lets you retrieve a single value using a Select statement; and ExecuteNonQuery, which lets you execute an Insert, Update, or Delete statement. You'll learn how to use all three of these methods in the topics that follow.

How to create and work with a data reader

To execute a command that contains a Select statement that returns a result set, you use the ExecuteReader method as shown in figure 12-8. This method executes the Select statement and creates a data reader object. Then, you can use the properties and methods of the data reader to work with the result set.

Notice that when you execute the ExecuteReader method, you can specify a behavior. The behavior you specify must be a member of the Command-Behavior enumeration. Some of the most common members of this enumeration are listed in this figure. You can use these members to simplify your code or to improve the efficiency of your application.

After you create a data reader, you use the Read method to retrieve the next row of data in the result set. Note that you must also execute the Read method to retrieve the first row of data. It's not retrieved automatically when the data reader is created.

To retrieve a column from a data reader, you use the Item property. Like many of the other objects you've seen previously, the Item property is the default property of a data reader. Because of that, you can omit it.

The example in this figure illustrates how you use a data reader. For the purpose of this example, you can assume that the data command contains a Select statement that retrieves data from the Categories table. Then, this code creates a data reader object and opens the connection used by the data command. Next, it executes the ExecuteReader method of the command to retrieve the data specified by the Select statement. Because the CloseConnection behavior is included on this method, the connection will be closed automatically when the data reader is closed. The ExecuteReader method also opens the data reader and positions it before the first row in the result set.

Next, a Do loop is used to loop through the rows in the result set. The condition on this statement executes the Read method of the data reader. This works because the Read method returns a Boolean value that indicates whether the result set contains additional rows. As long as this condition is true, the program processes the row that was retrieved. In this case, the program creates a new list item object using the values of the ShortName and CategoryID columns and adds this object to the list of items in a list box. After all of the rows have been processed, the data reader is closed.

Two ways to create a SqlDataReader object

```
sqlDataReader = sqlCommand.ExecuteReader()
sqlDataReader = sqlCommand.ExecuteReader(behavior)
```

Common CommandBehavior enumeration members

Member	Description
CloseConnection	Closes the connection when the data reader is closed.
Default	Equivalent to specifying no command behavior.
SingleResult	Only a single result set is returned.
SingleRow	Only a single row is returned.

Common properties and methods of a SqlDataReader object

Property	Description
IsClosed	Gets a value that indicates if the data reader is closed.
Item	Gets the value of the column with the specified name or position in the row.

Method	Description
Close	Closes the data reader. If the command executed a stored procedure that included output parameters or a return value, this method also sets these values.
Read	Retrieves the next row and returns a Boolean value that indicates whether there are additional rows.

Code that uses a data reader to populate a list box with categories

```
Dim rdrCategory As SqlDataReader
conHalloween.Open()
rdrCategory = cmdSelect.ExecuteReader(CommandBehavior.CloseConnection)
Dim liCategory As ListItem
Do While rdrCategory.Read()
    liCategory = New ListItem(rdrCategory("ShortName"), _
        rdrCategory("CategoryID"))
    lstCategories.Items.Add(liCategory)
Loop
rdrCategory.Close()
```

Description

- A data reader lets you read rows from the result set defined by a command object. To create a data reader object, you use the ExecuteReader method of the command. Before you execute this method, you must open the connection that's used by the data reader.

- The data reader is opened automatically when it's created. While it's open, no other data readers can be opened on the same connection. The exception is if you're using an Oracle data reader, in which case other Oracle data readers can be open at the same time.

- When you first create a data reader, it's positioned before the first row in the result set. To retrieve the first row, you have to execute the Read method.

- You can specify two or more command behavior members by combining them using the And operator.

Figure 12-8   How to create and work with a data reader

How to execute queries that return a single value

The first example in figure 12-9 shows you how to execute a command that returns a single value, called a *scalar value*. To do that, you execute the ExecuteScalar method of the command. In this case, the command contains a Select statement that retrieves a count of the number of products for a given category. This type of summary value is often called an *aggregate value*. A scalar value can also be the value of a single column, a calculated value, or any other value that can be retrieved from the database.

Before I go on, you should realize that you can use the ExecuteScalar method with a Select statement that retrieves more than one value. In that case, though, the ExecuteScalar method returns only the first value and the others are discarded.

How to execute action queries

As you should know, you can use an Insert, Update, or Delete statement to perform actions against a database. For that reason, these statements are often referred to as *action queries*. To execute an action query, you use the ExecuteNonQuery method of a data command as shown in the second example in figure 12-9.

This example executes a command that contains an Insert statement that adds a row to the Categories table. Notice that the ExecuteNonQuery method returns an integer that indicates the number of rows in the database that were affected by the operation. You can use this value to check that the operation was successful.

Code that creates and executes a command that returns an aggregate value

```
Dim cmdSelect As New SqlCommand()
cmdSelect.Connection = conHalloween
cmdSelect.CommandText _
    = "Select Count(*) As ProductCount " _
    & "From Products " _
    & "Where CategoryID = @CategoryID"
Dim prmCategoryID As New SqlParameter("@CategoryID", SqlDbType.VarChar)
cmdSelect.Parameters.Add(prmCategoryID)
...
cmdSelect.Parameters("@CategoryID").Value = ddlCategories.SelectedValue
conHalloween.Open()
Dim iProductCount As Integer = cmdSelect.ExecuteScalar
conHalloween.Close()
```

Code that creates and executes a command that inserts a row

```
Dim iRowCount As Integer
Dim cmdInsert As New SqlCommand
cmdInsert.Connection = conHalloween
cmdInsert.CommandText = "Insert Into Categories " _
    & "(CategoryID, ShortName, LongName) " _
    & "Values(@CategoryID, @ShortName, @LongName)"
Dim prmCategoryID As New SqlParameter("@CategoryID", SqlDbType.VarChar)
cmdInsert.Parameters.Add(prmCategoryID)
Dim prmShortName As New SqlParameter("@ShortName", SqlDbType.VarChar)
cmdInsert.Parameters.Add(prmShortName)
Dim prmLongName As New SqlParameter("@LongName", SqlDbType.VarChar)
cmdInsert.Parameters.Add(prmLongName)
...
prmCategoryID.Value = txtCategoryID.Text
prmShortName.Value = txtShortName.Text
prmLongName.Value = txtLongName.Text
conHalloween.Open()
iRowCount = cmdInsert.ExecuteNonQuery()
conHalloween.Close()
```

Description

- You use the ExecuteScalar method of a command object to retrieve a single value, called a *scalar value*.

- The value that's returned can be the value of a single column and row in the database, a calculated value, an *aggregate value* that summarizes data in the database, or any other value that can be retrieved from the database.

- If the Select statement returns more than one column or row, only the value in the first column and row is retrieved by the ExecuteScalar method.

- You use the ExecuteNonQuery method of a command object to execute an Insert, Update, or Delete statement, called an *action query*. This method returns an integer that indicates the number of rows that were affected by the query.

- You can also use the ExecuteNonQuery method to execute statements that affect the structure of a database object. For more information, see the documentation for your database management system.

Figure 12-9   How to execute queries that don't return a result set

A Product Maintenance application that uses command objects

The remaining topics of this chapter present an application that lets the user maintain the Products table of the Halloween database. To do that, it uses command objects to retrieve, insert, update, and delete rows. Although this application is relatively simple, it will show you how you can use command objects when you develop more complex database applications.

The design of the Product Maintenance application

The Product Maintenance application consists of the single page shown in figure 12-10. When this page is first displayed, only the Product drop-down list, Get Product button, and New Product button are enabled, as you can see in the first page shown here. To update or delete an existing product, the user selects the product from the drop-down list and clicks the Get Product button. Then, the application retrieves the data for the selected product, displays it on the page, and enables the appropriate controls as shown in the second page in this figure. The user can then modify the data and click the Update button or click the Delete Product button to delete the product. The user can also click the Cancel button to cancel the operation.

To add a new row, the user clicks the New Product button. Then, the application enables the input controls so the user can enter the data for the new product and disables the Product drop-down list, Get Product button, and New Product button. It also changes the text that's displayed on the Update button to "Add" so the user will know to click this button to add the new row.

The page for the Product Maintenance application

Description

- The Product Maintenance application lets users add, update, and delete rows in the Products table of the Halloween database.

- To add a product, the user clicks the New Product button and then provides the required information. To update or delete a product, the user selects the product from the drop-down list and clicks the Get Product button to display the product information.

- The user can click the Cancel button during any operation to cancel that operation.

Figure 12-10   The design of the Product Maintenance application

The code for the database classes

Figure 12-11 shows the code for the database classes used by the Product Maintenance application. The first class, ProductDB, provides the methods used to access the Halloween database. I'll describe it in detail in just a moment. The other class, Product, represents a single product. If you look at the definition of this class on page 3 of this listing, you'll see that it consists entirely of public variables.

The first two methods in the ProductDB class, GetCategories and GetProducts, return datasets that contain information from the Categories and Products tables. These methods use the database handling techniques you learned in chapter 4, so you shouldn't have any trouble understanding how they work.

The next method, GetProduct, retrieves a single row from the Products table. To do that, it defines a command object with a Select statement that uses a parameter for the product ID of the product to be retrieved. The product ID is provided as an argument to the GetProduct method.

After the command and parameter are created, the ExecuteReader method is used to execute the command and create a data reader object. Notice that the ExecuteReader method specifies the SingleRow command behavior because the query will return just one row. Then, the Read method of the data reader is used to retrieve that row, the values of that row are assigned to a new Product object, and the Product object is returned to the calling procedure. Notice that if the Select statement doesn't return a row, a value of Nothing is returned to the calling procedure. That could happen if another user deleted the requested product.

The code for the ProductDB class   Page 1

```
Imports System.Data.SqlClient
Public Class ProductDB

    Public Shared Function GetCategories() As DataSet
        Dim sSelect As String = "SELECT CategoryID, ShortName FROM Categories"
        Dim cmdCategories As New SqlCommand(sSelect, Connection)
        Dim daCategories As New SqlDataAdapter
        daCategories.SelectCommand = cmdCategories
        Dim dsCategories As New DataSet
        daCategories.Fill(dsCategories, "Categories")
        Return dsCategories
    End Function

    Public Shared Function GetProducts() As DataSet
        Dim sSelect As String = "SELECT ProductID, Name FROM Products"
        Dim cmdProducts As New SqlCommand(sSelect, Connection)
        Dim daProducts As New SqlDataAdapter
        daProducts.SelectCommand = cmdProducts
        Dim dsProducts As New DataSet
        daProducts.Fill(dsProducts, "Products")
        Return dsProducts
    End Function

    Public Shared Function GetProduct(ByVal ProductID As String) As Product
        Dim sSelect As String = "SELECT ProductID, CategoryID, Name, " _
            & "ShortDescription, LongDescription, ImageFile, " _
            & "UnitPrice, OnHand " _
            & "FROM Products " _
            & "WHERE ProductID = @ProductID"
        Dim DBConnection As SqlConnection = Connection()
        DBConnection.Open()
        Dim cmdProducts As New SqlCommand(sSelect, DBConnection)
        cmdProducts.Parameters.Add("@ProductID", ProductID)
        Dim drProducts As SqlDataReader
        drProducts = cmdProducts.ExecuteReader(CommandBehavior.SingleRow)
        If drProducts.Read() Then
            Dim Product As New Product
            Product.ProductID = drProducts.Item("ProductID")
            Product.CategoryID = drProducts.Item("CategoryID")
            Product.Name = drProducts.Item("Name")
            Product.ShortDescription = drProducts.Item("ShortDescription")
            Product.LongDescription = drProducts.Item("LongDescription")
            Product.ImageFile = drProducts.Item("ImageFile")
            Product.UnitPrice = drProducts.Item("UnitPrice")
            Product.OnHand = drProducts.Item("OnHand")
            Return Product
        Else
            Return Nothing
        End If
        DBConnection.Close()
    End Function
```

Figure 12-11   The code for the database classes (part 1 of 3)

On page 2 of this listing, you can see the AddProduct method that's used to add a new row to the Products table. This method receives a Product object that contains the data for the new row. Then, a command object that contains an Insert statement with a parameter for each column in the row is created, and the values in the Product object are assigned to these parameters. Next, the ExecuteNonQuery method of the command object is executed within a Try…Catch statement that catches SQL Server exceptions. That way, if the specified product ID already exists, this AddProduct method will catch the exception that's thrown and return a value of False to the calling procedure to indicate that the operation was unsuccessful. (Although other SQL Server exceptions can occur, this is the most likely one.) Otherwise, this method returns a value of True.

Notice that the value that's returned from the ExecuteNonQuery method isn't assigned to a variable since this value isn't used by the program. In that case, the return value is discarded.

Like the AddProduct method, the UpdateProduct method receives a Product object as an argument. This object is used to set the values of the parameters defined by the Update statement associated with the command object. Then, the value that's returned by the ExecuteNonQuery method is tested to determine whether the update was successful (see page 3). If it wasn't, it probably means that the specified product has been deleted by another user. In that case, a value of False is returned to the calling procedure. Otherwise, a value of True is returned.

Note that this code doesn't check whether another user has modified the same row before the changes are written to the database. To do that, a program needs to provide for *concurrency control*. You'll learn more about concurrency control and how you can implement it in the next chapter.

The code for the ProductDB class (continued)   Page 2

```
Public Shared Function AddProduct(ByVal Product As Product) As Boolean
    Dim sInsert As String _
        = "INSERT Products (ProductID, Name, CategoryID, " _
        & "ShortDescription, LongDescription, ImageFile, " _
        & "UnitPrice, OnHand) " _
        & "Values (@ProductID, @Name, @CategoryID, " _
        & "@ShortDescription, @LongDescription, @ImageFile, " _
        & "@UnitPrice, @OnHand)"
    Dim DBConnection As SqlConnection = Connection()
    Dim cmdProducts As New SqlCommand(sInsert, DBConnection)
    cmdProducts.Parameters.Add("@ProductID", Product.ProductID)
    cmdProducts.Parameters.Add("@Name", Product.Name)
    cmdProducts.Parameters.Add("@CategoryID", Product.CategoryID)
    cmdProducts.Parameters.Add("@ShortDescription", _
        Product.ShortDescription)
    cmdProducts.Parameters.Add("@LongDescription", _
        Product.LongDescription)
    cmdProducts.Parameters.Add("@ImageFile", Product.ImageFile)
    cmdProducts.Parameters.Add("@UnitPrice", Product.UnitPrice)
    cmdProducts.Parameters.Add("@OnHand", Product.OnHand)
    AddProduct = True
    DBConnection.Open()
    Try
        cmdProducts.ExecuteNonQuery()
    Catch e As SqlException
        AddProduct = False
    End Try
    DBConnection.Close()
End Function

Public Shared Function UpdateProduct(ByVal Product As Product) As Boolean
    Dim sUpdate As String = "UPDATE Products SET " _
                          & "CategoryID=@CategoryID, " _
                          & "Name=@Name, " _
                          & "ShortDescription=@ShortDescription, " _
                          & "LongDescription=@LongDescription, " _
                          & "ImageFile=@ImageFile, " _
                          & "UnitPrice=@UnitPrice, " _
                          & "OnHand=@OnHand " _
                          & "WHERE ProductID=@ProductID"
    Dim DBConnection As SqlConnection = Connection()
    Dim cmdProducts As New SqlCommand(sUpdate, DBConnection)
    cmdProducts.Parameters.Add("@ProductID", Product.ProductID)
    cmdProducts.Parameters.Add("@CategoryID", Product.CategoryID)
    cmdProducts.Parameters.Add("@Name", Product.Name)
    cmdProducts.Parameters.Add("@ShortDescription", _
        Product.ShortDescription)
    cmdProducts.Parameters.Add("@LongDescription", _
        Product.LongDescription)
    cmdProducts.Parameters.Add("@ImageFile", Product.ImageFile)
    cmdProducts.Parameters.Add("@UnitPrice", Product.UnitPrice)
    cmdProducts.Parameters.Add("@OnHand", Product.OnHand)
    DBConnection.Open()
    Dim iCount As Integer
    iCount = cmdProducts.ExecuteNonQuery()
    DBConnection.Close()
```

Figure 12-11   The code for the database classes (part 2 of 3)

The DeleteProduct method on page 3 of this listing receives a product ID as an argument. Then, it defines a command object that contains a Delete statement with a parameter for the product ID. Next, the ExecuteNonQuery method of this command is executed within a Try...Catch statement. The Catch clause on this statement catches any SQL error that occurs. The most likely error is a foreign key constraint error, which indicates that one or more rows exist in the LineItems table for that product. In that case, the return value of the DeleteProduct method is set to False. The return value of this method is also set to False if the return value of the ExecuteQuery method indicates that the Delete operation was unsuccessful. That can happen if the product has already been deleted by another user.

The last procedure in the ProductDB class, Connection, returns a connection object that the methods in this class can use to access the database. Notice that the Connection procedure retrieves the connection string it uses to create the connection from the application's Web.config file.

The code for the ProductDB class (continued)   **Page 3**

```vb
            If iCount > 0 Then
                Return True
            Else
                Return False
            End If
        End Function

        Public Shared Function DeleteProduct(ByVal ProductID As String) As Boolean
            Dim sDelete As String = "DELETE FROM Products " _
                            & "WHERE ProductID=@ProductID"
            Dim DBConnection As SqlConnection = Connection()
            Dim cmdProducts As New SqlCommand(sDelete, DBConnection)
            cmdProducts.Parameters.Add("@ProductID", ProductID)
            DBConnection.Open()
            Dim iCount As Integer
            iCount = cmdProducts.ExecuteNonQuery
            DeleteProduct = True
            Try
                iCount = cmdProducts.ExecuteNonQuery
                If iCount = 0 Then
                    DeleteProduct = False
                End If
            Catch e As SqlException
                DeleteProduct = False
            End Try
            DBConnection.Close()
        End Function

        Private Shared Function Connection() As SqlConnection
            Dim sConnectionString As String
            sConnectionString _
                = ConfigurationSettings.AppSettings("ConnectionString")
            Return New SqlConnection(sConnectionString)
        End Function

    End Class
```

The code for the Product class

```vb
Public Class Product
    Public ProductID As String
    Public Name As String
    Public ShortDescription As String
    Public LongDescription As String
    Public CategoryID As String
    Public ImageFile As String
    Public UnitPrice As Decimal
    Public OnHand As Integer
End Class
```

Figure 12-11   The code for the database classes (part 3 of 3)

The code for the Product Maintenance form

Figure 12-12 presents the code for the Product Maintenance form. At the beginning of this listing, you can see an enumeration named ControlState. As you'll see, this enumeration is used to manage the state of the form controls.

The first time the page is loaded, the Load procedure calls the BindProducts and BindCategories procedures to bind the Product and Category drop-down lists to datasets retrieved by the GetProducts and GetCategories methods of the ProductDB class. Since you learned how to bind drop-down lists in chapter 4, you shouldn't have any trouble understanding these procedures.

After it binds the drop-down lists, the Load procedure calls the SetControlState procedure. This procedure consists of a Select Case statement that sets the Enabled properties of the form's controls based on the ControlState value that's passed as an argument.

The code for the Product Maintenance form   **Page 1**

```
Public Class WebForm1
    Inherits System.Web.UI.Page

    Private Enum ControlState
        NoSelection
        NewProduct
        EditProduct
    End Enum

    Private Sub Page_Load(ByVal sender As System.Object, _
            ByVal e As System.EventArgs) Handles MyBase.Load
        'Put user code to initialize the page here
        If Not IsPostBack Then
            Me.BindProducts()
            Me.BindCategories()
            Me.SetControlState(ControlState.NoSelection)
        End If
    End Sub

    Public Sub BindProducts()
        Dim dsProducts As DataSet
        dsProducts = ProductDB.GetProducts()
        ddlProducts.DataSource = dsProducts
        ddlProducts.DataTextField = "Name"
        ddlProducts.DataValueField = "ProductID"
        ddlProducts.DataBind()
    End Sub

    Public Sub BindCategories()
        Dim dsCategories As DataSet
        dsCategories = ProductDB.GetCategories()
        ddlCategory.DataSource = dsCategories
        ddlCategory.DataTextField = "ShortName"
        ddlCategory.DataValueField = "CategoryID"
        ddlCategory.DataBind()
    End Sub

    Private Sub SetControlState(ByVal cs As ControlState)
        Select Case cs
            Case ControlState.NoSelection
                ddlProducts.Enabled = True
                btnGetProduct.Enabled = True
                btnNew.Enabled = True
                btnDelete.Enabled = False
                btnUpdate.Enabled = False
                btnUpdate.Text = "Update"
                btnCancel.Enabled = False
                txtProductID.Enabled = False
                Me.EnableEntryControls(False)
```

Figure 12-12   The code for the Product Maintenance form (part 1 of 4)

If the user clicks the Get Product button, the Click event procedure for that button, shown on page 2 of this listing, executes the GetProduct method of the ProductDB class to retrieve the selected row. If the row is found, it displays the values from that row on the form and executes the SetControlState procedure to enable the appropriate controls so the user can update or delete the product. Notice that before the item in the Category drop-down list that's associated with the selected product is selected, the Selected property of the currently selected item is set to False. That's necessary because only one item can be selected in a drop-down list at a time.

If the selected row wasn't found, the GetProduct procedure displays an error message indicating that the product has been deleted. Then, it executes the BindProducts procedure so that the deleted product is removed from the Product drop-down list.

If the user clicks the New button, the New procedure shown on page 3 executes the ClearFields procedure to clear the input controls. Then, it executes the SetControlState procedure to enable the appropriate controls so the user can enter the data for a new product.

If the user clicks the Update button, the Update procedure creates a new Product object using the values in the form controls. Then, the Text property of the Update button is tested to determine if a product is being added or updated. If it's being added, the AddProduct method of the ProductDB class is executed. If the return value from this method indicates that the product was added successfully, the input controls are cleared. Otherwise, a message is displayed indicating that the product ID already exists.

If the product is being updated, the UpdateProduct method of the ProductDB class is executed to update the product. Then, if the update is successful, the input controls are cleared. Otherwise, a message is displayed indicating that the product has been deleted.

The next to last statement in the Update procedure executes the BindProducts method to rebind the Product drop-down list. That way, the list is updated to reflect new, modified, or deleted products. Finally, the Update procedure executes the SetControlState procedure to prepare for the next user selection.

If the user clicks the Delete button, the Delete procedure shown on page 4 executes the DeleteProduct method of the ProductDB class to delete the selected product. If the delete operation is successful, the input controls are cleared. Otherwise, an error message is displayed indicating that the product has already been deleted or is in use. Then, the SetControlState procedure is executed and the Product drop-down list is rebound so that the deleted product is omitted from the list.

The last procedure is executed if the user clicks the Cancel button. It simply clears the input controls and executes the SetControlState procedure.

The code for the Product Maintenance form   **Page 2**

```vbnet
            Case ControlState.NewProduct
                ddlProducts.Enabled = False
                btnGetProduct.Enabled = False
                btnNew.Enabled = False
                btnDelete.Enabled = False
                btnUpdate.Enabled = True
                btnUpdate.Text = "Add"
                btnCancel.Enabled = True
                txtProductID.Enabled = True
                Me.EnableEntryControls(True)
            Case ControlState.EditProduct
                ddlProducts.Enabled = False
                btnGetProduct.Enabled = False
                btnNew.Enabled = False
                btnDelete.Enabled = True
                btnUpdate.Enabled = True
                btnUpdate.Text = "Update"
                btnCancel.Enabled = True
                txtProductID.Enabled = False
                Me.EnableEntryControls(True)
        End Select
    End Sub

    Private Sub EnableEntryControls(ByVal Enabled As Boolean)
        ddlCategory.Enabled = Enabled
        txtName.Enabled = Enabled
        txtShortDescription.Enabled = Enabled
        txtLongDescription.Enabled = Enabled
        txtImageFile.Enabled = Enabled
        txtUnitPrice.Enabled = Enabled
        txtOnHand.Enabled = Enabled
    End Sub

    Private Sub btnGetProduct_Click(ByVal sender As System.Object, _
            ByVal e As System.EventArgs) Handles btnGetProduct.Click
        Dim Product As Product
        Product = ProductDB.GetProduct(ddlProducts.SelectedItem.Value)
        If Not Product Is Nothing Then
            txtProductID.Text = Product.ProductID
            ddlCategory.SelectedItem.Selected = False
            ddlCategory.Items.FindByValue(Product.CategoryID).Selected = True
            txtName.Text = Product.Name
            txtShortDescription.Text = Product.ShortDescription
            txtLongDescription.Text = Product.LongDescription
            txtImageFile.Text = Product.ImageFile
            txtUnitPrice.Text = FormatNumber(Product.UnitPrice, 2)
            txtOnHand.Text = Product.OnHand
            Me.SetControlState(ControlState.EditProduct)
        Else
            lblProductError.Text = "That product has been deleted."
            Me.BindProducts()
        End If
    End Sub
```

Figure 12-12   The code for the Product Maintenance form (part 2 of 4)

The code for the Product Maintenance form

```
Private Sub btnNew_Click(ByVal sender As System.Object, _
        ByVal e As System.EventArgs) Handles btnNew.Click
    Me.ClearFields()
    Me.SetControlState(ControlState.NewProduct)
End Sub

Private Sub ClearFields()
    ddlProducts.SelectedIndex = 0
    txtProductID.Text = ""
    ddlCategory.SelectedIndex = 0
    txtName.Text = ""
    txtShortDescription.Text = ""
    txtLongDescription.Text = ""
    txtImageFile.Text = ""
    txtUnitPrice.Text = ""
    txtOnHand.Text = ""
End Sub

Private Sub btnUpdate_Click(ByVal sender As System.Object, _
        ByVal e As System.EventArgs) Handles btnUpdate.Click
    Dim Product As New Product
    Product.ProductID = txtProductID.Text
    Product.CategoryID = ddlCategory.SelectedItem.Value
    Product.Name = txtName.Text
    Product.ShortDescription = txtShortDescription.Text
    Product.LongDescription = txtLongDescription.Text
    Product.ImageFile = txtImageFile.Text
    Product.UnitPrice = txtUnitPrice.Text
    Product.OnHand = txtOnHand.Text
    If btnUpdate.Text = "Add" Then
        If ProductDB.AddProduct(Product) Then
            Me.ClearFields()
        Else
            lblIDError.Text = "That ProductID already exists."
        End If
    Else
        If ProductDB.UpdateProduct(Product) Then
            Me.ClearFields()
        Else
            lblIDError.Text = "This product has been deleted."
        End If
    End If
    Me.BindProducts()
    Me.SetControlState(ControlState.NoSelection)
End Sub
```

Figure 12-12   The code for the Product Maintenance form (part 3 of 4)

The code for the Product Maintenance form   **Page 4**

```
Private Sub btnDelete_Click(ByVal sender As System.Object, _
        ByVal e As System.EventArgs) Handles btnDelete.Click
    If ProductDB.DeleteProduct(txtProductID.Text) Then
        Me.ClearFields()
    Else
        lblIDError.Text = "This product has already been deleted " _
                    & "or the product is in use."
    End If
    Me.SetControlState(ControlState.NoSelection)
    Me.BindProducts()
End Sub

Private Sub btnCancel_Click(ByVal sender As System.Object, _
        ByVal e As System.EventArgs) Handles btnCancel.Click
    Me.ClearFields()
    Me.SetControlstate(ControlState.NoSelection)
End Sub

End Class
```

Figure 12-12   The code for the Product Maintenance form (part 4 of 4)

Perspective

In this chapter, you've learned the basic skills for using ADO.NET data commands. Although there's a lot more you can do with data commands than what's presented here, the information in this chapter will get you off to a good start. Then, for a more complete treatment of data commands and ADO.NET, please refer to *Murach's VB.NET Database Programming with ADO.NET*.

Terms

connection pool
connection pooling
parameterized query
parameter
named variable
scalar value
aggregate value
action query
concurrency control

13

How to use datasets with bound and unbound controls

In chapter 4, you learned some basics skills for working with the data in a dataset. This chapter expands on those skills by teaching you how to work with datasets using both bound and unbound controls. But first, it presents some concepts and skills you'll need regardless of whether you're using bound or unbound controls.

How to work with a dataset

Before you can use a dataset, you need to become familiar with the classes it contains and the properties and methods you can use with those classes. You also need to know how to create a data adapter and use it to fill a dataset with data from a database. Besides that, you should know how to cache data objects so you don't have to retrieve them from the database each time they're needed. And you should know how to use a data view to sort and filter the data in a data table. That's what you'll learn in the topics that follow.

The dataset classes

As you should know, a dataset is organized as a hierarchy of collections. For example, a dataset has a collection of one or more tables, and each table has a collection of one or more rows and a collection of one or more columns. Figure 13-1 presents some of the properties and methods of the four main classes that make up this hierarchy.

As you can see, you can refer to a collection in the dataset hierarchy using a property of the parent object. For example, you can refer to the collection of data tables in a dataset using the Tables property of the DataSet object. Similarly, you can refer to the collections of data rows and data columns in a data table using the Rows and Columns properties of the DataTable object. These are the properties you're most likely to use as you work with these objects.

Although they're not shown in this figure, the collections you refer to through the Tables property of a dataset and the Columns and Rows properties of a data table have properties and methods of their own. For instance, each collection has a Count property that you can use to determine how many items are in the collection. To get the number of tables in a dataset named dsProducts, for example, you can use code like this:

```
dsProducts.Tables.Count()
```

To access a specific item in a collection, you use the Item property. On that property, you specify the index value or name of the item you want to access. To access the Products table in the dsProducts dataset, for example, you can use code like this:

```
dsProducts.Tables.Item("Products")
```

Since Item is the default property of the collection class, however, you can omit it like this:

```
dsProducts.Tables("Products")
```

The first code example in this figure shows how you can use a For Each statement to loop through the items in a collection. Here, the statement loops through the rows in the Products table. To do that, it uses a variable that's declared as a DataRow object. Then, the For Each...Next statement uses this variable to retrieve the value of the ProductID column in each row. You can use similar code to loop through the columns in a table or the tables in a dataset.

Common properties of the DataSet class

Property	Description
DataSetName	The name of the dataset.
Tables	A collection of the DataTable objects contained in the dataset.
Relations	A collection of the DataRelation objects contained in the dataset.

Common properties and method of the DataTable class

Property	Description
TableName	The name of the table.
Columns	A collection of the DataColumn objects contained in the data table.
Rows	A collection of the DataRow objects contained in the data table.
Constraints	A collection of the Constraint objects contained in the data table.

Method	Description
NewRow	Creates a new row in the table.

Common property of the DataColumn class

Property	Description
ColumnName	The name of the column.

Common property and method of the DataRow class

Property	Description
Item	Accesses the specified column of the row.

Method	Description
Delete	Deletes a row.

Code that populates a drop-down list from rows in a data table

```
Dim dr As DataRow
For Each dr In dsProducts.Tables("Products").Rows
    ddlProducts.Items.Add(dr.Item("ProductID"))
Next
```

A statement that refers to a table in the dataset by its index

```
ddlProducts.DataSource = dsProducts.Tables(0)
```

Description

- A dataset can contain one or more data tables, and each data table can contain one or more data rows and data columns. The data tables, data rows, and data columns are stored in collections that you can access through a property of the parent object.

- You can refer to a specific object in a collection using a string with the object's name or its index value. All of the ADO.NET collections are zero-based.

Figure 13-1   The dataset classes

How to create and work with data adapters

You can use two techniques to create SqlDataAdapter objects, as illustrated by the syntax at the top of figure 13-2. If you use the first technique, you don't pass an argument to the constructor. In that case, you have to set the value of the SelectCommand property after you create the object as illustrated by the first example in this figure. The SelectCommand property identifies the command object that will be used to retrieve data when the Fill method of the data adapter is executed. If you use the second format, you can pass the value of the SelectCommand property to the constructor as illustrated by the second example.

If you will be updating the data that's retrieved by a data adapter, you'll need to create command objects that contain Insert, Update, and Delete statements and assign them to the InsertCommand, UpdateCommand, and DeleteCommand properties of the data adapter. Although you can create these objects yourself, ADO.NET provides a command builder object to do it for you. You'll learn how to use a command builder later in this chapter.

This figure also presents the two methods of a data adapter that you're most likely to use. You use the Fill method to load a data table with data from a database, and you use the Update method to update a database with changes made to a data table. You'll learn more about the Fill method in the next figure, and you'll learn more about the Update method later in this chapter.

The MissingSchemaAction property tells the data adapter how to create the columns in the dataset when you use the Fill method. The default value is MissingSchemaAction.Add, which creates a schema column for each column selected by the data adapter's Select command. If you need to include a primary key in the data table, you should specify the MissingSchemaAction.Add-WithKey constant for this property. Later in this chapter, for example, you'll learn about a method you can use to search for key data in a table. To use this method, the table you're searching must have a primary key.

Two ways to create a SqlDataAdapter object

```
dataAdapter = New SqlDataAdapter()
dataAdapter = New SqlDataAdapter(selectCommand)
```

Common properties and methods of a data adapter

Property	Description
SelectCommand	The command object used to retrieve data from the database.
InsertCommand	The command object used to insert new rows into the database.
UpdateCommand	The command object used to update rows in the database.
DeleteCommand	The command object used to delete rows from the database.
MissingSchemaAction	A member of the MissingSchemaAction enumeration that determines the action that's taken when the data retrieved by a Fill method doesn't match the schema of a table in the dataset.

Method	Description
Fill	Retrieves rows from the database using the command specified by the SelectCommand property and stores them in a data table.
Update	Saves changes made in the data table to the database using the commands specified by the InsertCommand, UpdateCommand, and DeleteCommand properties.

MissingSchemaAction enumeration members

Member	Description
Add	Adds the columns in the source table to the schema. This is the default.
AddWithKey	Adds the columns and primary key in the source table to the schema.
Error	A SystemException is generated.
Ignore	The columns that don't match the schema are ignored.

Code that creates a SqlDataAdapter object

```
Dim daProducts As New SqlDataAdapter()
daProducts.SelectCommand = cmdSelect
```

Another way to create a data adapter

```
Dim daProducts As New SqlDataAdapter(cmdSelect)
```

Description

- The SelectCommand property is set to the value you pass to the constructor of the data adapter. If you don't pass a Select command to the constructor, you must set this property after you create the data adapter.

- Although you can set the InsertCommand, UpdateCommand, and DeleteCommand properties directly, you can also use a command builder to build these commands for you. See figure 13-15 for more information.

Figure 13-2   How to create and work with data adapters

How to fill and clear a dataset

Before you can work with a dataset, you have to load data into it. To do that, you use the Fill method of the data adapter as shown in figure 13-3. The first statement in this figure, for example, loads the data defined by a data adapter named daProducts into a dataset named dsProducts. Notice that only the name of the dataset, and not the name of the data table, is used in this method. That's because a data adapter defines a single table even though a dataset can contain more than one data table. By default, the data adapter creates a table named "Table." You can change the name of this table by specifying the table name as the second argument of the Fill method, as illustrated by the second statement in this figure.

If you want to know how many rows were loaded into a dataset, you can retrieve the return value of the Fill method as illustrated in the third statement. Here, the return value is assigned to an integer variable. Then, you can use this variable any way you like within your program. For example, you might want to use it to keep a count of the number of rows in the dataset as the user adds, modifies, and deletes rows.

You can also use the Fill method to refresh the contents of a dataset during the execution of a program. To do that, you can use one of two techniques. First, you can use the Clear method of the dataset or a data table within the dataset to remove all the rows from that dataset or data table as illustrated in the last two statements in this figure. Then, you can use the Fill method to load the table with new data. This is the preferred method, and it's usually the most efficient.

Second, you can use the Fill method without clearing the dataset or data table. Then, if the table being refreshed is defined with a primary key, the rows in the existing table are updated by the rows in the database table. That, however, can be a time-consuming process if the table contains a large number of rows. That's why we recommend that you clear the table first. Also, if the table isn't defined with a primary key, the newly retrieved rows are appended to the existing rows, which isn't usually what you want. In that case, you'll want to be sure to clear the dataset or data table before executing the Fill method.

How to fill a data table

Two ways to use the Fill method

```
dataadapter.Fill(dataset)
dataadapter.Fill(dataset, "tablename")
```

A statement that fills a dataset using the default table name ("Table")

```
daProducts.Fill(dsProducts)
```

A statement that names the table to be created

```
daProducts.Fill(dsProducts, "Products")
```

A statement that retrieves the return value from the Fill statement

```
iRowCount = daProducts.Fill(dsProducts, "Products")
```

How to clear a dataset or table

The syntax of the Clear method for a dataset or table

```
dataset.Clear()
dataset.Tables("tablename").Clear()
```

A statement that clears all the tables in a dataset

```
dsProducts.Clear()
```

A statement that clears a single data table

```
dsProducts.Tables("Products").Clear()
```

Description

- The Fill method retrieves rows from the database using the Select statement specified by the SelectCommand property of the data adapter. The rows are stored in a data table within the dataset you specify.

- By default, the Fill method stores the data in the source table to a data table named "Table." Since that's usually not what you want, you should include the name of the data table as the second argument of the Fill method.

- When the Fill method is executed, the connection object that's associated with the SelectCommand object is opened automatically. After the dataset is filled, the connection object is closed.

- If you use the Fill method to refresh a table that already contains data, it will merge the rows retrieved from the database with the existing rows in the dataset based on the table's primary key. If the table isn't defined with a primary key, the Fill method appends the rows to the end of the table.

- The Fill method is implemented as a function that returns an integer value with the number of rows that were added or refreshed.

- The Clear method removes all the data from the table or dataset you specify. You can use this method to clear the data from a table that isn't defined with a primary key before you refresh that table. You can also use it to improve the efficiency of a retrieval operation for a table with a primary key.

Figure 13-3   How to fill and clear a dataset

How to cache data objects

ASP.NET's *application cache* is a feature that lets you save objects such as datasets in server memory so they can be retrieved quickly when they're needed. Datasets that contain data that doesn't change frequently are ideal for saving in the application cache. When a dataset has been stored in the application cache, an application can retrieve the dataset without having to access the underlying database. Figure 13-4 shows how the application cache works.

To start, you should realize that ASP.NET maintains a single cache for each application. Because of that, two or more users running the same application can access the same cache. As you can imagine, that can improve the efficiency of database operations. Regardless of the number of users who are running the application, however, keep in mind that all the pages in the application have access to the cache. Because of that, you'll want to be sure you carefully coordinate the contents of the cache and the names used for the cache objects from one page to the next.

To work with an application cache, you use the Cache class. To refer to the Cache object for an application from the code-behind file for a web form, you use the Cache property of the page. To refer to the Cache object from a class other than the code-behind file for a web form, you use the Cache property of the current HttpContext object.

You can see some of the common properties and methods of the Cache class at the top of this figure. To add an object to the cache, for example, you use the Insert method as illustrated in the first example. This method accepts two arguments. The first one is a string that contains the name of the object, and the second one is the object itself. In this case, the dsProducts dataset is added to the cache with a name of dsProducts.

After you place an object in the cache, it remains there even after the application that created the cached object ends. After the application that added the dsProducts dataset to the cache ends, for example, the page that's generated is sent back to the browser. Then, when the page is posted back to the server, the application can use a statement like the second one in this figure to retrieve the dataset from the cache and process the user request. Here, the Item property (the default) is used to retrieve the object named dsProducts.

When you add an object to the cache, it remains there until you delete it or until ASP.NET deletes it. This brings up an important point: ASP.NET can remove objects from the cache at any time to free up memory for other objects. As a result, adding an object to the cache doesn't guarantee that the object will be there the next time you need it. Before you retrieve an object from the cache, then, you should always check if it exists. To do that, you can use code like that in the third example. Here, an If statement tests if the dsProducts object is equal to Nothing. If it is, it means that the object doesn't exist. In that case, a procedure is called to create the dataset, and the dataset is added to the cache. Otherwise, the dataset is retrieved from the cache.

Before I go on, you should realize that you can store any type of object in the cache, including simple variables and arrays. However, the cache is used most often to store database data.

Common properties and methods of the Cache class

Property	Description
Item(key)	Gets the value of the cache object with the specified key, or adds an object with the specified key.
Count	Gets the number of objects in the cache.

Method	Description
Insert(key, value)	Inserts or replaces the cache object with the specified key with the specified value. See online help for this method for information about overloads that provide greater control over cached objects.
Remove(key)	Removes the object with the specified key from the cache.

A statement that adds a dataset to the cache

```
Cache.Insert("dsProducts", dsProducts)
```

A statement that retrieves the dataset from the cache

```
dsProducts = Cache("dsProducts")
```

Code that retrieves a dataset from the cache or creates a new dataset

```
If Cache("dsProducts") Is Nothing Then
    Me.FillProductsDataSet()
    Cache("dsProducts", dsProducts)
Else
    dsProducts = Cache("dsProducts")
End If
```

A statement that removes the dataset from the cache

```
Cache.Remove("dsProducts")
```

Description

- ASP.NET provides an *application cache* that you can use to store objects in server memory. Because the objects remain in memory until they're explicitly deleted or until ASP.NET deletes them, they can be accessed across sessions.

- The objects in the cache can also be accessed by two or more users running the same application. Because ASP.NET provides a separate cache for each application, the objects in the cache can't be shared between applications.

- You can add, modify, and delete cache objects using the properties and methods of the Cache class. To access the cache from a web page, use the Cache property of the page. To access the cache from outside a web page, use the Cache property of the current HttpContext object (HttpContext.Current).

- ASP.NET can remove an object from the cache at any time to make room for other objects. As a result, your applications should check to see if an object is available from the cache before trying to use it. Then, if the object isn't available, it can be recreated.

- To avoid repeated database access, it's common to store datasets in the cache. However, the cached dataset must be removed or refreshed whenever the underlying database tables are updated so it doesn't contain outdated data.

Figure 13-4   How to cache data objects

How to use data views

As figure 13-5 shows, a *data view* lets you sort and filter the rows in a data table. For example, you can use a data view to filter the Products table so only the rows in a given category are available. Or, you can use a data view to sort the rows in the Products table so they're available in alphabetical order based on the Name column. Note that a data view doesn't change the data in the data table in any way. Instead, it simply presents a "view" of the data in the table.

To create a data view, you can use one of the formats shown at the top of this figure. The first format simply creates the data view with its default settings. The second format sets the Table property of the data view to the data table you specify. The first statement in this figure, for example, creates a data view named dvProducts and sets its Table property to the Products table in the dataset named dsProducts.

To sort the rows in a data view, you assign a *sort expression* to its Sort property. To code a sort expression, you list one or more column names separated by commas. After each column name, you can code Asc or Desc to indicate whether the column values should be sorted in ascending or descending sequence. If you omit these keywords, the column values are sorted in ascending sequence.

The three sort expressions in this figure illustrate how this works. Here, the first sort expression consists of a single column name, so the data view will be sorted by that column in ascending sequence. The second expression consists of a single column name followed by Desc, so the data view will be sorted by that column in descending sequence. The third expression names two columns. In this case, the data view will be sorted by the first column in ascending sequence. Then, within that sequence, the data view will be sorted by the second column, also in ascending sequence.

To filter the rows in a data view, you assign a *filter expression* to the RowFilter property. A filter expression is a conditional expression that evaluates to a True or False value. The first filter expression in this figure, for example, tests if the ProductID column is equal to fox01. The second expression tests if the CategoryID column is equal to FX. And the third filter expression tests if the OnHand column is greater than 0. Notice in the first two examples that the string literal is enclosed in single quotes. That's because the entire filter expression is enclosed in double quotes.

Although the values used in the filter expressions shown here are coded as literals, you'll typically specify these values based on selections made by the user. To do that, you use code like that shown in the next example in this figure. Here, the RowFilter property is set to an expression that filters for all products that match a given category ID, which is specified as a string variable.

When you retrieve rows from a data view object, you should realize that each row is returned as a DataRowView object rather than as a DataRow object. Like the DataRow class, however, the DataRowView class has an Item property you can use to access the value of a specific column in the row. This is illustrated in the last example in this figure.

Two ways to create a data view

```
dataview = New DataView()
dataview = New DataView(table)
```

Common properties of the DataView class

Property	Description
Table	The table that the view is associated with.
Sort	An expression that determines the order of the rows in the view.
RowFilter	An expression that determines the rows that are included in the view.
Count	The number of rows in the view.

A statement that creates a data view

```
Dim dvProducts As New DataView(dsProducts.Tables("Products"))
```

Typical expressions for the Sort property

```
"Name"
"OnHand Desc"
"Category, Name"
```

Typical expressions for the RowFilter property

```
"ProductID = 'fox01'"
"CategoryID = 'FX'"
"OnHand > 0"
```

A statement that sets the row filter

```
dvProducts.RowFilter = "CategoryID='" & sCategoryID & "'"
```

Code that retrieves rows using a view

```
Dim drvProduct As DataRowView
For Each drvProduct In dvProducts
    ddlProducts.Items.Add(drv.Item("ProductID"))
Next
```

Description

- A *data view* provides a customized view of the data in a data table. Data views are typically used to sort or filter the rows in a data table.

- A *sort expression* is a string that consists of the names of one or more columns separated by commas. You can control the sort order by specifying Asc or Desc after each column name.

- A *filter expression* is a string that consists of a conditional expression. A row from the underlying data table is included in the data view only if the filter expression evaluates to True for that row.

- Each row in a data view is represented by a DataRowView object. You can use the Item property of this object to refer to a column in the row.

Figure 13-5   How to use data views

How to use bound controls to display data

In chapter 4, you learned how to bind a list control like a drop-down list or list box to a data table so it displays all the rows in that table. Because this technique is used frequently with web forms, I'll repeat that information here. In addition, I'll show you how to bind list controls to other sources of data, such as data views. I'll also show you how to bind other types of controls so they display a single data value. Then, I'll present an application that uses all of these binding techniques.

How to bind a Web Server control to multiple rows of a data source

To bind list controls, such as drop-down lists and list boxes, to multiple rows of a data source, you set the properties shown in figure 13-6. The two code examples in this figure illustrate how this works.

The first example binds a drop-down list to a data table. To do that, it sets the DataSource property to the dataset that contains the table (dsProducts), and it sets the DataMember property to the name of the data table (Products). Then, it sets the DataTextField property to the column named Name. The data in this column will be displayed in the list. Finally, it sets the DataValueField property to the column named ProductID. The data in this column will be stored in the list. That way, when the user selects an item from the list, the application can use the ProductID value to identify the related row in the data table.

The second example binds a drop-down list to a data view. Note that because a data view represents a single table, you don't have to assign a value to the DataMember property. Instead, you set the DataSource property to the data view. Then, you set the DataTextField and DataValueField properties to the columns you want to display and store in the list.

After you set the binding properties, you must use the DataBind method of the control to bind it to the data source specified by those properties. That's what the last statement in the first two examples do. Alternatively, you can bind all of the controls on a page at once. To do that, you execute the DataBind method of the page as shown in the third example.

The properties and method for binding a list control to a data source

Property	Description
DataSource	A data source, such as a dataset.
DataMember	The name of a member associated with the data source, such as a data table. If the data source contains only one bindable member, you don't need to set this property.
DataTextField	The name of the column in the data member whose value is displayed in the list.
DataValueField	The name of the column in the data member whose value is stored in the list.
DataTextFormatString	The format of the items displayed in the list.

Method	Description
DataBind()	Binds the control to its data source.

Code that binds a drop-down list to a data table

```
ddlProducts.DataSource = dsProducts
ddlProducts.DataMember = "Products"
ddlProducts.DataTextField = "Name"
ddlProducts.DataValueField = "ProductID"
ddlProducts.DataBind()
```

Code that binds a drop-down list to a data view

```
ddlProducts.DataSource = dvProducts
ddlProducts.DataTextField = "Name"
ddlProducts.DataValueField = "ProductID"
ddlProducts.DataBind()
```

A statement that binds all the controls on a page

```
Me.DataBind()
```

Description

- You can display the data in a data source in a list control by binding the control to the data source. To do that, you set the binding properties of the control and then execute the DataBind method of the control. You can also bind all of the controls on a page at once using the DataBind method of the page.

- If the data in the data source that a control is bound to changes, you must rebind the control before the changes in the data source are reflected in the control.

Figure 13-6   How to bind a Web Server control to multiple rows of a data source

How to bind a Web Server control to a single data value

You can also bind some of the Web Server controls, including the text box control, to a single data value. To do that, you create a *data binding expression* for the control as described in figure 13-7. A data binding expression contains information about the data you want to bind a control to.

To illustrate how this works, take a look at the three data binding expressions at the top of this figure. The first expression indicates that the control it's assigned to will be bound to the Value property of the item that's selected in a drop-down list. The second expression indicates that the control it's assigned to will be bound to the ProductID property of an object named Product. And the third expression indicates that the control it's assigned to will be bound to the result of a function named DaysUntil.

To use a data binding expression, you assign it to the attribute of the control you want to bind. This is illustrated by the aspx code for the first text box shown in this figure. Here, the Text attribute of the text box will be bound to the Name property of the Product object. Although you can assign a data binding expression to any attribute of a control, you're most likely to assign an expression to the Text attribute.

A data binding expression is evaluated when the DataBind method of the control it's assigned to or the DataBind method of the page that contains the control is executed. When the DataBind method of this text box is executed, for example, the value of the Name property of the Product object is retrieved and assigned to the Text attribute of the text box. Then, that value is displayed in the text box on the page.

You can also bind a control to a column in a data row. To do that, you use the Eval method of the DataBinder class as shown in this figure. The first argument of this method is the data source you want to bind to. The data source of the first two binding expressions shown here, for example, is a dataset. The data source of the third binding expression is a data view.

The second argument is a string value that consists of the properties that identify a data column in the data source. The string in the first expression shown here, for example, identifies the Name column in the first row of the first table of the dataset. The string in the second expression identifies the same column, but it refers to the table using its name rather than its index. The string in the third expression identifies a column named UnitPrice in the first row of a data view.

The third expression also passes a third argument to the Eval method. This argument specifies the format you want to use to display the data in the column. You can code any of the standard .NET format strings for this argument.

One peculiarity about the Eval method is that you can't include the names of default properties in the second argument. For example, you can't use the Item property to refer to a column in a data row, even though Item is the default property. Similarly, you can't use the Rows property of a data view to refer to a row in that view. If you do that, a runtime error will occur. To avoid this error, you should code the string values as shown here.

Examples of data binding expressions

A data binding expression that specifies the value of another control

```
<%# ddlProducts.SelectedItem.Value %>
```

A data binding expressing that specifies a property of a class named Product

```
<%# Product.ProductID %>
```

A data binding expression that calls a function in the code-behind file

```
<%# DaysUntil(10, 31) %>
```

A text box control that includes a data binding expression

```
<asp:TextBox id="txtName" Text='<%# Product.Name %>'></asp:TextBox>
```

Two ways to execute the DataBinder.Eval method

```
DataBinder.Eval(datasource, "navigation-path")
DataBinder.Eval(datasource, "navigation-path", "format-string")
```

Examples of binding expressions that call the DataBinder.Eval method

```
<%# DataBinder.Eval(dsProducts, "Tables(0).Rows(0).(Name)") %>
<%# DataBinder.Eval(dsProducts, "Tables(Products).Rows(0).(Name)") %>
<%# DataBinder.Eval(dvProducts, "(0).(UnitPrice)", "{0:c}") %>
```

A text box control with a binding expression that calls DataBinder.Eval

```
<asp:TextBox id="txtName"
Text='<%# DataBinder.Eval(dsProducts, "Tables(0).Rows(0).(Name)") %>' >
</asp:TextBox>
```

Description

- A *data binding expression* is an expression that contains information about the data you want to bind to. You assign a data binding expression to the control attribute you want to bind in the aspx file for a form. In most cases, you'll bind the Text attribute of a control.

- Data binding expressions consist of the characters <%#, followed by the binding information, followed by the characters %>.

- A data binding expression can specify any object property or method. For example, you can bind to a property of another control on the same page or a property of an object created in the code-behind file. You can also bind to a public function that's defined in the code-behind file.

- Data binding expressions are evaluated and replaced with the results of the expression when you execute the DataBind method for the control that contains the expression or when you execute the DataBind method for the entire page.

- You can use the Eval method of the DataBinder class to bind a control to a column in a data row. This method accepts the name of the data source and a string of properties that identify the column to be bound to as arguments. You can also code an optional third argument to specify how you want the data in the column formatted.

- To bind a control to a row in a data table, you have to fill the table with a single row, or you have to filter the table so it contains a single row. That's because the row is specified as a string value, which can't be changed as the program executes.

Figure 13-7   How to bind a Web Server control to a single data value

Before I go on, you should realize that the source of data you specify for the Eval method must consist of a single data row. That's because you specify the row as a string value, which means it can't vary from one execution of the program to the next. If the source of data for a binding expression is a table, that means that the data table must be filled with a single row. If the source of data is a data view, the data view must filter the data table to a single row.

A Product Display application that uses bound controls

Figure 13-8 presents the design of a Product Display application that uses bound controls. The Category drop-down list on the web page for this application is bound to a data table that contains information from the Categories table in the Halloween database. The Product drop-down list is bound to a data view that's associated with a data table that contains information from the Products table in the Halloween database. This data view filters the data table so that only the products for the selected category are displayed in the list. Finally, the label and image controls are bound to individual columns in a data view that's associated with the Products data table. This data view filters the table so that only the row for the selected product is available.

Because this application doesn't provide for modifying any of the data in the Categories and Products tables, it stores the datasets that contain these tables in the application cache. That way, the application must retrieve the data for these datasets from the database only if ASP.NET deletes the datasets from the cache.

The page for the Product Display application

Description

- The Product Display application displays information about the product selected by the user. To display a product, the user selects a category from the Category drop-down list to display all the products in that category in the Product drop-down list. Then, the user chooses a product from the Product list.

- This application uses two datasets: one to hold the category information and one to hold the product information. Both of these datasets are stored in the cache, so the database is accessed only if the data isn't available in cache.

- The Product drop-down list is bound to a data view that filters the Products data table based on the selected category.

- The label and image controls that display product information are bound to a second data view that filters the Products data table based on the selected product.

Figure 13-8   A Product Display application that uses bound controls

The code for the ProductDB class

Figure 13-9 presents the code for the ProductDB class that's used by the Product Display application. This class includes a private function named Connection that gets a SqlConnection object for the Halloween database. This function is identical to the one you saw in the last chapter, so you shouldn't have any trouble understanding how it works.

The GetCategories and GetProducts functions are also similar to the ones you saw in the last chapter. They return the datasets that contain the Categories and Products tables used by the application. The main difference between these functions and the ones in the last chapter are that the ones shown here check the application cache to determine if the datasets have been stored there. If so, the datasets are retrieved from the cache. Otherwise, a data adapter is created and the dataset is filled. Notice that these functions don't explicitly create the data commands that contain the Select statements. Instead, the string that contains the Select statement is specified on the constructor for the data adapter along with the connection object.

The code for the ProductDB class

```
Imports System.Data.SqlClient
Public Class ProductDB

    Private Shared Function Connection() As SqlConnection
        Dim sConnectionString As String
        sConnectionString _
            = ConfigurationSettings.AppSettings("ConnectionString")
        Return New SqlConnection(sConnectionString)
    End Function

    Public Shared Function GetCategories() As DataSet
        Dim dsCategories As New DataSet
        If HttpContext.Current.Cache("dsCategories") Is Nothing Then
            Dim sSelect As String = "Select CategoryID, ShortName " _
                & "From Categories"
            Dim daCategories As New SqlDataAdapter(sSelect, Connection())
            daCategories.Fill(dsCategories, "Categories")
            HttpContext.Current.Cache("dsCategories") = dsCategories
        Else
            dsCategories = HttpContext.Current.Cache("dsCategories")
        End If
        Return dsCategories
    End Function

    Public Shared Function GetProducts() As DataSet
        Dim dsProducts As New DataSet
        If HttpContext.Current.Cache("dsProducts") Is Nothing Then
            Dim sSelect As String = "Select ProductID, CategoryID, Name, " _
                & "ShortDescription, LongDescription, ImageFile, " _
                & "UnitPrice, OnHand " _
                & "From Products Order By ProductID"
            Dim daProducts As New SqlDataAdapter(sSelect, Connection())
            daProducts.Fill(dsProducts, "Products")
            HttpContext.Current.Cache("dsProducts") = dsProducts
        Else
            dsProducts = HttpContext.Current.Cache("dsProducts")
        End If
        Return dsProducts
    End Function

End Class
```

Figure 13-9   The code for the ProductDB class

The aspx code for the Product Display form

Figure 13-10 presents the aspx code for the Product Display form. Notice here that the AutoPostBack properties of both the drop-down lists are set to True. That way, the page will be posted whenever the user selects a different category or product. As you'll see in a minute, when the user selects a different category, the application filters the Product drop-down list so it includes just the products for the selected category and then displays the information for the first product in that category. Similarly, when the user selects a different product, the application displays the information for that product.

You should also notice the data binding expressions that are used for the label controls. These expressions all use the Eval method of the DataBinder class to bind the Text properties of the controls to a column in a data view named dvProducts. The expression for the Unit Price text box also includes a format string so the unit price will be formatted as currency.

The data binding expression for the image control is similar, but it's used to bind the ImageUrl property of the control. In addition, the result of the data binding expression is passed to a function named GetImageURL. This function is defined in the code-behind file for the form. You'll see what it does in just a moment. The result of this function is then assigned to the ImageUrl property.

The aspx code for the Product Display form

```
<%@ Register TagPrefix="ucl" TagName="Banner" Src="Banner.ascx" %>
<%@ Page Language="vb" AutoEventWireup="false" Codebehind="WebForm1.aspx.vb"
Inherits="ProductDisplay.WebForm1"%>
<!DOCTYPE HTML PUBLIC "-//W3C//DTD HTML 4.0 Transitional//EN">
<HTML>
  <HEAD>
    <title>WebForm1</title>
      <meta content="Microsoft Visual Studio .NET 7.1" name="GENERATOR">
      <meta content="Visual Basic .NET 7.1" name="CODE_LANGUAGE">
      <meta content="JavaScript" name="vs_defaultClientScript">
      <meta content="http://schemas.microsoft.com/intellisense/ie5"
            name="vs_targetSchema">
  </HEAD>
  <body>
    <form id="Form1" method="post" runat="server">
      <ucl:banner id="Banner1" runat="server"></ucl:banner>
      <BR><BR>
      <TABLE id="Table1" style="WIDTH: 372px; HEIGHT: 72px" cellSpacing="5"
             cellPadding="0" width="372" border="0">

        <TR>
          <TD style="HEIGHT: 28px" align="right">Choose a category:</TD>
          <TD style="HEIGHT: 28px">
            <asp:DropDownList id="ddlCategory" runat="server" Width="232px"
                AutoPostBack="True"></asp:DropDownList></TD>
        </TR>
        <TR>
          <TD style="HEIGHT: 28px" align="right">Choose a product:</TD>
          <TD style="HEIGHT: 28px">
            <asp:dropdownlist id="ddlProduct" runat="server" Width="232px"
                AutoPostBack="True"></asp:dropdownlist></TD>
        </TR>
      </TABLE>
      <BR>
      <asp:label id=lblName runat="server" Font-Size="Medium"
        Text='<%# DataBinder.Eval(dvProducts, "(0).(Name)") %>' >
      </asp:label><BR>
      <asp:image id=imgProduct runat="server" Height="150px"
        ImageUrl='<%# GetImageURL(DataBinder.Eval(dvProducts, "(0).(ImageFile)")) %>'>
      </asp:image><BR><BR>
      <asp:label id=lblShortDescription runat="server" Font-Size="Medium"
        Text='<%# DataBinder.Eval(dvProducts, "(0).(ShortDescription)") %>' >
      </asp:label><BR><BR>
      <asp:label id=lblLongDescription runat="server"
        Text='<%# DataBinder.Eval(dvProducts, "(0).(LongDescription)") %>'>
      </asp:label><BR><BR>
      <asp:label id=lblUnitPrice runat="server" Font-Size="Medium"
        Text='<%# DataBinder.Eval(dvProducts, "(0).(UnitPrice)","{0:c}") %>' >
      </asp:label>
    </form>
  </body>
</HTML>
```

Figure 13-10   The aspx code for the Product Display form

The Visual Basic code for the Product Display form

Figure 13-11 presents the code for the Product Display form. At the top of this form class, you can see the declarations for the two variables that will hold the datasets used by this application. In addition, you can see the declaration for the variable that will hold the data view that the label and image controls on the form are bound to. Notice that this variable is declared as Public. That's necessary because this variable must be visible to the aspx file for the form, since the data view is used in the data binding expressions in that file.

Each time this form is loaded, the Load procedure starts by executing the GetProducts method of the ProductDB class to get the Products dataset. Then, if the page is being loaded for the first time, the GetCategories method is executed to get the Categories dataset, and the BindCategoryDropDownList, BindProductDropDownList, and BindProduct procedures are executed to bind the controls on the form.

The BindCategoryDropDownList procedure sets the binding properties of the Category drop-down list so it will list the category names and store the category IDs. Then, it executes the DataBind method of that control. Similarly, the BindProductDropDownList procedure sets the binding properties of the Product drop-down list so it will list the product names and store the product IDs and then executes the DataBind method. But first, it creates a data view that includes only the products in the selected category, and it uses that data view as the data source for the control.

The BindProduct procedure also creates a data view. This data view includes just the row for the selected product. This is the data view that's used in the data binding expressions for the label and image controls. The BindProduct method then executes the DataBind method of each of these controls.

Notice that the BindProduct procedure binds the controls only if the Count property of the data view is greater than zero. This test is necessary because when a category is selected, the information for the first product in the Product drop-down list is displayed. If the selected category doesn't contain any products, however, the Product drop-down list will be empty. In that case, the Text property of the Name label is set to a message that indicates that there aren't any products for the selected category, and the other controls are cleared.

The Visual Basic code for the Product Display form

```
Public Class WebForm1
    Inherits System.Web.UI.Page

    Dim dsProducts As DataSet
    Dim dsCategories As DataSet
    Public dvProducts As DataView

    Private Sub Page_Load(ByVal sender As System.Object, _
            ByVal e As System.EventArgs) Handles MyBase.Load
        'Put user code to initialize the page here
        dsProducts = ProductDB.GetProducts
        If Not IsPostBack Then
            dsCategories = ProductDB.GetCategories
            Me.BindCategoryDropDownList()
            Me.BindProductDropDownList()
            Me.BindProduct()
        End If
    End Sub

    Private Sub BindCategoryDropDownList()
        ddlCategory.DataSource = dsCategories
        ddlCategory.DataMember = "Categories"
        ddlCategory.DataTextField = "ShortName"
        ddlCategory.DataValueField = "CategoryID"
        ddlCategory.DataBind()
    End Sub

    Private Sub BindProductDropDownList()
        Dim dvProductCategory As New DataView(dsProducts.Tables("Products"))
        dvProductCategory.RowFilter _
            = "CategoryID='" & ddlCategory.SelectedValue & "'"
        ddlProduct.DataSource = dvProductCategory
        ddlProduct.DataTextField = "Name"
        ddlProduct.DataValueField = "ProductID"
        ddlProduct.DataBind()
    End Sub

    Private Sub BindProduct()
        dvProducts = New DataView(dsProducts.Tables("Products"))
        dvProducts.RowFilter = "ProductID='" & ddlProduct.SelectedValue & "'"
        If dvProducts.Count > 0 Then
            lblName.DataBind()
            lblShortDescription.DataBind()
            imgProduct.DataBind()
            lblLongDescription.DataBind()
            lblUnitPrice.DataBind()
        Else
            lblName.Text = "There are no products for this category."
            lblShortDescription.Text = ""
            imgProduct.ImageUrl = ""
            lblLongDescription.Text = ""
            lblUnitPrice.Text = ""
        End If
    End Sub
```

Figure 13-11   The Visual Basic code for the Product Display form (part 1 of 2)

If the user selects a different category from the Category drop-down list, the SelectedIndexChanged procedure for that control executes the BindProductDropDownList procedure. That causes the Product drop-down list to be filtered by the selected category. Then, the SelectedIndexChanged procedure executes the BindProduct procedure to display the first product in that category. The BindProduct procedure is also executed when the user selects a different product from the Product drop-down list.

The last procedure for the Product Display form is the GetImageURL function that's executed from the aspx code for this form. This function adds "Images\" to the beginning of the file name that's passed to it. That's necessary because the image files for the products, whose names are stored in the ImageFile column of the Products table, are stored in a subdirectory named Images.

The code for the Product Display form   **Page 2**

```
    Private Sub ddlCategory_SelectedIndexChanged _
            (ByVal sender As System.Object, _
             ByVal e As System.EventArgs) _
             Handles ddlCategory.SelectedIndexChanged
        Me.BindProductDropDownList()
        Me.BindProduct
    End Sub

    Private Sub ddlProduct_SelectedIndexChanged _
            (ByVal sender As System.Object, _
             ByVal e As System.EventArgs) _
             Handles ddlProduct.SelectedIndexChanged
        Me.BindProduct()
    End Sub

    Public Function GetImageURL(ByVal sFileName As String) As String
        Return "Images\" & sFileName
    End Function

End Class
```

Figure 13-11   The Visual Basic code for the Product Display form (part 2 of 2)

How to use unbound controls to update data

Although you can use bound controls to display the data in a data table, you can't use them to update the data in a data table. To do that, you have to use unbound controls. In the topics that follow, then, you'll learn how to retrieve and work with the rows in a data table when you're using unbound controls, and you'll learn how to add, modify, and delete data rows. In addition, you'll learn how to update the database to reflect the changes that have been made to a dataset. Before you learn these skills, however, you need to understand how concurrency works in a disconnected data architecture.

Concurrency and the disconnected data architecture

In chapter 11, you'll learned about some of the advantages of ADO.NET's disconnected data architecture. This architecture also has some disadvantages, however. One of those is the conflict that can occur when two or more users retrieve and then try to update data in the same row of a table. This is called a *concurrency* problem. This is possible because once a program retrieves data from a database, the connection to that database is dropped. As a result, the database management system can't manage the update process.

To illustrate, consider the situation shown in figure 13-12. Here, two users have retrieved the Products table from a database, so a separate copy of the Products table is stored for each user. These users could be using the same program or two different programs. Now, suppose that user 1 modifies the unit price in the row for product cat01 and updates the Products table in the database. Next, suppose that user 2 modifies the short description in the row for the same product, then tries to update the Products table in the database. What will happen? That depends on the *concurrency control* that's used by the programs.

When you use ADO.NET, you have two choices for concurrency control. First, you can use *optimistic concurrency*. To use this type of concurrency, the application must check whether a row has been changed since it was retrieved. If it has, the update or deletion should be refused and the application should handle the situation. For example, it could display an error message that tells the user that the row could not be updated and then retrieve the updated row so the user can make the change again.

Second, you can use the *"last in wins"* technique. With this technique, no checking is done to ensure that a row hasn't changed since it was retrieved. Instead, the row that's updated by the last user overwrites any changes made to the row by a previous user. For the example above, the row updated by user 2 will overwrite the changes made by user 1, which means that the short description will be right but the unit price will be wrong. Since errors like this corrupt the data in a database, optimistic concurrency is used by most programs.

If you know that concurrency will be a problem, you can use a couple of programming techniques to limit concurrency problems. If a program uses a

Two users who are working with copies of the same data

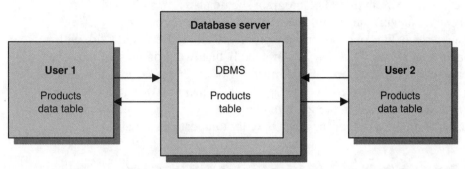

What happens when two users try to update the same row

- When two or more users retrieve the data in the same row of a database table at the same time, it is called *concurrency*. Because ADO.NET uses a disconnected data architecture, the database management system can't prevent this from happening.

- If two users try to update the same row in a database table at the same time, the second user's changes could overwrite the changes made by the first user. Whether or not that happens, though, depends on the *concurrency control* that the programs use.

- If a program uses *optimistic concurrency*, it checks to see whether the database row that's going to be updated or deleted has been changed since it was retrieved. If it has, the program must provide code to handle the situation.

- If optimistic concurrency isn't in effect, the program doesn't check to see whether a row has been changed before an update or deletion takes place. Instead, the operation proceeds without throwing an exception. This is referred to as "*last in wins*" because the last update overwrites any previous update. This leads to errors in the database.

How to avoid concurrency errors

- For many applications, concurrency errors rarely occur. As a result, optimistic concurrency is adequate because the users will rarely have to resubmit an update or deletion that is refused.

- If concurrency is likely to be a problem, a program that uses a dataset can be designed so it updates the database and refreshes the dataset frequently. That way, concurrency errors are less likely to occur.

- Another way to avoid concurrency errors is to design a program so it retrieves and updates just one row at a time. That way, there's less chance that two users will retrieve and update the same row at the same time.

Figure 13-12   Concurrency and the disconnected data architecture

dataset, one technique is to update the database frequently so other programs can retrieve the current data. The program should also refresh its dataset frequently so it contains the recent changes made by other programs.

Another way to avoid concurrency problems is to retrieve and work with just one row at a time. That way, it's less likely that two programs will update the same row at the same time. In contrast, if two programs retrieve the same table, they will of course retrieve the same rows. Then, if they both update the same row in the table, even though it may not be at the same time, a concurrency problem will occur when they try to update the database.

How to retrieve and work with a data row

After you fill a data table with data from a database, you can use the techniques in figure 13-13 to retrieve and work with the data in a data row. To start, you declare a variable that will hold the data row as illustrated by the first two examples in this figure. As you can see, you use the DataRow class to define the data row.

After you declare a variable to hold a row, you can retrieve a row and assign it to that variable. This figure shows two ways to do that. First, you can retrieve a row using its index as illustrated in the first example. Here, the Tables property of the dataset is used to get the table that contains the row, and the Rows property of the table is used to get the row with the specified index.

If you set the MissingSchemaAction property of the data adapter that was used to fill the data table to MissingSchemaAction.AddWithKey, you can also use the Find method of the data rows collection to get a row with the key you specify. To do that, you specify the key value as an argument, as illustrated by the second example in this figure. In this case, the key value is identified using the SelectedValue property of a drop-down list.

After you retrieve a row from a data table, you can retrieve the values of individual columns in the row. To do that, you use the Item property of the row and specify the name of the column as an argument. This is illustrated by the third example in this figure. Here, the column values are assigned to the appropriate properties of controls on a form. Note that because the Item property is the default property of a row, it can be omitted as shown in this example.

You can use a similar technique to modify the values in a data row. Just assign the new values to the appropriate columns using the Item property of the row and the name of the column as illustrated in the last example. Just as when you retrieve column values from a data row, you can omit the Item property when you assign values to the columns in a data row.

Code that retrieves a row using its index and assigns column values to form controls

```
Dim drProduct As DataRow
Dim iCurrentRow As Integer
    .
    .
    .
drProduct = dsProducts.Tables("Products").Rows(iCurrentRow)
```

Code that retrieves a row with the selected key value

```
Dim drProduct As DataRow
drProduct = dsProducts.Tables("Products").Rows.Find _
            (ddlProduct.SelectedValue)
```

Code that assigns column values to form controls

```
txtName.Text = drProduct("Name")
txtShortDescription.Text = drProduct("ShortDescription")
txtLongDescription.Text = drProduct("LongDescription")
txtImageFile.Text = drProduct("ImageFile")
txtUnitPrice.Text = FormatCurrency(drProduct("UnitPrice"))
txtOnHand.Text = drProduct("OnHand")
```

Code that modifies the values in the data row

```
drProduct("Name") = txtName.Text
drProduct("ShortDescription") = ShortDescription.Text
drProduct("LongDescription") = txtLongDescription.Text
drProduct("ImageFile") = txtImageFile.Text
drProduct("UnitPrice") = txtUnitPrice.Text
drProduct("OnHand") = txtOnHand.Text
```

Description

- You can use the Rows property of a data table to retrieve a row using its index. Then, you can assign that row to a variable that's declared with the DataRow type.

- You can use the Find method of a data rows collection to get the row with the specified key. If the row doesn't exist, this method returns a null.

- To use the Find method, a primary key must be defined for the data table. To retrieve the primary key from the database, set the MissingSchemaAction property of the data adapter to MissingSchemaAction.AddWithKey.

- To get or set the value of a column in a row, you use the Item property of the row and specify the name of the column as the argument. Since Item is the default property of a data row, you can omit it as shown above.

Figure 13-13   How to retrieve and work with a data row

How to delete an existing data row

Figure 13-14 presents two techniques that you can use to delete a row from a data table. Both of the examples in this figure assume that you have already retrieved a row as described in the previous figure.

The first technique is to use the Delete method of the data row to mark the row as deleted, as illustrated by the first example. Then, the row isn't deleted permanently until you issue the Update method of the data adapter.

The second technique is to use the Remove method of the data rows collection to permanently remove a row from the table in the dataset, as illustrated in the second example. Note, however, that you should use this technique only if you don't need to delete the row from the database. This makes sense when you're working with a dataset that isn't related to a table in a database.

How to add a new data row

Figure 13-14 also shows how you add new rows to a data table. To do that, you use the NewRow method of the table, and you assign the result to a data row variable as shown in the third example in this figure. The NewRow method creates a row based on the schema of the data table you specify, but doesn't actually add the row to the table. To do that, you use the Add method of the data rows collection of the table after you assign appropriate values to each of the row's columns.

A statement that uses the Delete method to mark the row as deleted

```
drProduct.Delete()
```

A statement that uses the Remove method to delete the row

```
dsProducts.Tables("Products").Rows.Remove(drProduct)
```

Code that creates a new row, assigns values to it, and adds it to the dataset

```
Dim drProduct As DataRow
drProduct = dsProducts.Tables("Products").NewRow
drProduct("ProductID") = txtProductID.Text
drProduct("CategoryID") = ddlCategory.SelectedItem.Value
drProduct("Name") = txtName.Text
drProduct("ShortDescription") = txtShortDescription.Text
drProduct("LongDescription") = txtLongDescription.Text
drProduct("ImageFile") = txtImageFile.Text
drProduct("UnitPrice") = txtUnitPrice.Text
drProduct("OnHand") = txtOnHand.Text
dsProducts.Tables("Products").Rows.Add(drProduct)
```

Description

- The Delete method of a row marks the row for deletion. The row isn't actually deleted until the Update method of the data adapter is executed.

- The Remove method of the data rows collection of a table permanently removes a row from the table. To identify the row to be deleted, you code it as an argument on this method. You should use the Remove method only if you don't need to delete the related row in the database.

- To create a new row based on the schema of a table, use the NewRow method of the table and assign the result to a data row variable. Because the new row is based on the schema of the table, you can refer to the columns in the table by name as shown above.

- To set the value of a column in a new row, use the Item property of the row and the column name just as you do when you're working with an existing row.

- After you assign values to the columns in the row, you use the Add method of the data rows collection for the table to add the row to the table.

Figure 13-14   How to delete an existing row or add a new row

How to create and work with command builders

As you have learned, a data adapter includes four command objects: a Select command, an Insert command, an Update command, and a Delete command. The Select command is used by the data adapter's Fill method to retrieve data from the database and add it to the dataset. The other commands are used by the data adapter's Update method to post any changes that have been made to the dataset to the database.

Although you can create the Insert, Update, and Delete commands yourself, ADO.NET provides an object called a *command builder* that can automatically generate Insert, Update, and Delete statements based on the data adapter's Select statement. That way, you don't have to worry about coding these statements and creating these commands yourself.

Figure 13-15 shows the two ways you can create a SQL Server command builder. In the first example, you can see that no arguments are passed to the constructor of the SqlCommandBuilder class. Because of that, you must set the DataAdapter property of the command builder after you create it. In the second example, the data adapter is passed to the constructor of the command builder. Then, when an Update method is executed on the data adapter, the Insert, Update, and Delete statements are generated and executed.

The biggest benefit of using a command builder is that the SQL statements it generates automatically handle optimistic concurrency checking. Then, if a concurrency error occurs, the operation is cancelled and a *concurrency exception* is thrown. The application can then catch this exception and handle it in an appropriate way. To help you understand how concurrency checking is implemented by a command builder, I'll show you examples of the statements a command builder generates in the next figure.

Although a command builder can save you some coding effort, you can't always use one. Specifically, you can't use a command builder if the Select command for the data adapter contains the name of a stored procedure or if it contains a Select statement that retrieves data from more than one table. In those cases, you'll have to create the Insert, Update, and Delete commands yourself. In addition, you'll want to create your own commands if you want to use a method of concurrency checking other than the one that's used by the command builder.

Two ways to create a SqlCommandBuilder object

```
commandBuilder = New SqlCommandBuilder()
commandBuilder = New SqlCommandBuilder(dataAdapter)
```

Common property of a command builder

Property	Description
DataAdapter	The data adapter that contains the Select statement that will be used to generate Insert, Update, and Delete statements.

Code that creates a SqlCommandBuilder object

```
Dim cbProducts As New SqlCommandBuilder()
cbProducts.DataAdapter = daProducts
```

Another way to create a SqlCommandBuilder object

```
Dim cbProducts As New SqlCommandBuilder(daProducts)
```

Description

- You can use a command builder to generate Insert, Update, and Delete commands for a data adapter from the Select command for the data adapter. For this to work, the Select command must contain a Select statement.
- The DataAdapter property is set to the value that you pass to the constructor of the command builder. If you don't pass a value, you must set the DataAdapter property after you create the command builder.
- The Insert, Update, and Delete commands are generated when you execute the Update method of the data adapter.

Notes

- A command builder can't be used with a Select command that contains the name of a stored procedure or a Select statement that retrieves data from more than one table.
- The Select statement associated with the data adapter must include a primary key or a unique column from that table.

Figure 13-15   How to create and work with command builders

The Insert, Update, and Delete statements generated by a command builder

Figure 13-16 shows the Insert, Update, and Delete statements that were generated by a command builder from the Select statement shown at the top of this figure. This Select statement retrieves columns from all the rows in the Products table and sorts them by product ID. The key to understanding the Insert, Update, and Delete statements that are generated from this statement is the parameters that are used in each of these statements.

The Insert statement uses parameters to identify the values to be assigned to each column. When the Insert statement is executed, the values in the columns of the new data row are assigned to these parameters. Then, a new row with these values is added to the table in the database.

The Update statement is considerably more complex. It uses parameters for three distinct purposes. First, it uses parameters in the Set clause to identify the values to be assigned to each column. Second, it uses a parameter in the Where clause to identify the key value of the row to be updated. Third, it uses parameters in the Where clause to provide for optimistic concurrency.

To provide for optimistic concurrency, the Where clause uses two parameters for each column to be updated. The first parameter indicates whether the original value of the column was null. If so, this parameter is set to a value of 1. Otherwise, it's set to a value of 0. Then, it compares this value with the current value of the column in the database to determine if they're both null. If so, it indicates that the column value hasn't changed since it was retrieved. If the original value of the column wasn't null, the Where clause compares the current value of the column with another parameter that contains the original value of the column. If these values are the same, it indicates that the column value hasn't changed. If a row with the specified key value is found and all of the columns pass their tests, the update is performed. Otherwise, a concurrency exception is thrown.

The Delete statement also uses parameters in the Where clause to identify the row to be deleted and to provide for optimistic concurrency. Then, if the row with the specified key value isn't found or if any of the column values have changed since the row was retrieved, a concurrency exception is thrown. Otherwise, the row is deleted.

The Select statement used by a command builder

```
Select ProductID, CategoryID, Name, ShortDescription, LongDescription,
       ImageFile, UnitPrice, OnHand From Products Order By ProductID
```

The Insert statement generated by the command builder

```
INSERT INTO Products( ProductID , CategoryID , Name , ShortDescription ,
                      LongDescription , ImageFile , UnitPrice , OnHand )
          VALUES ( @p1 , @p2 , @p3 , @p4 , @p5 , @p6 , @p7 , @p8 )
```

The Update statement generated by the command builder

```
UPDATE Products
   SET ProductID = @p1 , CategoryID = @p2 , Name = @p3 ,
       ShortDescription = @p4 , LongDescription = @p5 ,
       ImageFile = @p6 ,  UnitPrice = @p7 , OnHand = @p8
 WHERE ( (ProductID = @p9)
   AND ((@p10 = 1 AND CategoryID IS NULL) OR (CategoryID = @p11))
   AND ((@p12 = 1 AND Name IS NULL) OR (Name = @p13))
   AND ((@p14 = 1 AND ShortDescription IS NULL) OR (ShortDescription = @p15))
   AND ((@p16 = 1 AND LongDescription IS NULL)  OR (LongDescription = @p17))
   AND ((@p18 = 1 AND ImageFile IS NULL) OR (ImageFile = @p19))
   AND ((@p20 = 1 AND UnitPrice IS NULL) OR (UnitPrice = @p21))
   AND ((@p22 = 1 AND OnHand IS NULL) OR (OnHand = @p23)) )
```

The Delete statement generated by the command builder

```
DELETE FROM Products
 WHERE ( (ProductID = @p1)
   AND ((@p2 = 1 AND CategoryID IS NULL) OR (CategoryID = @p3))
   AND ((@p4 = 1 AND Name IS NULL) OR (Name = @p5))
   AND ((@p6 = 1 AND ShortDescription IS NULL) OR (ShortDescription = @p7))
   AND ((@p8 = 1 AND LongDescription IS NULL) OR (LongDescription = @p9))
   AND ((@p10 = 1 AND ImageFile IS NULL) OR (ImageFile = @p11))
   AND ((@p12 = 1 AND UnitPrice IS NULL) OR (UnitPrice = @p13))
   AND ((@p14 = 1 AND OnHand IS NULL) OR (OnHand = @p15)) )
```

Description

- The Values clause of the Insert statement that's generated by a command builder uses parameters to identify the values for each column in the row that's being added.

- The Set clause of the Update statement that's generated by a command builder uses parameters to identify the values to be assigned to the columns in the row that's being updated. The Where clause uses parameters to identify the original values of the columns and to indicate whether the original values were null.

- The Where clause of the Delete statement that's generated by a command builder uses parameters to identify the original values of the columns in the row that's being deleted and to indicate whether the original values were null.

- If the value of one or more columns in a row that's being updated or deleted have changed since the row was retrieved, a *concurrency exception* occurs.

Figure 13-16   The Insert, Update, and Delete statements generated by a command builder

How to update the database with changes made to a dataset

To execute the Insert, Update, and Delete statements associated with a data adapter, you use the Update method shown in figure 13-17. On this method, you specify the name of the dataset you want to use to update the database, and, optionally, the name of the table within that dataset. If you don't specify a table name, the name "Table" is used by default. Since that usually isn't what you want, you'll typically code the Update method as shown in the first example in this figure. Here, the database will be updated with the changes that have been made to the Products table in the dsProducts dataset.

When you execute the Update method, each row in the table is checked to determine if the row is new, modified, or marked as deleted. If it's a new row, the Insert statement identified by the InsertCommand property of the data adapter is used to add the row to the table in the database. Similarly, the Update statement identified by the UpdateCommand property is used to update a modified row, and the Delete statement identified by the DeleteCommand property is used to delete a row.

If you want to know how many rows were updated, you can retrieve the return value of the Update method as illustrated by the second example in this figure. You might want to use this value to display a message to the user that indicates the number of rows that were updated. Or, you might want to use it to determine if the update completed successfully.

To be sure that changes have been made to a dataset before executing the Update method, you can use the HasChanges method of the dataset. This method returns True if the dataset has been updated and False if it hasn't. You can see how this method is used in the third example in this figure.

To catch any exceptions that occur during an update operation, you typically code the Update method within a Try...Catch statement as shown in the last example in this figure. Notice that this statement includes two Catch clauses. The first one catches any exceptions thrown by the data provider, in this case, SQL Server. This type of exception might be thrown if you try to add a new row with a key value that already exists in the table. The second Catch clause catches any concurrency exceptions that occur.

The syntax of the Update method for a data adapter

```
dataAdapter.Update(dataset)
dataAdapter.Update(dataset, "tablename")
```

A statement that updates a database with the data in a dataset

```
daProducts.Update(dsProducts, "Products")
```

A statement that retrieves the return value from an Update method

```
iUpdateCount = daProducts.Update(dsProducts, "Products")
```

Code that checks for changes to the dataset before updating the database

```
If dsProducts.HasChanges Then
    daProducts.Update(daProducts, "Products")
End If
```

Code that updates a database and catches exceptions

```
Try
    daProducts.Update(dsProducts, "Products")
    bUpdateSuccessful = True
Catch eSql As SqlException
    bUpdateSuccessful = False
Catch eConcurrency As DBConcurrencyException
    bUpdateSuccessful = False
End If
```

Description

- The Update method saves changes made in the data table to the database that the data was retrieved from. To do that, it checks each row in the data table to determine if the row has changed.

- If a row has been added, modified, or deleted, the data adapter's Insert, Update, or Delete command is executed for that row.

- By default, the Update method saves changes made to the data table named "Table." Since that usually isn't what you want, you should include the name of the data table as the second argument of the Update method.

- You can use the HasChanges method to check if any changes have been made to the dataset before you update it.

- When the Update method is executed, a connection to the database is opened automatically. The connection is closed when the update is complete.

- The Update method is implemented as a function that returns an integer value with the number of rows that were updated.

Figure 13-17   How to update the database with changes made to a dataset

A Product Maintenance application that uses unbound controls

The last two figures of this chapter present the code for a Product Maintenance application that uses unbound controls. Because the Product Maintenance
page looks and works just like the one you saw in figure 12-10 of chapter 12, I
won't present it again here. The main difference between these two applications
is that instead of using command objects to retrieve and update the products, the
application in this chapter uses a data adapter.

The code for the ProductDB class

Figure 13-18 presents the code for the ProductDB class used by this application. This class begins with a Public enumeration that's used by the
UpdateProducts method. It indicates the result of the update operation and is
defined as Public so it can also be used by the Product Maintenance form.

Like the other ProductDB classes you've seen in this book, this class
includes a Connection method that provides the SqlConnection object for the
Halloween database. It also includes a GetCategories method that gets a dataset
with the categories information used by the Category drop-down list. This
dataset is retrieved from the application cache if it exists. Otherwise, it's created
and stored in the cache.

Like the GetCategories procedure, the GetProducts procedure also stores
the product data in a dataset. Since the application lets the user change the data
in this dataset, however, it isn't stored in the application cache. To create the
data adapter that's used to fill the dataset, this procedure calls a private procedure named DataAdapter.

The DataAdapter procedure creates a new data adapter using a Select
statement that retrieves data from the Products table. Notice that the
MissingSchemaAction property of this data adapter is set to MissingSchema-
Action.AddWithKey so the primary key will be included in the schema for the
table. That's necessary because the Product Maintenance form will use the
primary key to retrieve existing rows. Also notice that a command builder is
used to create the Insert, Update, and Delete commands for the data adapter.

The UpdateProducts procedure also uses the DataAdapter procedure to
create the data adapter it will use to update the database. Then, it executes the
Update method of the data adapter to perform the update using the data in the
Products table. This statement is coded within a Try...Catch statement so that
exceptions that occur during the update can be handled by the procedure. If the
update is successful, the procedure returns the Success member of the
UpdateResult enumeration. If a concurrency exception occurs, however, the
procedure returns the ConcurrencyError member of the UpdateResult enumeration. And if a SQL Server exception occurs, the procedure returns the SqlError
member of the UpdateResult enumeration.

The code for the ProductDB class

```
Imports System.Data.SqlClient
Public Class ProductDB

    Public Enum UpdateResult
        Success
        ConcurrencyError
        SqlError
    End Enum

    Private Shared Function Connection() As SqlConnection
        Dim sConnectionString As String
        sConnectionString = _
            ConfigurationSettings.AppSettings("ConnectionString")
        Return New SqlConnection(sConnectionString)
    End Function

    Public Shared Function GetCategories() As DataSet
        Dim dsCategories As New DataSet
        If HttpContext.Current.Cache("dsCategories") Is Nothing Then
            Dim sSelect As String = "Select CategoryID, ShortName " _
                & "From Categories"
            Dim daCategories As New SqlDataAdapter(sSelect, Connection())
            daCategories.Fill(dsCategories, "Categories")
            HttpContext.Current.Cache("dsCategories") = dsCategories
        Else
            dsCategories = HttpContext.Current.Cache("dsCategories")
        End If
        Return dsCategories
    End Function

    Public Shared Function GetProducts() As DataSet
        Dim dsProducts As New DataSet
        Dim daProducts As SqlDataAdapter = DataAdapter()
        daProducts.Fill(dsProducts, "Products")
        Return dsProducts
    End Function

    Private Shared Function DataAdapter() As SqlDataAdapter
        Dim sSelect As String = "Select ProductID, CategoryID, Name, " _
            & "ShortDescription, LongDescription, ImageFile, " _
            & "UnitPrice, OnHand " _
            & "From Products Order By ProductID"
        Dim daProducts As New SqlDataAdapter(sSelect, Connection())
        daProducts.MissingSchemaAction = MissingSchemaAction.AddWithKey
        Dim cbProducts As New SqlCommandBuilder(daProducts)
        Return daProducts
    End Function

    Public Shared Function UpdateProducts(ByVal Products As DataSet) _
            As UpdateResult
        Dim daProducts As SqlDataAdapter = DataAdapter()
        Try
            daProducts.Update(Products, "Products")
            Return UpdateResult.Success
        Catch eConcurrency As DBConcurrencyException
            Return UpdateResult.ConcurrencyError
        Catch eSql As SqlException
            Return UpdateResult.SqlError
        End Try
    End Function
End Class
```

Figure 13-18   The code for the ProductDB class

Although the last Catch clause will catch any SQL Server errors that occur, you should realize that a production application would probably test for more specific errors. In this case, for example, you might test for a constraint error caused by trying to add a new product with a primary key value that already exists or by trying to delete a product that has related rows in another table. In fact, in the next chapter, you'll see an application that does just that.

The code for the Product Maintenance form

Figure 13-19 presents the code for the Product Maintenance form. If you study this code, you'll see that it's similar to the code for the Product Maintenance form you saw in chapter 12. Because of that, I'll focus mainly on the differences here.

To start, you should notice that the Load procedure stores the dataset that contains the products in session state. That's necessary because this dataset will be used not only to display the products in the Product drop-down list, but to record changes the user makes to the products.

When the user selects a product from the Product drop-down list, the GetProduct procedure shown on page 2 of this listing starts by declaring a data row variable. Then, it uses the Find method of the data rows collection of the Products table to retrieve the selected row and assign it to that variable. Once the row is retrieved, it assigns the values in the columns of that row to the appropriate controls on the form.

The Update procedure that's executed when the user clicks the Update button (see page 3) also starts by declaring a data row variable. Then, if a row is being added to the Products table, the NewRow method of the Products table is used to create a new row, and that row is assigned to the data row variable. If a row is being modified, however, the Find method of the data rows collection is used to retrieve the selected row, and that row is assigned to the variable.

After it creates a new row or retrieves the existing row, the values of the controls on the form are assigned to the columns of the data row. Then, if the row is being added, the Add method of the data rows collection is used to add the row to the data table. Notice that this method is coded within a Try...Catch statement that catches constraint errors. A constraint error will occur if the user tries to add a product with a product ID that already exists in the data table. Then, an error message is displayed to advise the user of the error.

If the Add method is successful, the UpdateDatabase method is executed to update the database. This method is also executed to update the database with the changes made to an existing row.

The code for the Product Maintenance form   **Page 1**

```
Public Class WebForm1
    Inherits System.Web.UI.Page

    Private Enum ControlState
        NoSelection
        NewProduct
        EditProduct
    End Enum

    Dim dsProducts As DataSet

    Private Sub Page_Load(ByVal sender As System.Object, _
            ByVal e As System.EventArgs) Handles MyBase.Load
        'Put user code to initialize the page here
        If Not IsPostBack Then
            dsProducts = ProductDB.GetProducts()
            Session("dsProducts") = dsProducts
            Me.BindProducts()
            Me.BindCategories()
            Me.SetControlstate(ControlState.NoSelection)
        Else
            dsProducts = Session("dsProducts")
        End If
    End Sub

    Public Sub BindProducts()
        ddlProducts.DataSource = dsProducts
        ddlProducts.DataTextField = "Name"
        ddlProducts.DataValueField = "ProductID"
        ddlProducts.DataBind()
    End Sub

    Public Sub BindCategories()
        Dim dsCategories As DataSet
        dsCategories = ProductDB.GetCategories()
        ddlCategory.DataSource = dsCategories
        ddlCategory.DataTextField = "ShortName"
        ddlCategory.DataValueField = "CategoryID"
        ddlCategory.DataBind()
    End Sub

    Private Sub SetControlstate(ByVal cs As ControlState)
        Select Case cs
            Case ControlState.NoSelection
                ddlProducts.Enabled = True
                btnGetProduct.Enabled = True
                btnNew.Enabled = True
                btnDelete.Enabled = False
                btnUpdate.Enabled = False
                btnUpdate.Text = "Update"
                btnCancel.Enabled = False
                txtProductID.Enabled = False
                Me.EnableEntryControls(False)
```

Figure 13-19   The code for the Product Maintenance form (part 1 of 4)

The code for the Product Maintenance form

```
            Case ControlState.NewProduct
                ddlProducts.Enabled = False
                btnGetProduct.Enabled = False
                btnNew.Enabled = False
                btnDelete.Enabled = False
                btnUpdate.Enabled = True
                btnUpdate.Text = "Add"
                btnCancel.Enabled = True
                txtProductID.Enabled = True
                Me.EnableEntryControls(True)
            Case ControlState.EditProduct
                ddlProducts.Enabled = False
                btnGetProduct.Enabled = False
                btnNew.Enabled = False
                btnDelete.Enabled = True
                btnUpdate.Enabled = True
                btnUpdate.Text = "Update"
                btnCancel.Enabled = True
                txtProductID.Enabled = False
                Me.EnableEntryControls(True)
        End Select
    End Sub

    Private Sub EnableEntryControls(ByVal Enabled As Boolean)
        ddlCategory.Enabled = Enabled
        txtName.Enabled = Enabled
        txtShortDescription.Enabled = Enabled
        txtLongDescription.Enabled = Enabled
        txtImageFile.Enabled = Enabled
        txtUnitPrice.Enabled = Enabled
        txtOnHand.Enabled = Enabled
    End Sub

    Private Sub btnGetProduct_Click(ByVal sender As System.Object, _
            ByVal e As System.EventArgs) Handles btnGetProduct.Click
        Dim drProduct As DataRow
        drProduct = dsProducts.Tables("Products").Rows. _
            Find(ddlProducts.SelectedItem.Value)
        txtProductID.Text = drProduct("ProductID")
        ddlCategory.SelectedItem.Selected = False
        ddlCategory.Items.FindByValue(drProduct("CategoryID")).Selected = True
        txtName.Text = drProduct("Name")
        txtShortDescription.Text = drProduct("ShortDescription")
        txtLongDescription.Text = drProduct("LongDescription")
        txtImageFile.Text = drProduct("ImageFile")
        txtUnitPrice.Text = FormatNumber(drProduct("UnitPrice"), 2)
        txtOnHand.Text = drProduct("OnHand")
        Me.SetControlstate(ControlState.EditProduct)
    End Sub

    Private Sub btnNew_Click(ByVal sender As System.Object, _
            ByVal e As System.EventArgs) Handles btnNew.Click
        Me.ClearFields()
        Me.SetControlstate(ControlState.NewProduct)
    End Sub
```

Figure 13-19   The code for the Product Maintenance form (part 2 of 4)

The code for the Product Maintenance form

```vb
Private Sub ClearFields()
    txtProductID.Text = ""
    ddlCategory.SelectedIndex = 0
    txtName.Text = ""
    txtShortDescription.Text = ""
    txtLongDescription.Text = ""
    txtImageFile.Text = ""
    txtUnitPrice.Text = ""
    txtOnHand.Text = ""
End Sub

Private Sub btnUpdate_Click(ByVal sender As System.Object, _
        ByVal e As System.EventArgs) Handles btnUpdate.Click
    Dim drProduct As DataRow
    If btnUpdate.Text = "Add" Then
        drProduct = dsProducts.Tables("Products").NewRow
    Else
        drProduct = dsProducts.Tables("Products").Rows. _
            Find(ddlProducts.SelectedItem.Value)
    End If
    drProduct("ProductID") = txtProductID.Text
    drProduct("CategoryID") = ddlCategory.SelectedItem.Value
    drProduct("Name") = txtName.Text
    drProduct("ShortDescription") = txtShortDescription.Text
    drProduct("LongDescription") = txtLongDescription.Text
    drProduct("ImageFile") = txtImageFile.Text
    drProduct("UnitPrice") = txtUnitPrice.Text
    drProduct("OnHand") = txtOnHand.Text
    If btnUpdate.Text = "Add" Then
        Try
            dsProducts.Tables("Products").Rows.Add(drProduct)
            Me.UpdateDatabase()
        Catch eConstraint As ConstraintException
            lblError.Text = "A product with the ID '" _
                        & txtProductID.Text & "' already exists."
        End Try
    Else
        Me.UpdateDatabase()
    End If
    Me.BindProducts()
    Me.ClearFields()
    Me.SetControlstate(ControlState.NoSelection)
End Sub
```

Figure 13-19   The code for the Product Maintenance form (part 3 of 4)

The UpdateDatabase procedure starts by executing the UpdateProducts method of the ProductDB class. Notice that the dataset that contains the Products table is passed to this method. Then, the procedure tests the value returned by this method to determine if an error occurred. If so, it sets the Text property of the error label to an appropriate error message.

After the update operation is performed, the UpdateDatabase procedure executes the GetProducts method of the ProductDB class to recreate the dataset and then stores the dataset in session state. That way, if a new row was added to the dataset, it will appear in the correct sequence in the Product drop-down list. In addition, if the update operation failed, the dataset will be updated to reflect the data in the database.

To delete the selected data row, the Delete procedure starts by executing the Delete statement to mark the row for deletion in the data table. Then, it executes the UpdateDatabase method to delete the row from the database.

The code for the Product Maintenance form   **Page 4**

```
Private Sub UpdateDatabase()
    Select Case ProductDB.UpdateProducts(dsProducts)
        Case ProductDB.UpdateResult.ConcurrencyError
            lblError.Text = "Another user has modified or deleted " _
                        & "the product '" & txtName.Text & "'."
        Case ProductDB.UpdateResult.SqlError
            lblError.Text = "A SQL Server error has occurred."
    End Select
    dsProducts = ProductDB.GetProducts()
    Session("dsProducts") = dsProducts
End Sub

Private Sub btnDelete_Click(ByVal sender As System.Object, _
        ByVal e As System.EventArgs) Handles btnDelete.Click
    dsProducts.Tables("Products").Rows. _
        Find(ddlProducts.SelectedItem.Value).Delete()
    Me.UpdateDatabase()
    Me.ClearFields()
    Me.SetControlstate(ControlState.NoSelection)
    Me.BindProducts()
End Sub

Private Sub btnCancel_Click(ByVal sender As System.Object, _
        ByVal e As System.EventArgs) Handles btnCancel.Click
    ddlProducts.SelectedIndex = 0
    Me.ClearFields()
    Me.SetControlstate(ControlState.NoSelection)
End Sub

End Class
```

Figure 13-19   The code for the Product Maintenance form (part 4 of 4)

Perspective

In this chapter, you've learned how to use bound controls to display data from a dataset, and you've learned how to use unbound controls to update the data in a dataset. Now, you might want to consider when it makes sense to use a dataset and when it makes sense to use data commands as shown in chapter 12.

In general, it makes sense to use data commands if you only need to work with one row of data at a time. However, you should also consider the amount of data you'll be working with. If, for example, you're working with a small amount of data such as the data in the Products table of the Halloween database, it can be more efficient to retrieve all of the data into a dataset when the application starts.

Also keep in mind that if you use data commands to update the data in a database, you have to provide for your own concurrency control. To do that, you can use code like the code you saw in this chapter that's generated by a command builder. Alternatively, if a table contains a column with a date/time stamp or a version number, you can use that column to determine whether a row has been changed since it was retrieved. For more information on this technique, see online help.

One situation where you'll almost always use a dataset is when you need to display two or more rows from a data table at a time. You've seen several examples of how to do that with drop-down lists in this book. In the next chapter, you'll see how to use datasets to display multiple rows in Repeater, DataList, and DataGrid controls.

Terms

application cache
data view
sort expression
filter expression
data binding expression
concurrency
concurrency control
optimistic concurrency
"last in wins"
concurrency exception

14

How to use the Repeater, DataList, and DataGrid controls

In this chapter, you'll learn how to use three ASP.NET web controls that are designed specifically for working with the data in a data source such as a dataset. The Repeater and DataList controls display data from a data source in a list, and the DataGrid control displays data in a grid with columns and rows. As you'll see, you can customize the content, appearance, and operation of these controls in a variety of ways.

How to use the Repeater control

A repeater control displays items from a repeating data source such as a data table, a collection, or an array. In the following topics, you'll learn how to use this control and you'll see a simple application that uses it to display a list of products from the Halloween database.

An introduction to the repeater control

Figure 14-1 shows a simple list of products that was created by using a *repeater control*. To create a list like this, you define one or more *templates* within the repeater control that define the content and format of the list. In the aspx code shown in this figure, for example, you can see that a single Item template is used to create the product list. This template includes a bound column named Name, followed by a comma and a space, followed by another bound column named UnitPrice, followed by a Br element.

Note that to include bound data in a repeater control, you code data binding expressions like the ones you learned about in chapter 13. However, the data binding expressions for a repeater control aren't assigned to an attribute of the control. You'll learn more about how that works in the next figure.

Although you can create a repeater control by dragging it from the Toolbox just like any other control, Visual Studio doesn't provide a visual interface for creating the control's templates. To create the templates, then, you have to switch to HTML view and enter the code directly into the aspx file. Because of that, you're likely to use the repeater control only for simple lists. For more complicated lists, you can use the data list or data grid control as described later in this chapter.

To define the source of data for a repeater control, you use the DataSource and DataMember properties just as you do when you bind other list controls. Then, you use the DataBind method to bind the control to the data source as the program executes. When the repeater control is displayed, one row is displayed in the control for each row in the data source.

A simple list displayed by a repeater control

Austin Powers, $79.99
Frankenstein, $39.99
JarJar, $59.99
Martian, $69.99
Superman, $39.99

Properties and method for binding a repeater control

Property	Description
DataSource	A data source, such as a dataset.
DataMember	The name of a member associated with the data source, such as a data table. If the data source contains only one bindable member, you don't need to set this property.

Method	Description
DataBind	Binds the control to its data source. This method must be executed each time the data source changes.

The asp element for the repeater control

```
<asp:Repeater id="rProducts" runat="server">
  <ItemTemplate>
    <%# DataBinder.Eval(Container,"DataItem.Name") %>, 
    <%# DataBinder.Eval(Container,"DataItem.UnitPrice","{0:c}") %>
    <BR>
  </ItemTemplate>
</asp:Repeater>
```

Code that binds the repeater control

```
rProducts.DataSource = dsProducts
rProducts.DataMember = "Products"
rProducts.DataBind()
```

Description

- A *repeater control* displays a list of items from the data source that it's bound to. Typically, a data list is bound to a data table or a data view.

- To define the information that's displayed in a repeater control, you create one or more *templates* within the asp element for the control.

- To bind a repeater control to a data source, you set the DataSource and DataMember properties and then execute the DataBind method.

- To display the data from a column in the data source in a repeater control, you code a data binding expression that includes a call to the Eval method of the DataBinder class. See figure 14-2 for more information.

Figure 14-1   An introduction to the repeater control

How to define the templates for a repeater control

As the table in figure 14-2 shows, you can create five different templates for a repeater control. An Item template is always required. It specifies how each item from the data source is displayed. The AlternatingItem template is similar. If you create this template, it's used to display every other row in the data source. You'll typically apply a different style to this template than you do to the Item template to give a list a more graphic appearance. You'll see how this works in the application that's presented in the next three figures.

The Header and Footer templates let you specify content that's displayed before or after the items in the list. You'll typically use the Header template to create descriptive headings for the data that's displayed in the list. In addition, you can display a separator, such as a blank line, between each row in the list by defining a Separator template. For example, instead of including a Br element at the end of the Item template in the example in the previous figure, I could have coded this element within a Separator template.

To align the data in the templates, you typically use a table as illustrated by the code in this figure. Here, the Header template includes the <table> tag that marks the beginning of the table. Then, one row is defined within the header template with two cells that contain the text "Product" and "Unit Price."

Another row is defined within the Item template. It contains two cells with the data in the Name and UnitPrice columns of the data source. Finally, the Footer template includes the </table> tag that marks the end of the table.

You should know that when you code a table within the templates of a repeater control like this that the HTML editor will indicate that there are syntax errors. That's because of the way the table is nested within the templates. The repeater control will be rendered correctly regardless of these errors, however, so you can ignore them.

How to display bound data

To display bound data within a template of a repeater control, you code a binding expression like those shown in figure 14-2. Like the binding expressions you learned about in chapter 13, you use the Eval method of the DataBinder class to bind to a column in a data row. The arguments you specify on this method, however, are somewhat different from the arguments you use with other controls.

For the first argument of the Eval method, you specify the Container object, which refers to the repeater control itself. Then, when the Eval method is executed, the data source you specify on the DataSource and DataMember properties of this control will be used as the data source for this method. For the second argument, you specify a string that refers to a column in the current row of the data source that you want to bind to. To refer to the current row of the data source, you use the DataItem object. Then, when the Eval method is executed, the rows in the data source are processed one at a time, and the value of the column in the current row is displayed.

The templates for a repeater control

Template	HTML element	Description
Header	HeaderTemplate	Displayed before the first item in the data source.
Footer	FooterTemplate	Displayed after the last item in the data source.
Item	ItemTemplate	Displayed for each item in the data source.
AlternatingItem	AlternatingItemTemplate	Displayed for alternating items in the data source.
Separator	SeparatorTemplate	Displayed between items.

Templates that render an HTML table

```
<HeaderTemplate>
  <table>
    <tr bgcolor="Black" style="COLOR: white">
      <td width="250"><b>Product</b></td>
      <td width="80"><b>Unit Price</b></td>
    </tr>
</HeaderTemplate>

<ItemTemplate>
  <tr bgcolor="WhiteSmoke">
    <td><%# DataBinder.Eval(Container,"DataItem.Name")%></td>
    <td align="right">
        <%# DataBinder.Eval(Container,"DataItem.UnitPrice","{0:c}")%>
    </td>
  </tr>
</ItemTemplate>

<FooterTemplate>
  </table>
</FooterTemplate>
```

Description

- The templates you define for a repeater control specify what content to display. At the least, you must create an Item template that defines the items from the data source that you want to display.

- To create templates for a repeater control, you must work in HTML view. Then, you enter the template elements between the start and end tags for the repeater control.

- You can use the Eval method of the DataBinder class to display individual columns of the data source within a template. The first argument you pass to this method should be an object named Container, which refers to the repeater control. The second argument should be a string that refers to the column in the current row of the data source. To refer to the current row, use the DataItem property of the repeater control.

- You can format the data in a repeater control using a table. To do that, code a Header template with a <table> tag and a Tr element for each header row. Code an Item template with a Tr element for each row of data. And code a Footer template with a Tr element for each footer row and a </table> tag to end the table.

Figure 14-2   How to define the templates for a repeater control

A Product List application that uses a repeater control

Figure 14-3 presents the design of a Product List application that uses a repeater control to display a list of products from the Halloween database. To select the products that are displayed, the user chooses a category from the drop-down list. Then, the application uses a data view to filter the products so only the ones in the selected category are displayed.

The aspx code for the form

The repeater control that's used to display the products is defined with four templates. You can see the definition of these templates in the aspx code for the Product List form in figure 14-4. There, the Header template begins the definition of a table that's used to align the columns of the control. Then, it defines a row with two columns that contain the text for the column headings.

The Item and AlternatingItem templates define a single row with two columns that display the bound data. In this case, the data binding expressions refer to the Name and UnitPrice columns of the data source. Note that the only difference between these two templates is the background color they use. Finally, a Footer template is used to end the table.

The Visual Basic code for the form

Figure 14-5 presents the Visual Basic code for the Product List form. To start, you can see that the products and the categories are stored in datasets. These datasets are retrieved in the Load event procedure for the page using methods of the ProductDB class. Although the code for this class isn't presented here, it's similar to the code for the ProductDB class of the Product Display application you saw in chapter 13. The exceptions are noted in this figure. If you want to review the code in chapter 13, you can refer to figure 13-9.

If the page is being loaded for the first time, the Load procedure also calls the BindCategoryDropDownList procedure. This procedure sets the data binding properties of the drop-down list and then executes the DataBind method of this control.

Next, the Load procedure calls the BindProductRepeater procedure. This procedure starts by creating a data view that filters the rows in the Products table so only the products in the selected category are displayed. Then, it sets the DataSource property of the repeater control to the data view, and it executes the DataBind method of this control.

The last procedure for this form is executed when the user selects a category from the drop-down list. This procedure simply calls the BindProductRepeater procedure to bind the repeater control. Then, this procedure recreates the data view for the Products table based on the selected category and binds the repeater control to this data view.

The page for a Product List application that uses a repeater control

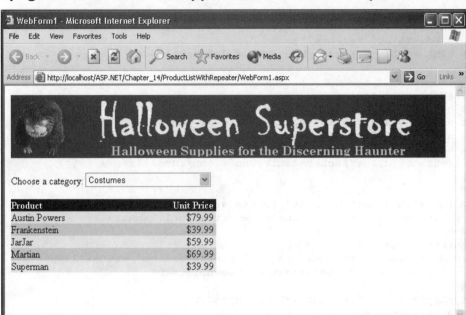

Description

- The Product List application lets the user select a category from a drop-down list and then displays the products in that category in a repeater control. The products are filtered using a data view and are listed in alphabetical sequence by name.

- The repeater control uses four templates. The Item and AlternatingItem templates contain binding expressions that display the data in the Name and UnitPrice columns. They differ only in their background colors. The Header template contains text that identifies the columns. The Footer template contains the </table> tag that ends the table that's used to format the columns in the control.

Figure 14-3   A Product List application that uses a repeater control

The aspx code for the Product List form

```
<%@ Register TagPrefix="ucl" TagName="Banner" Src="Banner.ascx" %>
<%@ Page Language="vb" AutoEventWireup="false" Codebehind="WebForm1.aspx.vb"
Inherits="ProductList1.WebForm1"%>
<!DOCTYPE HTML PUBLIC "-//W3C//DTD HTML 4.0 Transitional//EN">
<HTML>
  <HEAD>
    <title>WebForm1</title>
    <meta name="GENERATOR" content="Microsoft Visual Studio .NET 7.1">
    <meta name="CODE_LANGUAGE" content="Visual Basic .NET 7.1">
    <meta name="vs_defaultClientScript" content="JavaScript">
    <meta name="vs_targetSchema"
          content="http://schemas.microsoft.com/intellisense/ie5">
  </HEAD>
  <body>
    <form id="Form1" method="post" runat="server">
      <ucl:Banner id="Banner1" runat="server"></ucl:Banner><BR>
      <BR>
      Choose a category:
      <asp:DropDownList id="ddlCategory" runat="server" Width="200px"
          AutoPostBack="True"></asp:DropDownList><BR>
      <BR>
      <asp:Repeater id="rProducts" runat="server">
        <HeaderTemplate>
          <table cellpadding="0" cellspacing="0">
            <tr bgcolor="Black" style="COLOR: white">
              <td width="250"><b>Product</b></td>
              <td width="80" align="right"><b>Unit Price</b></td>
            </tr>
        </HeaderTemplate>
        <ItemTemplate>
          <tr bgcolor="WhiteSmoke">
            <td><%# DataBinder.Eval(Container,"DataItem.Name")%></td>
            <td align="right">
              <%# DataBinder.Eval(Container,"DataItem.UnitPrice","{0:c}")%>
            </td>
          </tr>
        </ItemTemplate>
        <AlternatingItemTemplate>
          <tr bgcolor="Gainsboro">
            <td><%# DataBinder.Eval(Container,"DataItem.Name")%></td>
            <td align="right">
              <%# DataBinder.Eval(Container,"DataItem.UnitPrice","{0:c}")%>
            </td>
          </tr>
        </AlternatingItemTemplate>
        <FooterTemplate>
          </table>
        </FooterTemplate>
      </asp:Repeater>
    </form>
  </body>
</HTML>
```

Figure 14-4   The aspx code for the Product List form that uses a repeater control

The Visual Basic code for the Product List form

```
Public Class WebForm1
    Inherits System.Web.UI.Page

    Dim dsProducts As DataSet
    Dim dsCategories As DataSet

    Private Sub Page_Load(ByVal sender As System.Object, _
            ByVal e As System.EventArgs) Handles MyBase.Load
        'Put user code to initialize the page here
        dsProducts = ProductDB.GetProducts
        If Not IsPostBack Then
            dsCategories = ProductDB.GetCategories
            Me.BindCategoryDropDownList()
            Me.BindProductRepeater()
        End If
    End Sub

    Private Sub BindCategoryDropDownList()
        ddlCategory.DataSource = dsCategories
        ddlCategory.DataMember = "Categories"
        ddlCategory.DataTextField = "ShortName"
        ddlCategory.DataValueField = "CategoryID"
        ddlCategory.DataBind()
    End Sub

    Private Sub BindProductRepeater()
        Dim dvProducts As New DataView(dsProducts.Tables("Products"))
        dvProducts.RowFilter = "CategoryID='" _
                            & ddlCategory.SelectedValue & "'"
        rProducts.DataSource = dvProducts
        rProducts.DataBind()
    End Sub

    Private Sub ddlCategory_SelectedIndexChanged _
            (ByVal sender As System.Object, ByVal e As System.EventArgs) _
            Handles ddlCategory.SelectedIndexChanged
        Me.BindProductRepeater()
    End Sub

End Class
```

Note

- The ProductDB class used by this form is similar to the ProductDB class used by the Product Display form in chapter 13 (see figure 13-9). The differences are (1) that only the columns needed by this form are retrieved from the Products table, and (2) that the rows in the result set are sorted by the Name column.

Figure 14-5   The Visual Basic code for the Product List form that uses a repeater control

How to use the DataList control

Like a repeater control, a data list control displays a list of items from a bound data source. It provides features that aren't available with the repeater control, however, and it can be created using a visual interface.

An introduction to the data list control

Figure 14-6 shows a simple list that was created by using a *data list control*. This list is similar to the list you saw in figure 14-1, but the data is displayed in columns. As you can see from the aspx code in this figure, you can create these columns without coding table tags. You'll see how that's accomplished in the next figure.

Like a repeater control, a data list control relies on templates that define the content of the control. In this example, a single Item template is used to display the list of products. Note, however, that the data that's displayed isn't bound directly to the data list control as it is for a repeater control. Instead, to bind data to a data list control, you add controls to its templates and then bind those controls. In this case, two label controls are bound to the Name and UnitPrice columns of the data source. Note that just like the data binding expressions you code for a repeater control, you specify the Container object as the first argument of the Eval method, and you use the DataItem property of the control along with the column name as the second argument.

You can also see in this figure that the data list control uses the same data properties and methods for data binding as the repeater control. You use the DataSource and DataMember properties to set the control's data source, and you use the DataBind method to bind the control. Then, when the control is displayed, it will contain one row for each row in the data source.

A simple list displayed by a data list control

Austin Powers	$79.99
Frankenstein	$39.99
JarJar	$59.99
Martian	$69.99
Superman	$39.99

Properties and method for binding a data list control

Property	Description
DataSource	A data source, such as a dataset.
DataMember	The name of a member associated with the data source, such as a data table. If the data source contains only one bindable member, you don't need to set this property.

Method	Description
DataBind	Binds the control to its data source. This method must be executed each time the data source changes.

The asp element for the data list control

```
<asp:DataList id="dlProducts" runat="server">
  <ItemTemplate>
    <asp:Label id=lblName runat="server" Width="200px"
        Text='<%# DataBinder.Eval(Container,"DataItem.Name")%>'>
    </asp:Label>
    <asp:Label id=lblUnitPrice runat="server" Text=
      '<%# DataBinder.Eval(Container,"DataItem.UnitPrice","{0:c}")%>'>
    </asp:Label>
  </ItemTemplate>
</asp:DataList>
```

Code that binds the data list control

```
dlProducts.DataSource = dsProducts
dlProducts.DataMember = "Products"
dlProducts.DataBind()
```

Description

- A *data list control* displays a list of items from the data source that it's bound to. It is similar to a Repeater control, but it offers more control over the content and format of the list that's displayed.

- To define the information to be displayed in a data list control, you create one or more templates. Because Visual Studio provides a designer interface for creating the templates for a data list, you don't have to define them from HTML view like you do for a repeater.

- To bind a data list control to a data source, you set the DataSource and DataMember properties and then execute the DataBind method.

- To display the data from a column in the data source in a data list control, you add a control to a template and then bind that control. See figure 14-8 for more information.

- The DataList control can be used for edit operations as well as display operations. For more information, see online help.

Figure 14-6   An introduction to the data list control

How to define the templates for a data list control

Figure 14-7 shows you how to create the templates for a data list control. As the table at the top of this figure indicates, you can create seven different templates. Five of them are the same as the templates you use for a repeater control. The other two, SelectedItem and EditItem, provide for the user selecting and editing items in the list. Because these functions are easier to implement using a data grid control, I won't show you how to use those templates here.

Like the repeater control, the only template that's required is the Item template, which defines how each item in the data source is displayed. But depending on the requirements of your application, you may need to use one or more of the other templates as well. For example, you'll typically use a Header template to create headings that are displayed in the first row of the data list.

Unlike the repeater control, you don't have to define the templates for a data list control in HTML view. Instead, you can use the designer interface that this control provides. To display this interface, right-click the data list control and choose Edit Template. Then, choose Header and Footer Templates, Item Templates, or Separator Template from the menu that appears. When you choose one of these commands, the control is placed in *template-editing mode* and the templates you selected are displayed. If you select the Item Templates command, for example, the four item templates shown in this figure are displayed. And if you select the Header and Footer command, the Header and Footer templates shown here are displayed.

You can add text to a template by clicking in the template to select it, then typing the text you want to add. However, you're more likely to add controls to a template. To do that, simply drag a control from the Toolbox and drop it on the template. In the Item template in this figure, you can see that I've added four label controls. In figure 14-8, you'll learn how to bind those controls to columns from the data source.

When you add controls to two or more templates, you typically want the controls in each template to be aligned. To do that, you simply set the Width properties of the corresponding controls to the same value. In this illustration, for example, I set the Width properties of the corresponding labels in the Item and Header templates to the same values.

Although you can easily set the width of each control, there isn't an easy way to align the data within each control. For example, you'll typically want to align numeric data on the right. To do that, you have to switch to HTML view and add a Style attribute to the control that specifies the appropriate alignment.

Before I go on, you should realize that you use templates to define the content of a data list control and not its appearance. For example, you use the AlternatingItem template to display different content for every other row in a data list, not to shade or highlight every other row like you do for a repeater control. That's because Visual Studio provides an easier way to format data list controls, as you'll see in figure 14-9.

The templates for a DataList control

Template	Description
Header	Displayed before the first item in the data source.
Footer	Displayed after the last item in the data source.
Item	Displayed for each item in the data source.
AlternatingItem	Displayed for alternating items in the data source.
SelectedItem	Displayed for the selected item in the data source.
EditItem	Displayed when an item is edited.
Separator	Displayed between items.

The item templates

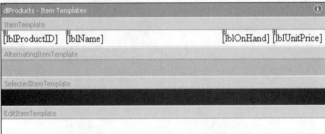

The Header and Footer templates

Description

- The templates you define for a data list control specify what content to display and what controls to use to display it. At the least, you must create an Item template that defines the items from the data source that you want to display.

- To create a template, right-click the data list control, choose Edit Template, then choose a command from the menu that appears. The control is displayed in *template-editing mode*.

- To add text to a template, select the template and begin typing. To add a control to a template, drag the control from the Toolbox onto the template, then use the Properties window to set the control's properties.

- You can create a data binding expression for a control in a template by entering it directly into the aspx code or by using the DataBindings dialog box described in figure 14-8.

- To line up the controls in two or more templates, set each control's Width property to the same value.

- To return to normal display mode, right-click the control and choose the End Template Editing command.

Figure 14-7　How to define the templates for a data list control

How to bind the controls within a template

After you add controls to a template, you can bind them to the data source by switching to HTML view and adding a data binding expression to the tags for the controls. Alternatively, you can use the DataBindings dialog box shown in figure 14-8. Here, you select the property you want to bind from the Bindable Properties list at the left of the dialog box. Then, you select the Custom binding expression option and enter a data binding expression in the text box. When you click OK, the binding expression is inserted into the HTML for the control.

The DataBindings dialog box for a control in a template

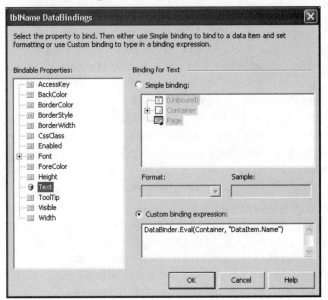

Description

- To bind a control in a template for a data list control, display the control in template-editing mode as described in figure 14-7. Then, select the control and click the ellipsis next to (DataBindings) in the Properties window to display the DataBindings dialog box.

- By default, the Text property is selected in the list of bindable properties. If that's not what you want, you can select any of the other properties in the list.

- To create a data binding expression, select the Custom binding expression option, then enter a data binding expression that uses the Eval method of the DataBinder class in the text box.

- The first argument you specify on the Eval method should be an object named Container, which refers to the data list control. The second argument should be a string that refers to the column in the current row of the data source. To refer to the current row, use the DataItem property of the data list control.

Figure 14-8   How to bind the controls within a template

How to format a data list control

To format a data list control, you can use one of the techniques presented in figure 14-9. The easiest way is to use the Auto Format dialog box. This dialog box lets you select one of 13 predefined schemes that use different combinations of colors and borders for the items in the data list.

Another way to format a data list control is to use the Format page of the Properties dialog box shown in this figure. This dialog box lets you set the colors, fonts, alignment, and other formatting options for the data list and each of its templates. Note that you can use this dialog box to customize an Auto Format scheme or to design your own scheme.

The Auto Format and Properties dialog boxes provide convenient ways to format a data list control. However, you can also apply formatting directly from the Properties window. To do that, you use the properties in the Appearance and Style sections of this window. The properties in the Appearance section apply to the data list as a whole, and the properties in the Style section apply to the templates that make up the data list. To set the properties for the Item template, for example, you can expand the ItemStyle group, and to set the properties for the Header template, you can expand the HeaderStyle group.

The Auto Format dialog box

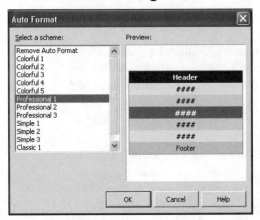

The Format page of the Properties dialog box

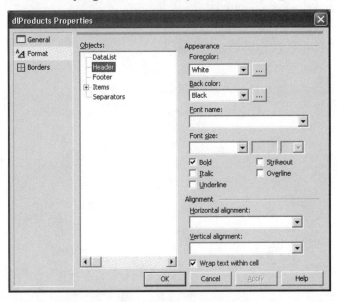

Three ways to format a data list control

- The easiest way to format the contents of a data list control is to use one of the built-in schemes. To apply a scheme, right-click the control and choose the Auto Format command. Then, choose the scheme you want to use.

- To manually set the formatting for a data list control, right-click the control and choose the Property Builder command. Then, click the Format tab and set the properties for the data list and its templates.

- You can also format a data list control and its templates from the Properties window. To display the formatting properties for a template, expand the style property for that template. To display the formatting properties for the Item template, for example, use the ItemStyle property.

Figure 14-9   How to format a data list control

A Product List application that uses a data list control

Figure 14-10 presents the specifications for a Product List application that uses a data list control. This application works just like the application you saw earlier in this chapter that uses a repeater control. However, it displays additional information for each product.

The data list control on this page uses just two templates. The Header template contains label controls that specify the text that's displayed at the top of each column. Then, the Item template contains label controls that are bound to the columns in the data source. The data binding expressions for these controls are listed in this figure, along with the width of each control. The corresponding controls in the Header template are set to the same widths.

As you can see in this page, the on hand and unit price columns have been aligned on the right. To do that, I added this style attribute to the asp tags for the label controls in the Header and the Item template:

```
style="TEXT-ALIGN: right"
```

The rest of the code for the data list control was generated using the designer interface.

The page for a Product List application that uses a data list control

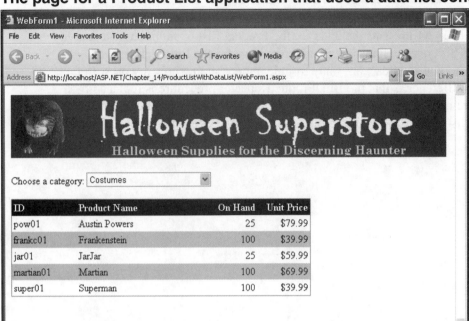

Controls in the Item template

Control	Binding Expression	Width
lblProductID	DataBinder.Eval(Container, "DataItem.ProductID")	100
lblName	DataBinder.Eval(Container, "DataItem.Name")	200
lblOnHand	DataBinder.Eval(Container, "DataItem.OnHand")	80
lblUnitPrice	DataBinder.Eval(Container, "DataItem.UnitPrice", "{0:c}")	80

Description

- The Product List application lets the user select a category from a drop-down list and then displays the products in that category in a data list control. The products are filtered using a data view and are listed in alphabetical sequence by name.

- The data list control uses two templates: an Item template and a Header template. The Item template contains label controls that are bound to the ProductID, Name, OnHand, and UnitPrice columns. The Header template contains labels that identify these columns.

- The widths of the labels in the Header template are set to the same widths as the corresponding labels in the Item template so the labels are aligned.

- Style attributes have been added to the on hand and unit price labels in the Header and Item templates to align their contents at the right side of the columns.

- The Professional 1 format has been applied to the data list control.

Figure 14-10   A Product List application that uses a data list control

The Visual Basic code for the form

Figure 14-11 presents the code for the Product List form that uses a data list control. This code is almost identical to the code for the form that used a repeater, so you shouldn't have any trouble understanding how it works. In fact, the only difference is that the BindProductRepeater procedure is replaced by a procedure named BindProductDataList, which sets the DataSource property of the data list control and then binds it.

The Visual Basic code for the Product List form

```
Public Class WebForm1
    Inherits System.Web.UI.Page

    Dim dsProducts As DataSet
    Dim dsCategories As DataSet

    Private Sub Page_Load(ByVal sender As System.Object, _
            ByVal e As System.EventArgs) Handles MyBase.Load
        'Put user code to initialize the page here
        dsProducts = ProductDB.GetProducts
        If Not IsPostBack Then
            dsCategories = ProductDB.GetCategories
            Me.BindCategoryDropDownList()
            Me.BindProductDataList()
        End If
    End Sub

    Private Sub BindCategoryDropDownList()
        ddlCategory.DataSource = dsCategories
        ddlCategory.DataMember = "Categories"
        ddlCategory.DataTextField = "ShortName"
        ddlCategory.DataValueField = "CategoryID"
        ddlCategory.DataBind()
    End Sub

    Private Sub BindProductDataList()
        Dim dvProducts As New DataView(dsProducts.Tables("Products"))
        dvProducts.RowFilter = "CategoryID='" _
                            & ddlCategory.SelectedValue & "'"
        dlProducts.DataSource = dvProducts
        dlProducts.DataBind()
    End Sub

    Private Sub ddlCategory_SelectedIndexChanged _
            (ByVal sender As System.Object, ByVal e As System.EventArgs) _
            Handles ddlCategory.SelectedIndexChanged
        Me.BindProductDataList()
    End Sub

End Class
```

Note

- The ProductDB class used by this form is similar to the ProductDB class used by the Product Display form in chapter 13 (see figure 13-9). The differences are (1) that only the columns needed by this form are retrieved from the Products table, and (2) that the rows in the result set are sorted by the Name column.

Figure 14-11   The Visual Basic code for the Product List form that uses a data list control

How to use the DataGrid control

Like the repeater and data list controls, the data grid control lets you display information from multiple rows of a data source. As you'll learn in the next few topics, however, the data grid control also provides a convenient way for letting users select and edit data. As a result, the data grid lends itself especially well to applications that let users maintain the data in small tables.

An introduction to the data grid control

Figure 14-12 presents a data grid control that lets the user maintain the data in the Categories table of the Halloween database. Because this table consists of just three columns (CategoryID, ShortName, and LongName), a data grid control works well for presenting its data.

The data grid control displays the data from a data source in a row and column format. As you'll see in the next figure, you can easily create columns that are bound to a column in the data source. When you do that, aspx code like that shown in this figure is generated. Notice in this code that data binding expressions aren't used to bind the columns. Instead, each column is defined with a DataField attribute that identifies the bound column.

In addition to data columns, you can create columns with buttons that let the user select, edit, and delete a row. The data grid in this figure, for example, contains two columns that let the user edit and delete rows. You'll learn how to create and work with columns like these later in this chapter.

Note that the data grid control doesn't provide for adding new rows. Because of that, you have to provide for adding rows yourself. One way to do that is to include a button control on the page that the user can click to add a new, blank row to the data grid. You'll see how this works later in this chapter when I present the complete application for maintaining the Categories table.

Another way to provide for adding a row to a data grid is to include a set of input controls where the user can enter the data for the new row along with an Add button. Then, when the user clicks the Add button, the program can add the new row to the data source and then rebind the data grid control so it displays that row. Although I won't present the code for this technique in this chapter, you shouldn't have any trouble figuring out how to implement it.

This figure also shows you how to bind a data grid control. As with the repeater and data list controls, you specify the data source for a data grid control using the DataSource and DataMember properties. Then, you bind the control using the DataBind method.

By the way, you can format a data grid control using the same techniques you use to format a data list control. That is, you can apply a built-in scheme, you can use the Properties dialog box, or you can use the Properties window. Because you already know how to use these techniques, I won't present them again here.

A data grid control that provides for maintaining a table

ID	Short Name	Long Name		
costumes	Costumes	Costumes	Edit	Delete
fx	FX	Special Effects	Update Cancel	Delete
masks	Masks	Masks	Edit	Delete
props	Props	Props	Edit	Delete

Properties and method for binding a data grid control

Property	Description
DataSource	A data source, such as a dataset.
DataMember	The name of a member associated with the data source, such as a data table. If the data source contains only one bindable member, you don't need to set this property.

Method	Description
DataBind	Binds the control to its data source. This method must be executed each time the data source changes.

The asp element for the data grid control

```
<asp:DataGrid id="dgCategories" runat="server" AutoGenerateColumns="False">
    <HeaderStyle Font-Bold="True"></HeaderStyle>
    <Columns>
        <asp:BoundColumn DataField="CategoryID" HeaderText="ID">
            <HeaderStyle Width="100px"></HeaderStyle></asp:BoundColumn>
        <asp:BoundColumn DataField="ShortName" HeaderText="Short Name">
            <HeaderStyle Width="150px"></HeaderStyle></asp:BoundColumn>
        <asp:BoundColumn DataField="LongName" HeaderText="Long Name">
            <HeaderStyle Width="200px"></HeaderStyle></asp:BoundColumn>
        <asp:EditCommandColumn ButtonType="PushButton" UpdateText="Update"
            CancelText="Cancel" EditText="Edit"></asp:EditCommandColumn>
        <asp:ButtonColumn Text="Delete" ButtonType="PushButton"
            CommandName="Delete"></asp:ButtonColumn>
    </Columns>
</asp:DataGrid>
```

Code that binds the data grid control

```
dgCategories.DataSource = ProductDB.GetCategories
dgCategories.DataMember = "Categories"
dgCategories.DataKeyField = "CategoryID"
dgCategories.DataBind()
```

Description

- A *data grid control* can display bound data in a row and column format. In addition, it can include button columns that let you select, edit, and delete data in the data source. A data grid doesn't provide for adding rows, so you have to use other techniques to do that.
- To define the columns in a data grid control, you use the Properties dialog box shown in figures 14-13 and 14-14.

Figure 14-12   An introduction to the data grid control

How to define the data columns

By default, a data grid control displays one column for each column in the data source. If that's not what you want, you can change the columns that are displayed by using the Columns page of the Properties dialog box shown in figure 14-13. You can also use this dialog box to specify additional properties for each column.

When you first display the Columns page of this dialog box, the Create columns automatically at run time option is selected. This option causes a column to be added to the data grid for each column in the data source. Then, any additional columns you select are displayed after those columns. Since that's usually not what you want, you should deselect this option and select the columns you want to display manually.

To add a bound column to the data grid, select the Bound Column item in the Available Columns list and click the Add button (>). The column will appear in the Selected columns list. Then, type the name of the source column in the Data Field text box and set the other properties as appropriate. To specify the text that's displayed above a column, for example, you set the Header text property. If you don't specify a value for this property, the column name is displayed. To specify the format of the data in a column, enter a format string in the Data formatting expression text box. And to create a column that can't be changed, select the Read only option.

The Columns page of the Properties dialog box with bound columns

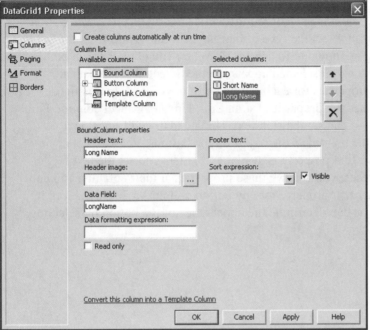

Description

- By default, a data grid control will display one column for each column in its data source. To define the data columns manually, you use the Columns page of the Properties dialog box. To display this dialog box, right-click the data grid and choose the Property Builder command. Then, click the Columns tab at the left side of the dialog box.

- If you define the data columns in a data grid control yourself, you should remove the check mark from the Create columns automatically at run time option. Otherwise, the columns you create will be added to those that are created by default.

- To add a bound column, select Bound Column from the Available Columns list and click the Add button (>). Then, type the name of the data column from the data source that you want to bind to into the Data Field text box.

- To change the order of the columns in the data grid, use the up and down arrows to the right of the Selected columns list. To delete a column from the data grid, select the column in the Selected columns list and then click on the Delete (X) button.

- To specify the text that's displayed above a column, enter the text in the Header text box. The default is the name of the bound column.

- To format the value that's displayed, enter a format string in the Data formatting expression text box.

- For more information about the other options that are available from this dialog box, click the Help button.

Figure 14-13   How to define the data columns

How to create button columns

You also use the Columns page of the Properties dialog box to create button columns. To do that, you select the type of button you want to add from the Button Column group as shown in figure 14-14. When you click the Add button, a column with the button you selected appears in the Selected columns list.

You can also set properties for each button column you add. In this figure, for example, you can see the properties for an Edit, Update, Cancel column. For this type of column, you can set the Edit text, Update text, and Cancel text properties to specify the text that's displayed on the buttons. For a Select or Delete button, a single Text property is available that lets you set the text for that button. In most cases, you'll leave these properties at their defaults. You can also change the Header text property for any button column to display text in its column header, and you can determine the appearance of the button by selecting a Button type option.

The Columns page of the Properties dialog box with the button columns displayed

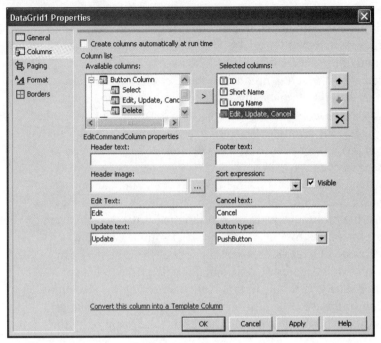

Description

- To add a button column to a data grid, display the Columns tab of the Properties dialog box and expand the Button Column group. Then, select the type of button column you want to add and click the Add button (>). The column is added to the Selected columns list.

- You can use the buttons to the right of the Selected columns list to change the order of the columns in the data grid or to delete columns from the grid.

- To display text at the top of the button column, enter the text in the Header text box.

- The Button type property determines the type of button that's displayed in the grid. The options are PushButton and LinkButton.

- The properties that are available change depending on the type of button column that's selected. For an Edit, Update, Cancel column, the Edit text, Update text, and Cancel text properties determine the text that's displayed on the corresponding button. See figure 14-15 for information on how these buttons work.

- For a Select or Delete column, the Text property determines the text that's displayed on the button.

Figure 14-14   How to create button columns

How to work with button columns

To work with the button columns in a data grid, you use the data grid events listed in figure 14-15. As you can see, the five events listed here correspond to the five possible buttons. When the user clicks on one of these buttons, the program should respond to the appropriate event. The exception is the SelectedIndexChanged event, which is fired when the user clicks on a Select button. In that case, that row is automatically selected and highlighted using the formatting specified by the SelectedItemStyle properties for the data grid. In the first data grid in this figure, for example, the third row is selected. If you want to perform any additional processing when a row is selected, you can respond to the SelectedIndexChanged event.

To illustrate how you use the events for the Edit, Update, and Cancel buttons, suppose the user clicks the Edit button in the fourth row of the first data grid shown here. Then, the program should respond to the EditCommand event of the data grid by displaying the row in *edit mode*. In this mode, the data columns are displayed as text boxes so the user can change the data they contain, and the Edit button is replaced by Update and Cancel buttons. This is illustrated by the second data grid in this figure. Note that to display a row in edit mode, the program simply sets the EditItemIndex property of the data grid to the appropriate row and rebinds the control. The rest is taken care of by the data grid control.

While a row is in edit mode, the user can click either the Update or Cancel button. If he clicks the Update button, the program should respond to the UpdateCommand event by saving the changes to the data source, exiting from edit mode, and then rebinding the control. To exit from edit mode, you set the EditItemIndex property of the data grid to -1. Similarly, if the user clicks the Cancel button, the program should respond to the CancelCommand event by exiting from edit mode and rebinding the control. However, it should not save any changes to the data source.

If the user clicks a Delete button, the DeleteCommand event is raised. The procedure that handles this event should delete the row from the data source and then call the DataBind method to update the data grid so the deleted row is no longer displayed.

Data grid events for working with buttons

Button	Event	Response
Edit	EditCommand	Place the row in edit mode and then rebind the control.
Update	UpdateCommand	Update the data source, exit from edit mode, and rebind the control.
Cancel	CancelCommand	Exit from edit mode and then rebind the control to display the original data.
Delete	DeleteCommand	Delete the row from the data source and then rebind the control.
Select	SelectedIndexChanged	No response is required.

A data grid with a row selected

ID	Short Name	Long Name			
costumes	Costumes	Costumes	Select	Edit	Delete
cute	Cute stuff	Non-scary stuff for kids	Select	Edit	Delete
fx	FX	Special Effects	Select	Edit	Delete
masks	Masks	Halloween masks	Select	Edit	Delete
props	Props	Props	Select	Edit	Delete

A data grid with a row in edit mode

ID	Short Name	Long Name				
costumes	Costumes	Costumes	Select	Edit		Delete
cute	Cute stuff	Non-scary stuff for kids	Select	Edit		Delete
fx	FX	Special Effects	Select	Edit		Delete
masks	Masks	Halloween masks	Select	Update	Cancel	Delete
props	Props	Props	Select	Edit		Delete

An event handler for the CancelCommand event

```
Private Sub dgCategories_CancelCommand(ByVal source As Object, _
        ByVal e As System.Web.UI.WebControls.DataGridCommandEventArgs) _
        Handles dgCategories.CancelCommand
    dgCategories.EditItemIndex = -1
    Me.BindDataGrid()
End Sub
```

Description

* If the user clicks an Edit, Update, Cancel, Delete, or Select button, the data grid events listed above are fired and the program should respond to them as indicated.

* To place a row in *edit mode*, set the EditItemIndex property of the data grid to the index of that row. Then, the bound columns become text boxes so the user can enter changes, and the Edit button is replaced by Update and Cancel buttons.

* To exit from edit mode, set the EditItemIndex property to -1 to indicate that no rows are being edited.

* If the user clicks a Select button, the SelectedIndex property of the data grid is automatically set to the selected row and the row is displayed with the formatting specified by the SelectedItemStyle properties.

Figure 14-15   How to work with button columns

A Category Maintenance application that uses a data grid control

To give you a better idea of how you can use a data grid control, figure 14-16 presents the specifications for a Category Maintenance application. This application lets the user edit or delete rows in the Categories table using a data grid control. In addition, the user can click the Add Item button to add a new row to this table.

The table in this figure lists the columns that I added to the data grid control. The first three columns are bound to the CategoryID, ShortName, and LongName columns of the data source. The last two columns are button columns. As you can see, I set the widths of the bound columns but not the button columns. That way, the bound columns will have fixed widths, but the widths of the button columns will change to accommodate the buttons they contain. If just Edit buttons are displayed in the fourth column, for example, that column will appear as shown here. But if Update and Cancel buttons are displayed in one of the rows in that column, the width of the column will increase so that both buttons are displayed. Also notice that I set the Button type property of the two button columns to PushButton so they appear as shown.

Although it isn't apparent in this figure, a label control is included on this form below the data grid. This label is used to display error messages if the program detects invalid data.

The page for the Category Maintenance application

Columns in the data grid control

Column type	Data Field	Header text	Button type	Width
Bound	CategoryID	ID		100
Bound	ShortName	Short Name		150
Bound	LongName	Long Name		200
Edit, Update, Cancel			PushButton	
Delete			PushButton	

Description

- The Category Maintenance program lets the user modify or delete rows in the Categories table of the Halloween database using a data grid control.
- To add a new row to the Categories table, the user clicks the Add Item button. Then, a new row is added at the bottom of the grid and that row is placed in edit mode.
- The Professional 1 format has been applied to the data grid control.
- A label control that will be used to display error messages is included below the data grid control.

Figure 14-16   A Category Maintenance application that uses a data grid control

The Visual Basic code for the CategoryDB class

Figure 14-17 presents the code for the CategoryDB class that's used by the Category Maintenance application. This class begins with a Public enumeration that's used by the UpdateCategories method. It indicates the result of the update operation and is defined as Public so it can also be used by the Category Maintenance form.

The CategoryDB class also includes two public procedures. The GetCategories procedure returns a dataset that includes all the rows and columns in the Categories table of the Halloween database. It uses the DataAdapter procedure to create the data adapter that's used to fill the dataset and update the database. Notice that this procedure uses a command builder (see chapter 13) to create the Insert, Update, and Delete commands.

The other public procedure, UpdateCategories, performs the update operation by executing the Update method of the data adapter. The Update method is called within a Try…Catch statement so that any exceptions that occur during the update can be handled by the procedure. In practice, every database application needs to catch all of the possible exceptions this way and handle them appropriately.

In this case, the first exception that's handled is a concurrency exception. If a concurrency exception occurs, the procedure returns the ConcurrencyError member of the UpdateResult enumeration.

The second exception this procedure handles is SQL Server exception number 547. This exception occurs if you try to delete a row from the Categories table when related rows exist in the Products table. If this exception occurs, the procedure returns the ForeignKeyError member of the UpdateResult enumeration.

This procedure also handles SQL Server exception 2627. This exception occurs if you try to add a row with a primary key value that already exists in the table. That can happen if another user adds a row with that value after you retrieve the data from the Categories table. If this exception occurs, the procedure returns the PrimaryKeyError member of the UpdateResult enumeration.

Finally, the procedure handles any other SQL Server exceptions that may occur. To do that, it returns the OtherSqlError member of the UpdateResult enumeration.

Incidentally, one way to find out the exception number for a specific exception is to force the exception during testing. To force a concurrency exception, for example, you can open two browsers and try to update the same row. Then, when the exception occurs, your code can catch the exception and use the Number property of the exception object to display the exception number.

The Visual Basic code for the CategoryDB class

```
Imports System.Data.SqlClient
Public Class CategoryDB

    Public Enum UpdateResult
        Success
        ConcurrencyError
        PrimaryKeyError
        ForeignKeyError
        OtherSqlError
    End Enum

    Private Shared Function Connection() As SqlConnection
        Dim sConnectionString As String
        sConnectionString _
            = ConfigurationSettings.AppSettings("ConnectionString")
        Return New SqlConnection(sConnectionString)
    End Function

    Public Shared Function GetCategories() As DataSet
        Dim dsCategories As New DataSet
        Dim daCategories As SqlDataAdapter = DataAdapter()
        daCategories.Fill(dsCategories, "Categories")
        Return dsCategories
    End Function

    Public Shared Function UpdateCategories(ByVal Categories As DataSet) _
            As UpdateResult
        Dim daCategories As SqlDataAdapter = DataAdapter()
        Try
            daCategories.Update(Categories, "Categories")
            Return UpdateResult.Success
        Catch eConcurrency As DBConcurrencyException
            Return UpdateResult.ConcurrencyError
        Catch eSql As SqlException
            If eSql.Number = 547 Then
                Return UpdateResult.ForeignKeyError
            ElseIf eSql.Number = 2627 Then
                Return UpdateResult.PrimaryKeyError
            Else
                Return UpdateResult.OtherSqlError
            End If
        End Try
    End Function

    Private Shared Function DataAdapter() As SqlDataAdapter
        Dim sSelect As String = "Select CategoryID, ShortName, LongName " _
            & "From Categories Order By CategoryID"
        Dim daCategories As New SqlDataAdapter(sSelect, Connection())
        daCategories.MissingSchemaAction = MissingSchemaAction.AddWithKey
        Dim cbCategories As New SqlCommandBuilder(daCategories)
        Return daCategories
    End Function

End Class
```

Figure 14-17   The code for the CategoryDB class

The Visual Basic code for the Category Maintenance form

Figure 14-18 presents the code for the Category Maintenance form. As you'll see, most of this code responds to the events that occur on the buttons of the data grid control.

The Load procedure for this page is responsible for managing the dataset used by this program. When this procedure is run for the first time, it calls the GetCategories method of the CategoryDB class to get the data from the database and fill the Categories data table. Then, it calls the BindDataGrid procedure to set the binding properties for the data grid control and bind the control. Finally, the Load procedure saves the dataset in session state. When the Load procedure is run after the first time, it simply retrieves the dataset from the session state object.

If the user clicks on the Add Item button, the Click event procedure for this button starts by adding a blank row to the Categories table. Then, it sets the EditItemIndex property of the data grid to the index of the newly created row, which is equal to the Count property of the Rows collection of the Categories table minus 1. That places the new row in edit mode. Finally, it calls the BindDataGrid procedure to rebind the data grid and sets a session state item named AddMode to True to indicate that the user is adding a row.

If the user clicks an Edit button, the procedure for the EditCommand event is executed. This procedure starts by checking the AddMode session state item to see if a new row is being added. If so, that row must be deleted and the AddMode session state item must be changed to False before another row can be edited. (Another way to handle this would be to ask the user if the new row should be saved before the next row is edited.) Next, the EditItemIndex of the data grid is set to the index of the row that contains the Edit button that was clicked, so that row is placed in edit mode. To get the index of that row, the procedure uses the Item property of the e argument that's passed to it to get the Item object. Then, the ItemIndex property of the Item object gets the index of that object. Finally, the Edit procedure calls the BindDataGrid procedure to rebind the data grid.

The Visual Basic code for the Category Maintenance form   Page 1

```
Public Class WebForm1
    Inherits System.Web.UI.Page

    Dim dsCategories As DataSet

    Private Sub Page_Load(ByVal sender As System.Object, _
            ByVal e As System.EventArgs) Handles MyBase.Load
        'Put user code to initialize the page here
        If Not IsPostBack Then
            dsCategories = CategoryDB.GetCategories
            Me.BindDataGrid()
            Session("dsCategories") = dsCategories
        Else
            dsCategories = Session("dsCategories")
        End If
    End Sub

    Private Sub BindDataGrid()
        dgCategories.DataSource = dsCategories
        dgCategories.DataMember = "Categories"
        dgCategories.DataKeyField = "CategoryID"
        dgCategories.DataBind()
    End Sub

    Private Sub btnAdd_Click(ByVal sender As System.Object, _
            ByVal e As System.EventArgs) Handles btnAdd.Click
        Dim dr As DataRow
        dr = dsCategories.Tables("Categories").NewRow
        dr("CategoryID") = ""
        dr("ShortName") = ""
        dr("LongName") = ""
        dsCategories.Tables("Categories").Rows.Add(dr)
        dgCategories.EditItemIndex _
            = dsCategories.Tables("Categories").Rows.Count - 1
        Me.BindDataGrid()
        Session("AddMode") = True
    End Sub

    Private Sub dgCategories_EditCommand(ByVal source As Object, _
            ByVal e As System.Web.UI.WebControls.DataGridCommandEventArgs) _
            Handles dgCategories.EditCommand
        If Session("AddMode") = True Then
            Dim i As Integer _
                = dsCategories.Tables("Categories").Rows.Count - 1
            dsCategories.Tables("Categories").Rows(i).Delete()
            Session("AddMode") = False
        End If
        dgCategories.EditItemIndex = e.Item.ItemIndex
        Me.BindDataGrid()
    End Sub
```

Figure 14-18   The code for the Category Maintenance form (part 1 of 3)

The most complicated procedure in this application is the one that's executed when the user clicks the Update button. This procedure starts by declaring three string variables to hold the values of the category ID, short name, and long name entered by the user. Then, the next three statements retrieve the data for those columns from the three text box controls in the data grid. To do that, they use the Item property of the e argument that's passed to the procedure to refer to the row in the data grid that's being updated. Then, they use the Cells property to refer to the collection of cells within the row. Because the collection of cells is zero-based, the first cell has an index value of zero, the second cell has an index value of 1, and so on.

Although it's not discussed in this chapter, each cell can have one or more controls. To refer to a specific control within a cell, you have to use the Controls collection. Like the Cells collection, the Controls collection is zero-based. So to refer to the first control in the first cell, you use an expression like this:

```
e.Item.Cells(0).Controls(0)
```

You can see this expression in the first of the three assignment statements in this procedure. Finally, the procedure uses the CType function to cast the resulting control to a text box so that its Text property can be assigned to the appropriate variable.

After the values have been extracted from the text boxes, the procedure calls the ValidCategory procedure to validate the input data. This procedure checks that the user entered a value into each text box. In addition, it checks that the values aren't longer than the Categories table in the Halloween database provides for. If invalid data is detected, the Text property of the message label on the page is set to an error message so that message will be displayed when the page is sent back to the browser.

If the data is valid, the UpdateCommand procedure creates a DataRow variable named dr to access the data row that corresponds to the row being edited. Then, it sets the columns to the values entered by the user. Notice that these statements are coded within a Try...Catch statement. That's because a constraint error will occur if the user enters a category ID that already exists in the table. In that case, the Text property of the message label is set to an appropriate error message.

If the column values are assigned successfully, the UpdateCommand procedure continues by calling the UpdateDataBase procedure to update the database with the changed row. Finally, the procedure sets the EditItemIndex property to -1 to exit from edit mode, calls the BindDataGrid procedure to rebind the data grid, and changes the AddMode session state item to False in case a row was being added to the dataset.

The Visual Basic code for the Category Maintenance form   Page 2

```vb
Private Sub dgCategories_UpdateCommand(ByVal source As Object, _
        ByVal e As System.Web.UI.WebControls.DataGridCommandEventArgs) _
        Handles dgCategories.UpdateCommand
    Dim sCategoryID, sShortName, sLongName As String
    sCategoryID = CType(e.Item.Cells(0).Controls(0), TextBox).Text
    sShortName = CType(e.Item.Cells(1).Controls(0), TextBox).Text
    sLongName = CType(e.Item.Cells(2).Controls(0), TextBox).Text
    If ValidCategory(sCategoryID, sShortName, sLongName) Then
        Dim dr As DataRow _
            = dsCategories.Tables("Categories").Rows(e.Item.ItemIndex)
        Try
            dr("CategoryID") = sCategoryID
            dr("ShortName") = sShortName
            dr("LongName") = sLongName
            Me.UpdateDataBase()
            dgCategories.EditItemIndex = -1
            Me.BindDataGrid()
            Session("AddMode") = False
        Catch eConstraint As ConstraintException
            lblMessage.Text = "A category with that ID already exists."
        End Try
    End If
End Sub

Private Function ValidCategory(ByVal CategoryID As String, _
        ByVal ShortName As String, ByVal LongName As String) As Boolean
    ValidCategory = True
    If CategoryID = "" Then
        ValidCategory = False
        lblMessage.Text = "Category ID is required."
    ElseIf Len(CategoryID) > 10 Then
        ValidCategory = False
        lblMessage.Text = "Category ID must be 10 characters or less."
    ElseIf ShortName = "" Then
        ValidCategory = False
        lblMessage.Text = "Short name is required."
    ElseIf Len(ShortName) > 15 Then
        ValidCategory = False
        lblMessage.Text = "Short name must be 15 characters or less."
    ElseIf LongName = "" Then
        ValidCategory = False
        lblMessage.Text = "Long name is required."
    ElseIf Len(LongName) > 50 Then
        ValidCategory = False
        lblMessage.Text = "Long name must be 50 characters or less."
    End If
End Function
```

Figure 14-18   The code for the Category Maintenance form (part 2 of 3)

The UpdateDatabase procedure calls the UpdateCategories method of the CategoryDB class to update the Categories table. Then, it tests the value returned by this method to determine if an error occurred. If so, it sets the Text property of the message label to an error message. Then, this procedure executes the GetCategories method of the CategoryDB class to retrieve a fresh copy of the dataset, and it saves that dataset in session state.

If the user clicks the Cancel button while a row is being added or changed, the CancelCommand procedure is executed. This procedure starts by checking the AddMode session state item to determine if a row was being added. If so, the procedure deletes the row and sets the AddMode item to False. Then, it sets the EditItemIndex property of the data grid to -1 to exit from edit mode, and it calls the BindDataGrid procedure to rebind the data grid.

The DeleteCommand procedure is executed if the user clicks the Delete button for a row. This procedure also checks the AddMode session state item to determine if a row is being added. If so, it must then determine if the Delete button that was clicked is in the new row or another row. To do that, it compares the index of the row that contains the Delete button that was clicked with the index of the new row. If the button wasn't in the new row, the procedure deletes the new row. In either case, it sets the AddMode session state item to False.

Next, the DeleteCommand procedure deletes the row that contains the Delete button that was clicked. Then, it calls the UpdateDatabase procedure to update the database, and it calls the BindDataGrid procedure to rebind the data grid.

The Visual Basic code for the Category Maintenance form   Page 3

```vbnet
Private Sub UpdateDataBase()
    Select Case CategoryDB.UpdateCategories(dsCategories)
        Case CategoryDB.UpdateResult.ConcurrencyError
            lblMessage.Text = "Another user has updated that category. " _
                            & "Please try again."
        Case CategoryDB.UpdateResult.ForeignKeyError
            lblMessage.Text = "That category is in use."
        Case CategoryDB.UpdateResult.PrimaryKeyError
            lblMessage.Text = "Another user has added a category " _
                            & "with that ID."
        Case CategoryDB.UpdateResult.OtherSqlError
            lblMessage.Text = "An unspecified SQL Server error " _
                            & "has occurred."
    End Select
    dsCategories = CategoryDB.GetCategories
    Session("dsCategories") = dsCategories
End Sub

Private Sub dgCategories_CancelCommand(ByVal source As Object, _
        ByVal e As System.Web.UI.WebControls.DataGridCommandEventArgs) _
        Handles dgCategories.CancelCommand
    If Session("AddMode") = True Then
        Dim i As Integer _
            = dsCategories.Tables("Categories").Rows.Count - 1
        dsCategories.Tables("Categories").Rows(i).Delete()
        Session("AddMode") = False
    End If
    dgCategories.EditItemIndex = -1
    Me.BindDataGrid()
End Sub

Private Sub dgCategories_DeleteCommand(ByVal source As Object, _
        ByVal e As System.Web.UI.WebControls.DataGridCommandEventArgs) _
        Handles dgCategories.DeleteCommand
    If Session("AddMode") = True Then
        Dim i As Integer _
            = dsCategories.Tables("Categories").Rows.Count - 1
        If e.Item.ItemIndex <> i Then
            dsCategories.Tables("Categories").Rows(i).Delete()
        End If
        Session("AddMode") = False
    End If
    dsCategories.Tables("Categories").Rows(e.Item.ItemIndex).Delete()
    Me.UpdateDataBase()
    Me.BindDataGrid()
End Sub

End Class
```

Figure 14-18   The code for the Category Maintenance form (part 3 of 3)

Perspective

With the techniques you've learned in this chapter, you can create sophisticated ASP.NET database applications. However, you should realize that you can do a lot more with the repeater, data list, and data grid controls than what's presented in this chapter.

For instance, you can use a repeater control to create a menu that consists of Anchor elements that use binding expressions to identify the content of each element. You can edit the HTML for a data grid control to create command buttons in addition to the Select, Edit, Update, and Cancel buttons that are available from the Properties dialog box. And you can use command buttons in a data list control to include additional functionality.

But even without these enhancements, the database programming techniques you've learned in the last three chapters should get you well on your way toward developing professional ASP.NET database applications. Then, to take yourself to another level, you can get our ADO.NET book.

Terms

repeater control
template
data list control
template-editing mode
data grid control
edit mode

Section 4

Other ASP.NET skills

This section contains six chapters that present other ASP.NET skills that you may need for some of your web applications. In particular, chapter 15 shows you how to use a secure connection for an application and how to authenticate the users of an application; chapter 16 shows you how to create and use web services; chapter 17 shows you how to create and use custom server controls; and chapter 18 shows you how to use Crystal Reports with a web application. Then, chapter 19 shows you how to use email and custom error pages with a web application as well as how to deal with the problems that can occur when users click the Back buttons in their browsers. Last, chapter 20 shows you how to deploy a web application when it's ready for use.

Because each of these chapters is written as an independent module, you can read these chapters in whatever sequence you prefer. If, for example, you want to learn how to use Crystal Reports in one of your applications, you can skip directly to chapter 18. Or, if you want to learn how to deploy a web application, you can skip to chapter 20. Eventually, though, you should read all of the chapters in this section because you should at least be aware of the capabilities that these chapters present.

15

How to secure a web application

Security is one of the most important concerns for any developer of web applications. To secure a web application, you must make sure that unauthorized users don't have access to it. In addition, you must make sure that private data that's sent between the client and the server can't be intercepted.

In this chapter, you'll learn how to use an Internet protocol called SSL to secure the transmission of data between the client and the server. In addition, you'll learn how to prevent unauthorized users from accessing your applications using a technique called forms-based authentication. When you complete this chapter, you'll have the basic skills you need to secure any application.

How to use SSL

To prevent others from reading data that's transmitted over the Internet, you can use the *Secure Sockets Layer*, or *SSL*. SSL is an Internet protocol that lets you transmit data over the Internet using data encryption. The topics that follow explain how SSL works and show you how to incorporate it into your ASP.NET applications.

An introduction to SSL

Figure 15-1 shows a web page that uses SSL to transfer data between the server and the client over a *secure connection*. To determine if you're transmitting data over a secure connection, you can read the URL in the browser's address bar. If it starts with https rather than http, then you're transmitting data over a secure connection. In addition, a small lock icon appears in the lower right corner of the browser window.

With regular HTTP, all data is sent as unencrypted plain text. As a result, if a hacker intercepts this data, it is easy to read. With a secure connection, however, all data that's transferred between the client and the server is encrypted. Although a hacker can still intercept this data, he won't be able to read it without breaking the encryption code.

A page that was requested with a secure connection

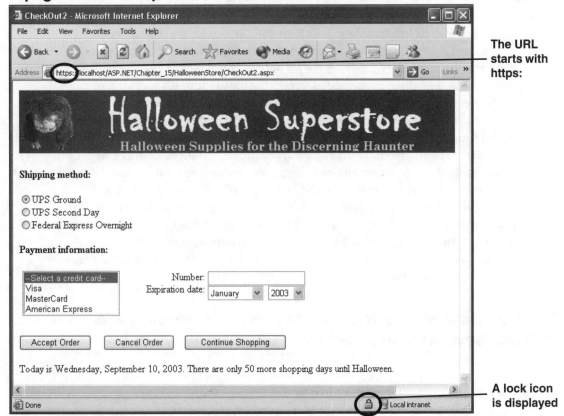

The URL starts with https:

A lock icon is displayed

Description

- The *Secure Sockets Layer*, or *SSL*, is the protocol used by the World Wide Web that allows clients and servers to communicate over a *secure connection*.
- With SSL, the browser encrypts all data that's sent to the server and decrypts all data that's received from the server. Conversely, the server encrypts all data that's sent to the browser and decrypts all data that's received from the browser.
- SSL is able to determine if data has been tampered with during transit.
- SSL is also able to verify that a server or a client is who it claims to be.
- The URL for a secure connection starts with HTTPS instead of HTTP.
- A web browser that is using a secure connection displays a lock in the lower right corner.

Figure 15-1   An introduction to SSL

An introduction to digital secure certificates

To use SSL to transmit data, the client and the server use *digital secure certificates* like the one shown in figure 15-2. Digital secure certificates serve two purposes. First, they establish the identity of the server or client. Second, they provide the information needed to encrypt data before it's transmitted.

By default, browsers are configured to accept certificates that come from trusted sources. If a browser doesn't recognize a certificate as coming from a trusted source, however, it informs the user and lets the user view the certificate. Then, the user can determine whether the certificate should be considered valid. If the user chooses to accept the certificate, the secure connection is established.

Sometimes, a server may want the client to authenticate itself with *SSL client authentication*. Although this isn't as common as *SSL server authentication*, it is used occasionally. For example, a bank might want to use SSL client authentication to make sure it's sending sensitive information such as account numbers and balances to the correct person. To implement this type of authentication, a digital certificate must be installed on the client.

How to determine if a digital secure certificate is installed on your server

In the topics that follow, you'll learn how to obtain and install digital secure certificates and trial certificates. Before you do that, however, you may want to check if a certificate is already installed on your server. If IIS is running on your local machine, chances are that a certificate hasn't been installed. If IIS is running on a server on a network, however, you can use the procedure in figure 15-2 to determine if a certificate has been installed and to view the certificate.

The Certificate dialog box for a digital secure certificate

Types of digital secure certificates

Certificate	Description
Server certificate	Issued to trusted servers so that client computers can connect to them using secure connections.
Client certificate	Issued to trusted clients so that server computers can confirm their identity.

Concepts

- *Authentication* is the process of determining whether a server or client is who and what it claims to be.
- When a browser makes an initial attempt to communicate with a server over a secure connection that uses SSL, the server authenticates itself by sending its *digital secure certificate* to the browser.
- In some instances, the server may also request that a browser authenticate itself by presenting its own digital secure certificate. This is uncommon, however.

How to determine if a digital secure certificate is installed on your server

1. Start the Internet Information Services program by clicking the Start button and then choosing All Programs→Administrative Tools→Internet Information Services (Windows XP) or Programs→Administrative Tools→Internet Services Manager (Windows 2000).
2. Expand the node for the server and the Web Sites node and then right-click on the Default Web Site node and select Properties to display the Properties dialog box.
3. Click the Directory Security tab. If a digital secure certificate is installed, the View Certificate button will be enabled. Click this button to display the dialog box shown above.

Figure 15-2   An introduction to digital secure certificates

How to obtain a digital secure certificate

If you want to develop an ASP.NET application that uses SSL to secure client connections, you must first obtain a digital secure certificate from a trusted source such as those listed in figure 15-3. These *certification authorities*, or *CAs*, verify that the person or company requesting the certificate is a valid person or company by checking with a *registration authority*, or *RA*. To obtain a digital secure certificate, you'll need to provide a registration authority with information about yourself or your company. Once the registration authority approves the request, the certification authority can issue the digital secure certificate.

A digital secure certificate from a trusted source isn't free, and the cost of the certificate will depend on a variety of factors such as the level of security. As a result, when you purchase a digital certificate, you'll want one that fits the needs of your web site. In particular, you'll need to decide what *SSL strength* you want the connection to support. SSL strength refers to the level of encryption that the secure connection uses when it transmits data.

If you use a 40-bit SSL strength, it might be possible for a determined hacker to break the encryption code. If your site requires a higher level of security, then, you can purchase a certificate that uses 128-bit SSL strength. Although these certificates are more expensive than 40-bit certificates, it's almost impossible for a hacker to break the encryption code. On the other hand, only the most current browsers support 128-bit strength, but most browsers support 40-bit strength. In most cases, then, you'll use 40-bit strength.

Common certification authorities that issue digital secure certificates

```
www.verisign.com
www.geotrust.com
www.entrust.com
www.thawte.com
```

SSL strengths

Strength	Pros and Cons
40-bit	Most browsers support it, but it's easier to break the encryption code.
128-bit	It's trillions of times stronger than 40-bit strength, but it's more expensive and only the most current browsers support it.

Description

- *SSL strength* refers to the length of the generated key that is created during the encryption process. The longer the key, the more difficult it is to break the encryption code.

- To use SSL in your web applications, you must first purchase a digital secure certificate from a trusted *certification authority*, or *CA*. Once you obtain the certificate, you send it to the people who host your web site so they can install it on the server.

- A certification authority is a company that issues and manages security credentials. To verify information provided by the requestor of the secure certificate, a CA must check with a *registration authority*, or *RA*. Once the registration authority verifies the requestor's information, the certification authority can issue a digital secure certificate.

- Since SSL is built into all major browsers and web servers, installing a digital secure certificate enables SSL.

Figure 15-3   How to obtain a digital secure certificate

How to obtain a trial certificate for testing

Most certification authorities will provide you with a free trial certificate you can use for testing purposes. The trial certificate typically expires after a relatively short period of time, such as two weeks or a month. Although you can continue to use the trial certificate after the testing period expires, the dialog box shown at the top of figure 15-4 will appear each time you enter a secure connection. This dialog box simply informs you that the certificate has expired and shouldn't be trusted.

Of course, you shouldn't run an ASP.NET application in a production environment using an expired certificate. When you're ready to deploy your application, then, you should contact the certification authority to obtain a valid certificate.

Another way to obtain certificates for testing purposes is to set up your own certification authority using Microsoft Certificate Server, which comes with Windows 2000 Server and Windows Server 2003. You can then use the certificate server to issue certificates for testing purposes. Because installing and configuring Microsoft Certificate Server is beyond the scope of this book, I won't describe it here. If you need to learn more about it, you can review the online help for Windows 2000 Server or Windows Server 2003 or you can visit Microsoft's web site.

The dialog box that's displayed when your trial certificate has expired

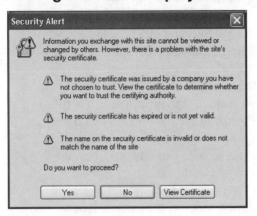

Description

- To test SSL connections in a local environment, you can request a free trial certificate from an established certification authority. The certificate typically expires in 14 to 30 days.

- After the certificate expires, you can still use it for testing purposes. When you switch to a secure connection and the certificate has expired, the dialog box shown above will be displayed. Then, you can click Yes to proceed with the secure connection even though the certificate has expired.

- The certification authority's web site will have detailed instructions you can follow to request, download, and install a trial certificate.

- An alternative to requesting a trial certificate from a certification authority is to become your own certification authority. To do that, you need to install Microsoft Certificate Server on a separate server computer on your network. Then, you can use the certificate server to create certificates you can use for testing.

- Certificates issued by a certification authority on a local network won't be trusted outside of your network, but they will be adequate for testing ASP.NET applications that use SSL.

Figure 15-4   How to obtain a trial certificate for testing

How to use the Web Server Certificate Wizard

Microsoft's web server, Internet Information Services (IIS), includes a Web Server Certificate Wizard you can use to manage digital certificates. Figure 15-5 describes how you use this wizard.

If your IIS server doesn't have a certificate installed, the Wizard walks you through the steps needed to create a file that contains the information a certification authority needs to issue a certificate. Once you create this file, you'll need to go to the certification authority's web site for instructions on how to request a certificate. Then, when you receive the certificate, you can return to the Certificate Wizard to install it.

You can also use the Certificate Wizard to manage existing certificates for your IIS server. For example, you can use it to remove certificates or renew expired certificates. You can also use it to assign a certificate that was previously installed but has been removed or to import a certificate used by another server.

The Certificate Wizard options for an IIS server that doesn't have a certificate installed

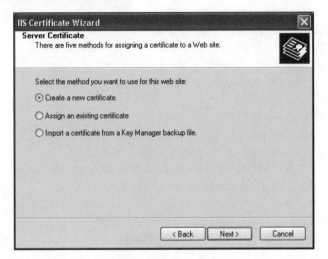

How to start the Web Server Certificate Wizard

1. Display the Properties dialog box for the Default Web Site node of the server as described in figure 15-2 and display the Directory Security tab.
2. Click the Server Certificate button to display the first Certificate Wizard dialog box. This dialog box indicates whether a certificate is installed or a request is pending and summarizes the functions the wizard can help you perform.

Description

- The Web Server Certificate Wizard manages the process of requesting certificates from certification authorities and installing certificates in IIS.
- If a certificate is already installed on your IIS server, the Wizard lets you renew the certificate if it's expired, remove the certificate, or replace it with another certificate.
- If no certificate is installed, the Wizard lets you create a certificate file that you can use to request a certificate from a certification authority, assign a certificate that was previously installed, or import a certificate from a copy exported from another server.
- If you have requested a certificate from a certification authority but haven't installed the resulting certificate, the Wizard lets you complete the request and install the certificate or cancel the request.

Note

- When you request a certificate from a certification authority, it's usually sent to you as an email attachment. Then, you can save the attachment on your hard drive and use the Wizard to install it. If the certificate is sent as text within the email instead, you'll need to copy and paste it into a file using a program such as WordPad and then save it with the extension *cer*.

Figure 15-5   How to use the Web Server Certificate Wizard

How to use a secure connection

Figure 15-6 shows how to request a secure connection in an ASP.NET application. To do that, you simply execute a Response.Redirect method with a URL that specifies HTTPS as the protocol rather than HTTP. Then, depending on how the user's browser is configured, the user may see a dialog box similar to the one shown in this figure before the application enters the secure connection.

To request a secure connection using HTTPS, you must use an absolute URL. That means that the URL must include the complete application path, including the web server's domain name and the directory path that leads to the application. For example, the first URL in this figure specifies //localhost as the web server's domain name and /ASP.NET/Chapter_15/HalloweenStore as the directory path.

Rather than coding this information into each URL, you may want to store the application path in the Web.config file as shown in the second coding example in this figure. As you can see, you store this information as an element within the <appSettings> section of this file. Then, you can use the AppSettings property of the ConfigurationSettings class to retrieve the value of the element that contains the path. This is illustrated in the third coding example. If you use this technique, you'll only need to change the application path in the Web.config file if you deploy the application to a different location.

Once your application has established a secure connection, it can navigate to other pages using relative URLs while maintaining the secure connection. To close the secure connection, the application must navigate to another page by specifying an absolute URL with HTTP rather than HTTPS as the protocol. This is illustrated in the last coding example in this figure.

A dialog box that may be displayed for secure connections

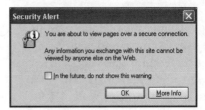

A URL that requests a secure connection

```
https://localhost/ASP.NET/Chapter_15/HalloweenStore/Checkout1.aspx
```

A Web.config file that defines the AppPath setting

```
<?xml version="1.0" encoding="utf-8" ?>
<configuration>
  <appSettings>
    <add key="AppPath"
         value="//localhost/ASP.NET/Chapter_15/HalloweenStore/" />
  </appSettings>

  <system.web>
  .
  .
```

Code that retrieves the application path from the Web.config file

```
Dim sURL As String
sURL = "https:" _
     & ConfigurationSettings.AppSettings("AppPath") _
     & "Checkout1.aspx"
Response.Redirect(sURL)
```

Code that returns to an unsecured connection

```
Dim sURL As String
sURL = "http:" _
     & ConfigurationSettings.AppSettings("AppPath") _
     & "Order.aspx"
Response.Redirect(sURL)
```

Description

- To request a secure connection, you must use an absolute URL that specifies https as the protocol. Once you establish a secure connection, you can use relative URLs to continue using the secure connection.

- To return to an unsecured connection after using a secure connection, you must code an absolute URL that specifies the http protocol.

- Instead of coding the application's path into each URL, you can store it in the <appSettings> section of the Web.config file. That way, if the path changes, you can change it in just one location.

- Depending on the security settings in your browser, a dialog box may be displayed before a secure connection is established. A dialog box may also be displayed before a secure connection is closed.

Figure 15-6   How to use a secure connection

How to force a page to use a secure connection

When you build a complete web application, you usually include navigation features such as menus or hyperlinks that guide the user from page to page. Unfortunately, users sometimes bypass your navigation features and access pages in your application directly. For example, a user might bookmark a page in your application and return to it later. Other users might simply type the URL of individual pages in your application into their browser's address bar. Some users do this innocently; others do it in an attempt to bypass your application's security features.

Because of that, a page that should use SSL to send or receive sensitive information shouldn't assume that a secure connection has been established. Instead, it should check for a secure connection and establish one if necessary. To do that, you can use the properties of the HttpRequest class shown in figure 15-7.

To check for a secure connection, you use the IsSecureConnection property. Then, if the connection isn't secure, you can use the Url property to retrieve the URL for the page and modify that URL so it uses the HTTPS protocol. After you do that, you can use the Redirect method to redirect the browser using the new URL. Notice that you typically include this code at the beginning of the Load procedure for the page. That way, you can be sure that no other code is executed until a secure connection is established.

Properties of the HttpRequest class for working with secure connections

Property	Description
IsSecureConnection	Returns True if the current connection is secure. Otherwise, returns False.
Url	The URL of the current request.

A Load procedure for a page that forces the page to use a secure connection

```
Private Sub Page_Load(ByVal sender As System.Object, _
        ByVal e As System.EventArgs) Handles MyBase.Load
    If Not Request.IsSecureConnection Then
        Dim sURL As String
        sURL = Request.Url.ToString.Replace("http:", "https:")
        Response.Redirect(sURL)
    End If
End Sub
```

Discussion

- If a page requires the user to enter sensitive information, such as passwords or credit card data, it should make sure that it's operating on a secure connection. To do that, the page should check the IsSecureConnection property of the HttpRequest object in its Load procedure.

- If the page isn't using a secure connection, it should switch to a secure connection to protect the privacy of the user's data. To do that, it can replace the http protocol in the URL to https and then redirect the browser to the new URL.

Figure 15-7   How to force a page to use a secure connection

A Halloween Store application that uses SSL

To show how secure connections are used in a typical application, the next two topics present a version of the Halloween Store application that uses SSL.

The operation of the Halloween Store application

Figure 15-8 shows the five pages of the Halloween Store application. As you can see, the application lets the user select products and display the shopping cart without establishing a secure connection. When the user clicks the Check Out button from either the Order page or the Shopping Cart page, however, a secure connection is established. The secure connection is then maintained while the two Check Out pages and the Confirmation page are displayed. When the user clicks the Return to Order Page button, however, the Order page is redisplayed with an unsecured connection.

The code for the Halloween Store application

Figure 15-9 presents the code for using SSL in the Halloween Store application. At the top of the first page of this figure, you can see the code for the Click event of the Check Out button on the Shopping Cart page. (The code for the Click event of the Check Out button on the Order page is identical.) This code creates a URL that uses the HTTPS protocol and the path that's specified in the <appSettings> section of the Web.config file. Then, it redirects the browser to the first Check Out page using a secure connection.

In the code for the first Check Out page, you can see that the Load event procedure checks if a secure connection has been established. If not, the URL is retrieved from the request and the HTTP protocol is replaced with HTTPS. Then, the browser is redirected to the page using a secure connection.

If the user clicks the Continue Checkout button, a relative URL is used to display the second Check Out page, which means that the secure connection is maintained. If the user clicks the Cancel or Continue Shopping button, however, the browser is redirected to the Order page with an unsecured connection.

The code for the second Check Out page is shown in part 2 of this figure. Like the first Check Out page, its Load event procedure makes sure that a secure connection is established before proceeding. In addition, if the user clicks the Cancel or Continue Shopping button, the Order page is redisplayed with an unsecured connection. If the user clicks the Accept Order button, however, the secure connection is maintained and the Confirmation page is displayed.

The code for the Confirmation page is also shown in this figure. As you can see, if the user clicks the Return to Order Page button on this page, the Order page is redisplayed with an unsecured connection.

How security is used by the Halloween Store application

ShoppingCart.aspx

Checkout1.aspx

Secure

Checkout2.aspx

Order.aspx

Confirmation.aspx

Unsecure

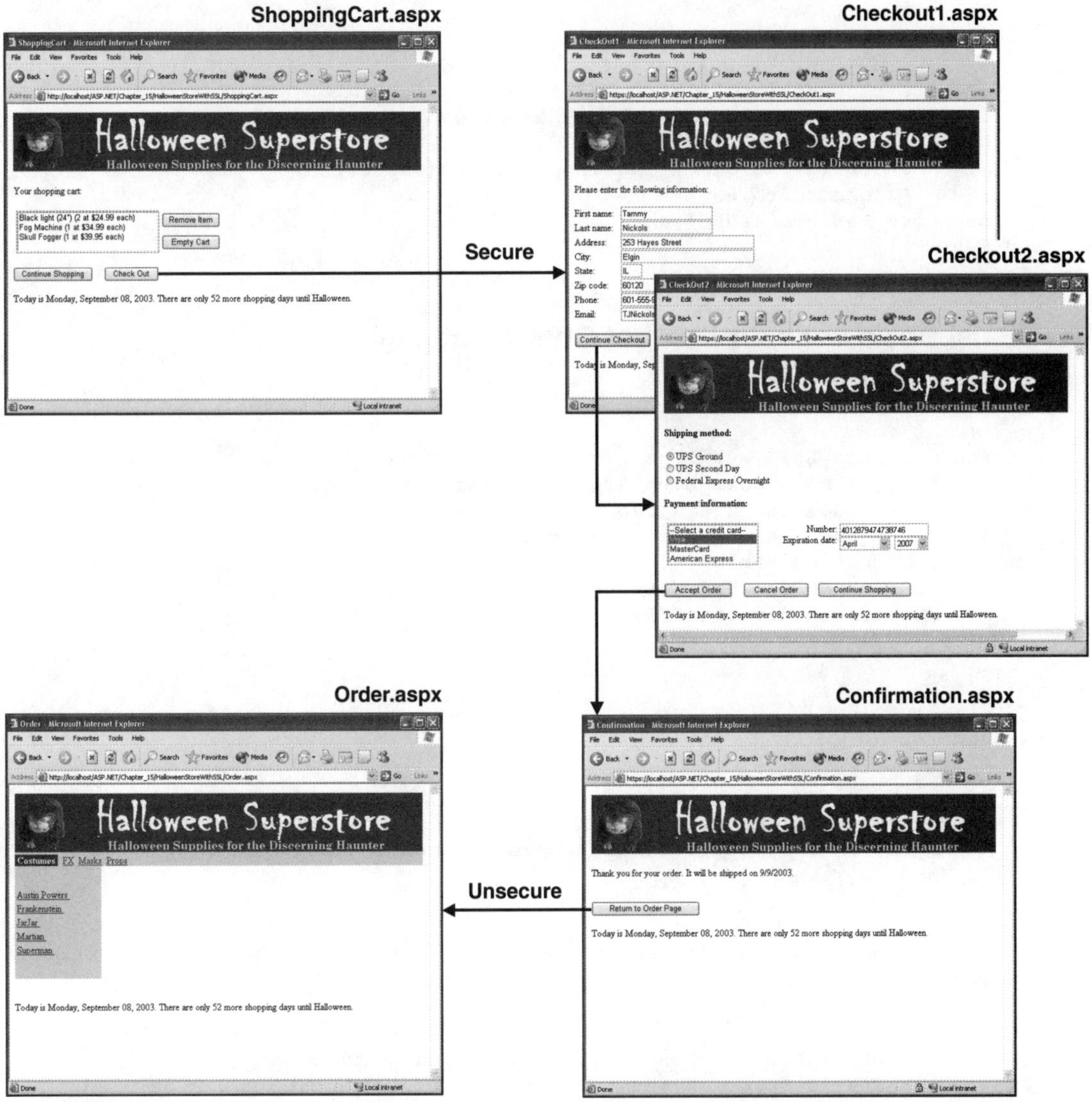

Description

- When the user clicks the Check Out button from the Shopping Cart page, the browser is redirected to the first Check Out page using a secure connection. (The Check Out button is also available from the Order page if the shopping cart contains one or more items.)

- When the user clicks the Continue Checkout button from the first Check Out page, the browser is redirected to the second Check Out page and remains in the secure connection.

- When the user clicks the Accept Order button from the second Check Out page, the browser is redirected to the Confirmation page and again remains in the secure connection.

- When the user clicks the Return to Order Page button from the Confirmation page, the browser is redirected to the Order page in an unsecured connection.

Figure 15-8   The operation of the Halloween Store application that uses SSL

The Visual Basic code for the Shopping Cart page

```
Public Class ShoppingCart
    .
    .
    Private Sub btnCheckOut_Click(ByVal sender As System.Object, _
            ByVal e As System.EventArgs) Handles btnCheckOut.Click
        Dim sURL = "https:" _
                & ConfigurationSettings.AppSettings("AppPath") _
                & "CheckOut1.aspx"
        Response.Redirect(sURL)
    End Sub
End Class
```

The Visual Basic code for the first Check Out page

```
Public Class CheckOut1
    .
    .
    Private Sub Page_Load(ByVal sender As System.Object, _
            ByVal e As System.EventArgs) Handles MyBase.Load
        'Put user code to initialize the page here
        If Not Request.IsSecureConnection Then
            Dim sURL As String
            sURL = Request.Url.ToString.Replace("http:", "https:")
            Response.Redirect(sURL)
        Else
            .
            .
        End If
    End Sub
    .
    .
    Private Sub btnCheckOut_Click(ByVal sender As System.Object, _
            ByVal e As System.EventArgs) Handles btnCheckOut.Click
        If IsValid Then
            .
            .
            Response.Redirect("CheckOut2.aspx")
        End If
    End Sub

    Private Sub btnCancel_Click(ByVal sender As System.Object, _
            ByVal e As System.EventArgs) Handles btnCancel.Click
        Session.Remove("Cart")
        Dim sURL = "http:" _
                & ConfigurationSettings.AppSettings("AppPath") _
                & "Order.aspx"
        Response.Redirect(sURL)
    End Sub

    Private Sub btnContinue_Click(ByVal sender As System.Object, _
            ByVal e As System.EventArgs) Handles btnContinue.Click
        Dim sURL = "http:" _
                & ConfigurationSettings.AppSettings("AppPath") _
                & "Order.aspx"
        Response.Redirect(sURL)
    End Sub
End Class
```

Figure 15-9   The code for the Halloween Store application (part 1 of 2)

The Visual Basic code for the second Check Out page

```vb
Public Class CheckOut2
    .
    .
    Private Sub Page_Load(ByVal sender As System.Object, _
            ByVal e As System.EventArgs) Handles MyBase.Load
        'Put user code to initialize the page here
        If Not Request.IsSecureConnection Then
            Dim sURL As String
            sURL = Request.Url.ToString.Replace("http:", "https:")
            Response.Redirect(sURL)
        Else
            .
            .
        End If
    End Sub
    .
    .
    Private Sub btnAccept_Click(ByVal sender As System.Object, _
            ByVal e As System.EventArgs) Handles btnAccept.Click
        If IsValid Then
            .
            .
            Response.Redirect("Confirmation.aspx")
        End If
    End Sub
    .
    .
    Private Sub btnCancel_Click(ByVal sender As System.Object, _
            ByVal e As System.EventArgs) Handles btnCancel.Click
        Session.Remove("Cart")
        Dim sURL = "http:" _
                & ConfigurationSettings.AppSettings("AppPath") _
                & "Order.aspx"
        Response.Redirect(sURL)
    End Sub

    Private Sub btnContinue_Click(ByVal sender As System.Object, _
            ByVal e As System.EventArgs) Handles btnContinue.Click
        Dim sURL = "http:" _
                & ConfigurationSettings.AppSettings("AppPath") _
                & "Order.aspx"
        Response.Redirect(sURL)
    End Sub
End Class
```

The Visual Basic code for the Confirmation page

```vb
Public Class Confirmation
    .
    .
    Private Sub btnReturn_Click(ByVal sender As System.Object, _
            ByVal e As System.EventArgs) Handles btnReturn.Click
        Dim sURL = "http:" _
            & ConfigurationSettings.AppSettings("AppPath") _
            & "Order.aspx"
        Response.Redirect(sURL)
    End Sub
End Class
```

Figure 15-9　The code for the Halloween Store application (part 2 of 2)

How to use forms-based authentication

If you want to limit access to your ASP.NET application to certain users, you can use *authentication* to validate each user's identity and prevent unauthorized users from accessing your application. The topics that follow introduce you to several types of authentication and show you how to use one of the most common types, called forms-based authentication.

An introduction to authentication

Figure 15-10 describes three types of authentication you can use in ASP.NET applications. The first, called *Windows-based authentication*, requires that you set up a Windows user account for each user. Then, you use standard Windows security features to restrict access to the application folder to certain users. When a user attempts to access the application, Windows displays a login dialog box that asks the user to supply the user name and password of the Windows account.

Passport authentication relies on the *Microsoft Passport* service to authorize users. Passport is a centralized account management service that lets users access multiple web applications with a single user account. Unfortunately, you must pay Microsoft a hefty fee for the right to use Passport in your applications.

To use *forms-based authentication*, you add a login page to your application that typically requires the user to enter a user name and password. Then, ASP.NET displays this page automatically when it needs to authenticate a user who's trying to access the application. Because you code this login page yourself, you can use any technique you want to determine which users are allowed to access the application. If you have a large number of users, for example, or if you allow users to register themselves, you can store the user names and passwords in a database. However, if you have a small number of users and don't want users to create their own accounts, you can store the user names and passwords in the Web.config file. You'll see how to use both of these techniques later in this chapter.

Windows-based authentication

- Causes the browser to display a login dialog box when the user attempts to access a restricted page.
- Is supported by most browsers.
- Is configured through the IIS management console.
- Uses Windows user accounts and directory rights to grant access to restricted pages.

Passport authentication

- *Passport* is a centralized authentication service offered by Microsoft.
- Passport lets users maintain a single user account that lets them access any web site that participates in Passport. The advantage is that the user only has to maintain one user name and password.
- Passport authentication is not free. You must sign up for Passport authentication and pay a significant fee to use it in your application. For more information, visit www.passport.com.

Forms-based authentication

- Lets developers code a login form that gets the user name and password.
- The user name and password entered by the user are encrypted if the login page uses a secure connection.
- Doesn't rely on Windows user accounts. Instead, the application determines how to authenticate users.

Description

- *Authentication* refers to the process of validating the identity of a user so the user can be granted access to an application. A user must typically supply a user name and password to be authenticated.
- After a user is authenticated, the user must still be authorized to use the requested application. The process of granting user access to an application is called *authorization*.

Figure 15-10   An introduction to authentication

How forms-based authentication works

To help you understand how forms-based authentication works, figure 15-11 shows a typical series of exchanges that occur between a web browser and a server when a user attempts to access a page that's protected by forms-based authentication. The authentication process begins when a user requests a page that is part of a protected application. When the server receives the request, it checks to see if the user has already been authenticated. To do that, it looks for a cookie that contains an *authentication ticket* in the request for the page. If it doesn't find the ticket, it redirects the browser to the login page.

Next, the user enters a name and password and posts the login page back to the server. Then, if the user name and password are valid, the server creates an authentication ticket and redirects the browser back to the original page. Note that the redirect from the server sends the authentication ticket to the browser as a cookie. As a result, when the browser requests the original page, it sends the cookie back to the server. This time, the server sees that the user has been authenticated and the requested page is sent back to the browser.

By default, the authentication ticket ASP.NET creates is sent as a session cookie. In that case, the user is authenticated only for that session. However, you also can specify that the ticket be sent as a persistent cookie. Then, the user will be authenticated automatically for future sessions, until the cookie expires.

HTTP requests and responses with forms-based authentication

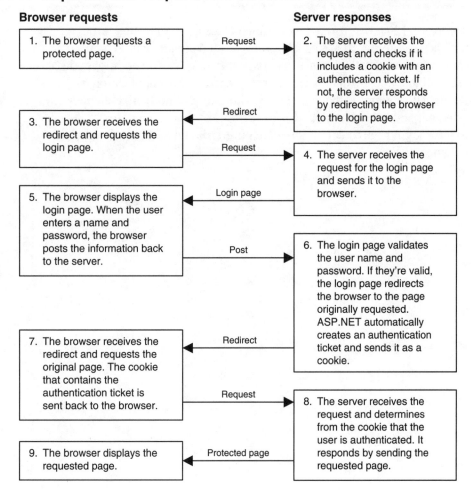

Browser requests

1. The browser requests a protected page.

3. The browser receives the redirect and requests the login page.

5. The browser displays the login page. When the user enters a name and password, the browser posts the information back to the server.

7. The browser receives the redirect and requests the original page. The cookie that contains the authentication ticket is sent back to the browser.

9. The browser displays the requested page.

Server responses

2. The server receives the request and checks if it includes a cookie with an authentication ticket. If not, the server responds by redirecting the browser to the login page.

4. The server receives the request for the login page and sends it to the browser.

6. The login page validates the user name and password. If they're valid, the login page redirects the browser to the page originally requested. ASP.NET automatically creates an authentication ticket and sends it as a cookie.

8. The server receives the request and determines from the cookie that the user is authenticated. It responds by sending the requested page.

Request · Redirect · Request · Login page · Post · Redirect · Request · Protected page

Discussion

- When ASP.NET receives a request for a page that's protected using forms-based authentication from a user who has not been authenticated, the server redirects the user to the login page.

- To be authenticated, the user's computer must contain an *authentication ticket*. By default, this ticket is stored as a session cookie.

- ASP.NET automatically creates an authentication ticket when the application indicates that the user should be authenticated. ASP.NET checks for the presence of an authentication ticket any time it receives a request for a protected page.

- The authentication ticket cookie can be made persistent. Then, the user will be authenticated automatically in future sessions, until the cookie expires.

Figure 15-11   How forms-based authentication works

How to enable forms-based authentication

As figure 15-12 shows, forms-based authentication is controlled through settings in the Web.config file. To enable forms-based authentication, you set the Mode attribute of the Authentication element to "Forms." In addition, you specify that all unauthenticated users be denied access to the application by changing the Allow element that's included within the Authorization element to a Deny element and then setting the Users attribute of that element to "?". Then, it's up to your login page to determine which users should be granted authentication tickets.

A Web.config file that enables forms-based authentication

```xml
<?xml version="1.0" encoding="utf-8" ?>
<configuration>

  <system.web>
    .
    .
    .
    <authentication mode="Forms" />

    <authorization>
      <deny users="?" />
    </authorization>
    .
    .
    .
  </system.web>

</configuration>
```

Wildcard specifications in the users attribute

Wildcard	Description
*	All users, whether or not they have been authenticated.
?	All unauthenticated users.

Discussion

- You use settings in an application's Web.config file to enable forms-based authentication and authorize users to access the application.

- To enable forms-based authentication, set the Mode attribute of the <authentication> element to "Forms." This attribute is set to "Windows" by default.

- To deny access to all unauthenticated users, replace the <allow> element within the <authorization> element with a <deny> element, and set the Users attribute of that element to "?" as shown above.

Figure 15-12   How to enable forms-based authentication

How to use the FormsAuthentication class

To authenticate a user, a login page can use the methods of the FormsAuthentication class shown in figure 15-13. This class is in the System.Web.Security namespace, so you'll want to include an Imports statement for this namespace in any class that uses it.

When a login page has established that a user has entered a correct user name and password, it should execute the RedirectFromLoginPage method. This method creates an authentication ticket for the user, and then redirects the browser to the page that the user originally tried to access. The two arguments on this method specify the user's name and whether or not the authentication ticket should be saved in a persistent cookie. The first statement shown in this figure, for example, specifies False for the second argument. Because of that, the authentication ticket will be saved in a session cookie.

Regardless of whether the authentication ticket is saved in a session cookie or a persistent cookie, you can use a SignOut method like the one shown in the second statement to log a user off your application. This method removes the authentication ticket from the user's computer. Then, the user will have to be authenticated again the next time the application is accessed.

I mentioned earlier in this chapter that you can store user names and passwords in the Web.config file. If you use this technique, you can use the Authenticate method to determine if the user name and password entered by a user is included in this file. And to create secure passwords, you can use the HashPasswordForStoringInConfigFile method. You'll learn how to use both of these methods later in this chapter.

Common methods of the FormsAuthentication class

Method	Description
`RedirectFromLoginPage(userName, createPersistentCookie)`	Issues an authentication ticket for the user and redirects the browser to the page it was attempting to access when the login page was displayed. *Name* is the authenticated name of the user, and *createPersistentCookie* is a Boolean value that indicates whether or not the cookie that contains the authentication ticket should be made persistent so the user can be logged in automatically on future requests.
`SignOut()`	Logs the user off by removing the cookie that contains the authentication ticket.
`Authenticate(name, password) As Boolean`	Indicates whether the user name and password combination exists in the <credentials> element of the Web.config file. See figure 15-15 for more information on storing user credentials in the Web.config file.
`HashPasswordForStoringInConfigFile (Password, Format)`	Returns an encrypted value for the specified password. See figure 15-16 for more information on encrypting passwords.

A statement that redirects the browser to the originally requested page

```
FormsAuthentication.RedirectFromLoginPage(txtUserName.Text, False)
```

A statement that logs a user off

```
FormsAuthentication.SignOut()
```

Discussion

- After you authenticate a user, you use the RedirectFromLoginPage method of the FormsAuthentication class to redirect the browser to the page that was originally requested. This method creates an authentication ticket that's passed as a cookie to the browser.

- The FormsAuthentication class is in the System.Web.Security namespace, so you should include an Imports statement for this namespace in any class that uses it.

- You use the Authenticate and HashPasswordForStoringInConfigFile methods when you store user credentials in the Web.config file. See figures 15-15 and 15-16 for details.

Figure 15-13   How to use the FormsAuthentication class

How to create a login page

Figure 15-14 shows how to create a login page. First, you should realize that a login page must always be named Login.aspx. That's because ASP.NET looks for a page with this name when it needs to authenticate a user.

Like the login page shown here, most login pages include two text boxes that let the user enter a user name and a password. In addition, they include a check box that lets the user indicate whether or not they want to be logged in automatically the next time the application is accessed. Then, if the user selects this check box, the application can create a persistent cookie that contains the authentication ticket.

When the user clicks the Log In button on this page, the Click event procedure for this button starts by executing the ValidateUser method of the UsersDB class. This class contains methods that access the Users table of the Halloween database. The ValidateUser method of this class checks that the Users table contains a row with the user name and password that are passed to it as arguments. If it does, this method returns a value of True to indicate that the user is valid. Otherwise, it returns a value of False.

If the user name and password are valid, the procedure continues by executing the RedirectFromLoginPage method of the FormsAuthentication class to redirect the browser to the page that was originally requested. Notice that the Checked property of the check box is passed as the second argument of this method. That way, if the check box is checked, a persistent cookie will be created. Otherwise, a session cookie will be created.

Although it's not shown in this figure, the Load event for a login page should always force the page to use a secure connection using the technique that was presented in figure 15-7. That's because the login page posts the user's name and password to the server. Then, if a hacker manages to intercept this information, your application won't be compromised.

Before I go on, take a look at the URL that's used to display the login page. As you can see, it includes a query string that defines an attribute named ReturnUrl. The value of this attribute is the path and file name of the page that was originally requested. (The slashes in the path are represented by the characters %2f.) ASP.NET uses this value to determine what page to redirect the browser to when the user is authenticated.

A Login page

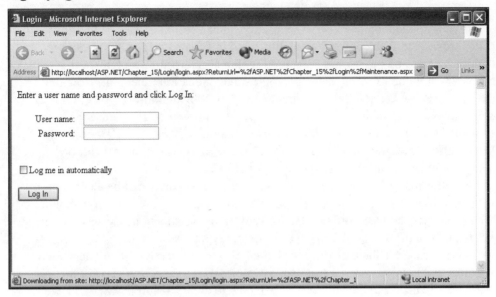

Code that authenticates the user

```
Imports System.Web.Security
Public Class Login
    Inherits System.Web.UI.Page

    Private Sub btnLogin_Click(ByVal sender As System.Object, _
            ByVal e As System.EventArgs) Handles btnLogin.Click
        If UsersDB.ValidateUser(txtUserName.Text, txtPassword.Text) Then
            FormsAuthentication.RedirectFromLoginPage(txtUserName.Text, _
                chkAutomatic.Checked)
        Else
            lblError.Text = "Incorrect user name or password. " _
                            & "Please try again."
        End If
    End Sub

End Class
```

Discussion

- When a user attempts to access a page that he's not authorized to access, ASP.NET automatically redirects the user to the application's login page. This page must be named Login.aspx.

- The login page should require the user to enter a name and password. Then, it can use any method it chooses to validate the name and password.

- To authenticate a user, the Login page should execute the RedirectFromLoginPage method of the FormsAuthentication class.

Figure 15-14   How to create a login page

How to store user credentials in the Web.config file

If your application has just a few users, you can store the user names and passwords in the Web.config file, as illustrated in figure 15-15. As you can see, the user names and passwords are stored within a <credentials> element that appears within the <forms> element of the <authentication> element. Note that the <forms> and <credentials> elements don't exist by default, so you'll need to create them. Then, within the <credentials> element, you create a <user> element for each user that provides the user's name and password. The first Web.config file shown in this figure, for example, defines two users with the names Doug and Anne and the passwords Jk43bK2 and a8KWE8n.

Because the Web.config file is a simple text file, security can be a concern when you use it to store user names and passwords. For this reason, you should always encrypt the passwords in the Web.config file as shown in the second example. To indicate that the passwords are encrypted, you set the passwordFormat attribute of the <credentials> element to one of two encryption schemes that your passwords can use: MD5 or SHA1. Then, you specify the passwords in encrypted form. You'll learn how to create a simple ASP.NET web page that encrypts passwords that you can use in the Web.config file in the next figure.

When you store user names and passwords in the Web.config file, you can use the Authenticate method of the FormsAuthentication class to determine whether a user has entered a valid user name and password. To do that, you pass the name and password entered by the user as arguments to this method, as illustrated in the last example in this figure. Then, the Authenticate method returns a Boolean value that indicates whether the name and password are valid. If they are valid, the RedirectFromLoginPage is called. Otherwise, an error message is displayed.

The <authentication> element of a Web.config file that includes user credentials with unencrypted passwords

```
<authentication mode="Forms" >
  <forms>
    <credentials passwordFormat="Clear">
      <user name="Doug" password="Jk43bK2" />
      <user name="Anne" password="a8KWE8n" />
    </credentials>
  </forms>
</authentication>
```

The <authentication> element of a Web.config file that includes user credentials with encrypted passwords

```
<authentication mode="Forms" >
  <forms>
    <credentials passwordFormat="SHA1">
      <user name="Doug" password="E61B042D983125C64727B426DA4E04293C2F0DFA" />
      <user name="Anne" password="944C899013FCB04F4D43E00A4A681919FFE853E1" />
    </credentials>
  </forms>
</authentication>
```

Code that authenticates users using the Web.config file

```
If FormsAuthentication.Authenticate(txtUserName.Text, txtPassword.Text) Then
    FormsAuthentication.RedirectFromLoginPage _
        (txtUserName.Text, chkAutomatic.Checked)
Else
    lblError.Text = "Incorrect user name or password. Please try again."
End If
```

Options for the passwordFormat attribute

Option	Description
Clear	The passwords are stored in clear text. In other words, they're not encrypted. This is the default.
MD5	The passwords are encrypted using an algorithm called MD5 (the *MD* stands for *Message Digest*). This algorithm is faster than the SHA1 algorithm, but the encrypted passwords are not as secure.
SHA1	The passwords are encrypted using an algorithm called *Secure Hash Algorithm*. SHA1 is slower than MD5 but more secure. SHA1 is the preferred encrypting algorithm.

Discussion

- If only a few users will be authorized to access an application, you can store the user names and passwords in the <credentials> element of the Web.config file.

- You use the Authenticate method of the FormsAuthentication class to validate a user's name and password against the names and passwords in the Web.config file.

- The passwordFormat attribute of the <credentials> element specifies how passwords are stored. If you're concerned about the security of the Web.config file, you can store the passwords in encrypted form by specifying MD5 or SHA1.

- For information on how to create a web page that encrypts passwords, see figure 15-16.

Figure 15-15   How to store user credentials in the Web.config file

How to encrypt passwords

Figure 15-16 shows how you can create a page that encrypts passwords for use in the Web.config file. This page contains a text box where you can enter an unencrypted password and two option buttons that let you select the encryption algorithm. Then, when you click the Encrypt button, the Click event procedure for this button is executed.

As you can see, the Click event procedure starts by checking to see which option button was selected and then setting a string variable to the appropriate value. Then, the HashPasswordForStoringInConfigFile method of the FormsAuthentication class is used to encrypt the password. The result is displayed in a label on the page, and you can copy and paste it into your Web.config file.

Although encrypting passwords makes them difficult to hack, please realize that a skilled hacker might still be able to discover some of your passwords. In particular, the encryption used by the HashPasswordForStoringInConfigFile method is vulnerable to a hacking technique called *dictionary lookup*. With this technique, the hacker encrypts all of the words in a large dictionary of common passwords, then looks for matches in your Web.config file. For this reason, you should prohibit your users from using common words as passwords. In addition, you should use normal Windows security features to protect the Web.config file from unauthorized users.

The Password Encrypter page

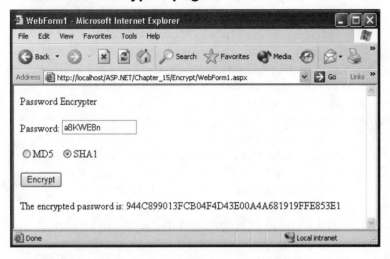

The code for the Password Encrypter page

```vb
Imports System.Web.Security
Public Class WebForm1
    Inherits System.Web.UI.Page

    Private Sub Page_Load(ByVal sender As System.Object, _
            ByVal e As System.EventArgs) Handles MyBase.Load
        'Put user code to initialize the page here
    End Sub

    Private Sub btnEncrypt_Click(ByVal sender As System.Object, _
            ByVal e As System.EventArgs) Handles btnEncrypt.Click
        Dim sPW, sAlgorithm As String
        If rdoSHA1.Checked Then
            sAlgorithm = "SHA1"
        Else
            sAlgorithm = "MD5"
        End If
        sPW = FormsAuthentication.HashPasswordForStoringInConfigFile _
            (txtPassword.Text, sAlgorithm)
        lblPassword.Text = sPW
    End Sub
End Class
```

Description

- After the password you enter is encrypted, you can copy and paste the encrypted password into your Web.config file.

Warning

- You shouldn't consider passwords encrypted by the HashPasswordForStoringInConfigFile method to be totally secure. A skilled hacker may be able to break its encryption algorithm and gain access to your application.

Figure 15-16   How to encrypt passwords

How to get information about the user

If you need to get information about the user that requested a page, you can use the FormsIdentity class to do that. Figure 15-17 shows the two properties of this class that you're most likely to use. As you can see, you can use the IsAuthenticated property to determine if the user has an authentication ticket, and you can use the Name property to get the user's name. Note that because the Name property retrieves the name from the authentication ticket, you can only get the name of a user who's been authenticated.

The two examples in this figure illustrate how you might use the Name and IsAuthenticated properties. In both examples, the IsAuthenticated property is used to determine if the user has been authenticated. If so, the Identity property is used to assign the user's name to a label. Note that to refer to the FormsIdentity object for the page, you use the Identity property of the IPrincipal object. This object represents the security context of the user and is accessed through the User property of the page.

The difference between these two examples is that the first one is coded within a page class, so the Page object doesn't need to be referred to explicitly. In contrast, if you want to refer to the FormsIdentity object from a user control, you have to use the Page property of the control to get the page that contains it.

Common properties of the FormsIdentity class

Property	Description
IsAuthenticated	A Boolean value that indicates whether the user has been authenticated.
Name	The user's name as specified in the authentication ticket.

Code that gets an authenticated user's name in a page class

```
If User.Identity.IsAuthenticated Then
    lblUserName.Text = User.Identity.Name
End If
```

Code that gets an authenticated user's name in a user control

```
If Page.User.Identity.IsAuthenticated Then
    lblUserName.Text = Page.User.Identity.Name
End If
```

Description

- A FormsIdentity object represents the user who requested the current page.

- If the user has been authenticated by forms, Passport, or Windows authentication, the IsAuthenticated property is set to true. Then, you can use the Name property to get the user's name.

- To access a FormsIdentity object from the code-behind file for a web form, use the Identity property of the IPrincipal object that's returned by the User property of the page. The IPrincipal object represents the security context of the user.

- To access the FormsIdentity object from the code-behind file for a user control, you must use the Page property of the control to get the Page object for the page that contains the control.

Figure 15-17   How to get information about the user

The Halloween Maintenance application

To show how you can use forms-based authentication to restrict access to a web application, the next two figures show portions of a maintenance application that lets users maintain the Categories and Products tables of the Halloween database. This application uses forms-based authentication so that only selected company employees can modify these tables.

The design of the Halloween Maintenance application

Figure 15-18 shows two of the pages of the Halloween Maintenance application. As you can see, the Maintenance page lets the user click on one of two links to maintain either the Categories table or the Products table. Because you saw pages that maintained these tables in chapters 12, 13, and 14, I won't present them again here.

The first time a user attempts to access the Maintenance page, the browser is redirected to the Login page. Then, the user can enter a name and password and indicate whether a persistent cookie should be created. When the user clicks the Log In button, the Maintenance page is displayed if the user name and password are valid. Otherwise, a message is displayed indicating that the name or password is invalid.

Notice that the footer that's displayed at the bottom of the Maintenance page includes the user's name. Also notice that the Maintenance page includes a Log Off button. If the user clicks this button, he or she is logged off and the Login page is redisplayed.

The Login and Maintenance pages of the Halloween Maintenance application

Description

- The Maintenance page of the Halloween Maintenance application contains two links that the user can click to maintain the Categories and Products tables in the Halloween database.

- This application uses forms-based authentication. The authorized users are specified in the Web.config file, and the passwords are encrypted using the SHA1 algorithm.

- After a user is authenticated, the user's name is displayed in the PageFooter user control.

Figure 15-18   The design of the Halloween Maintenance application

The code for the Halloween Maintenance application

Figure 15-19 shows the code for implementing forms-based authentication in the Halloween Maintenance application. First, it shows the code for the Login form. As I mentioned earlier, a login form should always be sure that it uses a secure connection, and that's what the code in the Load event procedure does. Then, the code in the Click event procedure for the Log In button uses the Authenticate method to authenticate the name and password entered by the user against the names and passwords defined in the Web.config file. If the user name and password are found, the RedirectFromLoginPage method is used to redirect the browser to the Maintenance page.

The Load event procedure for the Maintenance page includes code that forces the page to use an unsecured connection if the current connection is secure. This code is necessary because when the Login page redirects the browser to the Maintenance page, the secure connection remains active. As a result, it's up to the Maintenance page to close the secure connection.

The other procedure in the Maintenance page handles the Click event of the Log Off button. If the user clicks this button, the SignOut method is executed so the cookie that contains the user's authentication ticket is deleted. Then, the browser is redirected to the Maintenance page, which causes the Login page to be redisplayed since an authentication ticket is no longer available.

Note that if the user ends the application by closing the browser window instead of clicking the Log Off button, the authentication ticket is maintained if it was stored in a persistent cookie. In other words, it's maintained if the user checked the Log me in automatically check box on the Login page. If you want the authentication ticket to be maintained anytime the user selects this option, you can omit the Log Off button from the Maintenance page.

The Visual Basic code for the Login page

```vb
Imports System.Web.Security
Public Class Login
    Inherits System.Web.UI.Page

    Private Sub Page_Load(ByVal sender As System.Object, _
            ByVal e As System.EventArgs) Handles MyBase.Load
        If Not Request.IsSecureConnection Then
            Dim sURL As String
            sURL = Request.Url.ToString.Replace("http:", "https:")
            Response.Redirect(sURL)
        End If
    End Sub

    Private Sub btnLogin_Click(ByVal sender As System.Object, _
            ByVal e As System.EventArgs) Handles btnLogin.Click
        If FormsAuthentication.Authenticate _
                (txtUserName.Text, txtPassword.Text) Then
            FormsAuthentication.RedirectFromLoginPage(txtUserName.Text, _
                chkAutomatic.Checked)
        Else
            lblError.Text = "Incorrect user name or password. " _
                            & "Please try again."
        End If
    End Sub

End Class
```

The Visual Basic code for the Maintenance page

```vb
Imports System.Web.Security
Public Class Maintenance
    Inherits System.Web.UI.Page

    Private Sub Page_Load(ByVal sender As System.Object, _
            ByVal e As System.EventArgs) Handles MyBase.Load
        'Put user code to initialize the page here
        If Request.IsSecureConnection Then
            Dim sURL As String
            sURL = Request.Url.ToString.Replace("https:", "http:")
            Response.Redirect(sURL)
        End If
    End Sub

    Private Sub btnLogOff_Click(ByVal sender As System.Object, _
            ByVal e As System.EventArgs) Handles btnLogOff.Click
        FormsAuthentication.SignOut()
        Response.Redirect("Maintenance.aspx")
    End Sub

End Class
```

Figure 15-19   The code for the Halloween Maintenance application (part 1 of 2)

On page 2 of this figure, you can see the code for the PageFooter user control that's displayed at the bottom of the Maintenance page. The first time this page is displayed, the Load procedure checks if the user has been authenticated. If so, a value that includes the user's name is assigned to the Text property of the label in the user control. You can look back to figure 15-18 to see the complete content of this label.

You can also see the Web.config file for this application in part 2. This file defines two users who are authorized to access the application. As you can see, the passwords are encrypted using the SHA1 algorithm to protect the file against hackers.

The Visual Basic code for the PageFooter user control

```vb
Imports System.Web.Security
Public Class PageFooter
    Inherits System.Web.UI.UserControl

    Private Sub Page_Load(ByVal sender As System.Object, _
            ByVal e As System.EventArgs) Handles MyBase.Load
        'Put user code to initialize the page here
        If Not IsPostBack Then
            If Page.User.Identity.IsAuthenticated Then
                lblFooter.Text = "Hello "
                lblFooter.Text &= Page.User.Identity.Name & ".  "
            End If
            lblFooter.Text &= "Today is " & Now().ToString("D")
            lblFooter.Text &= ". There are only "
            lblFooter.Text &= Me.DaysToHalloween
            lblFooter.Text &= " more shopping days until Halloween."
        End If
    End Sub
    .
    .
End Class
```

The Web.config file for the Halloween Maintenance application

```xml
<?xml version="1.0" encoding="utf-8" ?>
<configuration>

  <system.web>
    .
    .
    <authentication mode="Forms" >
      <forms>
        <credentials passwordFormat="SHA1">
          <user name="Doug" password="E61B042D983125C64727B426DA4E04293C2F0DFA" />
          <user name="Anne" password="944C899013FCB04F4D43E00A4A681919FFE853E1" />
        </credentials>
      </forms>
    </authentication>

    <authorization>
        <deny users="?" />
    </authorization>
    .
    .
  </system.web>

</configuration>
```

Note

- The DaysToHalloween function that's called by the Load procedure of the PageFooter user control has been omitted from this figure. To see the code for this procedure, please refer to figure 10-5.

Figure 15-19   The code for the Halloween Maintenance application (part 2 of 2)

Perspective

This chapter has presented the basic skills for using SSL encryption to secure data transmissions and for using forms-based authentication to restrict access to a web application. These are the only skills you'll need for many of the applications you develop.

You should realize, however, that there's more to securing applications than what's presented in this chapter. For example, you can use .NET encryption classes to encrypt sensitive data before you store it in a database, and you can use advanced features of forms-based authentication to grant access to certain pages of an application to specific users. With the knowledge you've gained from this chapter, though, you should be able to learn how to use these and other advanced security features on your own.

Terms

Secure Sockets Layer (SSL)
secure connection
server authentication
client authentication
digital secure certificate
SSL strength
certification authority (CA)
registration authority (RA)
authentication
authorization
Windows-based authentication
Passport authentication
Microsoft Passport
forms-based authentication
authentication ticket
MD5 algorithm
Secure Hash Algorithm (SHA1)

16

How to create and use web services

In addition to web applications, you can use Visual Basic .NET to create web services. Web services allow you to store common processing routines on a web server, where they're available to other programmers who need to use the routines in their applications. In this chapter, you'll learn the basic concepts and skills you need to create and use web services.

An introduction to web services

Simply put, a *web service* is a class that resides on a web server and can be accessed via the Internet or an intranet. As a result, ASP.NET applications or other types of web applications can access the web service from any computer that's connected to the Internet or a local intranet.

What web services are used for

Web services are becoming an integral part of web development. One use of web services is to develop *distributed web applications* in which portions of an application can reside on different servers. For example, you might implement the business logic and database processing code for an application as a web service that runs on one server. Then, the user interface portion of the application can run on another server and call on the web service whenever business logic or database features are needed. It's even possible to provide two interfaces to the same web service: a web interface provided by an ASP.NET application that can be run from any computer that has a browser and Internet access, and a Windows interface provided by a Windows application that's installed on the user's computer.

Another use for web services is to allow applications developed by different companies or organizations to interact with one another. For example, the United States Postal Service has web services that let you calculate shipping rates, correct addresses, and track packages. You can use web services like these to incorporate the features they provide into your applications. Similarly, the popular search site Google offers web services that let you incorporate Google searches into your applications. As more companies create web services and publish them on the Internet, applications that use these services will become more popular.

How web services work

Figure 16-1 illustrates how web services work. As you can see, the web service is accessed from a web page running on a web server. In this example, the web service and the application's web pages reside on two different web servers. Although that doesn't have to be the case, this arrangement illustrates how web services can be used to create distributed applications. The server that hosts the web service must have both IIS and the .NET Framework installed.

Notice that the web page and the web service communicate using XML. Actually, web services use a rather complicated collection of protocols that are built on XML. These protocols include *WSDL*, which stands for *Web Services Description Language,* and *SOAP*, which stands for *Simple Object Access Protocol*. Fortunately, all of this is taken care of for you when you create and use a web service. As a result, you don't usually have to deal directly with XML, WSDL, or SOAP.

The operation of a distributed ASP.NET web application

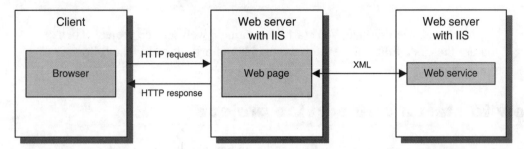

Description

- A *web service* is a class that resides on a web server and can be accessed by web applications or other web services to implement distributed ASP.NET web applications. A web service can also be accessed by Windows applications.

- Web services typically contain business logic that's coded as a collection of public methods.

- Like web applications, web services must reside on a web server with IIS. Although they can reside on the same server as the web applications that use them, they can also reside on a separate server.

- Information is passed between a web page and a web service using XML. Each web service must contain an XML document written in the *Web Services Description Language* (*WSDL*) that describes how the web service works and how clients can interact with it.

- If the web page and web service reside on the same server, the XML is passed as part of an HTTP request or response. If the web service resides on a different web server, the *Simple Object Access Protocol*, or *SOAP*, is used to facilitate the HTTP request and response.

- Because web services aren't tied to a proprietary technology, programs written in any language and running on any operating system can access a web service.

Figure 16-1   How web services work

How to create a web service

To create a web service, you start by creating a web service project. Then, you use the Code Editor to develop the public and private code. The following topics show you how.

How to start a web service project

Figure 16-2 shows the New Project dialog box for creating a web service. From this dialog box, you identify the location of the web server and the name of the directory where the web service will reside just as you do for a web application. Then, all of the files for the project are stored in that directory on the web server, and the solution file is stored in a directory with the same name within the default Visual Studio directory.

When you first start a web service project, it contains a single web service named Service1. The definition of this service is stored in a file with the extension *asmx*, as you can see in this figure. Like the aspx extension that's used for web pages, the asmx extension tells IIS that the file should be processed by ASP.NET.

As you can see in this figure, the default web service is displayed in a Component Designer window. This window is used to hold any non-visual components you add to the web service. If you use database components to access a database, for example, the components will appear in this window. Because a web service doesn't have a visual interface, however, no design surface is provided.

The New Project dialog box and a new ASP.NET Web Service project

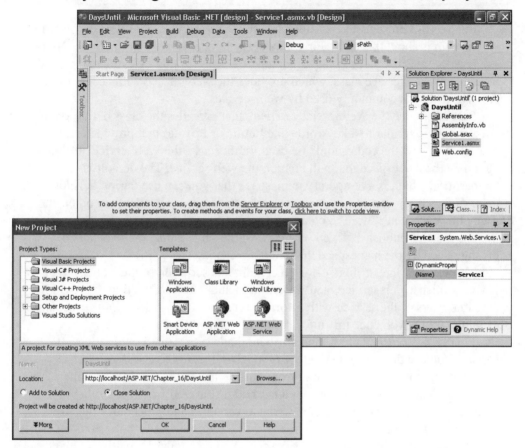

Description

- To start a web service project, display the New Project dialog box and select the ASP.NET Web Service template. Then, select the IIS server and enter the name of the directory where you want the project files stored. Visual Basic creates this directory in the Inetpub\wwwroot directory of the IIS server by default.

- Visual Basic also creates a directory with the name you specify in the default directory for Visual Studio and stores the solution file there.

- By default, a web service project consists of a single web service named Service1. This web service appears in the Solution Explorer with the *asmx* extension.

- When you start a new web service project, a Component Designer window is displayed for the default web service. You can use this window to add components (such as ADO.NET components) to the web service.

Figure 16-2   How to start a web service project

How to develop the code for a web service

Figure 16-3 presents the starting code for a web service. You'll want to note several things about this code. First, like everything else that's built on the .NET Framework, a web service is implemented as a class. In this case, the class inherits the WebService class, which provides the web service with access to the ASP.NET objects commonly used by web services.

Second, notice the WebService *attribute* that precedes the class definition. An attribute is similar to a keyword (like Public or Private) that provides information as to how the code should be used. In this case, the WebService attribute identifies the namespace that will contain the web service. The default is tempuri.org, which is a temporary namespace that you can use during development of a web service. If you publish a web service so it's available to other users, however, you'll want to change this name to something unique. That way, if someone else publishes a web service with the same name, the two can be distinguished by the namespace that contains them.

The WebService attribute can also contain a description of the web service. If you publish a web service, you'll want to include this information to provide potential users of the service with information about what it does. You'll see an example of how you code this information in the next figure.

Finally, notice the WebMethod attribute that's commented out in the web service. You use this attribute to identify a public method as a *web method*, which is a method that's accessible from outside the service. Aside from the WebMethod attribute, you code a web method just as you would any other method. In addition, you can include private variables and procedures that are used by the web method.

One key difference between a web service and a regular Visual Basic class is that a web service can't have properties. You can define public variables, but those variables aren't accessible to clients that use the web service. As a result, web methods are the only interface a client has to a web service.

You can still implement the equivalent of properties using web methods, though. For example, to retrieve the value of a property, use a web method that's coded as a function that returns the value of the variable for the property. And to set the value of a property, use a Sub procedure that accepts the value of the property and assigns it to a variable.

The starting code for a web service

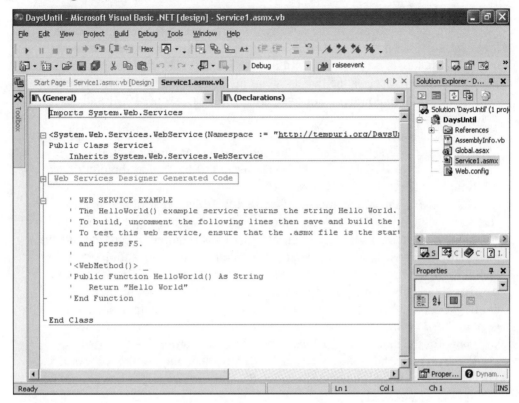

Description

- A web service is implemented as a class that inherits the WebService class of the System.Web.Services namespace. This class provides the basic functionality for all web services.

- You develop the code for a web service by coding *web methods*. A web method is a Public procedure with the WebMethod *attribute* (<WebMethod()>). A web service can also include private code that's not available from outside the service.

- Web services don't support property declarations or public variables. Instead, you can use public functions to get the values of private variables, and you can use public Sub procedures to set the values of private variables.

- You can use the WebService attribute (<System.Web.Services.WebService()>) to identify the namespace for the web service. The default namespace is http://tempuri.org. If a web service is made public, it must have a unique namespace to distinguish it from other web services with the same name.

- The WebService attribute can include a description of the web service. This description is displayed on the help and service description pages for the service.

Figure 16-3   How to develop the code for a web service

The code for the DaysUntil web service

To illustrate how you can use a web service, figure 16-4 presents the code for a web service named DaysUntil. This service contains three web methods that calculate the days remaining until a specified date. The first method, named simply DaysUntil, accepts the target date as an argument. The other methods, named DaysUntilHalloween and DaysUntilChristmas, assume 10/31 and 12/25 as the target date.

As you can see, the methods are coded as public functions that use a private function named DaysUntilDate to calculate the days remaining until the target date. Since you've seen this calculation earlier in this book, you shouldn't have any trouble understanding how it works.

Notice that each web method starts with a WebMethod attribute. In this case, the attribute is coded on a separate line that's continued to the line that contains the Function statement. Although that's not required, it can improve the readability of a web service that contains private procedures in addition to web methods. So we recommend that you use this format for all your web services.

You should also notice that the Date argument that receives the date used by the DaysUntil method is enclosed in brackets. These brackets indicate that Date is an *escaped identifier*. Escaped identifiers allow you to use Visual Basic keywords for the names of variables, procedures, and properties.

Finally, notice the WebService attribute at the beginning of the web service. This attribute identifies the namespace for the web service as

```
http://murach.com
```

This namespace is used to uniquely identify the web service. Although it isn't required, it is common practice to use an Internet domain name to help ensure that the namespace is unique.

The WebService attribute in this example also includes a brief description of the web service. You'll see one way this information is used in the next figure.

The Visual Basic code for the DaysUntil web service

```
Imports System.Web.Services

<System.Web.Services.WebService(Namespace:="http://murach.com", _
    Description:="Calculates the number of days until a given date")> _
Public Class DaysUntil
    Inherits System.Web.Services.WebService

    <WebMethod()> _
    Public Function DaysUntil(ByVal [Date] As Date) As Integer
        Return DaysUntilDate([Date].Month, [Date].Day)
    End Function

    <WebMethod()> _
    Public Function DaysUntilHalloween() As Integer
        Return DaysUntilDate(10, 31)
    End Function

    <WebMethod()> _
    Public Function DaysUntilChristmas() As Integer
        Return DaysUntilDate(12, 25)
    End Function

    Private Function DaysUntilDate(ByVal Month As Integer, ByVal Day As Integer) _
            As Integer
        Dim TargetDate As DateTime
        TargetDate = DateTime.Parse(Month.ToString & "/" & _
            Day.ToString & "/" & Now.Year)
        If Today() > TargetDate Then
            TargetDate = TargetDate.AddYears(1)
        End If
        Return DateDiff(DateInterval.Day, Today(), TargetDate)
    End Function

End Class
```

Note

- The Date argument used by the DaysUntil method is enclosed in square brackets to distinguish it from the Date keyword. This construct, called an *escaped identifier*, lets you use a Visual Basic keyword as a variable, procedure, or property name.

Figure 16-4   The code for the DaysUntil web service

How to test a web service

After you develop a web service, you can test it without having to create a client program that uses it. To do that, you simply build and run the web service in your default browser or in a Browse window just as you would a web application. When you do that, a *Service help page* like the first one shown in Figure 16-5 is displayed.

The Service help page identifies the web service and displays the description you specified in the WebService attribute. It also includes a link to the *service description* for the web service. This is the XML document you learned about in figure 16-1 that contains the Web Services Description Language (WSDL) that describes the web service. If you're interested in what this document looks like, you can click on this link to display it.

Finally, the Service help page lists the web methods that are available from the web service. If you click on the link for one of these methods, a *Service Method help page* for that method is displayed. The second screen in this figure, for example, is the help page for the DaysUntil method.

If a method requires arguments, the Service Method help page lists them by name and lets you enter values for them. Then, when you click the Invoke button, the method is executed and the XML that's generated as a result is displayed. In this figure, for example, you can see the XML that's generated when the DaysUntil method is executed using 05/16 as the value of the Date argument. If you're familiar with XML, you can see that the actual result of the calculation is contained within <int> and </int> tags. These tags are generated based on the return type of the method.

Although you can't see it in this figure, the Service Method help page also contains sample SOAP and HTTP requests and responses. If you're interested in what this code looks like, you may want to scroll down so you can see it. In general, though, you don't need to worry about how it works.

When you test a web service in your browser as shown in this figure, you can use the Visual Studio debugging tools you learned about in chapter 5 to debug it. To do that, just set one or more breakpoints before you run the web service. Then, the web service will enter break mode before it executes a statement that has a breakpoint, and you can use the tools that are available from break mode to debug the web service.

Help pages for the DaysUntil web service

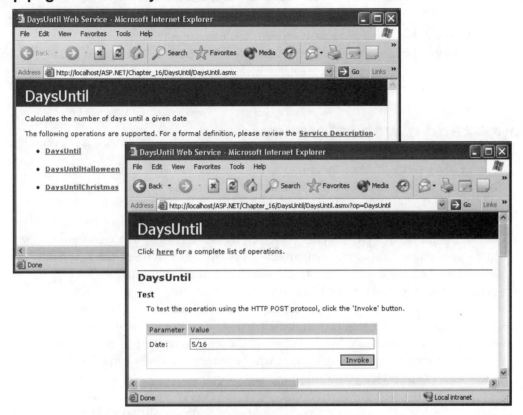

XML output for the DaysUntil web method

Description

- To test a web service in your default browser, click the Start button in the Standard toolbar. A *Service help page* like the first one shown above is displayed.

- To test a web method, click the link for that method. Then, enter any required parameters in the *Service Method help page* that's displayed and click the Invoke button. A page that shows the XML output for the method is displayed.

- When you use your browser to test a web service, you can set breakpoints and debug the web service just as you do for a web application.

Figure 16-5   How to test a web service

How to consume a web service

After you build and test a web service, you can use it from any project that requires the services it provides. To do that, you first have to add a reference to the web service. Then, you can create an instance of it and use it like any other class.

How to add a web reference

To add a web reference to a project, you use the Add Web Reference dialog box shown in figure 16-6. From this dialog box, you can enter the address of the asmx or wsdl file for the web service into the URL box. A wsdl file is an XML document that describes the web service and contains information on how a client can interact with it. This file is created by the developer of a web service that's available to the public so clients can "discover" the web service. It can be helpful for figuring out how to interact with a web service if you find that the documentation for the service is incomplete or confusing.

You can also locate a web service using the links that are available from the Add Web Reference dialog box. If the service is on your local server, for example, you can click the Web services on the local machine link and a list of all the web services on the local server will be listed. Then, you can click the link for the web service you want to add.

After you identify the web service, its description is displayed in the left pane of the dialog box. This is the same information that's displayed in the Service help page you saw in the last figure. You can use it to test or review the available web methods or to display the service description for the web service. When you're sure you've located the web service you want, you can click the Add Reference button to add a reference to the service to the project.

The dialog box for adding a web reference

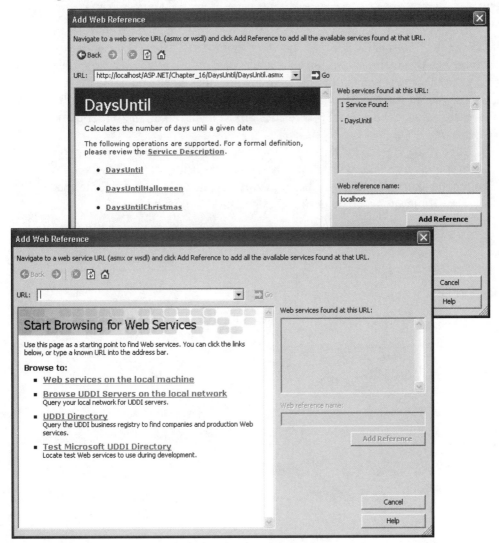

Description

- To add a reference to a web service to a project, right-click the project file in the Solution Explorer and select the Add Web Reference command from the shortcut menu to display the Add Web Reference dialog box.

- To locate a web service, enter the address of its aspx or wsdl file in the URL box and press Enter or select the URL from the drop-down list. Then, information about the service is displayed, and you can click the Add Reference button to add a reference to the web service to your project.

- You can also use the links in the Add Web Reference dialog box to locate web services on your local machine or a local network or to locate web services that have been made public by Microsoft or other companies.

Figure 16-6   How to add a web reference

How to use a web service

After you add a reference to a web service, it appears in the Web References folder in the Solution Explorer as shown in figure 16-7. Then, you can use the web service by creating an instance of it and assigning it to an object variable as shown in the first statement in this figure. Notice that when you name the web service, you must qualify it with the name of the server where it's located. In this case, because the web service resides on the local server, the server name is localhost.

After you assign an instance of the web service to an object variable, you can refer to any web method defined by the service using standard techniques. The second statement in this figure, for example, shows how you refer to the DaysUntilHalloween method defined by the DaysUntil web service.

The Solution Explorer with a web service reference

A statement that creates an instance of the DaysUntil web service

```
Private DaysUntil As New localhost.DaysUntil()
```

A statement that executes the DaysUntilHalloween method of this web service

```
iDaysUntilHalloween = DaysUntil.DaysUntilHalloween()
```

Description

- After you add a reference to a web service to a project, the name of the server where it's located is listed under the Web References folder in the Solution Explorer. To display the individual files for the web service, click the Show All Files button and then expand the server node.

- The disco file contains the address of the asmx file for the web service. The wsdl file contains a description of the web service. And the Reference.vb file contains the Visual Basic code that implements the web service.

- To use a web service in an application, you can create an instance of it using a declaration statement with the New keyword like the one shown above. The reference to the web service must include the name of the server where it resides.

- After you create an instance of a web service, you can execute its web methods using the same techniques you use to execute a method of any object.

Figure 16-7   How to use a web service

Perspective

Although the web service presented in this chapter is trivial, it demonstrates the techniques you can use to develop more substantial web services. As a result, the basic skills you've learned here are enough to get you started developing your own web services. In addition, you'll be prepared to learn the more complicated aspects of web services programming when the need arises.

Terms

web service
distributed web application
WSDL (Web Services Description Language)
SOAP (Simple Object Access Protocol)
attribute
web method
escaped identifier
Service help page
service description
Service Method help page

17

How to develop custom server controls

In this chapter, you'll learn how to create custom server controls. Custom server controls are similar to user controls, but are more powerful. They're also considerably more difficult to develop than user controls.

An overview of custom server controls

Before I show you how to create and use custom server controls, you need to understand what these controls are and how you work with them. That's what you'll learn in the topics that follow.

An introduction to custom server controls

Figure 17-1 presents an introduction to *custom server controls*. These controls are similar to the server controls that come with ASP.NET. Because you create custom server controls yourself, however, they can include features that aren't available with the standard ASP.NET Server controls.

For example, the form shown at the top of this figure includes four custom server controls. The first two, called CaptionedBox controls, are similar to a text box control but include a caption to the left of the text box. The second control, called a DateDDL control, consists of three drop-down lists that let the user select a month, day, and year. Like the CaptionedBox control, the DateDDL control also includes a caption. The third control, called a DaysUntil control, calculates the number of days until a specified date. In addition, text can be displayed before and after the calculated days.

When you create a custom server control, you base it on the WebControl class or a class that's derived from this class. That way, the control inherits the properties, methods, and events of that class. The DateDDL and DaysUntil controls, for example, are based on the WebControl class. In contrast, the CaptionedBox control is based on the TextBox class so it has access to the additional properties, methods, and events defined by that class.

In addition to the properties, methods, and events that are inherited from the base class, a custom server control can define its own custom properties, methods, and events. For example, the DaysUntil control has properties that let you set the month and day that's used in the calculation, as well as properties that let you specify the text that's displayed before and after the calculated number of days. You can also override the properties, methods, and events defined by the base class.

Custom server controls are typically stored in a *web control library*. Then, you can add the controls to the Toolbox as shown in this figure. To use a control, you simply drag it to a web form just as you would any other control. When you do, the control is displayed in the designer window just as it will appear in the form when it's displayed. (You can also use custom controls within user controls, but I'll focus on using them in web forms in this chapter.)

Although custom server controls are easy to use, they can be difficult to develop. That's because Visual Studio doesn't provide a designer interface to help you create them. Instead, you have to develop custom server controls entirely in code. As a result, you can't see how the control will appear until you build it and add it to a web form.

Four custom server controls displayed in the Web Forms Designer

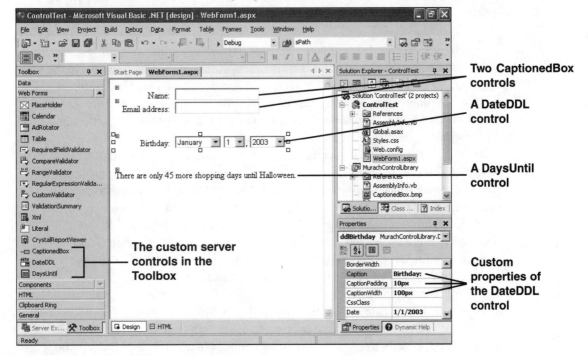

How custom controls are created

- A *custom server control* is a class that inherits the System.Web.UI.WebControls.WebControl class or a class that derives from this class.

- Visual Studio doesn't have a designer to help you create custom server controls. As a result, you must create them using code.

- Visual Studio includes a Web Control Library template you can use to create libraries of custom server controls. You can then distribute the library to other developers.

How custom server controls work with designers

- Custom server controls work just like the server controls that come with ASP.NET, but they can be customized with additional features.

- You can add custom server controls to the Visual Studio Toolbox. Then, you can add a custom server control to an ASP.NET web form by dragging it from the Toolbox just like any other ASP.NET control.

- Custom server controls have a visual interface you can use to work with them when you add them to an ASP.NET web form. For example, you can set the properties of a custom server control by selecting it in the designer and then using the Properties window.

Figure 17-1   An introduction to custom server controls

How custom server controls compare with user controls

In chapter 10, you learned how to create user controls that you can use within an application to maintain consistent appearance and functionality in the web pages it contains. In some ways, custom server controls are similar to user controls. In other ways, though, they're quite different. To help you understand how these two types of controls compare, figure 17-2 lists their similarities and differences and describes when you should use each type.

The main difference between custom server controls and user controls is that custom server controls are more difficult to develop than user controls but are easier to use once you've created them. As you know, Visual Studio provides a designer that you use to develop user controls. When you add a user control to a web form, however, the content of the user control isn't displayed in the designer. In contrast, Visual Studio doesn't provide a designer to help you develop custom server controls, but it does display the content of a custom server control when you add the control to a web form.

User controls tend to be application-specific. For example, a typical use of user controls is to create the banner, navigation menu, and footer for an application. Then, you can include those user controls in each page of the application. Since you're unlikely to use the same user controls in another application, you usually add them directly to the application that uses them.

Custom server controls usually provide more general-purpose functions than user controls. For example, the CaptionedBox and DateDDL user controls shown in the previous figure could be useful in a variety of applications. To make them available to other applications, custom server controls are usually created in a separate Web Control Library project. Then, Visual Studio lets you add the controls in the library to the Toolbox so they're available to any application.

Custom server controls...

- Are best used to create general-purpose controls you want to reuse in several applications.
- Are more difficult to develop than user controls but are easier to use once they're created.
- Are created entirely in code and consist of a single vb class file.
- Are rendered in the Web Forms Designer, so you can see how they appear at design time.
- Are usually created in Web Control Library projects.
- Can be added to the Toolbox.

User controls...

- Are best used when you want to create elements you can reuse on several pages within the same application.
- Are easier to develop than custom server controls but are more difficult to use once they're created.
- Are created with the User Control Designer and consist of an ascx file that defines the control's user interface along with a code-behind file.
- Appear as a simple button in the Web Forms Designer, so you can't see how they're rendered until you run the application and view the page in a web browser.
- Can't be added to the Toolbox.

Figure 17-2   How custom server controls compare with user controls

Three types of custom server controls

Figure 17-3 describes the three basic types of custom server controls. As you'll learn in this chapter, you implement each of these controls using different programming techniques. Keep in mind as you learn these techniques, however, that they're not mutually exclusive. In other words, you can use one or more of these techniques within the same custom server control.

A *rendered control* is a control that contains code that generates all or most of the HTML that's used to render the control. The rendered control shown in this figure is the DaysUntil control you saw in figure 17-1. Rendered controls are usually based on the WebControl class, which provides the basic functionality of an ASP.NET Server control. Then, the custom control overrides the Render method of this class to generate its own HTML. You'll see how that works in just a minute.

A *superclassed control* is a control that adds functionality to an existing ASP.NET Server control. The CaptionedBox control you saw in figure 17-1, for example, adds a caption to a text box control. Because this control is based on the TextBox class rather than the WebControl class, it has all the properties, methods, and events of a standard text box control.

A *composite control* is a control that's made up of two or more ASP.NET Server controls. For example, the DateDDL control consists of three drop-down list controls. Composite controls are based on the WebControl class. Then, the *child controls* that make up the control are added to the collection of controls defined by the WebControl class.

Note that a control can sometimes be implemented using more than one of the control types. For example, you could implement the DaysUntil control using any three of the control types. To implement it as a superclassed control, you would base it on a label control. Then, you would calculate the days remaining until the target date and assign the result to the Text property of the control, along with the text you want to display before and after the calculated days. To implement this control as a composite control, you could use three label controls: one for the text you want to display before the calculated value, one for the calculated value, and one for the text you want to display after the calculated value. Before you create a control, then, you should consider which type will provide the greatest flexibility and ease of use.

A rendered control that calculates the days until a specified date

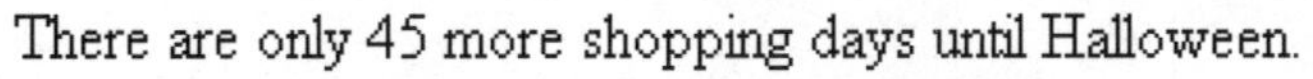

There are only 45 more shopping days until Halloween.

Two superclassed controls that add a caption to a text box

Name: [   ]
Email address: [   ]

A composite control that consists of three drop-down lists with a caption

Birthday: [January ▼] [1 ▼], [2003 ▼]

Description

- A *rendered control* is a control that inherits the System.Web.UI.WebControls.Web-Control class and handles the details of rendering its own HTML.

- Rendered controls are the most flexible type of custom control because they aren't bound by the predefined behavior of any existing controls. However, they can also be the most difficult to create.

- A *superclassed control* inherits the class for an existing control, such as a text box, and adds additional features, such as a caption.

- A *composite control* is made up of two or more standard control types. Composite controls inherit the WebControl class and add *child controls* to the collection of controls for that class.

- A custom server control can sometimes be implemented as two or more of the control types. In that case, you'll need to decide which type works best.

Figure 17-3   Three types of custom server controls

How to create a simple custom server control

In the topics that follow, you'll learn how to create a simple rendered control. First, I'll describe the default class that provides a template for creating a custom control. Then, you'll learn how to override the Render method in this class so you can control the HTML that's generated when the control is rendered. Finally, you'll see the design and code for the DaysUntil control.

The default class for a custom server control

When you add a custom server control to a project, Visual Studio creates a class like the one shown in 17-4. (The class shown here, WebCustomControl1, is created by default when you create a web control library. You'll learn more about that later in this chapter.) This class inherits the WebControl class and contains a single property named Text that gets and sets the value of a class variable. This class also contains a procedure named Render that overrides the Render method of the WebControl class. The Render procedure simply writes the value of the Text property to the HTML document for the web page.

As it is, the default class doesn't provide a useful function. However, it does provide a good starting point for building useful controls. Before you use this class, though, you need to understand how it works. If you've created your own class files using Visual Basic, you shouldn't have much trouble understanding most of this code. However, a few of the details might be confusing.

To start, notice the code within the angle brackets at the beginning of the Class and the Property statements. This code defines *designer attributes* that supply the Web Forms Designer with information about the control when it's used on a web form. You'll learn more about these designer attributes later in this chapter.

Next, notice that the class overrides the Render method of the WebControl class that it inherits. That way, it can generate the HTML needed to display the control. In this case, the Render method uses the Write method of the HtmlTextWriter object that's passed to it to write the value of the Text property to the control's HTML output stream. You'll learn more about the Write method and the other methods of the HtmlTextWriter class later in this chapter.

You should realize that because the Render method in the default class overrides the Render method of the WebControl class, the properties of the WebControl class that the default class inherits, such as Id, Height, Width, and BorderStyle, never get rendered. To render these properties, you have to call one of the render methods of the WebControl class. You'll learn how to do that in the next figure.

Finally, notice that the name of the Text property is enclosed in brackets. These brackets indicate that Text is an *escaped identifier*. Escaped identifiers provide a way to use Visual Basic keywords as identifier names. Although Text isn't a Visual Basic keyword, Microsoft used the brackets here to show you how you can create a property with the same name as a Visual Basic keyword, such as Date or Select.

The starting code for a custom server control

```
Imports System.ComponentModel
Imports System.Web.UI

<DefaultProperty("Text"), ToolboxData("<{0}:WebCustomControl1 _
runat=server></{0}:WebCustomControl1>")> _
Public Class WebCustomControl1
    Inherits System.Web.UI.WebControls.WebControl

    Dim _text As String

    <Bindable(True), Category("Appearance"), DefaultValue("")> _
    Property [Text]() As String
        Get
            Return _text
        End Get

        Set(ByVal Value As String)
            _text = Value
        End Set
    End Property

    Protected Overrides Sub Render _
            (ByVal output As System.Web.UI.HtmlTextWriter)
        output.Write([Text])
    End Sub

End Class
```

Designer attributes

- The code that appears within angle brackets (< and >) before the Class and Property statements defines *designer attributes* that specify how the control and its properties work with the Web Forms Designer. See figure 17-14 for more information.

- The designer attributes must appear on the same line as the Visual Basic element they apply to. If you want to place the Class or Property statement on a separate line, be sure to use a continuation character after the attribute's closing bracket as shown above.

Description

- A class like the one above is created by default when you add a control to a project using the Web Custom Control template or when you create a new Web Control Library project. It defines a simple rendered control that exposes a property named Text.

- The Render method receives an argument named output that's declared as an HtmlTextWriter object. This object is created by ASP.NET when it receives a request for a page. You can use it to write output to the HTML document for the web page.

- To create a useful custom server control from the default class, you must add code to define custom properties, modify the Render method, and add any other code necessary to implement the features your control will provide.

- The property name Text is enclosed in square brackets, which is a Visual Basic construct called an *escaped identifier*. An escaped identifier allows you to use a Visual Basic keyword as a variable, procedure, or property name

Figure 17-4   The default class for a custom server control

How to override the Render method for a custom control

Every ASP.NET server control has a Render method that's responsible for generating the HTML that's sent to the browser to display the control. In a custom server control, you usually override this method so you can generate the HTML that renders the control. Figure 17-5 shows how you do that.

When ASP.NET receives a request for a web page, it creates an HtmlTextWriter object that's used to write HTML to the output stream. This object is passed to the Render method, and you can use it within this method to write the HTML that renders the control. The examples in this figure show two ways you can do that.

First, you can execute the Render method of the base class (MyBase) to render the control that the custom control inherits without modification. Notice in this example that before the Render method is executed, a private procedure named RenderCaption is executed. As you'll see later in this chapter, you can use a procedure like this to add HTML to the output stream in addition to the HTML for the base class. In this case, the RenderCaption procedure renders a caption like the one used in the custom CaptionedBox control you saw earlier.

Second, you can use the RenderBeginTag and RenderEndTag methods of the base class to render the start and end tags of the control separately. Then, you can use the Write methods of the HtmlTextWriter object to include content between these tags. In this example, the Write method is used to include the value of the Text property between the start and end tags. Note that the start tag that's generated will include attributes that correspond to any control properties you set as you work with the control in the designer. In other words, by using the RenderBeginTag and RenderEndTag methods, you can render the properties the custom control inherits from its base class.

Methods of the WebControl class for rendering controls

Method	Description
`Render(output)`	Renders the HTML for the control to the specified HtmlTextWriter object.
`RenderBeginTag(output)`	Renders the begin tag for the control to the specified HtmlTextWriter object.
`RenderEndTag(output)`	Renders the end tag for the control to the specified HtmlTextWriter object.

A Render method that adds a caption to a superclassed control that's based on a text box

```
Protected Overrides Sub Render _
        (ByVal output As System.Web.UI.HtmlTextWriter)
    Me.RenderCaption(output)
    MyBase.Render(output)
End Sub
```

A Render method that adds text content to a control

```
Protected Overrides Sub Render _
        (ByVal output As System.Web.UI.HtmlTextWriter)
    MyBase.RenderBeginTag(output)
    output.Write([Text])
    MyBase.RenderEndTag(output)
End Sub
```

Description

- A custom control that inherits System.Web.UI.WebControls.WebControl can execute the Render method of the base class to render a Span element that implements the basic properties of a web control, such as the control's height and width.

- If a custom control inherits a specific control class, you can execute the Render method of the base class to render all the properties of that control. You can also include additional output in the HTML document by using the Write methods of the HtmlTextWriter class. See figure 17-13 for details.

- If you want to render additional information between the begin and end tags for a control, you can use the RenderBeginTag and RenderEndTag methods of the base class instead of the Render method. Then, you can add text between the start and end tags for the control by using the Write methods of the HtmlTextWriter class.

Note

- Web controls also have a RenderControl method, but you shouldn't execute this method from your overridden Render method. That's because the RenderControl method executes the overridden Render method, which would result in an infinite loop that will eventually terminate with a stack overflow error.

Figure 17-5   How to override the Render method

The design of the DaysUntil control

Figure 17-6 presents the design of the DaysUntil control you saw earlier in this chapter. As you'll recall, this control displays the number of days remaining until the target date specified by the Month and Day properties. Note that the default values for the Month and Day properties are 10 and 31, which means that this control displays the number of days until Halloween by default.

In addition to the Month and Day properties, the DaysUntil control includes TextBefore and TextAfter properties. These properties let you specify text that's displayed before and after the number of days. Because these properties don't have default values, no text is displayed by default.

The example in this figure shows how you could use the DaysUntil control on the Order page of the Halloween Store application. Here, this control is used in place of the PageFooter user control you saw in chapter 10. Notice that the Month and Day properties are left at their default values. In contrast, values are assigned to both the TextBefore and TextAfter properties so the control appears as shown here.

This figure also shows the aspx code that's generated for the control. Notice that this code includes Id and Runat attributes just as it would for any ASP.NET Server control. Also notice the tag prefix that's used for this control: CC1. This is the default prefix that's used for custom controls. Later in this chapter, you'll learn how to change this prefix.

The code for the DaysUntil control

Figure 17-7 presents the complete code for the DaysUntil control. The first thing you should notice is that this control inherits the WebControl class. That means that it can use any of the properties, methods, and events of that class.

On the first page of this listing, you can see the four properties of this control. Here, each property consists of simple Get and Set routines that retrieve and set the value of a class variable. If you're familiar with the techniques for coding Property procedures, you shouldn't have any trouble understanding how this code works.

On the second page of this listing, you can see the code for the overridden Render method. This code starts by executing the RenderBeginTag method of the base class to render the start tag of the base control. In this case, because the base class is WebControl, this method causes a <span> tag to be written to the HTML output stream. Next, the Write method of the HtmlTextWriter object is used to write the value of the TextBefore property, followed by the number of days remaining until the target date, followed by the value of the TextAfter property. Finally, the RenderEndTag method of the base class is executed to write the </span> tag that marks the end of the control.

To calculate the number of days remaining until the target date, the Render method executes the DaysUntilDate function. Because you saw code like this in the PageFooter user control in chapter 10, you shouldn't have any trouble understanding how it works.

A DaysUntil control on the Order page of the Halloween Store application

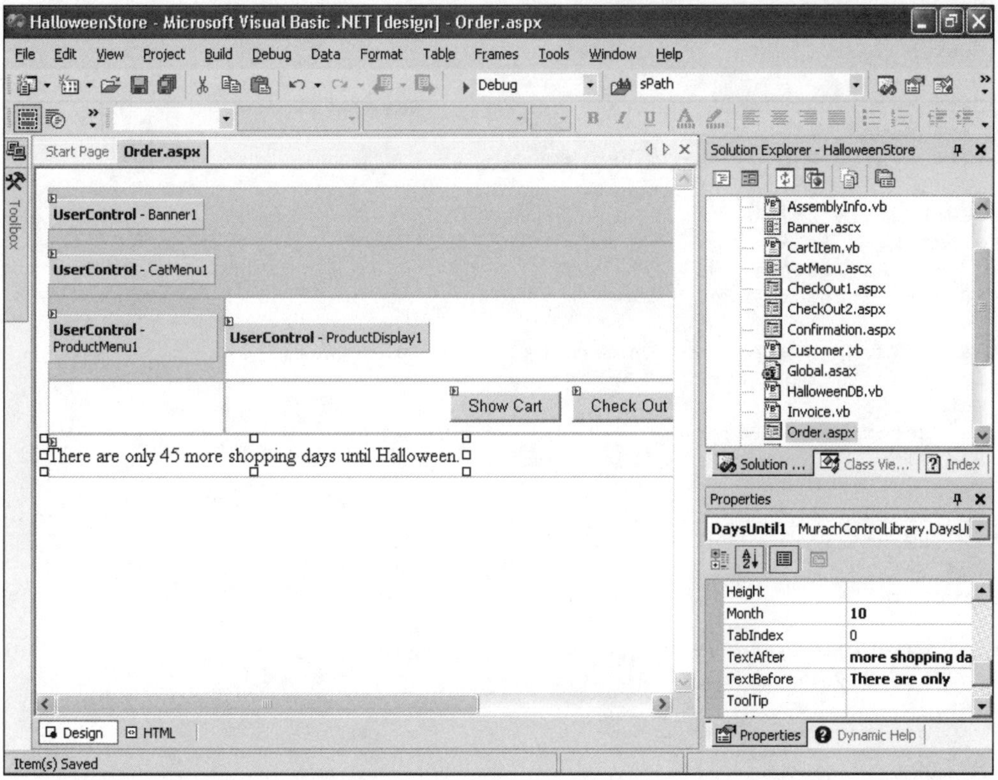

The aspx code for the control

```
<CC1:DaysUntil id="DaysUntil1" runat="server" TextBefore="There are only"
TextAfter="more shopping days until Halloween."></CC1:DaysUntil>
```

Properties of the DaysUntil control

Property	Description
Month	The target date's month. The default is 10.
Day	The target date's day. The default is 31.
TextBefore	The text that's displayed before the days until the target date.
TextAfter	The text that's displayed after the days until the target date.

Description

- The DaysUntil control is a rendered control that displays the number of days remaining until a target date and, optionally, text before and after the target date. The target date is specified by the Month and Day properties.

- By default, the Month and Day properties are set to display the number of days until Halloween. If that's not what you want, you can change these properties after you add the control to a web form.

Figure 17-6   The design of the DaysUntil control

The Visual Basic code for the DaysUntil control

```vb
Imports System.ComponentModel
Imports System.Web.UI

<ToolboxData("<{0}:DaysUntil runat=server></{0}:DaysUntil>")> _
Public Class DaysUntil
    Inherits System.Web.UI.WebControls.WebControl

    Dim sTextBefore As String
    Dim sTextAfter As String
    Dim iMonth As Integer = 10
    Dim iDay As Integer = 31

    <Bindable(True), Category("Appearance"), DefaultValue("")> _
    Public Property TextBefore() As String
        Get
            Return sTextBefore
        End Get

        Set(ByVal Value As String)
            sTextBefore = Value
        End Set
    End Property

    <Bindable(True), Category("Appearance"), DefaultValue("")> _
    Public Property TextAfter() As String
        Get
            Return sTextAfter
        End Get

        Set(ByVal Value As String)
            sTextAfter = Value
        End Set
    End Property

    <Bindable(True), Category("Appearance"), DefaultValue("")> _
    Public Property Month() As Integer
        Get
            Return iMonth
        End Get

        Set(ByVal Value As Integer)
            iMonth = Value
        End Set
    End Property

    <Bindable(True), Category("Appearance"), DefaultValue("")> _
    Public Property Day() As Integer
        Get
            Return iDay
        End Get

        Set(ByVal Value As Integer)
            iDay = Value
        End Set
    End Property
```

Figure 17-7   The code for the DaysUntil control (part 1 of 2)

The Visual Basic code for the DaysUntil control   **Page 2**

```
Protected Overrides Sub Render _
        (ByVal output As System.Web.UI.HtmlTextWriter)
    MyBase.RenderBeginTag(output)
    output.Write(sTextBefore & " ")
    output.Write(DaysUntilDate.ToString)
    output.Write(" " & sTextAfter)
    MyBase.RenderEndTag(output)
End Sub

Private Function DaysUntilDate() As Integer
    Dim TargetDate As DateTime
    TargetDate = DateTime.Parse(iMonth.ToString & "/" _
                & iDay.ToString & "/" & Now.Year)
    If Today() > TargetDate Then
        TargetDate = TargetDate.AddYears(1)
    End If
    Return DateDiff(DateInterval.Day, Today(), TargetDate)
End Function

End Class
```

Figure 17-7   The code for the DaysUntil control (part 2 of 2)

How to create and use a web control library

Now that you've seen the basic coding requirements for custom server controls, you're ready to learn how to create and use them in Visual Studio. To do that, you create a web control library that consists of one or more custom server controls. Then, you can add the controls to the Toolbox so you can use them in any application that requires them. In addition, you can distribute the library to other developers so they can use your controls. Note that if you're using the Standard Edition of Visual Basic .NET, you won't be able to create a web control library. However, you'll still be able to use the programming techniques presented in this chapter to create custom server controls so you can see how they work.

A procedure for creating and using a web control library

Figure 17-8 presents a procedure for creating and using a web control library. As you can see, you start by creating a Web Control Library project. Then, you modify the AssemblyInfo.vb file for the project to specify the tag prefix you want to use for the controls in the library. Next, you create the custom server controls, along with the icons you want to use for them in the Toolbox. Once you do that, you'll want to add an ASP.NET web application project to the solution that you can use to test the controls. Then, you can build the control library, add the controls in the library to the Toolbox, and then add the controls to a web form in the web application so you can test them. You'll learn the details of each of these steps in the topics that follow.

Step 1: Create a new Web Control Library project

The first step is to create a new Web Control Library project. To do that, you display the New Project dialog box as described in figure 17-8. Then, you select the Web Control Library template. When you do, you'll notice that the project isn't stored on the IIS server like Web Application projects are. That's because you can't execute the web control library directly. Instead, you add the controls it contains to other web projects.

A solution with a Web Control Library project

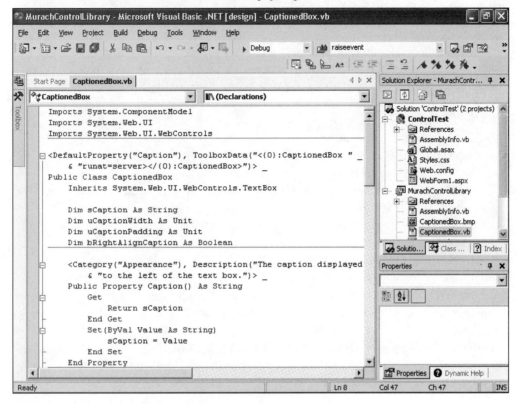

A procedure for creating a web control library

1. Create a new project using the Web Control Library template.
2. Edit the AssemblyInfo.vb file to specify the tag prefix for the controls in the library.
3. Create the custom server controls.
4. Create an icon for each control that you want to appear in the Toolbox.
5. Add an ASP.NET web application project to the solution that you can use to test the controls.
6. Build the web control library.
7. Add the controls in the library to the Toolbox.
8. Test the controls.

Description

- A *web control library* consists of one or more custom server controls. You build this library into a DLL that you can then distribute to other developers.

- To create a project for a web control library, you use the Web Control Library template that's available from the New Project dialog box (File→New→Project). Note that the project isn't stored on the IIS server, so you must enter the name and location for the project just as you do for a Windows project.

Figure 17-8   How to create and use a web control library

Step 2: Edit the AssemblyInfo.vb file to specify the tag prefix

After you create a new Web Control Library project, the next step is to edit the project's AssemblyInfo.vb file to specify the tag prefix you want to use for the controls in the library. This prefix will be used to identify the controls in the aspx code that's generated when you add the controls to a web form. Figure 17-9 shows how to edit the AssemblyInfo file.

To start, you need to add an Imports statement for the System.Web.UI namespace to this file. That's necessary because the TagPrefix attribute you'll add next is a member of this namespace. As you can see, you specify the TagPrefix attribute within a new Assembly element. This attribute includes two parameters. The first one specifies the name of the namespace for the web control library, and the second one specifies the tag prefix you want to use for the controls in the library.

By default, a web control library is stored in a namespace that has the same name as the project. Because of that, you can usually just code the project name for the first parameter of the TagPrefix attribute. If you change the project name, however, the name of the namespace isn't changed to match it. In that case, you may want to change the name of the namespace to match the project name. To do that, you can use the Properties dialog box for the project. You can also use this dialog box to verify the namespace name to be sure that you code it correctly in the TagPrefix attribute.

Step 3: Create the custom server controls

The next step is to create the custom server controls you want to include in the library. To create the first control, you can modify the WebCustom-Control1.vb file that's generated automatically when you create the Web Control Library project. Then, you can add additional controls to the library using the Project→Add New Item command and selecting the Web Custom Control template. This template generates the code you saw in figure 17-4, but uses the class name you specify in the Add New Item dialog box.

An AssemblyInfo.vb file for a web control library

```
Imports System
Imports System.Reflection
Imports System.Runtime.InteropServices
Imports System.Web.UI

' General Information about an assembly is controlled through the following
' set of attributes. Change these attribute values to modify the information
' associated with an assembly.

' Review the values of the assembly attributes

<Assembly: TagPrefix("MurachControlLibrary", "Murach")>
<Assembly: AssemblyTitle("")>
<Assembly: AssemblyDescription("")>
<Assembly: AssemblyCompany("")>
<Assembly: AssemblyProduct("")>
<Assembly: AssemblyCopyright("")>
<Assembly: AssemblyTrademark("")>
<Assembly: CLSCompliant(True)>
  .
  .
  .
```

Description

- Tag prefixes identify the source of the controls you add to a web form. The default tag prefix for custom controls is CC1, but you'll want to change the default to something that better identifies the source of the controls.

- To change the default tag prefix for a web control library, you add a TagPrefix attribute to the project's AssemblyInfo.vb file. This attribute specifies the name of the namespace for the control library and the tag prefix that will be used when a control in the library is added to a web form.

- Because the TagPrefix attribute is in the System.Web.UI namespace, you'll need to add an Imports statement for this namespace to the AssemblyInfo.vb file.

Note

- By default, the name of the namespace for a web control library is the same as the project name. To change this name, use the Project→Properties command to display the properties for the control library and then change the Root namespace specification.

Figure 17-9   How to specify the tag prefix for a web control library

Step 4: Create an icon for each control

The next step is to create an icon for each custom server control. These are the icons that will be displayed for the controls in the Toolbox. Because of that, you should try to create icons that represent the functions of the controls.

Figure 17-10 shows how to create an icon. To start, you use the Add New Item dialog box to add a bitmap file to the project with the same name as the custom control file. Then, you change the Build Action property of this file to Embedded Resource so that it's included in the assembly for the control library but not compiled. Next, you change the Height and Width properties of the icon to 16 so it has the same size as the other icons in the Toolbox.

After you change the Height and Width properties, you can use the Image Editor, the tools in the Image Editor toolbar, and the colors in the Colors tab to design the bitmap. Note that because of the size of the bitmap, the options for what you can draw are limited. Also note that the pixel in the bottom left corner of the image sets the color that will be transparent when the icon is displayed in the Toolbox. Because the image initially contains all white pixels, white is the default transparent color. If you want another color to represent transparency, then, you should change the color of this pixel.

Step 5: Add a test project to the solution

The easiest way to test your custom server controls is to add a web application project to the solution that contains the web control library. Then, after you add the custom server controls to the Toolbox, you can add them to a web form in this project to be sure they work properly.

To add a web application project, use the File→New→Project command to display the New Project dialog box. Then, select the ASP.NET Web Application template and enter the location for the project. Also, be sure to select the Add to Solution option so the project is added to the existing solution. If you don't select this option, a new solution will be started for the project.

At this point, you may be wondering why you add the test project before you build the control library and add its controls to the Toolbox. The answer is that when you add the controls to the Toolbox, you need to display the tab where you want the controls added. The only way to do that is to display a web form in the Web Forms Designer.

The bitmap editor with an icon for a custom control

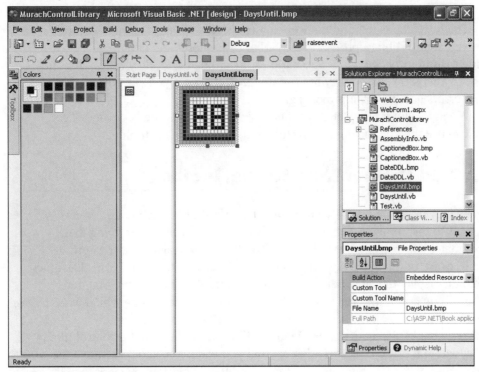

How to create an icon for a custom control

1. Highlight the Web Control Library project in the Solution Explorer, and then use the Project→Add New Item command to display the Add New Item dialog box. Select the Bitmap File template.

2. Give the bitmap the same name as the custom control you want to use it for, and then click the Open button.

3. Select the bitmap file in the Solution Explorer and change the file's Build Action property to Embedded Resource. This causes the bitmap file to be included in the assembly and used as an icon for the custom control.

4. Select the icon in the Image Editor and change its Height and Width properties to 16.

5. Use the tools in the Image Editor toolbar to draw the image.

Tips for drawing icons

*   Use the Zoom control (the one with the magnifying glass icon) to enlarge the image.

*   Because most of the tools in the Image Editor toolbar are impractical for a 16x16 bitmap, you'll use just the Pencil and Fill tools for most icons.

*   You can right-click a pixel with the Pencil tool to remove the color from the pixel.

*   The pixel in the bottom left corner of the icon sets the transparency color for the icon. Any pixels in the icon that use this color will allow the background of the Toolbox to show through when you add the control to the Toolbox.

Figure 17-10   How to create an icon for a custom control

Step 6: Build the web control library

The next step is to build the web control library. To do that, just highlight the web control library project in the Solution Explorer and choose Build→Build *projectname*. If any build errors are detected, they're listed in the Task List window just as they are for any project. Then, you can correct the build errors and build the project again.

When the build completes without any errors, a DLL file is created. Then, you can use this file to add the controls in the library to the Toolbox.

Step 7: Add the controls to the Toolbox

Once you've successfully built the web control library, you can add its controls to the Toolbox. Figure 17-11 presents the procedure for doing that. Note that when you add controls to the Toolbox, they're added to the current tab. Because of that, you'll want to open a web form in the Web Forms Designer and then display the tab where you want the controls added before you add them. If you don't, the controls will be added to the General tab, which isn't usually what you want.

You should also note that by default, all of the controls in the control library are added to the Toolbox. If that's not what you want, you should remove the check mark from any controls you don't want to add before you click the OK button in the Customize Toolbox dialog box. Alternatively, you can delete a control you don't want after it's added to the Toolbox by right-clicking on it and choosing the Delete command.

The Customize Toolbox dialog box

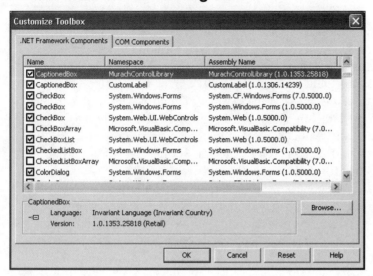

Procedure

1. Open the web form for your ASP.NET web application test project in the Web Forms Designer window and then display the Web Forms tab of the Toolbox.

2. Choose Tools→Add/Remove Toolbox Items to display the Customize Toolbox dialog box shown above.

3. Click the Browse button to display a standard Open dialog box.

4. Use the navigation controls to locate the Bin folder for the Web Control Library project.

5. Select the DLL file for the web control library and then click the Open button to return to the Customize Toolbox dialog box. All of the controls in the web control library will be selected and highlighted.

6. Remove the check mark from any of the controls in the library that you don't want to add to the Toolbox. Then, click the OK button to add the remaining controls.

Notes

- You can also add a custom tab to the Toolbox and then add your custom controls to that tab. To create a custom tab, right-click the Toolbox and select the Add Tab command. Then, enter a name for the tab in the text box that's displayed and press the Enter key. To add custom controls to the new tab, display that tab and then use the procedure above, or drag the controls from the Web Forms tab.

- If you need to delete a control from the Toolbox, you can do that by right-clicking on it and selecting the Delete command.

Figure 17-11   How to add custom controls to the Toolbox

Step 8: Test the custom controls

Figure 17-12 shows how you can test a custom server control. In general, you just drag the control from the Toolbox onto a web form in the test project. Then, you can set its properties using the Properties window to be sure that the control appears the way it should in the designer. At the top of this figure, for example, you can see three instances of the DaysUntil control with different property settings. Notice that to create the third control, I set not only the custom properties of the control, but several of the properties this control inherited from the WebControl class. You can see the settings for all of these properties in the aspx code for the controls shown here.

After you're sure that the controls appear correctly in the designer, you should run the test project to be sure they work properly at runtime. Before you do that, though, you should set this project as the startup project by highlighting it and then using the Project→Set as StartUp Project command. That's necessary because, by default, the first project you add to a solution is the startup project. In this case, that's the Web Control Library project, which isn't what you want.

When you test your custom controls, you should realize that coding errors sometimes manifest themselves in strange ways. Because of that, they can be difficult to debug. For example, if the Render method of a control generates invalid HTML, the control won't display correctly in the Web Forms Designer. Typically, the Designer will simply display the name of the control in brackets. In other cases, the control will appear correctly in the designer, but it won't display properly when you run the project. And in still other cases, the control will throw an exception when you run the application.

Fortunately, you can use the debugger to determine the cause of an error. If a control isn't being rendered properly, for example, you can set a breakpoint in the Render method. Then, you can review variable values and monitor program execution to determine the cause of the problem.

If the control displays in the browser but doesn't appear or work the way it should, you can also look at the HTML that's generated to be sure it's correct. To do that, use the View→Source command in your browser's menu.

Three instances of the DaysUntil control in the Web Forms Designer

```
45

45 days until Halloween

Christmas is only 100 days away!
```

The code generated in the .ascx file for these three controls

```
<%@ Register TagPrefix="murach" Namespace="MurachControlLibrary"
    Assembly="MurachControlLibrary" %>
    .
    .
    .
<murach:DaysUntil id="DaysUntil1" runat="server"></murach:DaysUntil><BR>
<BR>
<murach:DaysUntil id="DaysUntil2" runat="server"
        TextAfter="days until Halloween" Day="31" Month="10">
</murach:DaysUntil><BR>
<BR>
<murach:DaysUntil id="DaysUntil3" runat="server"
        TextBefore="Christmas is only" TextAfter="days away!"
        BorderColor="Transparent" BackColor="#E0E0E0" Font-Bold="True"
        Font-Italic="True" Month="12" Day="25">
</murach:DaysUntil>
```

Description

- To test a custom control, add it to a form in your web application test project. To do that, just drag it from the Toolbox.
- After you add the control to a form, you can set its properties in the Properties window to be sure that it appears as it should in the designer. You can also run the project to be sure that the control works properly at runtime.
- If you need to make changes to a control, you can do that and then rebuild the control library project using the Build→Rebuild *project name* command. The changes are automatically applied to the controls in the Toolbox and any controls you've added to the web form.

Notes

- Because the Month property of the DaysUntil control has a default value of 10 and the Day property has a default value of 31, the number of days until 10/31 is automatically calculated and displayed when you add the control to a web form as illustrated by the first control shown above.
- Because the DaysUntil control inherits the WebControl base class, you can also set properties of this class as illustrated by the third control shown above.

Figure 17-12   How to test a custom control

Additional programming techniques for custom controls

Now that you've learned how to create a web control library, you're ready to learn some additional programming techniques for creating custom server controls. That's what you'll learn in the topics that follow.

How to use the HtmlTextWriter class to render HTML

As you know, the Render method of a custom server control receives an HtmlTextWriter object named output as an argument. You use this object to generate the HTML needed to display the control. You've already seen how to use the Write method of this class to write simple text to the output stream. You can use this method to render all of the HTML for a custom server control by carefully constructing the HTML text using Visual Basic's string handling features. However, figure 17-13 presents some additional methods of the HtmlTextWriter class that make it easier to generate HTML output.

The methods shown in this figure simplify the process of creating valid HTML constructs. For example, the WriteBeginTag method writes an HTML start tag using the element name you supply. Note, however, that this method doesn't write the closing bracket for the start tag. That way, you can use the WriteAttribute method to add an attribute to the tag. Then, you can use the Write method to add the closing bracket for the tag by specifying HtmlTextWriter.TagRightChar for the string value.

You can also use the Write method to add content following the start tag. Then, you can use the WriteEndTag method to write the end tag. This is illustrated in the example in this figure. This code creates a Span element with a Style attribute that specifies the width and alignment of the content between the start and end tags.

If an element doesn't include any content, you can code the start tag as a *self-closing tag*. To do that, you use the HtmlTextWriter.SelfClosingTagEnd field to close the start tag instead of HtmlTextWriter.TagRightChar. This constant adds the characters "/>" to the output stream, which indicates the end of the element. Then, you can omit the end tag.

Common methods of the HtmlTextWriter class

Method	Description
`Write(string)`	Writes the specified string to the HTML output.
`WriteBeginTag(tagname)`	Writes the start tag for the specified HTML element. This method does not write the closing bracket (>) for the start tag. That way, you can include attributes within the tag.
`WriteAttribute(attribute, value)`	Writes the specified attribute and assigns the specified value. This method should be coded after the WriteBeginTag method but before the Write method that adds the closing bracket for the start tag.
`WriteEndTag(tagname)`	Writes the end tag for the specified HTML element.

Common fields of the HtmlTextWriter class

Field	Description
TagRightChar	The closing bracket of an HTML tag (>).
SelfClosingTagEnd	The closing slash and bracket of a self-closing HTML tag (/>).

A procedure that renders a Span element with text

```
Private Sub RenderCaption(ByVal output As System.Web.UI.HtmlTextWriter)
    output.WriteBeginTag("Span")
    Dim sStyle As String
    sStyle = "width: " & uCaptionWidth.ToString
    sStyle &= "; text-align: right"
    output.WriteAttribute("Style", sStyle)
    output.Write(HtmlTextWriter.TagRightChar)
    output.Write(sCaption)
    output.WriteEndTag("Span")
End
```

Description

- You can use the Write methods of the HtmlTextWriter class to create HTML for a custom control.

- To add the closing bracket for a start tag, you use the Write method and specify HtmlTextWriter.TagRightChar.

- If an element doesn't include any content, you can code the start tag as a *self-closing tag*. A self-closing tag ends with the characters />. To add these characters, use the HtmlTextWriter.SelfClosingTagEnd field.

Figure 17-13   How to use the HtmlTextWriter class to render HTML

How to use designer attributes

Figure 17-14 presents some of the designer attributes you can use with custom control classes and properties. The only two *class attributes* you'll typically use are the ones that are added by default to a custom control. As its name implies, the DefaultProperty attribute identifies the default property for the control. This attribute is set to Text by default since this is the only property that's defined for a control when you first create it. If you delete the Text property or change its name, you should delete the DefaultProperty attribute or change it to another property.

The second class attribute, ToolboxData, provides information that Visual Studio uses when you add the control to a form. Specifically, it provides the name of the tag that's used for the control. By default, this is the class name that you specify when you create the web control, which is usually what you want.

The *property attributes* provide the Visual Studio designer with additional information about the custom properties you define. For example, the attributes that are included on the Text property of a custom server control by default specify that the property can be used for binding (Bindable(True)), that the property should be listed in the Appearance category of the Properties window (Category(Appearance)), and that the property has no default value (Default("")). You can modify or delete any of these attributes or add any of the other attributes.

One property attribute you're likely to add is Description. The value you specify for this attribute is displayed in the Description pane at the bottom of the Properties window when you select the control in the designer window and then select the property. This is illustrated by the Month property from the DaysUntil control shown in this figure.

Common attributes for custom control classes

Attribute	Description
`DefaultProperty(name)`	The name of the default property for the control.
`ToolboxData(tagName)`	The name of the tag that's generated when the control is added to a web form from the Toolbox.

Common attributes for custom control properties

Attribute	Description
`Bindable(boolean)`	Specifies whether the property is typically used for binding.
`Browsable(boolean)`	Specifies whether the property should be visible in the Properties window. The default is True.
`Category(string)`	The category the property should appear under in the Properties window.
`DefaultValue(string)`	The default value for the property.
`Description(string)`	A description for the property.
`DesignOnly(boolean)`	Specifies whether the property is available only at design time. The default is False.

A property definition with property attributes

```
<Bindable(True), Category("Appearance"), DefaultValue("") _
 Description("The month used to determine the target date.")> _
Public Property Month() As Integer
    Get
        Return iMonth
    End Get

    Set(ByVal Value As Integer)
        iMonth = Value
    End Set
End Property
```

Description

- You can use *class attributes* and *property attributes* to add information to a control class or control property that makes the class or property easier to use in Visual Studio.

- Class attributes are coded at the beginning of a Class statement, and property attributes are coded at the beginning of a Property statement. The entire attribute list must be enclosed in angle brackets (<>).

- An attribute list consists of one or more attributes, separated by commas. Each attribute consists of an attribute name, followed by a value enclosed in parentheses.

Figure 17-14   How to use designer attributes

How to raise events in a custom control

In addition to defining custom properties, a custom server control can raise custom events. For example, the DateDDL control you saw earlier in this chapter raises an event named DateChanged whenever the user selects a different month, day, or year. A web form that uses this control can then include a handler for this event to provide special processing when the user changes the date. At the top of figure 17-15, for example, you can see a page that includes a DateDDL control and a label that displays a message when the DateChanged event occurs.

To define an event for a custom server control, you use an Event statement as shown in this figure. On this statement, you code the name of the event along with the definitions of any arguments you want to pass to the procedure that handles the event when it's raised. Then, to raise the event, you code a RaiseEvent statement. On this statement, you name the event you want to raise and you provide values for its arguments.

In this figure, you can see the Event statement that defines the DateChanged event and a Raise statement that raises the event. Notice that the Event statement defines two arguments. The first argument is an object named *sender*, and the second argument is an EventArgs object named *e*. Most events raised by custom controls should pass these two arguments. Then, the RaiseEvent statement should pass the control itself (Me) or a child control it contains as the sender argument so that the event handler can refer to this control. The event handler shown in this figure, for example, uses the Id property of the sender argument to display the name of the control.

For the e argument, the RaiseEvent statement typically passes a new EventArgs object. Because this object doesn't contain any event data, it serves no useful purpose to the event handler. If you develop more sophisticated controls, however, you can pass an event argument object that's based on the EventArgs object and that contains useful state information.

A page that tests the DateChanged event of the DateDDLExpires control

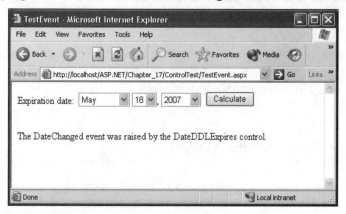

The syntax of the Event statement

```
[Public] Event name[(argumentlist)]
```

The syntax of the RaiseEvent statement

```
RaiseEvent name[(argumentlist)]
```

Code that defines the DateChanged event in the DateDDLExpires control

```
Public Event DateChanged(ByVal sender As Object, ByVal e As EventArgs)
```

Code that raises the event in the DateDDLExpires control

```
RaiseEvent DateChanged(Me, New EventArgs)
```

The event handler for the event in the web form

```
Private Sub DateDDLExpires_DateChanged(ByVal sender As Object, _
        ByVal e As System.EventArgs) _
        Handles DateDDLExpires.DateChanged
    lblEventRaised.Text = "The DateChanged event was raised by the " _
                        & sender.id & " control."
End Sub
```

Description

- To declare an event for a custom control, you code a Public Event statement at the class level. Then, you use a RaiseEvent statement in any method of the class to raise the event.

- The RaiseEvent statement for a control event should pass two arguments to the event handler: *sender* and *e*.

- The value of the sender argument should be the control that's raising the event (Me) or a child control that it contains. The event handler can use this argument to retrieve information about the control.

- The value of the e argument should be an EventArgs object. This is a base class that contains no event data and is used by events that don't need to pass state information to the event handler. You can use the New keyword to create an EventArgs object.

Figure 17-15   How to raise events in a custom control

How to create a superclassed control

As you know, a superclassed control is a control that inherits a specific ASP.NET server control rather than the generic WebControl class. The programming techniques for creating a superclassed control are similar to the techniques for creating a rendered control. However, you should be aware of a few coding details.

How to code a superclassed control

Before you create a superclassed control, you should carefully consider which control it inherits. In general, you'll want it to inherit the control that most resembles the appearance and function of the custom control you're creating. For example, if the primary purpose of the custom control is to display text, it should inherit the Label control. On the other hand, if the primary purpose of the control is to accept text input from the user, it should inherit the TextBox control.

How you code the Render method for a superclassed control depends on how you're extending the base control. If you're simply adding some HTML before or after the control, or if you're just changing some of the base control's property values before rendering the control, your Render method can call the Render method of the base class to render the entire base control. If your enhancements are more substantial, however, you may need to use the RenderBeginTag and RenderEndTag methods so you can render additional HTML between the control's start and end tags.

The design of the CaptionedBox control

To help you understand how superclassed controls work, figure 17-16 presents the design of the CaptionedBox control. This control adds a caption to a standard text box. Because it must provide all the standard features of a text box, it's based on the TextBox class.

To define the caption, this control uses four properties. The Caption property specifies the text to be displayed, the CaptionWidth property specifies the width of the caption, and the RightAlignCaption property determines whether the caption is right-aligned. Finally, the CaptionPadding property specifies how much space appears between the caption and the text box that follows it.

If you think about it, you'll see that the CaptionedBox control can be quite useful for aligning text boxes on a form. The web page in this figure illustrates how this works. As you can see, this page contains two CaptionedBox controls. To align the text box portions of these controls, the CaptionWidth and CaptionPadding properties of both controls are set to the same values. In addition, the RightAlign properties of the controls are set to True so that they appear as shown. This can be easier than using tables to align text boxes as you've seen throughout this book.

A web page with two CaptionedBox controls

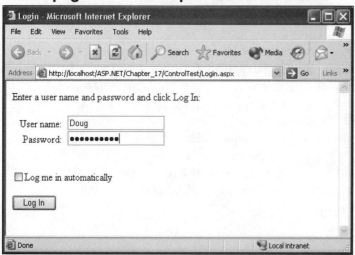

Properties of the CaptionedBox control

Property	Description
Caption	The text that's displayed to the left of the text box.
CaptionWidth	The width of the control's caption area.
CaptionPadding	The width of the area between the caption and the text box.
RightAlignCaption	Determines whether the caption text is right-aligned. The default is False.

The aspx code for the two CaptionedBox controls

```
<murach:CaptionedBox id="cbUserName" runat="server" Width="155px"
        Caption="User name:" CaptionPadding="10px" CaptionWidth="80px"
        RightAlignCaption="True"></murach:CaptionedBox>
<murach:CaptionedBox id="cbPassword" runat="server" Width="155px"
        TextMode="Password" Caption="Password:" CaptionPadding="10px"
        CaptionWidth="80px" RightAlignCaption="True"></murach:CaptionedBox>
```

Description

- The CaptionedBox control is a superclassed control that adds a text caption to the left of a text box. This control makes it easy to align text boxes without using tables.

Figure 17-16   The design of the CaptionedBox control

The code for the CaptionedBox control

Figure 17-17 presents the code for the CaptionedBox control. On the first page of this listing, you can see that the control inherits the TextBox class. In addition, you can see the custom properties that are defined for this class. Like the properties in the DaysUntil control, these properties simply retrieve and set the values of class variables. Notice that each of these properties includes a Description attribute that describes the property.

Also notice that the CaptionWidth and CaptionPadding properties and the class variables that hold their values are declared with the Unit data type. In case you aren't familiar with this data type, it represents a length measurement that consists of both the length and the unit of measure. By default, the unit of measure is a pixel, which is usually what you want.

The Visual Basic code for the CaptionedBox control   Page 1

```vb
Imports System.ComponentModel
Imports System.Web.UI
Imports System.Web.UI.WebControls

<DefaultProperty("Caption"), ToolboxData("<{0}:CaptionedBox " _
    & "runat=server></{0}:CaptionedBox>")> _
Public Class CaptionedBox
    Inherits System.Web.UI.WebControls.TextBox

    Dim sCaption As String
    Dim uCaptionWidth As Unit
    Dim uCaptionPadding As Unit
    Dim bRightAlignCaption As Boolean

    <Category("Appearance"), Description("The caption displayed " _
        & "to the left of the text box.")> _
    Public Property Caption() As String
        Get
            Return sCaption
        End Get
        Set(ByVal Value As String)
            sCaption = Value
        End Set
    End Property

    <Category("Appearance"), Description("The width of the caption.")> _
    Public Property CaptionWidth() As Unit
        Get
            Return uCaptionWidth
        End Get
        Set(ByVal Value As Unit)
            uCaptionWidth = Value
        End Set
    End Property

    <Category("Appearance"), Description("The space between the caption " _
        & "and the text box.")> _
    Public Property CaptionPadding() As Unit
        Get
            Return uCaptionPadding
        End Get
        Set(ByVal Value As Unit)
            uCaptionPadding = Value
        End Set
    End Property

    <Category("Appearance"), Description("Determines if the caption " _
        & "is right-aligned.")> _
    Public Property RightAlignCaption() As Boolean
        Get
            Return bRightAlignCaption
        End Get
        Set(ByVal Value As Boolean)
            bRightAlignCaption = Value
        End Set
    End Property
```

Figure 17-17   The code for the CaptionedBox control (part 1 of 2)

On the second page of this listing, you can see the overridden Render method. This method consists of just two statements. The first statement executes a private Sub procedure named RenderCaption. I'll describe this procedure in a moment. The second statement executes the Render method of the base class to render the base text box control.

The RenderCaption procedure is the only complicated procedure in this listing. It begins by rendering the start tag for a Span element. Within this tag, it renders a Style attribute that specifies the width of the caption using the CaptionWidth property. Notice that the ToString property of the uCaptionWidth variable is used to convert the length and unit of measure of this variable to a string value. If the caption width is set to 10 pixels, for example, the result is 10px.

Next, the RenderCaption method checks if the RightAlignCaption property is set to True. If so, it also adds a text-align property to the Style attribute. Then, it adds the closing bracket for the start tag.

The start tag for the Span element is followed by its content, which is the value of the Caption property. The content is then followed by an end tag for the Span element.

Next, the RenderCaption procedure renders another Span element to create the space between the caption and the text box. To do that, it includes a Style attribute in the start tag that specifies the value of the CaptionPadding property as the width of the element.

The Visual Basic code for the CaptionedBox control   Page 2

```
    Protected Overrides Sub Render _
            (ByVal output As System.Web.UI.HtmlTextWriter)
        Me.RenderCaption(output)
        MyBase.Render(output)
    End Sub

    Private Sub RenderCaption(ByVal output As System.Web.UI.HtmlTextWriter)
        output.WriteBeginTag("Span")
        Dim sStyle As String
        sStyle = "width=" & uCaptionWidth.ToString
        If bRightAlignCaption Then
            sStyle &= "; text-align: right"
        End If
        output.WriteAttribute("Style", sStyle)
        output.Write(HtmlTextWriter.TagRightChar)
        output.Write(sCaption)
        output.WriteEndTag("Span")
        output.WriteBeginTag("Span")
        output.WriteAttribute("Style", "width: " & uCaptionPadding.ToString)
        output.Write(HtmlTextWriter.TagRightChar)
        output.WriteEndTag("Span")
    End Sub
End Class
```

Figure 17-17   The code for the CaptionedBox control (part 2 of 2)

How to create a composite control

A composite control is a control that includes two or more child controls. Because of that, a composite control can be more difficult to create than rendered controls and superclassed controls. In the topics that follow, you'll learn the basic techniques for creating composite controls, and you'll see the design and code for the DateDDL control.

How to code a composite control

A composite control typically inherits the generic WebControl class. In addition, it should implement the INamingContainer interface as indicated by the first code example in figure 17-18. In case you're not familiar with interfaces, they define properties, methods, and events just like classes. Unlike classes, however, an interface doesn't include the details of how the properties, methods, and events are implemented. That's left to the classes that use them.

The INamingContainer interface is unusual in that it doesn't define any properties, methods, or events. Instead, it simply identifies the composite control as a container control, which ensures that its child controls will be unique. That way, you can include two or more instances of the control on the same page.

To work with the collection of child controls in a composite control, you use the Controls property of the WebControl class. To add a control to the collection, for example, you can use the Add method of the control collection object, and to remove all of the controls from the collection, you use the Clear method. This is illustrated by the second example in this figure. This procedure starts by clearing the controls collection. Then, it creates an instance of the Label class and an instance of the TextBox class and adds them both to the controls collection.

Notice that these statements are coded within a procedure named CreateChildControls. As you can see by the procedure declaration, this procedure overrides the CreateChildControls method of the base class. ASP.NET calls this method by default to create the child controls of the base control, if it has any. To create a composite control, then, you need to override this method to create the child controls you want to include in the composite control.

The last example in this figure shows how to add literal text to the controls collection. To do that, you use a literal control that specifies the text value you want to include. In this example, the literal control contains a single space ( ). Note that when you use a literal control, you can't apply a style to the text it contains. If you need to do that, you'll want to use a label control instead.

The most confusing aspect of creating composite controls is knowing when to use the EnsureChildControls method. This method ensures that the control's child controls have been created before the control is rendered in the designer. Because of that, you should execute this method from the overridden Render method. In addition, you should execute this method before executing any code that refers to the child controls.

A property and method of the WebControl class used with child controls

Property	Description
`Controls()`	Accesses the collection of controls contained by the web control.
Method	**Description**
`EnsureChildControls()`	Ensures that child controls have been created. You typically execute this method before performing any function on a child control, including rendering it.

Common methods of control collection objects

Method	Description
`Add(control)`	Adds the specified child control.
`Remove(control)`	Removes the specified child control.
`Clear()`	Removes all child controls.

The start of a class for a typical composite control

```
Public Class DateDDL
    Inherits System.Web.UI.WebControls.WebControl
    Implements INamingContainer
```

Code that adds a label and a text box to the collection of child controls

```
Public Overrides Sub CreateChildControls()
    Controls.Clear()
    Dim lbl As New Label()
    lbl.Text = sLabelText
    Controls.Add(lbl)
    Dim txt As New TextBox()
    Controls.Add(txt)
End Sub
```

Code that adds a literal control with a space to the controls collection

```
Controls.Add(New LiteralControl(" "))
```

Description

- A composite control is a custom control that has two or more child controls. The child controls are stored in a ControlCollection object, which you access through the Controls property of the composite control.

- A composite control typically inherits the System.Web.UI.WebControls.WebControl class, so it has access to all the properties and methods of that class.

- A composite control should include an Implements INamingContainer statement. This statement is required to ensure that the composite control's child controls will be unique.

- The EnsureChildControls method calls the control's CreateChildControls method if the child controls don't already exist. You should override the CreateChildControls method to create the composite control's child controls.

- When you execute the Render method of a composite control, it invokes the RenderChildren method to render the child controls. If you don't want the child controls to be rendered, you can override this method with an empty method.

Figure 17-18   How to code a composite control

The design of the DateDDL control

Figure 17-19 presents the design of the DateDDL control. This control includes three drop-down lists that let the user select a month, day, and year. When the control is displayed, the Month drop-down list is populated with the names of the months, the Day drop-down list is populated with the numbers 1 through 31, and the year drop-down list is populated with the 10 years that begin with the current year. This control also includes a caption just like the CaptionedBox control. In the page that's displayed at the top of this figure, you can see how this control is used to accept an expiration date from the user.

In addition to the Caption, CaptionWidth, CaptionPadding, and RightAlignCaption properties that are used to implement the caption, the DateDDL control has four properties that store date information. The first one, Date, stores the entire date. This property is updated any time the user selects a different month, day, or year. The other properties, Month, Day, and Year, store just the month, day, and year portion of the date and are updated any time the users changes that portion of the date. The last property, AutoPostBack, lets you specify whether the page that contains the control should be posted back to the server when the user selects a different month, day, or year.

The DateDDL control also raises an event named DateChanged whenever the user selects a different month, day, or year. Note that this event is raised only once each time the page is posted. That way, if the user selects a different item from two or more of the drop-down lists, the DateChanged event is only raised one time.

The code for the DateDDL control

Figure 17-20 presents the complete source code for the DateDDL control. Because this code is a bit complicated, you may have to study it awhile before you understand how this control works. I'll just describe some of the key portions of the code here.

First, notice that the three child controls that are included in this control are declared at the beginning of the class with the WithEvents keyword. That way, the class can use any of the events defined by the DropDownList class that these controls are based on. As you'll see in a minute, this control will use the SelectedIndexChanged event of each of these controls.

Next, notice that the EnsureChildControls method is executed each time the control needs to refer to one of its child controls. For example, this method is executed at the beginning of the Get and Set routines for the Month, Day, and Year properties shown on pages 2 and 3 of this listing. That's necessary because these procedures refer to the drop-down lists to get or set the month, day, and year. The EnsureChildControls method ensures that these drop-down lists exist before this code is executed.

A web page that uses a DateDDL control

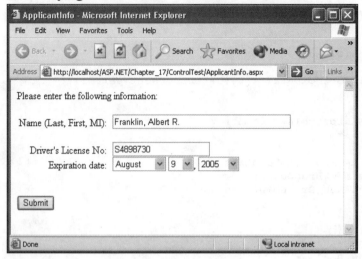

Properties of the DateDDL control

Property	Description
Caption	The text that's displayed to the left of the drop-down lists.
CaptionWidth	The width of the control's caption area.
CaptionPadding	The width of the area between the caption and the drop-down lists.
RightAlignCaption	Determines whether the caption is right-aligned. The default is False.
Date	The date selected by the user.
Month	An integer representing the month (1 to 12).
Day	An integer representing the day of the month (1 to 31).
Year	An integer representing the year.
AutoPostBack	Determines whether the page should be posted when the user selects a different month, day, or year. The default is False.

Event raised by the DateDDL control

Event	Description
DateChanged	Raised when the user selects a different month, day, or year.

The aspx code for the DateDDL control

```
<murach:dateddl id="DateDDLExpires" runat="server"
        Caption="Expiration date:" CaptionPadding="10px"
        RightAlignCaption="True" CaptionWidth="145px"></murach:dateddl>
```

Description

- The DateDDL control is a composite control that combines three drop-down lists that let the user select a date. It also includes a caption to the left of the drop-down lists.

Figure 17-19   The design of the DateDDL control

The Visual Basic code for the DateDDL control   **Page 1**

```
Imports System.ComponentModel
Imports System.Web
Imports System.Web.UI
Imports System.Web.UI.WebControls

<DefaultProperty("Caption"), ToolboxData("<{0}:DateDDL runat=server>" _
    & "</{0}:DateDDL>")> _
Public Class DateDDL
    Inherits System.Web.UI.WebControls.WebControl
    Implements INamingContainer

    Dim WithEvents ddlMonth As New DropDownList
    Dim WithEvents ddlDay As New DropDownList
    Dim WithEvents ddlYear As New DropDownList

    Dim sCaption As String
    Dim uCaptionWidth As Unit
    Dim uCaptionPadding As Unit
    Dim bRightAlignCaption As Boolean

    Dim iMonth As Integer
    Dim iDay As Integer
    Dim iYear As Integer
    Dim bAutoPostBack As Boolean
    Dim bDateChangedEventRaised As Boolean

    Public Event DateChanged(ByVal sender As Object, ByVal e As EventArgs)

    <Category("Appearance"), Description("The caption for the control.")> _
    Public Property Caption() As String
        Get
            Return sCaption
        End Get

        Set(ByVal Value As String)
            sCaption = Value
        End Set
    End Property

    <Category("Appearance"), Description("The width of the caption.")> _
    Public Property CaptionWidth() As Unit
        Get
            Return uCaptionWidth
        End Get
        Set(ByVal Value As Unit)
            uCaptionWidth = Value
        End Set
    End Property
```

Figure 17-20   The code for the DateDDL control (part 1 of 5)

The Visual Basic code for the DateDDL control   Page 2

```vb
<Category("Appearance"), Description("The space between the caption " _
    & "and the Month drop-down list.")> _
Public Property CaptionPadding() As Unit
    Get
        Return uCaptionPadding
    End Get
    Set(ByVal Value As Unit)
        uCaptionPadding = Value
    End Set
End Property

<Category("Appearance"), Description("Determines if the caption " _
    & "is right-aligned.")> _
Public Property RightAlignCaption() As Boolean
    Get
        Return bRightAlignCaption
    End Get
    Set(ByVal Value As Boolean)
        bRightAlignCaption = Value
    End Set
End Property

<Category("Misc"), Description("Gets or sets the date.")> _
Public Property [Date]() As Date
    Get
        Return CDate(Month & "/" & Day & "/" & Year)
    End Get
    Set(ByVal Value As Date)
        iMonth = Value.Month
        ddlMonth.SelectedIndex = Value.Month - 1
        iDay = Value.Day
        ddlDay.SelectedIndex = Value.Day - 1
        iYear = Value.Year
        ddlYear.SelectedValue = Value.Year
    End Set
End Property

<Category("Misc"), Description("Gets or set the month.")> _
Public Property [Month]() As Integer
    Get
        EnsureChildControls()
        iMonth = ddlMonth.SelectedIndex + 1
        Return iMonth
    End Get
    Set(ByVal Value As Integer)
        EnsureChildControls()
        iMonth = Value
        ddlMonth.SelectedIndex = iMonth - 1
        If Not bDateChangedEventRaised Then
            RaiseEvent DateChanged(Me, New EventArgs)
            bDateChangedEventRaised = True
        End If
    End Set
End Property
```

Figure 17-20   The code for the DateDDL control (part 2 of 5)

At the bottom of page 3 of this listing, you can see the Render method for this control. It, too, starts by executing the EnsureChildControls method to be sure that the child controls exist before they are rendered. Then, it executes the RenderCaption procedure, which works just like the procedure in the CaptionedBox control. Finally, the Render method for this composite control executes the Render method of the base class to render the control and its child controls.

On page 4 of this listing, you can see the overridden CreateChildControls method. This method is responsible for creating the month, day, and year drop-down lists and adding them to the controls collection. To do that, it starts by executing private procedures named MakeMonthList, MakeDayList, and MakeYearList to initialize the drop-down lists. Then, it clears the controls collection and adds the controls. Notice that literal controls that contain a space are added between the drop-down lists so that they don't appear right next to each other when they're displayed.

When the user selects a different month, day, or year from a drop-down list, the event handler for the SelectedIndexChanged event of that control is executed. The code for these event handlers is shown on page 5 of this listing. They simply set the Month, Day, and Year properties to the selection made by the user, and then call the AdjustDay procedure. If you look at the Set routines for the Month, Day, and Year properties in parts 2 and 3, you can see that they in turn raise the DateChanged event. Notice that a Boolean variable is used to keep track of whether the DateChanged event has already been raised to make sure it isn't raised more than once.

The AdjustDay procedure that's called by the SelectedIndexChanged procedure prevents the date from being set to an invalid date. If the user selects April 31, for example, this procedure adjusts the date to April 30 since April only has 30 days. Although this is the simplest solution to the problem, it's probably not the best solution. Another solution would be to post the page any time the user selected a different month and then load the appropriate days for that month into the Day drop-down list. Still another solution would be to raise an event or throw an exception if the user selects an invalid date. These are the types of coding decisions you'll need to make as you design your custom controls.

The Visual Basic code for the DateDDL control   **Page 3**

```vb
<Category("Misc"), Description("Gets or sets the day.")> _
Public Property [Day]() As Integer
    Get
        EnsureChildControls()
        iDay = ddlDay.SelectedIndex + 1
        Return iDay
    End Get
    Set(ByVal Value As Integer)
        EnsureChildControls()
        iDay = Value
        ddlDay.SelectedIndex = iDay - 1
        If Not bDateChangedEventRaised Then
            RaiseEvent DateChanged(Me, New EventArgs)
            bDateChangedEventRaised = True
        End If
    End Set
End Property

<Category("Misc"), Description("Gets or sets the year.")> _
Public Property [Year]() As Integer
    Get
        EnsureChildControls()
        iYear = ddlYear.SelectedValue
        Return iYear
    End Get
    Set(ByVal Value As Integer)
        EnsureChildControls()
        iYear = Value
        ddlYear.SelectedValue = iYear
        If Not bDateChangedEventRaised Then
            RaiseEvent DateChanged(Me, New EventArgs)
            bDateChangedEventRaised = True
        End If
    End Set
End Property

<Category("Misc"), Description("Determines whether a postback occurs " _
        & "when the selection is changed."), DefaultValue(False)> _
Public Property AutoPostBack() As Boolean
    Get
        Return bAutoPostBack
    End Get
    Set(ByVal Value As Boolean)
        bAutoPostBack = Value
    End Set
End Property

Protected Overrides Sub Render _
        (ByVal output As System.Web.UI.HtmlTextWriter)
    EnsureChildControls()
    Me.RenderCaption(output)
    MyBase.Render(output)
End Sub
```

Figure 17-20   The code for the DateDDL control (part 3 of 5)

The Visual Basic code for the DateDDL control

```vbnet
Private Sub RenderCaption(ByVal output As System.Web.UI.HtmlTextWriter)
    output.WriteBeginTag("Span")
    Dim sStyle As String
    sStyle = "width=" & uCaptionWidth.ToString
    If bRightAlignCaption Then
        sStyle &= "; text-align: right"
    End If
    output.WriteAttribute("Style", sStyle)
    output.Write(HtmlTextWriter.TagRightChar)
    output.Write(sCaption)
    output.WriteEndTag("Span")
    output.WriteBeginTag("Span")
    output.WriteAttribute("Style", "width: " & uCaptionPadding.ToString)
    output.Write(HtmlTextWriter.TagRightChar)
    output.WriteEndTag("Span")
End Sub

Protected Overrides Sub CreateChildControls()
    Me.MakeMonthList()
    Me.MakeDayList()
    Me.MakeYearList()
    Controls.Clear()
    Controls.Add(ddlMonth)
    Controls.Add(New LiteralControl(" "))
    Controls.Add(ddlDay)
    Controls.Add(New LiteralControl(", "))
    Controls.Add(ddlYear)
End Sub

Private Sub MakeMonthList()
    ddlMonth.Width = Unit.Pixel(85)
    ddlMonth.Items.Clear()
    ddlMonth.Items.Add("January")
    ddlMonth.Items.Add("February")
    ddlMonth.Items.Add("March")
    ddlMonth.Items.Add("April")
    ddlMonth.Items.Add("May")
    ddlMonth.Items.Add("June")
    ddlMonth.Items.Add("July")
    ddlMonth.Items.Add("August")
    ddlMonth.Items.Add("September")
    ddlMonth.Items.Add("October")
    ddlMonth.Items.Add("November")
    ddlMonth.Items.Add("December")
    ddlMonth.SelectedIndex = Me.Month - 1
    ddlMonth.AutoPostBack = bAutoPostBack
End Sub
```

Figure 17-20   The code for the DateDDL control (part 4 of 5)

The Visual Basic code for the DateDDL control   Page 5

```
Private Sub MakeDayList()
    ddlDay.Width = Unit.Pixel(40)
    ddlDay.Items.Clear()
    Dim i As Integer
    For i = 1 To 31
        ddlDay.Items.Add(i)
    Next
    ddlDay.SelectedValue = Me.Day
    ddlYear.AutoPostBack = bAutoPostBack
End Sub

Private Sub MakeYearList()
    ddlYear.Width = Unit.Pixel(65)
    ddlYear.Items.Clear()
    Dim i As Integer
    For i = Now().Year To Now().Year + 10
        ddlYear.Items.Add(i)
    Next
    ddlYear.SelectedValue = Me.Year
    ddlYear.AutoPostBack = bAutoPostBack
End Sub


Private Sub ddlMonth_SelectedIndexChanged(ByVal sender As Object, _
        ByVal e As System.EventArgs) Handles ddlMonth.SelectedIndexChanged
    Me.Month = ddlMonth.SelectedIndex + 1
    Me.AdjustDay()
End Sub

Private Sub ddlDay_SelectedIndexChanged(ByVal sender As Object, _
        ByVal e As System.EventArgs) Handles ddlDay.SelectedIndexChanged
    Me.Day = ddlDay.SelectedValue
    Me.AdjustDay()
End Sub

Private Sub ddlYear_SelectedIndexChanged(ByVal sender As Object, _
        ByVal e As System.EventArgs) Handles ddlYear.SelectedIndexChanged
    Me.Year = ddlYear.SelectedValue
    Me.AdjustDay()
End Sub

Private Sub AdjustDay()
    Select Case Me.Month
        Case 4, 6, 9, 11
            If Me.Day = 31 Then Me.Day = 30
        Case 2
            If Me.Mod 4 = 0 Then
                If Me.Day > 29 Then Me.Day = 29
            Else
                If Me.Day > 28 Then Me.Day = 28
            End If
    End Select
End Sub

End Class
```

Figure 17-20   The code for the DateDDL control (part 5 of 5)

Perspective

In this chapter, you've learned the basics of creating custom server controls that you can use in your ASP.NET web applications. You should realize, however, that there's a lot more to developing custom controls than what's presented in this chapter. For example, this chapter didn't show you how to bind data to custom controls, how to enable view state for custom controls, or how to create templated controls that work like the DataList or DataGrid controls. Nevertheless, the programming techniques you've learned in this chapter should give you a good start toward developing your own custom server controls.

Terms

custom server control
web control library
rendered control
superclassed control
composite control
child control
designer attribute
escaped identifier
self-closing tag
class attribute
property attribute

18

How to use
Crystal Reports
in a web application

Crystal Reports is a report-preparation program that's included as part of the
Visual Studio development environment. You can use it to retrieve data from a
database and create a report from that data. Then, you can use a web control to
display the report on a web page. This is a powerful feature for enhancing a
web application.

If you have the Standard Edition of Visual Basic .NET, you should know
that Crystal Reports isn't available to you. Even so, you may want to read
this chapter to get an idea of the functionality it provides.

An introduction to Crystal Reports

Before you learn how to create a Crystal report, you need to be familiar with the elements that make up a report and the two models you can use to provide data to a report. That's what you'll learn in the two topics that follow.

The three elements of a Crystal report

Figure 18-1 presents a Visual Basic application that contains a Crystal report. This report is made up of three elements. The *Crystal Report file* is a typed component that contains the definition of the report. The *Crystal Report Viewer control* provides the area where the report is displayed. And the *data source* provides the data that's displayed in the report. As you go through this chapter, you'll learn how to work with all three of these elements.

The two models for providing data to a report

Figure 18-1 also describes two ways you can provide the data for a Crystal report. The easier way is to "pull" it directly from a database. When you use the *pull model*, all of the information that's needed to connect to the database and retrieve the data is stored in the report file. In addition, Crystal Reports handles all of the data access for you, so no program code is required. To access the database, Crystal Reports uses the OLE DB or ODBC driver that you specify.

In contrast, when you use the *push model*, you specify a data source like an ADO.NET dataset. Then, the application is responsible for filling the dataset with data retrieved from the database. In other words, the application first retrieves the data, then "pushes" it into the report.

Because the pull model is the easier one to use, this chapter focuses on it. However, the basic techniques for creating a report are the same regardless of how the data is provided. As a result, you shouldn't have any trouble using the push model if that's what you need to do.

An application with a report created using Crystal Reports

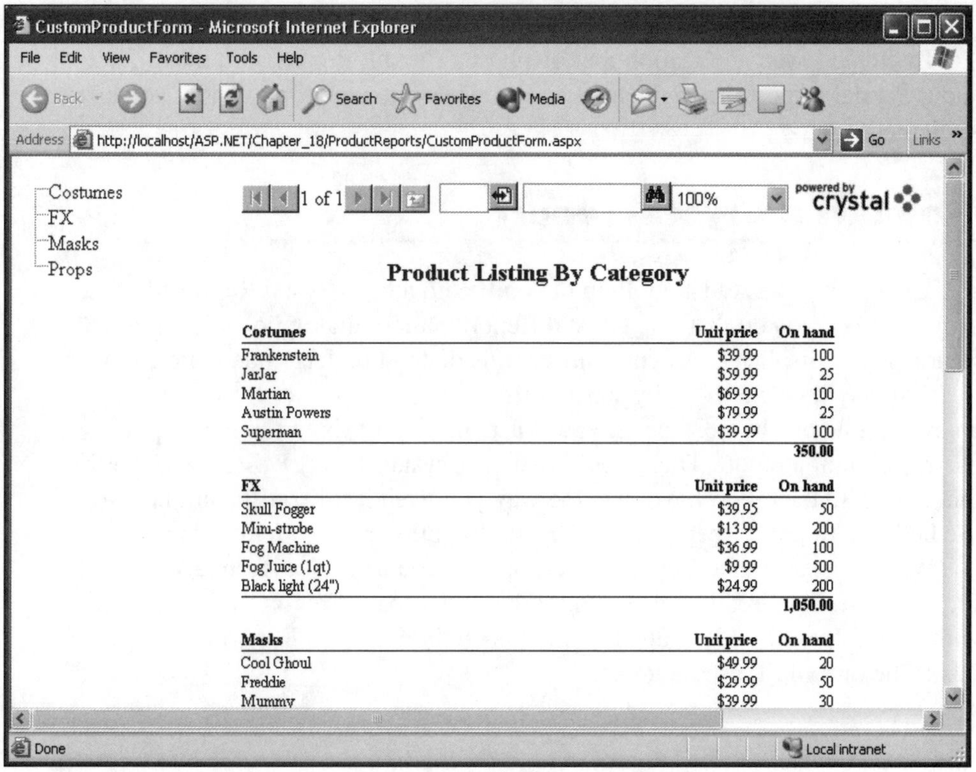

Three components of a Crystal Reports application

- A *Crystal Report file* provides the format of the report to be created.
- A *Crystal Report Viewer control* allows the user to view a report on a web page.
- A *data source* provides the data used to generate the report. The data source can be a database, an ADO.NET dataset, or some other type of file.

Two models for providing data to a report

- In the *pull model*, data is retrieved directly from the database. In this case, information about connecting to the database and the data to be retrieved is stored in the report file, and the database access is handled automatically by Crystal Reports.
- In the *push model*, the report uses a dataset as its data source. Then, the application is responsible for retrieving the data into the dataset.

Description

- Crystal Reports is a report writing tool that has been integrated into the Visual Studio environment.

Figure 18-1   An introduction to Crystal Reports

How to create a Crystal Report file

To create a web application that displays a Crystal Report, you must first add a Crystal Report file to the application. The following topics show you how to do that.

How to start a Crystal report

You can use the Add New Item dialog box to add a Crystal Report file to a project. When you do that, the Crystal Report Gallery dialog box shown in figure 18-2 is displayed. As you can see, this dialog box lets you create a report by using the *Report Expert*, by starting from a blank report, or by starting from an existing report. In most cases, you'll use the Report Expert to develop the basic design of a report. Then, you'll use the Crystal Report Designer to modify that design so the report looks just the way you want it to. You'll learn how to use both the Report Expert and the Crystal Report Designer in this chapter.

When you select the Report Expert option, you can select from a variety of Experts. The table in this figure summarizes the types of reports you can create with each Expert. In this chapter, I'll focus on the Standard Report Expert since this is the one you'll use the most.

The Crystal Report Gallery dialog box

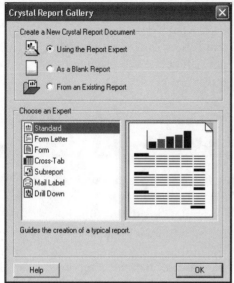

The Report Experts

Expert	Description
Standard	Creates a report with both detail and summary lines.
Form Letter	Creates a letter that combines text and data.
Form	Creates a report for use with preprinted forms.
Cross-Tab	Creates a report that cross-tabulates data.
Subreport	Creates a report with a subreport.
Mail Label	Creates mailing labels or other reports that require multiple columns.
Drill Down	Creates a report that lets you hide or display the details of summarized data.

Description

- To add a new Crystal Report file to a project, Select Project→Add New Item to display the Add New Item dialog box. Then, select the Crystal Report template, enter a name for the file, and click Open to display the Crystal Report Gallery dialog box.

- To use a *Report Expert*, select the Using the Report Expert option and then select the Expert you want to use.

- To start a new report based on an existing report, select the From an Existing Report option and use the resulting dialog box to choose the file for the existing report.

- To start a custom report, select the As a Blank Report option. This opens an unformatted report with placeholders for the most basic report information.

- You can also add an existing report file to a project by selecting Project→Add Existing Item and then locating and selecting the file.

Figure 18-2   How to start a Crystal report

How to use the Standard Report Expert

After you select the Report Expert you want to use, a tabbed dialog box appears to help you design your report. The topics that follow show you how to use the tabs for the Standard Report Expert. The report I'll create is a Product Listing report that lists all the products in the Products table, grouped by category.

How to select the data source for a report

The first tab of the Standard Report Expert lets you select the data source for the report. To use the pull model, expand the OLE DB (ADO) or ODBC (RDO) node in the Available Data Sources list, then complete the dialog boxes to select the database server, database, and tables you want to include in the report.

In contrast, if you're going to use a dataset as the source of data for a report, you must create that dataset before you create the report using the Report Expert. To create a Product Listing report, for example, you need to create a dataset that contains the data from the Products and Categories tables that will be used by the report. Once that's done, you can select the dataset tables you want to use in the Data tab of the Standard Report Expert dialog box.

Note, however, that the dataset you use with a Report Expert must be a *typed dataset*. Unlike the untyped datasets you've worked with in this book, a typed dataset is created from a custom dataset class that defines the schema of the dataset. That way, the Report Expert can display the tables and columns in the dataset so you can choose the ones you want to use in the report. If you want to learn more about how to create and use typed datasets, please refer to *Murach's VB.NET Database Programming with ADO.NET*.

The Data tab of the Standard Report Expert

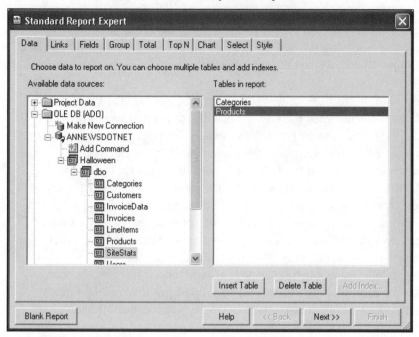

Description

- The Data tab of the Standard Report Expert lets you select the data source for the report.

- To use the pull model, click on the plus sign to the left of the OLE DB (ADO) or ODBC (RDO) folder and respond to the dialog boxes that are displayed to choose a driver and create a database connection. Then, expand the nodes for the database to display its tables and insert the tables you want to use.

- To use the push model with an ADO.NET dataset, expand the Project Data node, the ADO.NET DataSets node, and the dataset node you want to use. Then, select each table you want to use and click on the Insert Table button.

Notes

- When you use the pull model, the Report Expert uses either ADO or RDO as the data access method. These access methods were two of the predecessors to ADO.NET. You don't need to know anything about them, though, because the Report Expert does all of the data access for you.

- To use the push model with ADO.NET, you have to create a *typed dataset*. A typed dataset is created from a custom dataset class that defines the schema of the dataset.

Figure 18-3   How to select the data source for a report

How to complete the Standard Report Expert

Once you've selected the data source for the report, the remaining tabs of the Standard Report Expert dialog box let you specify the content, layout, and format of the report. Figure 18-4 describes the information you can complete on each of these tabs.

If you selected more than one table for a report, you can use the Links tab to specify the relationships between the tables. Usually, the Expert can figure out these relationships, so links are automatically created. However, you may need to add additional links for the relationships the Expert can't figure out.

The Fields tab lets you select the fields you want to appear on the report. The order in which the selected fields are listed on this tab will determine the order in which the fields appear in the report, so you should make sure the fields are listed in the proper sequence. The Fields tab includes controls that let you adjust the field sequence if necessary. The Fields tab also includes a Formula button that lets you create new fields that display the results of calculations.

The Group tab lets you create a report that groups related lines based on a Group By field. For example, the Product Listing report groups Product lines by the category name field. This tab also lets you specify a sort order for each group.

The Total tab lets you include summary totals for numeric data. You can use this tab to compute group totals as well as grand totals. By default, totals are calculated as simple sums. However, Crystal Reports provides other types of summary functions, including counts, averages, minimums, and maximums.

If a report is grouped by one or more fields and includes summary data for one or more fields, you can use the Top N tab of the Expert to sort the groups by the summary fields. For example, you can set up the Product Listing report to show those categories that have the greatest number of products first. Or, you can show the categories that have the most total on-hand units first.

The Chart tab lets you add a chart to a report. With this tab, you can create various types of charts, including bar charts, line charts, area charts, and pie charts.

The Select tab lets you filter the data that's included in the report by creating conditional expressions based on fields in the report or the data source. For example, you can set up the Product Listing report to show only those products whose quantity on-hand is zero.

The Style tab lets you add a title to the report and choose a style for the report. Once you've selected a report style, you can click the Finish button to end the Expert. Then, as you'll learn later in this chapter, you can use the Crystal Report Designer to modify the report so it looks just the way you want it to.

Although this has been a whirlwind trip through the nine tabs of the Standard Report Expert, you should be able to figure out how to use them if you take an hour or two to experiment with them. If you have our ADO.NET book, you can also refer to the Crystal Reports chapter for a more detailed visit to each of the tabs. Either way, though, you're going to need to experiment before you get comfortable with the Report Experts.

The Fields tab of the Standard Report Expert dialog box

The tabs of the Standard Report Expert

Tab	Description
Data	Specifies the data source for the report as described in figure 18-3.
Links	Creates relationships between tables. The Expert creates links automatically if it finds columns with the same name in two tables. You can also create links manually by dragging from one table to another.
Fields	Specifies the fields that are included in the report and the column heading used for each field. You can also create calculated fields based on formulas.
Group	Groups the rows of the report by one or more fields and specifies the sort order for each group.
Total	Specifies column totals that will appear in the report. By default, all numeric fields are totaled.
Top N	Specifies the sort order for each group as well as the top or bottom number or percent of each group that you want sorted. This overrides the sorting specified by the Group tab.
Chart	Adds a chart to the report.
Select	Filters the rows that appear in the report based on one or more fields.
Style	Specifies one of several predefined report styles, along with the report title.

Description

- The Standard Report Expert steps you through a series of tabs that let you specify the content and layout of the report.
- After you complete the information on each tab, you can click the Next button to advance to the next tab. Or, you can click the Back button to return to the previous tab.
- When you've completed all of the tabs for the report, click Finish.

Figure 18-4   How to complete the Standard Report Expert

How to use the Crystal Report Viewer control

To display a report in a Visual Basic application, you add a Crystal Report Viewer control to a form and bind the control to the report. Then, you can use the controls that are built into the viewer control to work with the report. You can also customize the viewer control so it provides just the features you want, and you can work with it in code.

How to bind a viewer control to a report

Figure 18-5 shows a viewer control after it's added to a web form. As you can see, the viewer resembles a user control in that it doesn't show the report's appearance in the designer. To see how the report appears, you have to build and run the application.

After you add a viewer control to a form, you have to specify the report that it will display. The technique you use to do that depends on whether you're using the push or the pull model. The examples in this figure show you how to use both of these models.

To use the push model, you start by creating an instance of the report. Then, you fill the dataset with the data that's used by the report, and you use the SetDataSource method of the report to bind the report to that dataset. Finally, you set the ReportSource property of the Crystal Report Viewer control to the report.

The coding is similar for the pull model, except that you don't have to fill the dataset because Crystal Reports will obtain the data directly from the database. Also, you don't have to use the SetDataSource method because the data source is specified in the report itself. So all you have to do is create an instance of the report class, then assign the report object to the viewer's ReportSource property.

A web form with a Crystal Report Viewer control

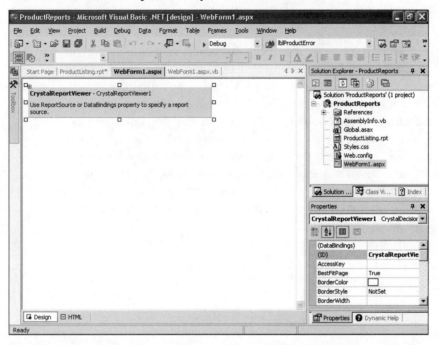

Code that binds a viewer control to a report that pushes data

```
Private Sub Page_Load(ByVal sender As System.Object, _
        ByVal e As System.EventArgs) Handles MyBase.Load
    Dim rpt As New ProductListing
    daProducts.Fill(dsProducts)
    rpt.SetDataSource(dsProducts)
    CrystalReportViewer1.ReportSource = rpt
End Sub
```

Code that binds a viewer control to a report that pulls data

```
Private Sub Page_Load(ByVal sender As System.Object, _
        ByVal e As System.EventArgs) Handles MyBase.Load
    Dim rpt As New ProductListing
    CrystalReportViewer1.ReportSource = rpt
End Sub
```

Description

- To add a Crystal Report Viewer control to a web form, drag it from the Web Forms tab of the Toolbox.

- If the data source is an ADO.NET dataset, you must fill the dataset and create an instance of the report class. Then, you use the SetDataSource method of the report to set its data source to the dataset, and you set the ReportSource property of the viewer to the report object.

- To bind a viewer control to a report that pulls data, create an instance of the report class, then set the viewer's ReportSource property to the report object.

Figure 18-5   How to bind a viewer control to a report

How to work with a report viewer using its built-in controls

Figure 18-6 shows how a report appears in a report viewer control at runtime. Here, the Product Listing report that's created by the Standard Report Expert is displayed along with some controls for working with the report.

If the report includes group fields, you can move directly to a group by clicking on that group in the *Group tree*. The Product Listing report, for example, is grouped by category, so the categories are listed in the Group tree. Then, you can click on a category to display the products for that category.

The report viewer also provides a variety of other tools that you can use to work with a report. For example, you can use the Zoom button to change the magnification of the report. And you can use the Search button to search for the text you specify within the report. If you experiment with these buttons, you shouldn't have any trouble figuring out how they work.

The report viewer with the Product Listing report displayed

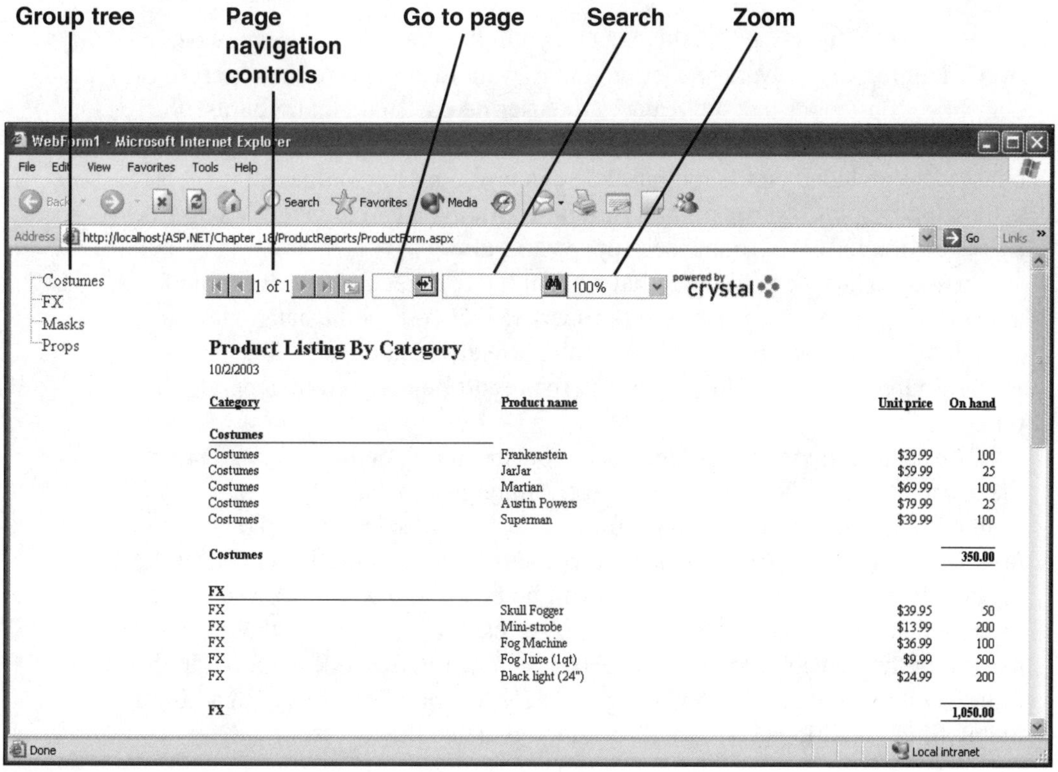

Description

- After you bind a report viewer to a report, you can build and run the application to display the report in the viewer as shown above.

- If a report includes grouping, the grouping fields are displayed in the *Group tree* at the left side of the viewer. To navigate to a particular group, click on it in the Group tree.

- To view the details for a single group, click the group name in the report. To return to the full report, click the Up button on the right side of the Page Navigation controls.

- To navigate through the pages of a report, use the Page Navigation controls.

- You can use the other toolbar buttons to go to a specific page, search for text, or zoom in or out.

Note

- The report shown in this figure is different from the report in figure 18-1 because this report has not yet been modified from its default appearance. In figures 18-9 through 18-12, you'll learn how to use the Report Designer to customize the appearance of a report.

Figure 18-6   How to work with a report viewer using its built-in controls

How to customize a report viewer

Because an interface like the one shown in the previous figure may be overwhelming to the average user, you may want to customize the report viewer control so it provides just the features the user needs. To do that, you use the properties listed in figure 18-7. Most of these properties determine which buttons are included on the toolbar. You can also omit the toolbar altogether by setting the DisplayToolbar property to False. And you can hide the Group tree by setting the DisplayGroupTree property to False.

In addition to the properties that control the features that are available from a report viewer control, you can set properties that control the data that's included in the report. For instance, you're already familiar with the ReportSource property, which specifies the report object used to generate the report.

The SelectionFormula property lets you specify a conditional expression that's used to filter the data in the report. Although you can set this property at design time, it's typically set at runtime to respond to selections made by the user. For example, suppose the form that contains the report viewer for the Product Listing report also contains a combo box that lets the user select a specific category. Then, the report could list just the products for that category by setting the SelectionFormula property as shown in the code example in this figure. Note that the condition you specify for this property is used in addition to any filter conditions you specify when you create the report.

Common properties of a report viewer

Property	Description
DisplayGroupTree	Determines whether the Group tree is displayed.
DisplayToolbar	Determines whether the toolbar is displayed.
HasGotoButton	Determines whether the Goto Page button is included on the toolbar.
HasPageNavigationButtons	Determines whether the page navigation buttons are included on the toolbar.
HasRefreshButton	Determines whether the Refresh button is included on the toolbar.
HasSearchButton	Determines whether the Search button is included on the toolbar.
HasZoomFactorList	Determines whether the Zoom control is included on the toolbar.
PageToTreeRatio	Species the size of the Group tree to the size of the report area. The default is 3, which means that the report area is three times larger than the Group tree.
ReportSource	The report to be displayed in the viewer. You typically set this property at runtime as shown in figure 18-5.
SelectionFormula	A formula that's used to filter the rows in the report. This formula is used in addition to any filter conditions you specify within the report.

Code that changes the selection formula

```
Private Sub ddlCategories_SelectedIndexChanged( _
        ByVal sender As System.Object, ByVal e As System.EventArgs) _
        Handles ddlCategories.SelectedIndexChanged
    CrystalReportViewer1.SelectionFormula = _
        "{Categories.ShortName} = '" & ddlCategories.SelectedValue & "'"
End Sub
```

Description

- You can set any of the properties shown above except for the last three to either True or False to indicate whether the associated feature is available.

- Although you can set the SelectionFormula property at design time, it's more common to set it at runtime based on selections made by the user. Any report fields referred to within the selection formula must be enclosed in braces as shown above.

Figure 18-7   How to customize a report viewer

How to work with a report viewer using its methods

If you customize a report viewer control by hiding the toolbar or removing toolbar buttons, you can add your own controls and code to provide for the functions the user needs. That way, you can design the user interface so it's consistent with other applications. To work with a report viewer in code, you use the methods listed in figure 18-8.

To let the user move from one page of a report to another, for example, you can add your own navigation buttons along with code like that shown in this figure. As you can see, this code executes the ShowFirstPage, ShowPreviousPage, ShowNextPage, or ShowLastPage method depending on which button the user clicks. Similarly, you can add a Search button and then use the SearchForText method to search the report for a given text string.

Common methods of a report viewer

Method	Description
RefreshReport	Refreshes the data used by the report by requerying the data source.
SearchForText	Searches the report for the specified text and returns a Boolean value that indicates whether the text was found.
ShowFirstPage	Shows the first page of the report.
ShowLastPage	Shows the last page of the report.
ShowNextPage	Shows the next page of the report.
ShowNthPage	Shows the specified page of the report. If the page number you specify is beyond the end of the report, the last page is shown.
ShowPreviousPage	Shows the previous page of the report.
Zoom	Changes the magnification percent for the report. You can also specify a value of 1 on this method to display the entire width of the page, and you can specify a value of 2 to display the entire page.

A procedure that uses form buttons to provide for navigation

```
Private Sub btnFirst_Click(ByVal sender As System.Object, _
    ByVal e As System.EventArgs) Handles btnFirst.Click
        CrystalReportViewer1.ShowFirstPage()
End Sub

Private Sub btnPrev_Click(ByVal sender As System.Object, _
        ByVal e As System.EventArgs) Handles btnPrev.Click
    CrystalReportViewer1.ShowPreviousPage()
End Sub

Private Sub btnNext_Click(ByVal sender As System.Object, _
        ByVal e As System.EventArgs) Handles btnNext.Click
    CrystalReportViewer1.ShowNextPage()
End Sub

Private Sub btnLast_Click(ByVal sender As System.Object, _
        ByVal e As System.EventArgs) Handles btnLast.Click
    CrystalReportViewer1.ShowLastPage()
End Sub
```

Description

- If you hide the toolbar on a report viewer or you remove some of the toolbar buttons, you can use some of the methods of the report viewer to provide the same functionality.

Figure 18-8   How to work with a report viewer using its methods

How to use the Crystal Report Designer

After you create a report using a Report Expert, you'll usually need to modify it so it works the way you want it to. To modify a report, you use the *Crystal Report Designer*. You can also use the designer to create a report from scratch if you choose to do that.

An overview of the Crystal Report Designer

Figure 18-9 shows the Product Listing report that was created by using the Standard Report Expert as it appears in the Crystal Report Designer. As you can see, the Crystal Report Designer includes a *Field Explorer* window and a *Report Designer* window. The Field Explorer window lists all of the fields that are available to the report. Note that the fields that are already included in the report have a check mark next to them. To add a field to the report, you can simply drag it from the Field Explorer window to the Report Designer window. You can also add text, lines, and boxes to a report by using the components in the Crystal Reports tab of the Toolbox.

To modify the layout of a report, you work in the Report Designer window. From this window, you can move and size a field using the mouse, you can change the font and alignment of a field using the toolbar buttons, and you can apply special formatting using the Format Editor dialog box.

You can also format the sections of a report from this window. At the least, each report includes five sections: report header and report footer sections that appear at the beginning and end of the report; page header and page footer sections that appear at the top and bottom of each page; and a details section that contains the fields from the data source as well as other fields you've created for the report. In addition, a report includes a group header and a group footer section for each group you define. You'll learn more about working with these sections in the next figure.

To make other changes to a report, you can use the commands in the menu that's displayed when you right-click on any section or field in the report. For example, if you want to add additional tables or datasets to a report or change the links between the tables you've selected, you can use the Add/Remove Database command in the Database submenu. This displays a Database Expert dialog box with the Data and Links tabs. Similarly, you can use commands in the Report submenu to change the selection criteria, grouping, and sorting for a report. And you can use the commands in the Insert submenu to add groups, totals, special fields, and charts. You can also use the buttons in the toolbar to perform some of these functions. The best way to find out what's available is to spend some time experimenting.

The Product Listing report in the Crystal Report Designer

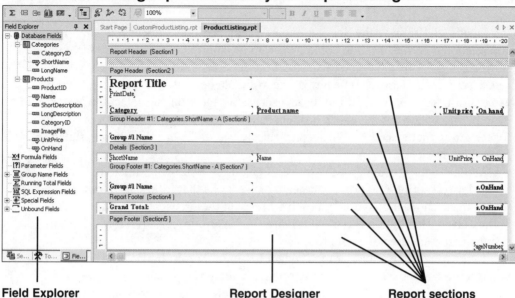

Field Explorer   **Report Designer**   **Report sections**

Description

- To modify the design of a report, you use the *Crystal Report Designer*. To open the designer for a report, double-click on the report file in the Solution Explorer.

- The Crystal Report Designer includes a *Field Explorer* that lists the fields that are available to the report; a *Report Designer* that you can use to work with the layout of a report; and toolbars that provide access to the most useful functions.

- Each report consists of five or more sections. The details section contains the data from each row in the data source, the report header and footer sections appear at the beginning and end of the report, and the page header and footer sections appear at the top and bottom of each page. Additional sections are included for each group you define.

- To add a field to a report, drag it from the Field Explorer to the Report Designer. The fields that are already included in the report have a check mark next to them in the Field Explorer. For more information on using the Field Explorer, see figure 18-11.

- To change the format of a report object, select it and use the toolbar buttons or right-click on it and select Format to display the Format Editor dialog box. You can also position and size an object using the mouse, and you can delete it by pressing the Delete key.

- To format the sections of a report, right-click in the Report Designer and select Format Section from the menu that's displayed. For details, see figure 18-10. You can also change the height of a section by dragging its bottom border.

- To change other aspects of a report, use the shortcut menu that's displayed when you right-click in the Report Designer.

- To add text, lines, and boxes, use the components in the Crystal Reports tab of the Toolbox.

- You can also design a new report that you create from scratch using these techniques.

Figure 18-9   An overview of the Crystal Report Designer

How to work with report sections

Figure 18-10 shows the Section Expert dialog box that's displayed when you select the Format Section command from the shortcut menu for any section. As you can see, this dialog box lists all of the sections in the report. Then, you can select a section and change any of the available options. For example, if you want to print each group of a report on a separate page, you can select the New Page Before option for the group header section or the New Page After option for the group footer section. This is particularly useful for printing on preprinted forms like invoices.

Another option you may want to use is Underlay Following Sections. This option lets you print a section underneath the sections that follow it. In other words, the sections are layered on each other, with the first section being the bottom layer. This option is particularly useful for printing group information on just the first detail line of each group.

To illustrate, take a look at the Product Listing report in figure 18-6. Here, you can see that the category name is printed in the group header for each group as well as in each detail line. Now, suppose you delete the category name from the detail section and select the Underlay Following Sections option for the group header section so that it will print beneath the detail section. Then, the category name will appear on the first detail line of each group along with the information for the first product. Of course, to get this to work right, you'll need to size the group header section just right and position and format the category name so it prints the way you want it too. If you experiment with this, however, I think you'll see how useful it can be.

The Section Expert

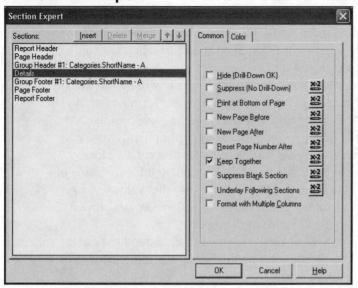

Options for formatting sections

Option	Description
Hide (Drill-Down OK)	Hides the section but makes it available for drill-down.
Suppress (No Drill-Down)	Suppresses printing of the section.
Print at Bottom of Page	The values for each group are only printed at the bottom of the page. This option is typically used with preprinted forms such as invoices where a single group prints on each page.
New Page Before	The section starts printing on a new page. Only available for a group section or the details section.
New Page After	The section that follows this section is printed on a new page.
Reset Page Number After	Resets the page number to 1 for the following page.
Keep Together	All lines for the section are kept together on the current page if they will fit or on multiple pages if they won't.
Suppress Blank Section	Suppresses printing of the section if it's blank.
Underlay Following Sections	The section is printed underneath the objects in the following sections.
Format with Multiple Columns	Displays the Layout Tab, which lets you format the report in multiple columns. This option is only available for the details section.
Reserve Minimum Page Footer	Minimizes the space that's reserved for the page footer section.

Description

- To format the sections of a report, you use the Section Expert. To display the Section Expert dialog box, right-click in the Report Designer and select Format Section.

Figure 18-10   How to work with report sections

How to work with fields in the Field Explorer

Figure 18-11 presents some information about working with fields in the Field Explorer. As you know, you can drag any field from this window to the Report Designer window to add the field to the report. You can also use the shortcut menus for field groups and individual fields to work with the fields as summarized in this figure. For example, you can create a new formula field by right-clicking on the Formula Fields group and selecting the New command.

In addition to the database fields, formula fields, and group fields you're already familiar with, you can also create parameter fields and running total fields. If you create a *parameter field*, the user will be prompted for the value of the parameter when the report is opened. Then, you can use that value within the report. For example, you might use it within the SelectionFormula property of the report to filter the data that's included in the report.

You can use a *running total field* to keep a running total of another field in the report. In this figure, for example, a running total field is being created to count the number of products for each category group.

The fields in the Special Fields group let you add common report information like page number and print date to a report. Note, however, that if you use a Report Expert to create a report, some of these fields may be added by default. When you use the Standard Report Expert, for example, a print date field is added below the report title and a page number field is added at the right side of the page footer.

The dialog box for creating a running total field

Toggle Field View

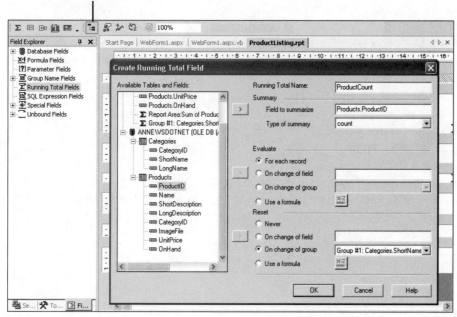

Field types

Type	Description
Database	Fields that are available from the database. You can add and remove fields and specify filter criteria using the Database Expert and the Select Expert.
Formula	Fields that are calculated from other fields in the report or database. You can create new fields and edit existing fields using the Formula Editor.
Parameter	Fields that prompt the user for values when the report is opened. You can create new fields and edit existing fields.
Group Name	Fields that are used for grouping in the report. You can add and delete groups and change grouping criteria using the Top N Expert and the Select Expert.
Running Total	Fields that are used to keep running totals of other fields in the report. You can create new fields and edit existing fields.
SQL Expression	Fields that query the database directly. You can create new fields and edit existing fields using the SQL Expression Editor. Only available with pulled data.
Special	Predefined fields such as print date and page number.
Unbound	Fields that contain expressions that aren't dependent on the data source.

Description

- You can use the Field Explorer to modify existing fields and to create new ones. To hide or show the Field Explorer, use the Toggle Field View toolbar button.
- To work with a field or field type, right-click on it and then select the appropriate item from the menu that's displayed.

Figure 18-11   How to work with fields in the Field Explorer

A custom Product Listing report

Figure 18-12 presents an improved version of the Product Listing report that I've customized using the Crystal Report Designer. If you compare this with the design in figure 18-6, you'll notice several differences.

To start, I sized, positioned, and formatted many of the fields so they appear just the way I want them to. In addition, I changed the height of some of the sections so that the lines are spaced out appropriately.

Next, I removed the category name from the details section of the report so that it doesn't print for every product for a category. Instead, I included the category name in the group header section. That way, the category name will be printed above each group.

You can see the result of these changes in the report shown in the report viewer in this figure. If you compare this report to the one back in figure 18-6, I think you'll see that the customized report has a more appealing format and is much easier to read.

The design of a custom Product Listing report

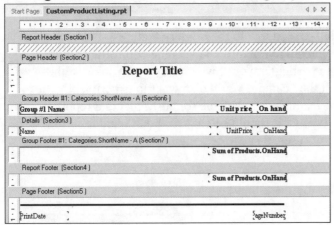

The report in a report viewer

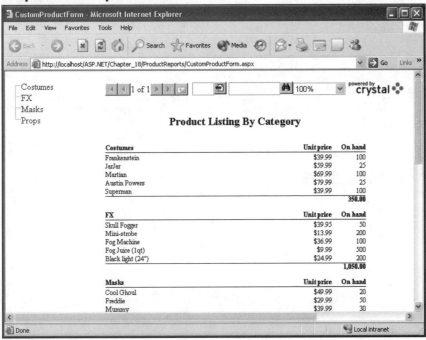

Figure 18-12   A custom Product Listing report

Changes made to customize this report

- The category name has been removed from the details and group footer sections of the report.

- The format of the On Hand total field has been changed to remove the unnecessary decimal positions.

- The heights of some of the sections have been changed and several of the fields have been sized, positioned, and formatted. In addition, lines have been added to clearly mark each group.

Perspective

Although this chapter has introduced you to the primary features of Crystal Reports, it will take some experimentation before you become comfortable with using it for generating reports. In particular, you'll want to try using some of the other Report Experts to see what they can do. You'll also want to experiment with the Report Designer to see what features are available for customizing a report.

Once you've mastered the Experts, it should be easy for you to add reporting to your web applications. In many cases, that can be a significant enhancement to your web applications.

Terms

Crystal Report file
Crystal Report Viewer control
data source
pull model
push model
Report Expert
typed dataset
Group tree
Crystal Report Designer
Field Explorer
Report Designer
parameter field
running total field

19

How to use email, custom error pages, and back-button control

Once you've got an application working the way it's supposed to, you can add enhancements that make it work even better. In this chapter, you'll learn how to add three of the most useful enhancements. First, you'll learn how to send email from an ASP.NET application. Then, you'll learn how to create and use custom error pages. And last, you'll learn how to handle the problems that can occur when the user uses the Back button to access a page that has already been posted.

How to send email

When you create a web application, you often need to send email messages from the application. For instance, when a user makes a purchase from an e-commerce site, a web application usually sends an email to the customer that confirms the order. Or, if a serious error occurs, the web application often sends an email message to the support staff that documents the error. In the topics that follow, you'll learn how to send email from your ASP.NET applications.

An introduction to email

You're probably familiar with *mail client* software such as Microsoft Outlook or Outlook Express that allows you to send and retrieve email messages. This type of software communicates with a *mail server* that actually sends and retrieves your email messages. Most likely, your mail server software is provided by your Internet Service Provider (ISP) or through your company.

The diagram in figure 19-1 shows how this works. The two protocols that are commonly used to send and retrieve email messages are *SMTP* and *POP*. When you send an email message, the message is first sent from the mail client software on your computer to your mail server using the SMTP protocol. Then, your mail server uses SMTP to send the mail to the recipient's mail server. Finally, the recipient's mail client uses the POP protocol to retrieve the mail from the recipient's mail server.

A third protocol you should know about is *MIME*, which stands for *Multipurpose Internet Message Extension*. Unlike SMTP or POP, MIME isn't used to transfer email messages. Instead, it defines how the content of an email message and its attachments are formatted. In this chapter, you'll learn how to send messages that consist of simple text as well as messages that use HTML format.

How email works

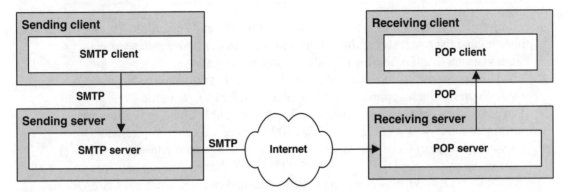

Three email protocols

Protocol	Description
SMTP	*Simple Mail Transfer Protocol* is used to send a message from one mail server to another.
POP	*Post Office Protocol* is used by mail clients to retrieve messages from mail servers. Currently, POP is in version 3 and is known as POP3.
MIME	The *Multipurpose Internet Message Extension* specifies the type of content that can be sent as a message or attachment.

Three common reasons for sending email from an ASP.NET application

- **To confirm receipt of an order.** When the user completes an order, the application can email a confirmation of the order to the user.
- **To remind a registered user of a forgotten password.** If the user forgets his or her password, the application can email the password to the email address that's on file for the user.
- **To notify support personnel of a problem.** If a problem like an unhandled exception occurs, the application can email a message that summarizes the problem to the appropriate support person.

Description

- When an email message is sent, it goes from the sender's *mail client* to the sender's *mail server* to the receiver's mail server to the receiver's mail client.
- *SMTP* and *POP* are the protocols that are commonly used for sending and retrieving email messages. *MIME* is the protocol for defining the format of an email message.

Figure 19-1   An introduction to email

How to configure the SMTP service in IIS

Before you can test an ASP.NET application that sends email messages, you must enable the email server that's built into IIS and configure it to send mail from your application. Figure 19-2 shows how to do that.

The first step is to start the SMTP service. You do that from the IIS management console, which you can reach in Windows XP by opening the Control Panel, and then opening Administrative Tools and double-clicking the Internet Information Services icon. (In Windows 2000, this icon is named Internet Services Manager.) Once you've opened the IIS management console, you can expand the tree to display the Default SMTP Virtual Server node. Then, you can start the SMTP service by selecting it in the tree and clicking the Start button in the toolbar.

Once you've started the SMTP service, you must configure it so that it allows your ASP.NET applications to send mail. To do that, you enable relaying for the local computer. This allows the mail server to accept mail from a specified computer and deliver it to the intended recipient. To configure the SMTP service to relay mail from the local computer, open the Relay Restrictions dialog box as described in this figure and add the localhost address (127.0.0.1) to the list of computers that the SMTP server will relay mail for.

How to make sure SMTP is running on your local server

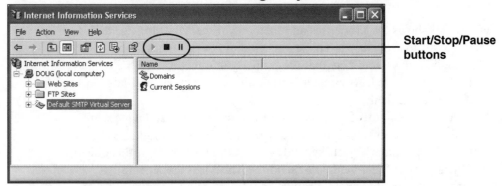

Start/Stop/Pause buttons

1. Open the Control Panel, double-click Administrative Tools, then double-click Internet Information Services (Windows XP) to open the IIS management console shown above.

2. Expand the tree to display your local computer's IIS server and the services running under it.

3. Select the Default SMTP Virtual Server service.

4. If the SMTP service is *not* running, the Stop button (■) will be disabled. In that case, click the Start button (▶) to start the SMTP service.

How to allow relaying for the local host

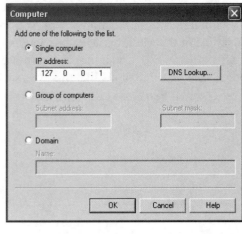

1. In the IIS management console, right-click the Default SMTP Virtual Server and choose the Properties command.

2. Click the Access tab, then click the Relay button. This displays the Relay Restrictions dialog box shown above.

3. Click the Add button to display the Computer dialog box shown above. Then, select Single Computer, type 127.0.0.1 into the IP address field, click OK to close the Computer dialog box, and click OK again to close the Relay Restrictions dialog box.

Figure 19-2   How to configure the SMTP service in IIS

How to send an email message

Figure 19-3 shows the properties and methods of the MailMessage and SmtpMail classes that you use to create and send email messages from ASP.NET applications. Note here that the property and methods of the SmtpMail class are shared. As a result, you don't have to create an SmtpMail object before you use them.

The first example in this figure shows how to create and send a message when you use the first format of the Send method of the SmtpMail class. First, you create a MailMessage object. Second, you set the properties of this object. And third, you use the Send method to send the MailMessage object.

In contrast, the second example shows how to create and send a message when you use the second format of the Send method. In this case, you just pass the four properties of a MailMessage object to the Send method. Then, the Send method creates the MailMessage object and sends it. You can use this format of the Send method if the message is in simple text format, you don't need to send copies of the message to anyone, and you don't need to send attachments with the message.

If you are using the SMTP service that's built into IIS to send the mail, you should set the SmtpServer property of the SendMail class to "localhost" before you send mail. This is illustrated by both examples. If you want to use a different mail server, though, you should set the SmtpServer property to the domain name of the server you want to use, like mail.myserver.com.

Although it's not illustrated here, you should note that the To, Cc, and Bcc properties of the MailMessage class let you send a message to one or more email addresses. To send a message to more than one address, just separate the addresses with semicolons like this:

```
msg.To = "doug@murach.com;anne@murach.com"
```

Common properties of the MailMessage class

Property	Description
From	The email address of the message sender.
To	The email address or addresses of one or more recipients.
Cc	The email address or addresses of one or more copy recipients.
Bcc	The email address or addresses of one or more blind copy recipients.
Subject	The subject line for the message.
Body	The body of the message.
BodyFormat	The format of the message body. The default is MailFormat.Text for a body that contains just text, but you can use MailFormat.HTML if the body contains HTML.
Attachments	A collection of MailAttachment objects.

Shared property and methods of the SmtpMail class

Property	Description
SmtpServer	The domain name of the SMTP server that will be used to send the message. If you use the default server that's built into IIS, this property should be set to "localhost."

Method	Description
Send(message)	Sends the specified email message.
Send(from, to, subject, body)	Creates and sends an email message using the specified From, To, Subject, and Body text.

A Sub procedure that sends an email message

```
Private Sub SendTextMessage(FromAddress As String, ToAddress As String, _
        Subject As String, Body As String)
    Dim msg As New MailMessage
    msg.From = FromAddress
    msg.To = ToAddress
    msg.Subject = Subject
    msg.Body = Text
    SmtpMail.SmtpServer = "localhost"
    SmtpMail.Send(msg)
End Sub
```

A Sub procedure that uses the second format of the Send method

```
Private Sub SendTextMessage(FromAddress As String, ToAddress As String, _
        Subject As String, Body As String)
    SmtpMail.SmtpServer = "localhost"
    SmtpMail.Send(FromAddress, ToAddress, Subject, Body)
End Sub
```

Description

- To send an email message, you use the properties and methods of the MailMessage and SmtpMail classes that are in the System.Web.Mail namespace.

- When you use the first format of the Send method of the SmtpMail class, you must first create a MailMessage object and set its properties. When you use the second format, the Send method both creates and sends the MailMessage object.

Figure 19-3   How to send an email message

How to add an attachment to an email message

An *attachment* is a file that's sent along with an email message. The most common types of attachments are text files, word processing documents, spreadsheets, pictures, and other media files such as sound and video files.

Figure 19-4 shows how you can create an attachment and add it to an email message. After you create an attachment object using the MailAttachment class, you add the object to the mail message's Attachments collection. Then, you can send the message.

Since the SMTP protocol is designed to send text messages, not binary files, any email attachment for a binary file must be converted to text format before it can be sent. Then, the text attachment must be converted back to a binary file when it's received. The most common format for converting attached binary files to text and back to binary files again is called *UUEncode*, and it's used by default. The other available format for converting binary files is called *Base64*. Since you shouldn't need to use this format, I haven't shown you how to create an attachment that uses it here.

The syntax for creating an attachment

```
New MailAttachment(filename)
```

One way to create a new attachment and add it to a message

```
Dim sFileName As String
sFileName = "C:\HalloweenStore\Attachments\ReturnPolicy.doc"
Dim ma As New MailAttachment(sFileName)
Dim msg As New MailMessage
msg.Attachments.Add(ma)
```

Another way to create a new attachment and add it to a message

```
Dim sFileName As String
sFileName = "C:\HalloweenStore\Attachments\ReturnPolicy.doc"
msg.Attachments.Add(New MailAttachment(sFileName))
```

Description

- An *attachment* is a file that is sent along with an email message. When the recipient receives the email message, he or she can open or save the attachment.

- To add an attachment to an email message, you create the attachment using the MailAttachment class. Then, you add the attachment to the message using the Add method of the Attachments collection of the MailMessage class.

- If an email attachment contains a binary file, it must be converted to text before it can be sent, and it must be converted back to binary when it's received. By default, binary files are converted to a format called *UUEncode*. However, you can also use a format called *Base64*.

Figure 19-4   How to add an attachment to an email message

How to send an HTML message

By default, email messages consist of plain text with no formatting. However, you can create a formatted message by using HTML as the MIME type, as described in figure 19-5. When you set the BodyFormat property of the MailMessage object to MailFormat.Html, you can use HTML formatting tags in the body of the message.

The example in this figure calls a private function named ConfirmationMessage to format the HTML for the body of an order confirmation message. This function uses basic HTML formatting tags to create a message that includes an image and some text. Note that if you refer to an image in the body by including an <img> tag, you must include the image file as an attachment as shown here. Otherwise, the recipient won't be able to see the image.

How an HTML message appears in an email client

A procedure that creates and sends a simple HTML message

```
Private Sub SendConfirmation()
    Dim msg As New MailMessage
    msg.From = "Doug@Murach.com"
    msg.To = sEmail
    msg.Subject = "Order Confirmation"
    msg.Body = Me.ConfirmationMessage()
    msg.BodyFormat = MailFormat.Html
    Dim sFile As String = "C:\Inetpub\wwwroot\HalloweenStore\images\banner.jpg"
    msg.Attachments.Add(New MailAttachment(sFile))
    SmtpMail.SmtpServer = "localhost"
    SmtpMail.Send(msg)
End Sub

Private Function ConfirmationMessage() As String
    Dim sName As String = HalloweenDB.GetCustomerName(sEmail)
    Dim sMsg As String
    sMsg = "<HTML><head><title>Order confirmation</title></head>" _
        & "<body><img src='banner.jpg' /><BR><BR>" _
        & "<h3>Thanks for your order, " & sName & "!</h3>" _
        & "Your order total is " & FormatCurrency(Invoice.Total) & "." _
        & "</body></HTML>"
    Return sMsg
End Function
```

Description

- HTML format lets you use all the HTML formatting that's available for web applications in your email. All modern email client programs can send and receive mail messages in HTML format.

- To send an email message in HTML format, set the BodyFormat property to MailFormat.Html. Then, you can use HTML in the message that you assign to the Body property.

- An HTML email message can include links to your web site. However, you should avoid sending HTML that includes scripts or web form controls. Many mail servers will reject them because they might be malicious.

- If the HTML includes <img> tags, you should include the image files as attachments. Otherwise, the user won't be able to see the images when he or she views your mail.

Figure 19-5   How to send an HTML message

How to use custom error handling

When an error occurs in an ASP.NET application, an exception is thrown. Then, if the exception isn't handled by the application, an ASP.NET Server Error page is displayed. This page includes an error message, a portion of the source code that threw the unhandled exception, and other debugging information. Since this type of error page usually isn't appropriate for the users of an application, you usually need to replace the generic error pages with your own custom error pages.

An introduction to custom error handling

Figure 19-6 describes four techniques you can use to display your own custom error pages. Depending on the needs of your application, you may need to use one or more of these techniques.

The first technique is to enclose code that might generate exceptions in a Try...Catch block. Then, you can redirect to a custom error page if an exception does occur.

The second technique is to code a Page_Error procedure in the code-behind file for a page. This procedure is called whenever an unhandled exception occurs on a page. Then, in the Page_Error procedure, you redirect the user to a custom error page.

The third technique is to code an Application_Error procedure in the Global.asax file. This procedure is called whenever an unhandled exception occurs on a page that doesn't have a Page_Error procedure. Then, the Application_Error procedure can redirect the user to a custom error page.

The fourth technique is to use the <customErrors> element in the Web.config file to designate custom error pages. This technique is used to display custom error pages when common HTTP errors such as a 404 – Not Found error occur.

A custom error page in a browser

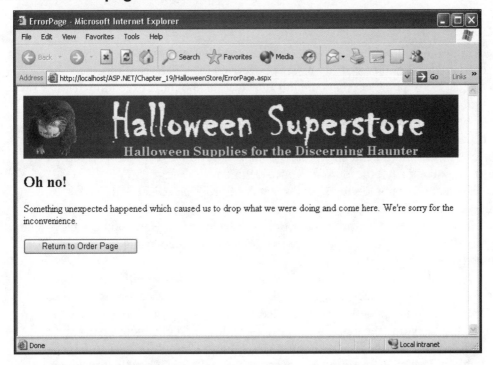

Four ways to display a custom error page when an exception occurs

- Use Try...Catch statements to catch exceptions as they occur, then redirect or transfer to a custom error page.
- Use the Page_Error procedure in a code-behind file to catch unhandled exceptions at the page level, then redirect or transfer to a custom error page.
- Use the Application_Error procedure in the Global.asax file to catch unhandled exceptions at the application level, then redirect or transfer to a custom error page.
- Use the <customErrors> element of the Web.config file to specify custom error pages that are displayed for specific types of HTTP errors.

Description

- If an unrecoverable error occurs, most applications display a custom error page to inform the user that a problem has occurred.
- Behind the scenes, the custom error page may also record the error in a log or send an email message to the application's support staff to notify them of the error.
- Custom error pages often use an Exception object to display a detailed message that describes the error.

Figure 19-6   An introduction to custom error handling

How to get and use the Exception object for an error

Figure 19-7 shows how you can use the properties and methods of the Exception and HttpServerUtility classes to get and use the Exception object for an error. This is the object that contains information about the exception that has occurred. The examples in this figure show how this works.

The first example shows how you can use a Try...Catch statement to get the Exception object. As you should know, the Catch clause catches the Exception object if any of the statements in the Try clause throw an exception. You can use this technique in any procedure of a code-behind file.

The second example shows how to get the Exception object within the Page_Error procedure. This procedure is executed automatically if an exception isn't handled by the other procedures of a code-behind file. Here, you use the GetLastError method of the Server object, which you access using the Server property of the page.

The third example shows how to get the Exception object within the Application_Error procedure of the Global.asax file. This procedure is executed automatically if an exception isn't handled by any of the procedures in the code-behind file including the Page_Error procedure. In the Application_Error procedure, however, the GetLastError method doesn't return the correct Exception object. That's because a second exception called HttpUnhandledException is thrown if an exception occurs and the exception isn't handled by a Try...Catch statement or a Page_Error procedure. As a result, the GetLastError method returns the HttpUnhandledException exception, not the exception that originally caused the error. To access the original exception, you must use the InnerException property of the Exception object that's returned by the GetLastError method.

Although you might think that you could use the ClearError method to clear the HttpUnhandledException exception and then use GetLastError to get the original exception, that won't work. That's because you can only use GetLastError to get the Exception object for the last exception that occurred. In this case, that's the HttpUnhandledException exception.

The fourth example shows how you might use the properties of an Exception object as you test an application. Here, the Write method of the HttpResponse object is used to display the Message and Source properties on the page. Notice that before this method is executed, the ClearError method of the Server object is used to clear the error. That way, the ASP.NET Server Error page won't be displayed.

Common properties of the Exception class

Property	Description
Message	A message that describes the error.
Source	The name of the application or object that caused the error.
InnerException	The Exception object that caused the exception at the application level.

Methods of the HttpServerUtility class for working with exceptions

Method	Description
GetLastError	Gets the most recent exception.
ClearError	Clears the most recent exception.

Code that gets the Exception object at the procedure level

```
Try
    statements that could throw an exception
Catch ex As Exception
    statements that use the Exception object named ex
End Try
```

Code that gets the Exception object at the page level

```
Dim ex As Exception
ex = Server.GetLastError()
```

Code that gets the Exception object at the application level

```
Dim ex As Exception
ex = Server.GetLastError.InnerException()
```

Code that displays the error message and source of the Exception object

```
Server.ClearError()
Response.Write(ex.Message & "<BR>" & ex.Source)
```

Description

- You can use a Try...Catch statement in any procedure of a code-behind file to get the Exception object for an error.

- In a Page_Error event procedure, which is executed when an unhandled exception occurs, you use the GetLastError method of the Server object to get the Exception object for the error.

- If you don't handle an exception with a Try...Catch statement or a Page_Error event procedure, an HttpUnhandledException is thrown. Then, you use the GetLastError method of the Server object in the Application_Error event procedure of the Global.asax file to get the Exception object for that exception, and you use the InnerException property of that exception to get the Exception object that actually caused the error.

- During testing, you may want to use the Write method of the HttpResponse object to write information about the exception to the page. Before you do that, you need to use the ClearError method to clear the error from the Server object so that the ASP.NET Server Error page isn't displayed.

Figure 19-7   How to get and use the Exception object for an error

How to code procedures that redirect to a custom error page

Figure 19-8 shows three ways to redirect to a custom error page when an exception occurs in an ASP.NET application. The first example shows how you can redirect to a custom error page from a Try…Catch statement. Here, a call to the Fill method of a data adapter is placed in a Try clause so any database exceptions can be handled in the Catch clause. If an exception occurs, the Catch clause adds the Exception object to session state and redirects to the error page. Then, the error page can use the Exception object to get information about the exception.

The second example shows how you can use a Page_Error procedure to catch all unhandled exceptions for a page and redirect to a custom error page. Here, the GetLastError method is used to get the Exception object. Then, the procedure adds the Exception object to session state and redirects to the custom error page.

The third example shows how you can use an Application_Error procedure in the Global.asax file to catch all unhandled exceptions for an entire application. Here, the GetLastError method is used to get the Exception object, and the InnerException property of the Exception object is used to get the exception that caused the error. Then, the procedure adds the Exception object to session state and redirects to the custom error page.

A Try…Catch statement that redirects to a custom error page if an exception occurs during a database operation

```
Try
    daProducts.Fill(dsProducts)
Catch ex As Exception
    Session("exception") = ex
    Response.Redirect("ErrorPage.aspx")
End Try
```

A Page_Error event procedure that redirects to a custom error page

```
Private Sub Page_Error(ByVal sender As Object, ByVal e As System.EventArgs) _
        Handles MyBase.Error
    ' Fires when an error occurs
    Dim ex As Exception
    ex = Server.GetLastError
    Session("exception") = ex
    Response.Redirect("ErrorPage.aspx")
End Sub
```

An Application_Error event procedure in the Global.asax file that redirects to a custom error page

```
Sub Application_Error(ByVal sender As Object, ByVal e As EventArgs)
    ' Fires when an error occurs
    Dim ex As Exception
    ex = Server.GetLastError.InnerException
    Session("exception") = ex
    Response.Redirect("ErrorPage.aspx")
End Sub
```

Description

- You can redirect to a custom error page from a Try…Catch statement, a Page_Error procedure, or an Application_Error procedure in the Global.asax file.
- Before redirecting to a custom error page, the Exception object should be added to session state so it can be used by the error page.

Figure 19-8   How to code procedures that redirect to a custom error page

The code for a custom error page

Figure 19-9 shows the aspx file and the code-behind file for the custom error page that's shown in figure 19-6. Here, the aspx file should be self-explanatory, because it simply displays a message and provides a button for returning to the Order page.

The code-behind file for the error page is more interesting, though, because it sends an email message to the support personnel that describes the error that has occurred. This assumes that the Try…Catch statement, Page_Error procedure, or Application_Error procedure that redirects to the error page has added the Exception object to session state. Then, the Load procedure for the error page gets the Exception object from session state and passes it to the SendEmail procedure, which sends the email message. After that, the Load procedure removes the Exception object from session state. This illustrates another common email use.

The aspx code for the ErrorPage form

```
<%@ Register TagPrefix="uc1" TagName="Banner" Src="Banner.ascx" %>
<%@ Page Language="vb" AutoEventWireup="false" Codebehind="ErrorPage.aspx.vb"
Inherits="HalloweenStore.ErrorPage" %>
<!DOCTYPE HTML PUBLIC "-//W3C//DTD HTML 4.0 Transitional//EN">
<HTML>
  <HEAD>
    <title>ErrorPage</title>
    <meta content="Microsoft Visual Studio .NET 7.1" name="GENERATOR">
    <meta content="Visual Basic .NET 7.1" name="CODE_LANGUAGE">
    <meta content="JavaScript" name="vs_defaultClientScript">
    <meta content="http://schemas.microsoft.com/intellisense/ie5"
          name="vs_targetSchema">
  </HEAD>
  <body>
    <form id="Form1" method="post" runat="server">
      <uc1:banner id="Banner1" runat="server"></uc1:banner>
      <H2>Oh no!</H2>
Something unexpected happened which caused us to drop what we were doing and
come here. We're sorry for the inconvenience.<BR><BR>
      <asp:button id="btnReturn" runat="server" Text="Return to Order Page">
      </asp:button></form>
  </body>
</HTML>
```

The Visual Basic code for the ErrorPage form

```
Imports System.Web.Mail
Public Class ErrorPage
    Inherits System.Web.UI.Page
    Private Sub Page_Load(ByVal sender As System.Object, _
            ByVal e As System.EventArgs) Handles MyBase.Load
        'Put user code to initialize the page here
        If Not IsPostBack Then
            Me.SendEmail(Session("exception"))
            Session.Remove("exception")
        End If
    End Sub
    Private Sub SendEmail(ByVal ex As Exception)
        Dim sBody As String
        sBody = "An exception occurred at " & Now.ToLongTimeString _
            & " on " & Now.ToLongDateString & "<br>" & ex.Message
        Dim msg As New MailMessage
        msg.To = "Support@Murach.com"
        msg.From = "Halloween@Murach.com"
        msg.Subject = "Exception in Halloween application"
        msg.Body = sBody
        msg.BodyFormat = MailFormat.Html
        SmtpMail.SmtpServer = "localhost"
        SmtpMail.Send(msg)
    End Sub
    Private Sub btnReturn_Click(ByVal sender As Object, _
            ByVal e As System.EventArgs) Handles btnReturn.Click
        Response.Redirect("Order.aspx")
    End Sub
End Class
```

Note

- This code assumes that the Exception object has been placed in session state.

Figure 19-9   The code for a custom error page

How to handle HTTP errors with the Web.config file

Not all unrecoverable errors cause ASP.NET to throw an exception. As figure 19-10 shows, some error conditions result in HTTP errors that are handled by the web server itself. For these errors, you can use the <customErrors> element in the Web.config file to specify custom error pages.

Although there are many different types of HTTP errors that can occur, the most common types are listed in this figure. Of these, the most common is the 404 error. This error occurs when a user attempts to retrieve a page that doesn't exist. In some cases, a 404 error is caused by a missing page or a page that has been renamed. In other cases, a 404 error is caused by an error in your application's navigation controls, such as a hyperlink control that uses an incorrect URL.

As this figure shows, you include an <error> element in the Web.config file for each HTTP error that you want to redirect to a custom error page. In the example, this is done for two types of errors. The first <error> element specifies that the page named E404.aspx should be displayed if a 404 error occurs. The second element specifies that the page named E500.aspx should be displayed if a 500 error occurs.

You can also specify a default error page that's displayed if an HTTP error that isn't specifically listed in an <error> element occurs. In the example in this figure, the defaultRedirect attribute specifies that a page named DefaultError.aspx should be displayed if any other HTTP error occurs.

A customErrors element in the Web.config file that designates custom error pages

```
<customErrors mode="On" defaultRedirect="DefaultError.aspx">
    <error statusCode="404" redirect="E404.aspx" />
    <error statusCode="500" redirect="E500.aspx" />
</customErrors>
```

Common HTTP error codes

Code	Description
401	Unauthorized request. The client must be authorized to access the resource.
403	Forbidden request. The client is not allowed to access the resource.
404	File Not Found. The resource could not be located.
500	Internal Server Error. This is usually the result of an unhandled exception.

Description

- The <customErrors> element in the Web.config file lets you designate custom error pages that are automatically displayed when unrecoverable HTTP errors occur. You don't have to write any code to redirect or transfer to these pages.

- To enable custom error pages, edit the <customErrors> element of the Web.config file and change the mode attribute to "On." Then, specify your generic error page in the defaultRedirect attribute.

- To associate a custom error page with an HTTP error, add an <error> element that specifies the HTTP error code in the statusCode attribute and the name of the custom error page in the redirect attribute.

Figure 19-10   How to handle HTTP errors with the Web.config file

How to handle the back-button problem

If the user clicks the Back button in the browser window to return to a previous ASP.NET form and then posts the form, the application's session state may not correspond to that form. In some cases, this can result in a problem that we refer to as the *back-button problem*. The topics that follow show you how to deal with it.

An introduction to the back-button problem

Figure 19-11 illustrates the back-button problem in a shopping cart application. Here, the contents of the user's shopping cart are stored in session state and displayed on the page. The user then deletes one of the two items, which changes the data in session state. At that point, the user changes his mind and clicks the Back button, which displays both items again, even though session state only includes one item.

If the user now proceeds to check out, the order is likely to show one item when the user thinks he has ordered two items. But that depends upon how the application is coded. In the worst cases, the back-button problem may cause an application to crash. In the best cases, clicking on the Back button won't cause a problem at all.

In general, there are two ways to handle the back-button problem. The first is to try to prevent pages from being saved in the browser's cache. Then, when the user clicks the Back button, the old page can't be retrieved. As you will see in the next figure, ASP.NET provides four methods for doing that, but they don't work if the user's browser ignores the page cache settings that are sent with a response.

The second way is to code critical web forms so they detect when the user attempts to post a page that isn't current. To do that, a form can use timestamps or random numbers to track the use of pages. Because there's no reliable way to prevent a page from being cached and retrieved via the Back button, you should use this second technique whenever possible.

An example of a back-button problem in the shopping cart page of the Halloween Store application

1. The user displays a shopping cart with two products. The shopping cart data is stored in session state and currently contains two items: one Cool Ghoul at $69.99 and one Deranged Cat at $19.99. The shopping cart displayed in the browser window looks like this:

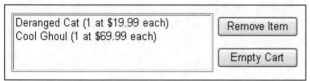

2. The user selects the first product and clicks the Remove Item button to delete it. The first line item is deleted from the shopping cart in session state and the updated page is sent to the browser:

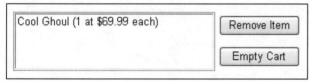

3. The user decides that he or she wants to purchase the Deranged Cat after all and clicks the browser's Back button, thinking this will undo the Delete action. The browser retrieves the previous page from its local cache:

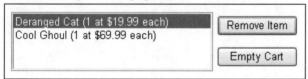

Because the browser redisplayed this page directly from its cache, the first line item was not added back to the shopping cart in session state. As a result, session state indicates that the user has ordered only one item even though the web page displays two items.

Two ways to handle the back-button problem

- Disable browser page caching for user input forms.
- Use timestamps or random numbers to track pages so you can detect when a page isn't current.

Description

- When a user clicks the browser's Back button, the browser retrieves a locally cached copy of the previous page without notifying the server. As a result, the information stored in session state can become out of sync with the data displayed in the browser window.

Figure 19-11   An introduction to the back-button problem

How to disable browser page caching

Figure 19-12 shows how you can use four ASP.NET methods to prevent a user's browser from caching pages. All of these methods work by adding information to the HTTP headers that are sent to the browser along with the page.

Unfortunately, some browsers ignore these headers, so these techniques don't guarantee that a page won't be cached. Still, it's not a bad idea to add the code in this figure to the Page_Load procedure of any ASP.NET page that gets important data like customer or product information.

The warning message that's displayed if the user returns to a page and caching is disabled

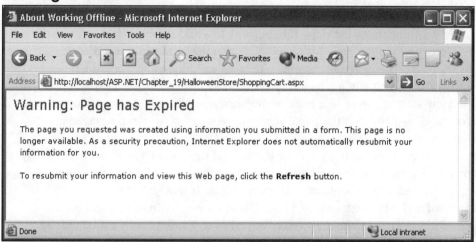

Methods that set page caching options

Method	Description
Response.Cache.SetCacheability	Indicates how the page should be cached. Specify HttpCacheability.NoCache to suppress caching.
Response.Cache.SetExpires	Specifies when the cached page should expire. Specify Now().AddSeconds(-1) to mark the page as already expired.
Response.Cache.SetNoStore	Specifies that the browser should not cache the page.
Response.AddHeader	Adds a header to the HTTP response object. Specifying "Pragma" for the key and "no-cache" for the value disables caching.

Code that disables caching for a page

```
Response.Cache.SetCacheability(HttpCacheability.NoCache)
Response.Cache.SetExpires(Now().AddSeconds(-1))
Response.Cache.SetNoStore()
Response.AddHeader("Pragma", "no-cache")
```

Description

- You can limit the effect of the Back button by directing the browser to not cache pages that contain state-sensitive forms. Then, when the user attempts to return to a page using the Back button, the warning message at the top of this figure is displayed.

- You can place the code to disable browser page caching in the procedure that handles the Load event of the form. This code should be executed each time the page is loaded.

- Unfortunately, the technique described in this figure doesn't ensure that the user's browser won't cache the page because the user's browser may ignore the page cache settings. As a result, you should use the technique in the next figure to prevent back-button problems.

Figure 19-12   How to disable browser page caching

How to use timestamps to avoid the back-button problem

Figure 19-13 illustrates the most reliable way to avoid the back-button problem. Here, you see the code for a web page that uses timestamps to determine whether the posted page is current. The basic technique is to record a timestamp in two places when a page is posted: view state and session state. Then, the view state stamp is sent back to the browser and cached along with the rest of the information on the page, while the session state stamp is saved on the server.

Later, when the user posts a page for the second time, the Page_Load event calls a private function named IsExpired. This function retrieves the timestamps from view state and session state and compares them. If they are identical, the page is current and IsExpired returns False. But if they are different, it indicates that the user has posted a page that was retrieved from the browser's cache via the Back button. In that case, the IsExpired function returns True. Then, the Page_Load procedure redirects to a page named Expired.aspx, which in turn displays a message indicating that the page is out of date and can't be posted.

Notice that before comparing the timestamp items in session state and view state, the IsExpired function checks that both of these items exist. If not, the function returns False so that current timestamps can be saved in both session state and view state.

Incidentally, this technique can also be used to deal with problems that occur when the user clicks the Refresh button. This posts the page to the server and gets a new response, which refreshes the page, so it has nothing to do with the browser's cache. However, this can cause problems like a user ordering a product twice without realizing it. Because most users tend to click the Back button far more than the Refresh button, though, the Refresh button causes far fewer errors. That's why most web developers ignore this problem.

A page that checks timestamps to avoid the back-button problem

```
Public Class ShoppingCart
    Inherits System.Web.UI.Page

    Dim ShoppingCart As SortedList

    Private Sub Page_Load(ByVal sender As System.Object, _
            ByVal e As System.EventArgs) Handles MyBase.Load
        'Put user code to initialize the page here
        If IsExpired() Then
            Response.Redirect("Expired.aspx")
        Else
            Me.SaveTimeStamps()
        End If
        ShoppingCart = Session("Cart")
        If Not IsPostBack Then
            Me.DisplayShoppingCart()
        End If
    End Sub

    Private Function IsExpired() As Boolean
        If Session("Cart_TimeStamp") Is Nothing Then
            Return False
        ElseIf ViewState("TimeStamp") Is Nothing Then
            Return False
        ElseIf ViewState("TimeStamp").ToString = _
                Session("Cart_TimeStamp").ToString Then
            Return False
        Else
            Return True
        End If
    End Function

    Private Sub SaveTimeStamps()
        Dim t As DateTime = Now()
        ViewState.Add("TimeStamp", t)
        Session.Add("Cart_TimeStamp", t)
    End Sub
    .
    .
    .
End Class
```

Description

- One way to avoid back-button problems is to use timestamps. The page saves two copies of a timestamp obtained via the Now() function: one in view state, the other in session state.

- The IsExpired function tests the view state and session state timestamps to make sure they are the same. If they aren't, the user has posted a page that has been retrieved from the browser's cache.

Note

- Some developers prefer to use random numbers rather than timestamps. Either technique will work.

Figure 19-13   How to use timestamps to avoid the back-button problem

Perspective

This chapter has presented three types of enhancements that you can add to an application once you've got the basic functions working right. In practice, most serious applications use both email and custom error pages to make an application more user friendly and less error prone.

In contrast, many serious applications ignore the back-button problem on the theory that the users should be smart enough to avoid that problem themselves. In fact, clicking on the Back button and re-posting a page will cause a problem on many e-commerce sites. That's why you may want to use the techniques in this chapter to handle that problem on your own web site.

Terms

Simple Mail Transfer Protocol (SMTP)
Post Office Protocol (POP)
Multipurpose Internet Message Extension (MIME)
mail client
mail server
attachment
UUEncode
Base64 encoding
back-button problem

20

How to deploy ASP.NET web applications

After you have completed a web application, you need to install it on the web server that will host the application. This chapter shows you how to do that. It begins with a brief overview of ASP.NET deployment. Then, it shows you how to create a custom Setup program that you can use to install an ASP.NET application on a web server.

Note that if you're using the Standard Edition of Visual Basic .NET, you won't be able to create a Setup program. Even so, you may want to read this chapter so you understand how these programs work.

An introduction to ASP.NET deployment

In the topics that follow, you'll learn how the files that make up an ASP.NET application are installed on an IIS server. You'll also learn the three techniques that you can use for installing an ASP.NET application on an IIS server.

How the files of an ASP.NET application are deployed on an IIS server

An application on an IIS server is installed in a *virtual directory*, as shown in figure 20-1. This virtual directory is sometimes called the *application root*. It contains all of the aspx and other content files that are required by the application, such as HTML or image files. In contrast, the application's executable files are located in a bin folder beneath the application root.

The first screen in this figure shows how an application appears when viewed with the IIS Manager that's used by IIS administrators. When IIS is initially configured, it consists of a single web site, named Default Web Site. Then, the ASP.NET applications typically reside in virtual directories beneath the default web site. In the IIS Manager in this figure, you can see that the Default Web Site contains a virtual directory named HalloweenStore.

To access a virtual directory from a browser, you specify the virtual directory name after the web site's domain name. If the Halloween Store application is installed on a web site with the domain name www.murach.com, for example, you can refer to it using this URL: www.murach.com/HalloweenStore. And to refer to the Order page for this application, you use www.murach.com/HalloweenStore/Order.aspx.

Note that the tree that appears at the left of the IIS Manager represents the logical structure of the IIS server, not the actual hierarchy of folders used to store the server's web sites on disk. Instead, IIS Manager lets you map the web sites and virtual directories on an IIS server to specific folders. Normally, Default Web Site is mapped to c:\Inetpub\wwwroot, and virtual directories within Default Web Site are mapped to subfolders of c:\Inetpub\wwwroot. However, you can map a virtual directory to any location that's accessible to the IIS server, including network drives.

The second screen in this figure shows how this works. Here, you can see that the files in the HalloweenStore virtual directory are located on the server's C drive in \Inetpub\wwwroot\HalloweenStore. As a result, when a user requests the URL at www.murach.com/HalloweenStore/Order.aspx, the IIS server retrieves the file at c:\Inetpub\wwwroot\HalloweenStore\Order.aspx.

Although it's possible to set up more than one web site on a single server, most servers are set up with just a single web site. For more information about how to configure multiple IIS web sites, though, you can refer to the online documentation.

An ASP.NET application as seen in the IIS Manager

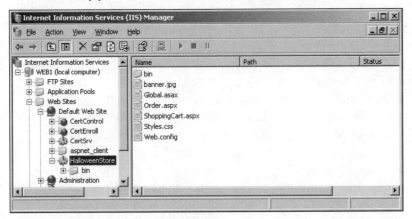

The application's folder as seen in the Windows Explorer

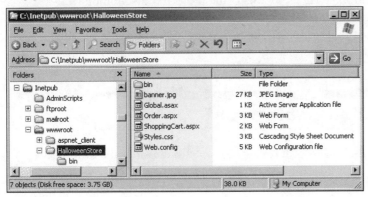

Description

- An IIS application resides in a *virtual directory* on the web server.
- Each virtual directory on an IIS server is mapped to a folder that's accessible to the server. By default, this folder is located in the c:\Inetpub\wwwroot folder.
- The content files for an application, such as aspx files, HTML files, and image files, are located in the application's virtual directory folder. The executable files are located in the bin folder beneath the application's virtual directory folder.
- You can use the IIS Manager to view an application's virtual directory and manage its settings. To start it on a Windows server, choose Start→All Programs→Adminstrative Tools→Internet Information Services (IIS) Manager.

Figure 20-1   How the files of an ASP.NET application are deployed on an IIS server

Three ways to install a web application

Figure 20-2 describes three ways to install web applications. First, you can use the Copy Project command to copy a project from your development computer to a production web server. Second, you can use the IIS Manager to manually create the application's virtual directory, then use the Xcopy command or the Windows Explorer to copy all of the project's files to the server. If you use one of these methods, you also have to copy any other files that the application requires, such as data files that reside in directories outside of the project. Nevertheless, either of these approaches is okay for small applications that require infrequent maintenance.

The third way to install a web application, though, is to create a Setup program that installs the application for you. To do that, you can use the Setup Wizard. This automates the task of installing an ASP.NET application and reduces the chance of installation problems. It also automates the task of uninstalling an application. That's why this is the preferred installation technique for most web developers, especially for large projects that require frequent maintenance. And that's why it's the technique that's presented in this chapter.

How web application deployment differs from Windows application deployment

Before I go on, I think it's worth taking a minute to consider the differences between how Windows applications are deployed and how ASP.NET web applications are deployed. To deploy a Windows application, you must install the application on each user's computer. As a result, if 100 people in your company are going to use the application, you need to install the application 100 times on 100 different computers.

In contrast, web applications don't have to be installed on each user's computer. Instead, you install the application just once on the web server. Then, each user can access the application using a browser. This deployment difference is one reason why many companies not only use web applications for e-commerce, but also for inhouse applications.

That doesn't necessarily mean that installing a web application on one server is easier than installing a Windows application on one client machine. In fact, installing a web application is often harder than installing a Windows application because it involves configuring an IIS server. The difference is that you only have to install a web application once.

The Copy Project command

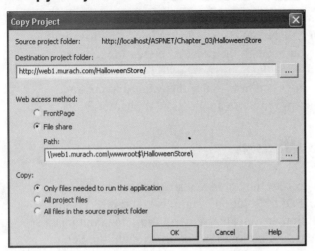

Three ways to install a web application

- Use Visual Studio's Copy Project command (Project→Copy Project) to copy a project to another location. This option is best for applications that will not be installed or upgraded frequently. To use this option, the web server you want to install the application to must have the FrontPage Server extensions installed or you must have file share access to the web server computer.

- Manually create the virtual directory needed for the application, then manually copy the application's files to the server using the Windows Explorer or the Xcopy command. Use this technique only if you don't have FrontPage or file share access to the web server.

- Create a Setup program that installs the application. This option is best for applications that will be installed at multiple sites or applications that you expect will have a short revision cycle, so they'll need to be upgraded frequently. This is the method that's preferred by most web developers, so it's the one described in this chapter.

Discussion

- There are several methods for deploying ASP.NET web applications. The method you use should depend on how often the application will need to be installed and what kind of access you have to the target server.

Figure 20-2   Three ways to install a web application

How to use the Setup Wizard

To make it easy to create an ASP.NET Setup project, Visual Studio comes with a Setup Wizard that walks you through the process of creating a basic Setup project. You can then customize the Setup project to include additional features. The topics that follow show you how to use this wizard to create a Setup project that installs the Halloween Store application of chapter 3.

How to start the Setup Wizard

Figure 20-3 shows you how to start the Setup Wizard. As you do this procedure, be sure to choose the Add to Solution option. If you don't, Visual Studio will close the current solution and create a new solution that contains just the Setup project. If you check the Add to Solution option, though, the Setup project will be created as a new project within the same solution as the application's project.

Note that because a Setup project isn't a web project, its files aren't stored in a project folder on the IIS server. Instead, the project files are stored by default in a folder within the folder where the solution is stored. If that's not what you want, you can change the folder in the New Project dialog box.

The dialog box for adding a Setup project to an existing solution

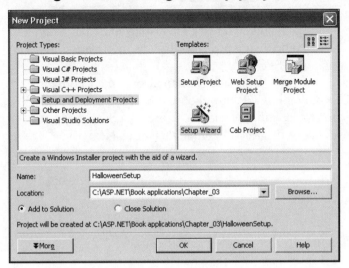

Description

- To create a Setup program for a web application, you add a Setup project to the solution that contains the application you want to deploy.

- To add a Setup project to a solution, choose the File→New→Project command to display the New Project dialog box. Then, click the Setup and Deployment Projects folder in the Project Types list, select the Setup Wizard template, enter a name for the Setup project, and select the Add to Solution option button. When you click on the OK button, the Setup Wizard is started.

- You can also add a Setup project by selecting the template for the type of project you want to create like a Web Setup Project. Because the Setup Wizard leads you through the creation of all of the project types, though, it's best to start all your Setup projects from this wizard.

Note

- Because a Setup project isn't a web project, its files aren't stored on the IIS server. Instead, when you select the Add to Solution option, the project location is set to the same folder where the solution is stored. If that's not what you want, you can change the location in the Location combo box.

Figure 20-3   How to start the Setup Wizard

How to choose the Setup project type

Figure 20-4 shows the first two dialog boxes that are displayed by the Setup Wizard. The first is simply a Welcome dialog box that displays information about what the wizard does and how to use it.

After you read the Welcome dialog box, click Next to display the Choose a Project Type dialog box. This dialog box lets you choose one of the four types of Setup projects that you can create with this wizard. To create a Setup project for an ASP.NET application, choose the second option, then click Next.

The first two Setup Wizard dialog boxes

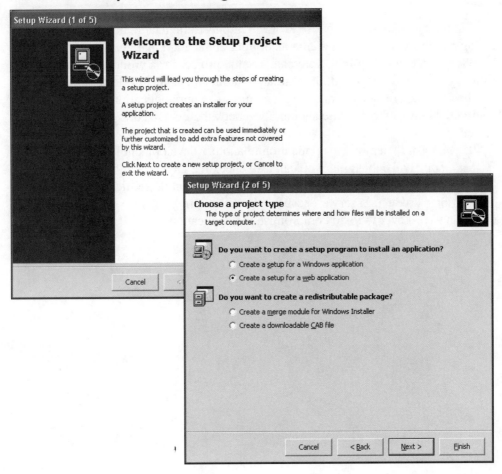

Description

- When you start the Setup Wizard, a Welcome dialog box is displayed. Then, you click the Next button to display the next dialog box, which lets you select the type of project you want to create.
- To create a Setup program for installing an ASP.NET application, select the second option to indicate that the application is a web application.

Figure 20-4   How to choose the Setup project type

How to add project files to a Setup project

Figure 20-5 shows the Choose Project Outputs to Include dialog box. This dialog box lets you select the elements of your application that you want to be installed on the target system. To create a Setup project for a production application, you should select both the Primary Output and Content Files options. If you have created resources for specific cultures so your application can be distributed internationally, you should also check the Localized Resources option.

If you want to deploy the application to another development server for further testing and debugging, you can also check the Debug Symbols and Source Files options. Note, however, that you don't want these files on the application's production server because a hacker might gain access to them and use them to discover ways to compromise the application.

The Setup Wizard dialog box for selecting project outputs

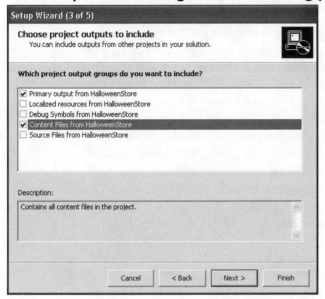

Output groups you can include in a Setup project

Name	Description
Primary Output	The assembly (DLL file) that's produced when the project is built, along with any dependency files required by the project.
Localized Resources	Assemblies that contain resources specific to the cultures that you've localized the application for.
Debug Symbols	Debugging files that contain symbolic information that can be used to debug the application.
Content Files	The HTML files, image files, and other files that make up the content of the web site.
Source Files	All of the source files for a selected project.

Description

- You use the project output check boxes to select the project files you want to install when you run the Setup program. If the solution contains more than one project, a set of check boxes will appear for each project.
- For most web projects, you only need to select the Primary Output and Content Files options.

Note

- You can specify additional output after you create the Setup project by selecting the Project→Add→Project Output command.

Figure 20-5   How to add project files to a Setup project

How to add other files to a Setup project

Besides the application's project files, you may want the Setup program to install additional files onto the target computer when a user installs your application. For example, the Halloween Store application requires two data files named categories.dat and products.dat and an image file named banner.jpg.

As figure 20-6 shows, the Choose Files to Include dialog box of the Setup Wizard lets you specify these additional files. To include a file, click the Add button. This brings up a dialog box that lets you select the file you want to add.

In most cases, the files you add to the setup project with the Choose Files to Include dialog box will reside in folders other than the application's project folder. That's the case for the two data files shown in this figure, which are stored in the c:\MurachData folder. In some cases, though, you also need to use this dialog box to include files that are stored in the project folder. If, for example, you use the Windows Explorer to copy a file to the application's project folder but you don't add it to the project from Visual Studio, the file isn't included in the Setup project. That's the case for the image file shown in this figure. Then, you have to add the file to the Setup project via the Choose Files to Include dialog box.

Note that the Choose Files to Include dialog box doesn't let you specify where the selected files will be installed on the target computer. Instead, all of the files for the project will be installed to the application root directory by default. In figure 20-9, though, you'll learn how to change the file locations.

The Setup Wizard dialog box for adding other files

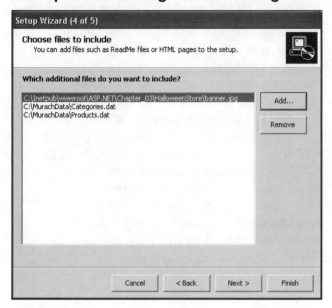

Description

- The Choose Files to Include page lets you add the files that you want installed along with the application but that aren't a part of the project, such as data files, images, or a ReadMe file.

- In most cases, files you add via the Choose Files to Include page are located outside of the application's project folder. For example, an application's data files may reside in a separate folder.

- If you add a file to the application's project folder outside of Visual Studio (for example, by copying the file to the project folder using Windows Explorer), you need to use the Choose Files to Include page to include the file in the Setup project.

- To include non-project files in the Setup project, click the Add button in the dialog box and then select the files.

Note

- If you need to add other files to a Setup project after you complete the Setup Wizard, you can do that by selecting the Project→Add→File command.

Figure 20-6   How to add other files to a Setup project

A basic Setup project for a web application

When you complete the Setup Wizard, the wizard creates a Setup project and adds it to the open solution as shown in figure 20-7. Here, the Solution Explorer window shows that the solution now has two projects. The HalloweenStore project is the Halloween Store application that the Setup program will install, and the HalloweenSetup project is the Setup project that will create the Setup program to install the Halloween Store application.

Notice that the HalloweenSetup project includes a folder named Detected Dependencies. A *dependency* is an item that an application requires in order to execute properly. For example, all .NET applications require that the target computer have the .NET Framework installed, and some applications may require that other components be installed. When you use the Setup Wizard, it automatically determines any dependencies that the application has and adds them to the Detected Dependencies folder. Then, the Setup program automatically installs any items that are missing from the target computer.

A new deployment project for a web application

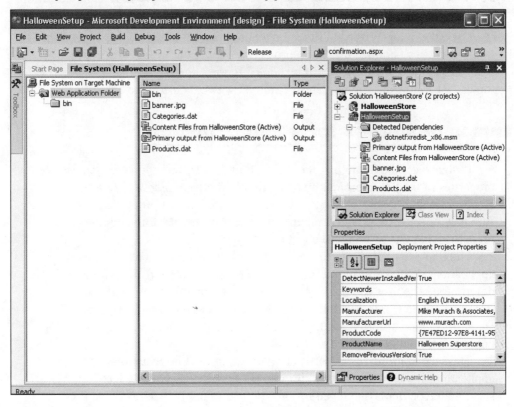

Description

- When you complete the Setup Wizard dialog boxes, a Setup project is added to the solution. This project includes any project output or other files that you selected in the Setup Wizard, along with any dependency files that were detected by the Setup Wizard.

- The dependency shown above is for a distributable version of the Common Language Runtime. This module is included by default in all Setup projects so the project being deployed can be installed on machines that don't already have the .NET Framework installed.

Figure 20-7   A basic Setup project for a web application

How to customize a Setup project

Once the Setup Wizard has created a Setup project based on your specifications, you can customize the Setup project by setting additional properties, adjusting the way the project will be copied to the target system, and so on. The topics that follow describe the most common ways to customize a Setup project.

Common properties for a Setup project

If you select the Setup project in the Solution Explorer, you can then set the properties of the Setup project by using the Properties window. Whenever you create a Setup project, you should review all of the project properties to make sure they're set appropriately. Figure 20-8 describes some of the common properties that you're likely to change.

The first group of properties provide support information about your application, such as the author, manufacturer, phone number, and a product description. The user can display this information by opening Add/Remove Programs in the Control Panel, selecting the application, and clicking the Click Here for Support Information link for the application. This brings up the dialog box that's shown in this figure.

The second group of properties provide additional information about the application. For example, the AddRemoveProgramIcon property lets you specify an icon that's displayed for the application in the Add/Remove Programs dialog box, and the ProductName icon lets you set the name of the product that's displayed by the Setup program and the Add/Remove Programs dialog box.

The Support Info dialog box displayed by Add/Remove Programs

Properties that are displayed in the Support Info dialog box

Property	Description
Author	The author of the product.
Description	Descriptive information about the product or the available support.
Manufacturer	The manufacturer of the product.
ManufacturerUrl	A URL for the manufacturer's web site.
SupportPhone	A phone number for product support.
SupportUrl	A URL for a web site that contains support information.
Version	The version number of the product.

Other common properties

Property	Description
AddRemoveProgramIcon	The icon that's displayed for the application in the Add/Remove Programs dialog box.
DetectNewerInstalledVersion	A Boolean value that specifies whether the installer should check for a newer version of the application on the target system. If a newer version is found, the application is not installed.
ProductName	The name that's used to identify the product during setup and in the Add/Remove Programs dialog box after installation.
RemovePreviousVersion	A Boolean value that specifies whether an earlier version of the application should be removed before the current version is installed.
Subject	Additional information about the product or installation.
Title	The title that's used to identify the product.

Description

- To change any of the properties for a project, select the Setup project in the Solution Explorer and use the Properties window.

Figure 20-8   Common properties for a Setup project

How to customize file system settings

One of the most important tasks of any setup routine is copying the application's files to the target computer's file system. The File System Editor, shown in figure 20-9, lets you specify how those files should be copied. Using this editor, you can change the default location where the application should be installed, change the names of the folders that should be created on the target system, and specify new folders that should be created on the target system when the application is installed.

By default, the entire application is installed in a virtual directory that's represented in the File System Editor as a folder called the Web Application Folder. The actual name of this virtual directory on the target system is specified by the VirtualDirectory property of the Web Application Folder. For example, you can see in this figure that this property is set to HalloweenStore for the Halloween Store's Setup project. As a result, a virtual directory named HalloweenStore will be created on the target system when you run the Setup program.

If you want the Setup program to create additional folders when the application is installed, you can add folders to the folder tree listed in the left pane of the File System Editor. For example, you can see in this figure that I added a folder named MurachData. Then, you can drag any files you want the Setup program to install in the new folder from Web Application Folder to the new folder. For example, to install the categories.dat and products.dat files in the MurachData folder, you can drag those files from the Web Application Folder to the MurachData folder.

Any new folder you create by using the File System Editor will be created in the application folder on the target computer by default. To change that, set the new folder's DefaultLocation property to the location where you want the folder to be created. The drop-down list for this property lists several generic locations, such as [TARGETDIR] (the default), [WindowsFolder], and [ProgramFilesFolder]. Then, you can choose one of these locations, or you can specify a complete path for the folder, such as C:\MurachData.

The File System Editor with a custom folder

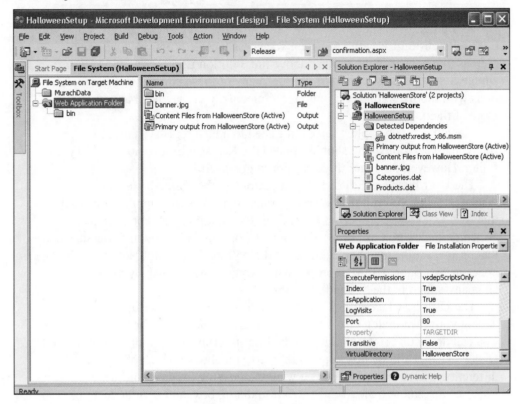

Description

- The File System Editor shows the folders where the application's files will be installed on the target system. The left pane lists the folders on the target system, and the right pane lists the files in the selected folder.

- To access the File System Editor, select the Setup project in the Solution Explorer and then click on that toolbar button at the top of the Solution Explorer window or select that editor from the View menu.

- The Web Application Folder represents the virtual directory on the IIS server where the application will be installed. You can specify the name that will be used for the application's virtual directory by setting the VirtualDirectory property of this folder, and you specify the page that's displayed by default by setting the DefaultDocument property.

- If you want the Setup program to create an additional folder, you can add a custom folder to the folder pane. To do that, right-click File System on Target Machine, then open the Add Special Folder submenu, choose Custom Folder, and type a name for the folder. To specify the location where the custom folder will be created, change its DefaultLocation property.

- By default, all of the project output and other files that you add to a Setup project are included in the Web Application Folder. To install a file to a different folder, drag it or cut and paste it to that folder.

Figure 20-9   How to customize the file system settings

How to use the other setup editors

As figure 20-10 shows, Visual Studio provides several other editors that you can use to customize Setup projects. To access these editors, you can use the buttons that appear in the toolbar above the Solution Explorer window. For simple Setup projects, you shouldn't need any of these editors. But for applications with more complicated setup requirements, you may need to use one or more of them.

Since most web applications don't need to adjust registry settings or create file type associations, you shouldn't need the Registry Editor or the File Types Editor. However, the other three editors can be useful.

The User Interface Editor lets you customize the dialog boxes that are displayed when you run the Setup program to install a web application. To do that, you just set the properties for each of the dialog boxes. For example, the Welcome dialog box has properties named CopyrightWarning and MessageText that let you set the text displayed in the dialog box. In addition, all of the dialog boxes have a BannerBitMap property that you can use to display your company's logo in the Setup dialog boxes.

The User Interface Editor also lets you customize the user interface by adding your own dialog boxes to those that are displayed by the Setup program. You can do that by right-clicking in the User Interface Editor and choosing Add Dialog. Then, a dialog box appears that lets you choose which of several different types of dialog boxes you want to add. Among the choices are a License Agreement dialog box, a ReadMe dialog box, and several generic dialog boxes that display various combinations of radio buttons, check boxes, and text boxes. Once you've added a dialog box, you can customize it by setting its properties.

The Custom Actions Editor lets you add actions to those that are performed by the Setup program. For example, you can use a custom action to create a SQL Server database when the application is installed. That might make sense when you're installing a new application that uses a new database that contains little or no data. Before you can add a custom action to a Setup project, though, you must first develop a batch file, script, or executable program that implements the action.

Finally, the Launch Conditions Editor lets you set conditions that must be met before the application can be installed. For example, you can use a launch condition to check the operating system version or to see if a particular file exists on the target system. If the condition isn't met, the Setup program aborts the installation.

The User Interface Editor for the HalloweenSetup project

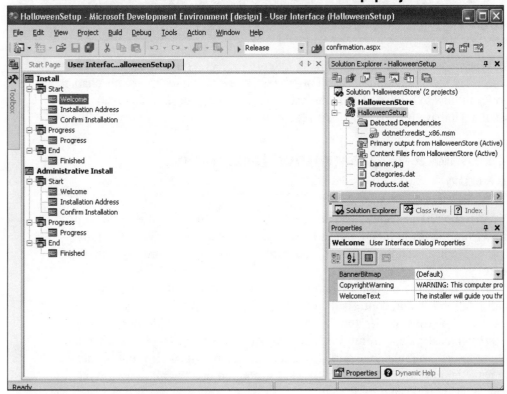

Other editors for a Setup project

Name	Description
Registry Editor	Specifies keys and values to be added to the registry on the target computer.
File Types Editor	Establishes a file association between a file extension and an application on the target computer. These associations aren't often used for web appplictions.
User Interface Editor	Customizes the setup dialog boxes. The Install dialog boxes are used when the application is installed to a web server. The Administrative Install dialogs boxes are used to upload the application's installer to a network server so the application can later be installed to multiple web servers.
Custom Actions Editor	Specifies additional actions to be taken during the install or uninstall process. For example, a custom action can call a SQL script to install a database on the target system.
Launch Conditions Editor	Specifies conditions that must be met by the target computer before the installation is run.

Description

- To access a setup editor, select the Setup project in the Solution Explorer and then click the appropriate button at the top of the Solution Explorer window or select an editor from the View menu.

Figure 20-10   How to use the other setup editors

How to build a Setup project and test the Setup program

When you're finished customizing a Setup project, you're ready to build the project and test the resulting Setup program. The next two topics in this chapter show you how to do that. Then, the last topic gives you some ideas on how to install a database if the application you're deploying uses one.

How to build a Setup project for a web application

As figure 20-11 shows, you build a Setup project by using the Build command from the Build menu, the same way you build any other Visual Studio project. Then, Visual Studio creates the three output files that are listed in this figure.

Setup.exe is the program you run to install the application; Setup.ini is a configuration file that controls the installation program; and the .msi file contains all of the files for the application, including the executable files, content files (such as .aspx and .html files), and any other files that you included in the Setup project. To make this work, the Setup.ini file provides information such as the name and location of the .msi file that's required and the minimum .NET Framework version required.

Installer files displayed in the Windows Explorer

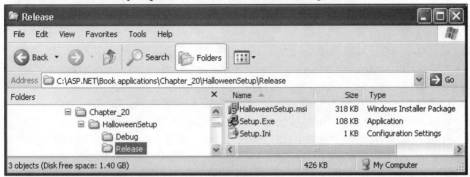

Common installer files for installing a web application

File name	Description
Setup.exe	The program you run to install the application.
Setup.ini	A configuration file that's used by Setup.exe.
projectname.msi	The Windows Installer file for the application. This file contains the assemblies and other files required by the application in compressed form.

Where the installer files are located

- By default, the Setup project is stored in a subfolder of the solution folder, but you can change that folder when you create the Setup project (see figure 20-3). Then, the installer files that are created when you build the Setup project are saved in the Debug or Release subfolder of the project folder.

Description

- Visual Studio lets you create both Debug and Release versions of your applications. The Debug version includes symbolic debugging information that allows you to use the .NET debugger to find and fix errors. The Release version doesn't include debugging information.

- To build a Setup project, first choose whether you want to build the Debug or Release version of the application by using the Solution Configurations drop-down list in the Standard toolbar. Then, select the Build command for the Setup project from the Build menu.

- By default, building a web Setup project creates the three files listed above. These files are stored in the Debug or Release subfolder of the project folder, depending on whether you selected the Debug or Release configuration when you built the project.

Figure 20-11   How to build a Setup project for a web application

How to run the Setup program for a web application

As figure 20-12 indicates, you can test a web Setup project from within Visual Studio by right-clicking the Setup project in the Solution Explorer and choosing the Install command. This installs the application on the web server that's running on your own computer so you can make sure that the Setup program has worked correctly. Then, when you're through testing, you can test the uninstall function by right-clicking the Setup project and choosing Uninstall.

To deploy a web application to another server, you must make the three setup files (Setup.exe, Setup.ini, and *projectname*.msi) available on that server. Then, you can run the Setup program from the server. If, for example, the server is on your local area network, you can copy the three setup files from your computer to a network folder and then run Setup.exe from that server. You can also copy the three files to a CD and then run the Setup program from the CD drive on the server where you want to install the application.

The screens in this figure show two of the dialog boxes that are displayed by the Setup program. The first one is simply the Welcome message that's displayed when the Setup program starts. The second one lets you override the default virtual directory where the application is installed.

If you later need to remove the application, you can use the Add or Remove Programs service in the Control Panel to do that. In fact, you should always remove an application before reinstalling it. That way, you can be sure that the new installation won't have any unwanted holdovers from the previous installation. Of course, if you know that an application will be upgraded frequently, you can set the RemovePreviousVersion property of the Setup project to True so that the previous version is removed automatically when the new version is installed.

How to handle database installation

Ideally, a Setup program should automatically install and configure an application's database. For example, a Setup project might include a custom action that calls a SQL Server script that creates a new database when the application is installed.

In many cases, though, database installation and configuration are done manually after the application is installed. If, for example, the application is going to use an existing database that's available on a database server, you just need to change the connection string that you used during development so it connects to the production database. If you saved that connection string in the Web.config file, that means you just need to edit that file on the web server.

Another alternative is to customize the Setup program to make the configuration change. For example, the Setup program could display a custom dialog box that asks for connection information, and then call a custom action to modify the Web.config file accordingly. Unless you're installing the application on more than one web server, though, this probably isn't worth the extra effort.

The first two screens of the Halloween Setup program

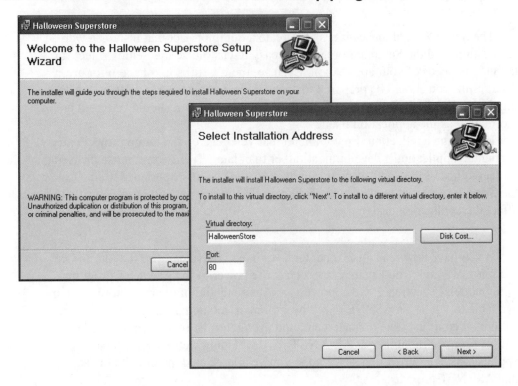

How to install and uninstall an application on your development computer

- To install an application from within Visual Studio, right-click on the Setup project in the Solution Explorer, and then select the Install command from the shortcut menu that's displayed. Or, select the Setup project in the Solution Explorer, and then select the Install command from the Project menu.
- To uninstall the application, use the Uninstall command in the Project menu or the project shortcut menu.

How to install and uninstall an application on the target web server

- Copy the three installer files to a CD or the target server. Then, execute the Setup.exe file from the target server.
- To uninstall the application, use the Add or Remove Programs service in the Control Panel.

Description

- When you run the Setup program, a series of screens is displayed. The second one lets you override the default virtual directory where the application is installed. After you complete these screens, the application is installed in the specified virtual directory.
- To execute the application once it's installed, open a web browser and enter the URL of the application's first page.

Figure 20-12   How to run the Setup program for a web application

Perspective

The Setup Wizard makes it easy to create a Setup project that installs a web application, and the Setup editors make it easy to customize the Setup project for the unique needs of your application. Even so, there's still a lot of room for error. As a result, you should be prepared to spend considerable time and effort developing the application's Setup project. Then, the Setup program should be tested as thoroughly as the application itself.

For a large application, I recommend that you develop the Setup project early during the application's development rather than later. Then, you can use the Setup project to install the application during testing and use the experience to fine tune the Setup project. As a side benefit, you may discover installation problems that affect the application design.

* * *

If you have now read all 20 chapters, we hope you've enjoyed the journey. In section 1, we hope you began to appreciate the power of the ASP.NET programming model. In section 2, we hope you saw the potential of the many tools that are available to you as an ASP.NET web programmer, including server controls, validation controls, state management, and user controls. In section 3, we hope you've seen the flexibility of ADO.NET for developing web-based database applications. And in section 4, we hope you've appreciated the breadth of features that ASP.NET provides.

Because ASP.NET is such a large subject, it may take a few years on the job before you truly master it. By that time, of course, Microsoft will probably have released a new version of ASP.NET that provides even more features to master. The good news is that you already know enough to develop professional e-commerce applications on your own. Besides that, you should have the concepts, skills, and perspective that you need for learning whatever else you need to know as you develop those applications. If that's the case, this book has done its job. And we thank you for reading it.

Terms

virtual directory
application root
dependency

Appendix A

How to install and use the software and downloadable files for this book

To develop web applications, you need to have Visual Studio .NET or the Standard Edition of Visual Basic .NET installed on your PC. If you want to run these applications from a web server on your own PC rather than a remote server, you need to install IIS. And if you want to access databases that are on your own PC rather than on a remote server, you need to install MSDE (Microsoft SQL Server 2000 Desktop Engine).

This appendix shows you how to install these products. It also describes the files for this book that can be downloaded from our web site and tells you how you can use them.

How to use the downloadable files

Throughout this book, you'll see complete applications that illustrate the material presented in each chapter. To help you understand how these applications work, you can download the source code and data for these applications from our web site. Then, you can open and run them in Visual Studio. These files come in a single download, as summarized in figure A-1. This figure also describes how you download, install, and use these files.

When you download the single install file and execute it, it will install all of the files for this book in the Murach\ASP.NET folder on your C drive. Within this folder, you'll find a folder named Book applications that contains the source code for all the applications in this book. The source code is organized in folders by applications within chapters. For example, the source files for the Halloween Store application in chapter 3 are stored in C:\Murach\ASP.NET\Book applications\Chapter_03\HalloweenStore. After you prepare these applications for use on your server, you can then use Visual Studio to open and run them.

The preferred sequence for software installation

Chances are that you already have the software you need for running ASP.NET web applications installed on your PC. But if you don't, figure A-1 shows you the preferred sequence for installing the required Microsoft software.

In particular, if you want to use the IIS web server on your own PC instead of on a remote server, you should install IIS before you install Visual Studio .NET and the .NET Framework. Otherwise, you will need to fix the .NET Framework as shown in figure A-2 and re-install Visual Studio .NET as shown in figure A-3. Once you've got IIS, Visual Studio, and the .NET Framework installed, you can install MSDE if you want to work with databases that are stored on your own PC, and you can prepare your PC for running the web applications that come with this book.

What the downloadable file for this book contains

- The source code for all of the applications presented in the book
- The Halloween database used in these applications
- A batch file that uses a SQL script to install the database as required

How to download and install the files for this book

- Go to www.murach.com, and go to the page for *Murach's ASP.NET Web Programming with VB.NET.*
- Click on the link for "FREE download of the book applications." Then, download "All book files." This will download one file named vasp_allfiles.exe to your C drive.
- Use the Windows Explorer to find the downloaded file on your C drive. Then, double-click on this file and respond to the dialog boxes that follow. This installs the files in folders that start with C:\Murach\ASP.NET.

The preferred sequence for software installation

1. If you want to run your web applications from a web server on your own PC, install IIS as shown in figure A-2.
2. Install Visual Studio .NET and the .NET Framework as shown in figure A-3.
3. If you want to work with databases on your own PC, install MSDE as shown in figure A-4.
4. Prepare your PC for running the applications that come with this book as shown in figure A-5.

Note

- If you're using Windows XP Home Edition, IIS is *not* available, so you won't be able to run web applications using just your PC. You'll need a separate web server.

Figure A-1   How to use the downloadable files for this book

How to install IIS

If you want to run ASP.NET web applications from a web server on your own PC, you need to install IIS as shown in figure A-2. Note, however, that you can't install IIS if you're using Windows XP Home Edition (in that case, IIS isn't available to you, and you'll have to have access to a separate web server).

To start the installation, you display the Add or Remove Programs dialog box and then click the Add/Remove Windows Components link as shown in this figure. When you do, the Windows Components Wizard starts and the second dialog box in this figure is displayed. This dialog box lists all the available Windows components. The components that are currently installed have a check mark in front of them. To install another component (in this case, IIS), just check it, click the Next button, and complete the dialog boxes that are displayed.

As I've already mentioned, if you're going to use IIS on your own PC, you should install it before you install the .NET Framework and Visual Studio .NET. If you've already installed the .NET Framework, though, you can repair it after installing IIS. To do that, you can execute the command shown in this figure. This command runs an executable file named dotnetfx.exe that can be found on one of the Visual Studio .NET installation CDs. In contrast, if you've installed Visual Studio before you install IIS, you'll need to re-install Visual Studio as described in the next figure.

In chapter 2 of this book, you'll learn how to open a web application from Visual Studio using the Open Project From Web dialog box. In some cases, we've found that this won't work without selecting an IIS option that isn't selected by default. If you have trouble using this dialog box, then, you'll need to use the Internet Information Services program to select this option.

Step 2 of figure A-5 describes how you start the Internet Information Services program. Once you start it, expand the server node and the Web Sites node (if necessary) as shown in that figure to display the Default Web Site node. Then, right-click the Default Web Site node and choose Properties from the menu that's displayed to display the Properties dialog box for the default web site. Next, click the Home Directory tab and check the Directory browsing option. Click the OK button to save the change. Now, the next time you start Visual Studio, the Open Project From Web dialog box should work properly.

The dialog boxes for installing IIS

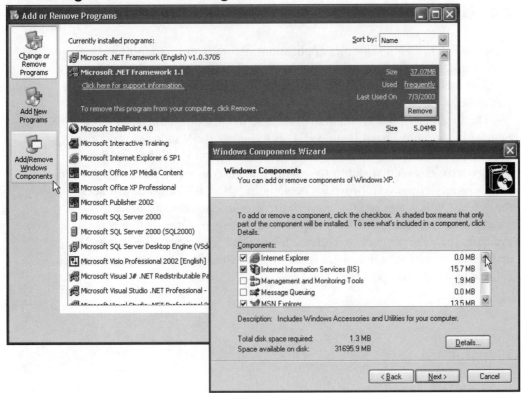

Description

- To install IIS, display the Windows Control Panel, and double-click on the Add or Remove Programs icon to display the Add or Remove Programs dialog box. Then, click on Add/Remove Windows Components to display the Windows Components Wizard, select Internet Information Services (IIS) from the list of components that are displayed, and click on the Next button to complete the installation.

When and how to repair the .NET Framework

- If you install IIS after installing the .NET Framework, you will need to repair the Framework. To do that, insert the Visual Studio .NET Windows Component Update CD. Then, click on the Start button in the Windows taskbar, choose the Run command, and enter this command:

```
<CD Drive>:\dotNetFramework\dotnetfx.exe /t:c:\temp /c:"msiexec.exe /fvecms
c:\temp\netfx.msi"
```

When and how to re-install Visual Studio .NET

- If you install IIS after installing Visual Studio .NET, you will need to re-install Visual Studio as described in the next figure.

Figure A-2   How to install IIS

How to install the .NET Framework and Visual Studio .NET

If you've installed Windows applications before, you shouldn't have any trouble installing Visual Studio .NET. You simply insert the first Visual Studio CD, and the setup program starts automatically. This setup program will lead you through the steps for installing Visual Studio as summarized in figure A-3.

The first step of the installation procedure for Visual Studio .NET (or the Standard Edition of Visual Basic .NET) is to update the Windows components. During this step, the components of the .NET Framework will be installed on your system. The second step is to install Visual Studio itself. Although you will have a variety of options for what's actually installed, it's safest to just accept the defaults unless you're familiar with the various components and know exactly what you need. The final step is to apply any updates that have become available since the product was released. Note that if you don't do that and updates are available, a link will appear on the Visual Studio Start page that you can use to install the updates.

The Visual Studio .NET setup program

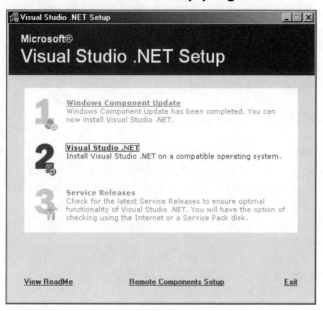

How to install Visual Studio .NET

- To install Visual Studio .NET, insert Disc 1 of the Visual Studio .NET CDs and the setup program will start automatically.

- If the .NET Framework has not been installed on your system, you will need to install it before installing Visual Studio .NET. To do that, click on the Windows Component Update link in the Setup dialog box.

- After the .NET Framework is installed, click on the Visual Studio .NET link and follow the instructions to install Visual Studio .NET. When the Options page is displayed, you can usually just accept the default options unless you have special requirements.

- After you install Visual Studio .NET, click on the Service Releases link to check for and install any updates that are available.

What if you're using Visual Basic .NET

- The setup program for the Standard Edition of Visual Basic .NET is similar to the setup program for Visual Studio .NET, but fewer options are available on the Options page.

When and how to re-install Visual Studio .NET

- If you installed Visual Studio .NET before you installed IIS, you need to re-install Visual Studio. To do that, display the Add or Remove Programs dialog box as described in figure A-Z. Then, highlight Visual Studio.NET and click the Change/Remove button to start the Visual Studio setup program. Click the Visual Studio.NET link, and then click the Repair/Reinstall link in the dialog box that's displayed.

Figure A-3   How to install the .NET Framework and Visual Studio .NET

How to install MSDE and use it with our databases

If you're using Visual Studio .NET 2002, the files you need to install MSDE are copied to your hard drive by default when you install Visual Studio. Then, you can simply run the Setup.exe program as described in figure A-4 to install MSDE. Otherwise, you can locate and run this program from the Visual Studio CDs as described in this figure. Note that this setup program doesn't display any dialog boxes or give any options like most setup programs do. In other words, it executes without interruption.

If you're using Visual Studio .NET 2003, you need to download the files for installing MSDE from Microsoft's web site as described in this figure. This web site also provides instructions for installing MSDE once you download these files. To do that, you have to run the Setup.exe program from the command prompt. To get to the command prompt, click the Start button, select Run, and enter cmd or command in the dialog box that's displayed.

After you install MSDE, you'll notice a server icon near the right side of the Windows taskbar. If you double-click this icon, the SQL Server Service Manager dialog box shown at the top of this figure is displayed. You can use this dialog box to start, continue, pause, or stop the SQL Server engine. By default, SQL Server is started each time you start your PC. If that's not what you want, you can remove the check mark from the Auto-start option in this dialog box. Then, you can start SQL Server whenever you need it using this dialog box.

Although you don't need to know much about how MSDE works to use it, you should know that when you run the setup program, it creates a copy of SQL Server and gives it a name. Then, you can use that name to create connections to the databases that are accessed by that server. For Visual Studio .NET 2002, the name is the name of your computer appended with VSdotNET. When I installed MSDE with Visual Studio .NET 2002, for example, the copy of SQL Server was named ANNE\VSdotNET as shown in this figure. For Visual Studio .NET 2003, the name depends on the name you enter for the INSTANCENAME parameter when you run the Setup.exe program. If you follow the instructions on the Microsoft web site, the name will be the same as if you had installed it from the 2002 CDs.

If you want to use the database that's available with the download for this book, you can do that without much trouble. Once you've installed the downloaded file, you can use the Windows Explorer to find and run the DB_Attach.bat file in the C:\Murach\ASP.NET\Database folder. This batch file runs a SQL Server script named DB_Attach.sql that attaches the database to the copy of SQL Server running on your computer. Note that this file assumes that the server name is the name of your computer appended with VSdotNET. If you specified a different name on the INSTANCENAME parameter when you installed MSDE, you can change the name in the DB_Attach.bat file using any text editor.

The SQL Server Service Manager

How to install and use MSDE

- If you're using Visual Studio .NET 2002, use Windows Explorer to navigate to this folder: C:\Program Files\Microsoft Visual Studio .NET\Setup\MSDE. Then, double-click on the Setup.exe file to run it and install MSDE. When you're done, restart your PC.

- If you're using Visual Studio .NET 2003, use Windows Explorer to navigate to this folder: C:\Program Files\Microsoft Visual Studio .NET 2003\Setup\MSDE. Then, double-click the msde_readme.htm document to display it in your browser. Click the link in that document to take you to the Microsoft web site, and follow the directions on the page that's displayed to download and install MSDE. When you're done, restart your PC.

- After you install MSDE, SQL Server will start automatically each time you start your PC. An icon will appear near the right side of the Windows taskbar to indicate that this service is running. To manage this service, double-click the icon or select the Start→Programs→MSDE→Service Manager command to display the dialog box shown above.

- The setup program creates a copy of SQL Server with a name that consists of your computer name followed by \VSdotNET. You can use this name to define connections to the databases that you use with this server.

How to attach the database for this book to MSDE

- If you're going to use the Halloween database used by the programs in this book on your own PC, you need to attach it to MSDE. To do that, you can use the batch file and SQL script that are downloaded and installed along with the other files for this book.

- To attach the database to MSDE, use the Windows Explorer to navigate to the C:\Murach\ASP.NET\Database folder, and double-click on the DB_Attach.bat file. That will run the batch file and attach the database.

Note

- If you didn't select the option to install MSDE when you installed Visual Studio .NET 2002, you can install it directly from Disc 3 of the Visual Studio .NET CDs. To do that, insert this CD, navigate to the Program Files\Microsoft Visual Studio .NET\Setup\MSDE folder, and double-click on the Setup.exe file to run it.

Figure A-4   How to install MSDE and use it with our databases

Before I go on, I want to make you aware of some problems you may encounter after installing the version of MSDE that's available from Microsoft's web site. First, the server may not appear in the SQL Server Service Manager dialog box. Then, if you need to start, stop, or pause the server, you'll have to type the server name into the Server combo box.

Second, you may not be able to see the server from the Server Explorer in Visual Studio. In that case, you can expand the Servers node, expand the node for your computer, right-click on the SQL Servers node, and select Register SQL Server Instance. Then, in the dialog box that's displayed, you can enter the name for your instance of SQL Server (the name you entered on the INSTANCENAME parameter). You may also be asked to enter the password you specified (SAPWD parameter) when you installed MSDE. At that point, you should be able to view and use the server.

How to use the downloaded web applications

Before you can open and run the web applications that you've downloaded for this book, you'll need to copy them to the web server. Then, you'll need to configure them for use with IIS. If IIS is installed on your own PC, you can do that by using the procedure in figure A-5.

When you install IIS on your system, it creates a folder named Inetpub on your C drive. Within this folder is a folder named wwwroot. This is where all of your web applications and services must be stored. To start, then, you'll need to copy the chapter folders that contain the web applications to this folder. You'll find the chapter folders in the C:\Murach\ASP.NET\Book applications folder that's created when you install the files for this book.

After you copy the folders to IIS, you'll need to configure each application for use by IIS. To do that under Windows XP, you use the Internet Information Services program shown in this figure. Under Windows 2000, the program name is Internet Services Manager, but you work with it the same way. When you first start this program, it will list the available web servers in the left side of its window. In most cases, this list will include just the web server on your PC. Then, you can expand the node for this server and then expand the node for the default web site to display the IIS applications.

Next, locate the chapter folder that contains the application you want to use, and expand it to display the application folder. Notice that it's displayed with a folder icon rather than an IIS icon like most of the other items in the list. In this figure, for example, you can see the folder for the HalloweenStore application for Chapter 4. To configure this application for IIS, display its properties as described in this figure, and then click the Create button in the Directory tab. When you do, you'll notice that the icon for the application changes from a folder icon to an IIS icon. To complete the configuration, click the OK button in the Properties dialog box.

The Internet Information Services program and the properties for an IIS application

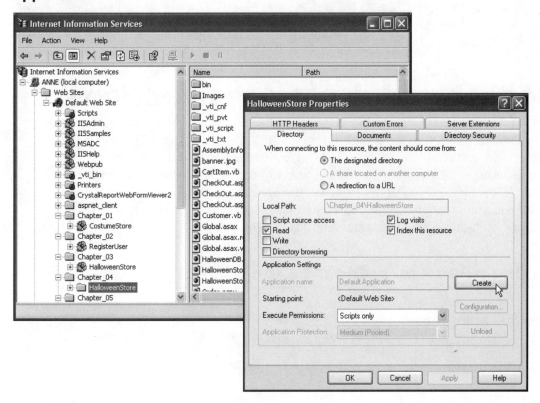

How to use the downloaded web applications

1. Use the Windows Explorer to navigate to the C:\Murach\ASP.NET\Book applications folder. Then, copy the chapter folder for the application you want to use to the C:\Inetpub\wwwroot folder.

2. In Windows XP, start the Internet Information Services program using the Start→All Programs→Administrative Tools→Internet Information Services command. In Windows 2000, use the Start→Programs→Administrative Tools→Internet Services Manager command.

3. Expand the server node (ANNE in the window shown above), the Web Sites node (if necessary), and the Default Web Site node to display the available applications. Then, expand the chapter folder you just copied so you can see the folder for the application you want to use. Right-click on that folder and select the Properties command from the menu that's displayed to display the Properties dialog box for that folder.

4. Display the Directory tab and then click on the Create button to configure the application for use with IIS. The icon in the Internet Information Services window will change from a folder to an IIS application icon like those shown above. Click on the OK button to accept the property changes, and then close the Internet Information Services program.

Figure A-5   How to use the downloaded web applications for this book

Appendix B

Coding and syntax conventions

Throughout this book, you've learned how to use ASP.NET and ADO.NET classes, methods, properties, and events. In most cases, we've shown you minimal syntax because when you work with Visual Studio, many of the coding details are taken care of for you by the Intellisense feature. However, this appendix summarizes the coding rules you have to follow and the syntax conventions that are used in the syntax summaries in the figures in case you ever have a question about them.

Coding rules and guidelines for VB.NET

General coding rules

1. Use spaces to separate the words and operators in each statement.
2. Indentation and capitalization have no effect on the operation of a statement.

Comments

1. Type an apostrophe followed by the comment.
2. A comment can be coded to the right of a statement or on a line with no statement.
3. A comment can't be coded to the right of a continuation character.

Continuations

To code a statement on more than one line so it's easier to read, type a space followed by an underscore (the continuation character) at the end of the first line. Then, type a return and continue the statement on the next line.

Coding recommendations

1. Use indentation and extra spaces to align statements and clauses within statements.
2. Use blank lines before and after groups of related statements.

Syntax conventions

Boldfaced element	Indicates that the element must be entered exactly as shown.
Regular-font element	Indicates that the element is provided by the programmer.
[option]	Indicates an option that may be coded but isn't required.
[option|option]	Indicates a set of alternative options, one of which may be coded.
{option|option}	Indicates a set of alternative options, one of which must be coded.
...	Indicates that the preceding option may be repeated multiple times.
<u>option</u>	Indicates the default value for an option.

A VB.NET coding example

Syntax: `cookie = New HttpCookie(name, value)`

Example: `NameCookie = New HttpCookie("UserName", sUserName)`

A SQL coding example

Syntax:
```
Select column-list
From table-1
    [Inner] Join table-2
    On table-1.column-1 {=|<|>|<=|>=|<>} table-2.column-2
[Where selection-criteria]
[Order By column-1 [Asc|Desc] [, column-2 [Asc|Desc]]...]
```

Example:
```
Select ShortName, ProductID, Name, UnitPrice
From Products Inner Join Categories
    On Categories.CategoryID = Products.CategoryID
Order By Categories.CategoryID
```

Index

What software you need for this book

- Any version of Microsoft Visual Studio .NET or the Standard Edition of Microsoft Visual Basic .NET (see the Introduction for more details).

- If you're going to use databases on your own PC, you need to install MSDE (Microsoft SQL Server 2000 Desktop Engine), which comes with both Visual Studio and Visual Basic 2002. For Visual Studio or Visual Basic 2003, you'll need to download the files for installing MSDE from the Microsoft web site.

- If you're going to use a web server that's on your own PC, you need to install IIS, which comes with Windows 2000 or XP (except the XP Home Edition).

- If you haven't installed these products yet, please read appendix A in this book. *It will probably save you some time.*

The downloadable files for this book

- Complete source code and data for the applications presented in this book

- Descriptions and data for practice exercises and new projects that you can develop on your own, along with additional instructional aids like chapter summaries and learning objectives

- Files that make it easy for you to set up the databases if you're going to use your own PC as a database server

How to download the application files

- Go to www.murach.com, and go to the page for *Murach's ASP.NET Web Programming with VB.NET*.

- Click on the link for "Free download of the book applications." Then, download "All book files." This will download one file named vasp_allfiles.exe to your C drive.

- Use the Windows Explorer to find the downloaded file (vasp_allfiles.exe). Then, double-click on it and respond to the dialog boxes that follow. This installs the application files and data in folders that start with C:\Murach\ASP.NET.

- From that point on, you can find the applications and data in folders like C:\Murach\ASP.NET\Book applications\Chapter_02 and C:\Murach\ASP.NET\Database.

- Go to appendix A for instructions on how to set up the database and web applications if you're going to have them reside on your own PC.

www.murach.com